THE BRITISH CABINET

THE
BRITISH CABINET

BY

JOHN P. MACKINTOSH

SECOND EDITION

METHUEN & CO LTD
11 New Fetter Lane EC4

First published 1962 by Stevens & Sons Ltd.
Second edition 1968
University Paperback edition 1968
© *1962 and 1968 by Stevens & Sons*
Type composed by The Eastern Press Limited, London & Reading
and machined and bound in Great Britain by
Cox and Wyman Limited, London, Reading & Fakenham

SBN   416   29670   X

Distributed in the U.S.A. by
Barnes   and   Noble   Inc.

PREFACE TO THE FIRST EDITION

IN 1958 Professor J. D. B. Mitchell of Edinburgh University was kind enough to ask me to join him in producing a third edition of Arthur Berriedale Keith's *British Cabinet System*. After some months' work both Professor Mitchell and Stevens and Sons agreed that an adequate revision would alter the original text to such an extent that the book could scarcely continue to be attributed to Keith. It seemed better to leave the second edition as it stood giving Keith's views and to bring out a new book. I am very grateful to Stevens and Sons for asking me to write this book and to Professor Mitchell for reading the manuscript and for his many helpful comments.

After an introductory survey and an attempt to trace the origins and early forms of the Cabinet in the eighteenth century, the main treatment is of the period since 1832. My method has been to read the first hand sources that are in print collecting all the relevant information. When these sources become scanty towards the end of the nineteenth century, I have supplemented them with manuscript collections, the Royal Archives at Windsor, and the papers of the Committee of Imperial Defence up to 1910. There is a wealth of material on the First World War and on some of the figures of the 1920s and 1930s but again I have tried to supplement these sources and bring the treatment up to date by means of a series of interviews with ex-Cabinet Ministers, civil servants, and others who have had opportunities for observing the Cabinet at work.

I have full notes of these interviews and in some cases of diaries and letters which I was allowed to read. The interviews were conducted on the understanding that I could incorporate information given me in the book provided I did not acknowledge the source. (Except in the cases of Earl Attlee's point on page 7 and an anecdote of the late Aneurin Bevan on page 402 where permission was given.) I have been allowed to quote from some of the diaries and letters on the same understanding. So in Part Five there are a few unsupported quotations whose authenticity will, I hope, be accepted since these were the only conditions on which

I could use the information, and I have no axe to grind! In assembling the material I tried to avoid the assumption that there was " a Cabinet System " whose various conventions and practices had simply to be illustrated. The object has been to try to establish how the Cabinet worked, its precise power and place in the machinery of government in each period, and the chapter divisions occur where there seemed to be a change of some significance.

My chief debt of gratitude is to the late Richard Pares whose standards as a teacher and an historian are a constant stimulus despite the knowledge that I can never attain them. I would like to thank Professor Andrew Browning and Professor Esmond Wright of Glasgow University for their kindness, which began in the short period when I taught at Glasgow University and has continued since then. Professor D. B. Horn of Edinburgh University encouraged and guided me as a student and then in my seven years as a member of his teaching staff. I am grateful for all his help and especially for his advice on every aspect of Part Two of this book. Dr. James Tumelty of Glasgow and Dr. John Hargreaves of Aberdeen gave me the benefit of their deep knowledge of the early and late nineteenth century while Mr. Graeme Moodie of Glasgow and Mr. Peter Heath of St. Andrews were good enough to advise me on the more modern sections of the book.

I must thank the following Cabinet and ex-Cabinet Ministers for according me an interview: Viscount Alexander, Earl Attlee, the late Aneurin Bevan, the Rt. Hon. R. A. Butler, M.P., Viscount Chandos, the Rt. Hon. J. Chuter Ede, M.P., Lord Crathorne, the Rt. Hon. A. Creech-Jones, M.P., Lord Dalton, the Rt. Hon. Hugh Gaitskell, M.P., the Rt. Hon. P. Gordon-Walker, M.P., the late Earl of Halifax, Viscount Head, the Rt. Hon. Thomas Johnston, Viscount Monckton, Lord Morrison, the Rt. Hon. P. J. Noel-Baker, M.P., Lord Pethick-Lawrence, the Rt. Hon. A. Robens, the Marquess of Salisbury, Viscount Samuel, the Rt. Hon. Emanuel Shinwell, M.P., the late Lord Stansgate, Viscount Stuart, the Earl of Swinton, the Rt. Hon. G. E. P. Thorneycroft, M.P., Lord Williams, the Rt. Hon. Harold Wilson, M.P., the Rt. Hon. Arthur Woodburn, M.P., and the Earl of Woolton. The many senior civil servants who gave me their impressions requested that I should not thank them personally but I would like to thank the

Cabinet Office collectively for their help at several stages and for the rapidity with which they granted " clearance " for the book.

On other aspects I was grateful for the advice of Lord Bridges, Sir E. A. Fellowes, Mr. Jo Grimond, Sir William Hayter, Mr. Francis Boyd of the *Guardian*, Mr. J. D. Margach of the *Sunday Times*, Mr. Hugh Massingham of the *Observer* and Mr. Francis Williams. My visits to London and the work they entailed were made infinitely easier and more enjoyable by the kindness and hospitality of my old friend David McW. Millar.

J. P. M.

UNIVERSITY COLLEGE, IBADAN.
    December, 1961.

PREFACE TO THE SECOND EDITION

BY 1968, ten years after this book was begun, there appeared to have been sufficient important developments to merit a second edition. There was considerable interesting evidence from the governments led by Macmillan, Douglas-Home and Wilson and also a controversy had developed over my conclusions which seemed to be worth discussing in its own right. In addition, I have had time to go into some aspects of the modern period more deeply and I have learned a great deal, particularly since being elected to Parliament myself in March 1966. In this edition the sections of the book up to 1922 have been revised, the historical material that has been published in the last ten years has been incorporated and the appropriate references have been added.

The special problems involved in the First World War and the personal impact of Lloyd George make it hard to decide whether this period should be treated as part of the contemporary situation. There were many developments under the pressure of war and post-war readjustment which pointed forwards, practices which were not revived till the 1940s. Yet these years have a certain unity and require such special attention that I decided to give them separate treatment in this edition.

In the final section on the modern Cabinet, I have revised the order of presentation and added a new final chapter. My reason is that in the original book, the work was done period by period and the material assembled and written up in this way. This explains why the theme picked out by commentators—the altered role of the Cabinet, the increasing power of the Prime Minister— did not emerge from the material or become clear to me until I was actually writing this last section. As a result, the argument emerges in a piecemeal fashion and I failed to give enough attention to the selection of a Prime Minister, his security in office and the difficulty of leading any kind of rebellion. Also the fact that I followed the pattern of some of the earlier sections and ended with a chapter on the influence of the Crown both obscured the argument and meant concluding on a negative note.

So the last section has been re-written, both to incorporate the large amount of new material I have collected and to present the theme in a more logical way. I begin with the role of the Crown which leads naturally to the problem of how a Prime Minister is chosen and his security in office. After examining the working of the central executive including the Cabinet, it is then possible and proper to look at the agencies through which government has to work and by which it may be limited: Parliament and the Civil Service. Then there are the external forces which may help or may act as checks, the pressure groups, the press and the public.

It is appropriate finally to draw the argument together in a concluding chapter explaining the conclusions. In this subject it is as important to avoid the overstatements (sometimes amounting almost to caricature) of those who say Britain has an " elected Monarch " or a presidential system as to expose the opposite error; the assertions that Harold Wilson has no more power than Gladstone or Campbell-Bannerman, and that " the Cabinet System " has not altered in any important sense in the last century. This last chapter reviews the controversy on this subject which has, in the last five years, spread from academic writing into the press, television and has even interested practising politicians.

I have omitted my original conclusion because, although I am still worried that democratic control is losing ground to the executive, I feel this is too large and serious a topic to be left to a few pages at the end of a book.

As before, I have supplemented the written sources with interviews with those who have served in Cabinets in recent years and with officials who have worked close to the Cabinet. I must particularly thank the Prime Minister, the Rt. Hon. Harold Wilson, for his help and the interest he has taken in my work. I am also grateful to Lord Aylestone, the Rt. Hon. Anthony Wedgwood Benn, Lord Blakenham, the Rt. Hon. John Boyd-Carpenter, the Rt. Hon. Sir Edward Boyle, Lord Brooke of Cumnor, Lord Carrington, the Rt. Hon. Anthony Crosland, the Rt. Hon. Richard Crossman, the Rt. Hon. Sir Alec Douglas-Home, Lord Eccles, the Rt. Hon. Tom Fraser, the Rt. Hon. Joseph Godber, the Rt. Hon. Patrick Gordon-Walker, the Rt. Hon. James Griffiths, the Rt. Hon.

Edward Heath, Lord Hill, the Rt. Hon. Quintin Hogg, the Rt. Hon. Douglas Houghton, the Rt. Hon. Cledwyn Hughes, the Rt. Hon. Roy Jenkins, the Rt. Hon. Sir Keith Joseph, the Rt. Hon. Selwyn Lloyd, the Rt. Hon. Iain Macleod, the Rt. Hon. Reginald Maudling, Lord Mills, Lord Muirshiel, the Rt. Hon. Michael Noble, the Rt. Hon. Charles Pannell, the Rt. Hon. Enoch Powell, the Rt. Hon. Geoffrey Rippon, the Rt. Hon. Duncan Sandys, the Rt. Hon. Christopher Soames, Lord Stow Hill, and Lord Watkinson. Among the senior civil servants who have worked in the Cabinet Secretariat or in No. 10 Downing Street, some have asked to be omitted even from this expression of general thanks but I can express my appreciation of the advice given to me by Mr. Frederick Bishop, Sir Timothy Bligh, Mr. Michael Hall, the late Lord Normanbrook and Sir Philip de Zulueta. I have kept notes of all these conversations but no quotations are used and none of the information is deployed in a manner which would reveal, even to those involved, the source of my information. The object of the interviews was to obtain the general impression of recent practice in the Cabinet rather than to elicit any secrets, and I hope the information and advice I received have enabled me to present a fair and balanced picture.

On a more personal level I would like to thank Miss Nora Beloff for many stimulating conversations on the political scene, Miss Norma Percy for her help and care in reading the proofs and compiling the index and my wife Una, for all her affection and support. The book is dedicated to her and to our son Stuart born in the week this edition went to press.

JOHN P. MACKINTOSH.

HOUSE OF COMMONS.
January, 1968.

CONTENTS

PART FOUR

THE TRANSITION TO A "CABINET SYSTEM"—1868–1914

PART FIVE

THE WAR AND POST-WAR COALITION—1914–1922

PART SIX

THE CABINET IN MODERN CONDITIONS

APPENDIX

Part One

An Introduction

CHAPTER 1

THE POSITION OF THE CABINET IN BRITISH GOVERNMENT

LIMITATIONS ON ITS POWERS

THE student of government is chiefly interested in power. His task is to discover where power lies in any society and to describe the government's share in its operation. In such a search the problem is complicated by the number of institutions and lack of knowledge of their working, and this multiplicity and obscurity may conceal the actual centres of power, since formal control may not coincide with real control. When Arthur Berriedale Keith began his *British Cabinet System* with the words: " The national government of Great Britain today is controlled by the Cabinet " he was stating that in his view the Cabinet was the effective centre of public or political power. Thus an analysis of the factors affecting the Cabinet and a description of its operation would reveal the process by which decisions were made and power exercised in this country.

This is still on the whole correct. Professor Keith went on to explain the limitations on the authority of the Cabinet. In the first place, it was chosen by a Prime Minister appointed by the Crown, though the occasions when the Crown could exercise any influence over the composition or conduct of the Cabinet were few and circumscribed by generally established rules. Secondly, the Cabinet's power was limited by its need to command a majority in the House of Commons. This, in turn, might involve concessions to a party organisation and adjustments to retain enough public support to win a general election. A final limitation was the ability of the Civil Service to frame and carry out the Cabinet's decisions. The existence of strong departmental attitudes or weaknesses might both bias the information on which the Cabinet relied in the formation of policy and affect the detailed execution of the final schemes.

The problem is to discover the extent of these limitations and to give a true account of the working of the Cabinet. The old picture of a structure so simple and straightforward, based on such clear principles that it could be labelled a " system," and be neatly wrapped up for export to the dominions and other countries, was largely drawn from the contemporary view of the situation between 1868 and 1914.

Then the Crown did have a certain advisory role and could be of help (*e.g.*, it could mediate in disputes between the Houses) but it never altered the decisions of the Cabinet. These decisions were taken with the knowledge that they would be subjected to the most careful examination both by Parliament and by a public opinion which had a great interest in politics. In this period, the activities of the government were concentrated on foreign affairs where Britain, as a leading power with ample resources, had a wide field of action, on questions concerned with the government of Ireland and the Empire, and to a small but growing extent on certain aspects of internal regulation where the major disputes were usually over matters of principle. It was still true that most policy decisions were executed either by positive action in foreign affairs or by the passage of laws enforced by the courts. Day-to-day administration involving constant relations with powerful groups in the community was a relatively new feature of government.

Under these conditions, the Cabinet operated in a delightfully simple manner. Including all the leading ministers, it discussed with little pre-digestion and no secretarial assistance all the issues of any importance and only in the restricted field of defence was the need for co-ordinated administration appreciated.

Provided that the conclusions were acceptable to the government party in the House of Commons (and if under a Liberal régime the House of Lords would let them pass), then these decisions were final. While it had the support of public opinion and the Commons, this Cabinet of men meeting in an informal atmosphere to settle the questions of the day was invested with all the apparently unlimited authority which commentators, such as Dicey, implied when they emphasised the sovereignty of Parliament.

Today, the Cabinet is still formally in the same supreme position. The decisions of the government are not said to be those of the Prime Minister or of the departmental ministers, Acts are not labelled with the names of politicians or civil servants or even held to be simply the work of Parliament; in theory they all emanate from the Cabinet.

However, the task of disentangling the actual limits of the power of the Cabinet and of describing its operation has become much more complex in the past twenty years. Now that the government is expected to supervise the economy of the country [1] and to run the welfare services, the area under its nominal control has grown enormously, and yet the task of living with the various power groups in the community has made the restrictions on the Cabinet's freedom of manoeuvre more and more evident. The existence of similar restrictions in foreign policy has been brought home by the loss of Britain's capacity on economic and military grounds to " go it alone " in world affairs.

It is true that even in the late nineteenth century, the theory of parliamentary sovereignty exaggerated the degree of freedom open to the legislature and therefore to the Cabinet. Gladstone fought the Midlothian campaign of 1880 on the assumption that a Liberal Cabinet could cast aside the whole of the previous government's foreign policy. But once in office he found that it is easier to undertake commitments in foreign countries than to abandon them and that world conditions might present alternatives which would drive the Liberals into actions (such as the occupation of Egypt) very similar to those which he had condemned in his election campaign. But even making these allowances, the freedom of action was much greater when Britain had a pre-eminent financial position with no ties to allies and no need even to consult the self-governing colonies. Since the policy of avoiding association with European alliances was abandoned after the turn of the century, the British Cabinet has steadily accumulated obligations. It is now expected to consult its allies in the NATO and SEATO pacts, to keep in touch with the members of the Commonwealth, and to remember its duties as a member of the United Nations Organisation.[2] Economic policies have to be reconciled with the needs of the Sterling Area, the General Agreement on Tariffs and Trade and will, in time, have to be adapted

---

[1] Sir Edward (now Lord) Bridges dates this from the publication of the *Employment Policy White Paper* in 1944 (Cmd. 6527). See his *Stamp Memorial Lecture on Treasury Control*, 1950, p. 19.

[2] Mr. Gaitskell, on May 20, 1960, called for a NATO " Cabinet " of ministers from each member country to sit permanently in Paris and control the policy of the Alliance. *The Guardian*, May 21, 1960.

to fit in with the European Common Market. The world is now so tightly organised that Britain's old independence of action has largely ceased and policy is normally confined to attempts at influencing a group of nations to move a little further in one direction or another.

The end of Britain's position as the world's creditor has had a similar effect. The Cabinet must now mould its policies with an eye to what the country can afford and to the probable trends in the economic climate of the world. It is open to argument whether Britain can support certain types of defence policy, the manufacture of some weapons or the maintenance of an army in Europe. Even minor military ventures outside the bounds of the primary diplomatic alignments may endanger the financial stability of the country.

Since 1918 the precarious state of Britain's balance of payments has frequently imposed restrictions on the internal policy of the Cabinet. A spectacular instance of such a restriction occurred on Sunday, August 23, 1931, when the Labour Cabinet paced the garden of No. 10 Downing Street waiting for Messrs. J. P. Morgan & Co. to let them know whether their proposed economy measures were sufficient for the New York bankers to feel justified in floating a loan. Another occurred on Tuesday, November 6, 1956, in the middle of the Suez War, when the Treasury found it could no longer support sterling at the current rate of exchange without an immediate loan from the International Monetary Fund and other sources of aid partly or largely under the control of the American government. In response to a telephoned request, the Cabinet was told that the loan could only be made available if Britain accepted the cease-fire proposals of the United Nations by midnight and " there seems little doubt that this bleak intelligence . . . almost instantaneously convinced everyone." [3] It is also certain that a sufficient if not the major reason why Britain did not use force to put down the Rhodesian rebellion after the illegal declaration of independence in 1965 was that this would have led to an immediate run on the pound. In fact since 1945

---

[3] Randolph Churchill, *The Rise and Fall of Sir Anthony Eden*, pp. 287–289. See also Anthony Nutting, *No End of a Lesson*, p. 146, and Hugh Thomas, *The Suez Affair*, p. 154. In this context, Lord Strang quotes Ernest Bevin as often remarking " if I could export so many million tons of coal a year, I could put our economy right and have an independent foreign policy." Lord Strang, *At Home and Abroad*, p. 287.

the British public has become accustomed to such major Cabinet decisions as the 1949 and 1967 devaluations, the credit squeezes of 1957, 1962 and 1966, defence cuts and the attempts to join the Common Market, being taken wholly or partly on the grounds of Britain's shaky balance of payments.

In the purely domestic field the one aspect of the relationships of the Cabinet which has become less complex is that of its connections with the Crown. Writing in 1865, Walter Bagehot gave a simple picture of the Crown as a figurehead with a few advisory functions. There has been a tendency to revise his account in the light of Queen Victoria's constant stream of comments on all public affairs, published in the nine volumes of her letters. It is clear that the Queen thought that in some sense she did govern the country and that ministers and policies did require her personal approval. On the other hand, when the Cabinet was set on a policy, that was the end of the matter and the Queen's authority was real only when her help was asked for by her ministers or on minor matters (such as the substitution of Campbell-Bannerman for Childers at the War Office in 1886) when the Prime Minister did not think the issue sufficiently important to take a stand. It is difficult however to make any swift or simple estimate of Queen Victoria's influence on her Cabinets and the question is discussed in detail in Chapters 4 and 9, below. Edward VII took both a less decided view of royal authority and a less active interest in politics but again his precise role in some of the major policies of his reign requires careful examination. Sir Harold Nicolson explains that George V fully accepted that, in Bagehot's words, his rights were only " to be consulted, to encourage, and to warn." [4] Yet there were instances such as the London Conference on Ireland in 1921, and the appointment of Lord Irwin as Viceroy of India in 1926, when the King's views or offers of mediation were of some help to the Cabinet or the Prime Minister. By the reign of George VI, however, the Crown's role had become purely that of a figurehead. Earl Attlee has said that " a conscientious, constitutional monarch is a strong element of stability and continuity in our constitution," [5] but by this he meant that the Crown attracts a great deal of the attention which might otherwise be

---

[4] Sir Harold Nicolson, *King George V*, p. 62.
[5] Earl Attlee on " The Art of Being Prime Minister," *The Times*, Saturday, June 15, 1957, p. 4.

lavished on the political leaders. Earl Attlee could not recall a single instance in his period as Prime Minister from 1945 to 1951 when the views of George VI had any effect on appointments or policies, imperial or domestic.[6] Lord Morrison (who when Home Secretary held a post involving close connections with the Crown) completed this picture by writing that Bagehot's description of the King accepting the Cabinet's policies, but exercising his right to warn ministers, was couched in stronger terms than he had ever experienced.[7] The adoption by the Conservatives in 1965 of a procedure for electing their leader removed the last situation in which a monarch had even to interpret rules or operate the machinery of consultation with party leaders.

It might be suggested that the Cabinet's relations with the House of Commons have been simplified by the increased rigidity of the party system. This is correct inasmuch as the ministers do not have to nurse their measures through the House and be prepared to defend and amend them at every turn. Governments with an assured majority in the House can risk short-term unpopularity provided they feel that their actions will be justified before the next election. Cabinets do adjust their policies to meet public opinion but such opinion makes itself felt in other ways than through M.P.s speaking and voting against the government. This development has also made the task of elucidating the various limitations on Cabinet authority harder. In 1867 the Second Reform Bill was the product of the decisions of the Cabinet, of amendments from the floor of the House and of a degree of public pressure so that it is possible, to some extent, to allocate credit for the measure. But now that support in the division lobbies is assured, pressure on and in the Cabinet is exercised by devious means and its weight is hard to assess. When Mr. Macmillan's government decided to amend its controversial Rent Act in 1958, was this because new factual evidence had come to light, because the balance of opinion in the Cabinet had altered, or were the " Rent Act Rebels " in the parliamentary Conservative Party responsible? When Mr. Wilson decided in 1967 to adopt a mild form of incomes policy was this because he felt a tough policy was unnecessary, because of the resistance of the T.U.C., had he

---

[6] This view was expressed by Earl Attlee in an interview on Tuesday, July 15, 1958, and one or two assertions to the contrary are discussed in Chapter 18.
[7] Herbert Morrison, *Government and Parliament*, p. 83.

heard that normally loyal trade union M.P.s would abstain or had the "doves" in the Cabinet had the best of the argument? In both these cases, the change of policy may have been due to a combination of the factors mentioned or to failures in the "trial by by-election" to which modern governments are subjected.

This latter possibility is a good example of the adaptation of British politics to new situations. When M.P.s were less rigidly controlled, the task of the Cabinet was to win and hold the confidence of the House. It was the poor showing of the front bench and the lack of enthusiasm among its supporters in the Commons that sapped the strength of the Liberal Ministry of 1868–74 rather than the loss of twenty-one by-elections in two years. But now that (despite occasional rebel groups) the support given by M.P.s in the House is no guide to the vigour of an administration or to feeling in the country, periodic tests of public opinion through by-elections have gained a far greater importance.

In any attempt to assess just how much power the Cabinet wields and how it operates in practice, it is hard to ascertain the relations of the Cabinet with the rest of the executive and with the many groups wielding power in the community. A proper account must try to estimate the degree of control the Cabinet exercises over the Civil Service, the public authorities, the trade unions and the various associations with which it must deal. The problem can be rephrased by asking how far the interconnections between the Cabinet and all these other institutions, public and private, with their own practical philosophies may condition or prescribe government action. The difficulty is accentuated in that many policy matters are settled in discussions with these bodies or within the government and consequently all these stages, as well as the final drafting of the legislation, are conducted in secret.

It is only safe to make one broad generalisation. Matters on which the political parties feel strongly—that is, policies which have been demanded by the government party or which will arouse opposition—are decided at a political level in the Cabinet or above. Clearly only a minority of the measures of any government arouse controversy either between or within the parties, and it is very hard to tell where the more administrative or routine decisions are taken. It is from the recommendations of the civil servant at the desk who encounters snags and discovers inadequacies in the current laws, that many new proposals are built up. Also it is at this level that the influence of the interested bodies is strongest. The *Report of the Committee on Intermediaries* explained (in 1949) that " the Ministry of Food . . . always dealt with the trade associations in formulating the basis of its policy." [8] The Select Committee on Delegated Legislation reported in 1953 that statutory instruments are almost always framed after consultation with the parties concerned. A study of the Agriculture Bill of 1947 led to the comment that " it was from the thought of the groups concerned as much as from the Ministry that the Bill emerged." [9] Thus, though the Cabinet occupies a much more commanding position in the life of the community than it did before 1914, the very pressure of work and the establishment of connections with so many other executive agencies has meant that more and more decisions have not only to be taken at lower levels but have to be shared. It is not even safe to assume that what appear to be purely political decisions taken by the Cabinet on the basis of party feeling are not, to some extent, determined by other factors, for there remains the (largely unexplored) field of the relations between the political leadership and powerful individuals, companies or unions which may be associated with or even be part of the party organisations contributing funds or ideas, thus gaining the ear of the politicians.

Finally, even when a decision has been tracked down to the Cabinet, this does not necessarily mean that it was reached by the body of ministers sitting round the table in the Cabinet room. The Cabinet itself has become a highly organised business meeting and a vast amount of work is done, but at the expense of much prior consultation and the delegation of many decisions to Cabinet committees. The arrangements have now become sufficiently formal for the Cabinet Office to compile a book of Cabinet committees giving the membership of each committee on the left-hand page and the terms of reference on the right, and a book of Cabinet precedents and procedure explaining how various types of business should be arranged and submitted. In such a highly organised body with a long agenda to be covered, there is little time for debate,[10] and as a result there has been a natural tendency for the

8 Cmd. 7904, p. 43.
9 J. D. Stewart, *British Pressure Groups*, p. 18.
10 Herbert Morrison, *op. cit.*, p. 5. Earl Attlee, *The Times*, June 15, 1957, p. 4.

influential members to have informal meetings with the Prime Minister or to settle matters at personal interviews with him. Normally these discussions are held to clear the ground and establish the actual points on which Cabinet decisions are required but, in the hands of some Prime Ministers the effect may be to weight the scales against possible criticism in the Cabinet and even, on some occasions, to withdraw matters from the purview of the Cabinet. Here again, the situation can only be conveyed by a description of the practice of recent Prime Ministers and their relations with their colleagues.[11]

Considering this complexity and the power of the Prime Minister, all that can be said is that the Cabinet is bound to be concerned in most major decisions during the lifetime of a government. It is the Cabinet that is the final court of appeal in inter-departmental disputes. If there is dissension between ministers, matters may be thrashed out in private and the contestants plead in turn with the Prime Minister, but it is in the Cabinet that the conflict must be formally solved, the minority either accepting the decision and assuming joint responsibility or, if they cannot tolerate it, tendering their resignations. If a minister is doing too much on his own, or even if the Prime Minister is acting too often without prior agreement, it is in the name of Cabinet responsibility that his colleagues will venture to object and request that the matter be reopened.

It is, then, as true today as it was in the late nineteenth century that in order to study the working of the Cabinet it is necessary to examine all the other institutions which participate in the decision-making process in the central government of Britain and that an accurate picture of the Cabinet should reveal how this process operates.

CONVENTIONS AND PRECEDENTS

Turning to the more technical problems of describing the role of the Cabinet, the most apparent is that its functions are not laid down. Save for the occasional allusion, as in the Ministers of the Crown Act of 1937, neither Prime Minister nor Cabinet is known to law.

The position of the Cabinet has been evolved out of the needs

[11] See Chapters 19 and 20 below.

of the British political system and these needs or practices are usually described as constitutional conventions. One way of arriving at some understanding of the Cabinet is to trace the historical development of these conventions—a method which is attempted in Parts 2, 3, 4 and 5 of this book. In each of these Parts the relations of the Cabinet with the rest of the governmental machine have been analysed and in Part 6 the same treatment has been applied to the contemporary period.

In using this method it is of some value to be clear about the nature of constitutional conventions and to realise how much (or how little) of the actual operation of the Cabinet is covered by the enumeration and explanation of these conventions.

There is a distinction between law and convention both from the view of the practical politician and the student of government, but in the long-term development of the constitution, it is of no great importance. Both rest on the necessities of political life. Laws can be repealed or conventions changed if this is found to be desirable. The difference between law and convention is just that there is no formal procedure for enacting or enforcing conventions, though some conventions (*e.g.*, the monarch shall not veto laws passed by both Houses; the Prime Minister shall resign if he is defeated on a major issue in the Commons) are as important as any laws and perhaps even more difficult to alter.

If, then, the Cabinet can only be described in terms of certain conventions and if these are not laid down in any authorised form, how can the commentator be sure that the correct conventions have been selected? Stanley Baldwin held that complete accuracy was unattainable.

" The historian can tell you probably perfectly clearly what the constitutional practice was at any given period in the past, but it would be very difficult for a living writer to tell you at any given period in his lifetime what the Constitution of the country is in all respects, and for this reason, that at almost any given moment . . . there may be one practice called ' constitutional ' which is falling into desuetude and there may be another practice which is creeping into use but is not yet constitutional." [12]

[12] Quoted by Sir W. Ivor Jennings in *Cabinet Government*, p. 12, from H.C. Debates, Vol. 261, col. 531, 1931–32.

It is certainly true that no writer could be "accurate in all respects" but Baldwin's statement is unduly pessimistic. A convention is simply a generally accepted political practice, usually with a record of successful applications or precedents. As all events in recent political history might be put forward as precedents, the term is reserved for deliberate actions taken in situations which required some judgment as to the wisdom of alternative courses of procedure. Even then, as Viscount Esher said, "precedent, like analogy, is rarely conclusive," [13] and by this he meant that it is rarely conclusive by itself. The added force arises from agreement that the actions quoted as precedents were correct and that the reasons for holding them correct are still applicable. This serves as a reminder that a precedent has no independent existence or validity, but is a correct decision or action in certain political circumstances. Thus searching for a precedent is really looking for a case where previous exponents of the constitution have solved a similar difficulty in an approved fashion.

So a new action and any precedents on which it may be based are correct for the same reason—that they are acceptable in the light of current political practice. George V fully realised this. In the election of December 1923, none of the three parties was returned with a clear majority and the King noted that "there are really no precedents for the present situation. I must use my own judgment as each case arises." [14] Thus a valid precedent and good judgment in a new situation both rest on an understanding of the facts of the case followed by the line of action which is best calculated to further the underlying principles of the current British political system.

These principles again are not formally declared but are the basic premises which the vast majority of those actively concerned with the government of Britain accept at any one time. By a process of observing and analysing the conduct of government and politics, these guiding themes can be deduced, though for most practising politicians they are known more by intuition. Whether implicitly understood or consciously set out, they become the principles underlying the formulation of new precedents. The essentially pragmatic nature of the British Constitution is that development

[13] Reginald, Viscount Esher, *The Influence of King Edward*, p. 67.
[14] Sir Harold Nicolson, *op. cit.*, p. 383.

comes not from departures of theory but from a gradual change in political feeling and practice which becomes accepted and is then registered in conventions (or in statutes like the Reform Acts or the Parliament Act of 1911) which in turn confirm and perhaps advance the original development.

In the contemporary constitution it is generally accepted that the prevailing political temper of the electorate, as it is revealed in our electoral system, should be given the fullest means of expression. It is necessary to phrase the principle in this way, as the simple statement that democracy must be maintained might be misleading. For example, in 1951 the Conservative Party had a narrow majority in the House of Commons returned on a total poll which was just a little smaller than the number of votes cast for Labour candidates. Yet there was no doubt that confidence in the 1950–51 Labour Government had declined and that this was further revealed by the results of the election, and few quibbled with the consequent installation of the Conservative Government. The idea that our electoral system should be altered so that M.P.s might be returned in the same proportion as the total of votes cast for the various parties has been canvassed as being more democratic, but on the whole rejected because the country prefers to adhere to our present method of registering electoral feeling.

Another guiding principle is that once the electorate has pronounced its verdict, the government that is formed should have every opportunity of carrying out its policy. The desirability of a strong government clearly responsible for all decisions has a deep hold in British politics. In most cases, harmony between this principle and the first one is easily achieved. The convention which guides the King in his selection of a Prime Minister is that he should seek to establish the strongest government possible in the circumstances. Normally this coincides perfectly with the duty of furthering the decisions of the electorate, as the strongest government is that which has won a majority of seats in the House of Commons. If three parties are returned, as in 1924 and 1929, the position is not so clear. However, in both cases the original question for the electorate was whether it wished to confirm the existing government in power and in each case the answer was " No." In 1924 disapproval of the Conservatives was revealed in practical terms by the Liberal M.P.s supporting a Labour motion of no confidence, and in 1929 by making it evident that they would rather support a Labour Government. Thus the King's decision to send for Ramsay MacDonald in each case both produced the only government possible in view of the political circumstances and reflected the leftward tendency of the electorate. There has been some criticism of the King's action in 1931 when he urged Mac-Donald to form a National Government. Most of the authorities have defended George V on the grounds that he sought and obtained the strongest government and that the overwhelming support of public opinion was recorded almost at once in the general election of October 1931. The criticism is examined in some detail in Chapter 16, but it suffices here to say that had the royal action been obviously contrary to either of these principles, it would have been much more open to attack. If after George V had urged MacDonald, Samuel and Baldwin to form a National Government, the other party leaders had been as decisively repudiated by their followers as was MacDonald, the notion of a National Government would have collapsed at once, or, if having been formed, the electors had declared in favour of a party—that is a Labour—government, then the whole proceedings of the previous August would have been exposed to grave criticism.

On certain issues, harmony between these two principles has depended on the explicit restriction of the will of the electorate to its manifestations in elections and to the general freedom to criticise the actions of the government in office. For example, asking parliamentary questions is one of the best-known methods of raising an issue and focusing criticism, but it rests solely on past practice regulated by the standing orders of the House of Commons. If the government so desires it can refuse to answer questions on the very vague ground that disclosure would be contrary to the public interest. In December 1957, the Prime Minister and the Foreign Secretary were due to attend a NATO Conference in Paris at which major defence matters including the establishment and siting of nuclear missiles in Europe were to be settled. There was plenty of time for the government both to inform the public of the issues at stake and to get some reaction from the electorate, yet it refused to contemplate any discussion in Parliament before the Conference had met and the decisions been taken. In this case, as over the refusal to answer questions, there is no suggestion that the government behaved unconstitutionally—it is expected to act as it sees fit and then to be judged on its general record.

In 1911 some Conservative leaders suggested a machinery for putting certain kinds of measures to a referendum so that major changes would not be made without the express approval of the electorate. There have also been suggestions that parties, in appealing to the electorate, are asking for a mandate to carry out the proposals contained in their election programmes and that they should not go beyond the specified programme when in office as they have no mandate for further actions. Neither of these suggestions has met with general approval as they concede powers to the electorate which are inconsistent with the principle that a government is free to run the country and to be judged on the merits of its total performance. Even when party spokesmen have taken specific stands during an election campaign (as in 1935 the Conservatives pledged support for the League of Nations or in 1951 when there were declarations that the food subsidies would not be cut) and have then altered their attitude after winning power, the suggestion that this was unconstitutional has carried no weight. The changes may have been necessary due to new circumstances or arguments which were only appreciated after office was attained but, whatever the explanation, the only answer is political criticism and the only retribution a change of mind by the electorate at the next election.

Most of the other constitutional conventions of today are derived from the working of these two basic principles in the environment of British institutions. The convention of collective responsibility has a mixed historical origin but its modern force derives from the insistence that it is essential for a strong government to show a united front in face of criticism. That this is its source is proved by the evidence that the limitations of the convention are determined on these very grounds. A minister in disagreement, even on such issues of conscience as the merits of capital punishment, may have to bow to the need for a single expression from the government. On the other hand, a minister may be pursuing what he has strong grounds for regarding as Cabinet policy, but if it rouses a great outcry he may not benefit from the doctrine of collective responsibility and may be dropped with the implication that the policy was his rather than that of the government. In December 1935, the Cabinet, having at first accepted Sir Samuel Hoare's agreement with Laval, then decided to repudiate it, and with it Sir Samuel Hoare, in the face of public criticism.[15]

These principles also explain the convention governing the Crown's right to refuse a Prime Minister's request for a dissolution. This request will never be refused if the Prime Minister can claim that an election will reveal a definite change of temper among the electorate or if he can show that the government is likely to be strengthened. The one case where the Crown could refuse is when an election would neither change party representation in the Commons to any appreciable extent nor aid the government. Let it be assumed that there are three parties well represented in the House so that a combination of any two of the parties would have an absolute majority, and that party A has formed a government relying on the support of party B in the division lobbies and opposed by party C. Then, if the government's stock was declining so that a general election would afford no chance of its winning an absolute majority, and yet if neither parties B nor C were eager to go to the country but were prepared to combine in support of an agreed Cabinet, the King would be entitled to refuse a dissolution and to commission a new Prime Minister. This situation almost arose on the defeat of the first Labour Government in 1924. Then George V only granted Mr. Ramsay MacDonald's request with " the utmost reluctance." The Labour Party had a reasonable claim to test the electorate's reaction to its first period of rule, and yet George V agreed only after he had ascertained that both the leaders of the Conservative and Liberal parties were unable or unwilling to combine in support of an administration formed out of the existing House.[16]

There are two further points on the question of conventions and the precedents which embody them. In the first place, as valid precedents exemplify the principles on which the political system is based, precedents can seldom be usefully drawn from

---

[15] Viscount Templewood, *Nine Troubled Years*, pp. 184–185.
[16] Sir Harold Nicolson, *op. cit.*, p. 400, and the note on the same page. Sir Harold Nicolson has confirmed that in the statement that George V had " ascertained from the leaders of the Conservative and Labour parties," etc., " Labour " is a misprint for " Liberal."

a period before these guiding themes were generally accepted. Sir W. Ivor Jennings makes this point and selects 1841 as the crucial date.[17] His reason is that in 1841, for the first time, the opposition won a general election and the Crown accepted the decision at the polls. But though this did mean that the result of an election had become a major factor in politics, the direct dependence of the Cabinet on the actions of the electorate was not established. With a wide variety among the types of constituency, with a number of political groups in the Commons especially between 1846 and 1859, and with no modern party organisations, the elections were concerned more with returning a specific M.P. than with which group of party leaders should be placed in power. The principle was not that the political temper of the electorate should have the prevailing influence on the choice of the Prime Minister but that it should be permitted to regulate the composition of the House of Commons. In such a situation, the process of selecting a Prime Minister owed something to popular acclaim, a great deal to the standing of the various leaders in the Commons and to the relations between these politicians while the Crown could still try, on occasion, to exercise some influence. A political system based on these principles is in some significant respects different from our own. The direct connection between the action of the electorate and the creation of a given Cabinet is broken by the intermediary of the House of Commons. In 1857, a Parliament elected on the single issue of " . . . were you, or were you not . . . for Palmerston," [18] began by supporting its hero but then ejected him and maintained a Tory Government for a further year. With governments dependent more upon relations between the various groups and personalities in the Commons than upon clear-cut decisions of the electorate, there was more scope for the Crown to act as an intermediary and to feel that its advice and support was a real factor in the life of a Cabinet. The notion that the character of the government should depend as directly as possible on the pronouncements of the electorate only arises after the electorate

[17] Sir W. Ivor Jennings, *op. cit.*, p. 9. In his third edition Sir W. Ivor Jennings modifies his earlier statement that " in that year (1841) the accession of the Tory Government marked the acceptance of the principles of democratic government" but he still considers that "most precedents since 1841 are relevant."

[18] Lord Shaftesbury quoted by E. L. Woodward, *The Age of Reform*, p. 162.

was almost doubled by the 1867 Reform Act. This measure created a more uniform constituency, and with a mass electorate, party organisations of a modern type were developed and the independence of M.P.s considerably reduced. It was "ever since Lord Beaconsfield's most unfortunate Act "[19] that Queen Victoria felt that her political freedom had gone and that the policy of the Liberals was reducing her to a machine for registering the results of general elections. So it would seem to be more accurate to say that, though many modern constitutional practices came into use after 1832, the principles underlying contemporary politics only really began to operate after the Reform Act of 1867 had had its effect and, for this reason, the historical chapters have a division at the General Election of 1868 and the analysis in Part 4 does not draw on precedents from the rather confused politics of the eighteen forties and fifties.

The second point is that conventions have differing degrees of force. Some are fundamental in that to break them would over-turn the basic principles of the constitution. Dicey defined a convention as a rule which, if broken, would lead to the violation of laws. This only applies in the case of the central conventions such as the obligation on a Cabinet to resign if it loses the confidence of Parliament. It is true that if this maxim was flouted, the Cabinet would soon be forced either to submit or to break the law by collecting unauthorised taxes and so on. But the force of the convention arises not from this legal sanction but from the fact that to make any such suggestion would be to violate the whole spirit and basis of the constitution. If a proposal of this kind was ever seriously put forward, it would be evidence that the conditions of politics in Britain were undergoing revolutionary changes.

Some conventions are of considerable force but might conceivably have altered by the year 2000, without totally changing the nature of the constitution. As the Civil Service grows in size and importance, it is possible that ministers might be held responsible to Parliament for only certain classes of action, and that civil servants might be called up to answer questions before standing committees of the House.

---

[19] Campbell-Bannerman's "Notes of a Conversation with the Queen," J. A. Spender, *Life of Campbell-Bannerman*, i. p. 171.

There are other conventions which are of less importance and merely indicate that certain practices are inadvisable or inappropriate. For example, it has often been said that the King's decision to ask Baldwin and not Lord Curzon to form a government in 1923 established the convention that a peer could no longer be Prime Minister. With the decision of the electorate being of such importance in forming a government, it was held that the Prime Minister should be a member of the elected House, thus being available there to answer the Labour opposition. Whatever the specific reasons for George V selecting Baldwin, these were taken to be his views and the precedent was accepted by the authorities on the constitution.[20] Yet Neville Chamberlain was prepared at one stage to advise the King that Lord Halifax was the most suitable person to lead a national government in May 1940.[21] Lord Halifax himself took the view that membership of the House of Lords made it impossible for him to be Prime Minister,[22] and this was clearly the attitude of promising young members of the Commons who were promoted to the Lords by the death of elder brothers before it was made possible to renounce a title under the Peerage Act of 1963. Thus even before this Act made certain that no future Prime Minister will sit in the Lords, the possibility was highly unlikely. (The reasons by 1963 may have been a little different from those quoted in 1940 which, like most of the anti-Curzon arguments in 1923, stressed the need for a Prime Minister to be available to face the opposition in the Commons. Though this was still important, it was possible for the Earl of Home to be Foreign Secretary from 1960 [23] and it may not have been so necessary for a Prime Minister to be present in person in the Commons, an additional powerful objection being the derision political opponents could heap on a party which could only find a suitable leader among its hereditary element.)

[20] Sir Harold Nicolson, *op. cit.*, pp. 376 and 377, and R. Blake, *The Unknown Prime Minister, The Life and Times of Andrew Bonar Law, 1858–1923*, pp. 513–527.
[21] Winston Churchill, *The Second World War*, Vol. I, pp. 523–524; Keith Feiling, *Life of Neville Chamberlain*, p. 441.
[22] Lord Halifax, *Fullness of Days*, pp. 219–220, and the Earl of Birkenhead, *Halifax*, pp. 453–455.
[23] As recently as 1955 Sir Anthony Eden had said: " I felt it impossible to ask a member of the House of Lords to be Foreign Secretary." Sir Anthony Eden, *Full Circle*, p. 274.

In other cases conventions may simply become out of date as the problems of politics change. In 1910 it was assumed that there were precedents establishing the right of the Prime Minister to ask the King to create sufficient peers to pass a measure that was clearly demanded by the electorate. But now that the Parliament Acts of 1911 and 1949 have laid down a procedure for circumventing the opposition of the House of Lords in a little over a year, the monarch might well be entitled to say that the precedents for the creation of peers no longer applied.

It has often been said that the problem of obtaining precise information about the working of the Cabinet and the real motives of the politicians is a grave handicap in any attempt to write about the British Constitution. The Official Secrets Acts prohibit the publication of Cabinet memoranda and the disclosure of any information which public servants or politicians have come by in the course of their duties. The meetings of the parliamentary parties, of the party executives and the relations of ministers and civil servants are all conducted in private, and only the proceedings of the first are sometimes leaked to the press and then often in a somewhat garbled fashion.

Nevertheless, this difficulty is not so serious if it is simply a matter of describing constitutional conventions. These conventions have a sound basis, even in the least important cases, in the system of politics and while new information may invalidate a precedent, it cannot create a convention that runs counter to current practice. If a single precedent creates a convention, it is because it is a very apt response to what has been a fairly evident constitutional tendency. To use the example given already, it was because the political status of the House of Lords was rapidly declining that the King's decision not to send for Lord Curzon in 1923 was taken to institute a convention. Had it later been proved from the archives that George V's selection of Baldwin was due, say, to a preference in times of doubt for men who smoked pipes, this would not create the convention that only pipe-smokers could become Premiers. On the other hand, even if the Curzon incident had not arisen, the fact that no peer had been Prime Minister since 1902 would leave the position much the same as it was before the 1963 Peerage Act:—extremely unlikely.

Thus the conventions of the British Constitution both guide and can be deduced from the form and practice of current politics. All that is required is careful observation together with a certain feeling for the system, and while inside information about the precise relations and activities of the politicians and civil servants would be most helpful, it is not indispensable for this purpose.

THE CABINET AT WORK—FOUR EXAMPLES

But even when an exhaustive description of the laws and conventions governing the Cabinet has been completed, all that has been explained is the outward relations of the Cabinet and its members with the other parts of the governmental machine. This type of formal treatment does not give a full answer to the essential questions of how much power the Cabinet wields, nor does it explain the manner in which it is exercised. Some of the conventions such as those of collective responsibility, Cabinet secrecy and Civil Service anonymity are intended precisely to prevent any such examination of the Cabinet.

Yet it is important to try to describe the content as well as the form of Cabinet government. Very occasionally the veil of secrecy is temporarily pulled aside as in the Parker Tribunal of inquiry into the allegations of a leak of information about the rise in the Bank Rate in 1957, or in the unusually frank series of letters exchanged on the resignation of Mr. Peter Thorneycroft as Chancellor of the Exchequer in January 1958, in the extended press conference called Prospect II given by the Air Ministry on May 6, 1958,[24] or in the writings and speeches of Mr. Christopher Mayhew after his resignation as Minister for the Navy in February 1966, especially *Britain's role Tomorrow*, pp. 131–153. For a few fleeting moments the public hears a fascinating snatch of the arguments that are actually going on in the government and gets a glimpse of how decisions are taken and it is sometimes possible to infer a little about the distribution of power. Some more information can be found in a few of the many biographies and autobiographies that are published. Thus a picture of the actual operation of Cabinet government can be built up if only in a

[24] See Professor Ely Devons, "Government on the Inner Circle," *The Listener*, March 27, 1958, for an interesting discussion of "government behind closed doors."

sketchy manner from a combination of newspaper reports, memoirs, government publications and interviews with politicians and civil servants.

The value of such an exercise and its capacity to put the institutions into proper perspective, to focus attention on the important points in the machinery and to underline the developing tendencies in the constitution is perhaps best brought out by giving four examples of Cabinet government at work. The choice is guided by the fact that it is easier to assemble information about legislative proposals than about the work of co-ordinating administration, by the fortunate existence of a wealth of evidence in the proceedings of the Parker Tribunal and by the recent studies of the Suez War.

The nationalisation of the iron and steel industry in 1951 is worth examining as an example of a major item of political policy involving a detailed measure and one which excited the most acute controversy. The first mention of such a proposal was when the 1933 Conference of the Labour Party carried a report on *Socialism and the Condition of the People* which included " ownership or control " of steel and other major industries and asked the executive to submit " a concise declaration of the measures which a Labour Government will endeavour to place on the Statute Book." As a result the 1934 Conference approved a series of proposals including one to set up an Iron and Steel Corporation " to take over all undertakings manufacturing iron and steel products " with Sectional Boards for the various branches of the industry.[25] This then became part of the 1935 election platform of the party though it was not emphasised and was omitted from both *Labour's Immediate Programme* and Mr. Attlee's short list of measures published in *The Labour Party in Perspective.* The proposal was reaffirmed by the Labour Party Conference in 1944, though in April 1945 Mr. Herbert Morrison and Arthur Greenwood wanted to omit it from the Policy Declaration for the forthcoming election.[26] After some dispute it was included as the last specific industry to be named for nationalisation in the Declaration called *Let Us Face the Future.* Meanwhile, the industry itself had suffered an acute decline between 1929 and 1931

---

[25] G. D. H. Cole, *A History of the Labour Party since 1914*, pp. 287 and 296.
[26] Hugh Dalton, *The Fateful Years*, pp. 432 and 433.

and had accepted a 33⅓ per cent. tariff in 1932 and reorganisation under the British Iron and Steel Federation after 1934. In 1955 it was revealed that in 1947 the Labour Cabinet had reached an agreement with the B.I.S.F. that nationalisation should take the form of " practical supervision of the industry " but that the ownership of the individual firms should not be disturbed.[27] There was a division of opinion over this in the Cabinet, the objecting minority including Ernest Bevin (because of old trade union recollections of the industry), Aneurin Bevan and Mr. Strauss, who was not in the Cabinet but was deeply concerned as Minister of Supply. The next stage is not quite clear, but the main features of the situation were " leaked " and it became generally known in the Parliamentary Labour Party that the Cabinet had decided on a modified scheme of public control. This information produced the expected agitation and sufficient pressure was built up to change the balance in the Cabinet. It was now agreed that nationalisation would have to involve actual public ownership of the shares though the various firms would retain their trade names and individual identities. The B.I.S.F. was incensed at this change of front, refused to co-operate any further, and boycotted the Iron and Steel Board when it was eventually set up. The rupture made it evident that the Lords would resist the measure and as there was not enough time both to prepare the new Bill and carry it through the procedure of the 1911 Parliament Act, the period of delay was shortened by the 1949 Parliament Act, a display of force which persuaded the Lords to let the Iron and Steel Bill pass though they gained the concession that no action could be taken till after the next general election.

Reviewing the factors influencing this decision perhaps the first point is that if the Labour Party had not written this item into its programme for twelve years before 1945, it would not have become a kind of touchstone of socialist intentions capable of rousing great feeling inside the party. Such a proposal could never have been made by the senior civil servants or by a working

[27] *The Manchester Guardian*, March 30, 1955. This account is built upon Sir Ellis Hunter's speech reported in *The Manchester Guardian* supplemented by the accounts of lobby correspondents, the recollections of private members of the Labour Party, the allusions in Herbert Morrison's *Autobiography*, p. 296, and the full account of the passage of the Bill in *Parliament at Work*, by A. H. Hanson and H. V. Wiseman, pp. 121–180.

party or committee of inquiry—it had to become a matter of political faith. On the purely practical level, the economic experiences of the nineteen thirties and the war, combined with the exigencies of post-war reconstruction and the export drive, all made some kind of government control inevitable and acceptable. The Labour Cabinet was naturally concerned to keep on good relations with the men who were playing a large part in Britain's industrial recovery and there was clearly heavy pressure to accept the terms they offered. It is interesting that the Conservative Government's Denationalisation Act in 1953 returned the industry to the degree of " practical supervision " originally negotiated with the Labour Cabinet in 1947. Yet the political pressure on the Labour Cabinet came from the most dangerous source, that is from within the party itself and it was not confined to the normally weak left wing. Some of the most senior ministers carrying great authority with the trade unions were behind it. Pressure from the Opposition was to be expected and was not a factor of importance. In situations such as this, the Cabinet is still the ultimate authority but its freedom of manoeuvre is narrow and the solution is worked out on what is almost a basis of joint consultation with the other interests involved.

The second example is the conduct of British foreign policy in the months leading up to the attempt to seize the Suez Canal in October 1956.[28] Hostility between the British Government and Colonel Nasser's government in Egypt had been increasing. Sir Anthony Eden (now Lord Avon) suspected Nasser of encouraging King Husain of Jordan to dismiss General Glubb, the British Commander of the Arab Legion. Four months later the U.S. and British Governments refused a loan for the construction of the Aswan High Dam in Egypt and Colonel Nasser, on July 26, 1956, nationalised the Suez Canal.

Sir Anthony Eden regarded the canal as essential to Britain's interests and was convinced that it was intolerable to allow Colonel Nasser " to have his thumb on our windpipe." [29] The Chiefs of Staff were instructed to prepare a plan to occupy the

---

[28] This account is based on Sir Anthony Eden, *Full Circle*; Randolph Churchill, *The Rise and Fall of Sir Anthony Eden*; Hugh Thomas, *The Suez Affair*; Anthony Nutting, *No End of a Lesson, The Story of Suez* and interviews with ex-ministers.

[29] Sir Anthony Eden, *op. cit.*, p. 426.

canal in conjunction with a French force and President Eisenhower was informed of these plans. On July 27 a Cabinet committee of seven had been formed " to keep in contact with the situation on behalf of the Cabinet." (The members besides the Prime Minister were Mr. Selwyn Lloyd, Mr. (now Lord) Butler, Mr. (now Lord) Head, Mr. Macmillan, Lord Salisbury and Mr. Duncan Sandys.) The detailed negotiations of the next few months lay with this group, though on key matters of arrangements with the French and through them with the Israelis, the Prime Minister acted with the Foreign Secretary or on his own.

In August the Government called a conference of twenty-two maritime Powers to concert diplomatic pressure. It proposed international control of the canal under a new convention but the United States would not support pressure in the form of a refusal to pay canal dues to Egypt and was by this time opposed to the use of force. The proposal (made by eighteen of the twenty-two nations) was refused by the Egyptians, and while the case was taken to the United Nations and the American idea of a " Users' Club " was explored, British and French military preparations continued. These were handled by the Prime Minister and the Foreign Secretary, the only meeting of the full Cabinet being on September 11, when it was agreed that the Canal Users' scheme should be given a trial. This foundered on the issue of to whom dues should be paid and the Russians vetoed an appeal to Egypt to negotiate on the basis of the eighteen Powers' proposals.

On October 14 the French acting Foreign Minister and the Deputy Chief of Staff came to Chequers, seeing only the Prime Minister and a Minister of State at the Foreign Office (Mr. Nutting). The plan of an Israeli attack in Sinai combined with an Anglo-French invasion in the canal area was explained. Nutting says that " I knew then that, no matter what contrary advice he might receive over the next forty-eight hours, the Prime Minister had already made up his mind to go along with the French plan." [30] Mr. Selwyn Lloyd returned from the United Nations and went to Paris with the Prime Minister to discuss the details. The broad outlines were explained to the Cabinet on October 18, after which meeting Sir Walter Monckton moved from Defence to " a back seat " as Paymaster-General. The full

[30] Anthony Nutting, *op. cit.*, p. 94.

Cabinet met again on October 24 to make the final decisions but these were not settled till a further meeting on October 25. Then it was agreed under what circumstance Britain would make war and an ultimatum was drawn up. It is doubtful whether the Cabinet knew that the date for the Israeli invasion was already fixed for October 29. On the day after the attack M. Mollet and M. Pineau came to London and the Cabinet met to authorise the dispatch of the ultimatum to Egypt to withdraw ten miles on each side of the Suez Canal. When this expired, the Cabinet authorised the opening of the air bombardment.

The interest of this episode is that it illustrates how, in time of pressure of events and when international negotiations are involved, the actual planning of action and taking of decisions is removed from the Cabinet to a committee of those most concerned and then, at special moments of stress or delicate negotiation, to one or two ministers or even to the Prime Minister alone. Yet Sir Anthony reported back at intervals to the Cabinet, they were carried along and a majority supported even if they were not fully aware of all the details of the policy. In the last resort, dissenting ministers—of whom there were at least three—could only agree, take " a back seat " or resign. At the meeting held to authorise the ultimatum a minister complained of the short time they had to make up their minds. " A lot of my present colleagues never served in a War Cabinet " was Sir Anthony Eden's comment. To this, Mr. Macleod who, with D. Heathcote Amory, had most doubts replied, " We didn't know we were at war." [31]

The third example is the decision to raise the Bank Rate from 5 per cent. to 7 per cent. announced on September 19, 1957.[32] During the summer of that year an inflationary situation was developing with some speculative selling of sterling. In the City of London there was alarm (perhaps more acute than Britain's trading position actually merited) and general talk of the need

[31] H. Thomas, *op. cit.*, p. 125, and Randolph Churchill, *op. cit.*, pp. 277–278.
[32] This description and analysis is based on the *Proceedings of the Tribunal appointed to Inquire into allegations that information about the raising of Bank Rate was improperly disclosed*, H.M.S.O. (Home Office) 1958, very helpful articles by E. Devons and H. J. Hanham in *The Manchester School*, January 1959, " The Bank of England from Within " in *The Banker*, March 1958 and " The Bank Rate Decision of September 19, 1957 " by Richard A. Chapman in *Public Administration*, Summer 1965 (Vol. 43).

for firm deflationary action on the part of the government. On August 7, 1957, Mr. Thorneycroft, the Chancellor of the Exchequer, asked the Treasury to consider methods of checking inflation. On August 12 a Treasury official informed the Governor of the Bank of England of " the way the Chancellor's mind was working." Discussions continued and on August 22, the Governor and Deputy Governor told the Treasury that they regarded a rise in the Bank Rate as desirable. Meanwhile other measures for a similar purpose were being prepared and concerted with the appropriate bodies. The Chancellor, Deputy-Governor (the Governor was on holiday) and a Treasury official agreed on September 13 that a rise in the Bank Rate should coincide with other deflationary measures, all of which would have to be announced before the Chancellor left for a meeting of the International Monetary Fund on September 20. The Governor and Deputy Governor of the Bank considered the matter on the 14th and suggested a rise to 7 per cent. to the Chancellor and Treasury on the 15th. Asked for a firm proposition by the Bank, the Governor consulted six of the twelve part-time directors next day and made his proposal definite.

Further discussions took place with the Treasury about the 7 per cent. rate on the 17th and on that date, when the Cabinet considered the terms on which the other economic measures (which it had already considered and approved) were to be announced, they were informed both about the Bank Rate and " that, by tradition, variation . . . is not a matter for decision by the Cabinet." It was agreed to leave this point to the Prime Minister, the Chancellor and the Governor. After various meetings Mr. Macmillan was reported as saying " he would not make up his mind whether the government should agree to the Bank Rate being raised and, if so, to what figure, until the following morning." Then, on the 18th, the Prime Minister saw the Chancellor again and they agreed on an increase to 7 per cent. The Governor proposed this figure to the committee of the Treasury and it was recommended to the Court of Directors of the Bank, who met on the morning of the 19th, gave their approval and made the announcement. On the same morning " that information was given to the Cabinet." " Did the Cabinet express approval of that conclusion? " " They took note of it."

Several interesting points emerge. The tradition that changes in the Bank Rate should not be discussed by the government arose in the last century when, both in theory and in law, the affairs of the Bank and monetary policy in general were not a normal part of the government's business. The theory is now altered and the Bank of England Act 1946 laid down that while the Court of Directors is responsible for fixing the Bank Rate, this is subject to any directions given by the Treasury. Thus there is the very curious situation that the traditional prohibition is broken through at two levels—the Treasury's power of direction means that it is consulted by the Court and its views carry the greatest weight while, on a higher level, the final decision rests with the Prime Minister and the Chancellor—but the prohibition is maintained against the Cabinet. The Cabinet, which contained ministers (Labour, Board of Trade, Home Secretary, Health, Education, etc.) whose departmental work would be profoundly affected by a sharp rise in the Bank Rate, was not encouraged to consider the merits of the proposal but was permitted to pass the matter on for decision to the Prime Minister, the Chancellor and the Governor of the Bank.

It is hard to determine the various degrees of influence exercised by the parties to the decision. The Chancellor obviously decided to take action against inflation. He was aided by the general temper of financial circles, the government and the City being fairly close in both their diagnosis and their remedies. The inclusion among the remedies of a rise in the Bank Rate was clearly regarded as likely, but it was first suggested by the Governor and he and his Deputy—fortified in the last stages by six of the directors—seem to have put forward the idea of an unusually sharp rise. Their advice convinced, and final authorisation was given by, the Prime Minister and the Chancellor. The Cabinet, under the guidance of the Chancellor, had discussed and approved of a series of deflationary measures. Had they opposed these measures, the decision about the Bank Rate would not have been made by itself. In the event of disagreement, the whole direction of economic policy would have been reconsidered by the Cabinet, as it was, four months later, when Mr. Thorneycroft wished to carry deflation a stage further, found no support and had to resign.

The final example is taken at random from among the minor items of routine legislation passed in 1958—the Land Drainage (Scotland) Act. It appears that with the desire to extend cultivation during the war, one problem was to prevent flooding and improve land drainage. An Act of 1941 provided for Treasury assistance but the Department of Agriculture for Scotland found that it was largely unworkable, as the Treasury grant was small and the consent of all proprietors had to be obtained before any scheme could be started. In 1947, the Secretary of State for Scotland appointed what became known as the Duncan Committee to investigate the problem. It consulted the Convention of Royal Burghs, the Association of County Councils, the National Farmers' Union of Scotland, the Scottish Land and Property Federation, and the Royal Institution of Chartered Surveyors. The Report stated that probably 200,000 acres were inadequately drained and recommended that a land drainage authority should be set up, covering urban as well as rural areas, with powers to proceed if two-thirds of the proprietors agreed, and with a Treasury grant.

The department proceeded to frame a Bill [33] in consultation with the interested bodies and the Treasury. The problem was that draining agricultural land into a fast river which already had a tendency to flood would only be satisfactory if bridges were widened and obstructions removed perhaps even in the next county. These operations would involve a considerable outlay for some county councils and they were only prepared to work such a measure if the cost was totally refunded by the Treasury. The Treasury refused this but the Scottish Department of Agriculture was eager to carry a comprehensive measure and pushed the proposal up to the Home Affairs Committee of the Cabinet. There the Chancellor of the Exchequer resisted the Secretary of State for Scotland's demands. The Bill was sent back to be re-negotiated by the department and various proposals for levying some general or special rate were considered, but none was acceptable to the Association of County Councils. In these circumstances the Bill was limited to merely strengthening

---

[33] The account of this measure is reconstructed from the *Report of the Duncan Committee* (Cmd. 7948), a careful reading of the government speeches on the " Consideration of Principle " stage in the Scottish Grand Committee (December 3, 1957) and the comments of the major pressure groups.

existing powers for the drainage of agricultural land and consultations were confined to the National Farmers' Union of Scotland
and the Scottish Landowners' Federation. The new measure gave
added powers to carry through schemes up to a cost of £20 an
acre. The Secretary of State said that there might be some argument as to whether this was the appropriate limit but "we have
adopted this figure in agreement with the organisations concerned." [34] When the draft went up to the Home Affairs Committee of the Cabinet, it was not opposed by the Treasury as,
like the existing Acts, it only called for grants of up to 50 per cent.
of the cost of approved schemes, and general approval was given.
Whether the Bill then went on in the form of an agreed
recommendation to the full Cabinet cannot be deduced, but it is
extremely unlikely. Most measures of this minor type only go to
the Cabinet if the members of the Home Affairs Committee
cannot resolve their differences. The final stage would be presentation to the Future Legislation Committee for a place in the
parliamentary time-table. The Bill was introduced in the House
of Commons in 1957 and criticised severely by the Opposition
for falling so far short of the Duncan Committee's proposals.
The public took virtually no interest in the Bill, the government
expressed its regrets that the opposition's appeal for a wider
measure could not be granted, set its face against any major
amendments and pointed out that the Scottish Grand Committee
would be wise to welcome even such a limited measure as it
would be fifteen years before this matter could be taken up again.

Here is an instance of the most common form of legislation,
that initiated by a department faced with a practical problem of
administration. To ventilate its proposals and give them weight,
a committee of inquiry was appointed. To obtain an agreed
measure it was necessary to get the acquiescence of those
affected—the local authorities, the farmers, the landowners, and
to settle the question of who was to provide the finance. Agreement was possible on one level if the Treasury met the full cost
and on another level if it would meet only half the cost—and its
insistence led to the second solution. The Cabinet does not need
to consider such matters. It has only to provide machinery to

[34] *Parliamentary Debates, Report of the Scottish Standing Committee,* December
3, 1957, p. 7.

ensure that those ministers concerned (Secretary of State for Scotland, Chancellor of the Exchequer, Home Secretary, Minister of Agriculture, etc.) are satisfied that the fundamental interests of their departments are reconciled and to permit the Cabinet to call up the matter if it produces an unexpected political storm or if the ministers will not accept the verdict of the Cabinet Committee.

It may be thought that these examples of the Cabinet at work have dwelt more than was necessary on the steel industry, on the details of the Suez conflict, on the Bank Rate and on land drainage. But the object of the illustrations was to correct the impression which books on the constitution have difficulty in avoiding, of a government machine working more or less in a vacuum. Every time the Cabinet or one of its committees moves from one item on its agenda to the next it is engaging gears with a complex machine that already has a momentum of its own. Each proposal has been pushed by some, resisted by others, has to be operated in practice, paid for and has been the subject of many meetings and memoranda long before it ever came near the Cabinet. Thus these illustrations help to show the increasing tendency of the Civil Service to consult outside bodies, the greater complexity of administration and the declining role of parliamentary initiative and criticism (though not of political pressure from within parties). They also reveal that many important decisions are taken above, below and alongside as well as in the Cabinet— all points which will be discussed in greater detail in the last two Parts of this book.

Part Two

The Origins of the Cabinet

CHAPTER 2

THE CABINET COUNCIL, 1660–1832

THE ORIGINS OF THE CABINET

A MAIN feature of the Cabinet system as it has developed in Britain is that the King's ministers number among them those members of the legislature who are most likely to command its confidence. So any discussion of the antecedents of such a Cabinet must centre round groups of men whose task was, in part at any rate, to help to create a harmony between the purposes of the executive and the decisions of the legislature. The Kings of England have always had advisers (sometimes called "favourites" by their opponents) and since the formative period of Parliament, there have always been councillors among its members who have conveyed the wishes of the sovereign to the two Houses.

This problem of maintaining harmony between Parliament and the Crown only became serious in the early seventeenth century when the House of Commons had acquired some legal rights and a degree of self-confidence and did not always trust royal policy. Attempts by the privy councillors to guide the debates and decisions were rejected and lack of confidence increased till a total breakdown was followed by civil war. When Charles II was restored to the throne in 1660, it was natural for the older statesmen to assume that, the ill-faith having presumably gone, the former relationship would be resumed.

Charles II's principal adviser in 1660 was Edward Hyde, who had definite opinions as to how the administration should be conducted. The King was to govern with the advice of a Privy Council including all the great officers of state, thus keeping a constant contact with all the departments.[1] If any finance or legislation was required to implement the decisions of the King and council, a request would be laid before Parliament and a lead given by one or two of the principal councillors.

At once this scheme ran into difficulties. The Privy Council

---

[1] E. I. Carlyle, "Clarendon and the Privy Council," *E.H.R.* (1912) p. 253.

began with twenty-seven members of mixed political leanings, and within three years the numbers had risen to between thirty and forty.[2] As Charles himself said in 1679, " the great Number of this Councill . . . made it unfit for the Secrecy & dispatch that are necessary in many great Affaires." [3] This must have been evident almost at once as in June 1660 " the Treasurer, the Marquis of Ormond, the General (Albemarle) with the two Secretaries of State (Nicholas and Morrice) were of that secret committee with the Chancellor which, under the notion of foreign affairs, was appointed by the King to consult all his affairs before they came to public debate." [4] Here then was a body whose numbers could be varied at pleasure and whose informal nature and powerful membership formed a latent threat to any notion of the supremacy of the Privy Council.

The second difficulty arose over relations with Parliament. Clarendon and the Treasurer, Southampton, " had every day conference with some select persons of the House of Commons, who had always served the King . . . in what method to proceed in disposing the House, sometimes . . . to assign parts to other men." [5] The weakness of running Parliament through such a steering committee was that the " select persons " might not have the ear of the members. By 1662–63 Clarendon had to admit to " these counsells " men who had more influence over the Commons (such as Bennet and Coventry) but once in this position, they were able to influence policy by declaring that unless certain steps were taken they could not guarantee adequate support in the House. By 1665 Coventry was admitted first to the Privy Council and then to the Foreign Committee, despite Clarendon's protestations that he held no great office of state and was therefore unsuitable.[6]

A further objection came from Charles. All ministers were dependent on him but Clarendon's formal attitude, with its great emphasis on the senior office-bearers, created an atmosphere

[2] E. I. Carlyle, *art. cit.*, pp. 257–258.
[3] Quoted by H. W. V. Temperley, " Inner and Outer Cabinet and Privy Council, 1679–1783," *E.H.R.* (1912) p. 684 from the Privy Council Register, April 21, 1679.
[4] Quoted by W. R. Anson, " The Cabinet in the Seventeenth and Eighteenth Centuries," *E.H.R.* (1914) p. 58, from Clarendon, *Continuation of Life*, i, 370, though he wrongly gives the date as 1667.
[5] E. I. Carlyle, *art. cit.*, quotes this from Clarendon, § 395.
[6] E. I. Carlyle, *art. cit.*, p. 261.

that was not altogether congenial. Charles preferred informality and flexible methods and placed a premium on successful management because it meant less disturbance. As Clarendon's political blunders increased opposition and led the Commons to appropriate moneys to specific purposes and then to inquire if the money had been spent as directed, Charles decided in 1667 to abandon him and turn to the men who promised the government an easier passage in Parliament.

A survey of the government in the late 1660s reveals that the Privy Council was the central clearing house of the administration, while certain branches such as the Treasury and Admiralty were being organised on a more distinct basis under commissions or boards. The King decided all major matters of policy with the aid of a small group of advisers. Originally the group was the Foreign Committee of the Privy Council but this title tends to decline in favour of words like Cabinet, council or junto. The qualifications for membership of the inner circle were a willingness to serve the Crown and the capacity to be of service. In some cases the service had no connection with Parliament (Lauderdale's task was to govern Scotland) but there had to be some members who were capable of political management. Clarendon had tried to mobilise, if not create, a steady support for royal policies in Parliament and his failures led to the formation of a more effective court party by Arlington and Clifford. Although frowned on, organisation seemed to be essential and a solid following was built up by granting the claims of old royalists, by enlisting family influence, by dinners and the award of lord-lieutenancies and excise pensions.[7]

The members of the inner group of ministers were not equally important or equally trusted by the King but there was, by the mid-1660s, a clear distinction between those in this position and the other privy councillors.[8] The reason was that there were

[7] A. Browning, " Parties and Party Organisation in the Reign of Charles II," *Transactions of the Royal Historical Society*, 4th Series, Vol. XXX, pp. 21–36, *passim*.

[8] This distinction is evident in several references to the Cabinet Council in the mid-1660s in *Pepys Diaries* (iv. 285; v, 411) and in the *Continuation of the Life of Edward, Earl of Clarendon* (ii, 150, 178, 384), but perhaps the contrast is revealed most succinctly in a letter from Henry Ball to Sir Joseph Williamson, June 27, 1673, when he says " This day the Cabinett rose not till 2 afternoone, having satt above 4 houres, so that there was no councell." (In *Letters Addressed to Sir Joseph Williamson*, Camden Society, Vol. I, p. 72.)

certain offices whose holders had to be aware of and therefore
to some degree be consulted about the overt acts of the government. It was almost impossible to take any major action (as
distinct from making secret plans or conditional agreements)
without the Lord Chancellor, the Treasurer, the two Secretaries
of State, the Lord High Admiral, and one or two leading courtiers
being informed and, on the whole, acquiescing. It became possible for those in political life, at any time, to list the members of
the Foreign Committee or Cabinet Council and to report when
any changes took place. For example, all those writing about
political developments in June 1673 stress that " the people are
extremely pleased to see the Duke of Ormond called into the
Cabinett Councell againe." [9]

This development of a Cabinet consisting of the major office-
bearers together with the most trusted courtiers has been obscured
and confused in that Charles often pursued or hankered after a
policy within a policy, the former being made known only to a
few of the ministers. When the political circles or Parliament
began to have suspicions, these few were hailed as the real
ministers. The best known example concerns the five men whose
initials could be arranged to form the word and have therefore
been referred to as *the* Cabal of the reign. Yet the only sense in
which they were united was that all five, for varying reasons,
signed the public Treaty of Dover of 1670 and its renewal in
1672. Of them, only Clifford and Arlington knew of the Secret
Treaty of Dover, while the day-to-day actions of the government
were discussed in a Cabinet which also included the Duke of
York as Lord High Admiral, Sir Orlando Bridgman as
Lord Keeper, Prince Rupert and Sir John Trevor, the second
Secretary of State.[10]

The policy of dispensing with the laws against Roman Catholics
and of allying with France between 1670 and 1673 broke up the
parliamentary following organised by Clifford and Arlington and
produced a strong opposition. The problem for these critics was
how to use the existing powers of Parliament to control Charles.

[9] Letter from Robert Yard to Sir Joseph Williamson, *op. cit.*, i, 61. See also
letters from Robert Yard, Sir Robert Southwell, J. Rosse, William Bridgeman
and Thomas Ross on pp. 48, 56, 58, 59 and 77. In these references to the
same event, three say he has been called into " the Cabinett," one into " the
juncto " and one " the Committee of Forreigne Affaires."
[10] W. D. Christie, Introduction to *Letters to Williamson, op. cit.*, p. vi.

The most obvious methods were to limit his finances and appropriate them to specific purposes and secondly to assume that he always acted on advice and to control the advisers. In the latter case the rather clumsy weapon of impeachment could be employed, but if the King acted with the aid of secret councillors, who was to be accused? This anonymity led Parliament to dislike the practice of maintaining an inner circle of advisers and members pressed for a return to the sole guidance of the whole Privy Council. Probably a further motive was that such a large body of leading statesmen was bound to lean more in the direction of the Protestant policy desired by Parliament.

Criticism was turned aside between 1674 and 1677 by some concessions and by the financial and political skill of the Earl of Danby, who became the leading member of the ministry. The position he had built up was only undone by the frenzy of the Popish Plot and in March 1679 Danby was driven from office. Charles, in grave difficulties, had to make concessions and one of them concerned the question of the royal advisers. On April 20 1679, he dismissed his old Privy Council and said " he hath resolved to lay aside the use he may have hitherto made of any single ministry of private advices or Foreign Committees for the conduct of his affairs." [11] On the same day a new Privy Council of thirty-three members was formed, a majority of whom had been opponents of the Crown.[12] The object was political—to gain time—and from the first Charles never trusted this Council. " God's fish! they have put a set of men about me, but they shall know nothing." [13] In May 1679 Charles prorogued Parliament without taking the advice of the Council and in July dissolved against their specific recommendation. When Shaftesbury protested the King replied " that in matters of this nature, which were so plain, and wherein he was so fully convinced, as of the necessity of dissolving this Parliament, he could not divest himself of that power of resolving without the plurality of votes in the Council." [14] When the council had been

[11] *Privy Council Register*, Vol. lxviii, printed in the works of Sir W. Temple, i, app. iii, and quoted in *English Historical Documents, 1660–1714*, ed. A. Browning, p. 101.
[12] E. R. Turner, " The Privy Council of 1679," *E.H.R.* (1915) p. 260. See also C. Roberts, " Privy Council Schemes in Stuart England," *American Historical Review*, Vol. 64.
[13] Quoted by E. R. Turner, *art. cit.*, from *Ailesbury's Memoirs*, i, 35–36.
[14] *Ormonde MSS.*, v, 530. Quoted by G. Davies, " Council and Cabinet, 1679–88," *E.H.R.* (1922) p. 52.

appointed, a Committee of Intelligence [15] was formed, consisting of the nine principal members. The King was often present and all major matters were considered by the Committee, so that it was to a large extent the old Foreign Affairs Committee under a new name. By October 1679 Charles had given up the Privy Council experiment and having overcome his financial and parliamentary difficulties in 1681 the Committee of Intelligence was purged of those who were not his personal supporters. From this time, till the end of his reign, Charles ruled with a small group of congenial advisers whose meetings were again referred to in contemporary papers as the Cabinet Council, the Cabinet or the Committee for Foreign Affairs.[16]

James II had a Cabinet including the Lord Chancellor, Jeffreys, Sunderland as Lord President (an office revived in 1679), Middleton as Secretary of State, the Treasurer, Rochester, Godolphin as Chamberlain to the Queen and the Lord Admiral Dartmouth.[17] It met on Sundays as the old Committee for Foreign Affairs or Cabinet had done under Charles II and employed the same clerk, William Bridgeman. As in the time of his brother, when James devised and began to implement schemes which were bound to alienate most of those concerned with public affairs, he fell back on private advice—in this case from Sunderland and the Jesuit, Edward Petre. It was evident that even the favourable Parliament of 1685 would not tolerate the King's attacks on the Church or his abrogation of anti-Catholic legislation. To try to overcome this obstacle, James was engaged in a drive to fill the borough corporations and pack the commissions of the peace and deputy-lieutenancies with men favourable to his policies (hoping thus to influence the elections) when the invitation was sent to William of Orange.

Thus the major constitutional lesson of 1688 was that there would have to be harmony between the Crown, the ministers and a majority in Parliament. The later Stuart expedients for avoiding this by doing without Parliament, ignoring legislation, manipulating the constituencies and bringing pressure to bear on the bench

---

[15] The minutes of the Committee of Intelligence are in *British Museum, Add. MSS.* 15643, fos. 1–52, and end on February 1, 1681. The clerk was William Bridgeman.

[16] G. Davies, *art. cit.*, p. 59.

[17] David Ogg, *England in the Reigns of James II and William III*, p. 335.

were now impossible. What was not laid down was how the harmony between Crown, ministers and Parliament was to be initiated and maintained—for the very good reason that the process was bound to consist of too fine a series of adjustments to be prescribed by law. It was assumed that the underlying unity, which Charles II had at times endangered and James II had finally disrupted, would be preserved by the Crown respecting and supporting the Church of England, maintaining Britain's prestige abroad, and conceding the political and social position won by the men of property and rank since 1642. But within this broad framework, the Crown was expected to choose its own ministers and to give a clear lead on all matters of policy. Support would normally be forthcoming but Parliament reserved its right to comment, the Commons had to agree to any grants of money and the convention was accepted that, if there were criticisms, these would be aimed at specific measures or at the advice of certain ministers but not at the Crown.

Such an informal method of maintaining the necessary degree of unity clearly meant that much depended on the personality of the monarch, on the capacity of the politicians, and on the temper of Parliament. Two of the chief tasks of the King and his advisers were the conduct of foreign policy and the command of the armed forces. It was in this field that personal capacity could make the difference between success and disaster—and these were the two subjects on which culpable failure could lead to a general withdrawal of support in Parliament. Many of the rather puzzling and subtle changes of political convention between 1688 and 1832 arise from the degree to which personalities and the pressures of war could affect the process of achieving harmony between Crown, ministers and a majority in Parliament.

William III accepted the invitation to invade Britain and decided to assume the Crown largely in order to engage the country in an anti-French alliance. A man of great determination and capacity, with a quite definite policy of his own, he took the major decisions throughout his reign, the best-known example being his negotiation and settlement of the two Partition Treaties without the knowledge of Parliament or of any of the British ministers.

The King's first inclination was to do without a Cabinet of advisers but when he left England for Ireland in the summer of

1690, he felt it was necessary to leave a group of senior office-holders to support Queen Mary and set up a Cabinet of nine.[18] The result was not entirely satisfactory. There was a dispute between the Cabinet and the Admiralty over the nomination of Haddock as a commander,[19] and a further wrangle over the orders to be sent to Admiral Torrington before the defeat at Beachy Head on June 30, 1690.[20] " I believe never any person was left in greater streights of all kinds," was the Queen's complaint.[21] Yet it was evidently impossible to leave the Queen without a council and such a body met regularly whenever William was abroad, the Queen attending most of the meetings, while Prince George was often present.[22]

The " Lords of the Committee " and the " Full Cabinet "

It may have been because of parliamentary objections or in order to try to keep a measure of secrecy that a change was made in the summer of 1694. The new secretary, Shrewsbury, writes that when William left, his " instructions to her (the Queen) were that there should be no cabinet council; but lords should be summoned, sometimes one, and sometimes another, as they should be judged most proper for the business they were to advise about." [23] It is fortunate that from the beginning of this experiment Shrewsbury's notes have been preserved.[24] He records twenty-one meetings with an average attendance of five ministers and on four occasions he refers to this group in letters as " the Lords of the Committee " as well using the more usual terms of cabinet and committee.[25] The Queen was not present, and on all matters of importance the

---

[18] *Memoirs of Mary . . .*, ed. R. Doebner, p. 28, quoted by David Ogg, *England in the Reigns of James II and William III*, p. 335, and *Finch papers, Historical MSS. Comm.*, Vol. II, p. 347 *et seq.* In the letters to William III Nottingham refers to the Queen acting on the advice of " the Committee " but William addresses a reply to " the Cabinet Council." Both titles are used in 1691. *Finch MSS.*, Vol. III, pp. 9, 113, 128 and 181.

[19] David Ogg, *op. cit.*, p. 336.

[20] *Ibid.*, p. 354.

[21] *Memoirs of Mary . . .*, p. 30, quoted by David Ogg, *op. cit.*, p. 336.

[22] Jennifer Carter, " Cabinet Records for the Reign of William III," *E.H.R.* (1963) pp. 95–114.

[23] W. Coxe, *Correspondence of Lord Shrewsbury*, p. 34.

[24] *Historical MSS. Comm. Buccleuch and Queensberry MSS.*, at Montagu House, Vol. II, Parts I and II. (The notes are mistakenly headed " Privy Council Minutes.")

[25] *Ibid.*, Part I, pp. 85, 107, 116, 122.

advice of the Lords was submitted to William for the final decision.

Even with this new method, the result was not altogether satisfactory. In June 1694 an attack on Brest was so delayed by lack of pay and provisions that the French knew all about it. Admiral Russell asked for permission to vary the plans and though Secretary Trenchard received letters to this effect and claimed to have sent the Queen's permission, Russell was not aware of it, the result being a costly failure.[26] The Lords of the Committee seem to have lacked the ability to think ahead—they just answered letters as they came from William or from commanders at sea. There was also some jealousy aroused. Lord Normanby complained that, though a member of the Cabinet, he was not asked to one of these meetings, and the Duke of Shrewsbury (communicating the complaint to William) confessed " that this manner we are now in, of holding secret councils will, most certainly, give the same reasons of discontent to my lord steward, chamberlain, and all the rest, who are not constantly admitted." William replied that those engaged were the Lord Keeper, the Lord President, the Lord Privy Seal and the two Secretaries of State and " assuredly that number is fully sufficient, and the meeting cannot be considered as a cabinet council, since they are distinguished, by their offices, from other counsellors of state, and therefore no one can find fault if they are more trusted and employed than others." [27]

When William went abroad again in April 1695, Mary had died, and the governing body left in England was the Cabinet nominated as Lords Justices. There are accounts of the meetings of the Lords Justices in the notes left by the two Secretaries of State, Sir William Trumbull and Lord Shrewsbury but there is no evidence that the smaller *ad hoc* body summoned in 1694 was still used.

On the return of the King in October 1695, the Lords Justices revert to being a Cabinet and now, for the first time under William III, it continued to meet when the King was in the country and he (sometimes accompanied by Prince George) attended a number of the meetings.[28] There is also evidence that smaller " working

---

[26] *Ibid.*, Part I, pp. 65–81.   [27] W. Coxe, *op. cit.*, pp. 35, 38.
[28] The references to the Cabinet notes taken by the Secretaries of State from 1690 to 1700, with the solitary exception of 1692 are in Jennifer Carter, *art. cit.*

parties " were selected from among the Cabinet to examine specific problems. The members of the smaller groups seem to have been merely the more active ministers; for instance, the Archbishop of Canterbury attended assiduously. Between October 1695 and November 1697, there are accounts of a hundred and ten meetings, fifty-three of them being smaller gatherings without the King. It is clear that the latter were not held to provide special advice for a secret royal policy, the notes taken at the Cabinet explaining that the smaller groups of Lords were commanded to investigate a precise question. In October 1695, " the Lords present are ordered to meet with the Lords of the Treasury, and endeavour, without altering the standard, to propose methods " for amending the coinage.[29] Later they were asked to report on some Irish Bills, to settle a matter about the consuls in Algiers and Tripoli, and to consider a Bill for the encouragement of seamen,[30] while in the early months of 1696 four or five Lords conducted an exhaustive examination of the suspects in the plot against the King's life.[31] This supplementary work of men usually referred to as the Lords of the Committee probably originated in the experiment of the summer of 1694. The problem was that the country was engaged in its first modern war as part of a European alliance involving complex questions of finance, military policy, the government of Ireland and Scotland and the preservation of internal security, so that it was essential to find men to conduct interviews and examinations at which it was neither suitable nor possible for the King to attend but which could not be left to minor officials. The number of these smaller meetings declined once the war was over and the internal situation more settled.

The full Cabinet meetings almost always took place on Sundays at a royal palace and the membership stabilised, usually including such officials as Lord Chancellor (called Lord Keeper, if a commoner), Lord President, Lord Privy Seal, the two Secretaries of State, household officers such as the Lord Steward and Lord Chamberlain and a few men of personal importance either in politics or by virtue of being Archbishop of Canterbury or the heir to the throne.

29 *Montagu MSS.*, Part I, p. 242.
30 *Ibid.*, pp. 242, 269, 275.
31 Trumbull's notes from February to April 1696, Berkshire Record Office.

The other feature of major interest in the reign is the relationship that developed between the Cabinet and Parliament. William III had as high a view of prerogative as his predecessors and intended, like them, to conduct his own policy and choose his ministers, with Parliament rendering support and granting finance. But he found that as Parliament drifted back into a generally critical attitude and as the regular adherents of the court were outnumbered, it might be worth reaching agreements with politicians who had some debating talent and family connections. In 1694, after the ministry (in which Danby played a leading part) had faced formidable opposition, William gave posts to a group of young Whig leaders known as the Junto. Macaulay has hailed this as the first example of the modern Cabinet because he held that the ministry owed its position to the existence of a Whig majority in the Commons,[32] and his view has been supported by the most recent authority, Mr. David Ogg.[33]

It is clearly impossible to stop at any point in time and select an occasion or an institution and announce that this is " The Cabinet." " The Cabinet system " is a phrase which has been used to describe a series of political practices and conventions which were observed in the latter part of the nineteenth century and it is almost certainly unwise to indulge in any search for a specific date of birth of the nineteenth-century Cabinet, especially at a time when the political conditions were so totally different from those obtaining under Queen Victoria. The Junto ministers were not a body put in power by the majority in the Commons. They were only four ministers among a Cabinet of nine when the executive authority was still, on all major matters, in the hands of the Crown. They were selected not as a result of a general election but because the government was in difficulties and it was only after taking office that they scored a success in the election of 1695. Finally, their inclusion did not guarantee the ministry a majority, it merely added to its voting and debating power.[34]

The importance of the selection of some ministers who had political connections like Harley's New Country group or the Junto is thus best appreciated simply in the light of political

[32] T. B. Macaulay, *History of England* (Everyman edition), Vol. III, pp. 248–250.
[33] David Ogg, *op. cit.*, p. 337.
[34] These points are all made by R. Walcott, *English Politics in the early Eighteenth Century*, p. 85.

developments in those decades. The change produced by the Revolution of 1688 was not so much an alteration of attitude on the part of Crown or Parliament as a greater necessity to evolve methods for retaining parliamentary support. The Crown found that besides the techniques of management built up under Charles II, successful ministries required a number of influential parliamentarians as well as administrators and courtiers. But these men were chosen by the Crown, not by Parliament, and with little cohesion governments were not even coalitions but collections of individuals who served for varying periods, the changes being between rather than as a result of elections.

The lack of any marked alteration in the Crown's attitude to its own prerogative or to relations with its ministers is matched by the continued parliamentary suspicion of Cabinets. The Privy Council was still formally at the centre of the administration, the Treasury, the Admiralty and the committees of trade and plantations all being offshoots of it. Though numbering sixty the Council, or those few that attended, was used to carry out many duties and no matters were formally excluded from its area of competence. This meant that Members of Parliament who were disposed to be critical of the court and who wished to point to genuine grievances over extravagance and over the misconduct of naval affairs, could lay the blame on contradictions between orders issued by the King, the Admiralty and the Cabinet of privileged advisers. There were also attacks on William and his advisers by groups whose main objective was to be taken into the government coalition. Both these latter and the genuine critics objected to the practice of Cabinet government and used the old weapon of impeachment against individual ministers. They inserted in the Act of Settlement of 1701 the provision that when the House of Hanover succeeded, all important matters of state should be dealt with in the Privy Council and that all resolutions were to be signed by the councillors who had indicated their agreement.

The clause did nothing to restore the position of the Privy Council and it became evident to Parliament that no King would accept and no councillor give advice on these conditions.[35] The

---

[35] This point is made by Betty Kemp in *The King and Commons, 1660–1832*, p. 119, and M. A. Thomson, *A Constitutional History of England, 1642–1801*, p. 217.

provision was repealed in 1706. By this stage in the reign of Queen Anne the full Cabinet and the smaller working parties of Lords had developed even further while the Privy Council was manifestly becoming honorary, as membership was not withdrawn from politicians when they had ceased to be ministers.

A major consideration in explaining the developments under Anne lies in the fact that though she had a mind of her own and some capacity, she was unable to give personal attention to the work of conducting foreign policy and the extra problems of the resumed war with France and so a larger part of the actual direction fell to the ministers. The Queen held Cabinets on Sundays as before, but often a second Cabinet meeting in the week was necessary, the membership being much the same as under her predecessor. Sometimes the First Lord of the Treasury, the First Lord of the Admiralty or the Lord Lieutenant of Ireland also attended while Archbishop Tenison became less active after 1710. Other ministers were called for their own importance rather than as a consequence of the posts they held.[36]

The working parties or committees of ministers which had supplemented the operations of the Cabinet under William became a more normal and more important feature of the government. Meeting in Whitehall, usually at the Cockpit, these working parties were now regularly known as the Lords of the Committee. All the members of the Cabinet could and on occasion did attend the Committee, but its numbers still averaged five or six as opposed to an average of eleven present at the Cabinet, and it now met about twice as often as the Cabinet. The greater frequency is almost certainly due simply to the increase in the war-time tasks of interviewing officers and diplomats and drafting dispatches, and to the fact that the Queen played a far less active role than her predecessor.[37]

[36] Geoffrey Holmes, *British Politics in the Age of Anne* notes that Sir Edward Seymour was a member from 1702 to 1704 and that " although he was only Comptroller of the Household in these years no politician of Seymour's stature holding office could conceivably have been excluded from the Cabinet," pp. 195–196.

[37] J. H. Plumb, " The Organisation of the Cabinet in the Reign of Queen Anne," *Transactions of the Royal Historical Society*, 5th Series, Vol. 7. See also I. F. Burton, " The Committee of Council at the War-Office: An Experiment in Cabinet Government under Anne," *The Historical Journal*, IV (1961), pp. 78–103, for an account of a short experiment of a committee of Cabinet ministers and generals in 1712 intended by Harley as a method of counteracting Marlborough's influence.

The final authority was still Queen Anne advised by her Cabinet and at its meetings the recommendations of the Committee were discussed and, if necessary, revised before action was taken. It appears that, as under William, very little parliamentary business was discussed in the Cabinet or in the Committee. In part this was because the Cabinet, then as now, was primarily an executive body arranging the business of the government. Also very little of its work required legislation, most of the important Acts of the period being promoted by factions or individuals in Parliament. But when new legal powers were required, for example to permit the pressing of seamen, the Cabinet arranged for the drafting and introduction of a Bill. Partly also parliamentary management was not the kind of business that could be arranged by discussion in the Cabinet, it required constant contact between ministers and members of the two Houses at Westminster and in private. Any connection between the membership of the Cabinet and the composition of the House of Commons was not acknowledged and existed only in that high office was an object of ambition and could be used to purchase or recognise the support of a group of members. Queen Anne had the traditional attitude that she would frankly state her wishes and expect both support and freedom in her choice of public servants.[38] She began her reign with a mixed ministry selected purely on a personal basis. It was backed by the government interest, the independent M.P.s who normally voted for the administration and the supporters of the two chief ministers, Godolphin and Marlborough. There followed a series of reconstructions caused in part by Anne's dislike of the conduct of the high Tories and in part by Godolphin's need to readjust in order to secure approval of finances for the war and of the Union with Scotland. Both the 1702 and 1705 elections strengthened the ministry, as a result of government exertions and the efforts of politicians who wanted to prove their value. But both the desires of Anne and the pressures on Godolphin had driven the ministry to lean more and more on the Whig group known as the Junto and they demanded a large share in office in return. Anne was most reluctant and only when faced with a threat of resignation from Godolphin did she admit the Junto leader, Sunderland, to the

---

[38] G. Holmes, *op. cit.*, p. 198, " She not only knew her mind but stubbornly adhered to it." Also p. 200.

Cabinet. This may seem to be an early example of the need for a majority in Parliament forcing the Crown to reconstruct the ministry, but the Queen was only temporarily circumscribed. Harley had been advising her to resist until Godolphin and Marlborough were forced to demand his dismissal. They just managed to carry their case at the price of Harley becoming private adviser to Queen Anne. Even when the government strengthened its position at the election of 1708, it would be incorrect to represent this as a party ministry.[39] It was still a mixed assembly of courtiers, the Churchill-Godolphin group, the Newcastle Whigs, the Junto and the pro-administration independent members. However, when the Queen had recovered from the death of her husband and decided that Godolphin and Marlborough could be dispensed with, she dismissed Sunderland and Godolphin in 1710 and installed Harley, St. John and Rochester in office. With the court, the clergy and a number of influential family groups all campaigning vigorously, government supporters won many of the contested seats [40] and the Queen was able to return to a ministry chosen by herself and backed by a loyal Parliament.

The hectic events of the last few days of the reign of Queen Anne afford an excellent illustration of the position of the Cabinet. Oxford (Harley) and Bolingbroke (St. John) developed a rivalry which reached such a pitch that the Queen, in rapidly failing health, was driven to choose between them. Oxford was dismissed and Bolingbroke prepared to advise the appointment of his supporters (and perhaps, by agreement, a few Whigs) to the vacant Cabinet posts. Yet not only appointments but the whole existence and vitality of the Cabinet consisted in the degree to which it was used by the sovereign. Unknown to law, it rested on no sure foundation of party support in the country or in Parliament and its authority was simply a reflection of such trust as the living monarch chose to repose in its members. As Anne's illness clearly entered its last stage, the divided ministry, in which she reposed no great confidence, faded into the background. At times like this, it was natural for the highest recognised official body to resume its old position. When the Privy Council was summoned, two

---

[39] R. Walcott, *op. cit.*, p. 160, and G. Holmes, *op. cit.*, p. 209.
[40] W. T. Morgan in *" An Eighteenth Century Election in England," Political Science Quarterly*, 1922, estimates the results of the 1710 election at: government 304, opposed 145, doubtful 38, not elected 26.

pro-Hanoverian lords appeared and carried the Council in favour of advising Anne to appoint the Hanoverian Shrewsbury as Lord Treasurer. This was Anne's last conscious act and the Privy Council arranged for the proclamation of King George the First.

The new King was advised by his envoy in London, Baron Bothmer, to appoint his Cabinet as soon as possible, and the first meeting took place on October 8, 1714, nine days after George had landed in Britain.[41] In the next two years the King (accompanied by the Prince of Wales) continued to summon and preside over Cabinet meetings at the royal palace while the Lords of the Committee met as before in Whitehall.[42] When George went to Hanover in the summer of 1716 he left the Prince of Wales, with whom his relations were already strained, as Guardian of the Realm and Lieutenant. In this capacity the Prince called a Cabinet every Thursday to consider business which had often been the subject of discussion and provisional decision at an earlier meeting of the Lords of the Committee.[43] In some cases, new issues were considered by the Cabinet and referred to the Lords.

GEORGE I CEASES TO ATTEND. THE RISE OF THE " INNER CABINET "

A week after the King returned in early 1717 he held a Cabinet and there were further meetings in the summer at Hampton Court, but Friedrich Bonet, the Prussian Resident in London, reported that " this custom is no longer adhered to in London, except, of course, when a definite day is arranged for a Cabinet meeting." [44] Meetings became irregular and the King's attendance infrequent and by the end of 1717 the Cabinet was being held in Whitehall without George being present. The royal withdrawal was never complete. George I called a meeting in March 1718 and may have attended once in 1721.[45] The Austrian ambassador, Count Kinsky, reported some conferences between George II and his ministers in

---

41 W. Michael, *Englische Geschichte im achtzehnten Jahrhundert*, Vol. iii, p. 559.
42 J. H. Plumb, *art. cit.*, p. 156. W. Michael, *op. cit.*, gives instances of these Cabinet meetings taken from the reports of Bonet, the Prussian Resident in London, and from the valuable letters between Methuen and Stanhope in *State Papers*, Dom. Entry Books, cclxvii.
43 W. Michael, *op. cit.*, p. 565. There is a good description of the process revealed in the negotiations with D'Iberville about the fortification of Mardyck.
44 Quoted by W. Michael, *op. cit.*, p. 568, from a despatch of Bonet, July 30/ August 10, 1717.
45 W. Michael, *op. cit.*, pp. 569–570.

1733 which might have been Cabinets. Certainly the King presided once in 1745 and perhaps on two other occasions, while George III made three appearances (in 1779, 1781 and 1784),[46] but for practical purposes after 1717 the Cabinet ceased to be a body meeting with the King.

The reasons for this change have not been pinpointed but a number of motives are fairly evident. The old explanation that George's inability to speak English led to the withdrawal has been abandoned since the problem of communication had evidently been overcome for the best part of three years after George's accession.[47] The chief reason was that George's personality altered the situation. He was both ignorant of English affairs and stupid [48] and could never be at ease presiding over a wide-ranging discussion among ten or twelve Cabinet ministers. Like many stupid men he was suspicious and preferred to lean on his German advisers and mistresses and perhaps on one or two Englishmen. The politicians, for their part, sensing this situation, preferred to consult with the King in private and not at the Cabinet where misunderstandings and animosities could so rapidly arise and flourish. An added motive was that if the King attended it was difficult to deny the Prince of Wales the right to attend and to preside as Regent in the King's absence. George and his son had not been on good terms in 1716 and the reports which reached Hanover of the Prince's activity in politics and popularity stung George till he was convinced that there was an attempt to discredit him and form a rival centre of attraction.[49] Even after the partial reconciliation in 1719 the Prince was neither made Regent nor nominated as one of the Lords Justices on George's subsequent visits to Hanover. Finally, the King did have certain very definite desires in foreign policy and while the Cabinet infuriated him with its reluctance to enter into

---

[46] H. W. V. Temperley, " Inner and Outer Cabinet," *E.H.R.* (1912) pp. 693–694.

[47] W. Michael, *op. cit.*, pp. 574–577, examines this legend and shows that there is no eighteenth-century evidence for the story. He suggests that it comes from Hallam's *Constitutional History* (published 1827), in which it is recorded that George left the Cabinet, and the next paragraph repeats Horace Walpole's story of conversations with Sir Robert in Latin. He suspects that subsequent writers have put the two together and attributed the first development to the next fact mentioned. George I could speak French and this was the language used in the Cabinet 1714–1717, the despatches of the English diplomats and the instructions that were drafted being translated into French for the occasion.

[48] J. H. Plumb, *Sir Robert Walpole*, p. 202.

[49] See J. M. Beattie, " The Court of George I and English Politics," *E.H.R.* (1966).

hostilities against Russia in 1716,[50] he (like his German advisers and mistresses) found individual ministers much more pliable in personal interviews.

Thus a complex of motives led George to formulate his dissatisfaction with the Cabinet system as it had operated under Queen Anne in a withdrawal from its meetings. There was no reason why this should have been permanent and George II might well have decided to return to the practice of the early years of his father's reign. However, the personal factors remained fairly constant for over twenty years. George II disliked the full Cabinets [51] and Sir Robert Walpole in 1725 declared that " no good ever came from them." [52] The original ejection of Townshend from the ministry in 1717 and Walpole's resignation had taken place largely because Sunderland and Stanhope had the ear of the King and Walpole's chief problem after he was taken back into the Cabinet in 1720 was not finance or the opposition in Parliament but the credit that the Sunderland group in the Cabinet still enjoyed with George I.[53] Whether Walpole's opponent was Sunderland or Carteret, the solution was to prevent him bidding for royal favour. The task of holding the approval of George I and his intimates, of George II and Queen Caroline, could be simplified by keeping the number of close advisers at a minimum.

The diary of Lord King gives a good picture of the working of the Cabinet between 1725 and 1730, and the details can be picked up after 1739 in the Newcastle papers [54] supplemented for two years by Hervey's memoirs and Admiral Norris's diary.[55]

In the first place, the King decided on the composition of the ministry and a list of Cabinet Council posts was filled. The offices which carried Cabinet rank were fairly definite. The Archbishop of Canterbury was automatically a member, and still attended on occasion.[56] The Lord President, Lord Chancellor, Lord Privy Seal, Lord Steward, Lord Chamberlain, the Groom of the Stole,

50 W. Coxe, *Memoirs of Sir Robert Walpole*, Vol. I, p. 94.
51 J. H. Plumb, *op. cit.*, p. 75.
52 *Diary of Lord King* in *Life and Correspondence of Locke* (ed. 1830), p. 52.
53 C. B. Realey, *The Early Opposition to Sir Robert Walpole*, pp. 33–34.
54 *Newcastle MSS. British Museum, Add. MSS.* 32,993–33,002 and 33,004.
55 *Lord Hervey's Memoirs*, in 3 vols., edited by R. R. Sedgwick (London, 1931) and Admiral Norris's Diary in *Add. MSS.* 28132–5.
56 *Diary of Lord King*, Entry for July 1, 1725, p. 11. *Add. MSS.* 33,004 records that the Archbishop of Canterbury was present at 11 out of 78 meetings between 1739 and 1745.

Lord Treasurer, the Lord Lieutenant of Ireland, the Master of the Ordnance, the First Lord of Admiralty and the two Secretaries of State were almost certain to be members. Other posts that could carry Cabinet rank were the Master of the Horse, the Keeper of the Great Seal of Scotland, a third Secretary of State, the Chancellor of the Exchequer and very occasionally the Lord Chief Justice.[57] It was possible to be a member of the Cabinet without holding any office [58] and in some cases minor appointments carrying no real duties were considered suitable (including such unlikely ones as Constable of the Tower and Warden of the Isle of Wight). The Cabinet Council was formally nominated as the Lords Justices of the Regency on the King's regular visits abroad.

What had been known as the Lords of the Committee was referred to as "the Select Lords" or "Lords whom the King principally intrusts with his affairs," [59] and again the members were specifically nominated, as when George II, on his accession, said he "would not let it (a treaty with the Duke of Wolfenbuttel) be communicated to the whole Cabinet but would take the first three of the lay lords, viz., the Chancellor, the President, the Privy Seal, the two Secretaries and Sir Robert Walpole, the Chancellor of the Exchequer." [60]

The King also decided what items were to be submitted to the Select Lords. There was clearly no right to give collective advice and in the 1730s no obligation on the Crown to adopt recommendations that were not acceptable. Many matters were settled by the King acting with his German councillors or the one Secretary who accompanied him to Hanover. In 1725 George sent over a treaty to have the Great Seal affixed, and when the Chancellor asked Lord Somerset whether this should not have first been submitted to the Regency he was told that it was an absurd idea because the King had already agreed to and signed the treaty.[61] In the same year, when danger was apprehended from Spain, the

---

[57] Lord Chief Justice Mansfield was a member from 1757 to 1763. I. R. Christie, "The Cabinet during the Grenville Administration, 1763–1765," *E.H.R.* (1958) p. 89.

[58] For example Pulteney (Lord Bath) was a member of the Cabinet from the fall of Walpole till 1746, without holding any post.

[59] *Diary of Lord King*, pp. 88, 99.

[60] *Ibid.*, p. 50.

[61] *Ibid.*, p. 20.

King instructed that the matter be laid before the Select Lords.[62] The King also gave instructions when the full Cabinet was to be summoned, though this became more automatic during the regencies and on occasion the Lords, having given their opinion, suggested that a matter should or should not be laid before the full Cabinet.

Out of these arrangements arose the distinction made in the 1750s and 1760s between posts with or without the circulation of papers. Almost all information of importance originated in the form of dispatches to the two Secretaries and the First Lord of the Admiralty. If the King placed a matter before the inner Cabinet, he asked these ministers to read all the relevant papers to the members and in time this meant that on most matters, they were kept regularly informed. But all such questions were not put before the full or outer Cabinet and it only heard those letters or reports which were necessary in order to understand the proposals submitted. In 1740 Lord Harrington, who was the Secretary in attendance on George II in Hanover, wrote to approve of Newcastle's action in putting certain questions before the Lord Chancellor, the Lord President, Sir Robert Walpole (with, of course, Newcastle present) and said they should

> " continue to meet and confer upon all points of importance that may occur, as also upon the instructions you will from time to time receive from hence, and it is His Majesty's pleasure that you should communicate to them the letters I shall write to your Grace by his consent and those which you shall receive from the King's ministers abroad, and that you shall settle always previously amongst yourselves which of those dispatches may be proper to be laid before the Lords Justices and prepare such heads of business as are to be considered by their Excellencies." [63]

Lord Hardwicke, writing to the Duke of Bedford in 1748 says

> " I observe by your billet that your Grace makes a very proper

---

[62] *Ibid.*, p. 21. There is another description of this meeting of Sir Robert Walpole, Lord King, the Earl of Berkeley, the Duke of Newcastle and the Earl of Godolphin (Devonshire should have been called but was out of town) in W. Coxe, *Memoirs of Sir Robert Walpole*, Vol. III, pp. 474–479.

[63] Quoted by R. R. Sedgwick in " The Inner Cabinet from 1739 to 1741," *E.H.R.* (1919) p. 291, from *State Papers*, Dom. Regencies, 25, June 4–15, 1740, Separate and Private.

distinction between such papers as are proper to be read at the meeting of the Lords Justices and such as are not: from whence I took the hint of perusing them with that view, and beg leave to submit it to your consideration, whether those letters and papers which I have separated, by tying them together with red tape, should for the present at least be read there or not; for they all make some mention of those points which the King has directed should be particularly considered by such of his servants as are consulted on the most secret affairs." [64]

It is clear, then, that the withdrawal of the King led to a marked decline in the power of the Cabinet. This was only to be expected. The smaller " working parties " under William III or Lords of the Committee under Anne had always included " those more trusted and employed than others." These men occupying the senior offices, better informed and more active in government, were only kept subordinate to the Cabinet by the fact that the presence of the Crown enabled the larger body to alter and revise and issue the definitive orders. When the King was no longer present this superiority came to an end in practice, though the Cabinet (especially as the Regency) still carried more formal authority.

THE DECLINE OF THE " OUTER " OR " FULL " CABINET

The process by which the inner Cabinet became the directing body is revealed by Lord King's diary. When the Crown wanted advice on an important matter, it was referred to the Select Lords. Walpole would dine with one or two colleagues or call at their offices and thrash out the problem.[65] Then there would be a meeting of the inner Cabinet and the King informed of the consensus of opinion. On many occasions this concluded the matter, but if the King had asked for specific directions to be prepared for commanders or for foreign ambassadors or if a public announcement was required, then heads of business would be drawn up and a Cabinet summoned. At the meeting letters would be read explaining the problem and it was, on most occasions,

---

[64] *Correspondence of John, Fourth Duke of Bedford,* Vol. I, pp. 375–376.
[65] *Diary of Lord King,* pp. 14, 17, 21, 28, 50, 52 and *passim.*

to be expected that in the discussion the views of the Select Lords would become those of the Cabinet. Agreement having been reached, advice was tendered in the traditional form that "their lordships are humbly of opinion that . . ." [66] It was by no means certain in the 1730s and 1740s that the King would accept the advice, and this is why the most important discussions then took place in the closet as Walpole, Carteret or Newcastle sought the agreement of George II.[67]

It has often been argued that the chief effect of the King's quitting the Cabinet was to produce a Prime Minister in the person of the politician who was asked to preside. This is, however, purely a theoretical supposition and has no basis in practice. Who took the chair at the full Cabinet was not a matter of any importance. The order of business at the inner Cabinet is nowhere explicitly described and while at various times some ministers clearly carried more weight than others the question of formal precedence does not seem to have been of any importance. The determining factors were that the Crown both chose its principal ministers and decided what matters should be submitted to them in any collective capacity. Each minister was responsible for his own department and would resent any suggestion that the King was taking advice on departmental matters from other individuals. Parliament likewise understood the idea that it could criticise a minister for his departmental failings and was on guard lest this responsibility should be obscured by a premier or "sole minister" as Pitt called Carteret in 1743. Thus the development of the post of Prime Minister was hampered by the fact that in many ways the King was his own Prime Minister, and by opposition from the other members of the Cabinet and from the Commons.

The relations between the King and his ministers are well brought out by the process of forming an administration. This was not always carried out by the individual who was likely to be most prominent, as all the King needed was a trusted negotiator. Even when the ministry was in office it was not always clear

---

[66] Both the advice of the inner and the full Cabinet was often embodied in a formal minute, and if this was the case, the same phraseology was employed.

[67] There is an interesting case in June 1748, when the inner Cabinet agreed on instructions to Admiral Byng, with the solitary exception of Newcastle. "However, when it came to be submitted to his Majesty, the Duke of Newcastle's arguments prevailed." *Bedford Correspondence*, Vol. I, pp. 381–383.

who was the leading member. In 1721 and 1722 Walpole and Sunderland were in equal competition for power, and though Newcastle and Pelham and later Newcastle and the elder Pitt co-operated it was open to argument as to who was the senior partner. Finally, when a leading minister fell from power this did not mean the end of the government. Even when Walpole resigned in 1742, only three Cabinet posts changed hands.

Until the early years of George III there were three senses in which it was possible to describe a Cabinet member as Prime Minister. The first, and by far the most important, was that he was strongest in the closet. Walpole's claim to the title depends chiefly on the fact that from 1727 to 1739 George II, prompted by Queen Caroline, reposed complete trust in him. The second sense, which derives directly from the first, was that a strong minister could carry a number of his supporters into office with him, and, if gaining power, could in time exclude more and more of his opponents—this being probably the most evident feature of Walpole's ascendancy. Finally the term might be used to designate the minister on whose ability the government rested, sometimes in the prosecution of a war, but more often in the management of Parliament. It was because this latter task was of such importance, and because getting money Bills through Parliament was a major part of the work that the minister most likely to be described as the premier usually held the post of First Lord of the Treasury.

Despite the firm view that responsibility was owed only by individual ministers to the King and to Parliament, a slight suggestion of joint responsibility was beginning to develop simply because it was evident that some policies were the work of a group of ministers in the inner Cabinet. The Duke of Argyle, discussing events in 1721, declared that, though he had been commander-in-chief and a member of the Cabinet, he had never seen Admiral Vernon's instructions because he was not of what he described as " the ministers' council." [68] When Pitt told Newcastle in 1755 that " if it was expected that he should take an *active part* in support of measures, he must be enabled to do it, which he could not think the calling him to the Cabinet Council would, in any degree, do . . . he could not, and would not, take

[68] R. R. Sedgwick, *art. cit.*, p. 290.

an *active part* in the House of Commons without he had an *office of advice* as well as of *execution*," [69] he was simply saying that he would not take a share of responsibility unless he was a member of the inner Cabinet. Ministers on occasion asked for their dissent to be recorded on the minute in which the advice of the full Cabinet was conveyed to the King. More often they indicated their disapproval by ceasing to attend Cabinet meetings. All this was merely a recognition of the fact that a ministry had, on the whole, to present a united front in Parliament and that a degree of joint responsibility was involved. No modern doctrine of collective responsibility could arise while the Cabinet was not chosen by a Prime Minister on the basis of political principle, but members owed their places individually to a monarch who played a large part in determining policy.

Some previous writers have made the mistake of arguing that the regular use of an inner council of ministers only arose as late as 1745.[70] It is difficult, in any rapid treatment, to avoid conveying the impression that development was more deliberate and consistent than was the case. The creation of a Cabinet after the Restoration and its increasingly formal character after 1690 have been described. William III began the practice of using small working parties of the most important office-holders to deal with specific matters. Under Anne these Lords of the Committee met much more frequently to prepare material for the full Cabinet. After George I ceased to attend the full Cabinet, the inner council slowly moved into a commanding position and in the 1720s it has been noticed as the chief advisory body on important issues of foreign and military policy. Such a description might suggest that after this had happened, the full Cabinet was of little significance and there is a danger of ante-dating the final sloughing-off of the outer body.

While the inner Cabinet contained only the more powerful and expert advisers (and they alone, for example, considered the

---

[69] P. C. Yorke, *The Life of Lord Chancellor Hardwicke*, Vol. II, p. 238.

[70] Sir William R. Anson, "The Cabinet in the Seventeenth and Eighteenth Centuries," *E.H.R.* (1914) p. 56. It should be noted that H. W. V. Temperley, *art. cit.*, *E.H.R.* (1912) is entirely in accord with the modern interpretation on this point and that R. R. Sedgwick, *art. cit.*, *E.H.R.* (1919), though describing the inner Cabinet between 1739 and 1741, is not suggesting that it originated in these years. He points out (p. 300) that a similar system was in use in the late 1720s, but he is not concerned with the origin of the practice.

two major questions of 1740, the negotiations with Frederick of
Prussia and the plans for an expedition against Cartagena [71]) the
full Cabinet still had a place in political life. It seems difficult to
contend that a body which met forty-four times between 1739
and 1741 and thirty-four times in 1744 and 1745 was moribund.[72]
The attitude of some senior statesmen to the outer Cabinet until
at least the 1750s was that it had a semi-legal status [73] probably
because of its regular constitution as the Lords Justices of the
Regency. Membership was regarded as an honour and the list of
those to be included was carefully worked out in Newcastle's
various schemes for an administration in 1757,[74] similar lists
being drawn up as late as 1765 and 1767.[75] Though those in political life were well aware of the inner Cabinet, it was still a very
secret body.[76] While it would consider secret policies and plans,
the politicians seem to have felt that matters that were public
property or had to be announced in Parliament ought to be put
through the formal Cabinet of the King's advisers.[77]

The large numbers of meetings in 1739–41 and 1744–45 were
called to consider and endorse the detailed instructions needed in
time of war and complex foreign negotiations. The last occasion
recorded in the Newcastle papers on which the outer Cabinet
asserted its authority over the King's more intimate advisers was
in 1743, when it refused to back Carteret's offer of money to the
Emperor Charles VII and advised the King not to ratify Carteret's
Convention with the Queen of Hungary.[78] The interesting aspect

[71] R. R. Sedgwick, *art. cit.*, pp. 292–293.

[72] These figures are compiled from the *Newcastle MSS. Add. MSS.* 33,004.

[73] In 1753 one Fawcett was accused of Jacobitism and examined by the Cabinet
Council. The Duke of Bedford attacked such a procedure and said that " a
Cabinet Council is not recognised in our constitution." Hardwicke and Bath
clearly met with general sympathy in the Lords when they rebutted this suggestion but unfortunately it is not absolutely clear that they were referring
only to the outer Cabinet. Coxe, *Pelham Administration*, Vol. II, p. 257
et seq.

[74] *Add. MSS.* 32,997, fo. nos. 146, 148, 158, 160, 162, 164, 191, 195, 197, 199.

[75] *Add. MSS.* 33,001, fo. nos. 25, 382.

[76] As Pulteney said in 1738, " We have in this kingdom several councils; we
have a Privy Council, a Cabinet Council; and for all I know a more secret
and less numerous council still, by which the other two are directed." Quoted
from *Parl. Hist.*, x, 591, by R. R. Sedgwick, *art. cit.*, p. 290.

[77] For example, after the Convention of the Pardo was negotiated, it was submitted to the full Cabinet in January 1739 and they advised ratification. W.
Coxe, *Memoirs of Sir Robert Walpole*, Vol. III, pp. 513–514.

[78] *Add. MSS.* 33,004, fo. 57–58. The Cabinet on the Convention with the Queen
of Hungary was on November 24, 1743, in which eight were opposed, four
in favour and Argyle wanted further " explanations."

of this episode was that the proposals did not come from a united inner Cabinet but were the sole work of Carteret, who had been formulating and executing foreign policy with little reference to any of his colleagues. Their only redress lay when the final draft reached the Cabinet before public announcement.

After the Pelham-Newcastle administration was settled in office, the inner Cabinet operated satisfactorily again and the meetings of the full Cabinet declined in number. The complex foreign negotiations of 1746–48 were all discussed in the inner Cabinet.[79] For three months in the winter of 1747–48, Newcastle fought a rearguard action to prevent a quick peace settlement and once, in January 1748, when sore pressed, he reported a matter "upon which no resolution is taken, or as I hope will be before the opinion of the rest of the King's servants is also known."[80] But there is no record of any such appeal and the full Cabinet was summoned only to give its unanimous approval of the preliminaries of the Treaty of Aix-la-Chapelle[81] and later to consider arrangements for proclaiming peace.[82] The next instance of the outer Cabinet being called was in April 1749 to consider whether George II should undertake to direct the education of the Prince of Wales, and it was called again in June of the same year to approve the draft of a royal speech.[83] The tendency to refer to the full Cabinet only on semi-formal occasions or on issues of unusual significance became even more marked in the 1750s. The Newcastle papers record no full Cabinet meetings in 1750, 1751 or 1752. There was one meeting on February 6, 1753, to endorse a despatch to British ambassadors on negotiations with Prussia,[84] and then the well-known occasion when George II asked the full Cabinet to consider his suggestion that Newcastle should succeed Pelham at the Treasury.[85] The next meetings were in 1755. On April 21 the inner Cabinet "were humbly of opinion, that the Lords of His Majesty's Cabinet Council should be summoned to

[79] Sir Richard Lodge, *Studies in Eighteenth Century Diplomacy*, pp. 272, 273, 283, 284, 308 and 322.
[80] *Bedford Correspondence*, Vol. I, p. 306, Newcastle to Bedford, January 7, 1748.
[81] Sir Richard Lodge, *op. cit.*, p. 342.
[82] *Add. MSS.* 32,994, fo. 31. (And most of the time of this Cabinet was taken up with the question of prosecuting the Vice-Chancellor of Oxford.)
[83] *Ibid.*, fo. nos. 45 and 51.
[84] *Add. MSS.* 32,995, fo. 2.
[85] *Ibid.*, fo. 60.

meet tomorrow " to approve important naval instructions and a despatch either of which might have led to war with France.[86] Meetings of the full Cabinet sitting as Lords Justices on May 8 and July 1 again endorsed important naval orders and on November 6 the inner Cabinet requested a full meeting to ratify the treaty which had just been signed with Russia.[87] In 1756, the full Cabinet was assembled on January 14 to approve a refusal to release some French ships, on February 27 [88] and March 17 to request a royal message to Parliament [89] and on March 25 to hear that Byng was being sent to the defence of Minorca.[90] The last occasion noted in the Newcastle papers (the Holdernesse minutes stop in June 1756) when the full Cabinet was called on a matter of policy was on May 10, 1756, and then it recommended a declaration of war.[91] After the outbreak of hostilities, the only mention of the full Cabinet is when it met to hear the report of the Recorder of London on sentences of capital punishment (the Cabinet urged a delay in the execution of Admiral Byng in February 1757) or a royal message to Parliament.[92]

When it came to approving the Treaty of Paris at the end of the war in 1763, this was done by the inner Cabinet alone.[93] On these final occasions in the early 1750s when the full Cabinet was called, the effect was to supplement the inner group of five to eight members by the household officials, the Lord Lieutenant for Ireland and the Lord Privy Seal, raising the numbers to between ten and thirteen. The larger meetings seem to have added nothing

[86] *Add. MSS.* 32,996, fo. 87.
[87] These minutes of November 6 and 7 are on folios 7, 8 and 9 of a volume of minutes (wrongly called Privy Council Minutes) referred to in the *Hist. Man. Comm.*, 11th Report, Appendix VII, *Holdernesse Papers*, p. 53. I am indebted to Professor D. B. Horn for the reference and to the Duke of Leeds for giving me access to the volume.
[88] *Holdernesse Papers*, fos. 25 and 43.
[89] *Add. MSS.* 32,996, fo. 377 (March 17 minute is also in the *Holdernesse Papers*, fo. 48.)
[90] *Holdernesse Papers*, fo. 49.
[91] *Add. MSS.* 32,996, fo. 423, and *Holdernesse Papers*, fo. 53.
[92] *Add. MSS.* 32,997, fo. 127. The final meeting of the old grand Cabinet to hear the King's speech was in February 1921. Thereafter it was sent to the King in a box. See L. B. Namier, " The End of the Nominal Cabinet " in *In the Margin of History*. A list of those attending such a " Hanging " Cabinet in 1810 is printed in *English Historical Documents, 1783–1832* (Vol. XI) ed. Aspinall and Smith, pp. 86–87, while George III refers to the Cabinet meeting called to hear his speech to Parliament as " entirely a matter of form " in 1784. *The Later Correspondence of George III*, Vol. I, ed. Aspinall, p. 61.
[93] *Bedford Correspondence*, Vol. III, p. 204.

to the original deliberations and it is difficult to feel any surprise when they were abandoned under the pressure of war.

As late as the 1760s, when plans for ministries were drawn up, members of the old full Cabinet were listed and in 1795 when approving of the appointment of the Duke of Montrose as Lord Justice General, George III noted that " he ought to remain of the Nominal Cabinet," [94] but otherwise references to the old full, nominal or grand Cabinet cease. After the accession of George III the word " Cabinet " in practice was applied only to the actual or, as it has been called, inner Cabinet.[95] The tendency to regard the latter more as a secret committee faded and the Cabinet was recognised explicitly as the source of advice for the Crown. George III never acquired the habit of spending his summers in Hanover so there was no need to constitute a regency and appoint Lords Justices. Also George, though eager to take an interest in the politics of power and place, was less concerned, at first at any rate, with the details of foreign policy. He was constantly available in England to receive the advice of the Cabinet, and tended in the early 1760s to leave the conduct of business to the politicians.[96] In this way the operation of the Cabinet achieved such regularity that though the King still gave (or could withhold) permission to lay matters before his ministers, once he had asked for their advice there was hardly any doubt that he would accept their proposals. As Grenville said in 1761: " the King might take a foreign measure with his secretary of state only, but . . . if the King referred the matter to the Council the opinion of the majority of the council was the measure." [97] In the first half of the eighteenth century, the Cabinet had tendered its advice in a minute which was drawn up by one of the Secretaries of State and read over to the Lords present to know

[94] Aspinall, *op. cit.*, Vol. II, pp. 291 and 310.

[95] I. R. Christie, " The Cabinet During the Granville Administration," *E.H.R.* (1958) p. 91. In the period after 1763 there is only one effective body in regular use and it is to this that the word " Cabinet " always refers. Whereas in the 1740s and 1750s Cabinet minutes could describe a meeting of either the full or the inner Cabinet, by the 1760s there is no doubt. See the six Cabinet minutes in Fortescue, *The Correspondence of King George III*, Vol. V, 178–187, for January 1781.

[96] R. Pares, *King George III and the Politicians*, p. 173.

[97] Quoted by D. A. Winstanley, " George III and his First Cabinet," *E.H.R.* (1902) p. 691, from *Add. MSS.* 32,929.

whether it fully expressed their sentiments.[98] The minute began with the place of meeting, the date and a list of those present, followed by the recommendations usually supported by the leading arguments or explanations. A fair copy was made and sent to the King.[99] After the 1770s Cabinet minutes were still used but with increasing frequency the alternatives of a letter from the Prime Minister, or at times a verbal account, were adopted.[1] The King usually replied by letter signifying his assent or explaining his views. By the early nineteenth-century minutes were becoming infrequent and were reserved for the more solemn occasions or for matters on which it was important that the King should have the precise wording before him.[2]

RELATIONS BETWEEN THE CABINET, PARLIAMENT AND THE CROWN

Established in this way as a regular and recognised feature, the development of the Cabinet was governed by its relations with Parliament on the one side and the King on the other. On the parliamentary side there were only minor changes in the eighteenth century. Once a Cabinet was appointed and given royal support, it could normally rely on a majority in both houses and a victory at the next general election. As a result, till 1784 there was no need even to choose a suitable year for an election[3]

---

[98] Shelburne explained in 1767 that it was " the indispensable custom " to take and read over a minute at Cabinet meetings. *Calendar of Home Office Papers of the Reign of George III*, ed. J. Redington, pp. 212–213.

[99] In 1787 when Sir James Harris, the Ambassador at The Hague, had attended Cabinet meetings on British policy in Holland, he asked for a copy of the minute " as a voucher for my conduct." *Diaries and Correspondence of the Earl of Malmesbury*, Vol. II, p. 307.

[1] Examples of such minutes are printed in Aspinall, *op. cit.*, Vols. I and II, up to 1795.

[2] The last minutes under the Regency and reign of George IV were in May 1812 and concerned the terms under which ministers were willing to serve after the assassination of Perceval; in 1820 when the Cabinet refused to accept certain of George's amendments to the section of the King's speech dealing with the Civil List; in 1824 over the possibility of sending British troops to Portugal; in 1827 over the conditions on which the Cabinet took office and in 1828 when the rest of the Cabinet advised that Wellington, on becoming Prime Minister, had to resign as Commander-in-Chief. A. Aspinall, *The Letters of George IV*, 71, 78, 84, 806, 1170–1171, 1378, 1482.

[3] In 1774 when an election was due, George III urged North to choose an unexpected month, as the Nabobs, Planters, etc., were not ready for the battle. Donne, *Correspondence of George III with Lord North*, Vol. I, p. 201. Also in 1780 when an election had to come within a year some ministers were eager for a speedy dissolution when " our opponents are depressed, the nation is set against riots . . ., events have been favourable beyond conception." Lord Sandwich quoted by I. R. Christie, *The End of Lord North's Ministry, 1780–1782*, p. 30.

and there was no connection between the life of a Parliament (which ran close to its full seven years) and the life of a ministry. Opposition in Parliament was of two kinds. The first was the sporadic attacks of those who were interested in politics and belaboured the government in order to be bought off with office. The second was a more genuinely critical spirit amongst the country members who suspected the government of taxing them too heavily in order to have funds for its own purposes. When, on very rare occasions, these two types of opposition joined hands and were reinforced by patriotic alarm over defeats in foreign policy or in actual war, the ministers could be in genuine danger. During the century there was some development in the notion of what action it was proper for the critics to take. In 1741, facing a motion of censure, Walpole could say " that an address to His Majesty to remove one of his servants, without so much as alleging any particular crime against him, is one of the greatest encroachments that was ever made upon the prerogatives of the Crown." [4] By 1778, facing exactly the same challenge, Lord North accepted that an attempt to censure an individual minister was a legitimate method of attacking the policy of the Cabinet as a whole, and he kept insisting that the American War was the responsibility of all the King's servants.[5]

Such minor alterations in constitutional form did not change the fact that the relations between Cabinet and Parliament were primarily a matter of the management of members by the leading ministers. While the administration enjoyed royal confidence, a favourable majority in the House of Lords was so certain that the peers received little attention for their own sakes, the chief point of the 166 creations between 1784 and 1820 being to reward support in the Commons or at elections. Provided a Cabinet did not reveal marked incompetence, or impose apparently unwarrantable taxation, its position was unassailable in the Commons, and opponents disliked by the Crown could do nothing but seek the favour of the current Prince of Wales. This is not to deny that

[4] Yet at this time the practice of referring to " the Opposition " began and its members started to occupy the benches on the left of the Speaker. See A. S. Foord, *His Majesty's Opposition, 1714–1830*, pp. 151–159.

[5] D. B. Horn and M. Ransome, ed., *English Historical Documents*, Vol. X, print Walpole's speech on p. 129, and Costin and Watson, *The Law and Working of the Constitution*, print excerpts from North's speeches in 1778 and 1779 in Vol. I, pp. 238–239.

Cabinets had to work to maintain their position and that individual ministers often owed their places to the support they held either by virtue of their abilities or their connections. Even when the resources available for management had declined considerably by the 1820s,[6] Cabinets (though not all their measures) had little to fear from Parliament, and ministers after 1832 at times looked back in longing to the days when the executive was so much stronger.

This description of the relations between Cabinets and Parliament covers the influence of any external public opinion. Parliament in the late eighteenth century did represent the views of the politically interested classes. It was their loss of confidence, as manifested not in a few meetings of county associations but in the withdrawal of support by the non-political M.P.s, that forced North out of office in 1782 and made Pitt reverse his foreign policy in 1791. Commercial and industrial interests could exercise considerable pressure through sympathetic members [7]—as over the repeal of the Stamp Act,[8] the opposition to Pitt's economic policies towards Ireland in 1785,[9] and the constant activity of the East and West India interests. The Committee for the Abolition of the Slave Trade was ultimately successful in 1807 after repeated petitions and propaganda directed not only at Parliament but at all sections with any political influence. Though these external demands did on occasion buoy up opposition groups,[10] and in the elections of 1784 and 1807 there was some public reaction which served to confirm the result of the government's management,[11] the importance of such pressures rested almost entirely on the support they could muster inside Parliament. As the government was usually in a very strong position, it was in the interest of most groups to come to terms with the Cabinet and have their views considered in return for support. Thus,

[6] See below, p. 71.

[7] F. G. James, " The Irish Lobby in the Early Eighteenth Century," *E.H.R.*, Vo.1 81 (1966), pp. 543–557.

[8] L. S. Sutherland, " Edmund Burke and the First Rockingham Ministry," *E.H.R.* (1932) p. 46.

[9] W. Bowden, " Influence of the Manufacturers on some early Policies of William Pitt," *American Historical Review*, July 1924.

[10] L. S. Sutherland, *art. cit.*

[11] Mrs. E. George, " Fox's Martyrs: The General Election of 1784, *Transactions of the Royal Historical Society*, 4th Series, Vol. XXI, p. 133. C. E. Fryer, " The General Election of 1784," *History*, Vol. IX, and W. T. Laprade, " Public Opinion and the General Election of 1784," *E.H.R.* (1916) p. 224.

while the various movements of opinion among those sections with political influence might perhaps complicate the position and policies of the Cabinet on specific occasions, allowances were made for their effects in the normal calculations of the parliamentary managers.

The more important relationship was clearly that between the Cabinet and the Crown. The sovereign's choice of servants depended on his personal inclinations exercised among a series of oligarchic groups—and so left a great deal open to the capacity and persistence of the King, to the relations between the politicians and, as has been said, to their ability to sway the House of Commons. The first two Hanoverians had a wide field of choice among those claiming the title of Whigs, but George II was not heavily endowed with political acumen or persistence. While Queen Caroline lived he had an able counsellor, but after her death in 1737 and the fall of Walpole in 1742, he lacked the force to impose his decisions on the senior statesmen. George II would have liked to keep Carteret (Earl Granville) in 1744, but the Remonstrance presented by Newcastle, Pelham and Hardwicke made it clear that the King would have to choose between them (supported by the rest of the Cabinet) and Carteret.[12] Two years later, when the Pelhams decided to bring their disagreements with George to a head and persuaded their fellow ministers to resign collectively, the King was helpless. He tried to form an administration around Pulteney (Bath) and Granville but had to give up after a few days and accept the Pelhams' terms.[13] George revealed his weakness in 1754 when Pelham died in that he called a Cabinet to consider his tentative proposals for the redistribution of offices. Yet it would be a mistake to regard these signs of deference to the wishes of the ministers as anything more than a product of personal factors, and there were none of the alterations in basic conditions of politics which might have led to the growth of new conventions.

[12] The Remonstrance is printed in P. C. Yorke, *The Life of Lord Chancellor Hardwicke*, Vol. I, pp. 332–335. It is noteworthy that the paper never took the step, which would have been considered unconstitutional, of asking George to dismiss Carteret. It was purely a criticism of policies and it was assumed that if these were changed, Carteret would have in honour to resign.

[13] Even in this admittedly exceptional situation, J. B. Owen, in his *Rise of the Pelhams*, still stresses that George's " unhappy position was entirely of his own making " and that " the initiative was always in his hands," p. 299.

That George II retained all his powers, if he was bent on employing them, was brought out by the great difficulty in inducing him to accept Pitt as an inner Cabinet Minister in 1756–57. Thus though the accession of George III involved no more than a change in the central personality it was nevertheless an alteration in the most important single factor affecting the Cabinet. George III thought that amongst the prerogatives of the Crown were the right to veto legislation (which he never used) and the right to choose his ministers. The second he had the persistence and ability to carry through, though he confined himself to selecting the ministers and did not try to dictate policy. But between 1767 and 1770 George III's correspondence began to deal more and more with matters of administrative detail.[14] The reason was that Grafton and North were indecisive and George was driven to take an increasing part in government. By the end of Lord North's administration he might well be described as his own Prime Minister, holding together a tottering administration.[15] It was in these years that he twice attended the Cabinet to show his determination not to relent in the American war or in his support of Lord North.[16]

Yet George's very activity had an effect on the political atmosphere. His use of the royal power of appointment had inevitably to be directed against the old groups which had governed under his grandfather, and though prepared to take office on George's terms they had some propensity to criticise the royal powers which had been used against them. When this criticism was backed by disappointed office-seekers and by the genuine dissatisfaction over blunders in what was so clearly George III's war with the American colonies, it acquired a new flavour and a new intensity. The King was forced to accept the second Rockingham Cabinet (and with it some definite proposals for legislation) in 1782 and then the Fox-North coalition in 1783. This was not like Newcastle and Pelham using their scarcity value as governors to press the King into giving them precedence over their rivals. Fox probably hoped that his Cabinet would be

---

[14] R. Pares, *George III and the Politicians*, p. 174.
[15] It was, of course, always the case that the King did not need to refer all questions to the Cabinet and the most delicate and secret negotiations may only have been revealed to the leading minister and secretary of state. See Fortesque, *op. cit.*, Vol. IV, p. 473.
[16] R. Pares, *op. cit.*, p. 151.

strong enough for George ultimately to acquiesce—indeed this was its only chance of survival—but there was an extra ingredient of personal animosity which bore fruit in some new constitutional practices. Two changes which did not last were that Rockingham in 1782 made royal acceptance of the measures known as "Economical Reform" a condition of office and in 1783 Portland, as head of the Fox-North Coalition, was able to insist on the King accepting all seven of his nominations to the Cabinet.[17] The change which does appear to have persisted was that in both the Rockingham and Fox-North ministries matters were considered by the Cabinet without the King's permission being obtained. It was against this that George III was protesting when he wrote that "certainly it is quite new for business to be laid before the Cabinet and consequently advice offered by the Ministers to the Crown unasked."[18] As part of this process North agreed with Fox that "there should not be a Government of Departments . . . I think it a very bad thing,"[19] and by this he meant that departmental business should go to the King only after the Cabinet had declared its opinion.

It is true that George III emerged triumphant from the crisis of 1782–84, but his difficulties were a symptom of the very gradual arrival of some issues in politics. The reactions of his opponents, though exaggerated by the stresses of their position as unwanted servants of the Crown, pointed the direction of development. The Pelham-Newcastle-Hardwicke Cabinet of the 1740s and the Grenville Cabinet of 1763–65 had shown a tendency to see themselves as "a separate body standing over against the king."[20] In both these cases, there had been friction between the leading ministers and the Crown, but now, even after George had installed an entirely satisfactory Prime Minister in the person of the Younger Pitt, the tendency of the Cabinet to consider problems without previous royal permission continued.

In general the Cabinet gained strength under Pitt for a variety of reasons. Until after the outbreak of the war with Revolutionary France the only alternative to him was the detested Fox. Pitt had no desire to fortify his position against the Crown but he tended

---

17 Fortescue, *op. cit.*, Nos. 3648, 4268 and 4271.
18 Fortescue, *op. cit.*, Nos. 3699, 3700.
19 Betty Kemp, *op. cit.*, p. 126.
20 R. Pares, *op. cit.*, p. 167.

on all occasions to arrogate power to himself. It is well known that he forced George to dismiss Lord Thurlow in 1792 for opposing Cabinet measures, though the view that the Chancellor should be a royal nominee remained until 1830. At the same time the Crown's ability began to diminish after George had had his first bout of insanity in 1788. In the next year he wrote; " I must decline entering into a pressure of business, and indeed for the rest of my life shall expect others to fulfil the duties of their employments, and only keep that superintending eye which can be effected without labour or fatigue." [21] Despite this George was still fairly active and could argue with his ministers. When Grenville sent a Cabinet minute in July 1796 proposing what were in effect the outlines of a peace settlement with France, the King objected very strongly and summoned Pitt and Grenville to hear his views.[22] As he aged, however, George did have to leave more to his ministers, a trend which continued under George IV, who lacked both the capacity and courage of his father.

These tendencies in the direction of unity and collective responsibility on the part of the Cabinet, though important, did not alter the basic elements in the Constitution. The situation is well illustrated by Pitt's resignation in 1801. It seems evident that the Cabinet had laid its plans for carrying the Union with Ireland without getting George's permission or informing him of the prospect of some relief for Catholics. Such a practice had only arisen in the last twenty years, but once George was informed and declared his hostility Pitt's position collapsed. Pitt not only realised that George had transferred his confidence and was going to dismiss him, but accepted that this was quite legitimate. The subsequent history of the question is revealing. In the early eighteenth century the Cabinet would have been most reluctant to suggest a measure known to be obnoxious to the King and the latter would have felt free to ignore any such advice. By 1800 it was an open matter whether the monarch could reject advice or veto consideration of a question, so instead George III preferred to exact a promise from Pitt in 1804 that he would not

---

[21] Quoted by A. Aspinall, *The Cabinet Council, 1783–1835*, from Stanhope's *Pitt*, ii, Appx. vii.

[22] A. Aspinall, *The Later Correspondence of George III*, Vol. II, pp. 496–497 and *The Dropmore Papers*, Vol. III, pp. 227–230.

raise the problem. Yet in 1807 the Cabinet of All the Talents declared " the absolute impossibility of their thus fettering the free exertion of their judgment," [23] and in 1812 that high Tory, Lord Eldon, wrote:

> " As to the Proposal that the Roman Catholic claims should be taken into consideration by Cabinet, I conceive it to be the duty of Government to consider in Cabinet the claims of any body of His Majesty's subjects, and to decide upon them bonâ fide whenever the attention of Government is called to that consideration by any member of the Cabinet acting upon his sense of public duty." [24]

But despite these strong statements, Catholic Emancipation was kept an open question from 1812 to 1828 when, at any time, royal acquiescence would have ensured its passage, and George IV only consented to let Wellington make it a government measure under intense pressure including the threat of civil war.

Thus by 1830, the Cabinet was a long-standing feature of British government. Its numbers had slowly risen from five or six in the 1740s to between seven and nine in the 1760s. After the turn of the century, Cabinets varied between fifteen in 1818 and eleven in 1828, Earl Grey's total of thirteen in 1830 being a fair average for the period. This growth was largely due to the composite nature of the governments. It was often difficult to find adequate debating talent in the House of Commons, and cohesion was made harder by the reappearance of issues in politics.

The Household offices had ceased to carry Cabinet rank with the demise of the outer Cabinet, the last case of any importance being when Bute was put into the active part of the ministry as Groom of the Stole in 1760. In 1806 Lord Ellenborough was included in Grenville's Cabinet while Lord Chief Justice, but such an appointment was criticised in Parliament and did not recur. Some new departmental posts had arisen or achieved Cabinet rank, such as the President of the Board of Trade, the Secretary for War (and Colonies after 1801), the President of the Board of Control (India), First Commissioner of Woods and Forests

23 Lord Holland, *Memoirs of the Whig Party*, ii. The Cabinet minute is printed in the Appendix on p. 319 and this section is italicised.
24 *Correspondence of George IV*, ed. A. Aspinall, No. 90.

and the Irish Secretary, while appointments involving negligible duties like the Chancellor of the Duchy of Lancaster, Master of the Mint, Postmaster-General and Paymaster-General were on occasion used to confer membership of the Cabinet.

As has been said, the power of the Crown had been declining both in absolute terms and as against the ministers for fifty years. The decline was in part personal, in part due to the emergence of more definite political issues and of a public concerned about politics and in part to the process of administrative reform which slowly reduced the amount of money, patronage, contracts and favours through which the Crown could influence politics.[25]   The other product of these developments was the increased strength of the Cabinet. It now deliberated on all matters without royal permission and the Crown would have had great difficulty in ignoring its recommendations. Even on matters of patronage, the King was expected to take his ministers' advice and Liverpool offered to " recall to your Majesty's recollection cases in which it could not but be distinctly admitted that the expectation which might have been personally held out by the sovereign was subject to the responsibility of his ministers, and that it must be a sufficient answer on such an occasion that the appointment has been obstructed in a quarter which cannot by the laws of the country be passed by." [26]   The post of Prime Minister was more clearly recognised by the 1820s and it was possible for Liverpool to retain office, though often on very bad terms with George IV, because he had the loyalty of his colleagues. Cabinets, though still composed of various groups and neither taking nor leaving office as a body, were finding it more necessary to work as a unit. In 1801 when Lord Loughborough was replaced as Lord Chancellor, he kept his key to Cabinet boxes and went on attending meetings till the Prime Minister, Addington, procured his explicit dismissal from the King.[27] It was still assumed, even when a complete ministry

[25] See A. S. Foord, " The Waning of ' the Influence of the Crown,' " *E.H.R.* (1947) pp. 484–507.   The same process took place a little later in the House of Lords, largely as a reflection of the increasing number of political issues in the Commons.   See D. Large, " The Decline of ' the Party of the Crown ' and the Rise of Parties in the House of Lords, 1783–1837," *E.H.R.*, Vol. 78 (1963) pp. 669 695.

[26] Quoted by R. Pares, *op. cit.*, from *Correspondence of George IV*, ed. Aspinall, i, Nos. 910, 914, 916–921.

[27] John, Lord Campbell, *Lives of the Lord Chancellors*, Vol. VIII, p. 197.

was forced on the King in 1783, that the Lord Chancellorship remained a royal appointment but in 1830 Lyndhurst could not be accommodated in the Grey Cabinet and the appointment of Brougham indicated that all the offices in the Cabinet had become political and all were vacated when the Reform Ministry resigned in 1832.

Yet when all these tendencies have been noted, the major factor in politics was still that the Crown could hold and win (if with a smaller margin) an election. This meant that the choice of ministers still lay with the Crown rather than with the electorate or the House of Commons, and George IV was able to veto a Whig Government as long as he lived and to prevent legislation he disliked unless actually threatened with a major disturbance, as in Ireland in 1828 and 1829. Only when the Reform Act of 1832 swept away the worst of the rotten and nomination boroughs and widened the franchise did this royal power dissolve and the political conditions affecting Cabinet government undergo a radical alteration.

Part Three

The Early Victorian Cabinet 1832–68

CHAPTER 3

RELATIONS WITH PARLIAMENT AND THE PUBLIC

THE EFFECTS OF THE 1832 REFORM ACT

IN this chapter it is proposed to give a brief account of the effects of the Reform Act of 1832 on those aspects of politics which influenced the development of the Cabinet, and then to continue with a more detailed examination of the period till 1868.

The role of the Cabinet has always been too many-sided to permit of any short summary, but its position and power up to 1832 can be described largely in terms of the Cabinet's relations with the Crown on the one side, and with Parliament (and, in a limited sense, the public) on the other. Any factor which had an effect on the temper and practice of either the Crown or Parliament in some degree touched the Cabinet. Thus there were gradual readjustments to the decline in the capacity of George III, a tendency which was not interrupted by the accession of George IV. Similarly in these years, the growth and redistribution of population and increased industrial activity produced tensions which in time reached the surface of politics. Aided by an expanding newspaper press and combined with Irish and foreign problems, such tensions had an influence on Members of Parliament—and this influence had to be considered by Cabinets wishing to avoid difficulties in the House of Commons.

During the regency and reign of George IV, a demand for reform of the electoral system had become one of those issues which acted as a focus of interest and pressure (though till 1830 it was by no means the most prominent demand). The introduction of a Reform Bill in early 1831 was due to some fortuitous and some long-term factors, but its passage did much more than merely intensify the effect of existing tendencies. By abolishing the worst of the rotten boroughs, widening the franchise, and redistributing seats, the Reform Act changed the relationship between Members and their constituencies. It rapidly emerged that under the new electoral conditions the Member of Parliament had to take great care to conciliate local influences all of which had some interest in his political conduct. As a result, royal offers to help or reward were no longer major factors affecting the conduct of Members of Parliament. At the same time there were fewer resources available for patronage [1] and for both these reasons royal influence, which had been declining for the last thirty years, virtually came to an end in 1832.[2]

This meant that the Crown could no longer choose and maintain ministers. It might, by a happy accident, anticipate a change of mind on the part of Parliament or the public, but this was so unlikely and so uncomfortable if it failed (as William IV found out when he installed Peel in 1834 and held an election) that the Crown realised that it must restrict its selection to a search for the Prime Minister who was most likely to command the largest measure of support in the House of Commons. In these circumstances royal initiative was not removed but was reduced from the vital element to a minor influence.

But though the Crown no longer played the decisive part in choosing ministers, it did not follow that the Members of Parliament wanted or had evolved machinery which would permit them to do so. Parties existed in the sense that many could be described as Whigs, Tories or Radicals, though few liked to be termed " party men." The leaders of a party were those who entered the Cabinet and its adherents were such Members of Parliament as attended the meeting held at the start of the session and voted with the government on most occasions. Parties were thus loose entities which grew up around Cabinets rather than well-defined organisations which could produce them. Yet political feelings were clearly marked and it was usually evident that

---

[1] See above, p. 71 and note 25. It can be argued that the Crown lost the election of 1830 and that royal influence was no longer a decisive factor before the Reform Act. But in this case the situation was complicated by the fact that William IV was mildly pro-Whig and however far these trends had gone by 1832, the Reform Act set a seal on this development.

[2] N. Gash, *Politics in the Age of Peel*, p. 337, estimates that the court and government could between them exercise a strong influence in some 13 constituencies in England and Wales, but he agrees with F. R. Bonham, the Conservative electoral expert, that this would probably affect the result in not more than six seats. It is not clear whether Professor Gash is going back on these earlier estimates in his *Reaction and Reconstruction in English Politics, 1832–1852*, p. 23, when he repeats the exaggerated remarks made by Tory politicians about royal influence in the elections of 1837 and 1841. There is no evidence that his original calculations were wrong.

a given House of Commons was more likely to support ministers of a certain political colour. The actual formation of a Cabinet would then depend on the Crown selecting a leading politician of this political colour and on his capacity to obtain the assistance of sufficient prominent men to permit the construction of a Cabinet which would win the confidence of a majority in the House.

Once a group of politicians began the task of forming a Cabinet and conducting business, they had to deal with 658 Members in a House of Commons returned by and dependent on constituencies of very differing political complexions. As a result, the position of the Cabinet was a great deal weaker than before 1832. It could no longer rely on royal support to ensure a majority in the House and at elections: the old methods of controlling Members had largely disappeared. There were no blocks of seats in the gift of a single patron who could be conciliated.[3] It has been estimated that in some fifty constituencies the local magnate could exercise a powerful influence [4] and in most cases secure the return of one of the family (in rather fewer instances, of nominees), but the effect of such influence was to bind the Member to the patron, not to the ministry. Patronage at the disposal of the government had steadily declined and while minor posts were still filled on political recommendation,[5] jobs were not sufficiently numerous or attractive to affect the allegiance of Members of Parliament. Most patronage was a reward for support which had been rendered on other grounds and some patronage was so minor in significance that it was given to the local M.P. whatever his voting record might have been.[6] There were still seats which might be won by bribing the electors or using local patronage, but such activity usually caused more political trouble than it was worth. There was a growing feeling that attempts to gain seats in this way were illegitimate.[7] As political issues became more prominent M.P.s for every type of constituency found that

---

[3] The largest number was reputed to be three under the control of Lord Segrave but Professor Gash, *op. cit.*, pp. 211–213, has shown that only one seat was effectively retained by him.

[4] *Ibid.*, p. 211.

[5] E. Hughes, " Civil Service Reform, 1853–55," *History*, 1942, pp. 54–55.

[6] *Ibid.*, pp. 58–59.

[7] See the scandal that broke out over Conservative attempts to use government patronage in the dockyard seats in 1852. R. Blake, *Disraeli*, p. 321.

they had to declare their views and once these were established, Members expected the Cabinet to win rather than buy, coax or obtain their votes. The strongest pull on the Member was from his constituency and if he satisfied the patron in a close seat, paid the money to bribe a venal constituency, belonged to the local family in a small borough, or met with the approval of a wider electorate, he was secure. Cabinets were dependent on the good will of Members of Parliament and while fear of the dangers and costs of a dissolution at times acted as a restraint, the government could seldom directly dislodge opponents at an election.

The effect of the Reform Act on the House of Lords created a further difficulty for some Cabinets. The link between the Houses in the form of peers controlling groups of seats in the Commons was largely broken. The whole theory of representation which triumphed in 1832 served to raise the prestige of the Commons and though defeats in the Lords were serious matters, they were not taken to indicate a loss of public confidence and resignation was not a necessary consequence. Yet governments were still eager to defend themselves in the Lords and this task was now more difficult. The appeal to the peers had always been based on loyalty to the Crown supplemented by patronage but now that the latter had declined and loyalty did not necessarily involve supporting all the measures of a Cabinet, the Lords were ready to recast and reject legislation on a considerable scale.[8]

Thus the statesmen whose habits had been formed under the Georges had, after 1832, to adapt themselves to conditions which, despite many continuous features, did embody marked differences. Both Peel and Melbourne were worried by the weakness of the executive in the face of a House of Commons full of independent M.P.s (defined aptly by Lord Derby as Members who could not be depended on [9]). Both had difficulties with the House of Lords and both played important parts in helping the Crown to adapt to the new distribution of power.

---

[8] See D. Large, " The Decline of ' the Party of the Crown ' and the Rise of Parties in the House of Lords, 1783–1837," *E.H.R.*, Vol. 78 (1963) pp. 669–695.

[9] Memorandum of Lord Derby's visit by Prince Albert, February 1, 1855, *Queen Victoria's Letters*, Series I, Vol. III, p. 106. (Hereafter referred to as *Letters*.)

THE DEGREE OF CONTROL EXERCISED BY THE COMMONS

Turning to a closer discussion of the Cabinet, the first task is to examine its relations with the institution which affected it most—the House of Commons. It was this House which conditioned the life of a Cabinet and played a major part in shaping policy. But despite its pervasive influence, the Commons could not effectively choose a Prime Minister or start the process of forming a ministry; it could provide the background and make its prevailing temper felt. Directly the results of a general election were known, commentators could forecast the distribution of strength in the House since by the 1830s no one could play an effective part in public life without taking a stand on some political issues—the " non-political " Member had disappeared.

Thus it was clear, after the electoral landslide of December 1832, that the first reformed House of Commons would tolerate nothing but the continuation of Earl Grey's Cabinet. Even in these circumstances, had Earl Grey chosen to retire, the selection of a successor would have lain not with the House or with the Whig Party but would have depended on royal nomination and the co-operation of the leading Whigs. The influence of the House would still be felt, since prominence in a party was in many cases the reflection of prestige in the Commons. While men achieved Cabinet rank for a variety of reasons, it was impossible to form a ministry without an effective leader in the Commons and the support of most of the debating talent on the same side. When Melbourne resigned in 1839, Queen Victoria summoned the Duke of Wellington, but he declined in favour of Sir Robert Peel " on account of his advanced age and the necessity in his opinion of the Minister being in the House of Commons." [10] If the Conservative Prime Minister was not to be a peer, Peel's standing in the House made him the only possible choice and when, after the election of 1841, a Conservative majority defeated Melbourne, Peel received the royal commission.

In the late 1840s and 1850s, as political tension and nation-wide issues declined, the temper of the Commons became more indeterminate. After a study of the election results in 1847 and 1852 it was possible to forecast that Cabinets containing the

---

[10] Memorandum by Sir Robert Peel, May 8, 1839, in C. S. Parker, *Sir Robert Peel*, Vol. II, p. 390.

leading Whig statesmen were more likely to be acceptable, but the House was divided into too many political groups to permit of any confident prediction. The return of Whigs, Tories, Peelites, Irishmen and Radicals in numbers which gave no definite group an absolute majority left the formation of Cabinets more in the hands of the leading politicians and the Crown. But the lack of an absolute majority meant that a minor readjustment of relations in the House of Commons, the alienation of only a small number of M.P.s, could destroy a Cabinet. This situation constituted an indirect control over the formation of Cabinets in that politicians who could not collect a wider support than their own followers were reluctant to make the attempt—this being the reason why Derby declined the royal commission in 1851 and 1855. The alternative situation where several groups in the House were clearly turning for leadership in a certain direction occurred in 1854 and 1855 when growing support for Palmerston raised his prestige, led the other politicians to defer in his favour and enabled him to maintain a Cabinet composed only of Whigs.

The theory of the British Constitution in the mid-nineteenth century entirely accepted the idea that the representative House contained, criticised and could dismiss the executive but (although its reactions would obviously be a major consideration) could not actually take steps to form a new executive. The initiative was to come from the Crown but its duty was to select the Prime Minister who was most likely to win the support of a majority in the House of Commons. The dangers of attempting to impose a personal preference on a reluctant House was fully revealed in 1835 when Peel's ministry was defeated six times in six weeks and forced to retire despite the evident support of William IV, the House of Lords, the City and, Peel hinted on some issues, of public opinion.[11]

A much less clear-cut case occurred in May 1839. On that occasion Peel could probably have formed a government and then achieved a majority at an election, had he been prepared to overlook difficulties with the Queen. But when she made some objections, he was unwilling to act and unable to force her hand

---

[11] Parker, *op. cit.*, Vol. II, p. 300. It is only fair to add that Peel on the whole disapproved of the dismissal of Melbourne in 1834 and would have let this be known had he been in the country at the time.

as Melbourne had forced William's in 1835 simply because he did not have a majority in the House. Commenting on this at a later date, Wellington considered that the possession of a majority implied a duty to remain in office, since any other Cabinet was unlikely to last, and he doubted whether Melbourne was entitled to retire simply because his majority had fallen to five (on the decision of the government to suspend the constitution of Jamaica). Certainly, the continued support of the House from 1839 to 1841, if unenthusiastic, showed that most of the Members were still prepared to tolerate a Whig Cabinet. However, the revelation of the young Queen's partisanship in the Bedchamber crisis of 1839 alarmed Melbourne and in the next two years he frequently explained that if and when the balance in the House changed, she would have to accept a new ministry. In 1841 he reminded her " that Peel was in a very difficult position now, backed by a large majority, to when the other overture was made. He had the power *now* to extort what he pleased." [12]   For a government to remain in office, what was required was not a party majority but a majority of the Members in the House. It is often said that Lord Derby in 1852 and 1858–59, and even Lord John Russell from 1846 to 1852, led minority governments. But these governments had minority backing only in the sense that the Members who attended their occasional meetings of supporters and accepted their Whips could not outvote all other combinations. They could remain in office only so long as there was a favourable majority in the most important divisions in which the position of the Cabinet was at stake.

Criticism of a government tended to take the form of objections to specific proposals rather than of motions of no confidence or a refusal to vote supplies. The main reason for this lay in the character of the Commons, the undeveloped state of parties, the qualified nature of party allegiances, and the number of men with specific pledges or individual views. The result, in practice, was that groups were often prepared to unite in opposition to a given proposal but would not go to the length of a general motion of censure. Apart from the one instance when William IV dismissed Melbourne in 1834, governments changed when a major

[12] Memo. by Anson, Private Secretary to the Prince Consort, August 30, 1841, *Letters*, Series I, Vol. I, p. 384.

proposal rallied sufficient opponents to leave the ministers in a minority (or when internal dissension was intensified by pressure from the Commons). But, for the same reasons, a new government usually had a breathing space as opposition would not become formidable until the Cabinet's proposals had been matured and put before the House. Even in the most clear-cut case, when Peel had been installed and then defeated in the election of 1834–35 and many Whigs were eager " to demolish these men," [13] the opposition was in several minds as to the most expedient tactics. Lord Grey wrote that " my plan . . . would be to bring forward no direct question, unless something in the Address to which I could not assent forced me to an amendment, till the views of Ministers were fully developed." [14] Lord John Russell preferred a more direct attack. He got the government's nominee for the Speakership rejected, but an amendment regretting that the progress of reform " has been interrupted and endangered by the unnecessary dissolution " was carried by only seven votes.[15] The more moderate Whigs were sceptical about Lord John's idea of limiting the government by voting supplies for only three months, and so he decided to choose the issue which was best calculated to unite Peel's opponents. He moved for a Committee of the whole House on the Irish Church and steadily carried resolutions on this matter against the government till Peel resigned.

When Lord Melbourne's government was clearly declining and financial problems threatened further weakness in 1841, Peel was faced with rather a different situation. The government proposed a reduction in the timber and sugar duties, but was defeated by thirty-six votes and its resignation was generally expected. Instead Lord Melbourne remained in office in order to bring forward the Cabinet's scheme for a fixed duty on corn, before asking for a dissolution. Peel felt that having lost on such a major matter, the government should not be allowed an indefinite time for choosing the issues on which to appeal to the country. Yet when he moved his motion of lack of confidence, it was carried by only one vote. In the Whitsun recess of 1846 when the Protectionists were considering how to defeat Peel, Disraeli says " the

---

[13] Lloyd C. Sanders, ed., *Lord Melbourne's Papers*, p. 251.
[14] *Ibid.*, p. 242.
[15] S. Walpole, *Life of Lord John Russell*, Vol. I, p. 218.

impetuous demanded a formal vote of want of confidence in the government, but the objection to this suggestion was, that in all probability the vote would not have been carried." [16] They had to wait till an issue arose—the coercion Bill for Ireland—on which the government had decided to stand and which sufficient Protectionists and Whigs were prepared to oppose. With no cohesive absolute majorities in the House after 1846, attempts to defeat ministries in the 1850s all followed this pattern: the construction of motions on matters of substance which would unite as many of the political groups as possible.

Thus Cabinets depended for their existence on the support of a majority in the Commons, but they could usually rely on some time to settle into office, with the knowledge that when the challenge came it would be on a major matter of policy. And the support of the House did not have to be constant or unvarying. Governments could survive, though perhaps with diminishing prestige, a fair number of defeats provided that there was no sustained series of hostile votes revealing a continuing dissatisfaction (as Peel obviously faced in March and April 1835). If a Cabinet resigned or asked for a dissolution after a single defeat it was because the voting either registered changes brought about by a general election, or revealed an obvious loss of confidence (as in the defeat of Aberdeen's government by 305 to 148 in January 1855), or was held to touch upon the honour of the Cabinet. A change of attitude in the House was readily detected by both ministers and observers. It was much harder, however, to predict those issues on which the Cabinet would be prepared to trim its sails beforehand or to accept a rebuff and those issues on which it would decide to stand or fall.

In April 1833 Lord Grey was defeated on such a major matter as the malt tax but continued in office, as it was evident the objection was to this one item and his supporters were " sorry and repentant." [17] In contrast to Grey's mild, almost passive, leadership when Peel was beaten on the sugar duties in June 1844,

---

[16] B. Disraeli, *Lord George Bentinck*, 1905 edition, pp. 150 and 169.
[17] *Greville's Journals*, ed. Henry Reeve (1874), Series I, Vol. II, p. 368. Though it should be noticed that Grey's first reaction was to consider resignation and he was " very hurt " by his treatment. In effect the decision was reversed when the government pointed out that though there was a case for the repeal of both malt and assessed taxes, since the Revenue could not bear the loss, it was fairer to leave both.

he went down to the House and insisted on a reversal of the vote. "People of all parties were exasperated and disgusted "[18] but Peel got his way. In 1853 and early 1854, the Aberdeen government suffered a series of rebuffs in the Commons but remained in office because ministers felt that they might still gather sufficient strength.

Cabinets that were eager to cling to office could often sense changes in the reactions of Members of Parliament and adapt their policies so that, in extreme cases, the House could almost be said to be leading the government. After a long exchange of memoranda and discussion, Lord John Russell's Cabinet decided in January 1848 to raise expenditure on the Army and Navy by £508,000, which would involve an increase in income tax from 7d. to 1s. in the pound. The Prime Minister introduced the proposals but the dissatisfaction of the Commons was so evident that within a fortnight the estimates were decently buried in committee and the income tax left at its existing rate. While public attention was distracted by the European revolutions, the ministry retraced its steps and reduced expenditure on the services before the end of the session.[19] In early 1855 Palmerston was struggling to set up his government and wanted to put aside Roebuck's motion for a committee of inquiry on the Crimean War, but as the Commons were obviously intent on it, he gave way. Shaftesbury was not far wrong in the early stages of the ministry, when he wrote " I much doubt whether he has, since he became Premier, been able to do any one thing according to his own judgment and preference." [20] Even when Palmerston's government was much more secure in mid-1856 and a dispute arose with the United States over the Foreign Enlistment Act (passed during the Crimean War), the Prime Minister's desire to take what he regarded as a firm stand had to be abandoned.[21] Sidney Herbert said it was " most discreditable " for " no Government should take a reversal of a peace and war policy from the House of Commons." [22] In 1858 the Cabinet led by Lord Derby and Disraeli introduced an India Bill which was greeted with derision and,

18 *Ibid.*, Series II, Vol. II, p. 247.
19 S. Walpole, *op. cit.*, Vol. II, pp. 16–27.
20 H. C. F. Bell, *Life of Lord Palmerston*, Vol. II, p. 116.
21 *Ibid.*, Vol. II, p. 156.
22 Lord Stanmore, *Memoir of Sidney Herbert*, Vol. II, p. 46.

if persisted with, would certainly have been defeated. Lord John Russell offered to submit a series of resolutions to the House so that an alternative Bill could be based on acceptable principles. Disraeli was only too glad to agree, but pressed by Edward Ellice's remark that it is " better to have one Government at a time," [23] he undertook to bring in the resolutions himself. The introduction of preliminary resolutions occurred on other occasions when the government either wanted to ascertain the views of the House, though this expedient might also be adopted if the ministry was not clear in its own mind or, very infrequently, as a device for postponing a decision. All three motives were present in early 1867 when Disraeli wanted to approach the difficult subject of parliamentary reform by the method of introducing resolutions. Directly the Cabinet realised that the House and the public wanted the matter settled, they turned to the preparation of a Bill.

On other occasions, governments were prepared simply to abandon measures that ran into difficulties in Parliament. While this was understandable with minor items of legislation, Lord John Russell had to give up two Reform Bills (in 1854 and 1860) when the House showed a lack of interest which concealed a latent hostility. It is true that in these instances a majority of the ministers was lukewarm and whether a government was prepared to stake its existence on a proposal did in part depend on the degree of unanimity or enthusiasm for the measure within the Cabinet. In 1853, after a long battle, the Cabinet acquiesced in Gladstone's budget but only after Lansdowne and Palmerston had told the Prime Minister, Lord Aberdeen, that " they would also acquiesce in its defeat, so that they could be no party to a dissolution on it, against the verdict of the House of Commons." [24] In 1861, Palmerston as Premier made it clear that though the Cabinet had accepted the budget, he thought that the financial arrangements should have been framed upon a different principle and that " as far as I am concerned, I do not intend to make the Fate of my administration depend upon the Decision which

---

[23] Herbert Paul, *History of Modern England*, Vol. II, p. 160.
[24] *Autobiography and Memoirs of George Douglas, Eighth Duke of Argyll*, ed. the Dowager Duchess of Argyll, Vol. I, p. 433. See also John Morley, *Life of Gladstone*, Vol. I, p. 466.

Parliament may come to upon your Proposal." [25]   When Lord
John Russell's last Reform Bill was defeated in 1866, some of
the opposition expected the Cabinet to let the matter drop as
before, suffering perhaps a few changes of personnel in the
process.[26]   It was a sign of greater unity and determination in the
government and of the revival of political feeling in the country
that this possibility was not considered. The Cabinet discussed
only the alternatives of reintroducing the Bill, asking for a dissolution or resigning and decided in favour of resignation.

With all these possibilities of avoiding an issue, of adapting
policies to meet criticism or even of swallowing a rebuff, a government which had been enjoying the support of a majority of the
Commons was unlikely to resign unless it saw itself as not merely
defeated but in some measure discredited.[27]   And the dividing
line in such a subjective test was hard to determine. Lord
Derby's Government of 1852 held out no hope of reviving protection, but apparently it would have resigned if Charles Villiers'
motion describing the repeal of the Corn Laws as a " just, wise
and beneficial measure " had been passed. It was, however,
prepared to accept a motion which was substantially the same
omitting only the three " odious epithets." [28]   Some of the issues
on which Cabinets were prepared to stand or fall rested on the
narrowest of margins. The decision of Palmerston and his colleagues to resign after being defeated on the Conspiracy to
Murder Bill in February 1858 is a case in point. A majority
favourable to Palmerston had been returned in the election of
1857 and the first reading of the Bill was carried by 200 votes.
The amendment, which was carried by nineteen, did not destroy
the Bill but merely regretted that a French despatch of January
20 had not been answered. Both the Queen and Lord Derby
were quite prepared for Palmerston to continue despite this reverse
and Lord Derby asserted that if Clarendon's speech of explanation

[25] P. Guedalla, *Gladstone and Palmerston*, pp. 166–167 and Morley, *op. cit.*,
Vol. II, p. 39.
[26] Andrew Lang, *Life, Letters and Diaries of Sir Stafford Northcote, First Earl
of Iddesleigh*, p. 139.
[27] Discussing Lord John Russell's rebuff over Locke King's motion in 1851, Sir
T. Martin says " This defeat, had it stood alone, might have been retrieved,
but coupled as it was with other indications of loss of confidence, it was
conclusive." Sir T. Martin, *Life of the Prince Consort*, Vol. II, p. 346.
[28] Herbert Paul, *op. cit.*, Vol. I, p. 264.

had been made before rather than after the division, the government would not have been defeated. Yet the Cabinet agreed unanimously to resign because Palmerston's popularity had fallen, and in face of a calculated attempt to trip up the government they had lost. Prince Albert recorded that they had resigned "from the real conviction of the impossibility to go on with honour and success." [29]

The Cabinet's Capacity to Lead the Commons

If these were the ways in which the reactions of the House affected the Cabinet, it remains to examine the other side of the coin and consider how far the government was able to control the Commons. After the cement of patronage was gone, political or party feeling remained as the major connection between a Cabinet and its followers. The battles over reform between 1830 and 1832, the many items of controversial legislation in the 1830s, and Peel's celebrated 1841–46 ministry, have all helped to suggest that parties existed in a milder version of their late Victorian form; an impression which has been strengthened by the Protectionists' accusation that Peel "betrayed his party" and by Disraeli's well-known remark "that the first duty of an English minister is to be faithful to his party, and that good and honourable government in this country is not only consistent with that tie but in reality mainly dependent upon its sacred observance." [30]

But the nature of parties in this period did not imply any real control by leading ministers over their supporters. Candidates usually subscribed to some political principles and their views almost always played a part in returning them to Parliament, but as Members they felt bound to these principles and to the influential elements in their constituencies, not to unswerving support for a given ministry. If ever there was a party victory in these years, it was the Whig triumph at the first reformed election in

---

[29] *Letters*, Series I, Vol. III, pp. 337–340. The word "honour" occurs twice in Palmerston's explanation.

[30] B. Disraeli, *op. cit.*, pp. 253–254. Disraeli is here indulging in a partisan argument against Peel and he greatly exaggerates both the actual role of parties in this period and the strength and unity of the Conservative Party under Peel. On p. 201 he admits that Peel had never shown any interest in building up the Conservatives as a party before 1841 or in acting as a party leader when in office.

December 1832, but having had a look at Parliament, Lord Brougham wrote:

> " Our majority is not made up of men we can reckon upon as of old—nominees, and persons with few constituents, attached to us as members of a party. We talk of having it all our own way. True the Tories have none of their way, but does it follow that we have ours? Only if we go in one direction, and far enough. Of 'thick and thin men' in the old sense we have not many more than are in office; and the body of expectants is reduced to few indeed; partly because everything is cut down, partly because to take any place costs a troublesome election.
>
> Therefore we must make up our minds to give a large lump of reform and improvement with a good grace." [31]

On one of Hume's motions against sinecures in the Army and Navy departments (February 1833) Le Marchant observed that "many of our best friends voted against us" [32] and Althorp had to tell them that unless there was more regular and consistent support, the government could not be carried on.[33] Some commentators wondered whether the difficulties Lord Grey's government encountered in the Commons (such as the defeat on the Malt Tax already mentioned) were due to the size of its majority,[34] but while this may have increased the tendency to vote purely on the merits of an issue, the basic difficulty lay in the greater independence of Members.

Sir Robert Peel considered that the new conditions of politics left the executive so weak that party disputes of the old pre-1832 type could not be permitted. As he wrote to the Duke of Wellington in 1835, "We . . . feel much more interested in protecting the monarchy and the public interests involved in its security, than in fighting a mere party." [35] Professor Gash has shown conclusively that Peel did not set out to organise a party, the Conservative members gathered round him and were bitterly resentful when he insisted on a measure of allegiance in return

---

[31] Lord Brougham quoted in C. S. Parker, *Sir James Graham*, Vol. I, p. 170.
[32] A. Aspinall, *Three Early Nineteenth Century Diaries*, p. 303.
[33] Greville, *op. cit.*, Series I, Vol. III, p. 65.
[34] Queen Victoria thought that one of Peel's problems in 1844 was his nominal majority of 100. *Letters*, Series I, Vol. II, p. 19.
[35] C. S. Parker, *Sir Robert Peel*, Vol. II, p. 313.

for his leadership.[36]   While the 1841–45 ministry was indeed a great *tour de force* on Peel's part,[37] he felt the need to carry his supporters with him so irksome that there was almost an air of recklessness and relief in his announcement to his new Cabinet in December 1845.   Peel told them that " he was your Majesty's Minister, and whether supported or not, was firmly resolved to meet Parliament as your Majesty's Minister, and to propose such measures as the public exigencies required." [38]   Members would often be called upon to account for the votes they had cast in the House, but not by the party leaders.   They would have to explain their conduct to a variety of interests, political, personal and sectional in their constituencies.   The actions of any government cut across so many of these interests that it was usual to indicate support for protection rather than for anything a Derby Cabinet might do, for free trade rather than for a " thick and thin " backing of Peel or Russell.

But while support could not be commanded, Members were by no means indifferent to the fate of governments and would pause before they cast a vote which was certain to lead to a general resignation.   It was appreciated that there was a limit to the number of rebuffs a government could sustain and still carry on. In the 1830s and early 1840s when political issues (the aftermath of reform or dislike of radicalism) were fairly strong, there were absolute majorities in the House which regarded the defeat of the ministry as definitely undesirable.   The mass of reformers elected in 1832 were genuinely alarmed at the accumulating evidence of weakness in Lord Grey's Cabinet and when its mainstay in the Commons, Lord Althorp, resigned in July 1834, an address was rapidly signed by 206 Members asking him to remain in office.[39] The experience of the struggles of the winter of 1834–35, the rallying of Conservatives around Peel, Melbourne's need to pursue careful tactics, the Lichfield House compact between Whigs, Irish and Radicals, all did much to give precision to party feelings and

---

[36] N. Gash, " Peel and the Party System," *Transactions of the Royal Historical Society*, 5th Series, Vol. I, pp. 47–69.

[37] N. Gash, *art. cit.*, uses this phrase, p. 62.

[38] *Letters*, Series I, Vol. II, p. 74.

[39] Sir D. Le Marchant, *Viscount Althorp*, pp. 516–517.   It was noted " that a large number of the signatures were those of members who . . . prided themselves on their freedom from party ties and their thorough independence."

connections. With fewer Members, the Whigs had to re-adjust their Cabinet in 1839 and to take stands on issues of reform and free trade in order to hold their party together while Peel gathered his forces in preparation for office.[40]

Yet even the mild degree of constraint imposed by these conditions was resented by early Victorian M.P.s. They wanted to be able to reject a policy or a measure without having to consider whether they wished to see another Cabinet in power. In early 1847 " men complained of the unreasonable conduct of the ministers "[41] because they made major questions a matter of confidence for the second time in six months. Peel, as has been said, tended to assume support and insisted on the House reversing its adverse vote on the sugar duties in 1844, but his attitude exasperated many Conservatives. Sir James Graham wrote in March 1845 " that our country gentlemen are out of humour, and . . . the existence of the Government is endangered by their present temper."[42] After 1846 governments could seldom rely on even the nominal adherence of an absolute majority of the House and so executive weakness was even more evident in this period. Both ministers and leaders of the opposition had to move with care or they might find that even those who normally followed them had fallen away. In 1854, after the Aberdeen coalition had suffered a humiliating series of minor reverses, Lord John Russell held a meeting of supporters at the Foreign Office and told them " that, unless the Government were better supported, it could not go on."[43] Although the Protectionists were the most manageable of the major groups, Lord Derby had his difficulties and in February 1857 he had to summon his followers and announce that unless he was supported in a body (on the vote of censure over the Arrow affair), he would cease to be their leader. Disraeli often had to overlook criticism based on personal as much as political grounds but when, after special appeals for united resistance to Gladstone's 1861 budget, more than twenty Conservatives

---

40 N. Gash, *Reaction and Reconstruction in English Politics, 1832–1852*, Chapters V and VI.

41 B. Disraeli, *op. cit.*, p. 253. Greville (Series II, Vol. III, p. 324) records that when the government decided to make Mr. Hutt's motion against the African squadron in 1850 an issue of confidence " people . . . are excessively disgusted."

42 C. S. Parker, *Sir Robert Peel*, Vol. III, p. 172.

43 S. Walpole, *op. cit.*, Vol. II, p. 225.

abstained on a division, he withdrew from the House for three or four days till the malcontents had apologised.[44]

A factor which could, on occasion, help ministers and restrain their leading opponents was the difficulty of forming a new administration. Peel was reluctant to press home any attacks between 1835 and 1837, not only because he felt it was his duty to support the executive, if at all possible, but because a further resignation would only show that the Conservatives still had no majority and permit a triumphal return by the Whigs.[45] It was a serious embarrassment to Lord Derby (then Stanley) in February 1851 to confess that after helping to defeat Lord John Russell, he had not sufficient men of ability to form a Cabinet and could not persuade any other groups to join him. When he refused again on the same grounds in early 1855, he asked the Queen not to disclose the fact because, he said, there would be irritation when it was known that he had only consulted Disraeli.[46] But part of the reason was that it was hard to go on conducting an opposition if it was generally known that recently he had had to plead an inability to take office. Reflecting on the problems of constructing a Conservative Government in June 1866, Gathorne-Hardy observed that " the fatal thing will be if all combinations fail, and the old lot come back triumphant as dictators." [47]

In view of the problems of forming a ministry, especially when there appeared to be little chance of obtaining steady support, and considering the dangers of failure, the opposition on occasion preferred the kind of tacit backing which gave a measure of control over the government. A Cabinet with only a precarious majority might be able to resist motions of no confidence but find it difficult to carry even the essential financial measures of the year. In this case the offer of opposition aid was a considerable temptation although it involved a further sacrifice of power. Thus Peel, who had always refused to harry the Whigs, was on the whole content to aid and guide the Melbourne ministry between

44 Monypenny and Buckle, *Life of Disraeli*, Vol. IV, p. 300.
45 C. S. Parker, *Sir Robert Peel*, Vol. V, p. 315. It was also undesirable because it would permit the Whigs to " settle their relations to the king."
46 *Letters*, Series I, Vol. III, p. 106.
47 A. E. Gathorne-Hardy, ed., *Gathorne-Hardy, First Earl of Cranbrook*, Vol. I, p. 188.

1837 and 1841.[48]   In somewhat different circumstances, Peel steadily supported Lord John Russell from 1846 till 1850 and in return was consulted by the Whig Cabinet on many important matters.   After his defeat in 1859, Lord Derby and most of the Conservative Party agreed that it was better to let Palmerston administer the country free from the dangers of ultra-liberal pressure, and in 1860 and 1861 the Conservatives even went the length of letting Palmerston know that he would have their backing in the event of a showdown over Gladstone's financial proposals.[49]

These instances of partial co-operation between the leaders of the various parties or groups reveal another consideration which might limit the power of rank-and-file Members of Parliament. Backbench opinion could be muffled if it lacked a measure of leadership.   Any group wishing to have a serious impact had to have its quota of spokesmen at a time when the number of men capable of holding the House was limited.   Thus if most of the men of talent were agreed on certain issues, back-benchers might have no really satisfying alternative courses of action placed before them.   It will always be a matter of conjecture as to how many Members did actually desire the repeal of the Corn Laws in 1846. Certainly repeal was made feasible only because the recognised leaders on both sides favoured it and because the Protectionists could not throw up a potential ministry.[50]   Similarly, private M.P.s who genuinely desired an extension of the suffrage had little hope, since Tory Reform Bills could be outvoted and the Whig leadership was not prepared, before 1866, to stand or fall by such a measure.

In discussing this question of the Cabinet's capacity to influence or control the House of Commons, it is often asserted by later authorities that the government always had in reserve the power

---

[48] Peel had lent his support to the Whig Government on many occasions between 1832 and 1837; for example, when he offered to help them get out of a scrape over the malt tax. See Parker, *op. cit.*, Vol. II, p. 216.

[49] G. E. Buckle, pointing out that Disraeli realised that the opposition could influence, if not actually direct, affairs, says, " never was that control so brilliantly and so successfully exercised as during the six years of Palmerston's last administration." This is claiming too much, for the financial policy of the country was Gladstone's, its foreign policy that of Palmerston and Russell, though Disraeli may have helped Palmerston to see that little else was achieved. Monypenny and Buckle, *op. cit.*, Vol. IV, p. 378.

[50] G. Kitson Clark, " The Repeal of the Corn Laws and the Politics of the Forties," *Economic History Review*, 2nd Series, Vol. IV, mentions this point on p. 8.

to threaten a dissolution. It is true that Members had an acute dislike of unnecessary elections, not so much for fear of defeat but because of the considerable exertion and expenditure involved. Also, as Lord John Russell remarked, "nothing tends so much . . . to make members stand in servile awe of their constituents, as frequent General Elections." [51] But during this period it was not normal practice for the possibility of a dissolution to be used as a threat and to do so required a royal sanction which could not be taken for granted. Politicians usually considered that a government was responsible to Parliament and if defeated in the Commons, the correct procedure was for it to resign and permit the formation of another Cabinet. The idea that a ministry was the direct result of a general election and that defeat automatically entitled it to appeal once again to the people was the product of a later era. Parliaments were supposed to run for some five or six of their full seven years and the respectable reasons for holding an early election were either the appearance of a new major issue of policy which might be more fairly settled after an election or the conviction, when several combinations had failed, that greater stability was likely after an election.

In practice, this meant that a government which had won a recent general election and then suffered defeat was normally expected to resign. For instance, when Palmerston was beaten over the Conspiracy to Murder affair in 1858, his Cabinet was under a year old, his credit had fallen in the House and it appears that none of the politicians had any fear of a dissolution. On the other hand when the Liberal Government was defeated in 1866 it had only been in existence for a year, but there was a new Prime Minister in the person of Earl Russell and the defeat was over a Reform Bill which had not been an issue at the 1865 election. For these reasons the Cabinet did consider a dissolution as one of four lines of action open to it. The possibility does not seem to have worried Members because, as yet, few were convinced either that the government was determined to stand or fall by the measure or that it was likely to improve its position by an appeal to the electorate.

If a ministry had been ejected and a second Cabinet formed from among its leading opponents and then this government was

---

[51] *Letters*, Series I, Vol. II, p. 149.

in turn defeated, a dissolution was much more likely on the two-fold grounds that the new administration was entitled to test public support and that the existing Parliament did not offer a basis for stable government.[52]   It was on these grounds that the Conservatives asked for and obtained dissolutions in 1852, 1859 and 1868. In 1852 the likelihood of such a solution was appreciated because the Parliament had lasted since 1847, it had proved very difficult to maintain an executive and when Lord John Russell's Cabinet had been defeated earlier in the year, he and his colleagues had discussed the question of a dissolution and had preferred to leave the decision to their successors in office.[53]   Indeed, the Peelites were so impressed by these difficulties that they had informed Derby on the formation of his government that they would give their support on condition of a dissolution in the summer of 1852. In 1859 and 1868 the Parliaments were only two or three years old and alternative Cabinets were ready to take office, so that on these occasions there were doubts about the propriety of dissolution but not much surprise.   Gladstone maintained in both instances that the proper course was resignation,[54] and Speaker Denison went so far as to describe the 1859 dissolution as "a rash and mischievous act." [55]

When governments were defeated in 1841 and 1857, the Parliaments had lasted for four and five years and it was almost certain that either the outgoing or incoming Premier would ask for a dissolution.   Thus in all these cases when defeat was followed by dissolution (in 1841, 1852, 1857, 1859 and 1868) many Members must have been aware of the possibility when they decided which way to vote.   It was not usually necessary to threaten a dissolution. The political sense of the House was a fair guide as to the alternatives open to the government.   In 1834 the Grey Cabinet was in a precarious state and though it had not planned a course of

---

[52] There was also an old idea, of pre-1832 vintage, that since governments were the personal servants of the Crown and required its personal confidence, the defeat of these servants at an election was a humiliation for the Crown (*Letters*, Series I, Vol. II, p. 108, for Queen Victoria's well-known remarks describing the 1841 dissolution as "most lowering . . . and hurtful") but this notion was declining (see below, pp. 195–199, for a discussion of the Crown, the Cabinet and the royal prerogative of dissolution).

[53] *Letters*, Series I, Vol. II, pp. 445–446.

[54] W. D. Jones, *Lord Derby and Victorian Conservatism*, p. 255 and H.L. Debates, Vol. 191, col. 1710, May 4, 1868.

[55] Quoted by H. C. F. Bell, *op. cit.*, Vol. II, p. 207.

action in the event of a defeat, " the majority of the members dread a dissolution, knowing that the next elections must be fiercely contested, and be expensive and embarrassing in all ways." [56]   On other occasions, the government might intimate that it would stake its existence on the passage of a certain measure and Members could usually calculate whether this would be followed by an appeal to the electorate.[57]   When Lord John Russell announced that the Cabinet regarded the repeal of the Navigation Laws in 1849 (just two years after a general election) as a matter of confidence, Lord Campbell noted that " the dread of a change of Ministry and of a dissolution of Parliament has carried us over the second reading." [58]   The one occasion on which an explicit threat was made was in 1858, when Derby obtained royal permission to announce that if the motion of censure over Ellenborough's despatch to India was carried, he would go to the country.[59] Backing of this kind did not arise in 1859 when the Cabinet decided to introduce a Reform Bill, as it was accepted that if such a Bill passed there would have to be an appeal to the newly enfranchised electorate.   As both acceptance or rejection seemed likely to lead to a dissolution, the House was completely free to express its opinion and the Bill was rejected by thirty-nine votes.[60]

Compared with the five occasions between 1832 and 1868 when the defeat of the government was followed by a dissolution, there are eight instances when Cabinets preferred simply to resign.[61]   Thus voting against and defeating a government was by no means bound or even likely to lead to a dissolution, and dislike of a premature election could not be used as a regular means of

---

[56] Greville, *op. cit.*, Series I, Vol. III, pp. 97 and 104.

[57] Greville reported in 1844 " such a dread of a general election " that Peel was able to bring in the Sugar Duties Bill and insist on its passage, *ibid.*, Series II, Vol. II, p. 248.

[58] Hon. Mrs. Hardcastle ed., *Life of John, Lord Campbell*, Vol. II, p. 252.

[59] Lord Granville wrote to Lord Canning on May 24, 1858—" I believe that a hundred Radicals agreed at the last moment they must do everything to prevent a dissolution." But many other observers attribute the collapse of the Opposition to the general weakness of their case, Lord E. Fitzmaurice, *Life of Lord Granville*, Vol. I, p. 308.

[60] The same motive was a major obstacle to Lord John Russell's Reform Bill in 1860. Sir James Graham wrote to Sidney Herbert, " It is evident that the fear of dissolution predominates over every other fear in this House of Commons and nothing will appease this apprehension but the *postponement* of the Reform Bill." Lord Stanmore, *Life of Sidney Herbert*, Vol. II, p. 268.

[61] This does not include resignations in 1841 and 1859 when governments were defeated as the result of or soon after a general election.

controlling Members. Fears that the Cabinet might make such a recommendation only arose in certain situations and then only in the earlier years of a Parliament. If either the government's record was poor or its unity precarious or if the normal term of Parliament was not far away, these fears ceased to operate. So the desire to avoid a premature dissolution did act as a restraint on Members at certain times, but it was not possible to exploit this motive in a systematic manner and its existence did not materially alter the relations of the Cabinet and the Commons.

In this discussion of the relations of the Cabinet and the Commons, there is no intention of suggesting that parties did not exist or perform important functions—the point is merely that they did not exist in a form which enabled the Cabinet to discipline its supporters. Party organisation within Parliament consisted of the meetings (held at the start of the session) of Members who favoured the government,[62] together with the Whip and his efforts to persuade these Members to attend and give their support, backed by the community of feeling between the Cabinet and its back-benchers.

Outside Parliament, party organisation arose from the complicated process of registering voters.[63] In constituencies which were not controlled by one landowner or one section of the community, the desire to capture the seat for an interest or for certain principles led the individuals concerned to act together and in some cases form a committee. A part-time agent or lawyer was usually employed to see to the registration, while the local men of influence or the committee found a suitable candidate and perhaps collected a fund to cover expenses.[64]

National organisation, if it merited such a definite term, was simply the work of the Whip and, in the 1830s and 1840s, of one or two "election experts," who explained registration problems to local agents or committees and, if it was requested, suggested possible candidates. The best known of these experts were F. R.

---

[62] As Professor Gash points out, *art. cit.*, pp. 59–61, there was no recognised way of joining a party and the invitations were only sent to those whose past conduct showed that they wanted to be asked. "The question was one almost of punctilio rather than discipline."

[63] See J. Alun Thomas, "The System of Registration and the Development of Party Organisation, 1832–1870," *History*, New Series, Vol. XXXV (1950–51).

[64] There is an excellent description of a local organisation in F. M. L. Thompson, "Whigs and Liberals in the West Riding, 1830–60," *E.H.R.* (1959), p. 214.

Bonham, Edward Ellice and James Coppock. They could offer nothing except advice and contacts and, in a very few cases, some financial help, so that there was little they could threaten to withdraw.[65] Endorsement and all the important personal and financial backing came purely from within the constituency and if the group or committee was satisfied with its candidate or Member, he was entirely secure.

It may be wondered why these local groups did not insist on steady support for Grey or Peel, Derby or Palmerston. The reasons were that the 1832 Reform Act left so much diversity in the types and sizes of constituency so that there were still marked local and sectional divergencies. These different interests might have been overlaid or amalgamated by one or two national issues if the enfranchised classes had been acutely divided, as they were between 1830 and 1832.[66] But once parliamentary reform was achieved, even the major conflicts over the Irish Church, the Corn Laws, Palmerston's foreign policy and so on did not cut deeply across the constituencies. Such issues had to take their place alongside or among local divisions over personalities, family influence, and pressures from economic and religious bodies. Thus the primary desire of the constituency was to return a man who suited its precise needs, including perhaps the right family name, religious background and occupational interest and, while failure to serve these needs could lead to very serious repercussions,[67] their variety meant that the Cabinet could not readily or safely appeal to constituencies against the conduct of the local Member. In this "Golden Age of the Private M.P." there was often very close

[65] N. Gash, " F. R. Bonham, Conservative ' Political Secretary ' 1830–47," *E.H.R.* (1948), p. 502, gives a good picture of one of these experts. Professor Gash detects a " measure of control " in that Bonham's recommendation was " a badge of orthodoxy " for an unknown candidate. But it was not a prerequisite for any candidate and does not seem to have been used to obtain obedience between elections.

[66] Professor Gash in his article on " Peel and the Party System," p. 64, says " parties were disunited because the governing classes were disunited." While this is clearly true when disunity is taken to mean the variety of local particular interests, in a broader sense there was unity. There were no deep nation-wide divisions which would have recreated stronger party divisions.

[67] The electoral history of Edinburgh is an excellent example. A large, politically-conscious electorate in most years enthusiastically returned candidates presented by the Whig Committee but among the powerful local groups were the various Presbyterian churches, which combined to eject T. B. Macaulay in 1847 after he had voted for the grant to the Catholic College at Maynooth.

scrutiny and control from below.[68]   Freedom for the Member lay in the government's lack of power to coerce. It could only appeal to the House and leave each M.P. to react according to the merits of the case and the attitudes of his supporters in his own constituency.

The power which such a system left to the private Member did make the task of government very hard. But it must be emphasised that the formation of policy still lay almost entirely with the Cabinet. Parliament criticised, proposed changes and exercised a formative influence inasmuch as Cabinets had a fairly shrewd idea of what was likely to prove acceptable, but the House reacted to rather than formed or proposed positive lines of action. A major indication of the power of Parliament and a further reason for the efficacy of its criticism lay in the capacity of Members to extract information. Canning was the first Foreign Secretary to try to win the support of Parliament and the public by publishing collections of despatches on aspects of his policy. Palmerston continued this practice after 1830 but he (and other Foreign Secretaries) now found that, while prepared to table a considerable amount of material, they seldom cared to resist demands for further publication.[69]   The procedure was for a Member to move for an Address for papers to be laid before the House and if there was any show of reluctance, the government might lose votes which would not have been cast against the policy itself. So the House, the Press and the public had very full accounts of the Levant crisis of 1839–41, the origins of the Crimean War, the arguments over Italy, Schleswig-Holstein and all the other major questions laid before them more or less at once. The effect was not necessarily a weakening of the government's position. Several people said that if they had been able to read Malmesbury's Italian despatches before the critical division in June 1859, they would not have voted against the government.[70]

---

[68] As Greville observed in 1833, " the House of Commons is in such a state that it is next to impossible to say what Ministers can or ought to do . . . every man is thinking of what he shall say to his constituents, and how his vote will be taken, and everything goes on (as it were) from hand to mouth." Greville, *op. cit.*, Series I, Vol. III, p. 17.

[69] Temperley and Penson, *A Century of Diplomatic Blue Books*, 1814–1914, describes the situation in an introduction and comments on the attitude of each Foreign Secretary.

[70] Malmesbury, *Memoirs of an Ex-Minister*, p. 491. The Blue Book was ready but was not laid before the House of Commons. There were various specula-

On domestic matters, the same desire for information led to constant inquiries and reports but, as the government was not normally held responsible for any deficiencies outside its own field of action, there was less danger here than in foreign affairs. An investigation which revealed an undesirable situation might lead to a demand for legislation. Many of the major reforms of the period originated in this way and the Cabinet then had to consider whether it should adopt the measure, leave it an open question, or resist any action. The capacity to extract or collect information on every kind of foreign, colonial or internal problem was a direct consequence of the power of the private Members and contributed to their ability to contain and criticise the government. Roebuck's private motion for a Committee of Inquiry into the conduct of the Crimean War in January 1855 proved to be the last push for the tottering Aberdeen Cabinet. Gladstone and several of his Peelite colleagues felt that while Parliament was entitled to dismiss an unsatisfactory administration, to proceed to investigate the war while it was being carried on and then, presumably, to use the information to press alternative methods on the new administration, was an assumption of initiative which might, in time, make government impossible. Yet not even Palmerston was able to deny the House its committee, though firmer direction and better success in the war strengthened the Cabinet's position, and the House remained a well-informed and zealous critic of the government's policies.

THE PLACE OF PRESSURE GROUPS

Because the life of a Cabinet depended so much on its standing in the Commons, ministers tended to think of public opinion not so much as a separate entity but as it was revealed in Parliament. In the same way pressure groups usually concentrated on returning or interesting Members rather than on direct attempts to influence the government. Thus in the great battle over the repeal of the Corn Laws, the Anti-Corn Law League could score debating points but its real impact on politics began when it started to convert Members, to create forty-shilling freeholds in

tions as to why Disraeli did not bring forward the Book, the most probable being Malmesbury's explanation that " his real reason for this strange line was that he *had not read it*, and could not have fought it in debate."

winnable seats and to put up candidates. On the other side "it is probably true to say that the parliamentary organisation of the protectionist party was largely made possible by the Anti-League and that without some such basis Disraeli and Bentinck could never have carried on such a long struggle." [71]

But if the Cabinet was about to make specific proposals affecting certain groups, it was obviously wise to put one's case directly to the ministers. So when Gladstone was preparing his 1853 budget " soap deputations and post-horse deputations, representatives of tobacco and representatives of the West India interest, flocked to Downing Street," while in 1860 " he was besieged by delegates from the paper makers; distillers came down upon him; merchants interested in the bonding system, wholesale stationers, linen manufacturers, maltsters, licensed victuallers, all in turn thronged his ante-room." [72] On any subject connected with trade or religion, deputations would pour in. When Lord Granville considered adopting the Royal Commission's proposal for municipal rating for education in 1865, he realised the dangers. "Here they come in number about five thousand" was his Under-Secretary's description of a body of enraged clergy seeking an audience, and the proposal was ultimately abandoned. [73]

These deputations were significant in that they might put further evidence before the government and could give some measure of the potential opposition, but ministers were much more concerned about the reaction of Parliament. There is no evidence that Gladstone altered any of his financial proposals in response to the suggestions of the interest groups, but he was worried that sufficient M.P.s were either connected with the paper industry or were open to its influence to turn the tide in the House in 1860. [74] Sometimes the problem for the government was that Members feared the reaction of their constituents if they annoyed a powerful pressure group. The Sabbatarians scored a steady run of successes on this basis, [75] but more often the danger was that sufficient

[71] R. Blake, *op. cit.*, pp. 225 and 231.
[72] Morley, *op. cit.*, Vol. I, p. 464 and Vol. II, p. 28. Also P. Guedalla, *op. cit.*, p. 130, letter no. 72 and pp. 277–278, letter no. 223.
[73] Lord E. Fitzmaurice, *op. cit.*, Vol. I, p. 426.
[74] During the course of the debates the majority in favour of abolishing the excise duty on paper fell from 53 to nine.
[75] Sir Benjamin Hall, the Chief Commissioner of Works, had military bands playing in the London parks on Sundays. A motion was put down in May 1856 to stop this and the Cabinet was told that if they resisted " they

Members were personally affected by the proposed measures to cancel the small majorities of the period. It was natural that Members of Parliament should have close connections with specific trades or professions or be more impressed by the needs of the countryside as opposed to those of the towns and their reactions could, on occasion, be better forecast from this angle than from that of their party affiliations. Disraeli referred to the West Indies interest as " the sugar members " and alleged that they had voted for repeal of the Corn Laws because the government had promised not to touch the duties on slave-grown sugar.[76] There is not enough evidence to show whether the railway company directors, army officers and other occupational divisions of the House had any degree of organisation or informal contact. The East and West India merchants were probably the most close-knit of the groups.

One should not put too crude an interpretation on an analysis of politics in terms of economic or professional interests.[77] In 1846 the fifty-eight Members connected with banks or financial concerns voted forty-three to fifteen in favour of the repeal of the Corn Laws, but whether this reflected a calculation of personal or class benefit, or whether it was simply that these men were more open to the arguments of classical economics, would be hard to determine and of little value for our present purposes. The point is that with the weakness of party ties and the lack of government control over Members, any factor which could sway individuals and therefore votes was important. It was for this reason that interest groups preferred to help elect or win over M.P.s rather than to lobby government departments.

THE PRESS

The influence of the Press in this period arose from the same conditions. As some Members had to consider the views of their

would be beaten, and moreover that no man could support them in opposition to it without great danger of losing his seat at the next election." The Cabinet saved their faces by getting the Archbishop of Canterbury to request them to stop the bands, which they did. Greville, *op. cit.*, Series III, Vol. II, p. 46.   [76] B. Disraeli, *op. cit.*, pp. 213 and 187.

[77] J. A. Thomas in *Economica*, 1929 (" The Repeal of the Corn Laws ") and *Economica*, 1925 (" The House of Commons, 1832–1867 ") has produced some useful figures in what he calls " a functional analysis " though he grossly oversimplifies the dependence of political decisions on direct economic interests.

constituents while others (often in small boroughs) were relatively free to vote according to their convictions, those papers which were written exclusively for the educated and fairly narrow electorate and for the political circles mainly in London, could always attract immediate attention.[78]   Just how much power the various newspapers and political journals enjoyed is hard to assess, and this problem will be considered later, but what is evident is that the politicians (and most contemporary commentators) attached great importance to the Press.   Discussing the position of the Conservative Party in 1861, Prince Albert said: " But you have no newspapers " and " the country is governed by newspapers." [79] He also remarked that " when Parliament is sitting their influence is less," presumably because criticisms could be answered by speeches in the House which were then reported even in hostile papers.   Certainly Cabinets were willing to go to considerable lengths to get the best possible Press.   One method was to offer direct access to information.   In 1829 Croker had suggested to Wellington that a Cabinet Minister should have the regular task of briefing favourable journals,[80] and on occasion attempts were made to win over a specific paper, usually *The Times,* by providing exclusive news.[81]   Disraeli was so anxious to have the support of *The Times* in 1858 that he leaked news of Derby's interview with the Queen at which the membership of the Cabinet was discussed to the Editor, Delane, but this only led to a rebuff and a quarrel.[82]   If a party lacked support, leading politicians were not above starting or acquiring a newspaper.   In 1839, Lord Melbourne's Cabinet considered an open break with the *Morning Chronicle* and the foundation of a new Whig paper.[83]   Lord Clarendon as Lord Lieutenant of Ireland in 1850 felt it was important to have a paper putting the Whig Unionist case and provided the Editor of the *World* with £1,100 of secret service money, though all he gained was an attempt at blackmail and an embarrassing appearance in

---

[78] There is a good description of the influence of the Press on the London political coteries in Lord George Hamilton, *Parliamentary Reminiscences and Reflections, 1868–1885,* pp. 24–31.

[79] Monypenny and Buckle, *op. cit.,* Vol. IV, p. 295.

[80] *Croker Papers,* Vol. II, p. 22.

[81] Prince Albert alleged that Lord John Russell won over *The Times* in July 1846, by giving it private information about the formation and policies of the new Cabinet.

[82] Blake, *op. cit.,* pp. 381–382.

[83] *Lord Melbourne's Papers,* pp. 399–400.

court.[84]   After the split of 1846, the Protectionists had been left with only minor papers—the *Morning Post, Standard* and *Morning Herald* and the weekly *John Bull*.   To remedy this situation there was talk of buying and improving *John Bull* in 1850 and a year later Disraeli and Stanley were considering the foundation of a new journal.   The bitter experience of the first Derby-Disraeli ministry,[85] roughly handled by the newspapers, led Disraeli to put out a circular appeal for funds and start a new weekly, the *Press*, which he ran till 1858.[86]   Foreign governments seem to have attached an equal importance to British newspapers and in 1852 Walewski confessed that the French Government paid the *Morning Post* and that he saw the editor every day.[87]

It might be imagined that if the politicians did place such emphasis on the reactions of the Press, the result would be to give the papers at least a measure of the influence attributed to them. There is some evidence for this suggestion.   But while men read and were pleased or irritated by the political journals, their actions were usually based on more permanent and stable factors such as their own attitudes, the nature of the task in hand, and the state of the House of Commons.   It was natural that those who wrote for the papers and those whose activities were continually reported and discussed should tend to overestimate the impact of the Press.   In this century politicians and journalists have often overlooked the fact that the vast majority of readers are not interested in politics and have had their views formed by a long process which can scarcely be affected by a short newspaper campaign.   In the early Victorian era, the political opinions of Members of Parliament and of the circles which influenced them were equally the product of long-standing factors, of their personalities and their own experiences. It is, therefore, doubtful whether any considerable number of Members or electors changed their political opinions because of propaganda by the Press.   What was more likely was that fears about the wisdom of particular

---

[84] Sir H. Maxwell, *Life and Letters of the Fourth Earl of Clarendon*, Vol. I, p. 319.

[85] Lord Malmesbury noted in March 1852 that " the Opposition papers are loud in their abuse of us personally, to an amount of scurrility that does them no honour ": *op. cit.*, p. 237.

[86] Monypenny and Buckle, *op. cit.*, Vol. III, pp. 489–505.

[87] Malmesbury, *op. cit.*, p. 277.

policies may have been increased by new information and by evidence that others shared these fears. The influence of the papers was much more evident in arguments against and exposures of specific lines of action and from the sensitivity of ministers to this kind of attack. Lord Aberdeen feared that the public clamour over the Tahiti crisis, whipped up by the Press, might drive the Cabinet into precipitate action despite his threat to resign. The Duke of Newcastle's biographer considers that during the Crimean campaign, the Duke, who was Secretary of State for War, "watched its (the Press's) utterances with nervous anxiety, was sensitive to its attacks, and was inclined to listen, if not to defer, to its opinion even on questions as to which his own private sources of information were complete and reliable." [88]   It was these direct and detailed challenges that upset politicians and produced disturbing letters from their followers saying "we have no morning paper; general complaint is made by the party that they have no organ in the press of their opinions and feelings." [89]   While most public figures at this time had to develop the capacity to live with contemporary newspaper comment, allowing themselves an occasional letter or speech in reply, it was considered humiliating and damaging for the government or the opposition to be unable to present its views and answer attacks.

On the higher levels of government policy, just as there was little chance of newspapers converting Protectionists into free traders, there is little evidence of Cabinets changing direction in response to pressure from the papers. But with the tendency of M.P.s to reserve judgment till they saw how a new ministry or a new proposal was shaping, it was often of value to win a favourable reception from the Press. This was particularly so in the case of *The Times*, whose circulation at 40,000 in the 1850s far exceeded that of the other papers and whose influence was commensurate. The Editor, Delane, was closely connected with Lord Aberdeen over a number of years (Aberdeen even agreeing on Delane's advice to put a radical, Sir W. Molesworth, in his Coalition Cabinet) [90] but shifted to a support of Palmerston after *The Times*

---

[88] J. Martineau, *Life of Henry Pelham, 5th Duke of Newcastle*, p. 194.

[89] Poulett Thomson to Lord Melbourne, June 10, 1839, *Lord Melbourne's Papers*, p. 400.

[90] A. I. Dasent, *John Delane, 1817–1879*, Vol. I, pp. 51, 151–152. *Ibid.*, Vol. I, pp. 251, 257. Dasent asserts that Palmerston's appointment of Sir Robert Peel

had exposed the weaknesses in the conduct of the Crimean War. By 1857 Palmerston was giving Delane prior notice of the Government's intentions and was consulting him over such matters as the choice of a new Speaker.[91] Disraeli's efforts to win Delane's approval in 1858 only led to a quarrel and when Palmerston became Prime Minister once again, a regular correspondence resumed, though *The Times* often pressed the Government on particular issues such as the need for stronger defence forces and for neutrality over the Schleswig-Holstein dispute. After Palmerston died several of Lord Russell's colleagues were anxious to retain the goodwill of *The Times* by offering the able Member for Calne, Robert Lowe, who had written for the paper in the past, a seat in the Cabinet,[92] but Lord Russell preferred to offer the place to George Goschen. In February 1867 when Disraeli was struggling to formulate a creditable Reform Bill in the face of a divided Cabinet, Derby wrote: " It will be a crumb of comfort to you to know that I have had a most satisfactory interview with Delane. He is cordially with us, and will do all in his power to carry us through. He listened most attentively to the whole of our programme and pronounced oracularly 'I think it will do.' " [93] Disraeli was no doubt glad of this backing, but his Reform Bill arose directly from his desire to score a spectacular political stroke and was framed solely with reference to what the Cabinet (or most of them), his followers, and the House of Commons would accept. Where *The Times* may have helped was in contributing to the general opinion that something must be done to settle the Reform Question—though this sentiment would still have existed, if in a less general form, without the support of " The Thunderer." Thus the Press and particularly *The Times* could influence opinion in political circles and produce new evidence or give point to existing criticisms of a government. The most telling

as Irish Secretary in 1861 was due to Delane but the evidence only proves that he recommended Peel to the Prime Minister and was thanked for so doing by Peel. Vol. II, pp. 29–30.

[91] *Ibid.*, p. 251.

[92] Hon. Arthur D. Elliot, *Life of Lord Goschen*, Vol. I, p. 82. Lord Russell wrote to a friend: " I am aware that Mr. Delane is very angry that I did not ask to kiss his hand instead of the Queen's, when I was appointed to succeed Palmerston, but I would rather be out of office than hold it upon such humiliating conditions." Lord George Hamilton, *op. cit.*, p. 26.

[93] Monypenny and Buckle, *op. cit.*, Vol. IV, p. 492.

example was the picture of blundering and incapacity built up by
W. H. Russell's reports from the Crimea printed in *The Times*.
Yet even in this case the contribution of the papers was to
accelerate objections that would inevitably have arisen as failure
became evident. It is difficult to imagine the Aberdeen coalition
lasting much longer than it did whatever the attitude of the Press.

It must not be forgotten that even in this period, newspapers
were reacting to events and catering for as well as trying to mould
public opinion. There were occasions when a wave of popular
sentiment moved a Cabinet, especially if its members were divided
or undecided. The rising tide of Russophobia undoubtedly led
the Aberdeen coalition to take one step after another leading in the
direction of war in the winter of 1853–54.[94] It was the revival of
public interest in reform that made some broadening of the
franchise inevitable after 1865. In both these cases the movement
of opinion was started by events and speeches and was stimulated
and given a broader base by some newspapers. Public opinion as
revealed by meetings, demonstrations and petitions as well as in
the Press had its effect in part by creating an atmosphere and
raising arguments which influenced wavering ministers and in part
by leading some Members of Parliament to take a different view
of these particular policies. When Palmerston took office in 1855
or when Disraeli decided to go for household suffrage in 1867,
they had a sense of public backing which helped them to rally
their colleagues and hold the support of the House. The Press
contributed to this sensation but it was a product of many other
factors as well and it had meaning for the politicians only if it
could be measured in terms of numbers in the division lobbies
of the House of Commons.[95]

It would appear, then, that the papers played an important part
in political life in that they spread information and increased the
tempo of and interest in political conflict. Their views received
the greatest attention from all who were involved, but it would be
mistaken to regard the Press as an originating factor in political

---

[94] Sir Arthur Gordon, *The Earl of Aberdeen*, p. 256.
[95] Lady C. Cecil in her biography of her father (*The Life of Robert, Marquis
of Salisbury*) points out that after vague discussions in late 1866 " there is no
doubt that, from the moment that the Government came face to face with its
following in the House of Commons, the Cabinet atmosphere changed as if
by magic." Vol. I, p. 224.

life or as an agency which had any independent effect on the fate of Cabinets.

INTER-DEPENDENCE OF THE CABINET AND THE COMMONS

So far, this chapter has concentrated on the relations of the Cabinet and the House of Commons, including such factors as the effect of party ties, the Press and public opinion. Besides the primary question of how far the Cabinet, though dependent on the Commons, was able to guide and control the House, there were a few other ways in which the state of Parliament and the state of the government affected each other. Inasmuch as the Commons had to be convinced that the government was pursuing a wise policy, it was important to have able parliamentarians on the Treasury Bench. The leader of the House and his principal colleagues had to take their places in the late afternoon (usually just before 5 p.m.) when the sitting began and stay there, ready to answer every criticism, till Parliament rose at any time between eleven and the small hours. Thus a number of well-informed and respected spokesmen was a great asset. Yet the supply of front bench talent was never plentiful. Out of 658 Members only some 200 spoke or made any verbal contribution during the average session and few of these had the energy, persistence or weight for Cabinet office.

As a result the prospects of a Cabinet depended in part on the capacity of its members, and on their own morale as revealed by attendance at the House and a willingness to defend the government. Growing hostility in the Commons and divisions among those who were normally supporters dismayed the ministers and this in turn reduced their capacity to win over the House. The situation was summed up admirably by Brougham writing to Lord Grey in 1833:

"... I firmly believe the greater part of our unpopularity is owing to ourselves ... the Cabinet Ministers in the House of Commons either despise their adversaries or fear them; I should rather say they despise some and fear others—and the error is equally great, and will soon be equally fatal in both cases. Graham and Grant sit as if they had not the gift of one tongue apiece ... Palmerston I pass: it would be most unjust to expect anything from him, worked and worn to death as he has been; but Grant and Graham are wholly without excuse . . . I speak now of Cabinet Ministers. How can men in the back rows get up and take part in debate when the Government itself abandons its case? Althorp is admirable and invaluable, but he is also quite indifferent, and cares not how much either himself or anyone else is attacked. What with his indifference, Grant's indolence, and Graham's alarms, we are left entirely to Stanley and Spring Rice. The former is a host in himself; the latter is, next to him, by far our best man for debating. Lord John, too, is invaluable, and shows a spirit and debates with an effect, which are admirable. And in former times that force would have been quite enough, when there was but one debate in a week, and two or three speeches only were attended to. But now things are mightily changed. The debate ranges from Monday to Saturday, and twenty speeches are made in a night . . . Now to see two Cabinet Ministers *who can speak* sitting silent under an attack upon the Government, is enough to discredit any majority in the House, and I *know* it has that effect nightly at the present moment." [96]

There were complaints throughout the period that Cabinets contained too many mediocrities who could not or would not pull their weight.[97] Shortage of men of ability was a major reason for the weakness of the Conservatives after 1846. A new member had only to give the least indication of promise to be tipped for high office. Lord Clarendon returned from diplomatic service in 1839, gave one good speech in the Lords and was " marked out by public voice for the Foreign Office." [98] After only intermittent attendance in the House for six years and no speeches Lord Hartington was made Under-Secretary at the War Office and its spokesman in the Commons.[99] The rapid promotion to Cabinet

---

[96] *The Life and Times of Henry, Lord Brougham*, by Himself, Vol. III, pp. 266–267.

[97] This was said, among other occasions, of Melbourne's government in 1838 (Greville, *op. cit.*, Series II, Vol. I, pp. 53 and 177), of Peel's Cabinet in 1844 (*ibid.*, Series II, Vol. II, p. 267), while Lord John Russell complained of lack of front bench support in 1848 (Walpole, *op. cit.*, Vol. II, p. 90).

[98] Greville, *op. cit.*, Series II, Vol. I, p. 228.

[99] His biographer reflects that " his appointment shows the handicap then possessed . . . by . . . young men in high aristocratical positions . . . that things may be made too easy for them." B. Holland, *Life of the Duke of Devonshire*, Vol. I, p. 56.

rank of Sidney Herbert and Lord Lincoln (in January 1845) or of George Goschen (in early 1866) showed that there was no superfluity of talent available. Under these conditions it would be hard to overestimate the value of able and trusted exponents of government policy. Lord Althorp, though a pitiful speaker, was so widely respected that in many ways he held Lord Grey's government together and it was a kind of backhanded tribute to this fact that William IV chose to regard his retiral as a suitable moment to try and force a change of government. Orators like Stanley (before he became Lord Derby) or Palmerston were able on celebrated occasions to swing a critical House round to their opinion.[1] It is worth noticing that these victories were achieved by earnestness, command of detail and an appeal to the deeper patriotic and conservative instincts of Members, not by any attitude of condescension or command (as Stanley himself found out on the occasions when he took too high a line). In 1844, when Peel's tendency to high-handed leadership was becoming the subject of complaint, he took care " to disclaim the arrogant pretension of insisting on his party adopting every measure he thought fit to propose." [2] The House elected in 1857 was said to have been returned simply to give backing to Lord Palmerston, yet when he began to behave as if it owed him support and to ignore Members' feelings, he stored up resentment which culminated in his defeat in February 1858.[3]

Not only was the quality and conduct of the Cabinet scrutinised with great care but it was important to give the appearance of confidence and unanimity. Prime Ministers often echoed Lord Melbourne's remark: " for God's sake, let there be no resignations at all," fearing as he did that if one or two went, the whole government would collapse.[4] In 1859 the Derby Cabinet was

---

[1] On Irish Coercion in 1833, " Stanley in half an hour changed the whole state of affairs." W. M. Torrens, *Memoirs of Viscount Melbourne*, Vol. I, p. 419. Palmerston's achievement in the Don Pacifico Debate in 1850 is only the best known of his triumphs.

[2] Greville, *op. cit.*, Series II, Vol. II, p. 248.

[3] The irritation over Palmerston's allegedly high-handed treatment of Parliament arose over a number of quite trivial points, the most substantial being the appointment of Lord Clanricarde to a Cabinet vacancy despite general objections to Clanricarde's private character.

[4] Greville, *op. cit.*, Series II, Vol. I, p. 309, and Maxwell, *op. cit.*, Vol. I, p. 195. Amongst other instances, it was feared that the Whig Government would break up if there were resignations in 1839 or 1840, Graham feared a

acutely divided over a Reform Bill. Two members, Walpole and Henley, resigned in late January. But to prevent this news undermining the position of the Cabinet and the chances of the Bill, they continued to attend Cabinet meetings and delayed their explanations in Parliament till March 1.[5] On matters where feelings were strong, it was hard to maintain a government after doubts were increased and the opposition encouraged and augmented by ex-Cabinet Ministers. Peel felt he had to resign in December 1845 although only two members of his Cabinet refused to follow him. The danger of resignations could only be overcome if the individuals had rendered themselves unpopular (as Lord John Russell had in July 1855), if the opposition refused to press the point (as they had promised, should Gladstone resign in 1860 or 1861), or on the rare occasions when the government felt its record or its proposals were meeting with real and increasing popular support. Thus Palmerston's Cabinet survived the loss of three Peelites in early 1855 because the House felt that this government had to be given a trial, and Derby could face the resignations of Carnarvon and Cranborne in 1867 because of the growing Conservative demand for a measure of reform.

A final effect of the conditions in the House on the Cabinet lay in the strain which was imposed on ministers. These were men who, in most cases, had ample private means and lands and titles [6] which made them persons of distinction long before they considered any political office. The few who were engaged in industry or finance had to face the possibility that without personal supervision their businesses would decline, or that their own share in the profits would not increase.[7] As ministers, some had

general disintegration when Gladstone resigned over Maynooth in 1845, Palmerston derived strength from a similar apprehension in 1850, and the Aberdeen Coalition was never in a condition to face the resignations that were constantly threatened in 1853 and 1854.

[5] Monypenny and Buckle, *op. cit.*, Vol. IV, p. 199. W. D. Jones, *op. cit.*, p. 248. At this time at least one newspaper kept a man stationed in Downing Street to report the length of Cabinet meetings and implications were drawn if there were any persistent absentees.

[6] In 1851, Palmerston observed that Derby was not keen to take office and "perhaps . . . the possession of a large estate gives him as much employment as he wants." E. Ashley, *Life of Viscount Palmerston, 1846–1865*, Vol. I, pp. 264–265. Grey and Althorp are other examples of men who put their shoulders to the wheel with much reluctance.

[7] Cobden was only saved from bankruptcy by the generosity of his friends and George Goschen gave up the prospects of great wealth when he left Frühling

very heavy departmental work while all had to attend the long sittings of the House and face constant criticism, both political and personal, there and in the press. It was assumed that a close personal intimacy would exist between Cabinet Ministers who not only worked together but had a weekly dinner in each other's houses. Under this pressure and being so dependent on each other's performances, it was hard to maintain the necessary unanimity and mutual confidence. Ministers might rapidly feel that their colleagues were not helping them in the House or were committing the Cabinet to rash policies or were a liability in that they alienated the Radicals, the Peelites, or some other source of possible support. This explains the frequent stipulations by individual politicians that they would only join a Cabinet if it did or did not contain Radicals, or if a certain person was or was not Foreign Secretary. Once formed, there might be threats of resignation if changes were not made in certain posts. Dissensions about who would or would not serve with whom reached a climax in 1855, when the formation of a government in time of war was held up by the refusals of Gladstone and the Peelites to join without a declaration from Aberdeen that he approved of the new Cabinet.[8] For all these reasons there was often a genuine diffidence about accepting office [9] and a real longing for release. As Secretary for War, Sidney Herbert's heavy administrative burdens and his duties in the House of Commons, which forced him to speak 200 times in his last session, undoubtedly hastened his death.[10] Eight years earlier he had wondered why " men of fortune and station . . . undertake the labour and the cares, and face the abuse " [11] of

and Göschen for political life. On the other hand, when tempted with office, Lord Chandos made it clear that he preferred his duties as chairman of a railway.

[8] Mrs. Simpson commented in her diary that " there is a general impression that this discussion is discreditable to aristocratic institutions; that the Cabinet seem to think much more of their duty to each other than to the country." M. C. M. Simpson, *Many Memories of Many People*, p. 168.

[9] There is the well-known story of Lord Melbourne receiving the royal summons in 1834 with no enthusiasm. He talked about it with his valet, Tom Young. " I think it's a damned bore. I am in many minds as to what to do." Young replied " Why damn it all, such a position was never held by any Greek or Roman: and if it only lasts three months, it will be worth while to have been Prime Minister of England." " By God, that's true," said Melbourne, " I'll go." Lord David Cecil, *Lord Melbourne*, p. 111.

[10] Lord Stanmore, *op. cit.*, Vol. II, p. 403. In guiding the second Reform Bill through the House of Commons Disraeli spoke more than 300 times. Monypenny and Buckle, *op. cit.*, Vol. IV, p. 546.

[11] Lord Stanmore, *op. cit.*, Vol. I, p. 168.

political life. Peel told Hardinge in 1846 that " to be for five years the Minister of this country in the House of Commons, is quite enough for any man's strength. . . . But to have to incur the deepest responsibility, to bear the heaviest toil, to reconcile colleagues with conflicting opinions to a common course of action, to keep together in harmony the Sovereign, the Lords and the Commons; to have . . . to adopt the opinions of men . . . who spend their time in eating and drinking and hunting (he is referring to the backbenchers) (is) . . . an odious servitude." [12] Peel's relations with his backbenchers amply reveal that the problems of forming a Cabinet, agreeing on policy and carrying on the government arose from the conditions of politics; that is from the power of the House of Commons, the lack of any major issues dividing the electorate, and of any potent motives which would easily reconcile men to the burdens of office.

THE CABINET AND THE HOUSE OF LORDS

Having discussed the relations between the Cabinet and the House of Commons, it remains to consider the limitations imposed on Cabinets by the House of Lords. The precise powers enjoyed by the House of Lords before 1832 are hard to determine because they were seldom exercised in an independent fashion. So many members of the Commons had connections with peers that the two Houses were very similar in general outlook, and the process by which the government obtained a majority in the Commons applied equally well to the Lords. Since the seventeenth century it had been accepted that the fortunes of a government depended primarily on its performance in the Commons but the Lords were never explicitly relegated to a subordinate position. Some observers did notice that with the growth of the population and wealth of the country and with the increasing importance of an extra-parliamentary public opinion, the Lords were playing a diminishing role in the constitution.[13] This tendency was completed and made painfully evident when the contest over parliamentary reform was ended with the coercion of the Lords and

---

[12] Parker, *Sir Robert Peel*, Vol. III, p. 473.

[13] It was in 1817 that Wellington made his well-known remark: " Nobody cares a damn for the House of Lords; the House of Commons is everything in England and the House of Lords nothing." G. M. Trevelyan, *Lord Grey of the Reform Bill*, p. 163.

victory for a principle of representation which clearly relegated the Upper House to an inferior position. Also, the abolition of so many pocket and rotten boroughs reduced the connection between the two Houses [14] to such an extent that a Cabinet might now find it could rely on majority support in the Commons but not in the Lords.

In this situation, the problem arose of whether the government had to have the backing of a majority in the Upper House. The first clash after 1832 came when the Lords condemned Grey's policy towards Portugal in June 1833. Grey was correct to regard this as a vote of censure and he threw out some hints that he might resign. But after talking with the King and the Cabinet and in view of the fact that the Lords could not change his foreign policy, he agreed to remain in office on the strength of a vote of confidence by the House of Commons.[15] More serious the Lords went on in the next two years to reject several major government measures including the Irish Tithe, Irish Corporation and English Municipal Corporation Amendment Bills. These episodes revealed a rather curious state of affairs. The Lords could reject legislation (though they did not normally exercise this power over money Bills) and could thus make the life of a government unfruitful if not impossible, yet their support was not regarded as essential. The relationship was not stabilised till after the very strained relations of 1835–36 but thereafter it rested on an assumption that the Lords would not act in a wildly partisan fashion and attack government measures whatever their merits. This followed from the view that while a ministry retained the confidence of the elected representatives it was entitled to remain in office. The peers on the whole accepted these assumptions, though many found the explicit recognition of the situation hard to bear. As Wellington said " it is not so easy to make men feel that they are of no consequence in the country, who had heretofore had so much weight, and still preserve their properties and their stations in society and their seats in the House of Lords." [16] The remark

---

[14] N. Gash, *op. cit.*, has concluded that some 50 peers were left with a strong influence in about 60 constituencies.

[15] Greville, *op cit.*, Series I, Vol. II, pp. 376–377.

[16] Parker, *Sir Robert Peel*, Vol. II, p. 218.

also revealed a common tendency to exaggerate both the earlier importance of the Lords and its contemporary decline.[17]

Even in this secondary role, the Lords still had considerable power and could cause Cabinets many difficulties. The central problem was that while many amendments could be accepted and were even useful,[18] repeated rejections of major items of government policy caused acute embarrassment. The tension already mentioned in the mid-1830s when, as Greville said, " the Lords have been bowling down bills like ninepins," [19] led some Whigs to wonder whether a showdown and a positive definition of the secondary role of the House of Lords was necessary. Lord Melbourne preferred to take no strong action but the matter was raised in Cabinet in 1837 [20] and Lord John Russell prepared a memorandum on the problem suggesting that eight, ten or twelve Liberal peers should be created whenever the Lords acted in this fashion. Nothing came of this though the conduct of the Lords was adding to the dissensions within the government, discrediting it in the eyes of its more ardent supporters and, with all the other difficulties ministers had to face, might well have proved to be the last straw. The Lords relaxed a little with the accession of Queen Victoria and though they resumed their critical attitude towards the ministry in 1838 and 1839,[21] Melbourne was less concerned, perhaps because he had a more positive motive for enduring office—his desire to aid and accompany the young Queen.

Conservative Cabinets had few problems with the Lords and it was fortunate that Peel introduced and Wellington supported the Repeal of the Corn Laws or a serious crisis might have arisen.

---

[17] Examples are Disraeli's remark that he did not give a fig for the Lords (Jones, *op. cit.*, p. 206) and Shaftesbury's complaint that " it is allowed to debate, transact private business, and reject a few unimportant bills; but its vital powers are gone, and never will it dare to resist the House of Commons for two years on any point." E. Holder, *Life and Work of the Seventh Earl of Shaftesbury*, Vol. III, pp. 201–202.

[18] In 1839 Lord Melbourne told the Queen that the Lords had behaved quite well and that their alterations may have improved Bills. Viscount Esher, ed., *The Girlhood of Queen Victoria*, Vol. II, p. 241.

[19] Greville, *op. cit.*, Series I, Vol. III, p. 361.

[20] Parker, *Sir Robert Peel*, Vol. II, p. 335.

[21] In 1839 a motion by a peer, Lord Roden, calling for an inquiry into the condition of Ireland since 1835 was treated as a motion of censure by the government and lost. Melbourne once again affirmed his intention to carry on while he had a majority in the Commons. *Girlhood of Queen Victoria*, Vol. II, p. 134 and *Letters*, Series I, Vol. I, p. 188.

After 1846, with the Conservative peers divided into Protectionists and Peelites, the political attitudes of the Lords were less rigid. Lord John Russell's Cabinet (1846–52) had little to complain of, though again they realised that the Lords could defeat their proposals and make them appear foolish. In 1849, Lord John felt "that after having brought forward the Navigation Bill (for repeal of the remnants of the Navigation laws) in so solemn a manner for two sessions we ought to resign if we are beaten by a considerable majority in the Lords." [22]   The Court and Wellington both exerted their influence and after a tense debate in a crowded House, the government won. Another case of the Lords' power to frustrate a policy arose when Baron Rothschild was elected for the City of London in 1847. A minister introduced a Bill to alter that part of the installation of new M.P.s which requires them to swear allegiance "on the oath of a true Christian." The Bill (to remove Jewish Disabilities) passed the Commons in 1848 but was rejected by the Lords then and in subsequent sessions for ten years, till in 1858 Derby finally accepted a Bill to permit each House to alter its own form of oath by resolution. The Lords could also undertake useful preliminary skirmishing for their allies in the House of Commons. On the two occasions when Lord Palmerston's foreign policy came under heaviest criticism, the first rounds were fought out in the Lords. Defeated there on his handling of the Don Pacifico affair in 1850 and of the Schleswig-Holstein problem in 1864, Palmerston had to turn for vindication to the Commons with the stage already set for a showdown.

After 1841 Cabinets faced little in the way of systematic opposition from the Lords either because they were Conservative in name, or if they were called Whig or Coalition, were Conservative in tendency. The political gulf between the Houses which had opened between 1830 and 1832 was narrowed by the end of that decade and few governments took up issues which were likely to reopen the breach. The one indication that the situation could recur came in 1860 when the Lords rejected Gladstone's Bill to repeal the Paper Duty, but they were not willing to widen the conflict when he incorporated repeal with all his other financial proposals for 1861 in a single Bill.

[22] *Later Correspondence of Lord John Russell*, ed. G. P. Gooch, Vol. I, p. 194.

In their attempts to control the peers, Cabinets could appeal to several sentiments. One was that the Lords had a duty to see that the King's government could carry on even if this involved passing some measures which they might as individuals, dislike. Wellington was the most prominent exponent of this view though duty for him was almost a personal debt of honour to the Crown.[23] The difficulty of such an appeal was the growing evidence that these were not the King's ministers in the old sense. After 1832, it was possible to be a supporter of throne, church and constitution and yet to vote against the government. Another sentiment which Peel stressed in his dealings with the Lords was that of self-interest or common sense. He argued that moderate changes should be accepted even when they were not palatable as resistance would, in the long run, only encourage a destructive radicalism and damage the state while moderation would retain respect for the Lords and thus secure their position in the constitution.

A further possible appeal was to party feelings. Cabinets in this period usually contained a majority of peers and they attempted to gather support in the Lords in the same manner as their colleagues in the Commons. The task was much easier for the Conservatives as they started with the sympathy of the bulk of the House.[24] However, the peers were often of an independent mind and they faced no electorate, so that the Conservative leaders in the 1830s had some difficulty in controlling their supporters in the Lords.[25] When the Whigs were asked to form a government in late 1845, Lord John Russell explained that one reason why they could not proceed without Lord Grey was the extreme weakness of their party in the House of Lords though later Russell was able to persuade virtually all the Whig peers to vote for Peel's Bill.[26] After 1846, with the Conservative

---

[23] Among the instances of Wellington winning over the peers, one of the most remarkable was the occasion when he came down to the House and denounced the Bill dealing with Canada Clergy Reserves in 1840 and then let it pass almost unaltered.

[24] In the 1830s the Conservatives had a majority of about 100.

[25] See the Memo. by Peel of July 4, 1837, Parker, *Sir Robert Peel*, Vol. II, pp. 336–338.

[26] Maxwell, *op. cit.*, Vol. I, p. 260. This was not nearly such an important reason for refusing to form a government as the Whig minority in the House of Commons. See F. A. Dreyer, "The Whigs and the Political Crisis of 1845," *E.H.R.*, Vol. 80 (1965), pp. 514–537.

majority split into Protectionists and Peelites, the political situation in the Lords was more open. Lord Derby could rely on support when he was Prime Minister but not when he was in opposition.[27] The Aberdeen Coalition had ample backing in the Lords [28] and the Whigs in office, provided they had good spokesmen and a sound case, met little difficulty.[29] By the late 1850s the Lords were rapidly reverting to a predominantly Conservative outlook, so that the appeal to political feelings became a one-party weapon once again in the 1860s.[30]

It has sometimes been suggested that as the Lords had been relegated to a secondary role, their opposition was never taken too seriously. Such an attitude neglects their very definite powers and the reluctance of Whig statesmen to face anything like a showdown. In 1836 when Lord John Russell proposed regular retaliatory creations of Liberal peers, Melbourne had replied that to adopt such a policy would lead to the resignation of the government (presumably because William IV would have refused).[31] He was certainly correct that neither he nor the Whig Party wanted a major struggle over this issue. With the Lords strengthened by reluctance to face a showdown on the part of their few opponents and by a widespread positive desire for a reliable barrier against radicalism, they had to be accommodated by the Cabinets of the period. Such an accommodation was possible on the basis that the Lords could and would criticise, alter or reject government proposals. Their views had to be considered by Cabinets but the Lords would not attempt to use their powers in order to influence the composition or existence of a Cabinet or to reject measures simply because they emanated from a government disliked by the Lords.

---

[27] W. D. Jones, *op. cit.*, p. 206.

[28] *Argyll's Memoirs.* Vol. II, p. 50.

[29] The Whig peers held more proxy votes and were helped by the custom of calling for these votes—a practice which only declined between 1855 and 1858.

[30] Even then, it was still necessary to have adequate Conservative spokesmen. Disraeli observed in February 1868 that " our difficulty will be our more than debating weakness in the House of Lords " (Monypenny and Buckle, *op. cit.*, Vol. IV, p. 585), and Gathorne-Hardy made it a condition of joining the Cabinet that this weakness should be remedied by bringing in Lord Cairns. A. E. Gathorne-Hardy, *op. cit.*, Vol. I, p. 261.

[31] *Earlier Correspondence of Lord John Russell*, ed. Rollo Russell, Vol. II, p. 185 and Walpole, *op. cit.*, Vol. I, p. 267.

CHAPTER 4

THE INFLUENCE OF THE CROWN

AFTER discussing the relations between Cabinets and the two Houses of Parliament, and the effects of public opinion, one factor which influenced the life of a ministry still remains to be considered—its connection with the Crown. The sovereign had certain formal powers. He—or she—chose the Prime Minister and had to be consulted on and had to approve of all major appointments, foreign despatches, and important items of legislation. The Crown could withhold or grant permission to dissolve Parliament and finally, on very rare occasions, it might be asked to create peers so that government Bills could pass the House of Lords. The difficulty lies in assessing how much real control or influence these formal powers allowed the sovereign.

There is still a surprising discrepancy between the various estimates of royal power in this period. Most early views were based on Walter Bagehot's conclusion that merely for the effective working of Cabinet government "royalty is not essential; that upon an average, it is not even in a high degree useful." [1] A. L. Lowell carried this analysis a stage further in 1908 and produced the remarkably accurate assessment " that under ordinary circumstances the personal influence of the King in political matters is not likely to be very effectively asserted outside of foreign affairs, Church patronage, and some other appointments to office." [2] Later commentators, however, have accused Bagehot and his followers of underestimating the political role of the Crown, especially since the publication of the nine volumes of the *Letters of Queen Victoria* (completed in 1932) and some recent

---

[1] W. Bagehot, *The English Constitution* (first published 1867), 1928 edition in *The World's Classics*, p. 224. Bagehot in fact was prepared to concede rather more than this general conclusion suggests. He did not fail to see that an able or persistent monarch could make a good deal out of the rights " to be consulted, to encourage and to warn." " By years of discussion with ministry after ministry, the best plans of the wisest king would certainly be adopted " which explained why " Prince Albert really did gain great power."

[2] A. L. Lowell, *The Government of England*, Vol. 1, p. 43.

118

interpretations have ascribed quite amazing powers to the Crown.[3]

The reasons for these differences of interpretation lie in the difficulties of allocating influence. If several parties all urge a roughly similar policy, whose advice was decisive? Historians, reading the stream of instructions and comments poured forth by Queen Victoria and Prince Albert and noting that something very similar took place, have found it difficult to reach agreement on the measure of royal influence. In a study of the Cabinet what matters is not the number of occasions on which royal approval had to be obtained or the quantity of advice offered by William IV, Queen Victoria or Prince Albert. The questions one must pose are what part did the Crown play in the normal process by which political decisions were reached and to what extent was the position of Cabinets or of individual politicians affected by royal intervention.

The answers lie in the political conditions which arose after the passage of the 1832 Reform Bill. With the Court's influence over individual constituencies (never very great) reduced to some six seats and with the whole system of obtaining a favourable majority finally broken, the Crown could no longer choose and maintain its own ministers. If the House of Commons had a clear preference for ministers of a given political complexion, the Crown had to follow suit and if there was one man whom these politicians acknowledged as their leader then the Crown would ultimately have to commission him as Prime Minister. Backed by a majority of the House of Commons, a Prime Minister could, in the last resort, insist that his recommendations on personnel and policy should be accepted.

These limits on royal power were painfully learnt by William IV. He had formed his ideas in the reigns of his father and his brother and was quite consistent in his views after 1832. When William dismissed Lord Melbourne in late 1834 (and it was a dismissal) and installed Sir Robert Peel, he sent the latter a

---

[3] F. Hardie in *The Political Influence of Queen Victoria*, p. 18, says that if Albert had lived " it is possible to imagine a gradual Prussianisation of the British constitution, and, finally, an open conflict between the Crown and the forces of Radicalism." R. Fulford in *The Prince Consort*, p. 116, says: " the Prince enjoyed more political power and influence than any English sovereign since Charles II."

lengthy memorandum to justify his conduct.[4] In this he argued
that it was the King's task to choose the minister and, if necessary, to dismiss him. William said that the state of the House
of Commons and of the Lords should be considered as it was
desirable that an administration should last, but the chief qualification for office was royal confidence. His approval was necessary
also for appointments to every post in the ministry and for each
item of legislation.

William went on to explain that when Stanley's resignation
weakened the Cabinet in May 1834 he had considered changing
his ministers but decided that Lord Grey had " established strong
claims to his regard and confidence." [5] He recounted his attempts
to effect a union of parties on the retirement of Lord Grey in
July 1834 and only after this failed was Melbourne entrusted with
the task of forming a government. William reiterated his determination to protect the Anglican Establishment in Ireland and
made it clear that by consenting to a commission of inquiry he
had not pledged himself to permit the introduction of any legislation. When Althorp was elevated to the House of Lords in
November 1834 Melbourne had come to consult the King about
a new leader of the House of Commons, but William had decided
that it was time for a change. He regarded Lord John Russell as
a weak and dangerous successor to Althorp, the Whig policy on
Ireland as obnoxious, he felt that the Lord Chancellor, Brougham,
could not be trusted and so he had asked Peel to form a ministry.[6]

All this was reminiscent of the language of George III at the
turn of the century but now William found that after " his Government " had held an election, it was repeatedly defeated in the
House of Commons and he was driven to reappoint Melbourne.[7]
William still hankered after a coalition but the Whig leader,
irritated by the King's action and much less diffident than in
the previous year, demanded royal confidence. Before taking

---

4 *The Memoirs of Baron Stockmar*, ed. Baron E. Von Stockmar, Vol. 1,
pp. 312–350.
5 *Ibid.*, p. 324.
6 *Ibid.*, pp. 325–330, and Parker, *Sir Robert Peel*, Vol. II, pp. 252–256.
7 William originally sent for Grey who recommended him to see Melbourne
and Lansdowne. When they called, William still talked of a coalition and
did not ask either of them to form a government. The following day he had
to commission Melbourne. See the accounts in *Lord Melbourne's Papers*,
pp. 266–271, and Lord Broughton in the *Edinburgh Review* for 1871, pp.
315–316.

office Melbourne, though he had no particular attachment to such men as Lord John Russell, insisted on the principle that "he can neither acquiesce in any general or particular exclusions, and that he must reserve to himself the power of recommending for employment any one of your Majesty's subjects who is qualified by law to serve your Majesty." Moreover, as the Whig majority in the House of Commons had passed definite resolutions on the Irish Church, the Cabinet must be free to introduce similar Bills.[8]

Although ministers talked the old language of "requiring the royal confidence" this was manifestly a government imposed on the King by the House of Commons. Lord Gosford, departing for Canada, was told—"Mind me, my Lord, the Cabinet is not my Cabinet; they had better take care, or by G–d! I will have them impeached." [9] For the next two years William fulminated against "his servants." There were outbursts when Lord Glenelg read his instructions to the Governor-General of Canada; for long periods no members of the government were received at the Palace and on public occasions the King harangued them on such subjects as the Militia and the Russian menace. Yet none of this did the ministry any harm in the Commons—indeed evidence of threats to its existence did a good deal to keep its Irish and Radical supporters loyal in the division lobbies. In 1836 Melbourne suspected that there might be another attempt at dismissal [10] and had this happened the result would only have been a further demonstration that the King could not impose a Cabinet on the House of Commons.

Had the monarch who ascended the throne in June 1837 been another difficult and politically inept man, there might have been much more of the plain speaking William IV encountered and consequently much less disagreement today about the influence of the Crown. As it was, Queen Victoria encountered the same limitations on her actions, though her own approach to politics, the deference paid to her by the politicians and the decline of party issues after the 1840s all served to blur the edges a little.

Once on the throne, Queen Victoria was eager to be free of the oppressive control of her mother and her mother's adviser, Sir

---

[8] *Lord Melbourne's Papers*, pp. 274–275.
[9] Lord Broughton in the *Edinburgh Review*, Vol. 133 (1871), pp. 319–320.
[10] Lord Broughton, *Recollections*, Vol. V, p. 61.

John Conroy. She rapidly learnt to rely on Lord Melbourne, who retained the old conception that ministers ought to enjoy the personal confidence of the Crown. But if his assumption was accepted now that the ministry was dependent on the House of Commons, the Queen would find herself having to be partial to Whig, Conservative or coalition governments as they came about and the Crown would lose its independent position. Prince Albert realised this and he and his former tutor Stockmar had evolved their own theory of the position of a constitutional monarch, a theory which was adopted by the Queen as she and Albert entered into their complete working partnership in the early 1840s. In certain respects this theory fitted the new position of the Crown. Writing to Albert in 1841, Stockmar reiterated his belief that " the Crown supports frankly, honourably, and with all its might, the ministry of the time, whatever it be, so long as it commands a majority, and governs with integrity for the welfare and advancement of the country." [11] But support was to carry no partisan implications and Peel was told in 1845 that the Crown would not use its influence on behalf of the government candidate in a by-election at Windsor.[12]

To emphasise constitutional backing for the government of the day in the sense of supporting its decisions but not its candidates would seem to fit perfectly into the limits set by post-1832 conditions. But Prince Albert and the Queen did not want a position above the political battle in order to became impartial figureheads. The ambiguities about some of their actions after the late 1840s arose because they both believed that in a real sense the Queen governed the country and looked after its ultimate interests in a manner which short-term partisan political leaders could not emulate. Stockmar theorised on the point and said the sovereign should enjoy " the position of a permanent Premier, who takes rank above the temporary head of the Cabinet, and in matters of discipline exercises supreme authority." [13]

---

[11] Martin, *op. cit.*, Vol. II, p. 110.
[12] Gash, *op. cit.*, p. 382.
[13] To this very long letter, which was to console Albert for the attacks made on him in 1854, the Prince replied " I heartily agree with every word that you say." Martin, *op. cit.*, Vol. II, pp. 545–553. It is difficult to disagree with Gladstone's judgment that " a congeries of propositions stranger in general result never, in our judgment, was amassed in order to explain to the unlearned the more mysterious lessons embraced in the study of the British

Victoria and Albert attempted to fulfil this broad function on two levels. The first major theme was to insist on all their formal rights of prior consultation and approval.[14] While they remained on this ground, they were entirely within the limits open to the monarchy and were playing their expected part. There was great reverence for the Crown as an institution and, in time, considerable respect for the Queen as a person. No politician had a calculated objective of reducing or ending royal participation in government and if there was any evidence that the Queen had not been treated with respect or that her rights were not being observed she could always obtain immediate redress. Thus in the debate over his dismissal in 1851 Palmerston was quite confident that he could defend his reputation and the consistency of his attitude to France. The whole situation changed when Lord John Russell read out the Memorandum of August 12, 1850, which, in laying down two conditions for the Foreign Secretary to observe, indicated that Palmerston had recently been "failing in sincerity towards the Crown."[15] Once the Commons realised that this had been happening, that Palmerston had accepted the reproof and that now he was again guilty of acting without royal or Cabinet approval, his whole position collapsed.

The second level of royal activity developed out of these formal rights. Victoria and Albert commented on the documents and recommendations put before them and in time evolved certain opinions on matters of policy and, in some cases, on the fitness of certain individuals and of particular Cabinets to carry on a creditable government. Whenever these views came into conflict with the opinions of a united Cabinet or of the settled desires of a majority of the House of Commons, Victoria and Albert had to learn the lessons of William IV and give way. On the whole, they appreciated this point and though Victoria continually talked

Monarchy." W. E. Gladstone, *Gleanings of Past Years*, 1843–78, p. 76. Stockmar was putting this point of view to Albert from the time of the Prince's earliest interest in British government. Stockmar's *Memoirs*, Vol. I, p. 380. See also Albert's comments on Palmerston's fall in 1851. "Is the sovereign not the natural guardian of the honour of his country, is he not *necessarily* a politician? Has he no duties to perform towards his country?" B. Connell, *Regina* v. *Palmerston*, p. 242.

14 As early in the reign as April 1847 the Queen was asking both Lord John Russell and Palmerston "to see that the drafts to our foreign Ministers are not despatched previous to their being submitted to the Queen . . .," a request that was constantly repeated over the next four years. B. Connell, *op. cit.*, pp. 56, 107, 116. 15 *Letters*, Series I, Vol. II, p. 315.

as if she would not acquiesce,[16] she always did so in time and only in a few instances was there anything in the nature of a struggle. After the unfortunate dispute over the Ladies of the Household in 1839 and because she was infuriated by Peel's successful motion to reduce the Prince's annuity from £50,000 to £30,000, the Queen sometimes said she could never send for the Conservative leader. But when Peel won a majority in 1841 there was no alternative.

From 1846 onwards, when no single party was evidently in command of the Commons, the situation seemed to leave more scope for royal initiative. This was possible, but if most of the men capable of leading a government reached an agreement about the composition of a Cabinet, the Crown again played a purely formal part. In the process of choosing a Prime Minister the Queen's actions flowed along clearly prescribed channels. When a preponderantly Whig government was defeated, as in 1851, 1852, 1855 or 1858, she summoned Lord Derby as the leader of the largest group in the opposition. There would be a pause as Derby attempted to draw other elements into his cabinet or considered whether the Conservatives could risk trying to conduct a government alone. Both these possibilities really depended on whether the Whigs, Peelites and a few Radicals were able to reconcile their differences or whether their quarrels were sufficiently deep for some of them to prefer a short period of Conservative government. If Derby refused, the Queen turned back to the elements from which the previous governments had been formed. The choice would then lie between a leading Whig like Lord John Russell or Lord Palmerston, a Peelite, or a generally respected figure such as Lord Lansdowne who might preside over a combined Cabinet. This set of politicians were fully aware that if Derby " handed back " one of them would have to lead and distribute the other posts in an acceptable manner, so that they were always holding negotiations amongst themselves. When agreement was reached, or if one by virtue of his standing in the House had clear priority, the Queen found her offers declined

---

[16] W. E. Mosse in " The Crown and Foreign Policy. Queen Victoria and the Austro-Prussian Conflict, 1866," *Camb. Hist. Journal*, 1951, No. 2, somewhat overestimates royal influence because he places too literal an interpretation on Queen Victoria's remarks that it would " be impossible for her to consent " to one proposal and another " could not receive the Queen's approval."

and guided in the right direction till the designated person was approached. No agreement could be worked out between the Whigs and Peelites in 1851 because of their differences over the Ecclesiastical Titles Bill and after two full rounds of consultations the only alternative was to restore Lord John Russell. In 1855 after Derby's refusal, the Queen had, in time, to accept Palmerston as Prime Minister since he was the only member of Lord Aberdeen's coalition who had the confidence of the House.[17]

When the Conservatives accepted office in 1852 and 1858 it was clear that their tenure was precarious and that they would be in real danger once their various opponents agreed to combine. By the autumn of 1852 the Whig-Peelite controversy over the ecclesiastical titles question was less troublesome than it had been in early 1851. Antagonism had been reduced by their mutual exclusion from the government and their leaders were able to engage in renewed discussions in the hope of achieving an acceptable alternative should the Conservative Cabinet be defeated. The Court wanted a stable administration and realised that this could be best founded on a Peelite-Whig coalition. The royal desires assisted the process of negotiation and discussions among the politicians narrowed the choice for Prime Minister to Lansdowne or Aberdeen, with Lansdowne the more reluctant and Lord John Russell thinking he might accept office under Lord Aberdeen. So when Queen Victoria sent for both Aberdeen and Lansdowne, the latter's illness allowed him to leave the formation of the government to negotiations between Aberdeen and Lord John. In this instance the Crown had been of considerable help, but the decisive factors were the state of the House of Commons and the political and personal preferences of the non-Conservative politicians.[18] When the second Derby government fell in 1859 the situation was simpler because the two chief

---

[17] As the Queen wrote to King Leopold, " I had no other alternative." G. Henderson, " The Influence of the Crown, 1854–56," *Juridical Review*, 1936, p. 311.

[18] The most extreme claims for royal influence in the selection of a Prime Minister and formation of a government occur over the creation of the Aberdeen coalition. Roger Fulford in *The Prince Consort* calls the Peelites " a nineteenth-century version of the King's Party " and says the government was " the creation of Prince Albert " (pp. 146 and 152.) These views cannot be sustained without a serious distortion of the evidence. C. H. Stuart, " The Formation of the Coalition Cabinet of 1852," *Transactions of the Royal Historical Society*, 5th Series, Vol. 4, p. 45, shows how the political leaders

contenders, Palmerston and Lord John, were so equally balanced that they met and agreed to act together in forming a Cabinet, the premiership being left to whichever the Queen chose to summon. Victoria wanted neither of "the bad old men" and selected Granville, but he was forced to explain that he could not proceed without Palmerston and Russell, so the Queen had to accept them as the managing partnership in her new government and commission Palmerston. By the late 1860s party lines had grown more definite and the direct connection between winning a majority of the seats in the House of Commons and the royal request to form a government became even clearer than it had been in 1841.

In this matter of choosing a Prime Minister the politicians had no desire to diminish the royal prerogative or to dictate to the Queen. Each person commissioned to form a government considered the task and if he declined, it was because of the hard facts of the political situation. These men consulted or commissioned by the Queen would have to meet the heavy burdens of forming and maintaining a Cabinet and of facing the House of Commons. They would naturally discuss the possibilities long before the occasion arrived, not to coerce the Crown but to find the most workable combination and it was then hoped that by observation, consultation or trial and error Queen Victoria would soon arrive at the same conclusion.

The Crown's right to approve of the appointments to senior posts was similarly circumscribed. If the Prime Minister backed by the Cabinet insisted, the Queen had to agree. The best-known case occurred when Victoria and Albert became more and more dissatisfied with Palmerston as Foreign Secretary after 1846.[19] Much has been written about this most interesting encounter, but the central fact is that so long as Lord John Russell and the

had been moving in this direction for a considerable period though he lays too much stress on tactical considerations (*e.g.*, the suggestion that Peelite leaders opposed the Ecclesiastical Titles Bill to win Irish votes) and neglects the pervasive pressure of the need to form a government which could last in the Commons.

[19] From June 1848, Prince Albert had kept a dossier of Palmerston's misdemeanours, the Queen noting that certain of the Foreign Secretary's despatches were "almost a mockery of Lord John, the Cabinet, the country and herself" and that Palmerston "behaved . . . like a naughty child." B. Connell, *op. cit.*, pp. 78–80.

Cabinet were not prepared to dismiss Palmerston, his position was secure.[20] Queen Victoria told the Prime Minister of her total lack of confidence in her Foreign Secretary as early as September 1848,[21] but though she could stop Lord Normanby being sent to a conference in Brussels, she could delay or tone down some despatches, neither Palmerston nor the main lines of his policy were changed. On several occasions Lord John, for the sake of peace, asked Palmerston to move, but as he refused and neither the Cabinet nor Lord John would risk his resignation, the matter rested. When the government resigned and then returned to office in early 1851 none of the royal appeals could stop Palmerston resuming his post. By October relations were again at breaking point, but the Prime Minister reminded the Queen that any directions about Palmerston could only be given on the advice of the Cabinet.[22] The final decision to make a change was taken by Lord John Russell and confirmed by the Cabinet without the Court being consulted, the reason being that Palmerston had flouted the Cabinet's decision to remain neutral towards Louis Napoleon, not only in conversation with Walewski but later in a despatch to Paris. In later years Lord John considered that it would have been wiser to have overlooked Palmerston's transgression[23] and had he and the Cabinet agreed to do so, there would have been no change.

A few years earlier, had Palmerston moved, the successor was to have been either Lord Clarendon or Lord Minto, but by August 1850 Clarendon had declared a decided objection to taking the Foreign Office [24] and Lord John did not regard him as suitable. The Court preferred Lord Granville and so did the Prime Minister. The Cabinet, on the initiative of Sir George Grey, agreed that an offer should be made to Clarendon in view of the general opinion that he was " next on the list." [25] Lord John Russell sent the offer with a note saying he would rather have Granville, so that it would be helpful if Clarendon did not accept

---

20 B. Southgate makes the interesting suggestion " that Palmerston would not long have survived at the Foreign Office after 1848 if the Palace had tried less hard to get him out." *The Most English Minister*, p. 243.
21 *Letters*, Series I, Vol. II, p. 231.
22 *Ibid.*, p. 394.
23 Earl Russell, *Recollections and Suggestions*, p. 258.
24 *Letters*, Series I, Vol. II, p. 311.
25 *Ibid.*, pp. 418–419.

—which met with the latter's entire assent, though he passed some bitter remarks about the Queen and Prince preferring that " courtiers . . . should conduct the affairs of the country." [26] Thus Granville would not have become Foreign Secretary if Clarendon had wanted the post, or if Lord John had not actively preferred Granville, or if the Cabinet and Prime Minister had had any other politician in mind. Lord John was, no doubt, glad to choose someone acceptable to the Court, but it would be quite wrong to suggest that the appointment was dictated by Victoria and Albert [27] and they raised no objections when Aberdeen selected Clarendon as his Foreign Secretary in early 1853.

The same situation was true of appointments to minor offices. The Queen objected to Bernal Osborne becoming Under-Secretary at the Foreign Office under Aberdeen and, as it was a matter of little importance, he was moved to the Admiralty.[28] In 1855, just after Palmerston became Prime Minister, the Queen objected to the appointment of Sir R. Peel to the War Office with no effect.[29] Later, when Palmerston lost two powerful debaters with the elevation of both Sidney Herbert and Lord John Russell to the Lords, he suggested that Layard should be made Under-Secretary for Foreign Affairs. The Queen's first letter said " she cannot alter her determination " to refuse and the next that it would be " a serious evil," but Palmerston insisted and she had to give way.[30]

On matters of actual policy the Court took little interest in domestic affairs except that Albert favoured free trade and Victoria was prepared at such times as the reform agitation of 1866–67 to say that it would be in the general interest if the question was settled. The Queen and the Prince were, however, very well informed about and actively interested in foreign policy and defence, yet here also they encountered the same limitations. They seldom, in fact, recommended policies of their own, being content to comment on the proposals of the Foreign Secretary, and their activities in this sphere must be considered under the heading

[26] Maxwell, *op. cit.*, Vol. I, pp. 336–341. Russell had already sounded Clarendon about the F.O. and Clarendon's reply sent the day before he knew a formal offer of the Foreign Office was on its way, said: " I am exceedingly obliged to you for having thought of my objections to occupy P.'s place; which are as strong as ever." *Ibid.*, p. 336.

[27] R. Fulford, *op. cit.*, pp. 135–137.

[28] *Letters*, Series I, Vol. II, p. 514.

[29] B. Connell, *op. cit.*, p. 171.   [30] *Letters*, Series I, Vol. III, pp. 567–571.

of influence rather than of direct intervention. On all matters of policy, when the Cabinet was united on an issue the Crown's recommendations remained or were revealed in their proper light as being simply advice which need not be accepted.[31]

Thus the limits which the post-1832 conditions of political life imposed on William IV applied with equal force to Victoria and Albert, though there were fewer direct collisions and less need for blatant explanations. Within these limits, the formal rights of consultation and approval led to expressions of opinion which might have an effect on the politicians. One reason why such an influence could arise was that Cabinets were not always united or even clear in their minds as to the policies they wished to pursue. It is possible that in the diplomatic negotiations which took place in 1854 while the country was drifting into war with Russia, Prince Albert's advice may have affected the form of some of the steps taken, though not the general direction of policy.[32] Again, knowing the views of the Cabinet, the Court might suggest a better wording of despatches. When Clarendon wanted to say that Prussia was no longer adopting a purely neutral attitude over the Austrian, British and French ultimatum to Russia in December 1855, Prince Albert was able to point out that his words could be capable of a much stronger interpretation. In the famous case of the despatch to Washington asking for a return of the southern agents removed from the Trent in November 1861 and for an apology, the Prince performed the same service. Palmerston wanted a peaceful outcome but was prepared for anything. When Albert suggested a milder tone the Prime Minister readily accepted, apologising for a message drafted " by the help of fourteen people . . . each proposing verbal alterations." [33] The milder tone did help the American Government to withdraw with greater ease.[34]

---

[31] When Palmerston and Russell put forward a despatch asking both France and Austria not to intervene in Italy in January 1860, the Court protested and appealed but in the end " We could *not prevent* this *proposal* . . .—as the rest of the Cabinet thought it could *not* be opposed." *Ibid.*, p. 490.

[32] See G. Henderson, *art. cit.*, pp. 298–309. Although Henderson gives the maximum weight to every royal suggestion, he can only conclude that Prince Albert " sometimes exercised considerable influence," and it is noteworthy that such occasions were when the Cabinet had no settled policy or when it was a matter of form rather than of content.

[33] Quoted by H. C. F. Bell, *op. cit.*, Vol. II, p. 295.

[34] As Palmerston summed it up in a letter of condolence after the Prince's death : " There can be no doubt that, as your Majesty observes, the alteration made in the despatch to Lord Lyons contributed essentially to the satisfactory settlement of the dispute." B. Connell, *op. cit.*, p. 322.

On the occasions when the Court was dissatisfied with the government's foreign policy it found that the normal practice of hearing the Cabinet's opinion only through the Prime Minister or the Foreign Secretary was very frustrating. The Queen was not always sure that the papers put before her were a precise expression of the Cabinet's views or that her own reservations were fully reported to the Cabinet or, when she had made such a request, embodied in despatches. In order to try and prevent Palmerston acting on his own, Prince Albert in 1849 asked that all outgoing drafts should be sent through the Prime Minister. Even this did not solve the problem as the Cabinet, on the whole, were behind Palmerston, while the Court disliked his approval of nationalist movements and his consequent anti-Austrian bias. In June 1850, when Palmerston's policy over the Danish Protocol was suspected of being anti-German, Queen Victoria went a stage further and asked Lord John Russell to lay the correspondence before the Cabinet. She said she would " abide by their deliberate opinion." [35]

In the next series of battles with Palmerston during his second ministry from 1859 to 1865, the Cabinet was not always in sympathy with the policy he and his Foreign Secretary, Lord John Russell, wished to pursue and therefore royal influence was at its strongest in these years. Queen Victoria appreciated the situation and as she disagreed strongly with Palmerston over the Italian and Schleswig-Holstein affairs (again largely because the policies had appeared to Albert to be anti-German), she regularly asked to have her letters read to the Cabinet, or even for despatches to be resubmitted with her comments before being forwarded. At the same time the Court was receiving private reports of Cabinet discussions from Lord Granville and occasionally from Sir Charles Wood. On important occasions the Queen was prepared to ask for the support of individual Cabinet members [36]

---

[35] *Letters*, Series I, Vol. II, p. 298.

[36] She wrote to General Peel saying that " when the question of the Indian Army comes before the Cabinet " she relied on him to " stoutly defend the interests of the Crown "; February 13, 1859. *Letters*, Series I, Vol. III, p. 410. Most of Queen Victoria's lobbying in the Cabinet was in Palmerston's 1859–65 ministry, though she had appealed to Clarendon to support the royal view about the defences in 1857: Martin, *op. cit.*, Vol. IV, p. 91. She also used her Secretary, General Grey, to lobby ministers before a critical Cabinet. See W. E. Mosse, " Queen Victoria and her Ministers in the Schleswig-Holstein Crisis, 1863–4," *E.H.R.*, Vol. 78, p. 268.

and when the controversies were at a climax, she was requesting the Prime Minister to read memoranda to the Cabinet,
having already forewarned and primed Sidney Herbert, the Duke
of Newcastle and Sir Charles Wood through Lord Granville.
Having clandestine reports from other ministers, the Court was
able to insist that the policy of the whole Cabinet was adhered to
at least in the letter of the despatch. This watchfulness earned
the gratitude of some ministers. In 1859 Sidney Herbert said " it
was clear that the Queen had come to the assistance of the
Cabinet," [37] while after the dispute over the Danish problem in
1864 Gladstone reflected that " for the first time I think she takes
a just credit to herself for having influenced beneficially the course
of policy and of affairs in the late controversy." [38] Taking a broad
view of the Italian Question, royal intervention toned down some
of the British notes but on the whole Palmerston and Russell were
able to pursue their policies to a successful conclusion.[39] In the
involved discussions over Schleswig-Holstein, the Crown was able,
as Gladstone suggests, to help Palmerston's opponents curb his
actions, but the main reason why the Prime Minister lost was
that a majority of the Cabinet, of the House of Commons and
of the country did not endorse his policy.

Apart from any attempts to influence the conduct of the
government, the mere exercise of the formal rights of consultation
and approval meant that the Crown had to have constant and
close dealings with the leading ministers. At a time when governing
the country imposed heavy burdens and the prospect of office did

[37] *Letters*, Series I, Vol. III, p. 467. See also B. Connell, *op. cit.*, pp. 265–268,
273–275.
[38] Morley, *op. cit.*, Vol. II, pp. 104–105. The Prince could also score a few
points simply by asking for information such as detailed returns of the state
of fortresses, ships, stores, etc.: see Martin, *op. cit.*, Vol. IV, p. 123. The
most detailed treatment of royal action in the Schleswig-Holstein crisis is
W. E. Mosse's article (note 36 above). He uses such phrases as "the
Queen had carried the day" and says "she was, in fact, acting . . . as
head of the ' peace party ' in the Cabinet." Yet he refutes his own more
extreme suggestions by admitting that she "never clashed with the *majority*
of the Cabinet," that she accepted Cabinet decisions and never "swayed
the Cabinet as a whole," concluding that "it may be doubted whether . . .
(she) decisively influenced the course of events."
[39] W. E. Mosse in "The Crown and Foreign Policy," *Camb. Hist. Journal*,
1951, No. 2, put the Queen's influence at too high a level when he says
she "was . . . allowed a right of veto over policies which she considered
totally unacceptable." There was no veto if the Cabinet was united and, in
the case of Italy, nothing as strong as a veto though only the Prime Minister
and Foreign Secretary were in agreement.

not overcome all hesitations, the personal relations which developed between the sovereign and the minister could make a considerable difference to the atmosphere and morale in the top circles of the government.[40] Despite Lord Grey's great desire to return to private life, an appeal from William IV was able to persuade him not to resign in January 1834.[41] Later, though William could not get rid of Melbourne, his outbursts and obstruction did sour and depress the Cabinet. In 1837 the change that took place was not that the young Queen brought any accession of strength in the lobbies of the House of Commons,[42] but that Melbourne delighted in the association and thus had a positive desire to hold the Cabinet together and remain in office. The most effective single intervention of the Crown in political life during this period was when Queen Victoria put enough heart into Melbourne's Cabinet to keep them going for longer than they would have lasted had William lived. When their majority sank to five over the Jamaica Bill in 1839, Melbourne resigned and Peel was summoned. With a minority in the House and expecting in time to have to ask for a dissolution, Peel requested that the Queen should remove some of the Whig ladies of the Household as a sign of confidence in him. Victoria bridled and asked Melbourne and his Cabinet to stand by her. "The reading of these letters gave a new spirit to our waverers, and even Howick and Rice owned that it was impossible to abandon such a Queen and such a woman." [43] The Whigs had a majority albeit tenuous in the House and the Queen's appeals held them to their unwelcome duties.

---

[40] N. Gash, *Reaction and Reconstruction in English Politics, 1832–1852*, observes (p. 20) that " with a difficult measure or a tired Prime Minister, the flanking fire of royal criticism might be of some consequence."

[41] G. M. Trevelyan, *op. cit.*, p. 356. William's appeal was joined to that of the entire Cabinet.

[42] It has sometimes been suggested that the Queen's evident support for Lord Melbourne increased his following in the Commons. M. G. Brock, " Politics at the Accession of Queen Victoria," *History To-day*, Vol. 3, p. 330, says that " the knowledge that the ministry possessed, or were likely to win, the sovereign's confidence could be relied on to have a magnetic effect on . . . ' independent ' and wavering M.P.s." There is no evidence for this view. Contemporary estimates of party strength in the House are very detailed and give no category of " supporters of a government favoured by the Crown." Support for the Whigs varied, under both William IV and Victoria but not in accordance with the degree of favour shown by the monarch. The Whips and party leaders based all their (very accurate) calculations on the views of members who were independent in the sense of being uncommitted to " thick or thin " party voting, and on the issue in question.

[43] Lord Broughton, *op. cit.*, Vol. V, p. 193.

Some noblemen such as Palmerston and Russell seemed almost to take a Whiggish pleasure in a state of friction between themselves and the Queen, but for others royal approval was a great solace. Peel was buoyed up by the knowledge of royal confidence in his short ministry in 1846, and in 1855 the Queen was able to persuade Aberdeen and his colleagues not to run away but to meet Parliament and resist Roebuck's motion for a committee of inquiry. The same motive could influence some individual decisions; it was hearing of the Queen's approval that decided Lord Ellenborough to accept the post of Governor-General of India in 1841.[44]

The Crown could also assist ministers in several ways. A Prime Minister having difficulties with a colleague might find a word from the Queen helpful. Disraeli was a past master in the use of this weapon. He prepared the ground by reporting the dangers to the country should a split take place and later, when the calamity was imminent, warned the Queen—" it may be necessary that the thunder of Olympus should sound." Queen Victoria urged General Peel not to resign in January 1867. She also gave Disraeli permission to refer to ministers' duty to stand by her when some of them preferred to resign rather than wait, as Disraeli wished, for an election on the reformed register in late 1868.[45] It was possible for the Crown to sway a few votes in the House of Lords, though no matter what William IV or Victoria might have done the peers would still have created great difficulties in the 1830s. On rare occasions the Crown might be used as a link with the Opposition, as when Albert asked Aberdeen to moderate Peelite attacks on the government in June 1855.[46] As might be expected such appeals could only take effect if political feelings were not strongly engaged. In 1866 the Queen offered to use her influence on behalf of a Conservative Reform Bill, but Disraeli remarked (to Sir Stafford Northcote) that " the royal project of gracious interposition with our rivals is a mere phantom. It pleases the vanity of a Court deprived of substantial power, but we know, from the experience of similar sentimental schemes, that there is nothing practical in it." [47]

---

[44] *Letters*, Series I, Vol. I, p. 433.
[45] Monypenny and Buckle, *op. cit.*, Vol. V, p. 28.
[46] Martin, *op. cit.*, Vol. III, pp. 289–291.
[47] Monypenny and Buckle, *op. cit.*, Vol. IV, p. 455.

The one other power open to the Crown was that of granting or withholding a dissolution. There was, both then and since, considerable confusion about the circumstances in which the King or Queen could refuse a dissolution. The prevailing attitude before 1832, which lingered on for some twenty years afterwards, was based on the guiding principles of eighteenth-century politics. The King's task was to maintain a stable government and the ministers were men whom he had placed in power. The House of Commons was entitled to criticise the policies of the Cabinet, but if the latter decided to resign there was no question of appealing to the electorate—the King selected other ministers. Normally dissolutions took place when a Parliament was nearing the end of its seven-year term. The only reason for a premature dissolution was if stable government was proving difficult and the King and his ministers decided that an election would strengthen the executive. It would clearly be damaging if the result of the election was to weaken the government as this would cast a reflection on the ministers and on the King who had appointed them. It would also deprive the King of a most effective method of bolstering his Prime Minister and Cabinet. Both Peel and Melbourne, whose political instincts had been formed in the pre-reform era, held these views. Lord Melbourne was most reluctant to advise a dissolution in 1841 because he was not sure that it would strengthen the Queen's Ministers. Similarly Queen Victoria agreed with Peel's remark in 1846 that " the power of Dissolution is a great instrument in the hands of the Crown, and . . . there is a tendency to blunt that instrument if it be resorted to without necessity," and regretted having granted Melbourne's request on that occasion.[48]

After 1832 a number of these points still held good. Ministries were not selected and maintained by the Crown, but they were not yet directly dependent on the verdict of the electorate. It was still the normal assumption that if the House of Commons voted against government proposals and the result was the resignation of the Cabinet, a new ministry would be formed out of the existing House. In a period of much greater governmental instability, the Crown's obligation to seek a stable executive was naturally emphasised, despite the fact that its power to influence elections had virtually disappeared. Thus it was wrong for a Prime

Minister to threaten a dissolution, on the twofold grounds that this was an illegitimate attempt to coerce the Commons and that it was misusing a royal power best reserved for the solution of special difficulties.

On the other hand, the fact that the Crown could no longer ensure a definite increase in support for a government at a general election meant that it had become dangerous to act without or against the advice of its ministers. If a dissolution was requested and refused, it would be tantamount to a dismissal and the appointment of a new Cabinet by the Crown. The royal action would become the subject of political controversy and should the newly installed Cabinet be granted a dissolution and then suffer defeat at the hands of its predecessors in office, the result would be hailed as a party triumph over the Crown. Thus the old view that the King or Queen was entitled to refuse a dissolution, and that the request should only be granted in special circumstances when the executive both required and would obtain reinforcement, still had some relevance to political conditions. Yet it was limited or overlaid by the very serious consequences of independent royal intervention in the course of political conflict. The conflict between these positions came out quite clearly when Queen Victoria asked Lord Aberdeen if she had been correct in refusing to let Lord Derby threaten a dissolution should he suffer defeat over Ellenborough's despatch to India in 1858. Aberdeen replied that such a threat was improper and she was entitled to refuse, but if the request came after an actual defeat it would be quite unprecedented to deny the Prime Minister an appeal to the electorate.[49] In practice the conflict was minimised in that politicians preferred to resign if they thought they were unlikely to gain strength. A government which had won a recent general election but was then seriously defeated in the House of Commons usually took this as a sign of waning popularity and resigned.[50] In every instance when a Prime Minister did ask for a dissolution, it was granted

---

[49] *Letters*, Series I, Vol. III, p. 363. Faced with Derby's assurance that he would be beaten by between 15 and 35 votes and the prospect of Palmerston as Prime Minister, the Queen said she would grant a dissolution but she trusted Derby would not use this information dishonourably. *Ibid.*, pp. 367–368.

[50] See above, pp. 13–15, for a discussion of the effect of the power to advise a dissolution on the relations of the Cabinet and the House of Commons.

and the right to refuse did nothing to increase the Crown's share of political power.

In conclusion, the part played by the monarch in the regular flow of political decisions was very small. So much had to be put before the King and the contacts between William IV, Victoria, Albert and the politicians were so numerous that historians have been misled by their very bulk. An analysis of how many decisions would not have been taken or would have assumed another form but for royal intervention reveals a mere handful, and many of these cannot be reduced to definite terms. The Crown took up a great deal of the politicians' time, but in planning a course of action Cabinets gave far more thought to the actual complexity of the problem, to the anticipated response of foreign Powers, the views of the public and the Press, the attitude (on matters requiring legislation) of the Lords and, above all, to the reactions of the House of Commons, than to the royal views. Bagehot was correct in saying that for the efficient working of Cabinet government "royalty is not essential." A monarch capable of inspiring loyalty helped to convince ministers that it was worth assuming the burdens of political life, but had there been no Crown (say in the event of a nonentity on the throne or a long minority) other motives as simple as pride in Britain, the need to defend property and to conduct foreign affairs would have sufficed. The country would never have lacked an executive. The members and policies of the Cabinets would have had to be composed from the same materials, to face the same Parliaments and problems and to be acceptable to the same public.

*   *   *   *   *   *

This completes the description of the place of the Cabinet in the early Victorian political system. To give a proper account, the greatest difficulty is in presenting an accurate estimate of the balance between Cabinet and Parliament. Some writers on the modern constitution have tried to draw a sharp distinction between criticism and control. The task of Parliament in this respect, they argue, is to question and discuss, but the possession of real power to prevent government action and to force changes of policy would trespass on the function of the executive. In fact the two cannot be separated to this extent. Without the capacity to extract information, to delay action, to defeat proposals and even to propose and carry alternatives, parliamentary criticism loses most of its force and therefore much of its value. Yet even when Parliament was as powerful as in this period it was quite possible to retain the broad distinction between framing and bringing forward policies and the task of scrutinising, amending and accepting them. In the 1830s and 1840s parliamentary procedure was remodelled so that government business had priority on two days in the week and some restrictions were placed on the right to amend government orders. Parliament could institute inquiries, demand to see correspondence with foreign Powers and draw up and carry Bills, but it was now accepted that the initiative on matters of major importance came from the Cabinet. The final decision depended in large part on whether the government brought forward an issue and the terms in which it was presented to Parliament. On most of the major issues of the period—the dispute over appropriation of Irish Church funds in the 1830s, the fate of the Corn Laws, British policy in the Near Eastern crisis of 1839–41, Gladstone's great budgets, the attitudes to Italian unification and the Schleswig-Holstein question, the degree of Reform in 1867—the first and essential step was discussion and decision within the Cabinet.

CHAPTER 5

THE WORKING OF THE CABINET

FORMATION AND DISSOLUTION OF CABINETS

A STUDY of this kind must give not merely a picture of the power and position of the Cabinet in British government, but also a description of the process of forming and dissolving Cabinets and of their character and internal organisation.

In the decade after the passage of the Reform Bill, the first person summoned by the monarch might not always be expected to take the office of Prime Minister. In 1834 and 1841 Wellington was called as the senior Conservative statesman though those in political circles knew that he would immediately recommend Peel for the premiership. Grey was the first Whig to be consulted in 1835 despite his retirement in the previous year. However the practice of asking senior statesmen for advice in the 1850s had a slightly different aspect, as it was not always clear which party would ultimately be successful in forming a Cabinet. With the simplification of party divisions in the 1860s and the existence of more clearly designated leaders, it became customary to deal at once with the prospective Prime Minister.[1]

In view of the difficulties already described in forming and keeping a Cabinet together, politicians who expected to come into office were engaged in a more or less continuous process of adjusting their relations so that the outline of a new administration often took shape before the existing government was finally defeated. The evident weakness of the Whigs in May 1834 led Wellington and Peel to come together and discuss the distribution of offices in any administration they were called upon to form.[2] To comfort Gathorne-Hardy in April 1868, Disraeli wrote that "Gladstone, instead of wishing to upset us, has no Cabinet ready "[3] while Derby, after his defeat in 1859, contemplated a

---

[1] When, as in 1859 and on later occasions, the Queen summoned someone other than the clearly designated leaders of a party, it was not so much for advice as to try to avoid commissioning a person she disliked.
[2] Parker, *Sir Robert Peel*, Vol. II, pp. 240–242.
[3] A. E. Gathorne-Hardy, *op. cit.*, Vol. I, p. 275.

counter-attack on the grounds that Palmerston had dislodged him without having a Cabinet already prepared to take office.[4] If the politician commissioned by the monarch had not been able to ascertain whether his colleagues were ready to work together or whether they were willing to face the House of Commons, he had then to engage in rapid consultations. When Peel resigned in late 1845, Lord John Russell was asked to form a government on December 11. The next day he saw some leading Whigs, consulted a member of the outgoing Cabinet and wrote to the Queen asking how far he could expect support from Peel. On December 18 Peel's reply was read at a meeting of fifteen Whigs who voted ten to five in favour of accepting the royal commission only to find that the conditions under which Lord Grey was prepared to serve (the exclusion of Palmerston from the Foreign Office) made further progress impossible.[5] The trouble in this case was that besides their quarrels and reluctance to tackle the problem of the Corn Laws, the Whigs were in a minority in Parliament. In a similar situation in 1866, Derby called a meeting of twenty-two of his colleagues and asked them whether he should accept the royal commission and if so whether he should try to form an enlarged government or, if this failed, a purely Conservative administration.[6]

Even when the leaders of a party had reason to expect the support of a majority of the House and the co-operation of their colleagues in forming a Cabinet, the Prime Minister could not simply summon a number of men and offer each of them a specific post. Some of the most important politicians might make conditions before they would accept office. Lansdowne was a senior member of the Whig coterie and an essential part of any Cabinet they formed. In 1834 he announced that he would not enter a government which contained Lord Durham,[7] while in December 1845 he would only take office if the future Cabinet met and formally adopted a minute embodying a proposal to give landlords tax relief of about a million pounds.[8] Once the major appointments were settled, these men discussed the distribution of other offices. Sometimes leadership appeared to be concentrated

[4] Jones, *op. cit.*, p. 258.

[5] *Later Correspondence of Lord John Russell*, Vol. I, pp. 102–106.

[6] *Letters*, Series II, Vol. I, p. 344.

[7] Lord Broughton, *op. cit.*, Vol. IV, p. 357.

[8] *Later Correspondence of Lord John Russell*, Vol. I, pp. 93–94.

in a few hands as in 1859 when the new government was evidently to be led by Palmerston or Russell. " In either case," Lord John wrote, " the nomination to Cabinet offices ought to be concerted between us," [9] but this did not mean either had much freedom of action. The shape of the Cabinet was influenced by the views of the indispensable elements such as Gladstone (who accepted on condition that he went to the Exchequer) or Sidney Herbert (who made the proviso that he should go to the House of Lords if overworked) and Palmerston and Russell found themselves joined by five of their colleagues in the discussion over the remaining appointments.[10]   The numbers of this inner circle varied.   In 1852 Derby, Disraeli and Malmesbury were the only men of note in the government and they arranged the main offices,[11] while Lord John Russell, with more talent at his disposal, usually had to accept advice from a larger gathering.[12]   If the ministry was the product of a coalition, there would be bargaining among the leaders of the various sections.[13]   As the important offices were filled, the character of the government became more evident and those invited to accept the remaining posts might make further conditions or ask for assurances about policy.   The Peelites had been willing to work with the Whigs in a genuine coalition under Aberdeen but were full of misgivings about joining a very similar government led by Palmerston in January 1855.   Spring Rice had said he would enter Lord Melbourne's first Cabinet provided it contained no Radicals [14] and Disraeli showed his greater strength in 1866 by making Northcote's entry into the Cabinet a condition of his own acceptance of office.   A frequent condition was that Palmerston should be kept under control (on the part of Grey in June 1846 [15])

9 Parker, *Sir James Graham*, Vol. II, p. 385.
10 Lord Stanmore, *op. cit.*, Vol. II, p. 200. Palmerston was only too pleased about this. As he told Granville—" A pretty mess I should have been in with Johnny alone, and objecting to all his proposals with no-one to back me up . . ." Lord E. Fitzmaurice, *op. cit.*, Vol. I, p. 531.
11 Jones, *op. cit.*, p. 160.
12 In June 1846, for example, Lord John and five others met to discuss the composition of the government. Maxwell, *op. cit.*, Vol. I, p. 264.
13 After the protracted negotiations which settled the personnel of Aberdeen's Cabinet (7 Peelites, 5 Whigs, 1 Radical), Sir James Graham said " I have never passed a week so unpleasantly." Parker, *Sir James Graham*, Vol. I, p. 200.
14 *Lord Melbourne's Papers*, p. 266 and Torrens, *op. cit.*, Vol. II, p. 104.
15 Maxwell, *op. cit.*, Vol. I, p. 269.

or later, in 1855 and 1859 when he became Prime Minister, that all questions of foreign policy should be submitted to the Cabinet.[16]

Once a government was formed, a change of promotion was usually discussed among the same group of leading members. But since the effect could be almost as upsetting as that of a resignation, it was often wise to obtain a wider measure of consent. The Queen protested in 1851 " against the Cabinet's taking upon itself the appointment of its own Members, which rested entirely with the Prime Minister and the sovereign," but in matters as politically delicate as the removal of Palmerston and the appointment of Granville as his successor, the Premier had to be sure that his colleagues were in agreement.[17] The error of not doing so came out later in Palmerston's most unfortunate appointment of Clanricarde as Privy Seal. Then he only consulted Granville, perhaps because he knew it would be unpopular.[18] This mistake was all the more curious in view of Palmerston's previous experience, when he had been virtually pushed out of the Aberdeen Cabinet by a curt letter drafted for this purpose by the Prime Minister, Lord John Russell, Lord Clarendon and Sir James Graham. Once the Cabinet reassembled, it became evident that several members were unhappy about different aspects of this event and when an intermediary persuaded Palmerston to withdraw his resignation he had to be readmitted.[19] On becoming Prime Minister in 1855 Palmerston was well advised to consult the whole Cabinet about the vacancies left by the four retiring Peelites, as the character of the administration could not but be altered by such an extensive regroupment and the slightest dissension would have been fatal.[20] When Molesworth died later in the year, he again raised the question of a successor with the

[16] In 1855 this point was made in *Argyll's Memoirs*, Vol. I, p. 530 and Newcastle urged Gladstone to insist on the same condition if he joined. (Martineau, *op. cit.*, pp. 254–256.) Newcastle reiterated his opinion when he accepted office under Palmerston in 1859 (Martineau, *op. cit.*, p. 286). In 1865 Clarendon asked Lord Russell " not to make many *coups d'Etat* without consulting the Cabinet." Maxwell, *op. cit.*, Vol. II, p. 299.

[17] *Letters*, Vol. II, pp. 415–416.

[18] Lord Stanmore, *op. cit.*, Vol. II, p. 105.

[19] The best account of this incident is in H. C. F. Bell, *Lord Palmerston*, Vol. II, pp. 94–102, supplemented by Sir Arthur Gordon, *The Earl of Aberdeen*, p. 273, and Walpole, *op. cit.*, Vol. II, pp. 197–202.

[20] Argyll, *op. cit.*, Vol. I, p. 304.

Cabinet.[21]   On the other hand, where there were jealousies Melbourne told the Queen it was safer to discuss a reshuffle at separate interviews rather than in open Cabinet [22] and clearly only this method was possible if a minister was being asked to stand down.[23] Thus consultation on Cabinet changes was often widespread but the assurance that a minister's views would be considered was a sign that he was one of the men who mattered. To try to persuade Graham to take the Admiralty in 1849, Lord John Russell went over his policies in a two-hour talk and indicated his desire for further Peelite acquisitions by promising " to discuss in a confiding spirit" how vacancies in the Cabinet should be filled up.[24]

It was customary for the Cabinet to decide the manner of its demise. To some extent this was because it was not always clear whether a given defeat was to be accepted as showing a definite lack of confidence and even when this was decided, ministers had the alternatives of resigning or asking for a dissolution. But the main reason was that on all essential matters, the Cabinet acted collectively. On many occasions there was no doubt as to the correct course though, as Derby reported to the Queen in 1852, " as a matter of form, it is necessary that he should consult his colleagues." [25] When the situation was not so clear there was the normal process of discussion. On May 7, 1839, Melbourne opened Cabinet proceedings by raising the whole position of the government, its small majorities and the evident intention of the Radicals to desert, and after some talk there was a unanimous decision to resign.[26] Two years later the division between those who, like Melbourne, favoured resignation and those who preferred dissolution was not resolved till the Premier took his pen and noted ministers' opinions *seriatim*.[27] After passing the 1867 Reform Bill Disraeli had convinced his colleagues that they should hold on till they could dissolve on the reformed register, but when defeat came unexpectedly early, he thought it safer not to reopen the matter in the Cabinet before advising the

21 *Ibid.*, p. 590.   22 *The Girlhood of Queen Victoria*, Vol. II, p. 73.
23 As Brougham pointed out when he and Grey were considering asking
   Goderich to move. *Life and Times of Lord Brougham*, Vol. III, p. 243.
24 C. S. Parker, *Sir James Graham*, Vol. II, p. 74.
25 *Letters*, Series I, Vol. II, p. 500.
26 Lord Broughton, *op. cit.*, Vol. V, p. 188.
27 Lord Broughton in *Edinburgh Review*, 1871, p. 336.

Queen that he intended to remain in office till the new register was ready. Malmesbury reported that "the ministers are very angry with Disraeli for going to the Queen without calling a Cabinet and Marlborough wants to resign." [28]

FUNCTIONS OF THE CABINET

Not only did the formation, maintenance, and even on occasion the conclusion of Cabinets involve many problems, but it must also be remembered that this gathering of ministers had several different functions to perform. Most obviously, the Cabinet was the centre of political power; it was the body which determined policy. It was possible for Prime Ministers, Foreign Secretaries and even lesser ministers to take some decisions on their own, but if there was any dispute or challenge from Parliament or the Press, the matter had to be settled in the Cabinet. There was little point in a man of reputation joining a government if he was not in the Cabinet. In 1866 Derby wanted Shaftesbury to lend his prestige to the ministry but in order to avoid taxing his strength, offered him an office outside the Cabinet. Shaftesbury "answered, truly enough, that in that case the effect of his appointment would be lost." [29] When Lord Eliot proposed the abolition of his office of Chief Secretary for Ireland and the transfer of his functions to the Home Secretary, a major argument was that "Irish members would infinitely prefer communication with a Cabinet Minister." [30] The only occasion, in this period, on which the subordinate members of a government had any independent effect was in November 1855, when the Cabinet was prepared to stand by Lord John Russell but the junior ministers asked for his resignation and Lord John acquiesced.[31]

The knowledge that power was concentrated in this body explains the tendency to "count noses." [32] As Clarendon

---

[28] Malmesbury, *op. cit.*, p. 639.

[29] *Letters*, Series II, Vol. I, p. 349.

[30] Lord Eliot to Sir Robert Peel, Parker, *Sir Robert Peel*, Vol. III, p. 111.

[31] *Life of Lord Campbell*, Vol. II, p. 334 and *Letters*, Series I, Vol. III, p. 166. Even in this case Palmerston reported the junior ministers simply as conveying the desire of "the great bulk of the steadiest supporters of the Government."

[32] Sir James Graham used this expression in the negotiations of 1849, Parker, *Sir James Graham*, Vol. II, p. 74.

observed, " the composition of the Cabinet is of the utmost importance as indicative of . . . (the government's) policy " [33] and
Sidney Herbert felt that even one change in 1859 would lessen
its " too Italian complexion." [34]   Lord Derby's Ministry of 1858
had a highly conservative wing including Chelmsford, Walpole,
Henley, Hardwicke and Peel and a more liberal element composed
of Disraeli, Stanley, Pakington, Salisbury and Lytton, a situation
of which most of those involved in public life were aware.[35]
Because power depended on membership of and influence in the
Cabinet, attempts to build up a coalition or to draw in a parliamentary group (such as the Peelites in 1855 or the Adullamites
in 1866) [36] were usually based on the offer of so many seats
in the Cabinet. Besides the relative strength of political factions,
observers were careful to note any combinations based on other
grounds. When Lord John Russell found two of his Irish proposals rejected in 1848, he felt that the opposition, though taking
its stand on the laws of political economy, derived some strength
from family relationships. The leading opponent, Lord Grey, was
supported by his brother-in-law Sir Charles Wood, his cousin
Sir George Grey, and after January 1849, by Sir Francis Baring
who was the cousin by marriage of Lord Grey and Lady Wood
and Sir George Grey's brother-in-law.[37] Sometimes known as
" the phalanx," Prince Albert also referred to this " Grey Party "
(he included Lord Clarendon among its members), though their
views and their references to Lord John Russell's wing as " old
women " suggest that politics played as large a part in the align-
ment as family ties.[38] It is significant that Lord John's proposals
were defeated although the Grey Party mustered only four or
five votes in a Cabinet of fourteen. In general the issues coming
before governments were so varied and political thought was so

[33] Maxwell, *op. cit.*, Vol. I, pp. 265–267.
[34] Lord Stanmore, *op. cit.*, Vol. II, p. 200.
[35] Jones, *op. cit.*, p. 246.
[36] See James Winter, " The Cave of Adullam and Parliamentary Reform,"
E.H.R., Vol. 81, pp. 38–55. Disraeli offered the Adullamites two places and
later Lord Derby raised the offer to three. See also Maurice Cowling,
" Disraeli, Derby and Fusion, October 1865–July 1866," *The Historical
Journal*, Vol. 8, 1965, pp. 31–71, for a full account of offers of Cabinet
places both by the Conservative and the earlier Whig administration.
[37] Walpole, *op. cit.*, Vol. II, pp. 78–81.
[38] *Letters*, Series I, Vol. II, p. 102.

free of stereotyped reactions that divisions did not regularly occur along the lines of ideology, past connections or family ties.[39]

Besides determining policy, the Cabinet conducted such administration as was necessary and considered the items of legislation that it had decided to introduce. As always it was difficult to tell where administration stopped and policy began. The Cabinet settled the broad framework of British foreign policy, but since neither the House of Commons nor the public took a constant interest [40] in it, the details were left to the Foreign Secretary, sometimes aided or supervised by the Prime Minister; their relations depended on the interests and personalities of the two men. In financial affairs, likewise, the ministers met to hear the plans of the Chancellor of the Exchequer a few days before the announcement in Parliament. There was much more concern over financial policy and Cabinets could and did review the Chancellor's proposals, but the initiative in framing the scheme and preparing the arguments naturally lay with the minister. The only other subjects which required regular administration were defence and Ireland, though colonial affairs did take up some of the time of the Cabinet between 1830 and 1850.[41] On defence, much depended on the state of foreign relations and whether any money could be spent without raising taxes. Both these factors varied so much (revenue tended to fluctuate with the trade cycle) that a coherent long-term policy on defence never materialised and little was achieved. The regular administration of the Army was largely in the hands of the Commander-in-Chief at the Horse Guards and though he took orders from the Cabinet, most matters were left to him once the size and cost of the Army had been determined. The Cabinet took a little more interest in the Navy, but since the need to combine economy with a three-Power standard (a Navy as strong as the combined fleets of France, Russia and the United States) was generally recognised both by ministers and by the Admiralty, there was little left to settle except the disposition

[39] The best example is that in the disputes over parliamentary reform and diplomacy in 1853–54, the Aberdeen Cabinet never divided along Whig versus Peelite lines.

[40] Maxwell, *op. cit.*, Vol. I, p. 173. Greville pointed out to Clarendon that foreign affairs are seldom discussed except in the House of Lords.

[41] See H. T. Manning, " Colonial Crises before the Cabinet, 1829–1835," *Bulletin of the Institute of Historical Research*, Vol. 30 (1957).

of the fleet.[42]　The Prime Minister, the Foreign Secretary, the Chancellor of the Exchequer and the First Lord usually consulted on the main decisions. Ireland presented a long-term problem both of administration and remedial legislation. The government was conducted by Dublin Castle and the Cabinet had only to provide the legislation, though this task was beset with difficulties.[43]　The remedies for each of Ireland's troubles could be regarded as the thin end of a wedge which might later be inserted in the English social system. To deal with the Irish Church raised the bogies of disestablishment and the endowment of Popery, to tackle the land problem involved not only challenging the growing dogmas of *laissez-faire* but threatening landlords' rights, while any move to repeal the Act of Union would have been regarded as utterly retrograde and dangerous. As a result Ireland had some spells of good administration,[44] depending on the quality of the men in Dublin Castle, and some remedial legislation was passed though this usually had to be forced out of the British Cabinet. Either a desire for Irish votes in the Commons, the pressure of imminent disaster in Ireland, or threats of resignation from the Lord Lieutenant [45] were required before the Cabinet would act and successive British governments cannot be said to have tackled these persistent problems with success.

On the whole, the Cabinet was not a suitable instrument for preparing or conducting any continuous or detailed programme of administration. As Lord John Russell noted at the time of the Crimean War, it was " a cumbrous and unwieldy instrument. . . . It can furnish suggestions, or make a decision upon a measure submitted to it, but it cannot administer." [46]　The Cabinet's inadequacies were tolerated because there was little of this kind of work to be done and the Commons tended to judge governments

---

[42] Sir J. H. Briggs in his *Naval Administrations, 1827–1892* constantly laments the Cabinet's economical attitude towards the Navy, but in fact the Admiralty realised that it would never get more than just enough for its pressing needs.

[43] There was also some friction in the relations between the Lord Lieutenant who controlled the Government of Ireland and the Chief Secretary who managed parliamentary affairs at Westminster. See R. B. McDowell, " The Irish Executive in the Nineteenth Century," *Irish Historical Studies*, 1955, pp. 264–278.

[44] Especially under Thomas Drummond between 1835 and 1840.

[45] Clarendon, as Lord Lieutenant, frequently used this weapon. Greville, *op. cit.*, Series II, Vol. III, pp. 105–106 and 217.

[46] Quoted by Olive Anderson in " Cabinet Government and the Crimean War," *E.H.R.* (1964), Vol. 79, p. 549.

more by their handling of specific problems. The only other regular governmental task of the Cabinet was to decide on the principles of new legislation, which often involved framing the Bill concerned. Sometimes the burden was carried by commissions of inquiry (as with the Poor Law Amendment Bill, and the Municipal Reform Bill), or there had been a considerable measure of preparation by pressure groups or interested individuals. However, it was now accepted that most major items of legislation were drafted by the government under the supervision of the Cabinet, so that ministers had to have some criteria of judgment. If the Bill was the work of a department, such as the Treasury, the Home or the Colonial Office, it would have been prepared by the minister or by the Permanent Secretary on the basis of existing information. Some measures, such as the Repeal of the Corn Laws or the Ecclesiastical Titles Bill, could be drawn up by any competent politician. But when there was no obvious department and the Cabinet was breaking new ground, it was quite common to appoint an *ad hoc* committee from among the Cabinet members. References have been found to twenty-six committees.[47] The usual procedure was to ask five or six men to help the individual in charge of the measure collect information and frame the clauses before returning to the full Cabinet.[48] There was no need for anything like a standing future legislation committee, as the Cabinet held a series of meetings in the late autumn to arrange priorities and strategy for the coming parliamentary session, and on each Saturday during session it settled the tactics for the coming week.

Only during and just after the Crimean War was there any suggestion of a standing committee. (When Disraeli called for a War Cabinet in his paper, the *Press*, in January 1855, all he

[47] There were six committees to prepare reform Bills so that by 1866 Derby could declare that enough was known to make another committee unnecessary (Monypenny and Buckle, *op. cit.*, Vol. IV, p. 454). Three sat on Indian questions, and Bankruptcy, Patents, Law Reform, Church Reform, Army and Navy estimates, income tax, sugar duties and Irish discontents were all considered in this way. Occasionally other ministers or officials attended these committees—the Attorney-General on law reform, and the Duke of Cambridge on Army estimates.

[48] On one occasion, the 1868 Education Bill, the Cabinet began by agreeing on the principles and then left a committee to fill in the detailed proposals. Monypenny and Buckle, *op. cit.*, Vol. V, p. 581.

seems to have meant was a government led by Derby, Ellenborough, Palmerston and himself.[49]) An actual military or War
Committee of the Cabinet was established in August 1855 because
of the outcry against the inefficient prosecution of the war in late
1854 and the criticisms of the Select Committee into the state of
the Army before Sebastopol. The Select Committee pointed to
the fact that the Cabinet had been on holiday in August and September 1854 when the Army had moved to the Crimea, landed,
fought the battle of the Alma and began the siege of Sebastopol.[50]
Consisting of Palmerston, Panmure, Sir Charles Wood (the
heads of the naval and military departments) and Lord Granville,
the Cabinet Committee considered methods of relieving Kars,[51]
accepted General Simpson's resignation and decided to appoint
Sir W. Codrington in his place,[52] and also dealt with coastal
defences.[53] The committee was active through the remainder of
1855 but was suspended when the House rose in the summer
of 1856. All its decisions had to be endorsed by the full Cabinet.[54]
Its revival was announced in late 1856, under the title of the
Military and Defence Committee [55] when it met to consider the
fortifications of Plymouth, Portsmouth and Dover and in December 1857, assisted by the Commander-in-Chief, it discussed the
Navy.[56] The committee reappears during the Indian Mutiny [57]
and then in late 1859, presumably to support Palmerston in his
campaign for stronger defences, as Gladstone was most indignant
that he had never been informed of its existence.[58] Its final brief
appearance was in December 1861 when it met to concert preparations for a possible war with the United States after the Trent
incident.[59]

49 Monypenny and Buckle, *op. cit.*, Vol. III, p. 558.
50 Evidence of Lord Aberdeen before the Select Committee on the Army before
   Sebastopol, 1854–1855, IX, Part III, p. 290. See also Olive Anderson, *op. cit.*
51 Sir George Douglas and Sir George Ramsay, ed. *The Panmure Papers*, Vol.
   I, p. 374. Letter to General Simpson on September 3.
52 *Ibid.*, p. 421 and Martin, *op. cit.*, Vol. III, p. 382.
53 Fitzmaurice, *op. cit.*, Vol. I, p. 132. 54 *The Panmure Papers*, Vol. I, p. 431.
55 There has been some confusion as Queen Victoria's letter (Series I, Vol. III, p.
   269) refers to " committees " in the plural but the same letter in *The Panmure
   Papers*, Vol. II, p. 317 is in the singular and it is clearly a single body.
56 *Ibid.*, Vol. II, p. 459.
57 Palmerston refers to it in a letter to the Queen on July 15, 1858. B. Connell,
   op. cit., p. 218.
58 Lord Stanmore, *op. cit.*, Vol. II, pp. 270 and 279, and H. C. F. Bell, *op. cit.*,
   Vol. II, p. 238.
59 K. Bourne in " British Preparations for War with the North 1861–2," *E.H.R.*,
   Vol. 76 (1961) refers (p. 606) to two minutes of the committee in the papers

Despite the activities of the committee in 1855–56, the Crimean War was primarily conducted by the reorganised War Office at home in response to the requests and reports reaching them from the Crimea. The latter part of the war showed that a department under an energetic minister (such as Sidney Herbert) could be galvanised into doing competent work but that the Cabinet, while capable of major decisions of principle, was not a suitable instrument for conducting detailed administration over a long period.

In view of the reflections on the Civil Service implicit in the Northcote-Trevelyan Report and of the widespread criticism at the time of the Crimean War, it may be asked how far the Cabinet was limited by weaknesses in the machinery at its disposal.[60] The chief target of contemporary complaint was the arrangements for conducting military operations. The Army was under the nominal control of the Secretary of State for War and Colonies, its finances were managed by the Secretary *at* War, the actual conduct of the troops was directed by the Commander-in-Chief, while the Ordnance was under a Board, the commissariat was managed by the Treasury and the militia came under the authority of the Home Office.[61] But the fault really lay with the Cabinet, for an attempt to unify control in the 1830s had been abandoned as it aroused too much antagonism.[62] The powers of the Commander-in-Chief were not defined and Sir John Cam Hobhouse had resigned his post as Secretary of State for War when his colleagues would not support him in a dispute with Lord Hill over the abolition of flogging.[63] Even when the early failures

of Sir George Cornewall Lewis in the National Library of Wales. There is also a reference in a letter from Palmerston to Queen Victoria in B. Connell, *op. cit.*, p. 311.

[60] It was well known that the Colonial Office had sometimes taken two or more years to answer despatches from colonial governors and its defenders have pointed in turn to the tardiness of the Treasury and Board of Trade. See P. Knaplund, *James Stephen and the British Colonial System*, pp. 41–42. Sir J. H. Briggs, *op. cit.*, p. 35, complains of the " want of communication between the various departments of the State " and cites the decision as to which coaling stations were to be defended. This required communications between the Admiralty, the War Office, the Horse Guards, the Colonial Office, the Foreign Office and the Treasury and seven years elapsed before the matter could be settled. On the other hand the evidence in Sir Charles Trevelyan's Letter Books shows regular work and rapid replies, though dealings with Sir Charles may well have received a priority far above all other business. See J. Hart, " Sir Charles Trevelyan at the Treasury," *E.H.R.* (1960), p. 92.

[61] There is an excellent description of the pre-1854 arrangements in Sir Robert Biddulph, *Lord Cardwell at the War Office*, pp. 1–14.

[62] J. M. Stocqueler, *A Personal History of the Horse Guards*, p. 232.

[63] Lord Broughton, *op. cit.*, Vol. IV, p. 299.

in the Crimea and pressure from Parliament and from Lord John Russell led to the separation of War and Colonies and the abolition of a separate Secretary *at* War, there was no thorough overhaul of the department.[64] Sidney Herbert, who took over from the ineffective Duke of Newcastle in January 1855, did all he could, but complained that he lacked Cabinet backing and had to contend with the vis inertiae of subordinate officials.[65] When a crisis arose, a vigorous minister could chivy the office into action but no amount of energy could quite make up for the low capacity of the Army officers in the field and the inadequate information they provided. It required great exertions on the part of the Secretary of State to overcome the internal weaknesses of a department which, as Trevelyan observed in December 1858, " has not been reduced to order and is under no real control." [66]

In some offices, ministers were glad to have the advice of permanent officials. As First Commissioner of Works, Lord John Manners " depended fearlessly upon the knowledge and loyalty of Philipps, the permanent Secretary." [67] James Stephen, Permanent Secretary at the Colonial Office, had a reputation for deciding many questions of policy though the arrival of a vigorous Secretary of State or a parliamentary outcry (both of which occurred in 1833 when Stanley was appointed during a crisis over the abolition of slavery) could change the whole situation and Stephen was given forty-eight hours to draft a Bill based on a new scheme.[68] But the Office still had its own views and three years after Stephen retired, Palmerston remarked that the clerks entertained the foolish idea of getting rid of the Ionian Islands.[69]

The business of government was in fact sufficiently light and straightforward for one man to master and personally supervise the work of a department if he felt so inclined. During his tenure of the Foreign Office Palmerston read every incoming despatch and drew up all important outgoing messages. The Earl of Mayo as Chief Secretary for Ireland read, digested, minuted and, if necessary, answered every letter which came to his department.[70]

64 This point is well brought out by Sir R. Biddulph, *op. cit.*
65 Lord Stanmore, *op. cit.*, Vol. II, p. 202.
66 J. Hart, *art. cit.*, p. 105.
67 Charles Whibley, *Lord John Manners and His Friends*, Vol. II, p. 50.
68 H. T. Manning, *art. cit.*, pp. 53–58.
69 E. Ashley, *op. cit.*, Vol. I, p. 266.
70 W. W. Hunter, *Life of the Earl of Mayo*, p. 84.

When civil servants engaged in anything more than clerical functions, it was a sign that the affairs of that office were either routine or non-controversial or that the minister had a high respect for the experience and judgment of the official. In 1834 the Poor Law Commission had been set up as an independent body to prevent undue pressure from Parliament. Thirteen years later it was brought under the control of the Cabinet and the Commons were told that this was to establish a parliamentary spokesman for the Board whom they could question and criticise. But at least as strong a motive was the desire to extend the same direct ministerial control over the Board as existed over other departments. Responsibility to Parliament was a reasonable doctrine in as much as each minister could or should have supervised every important action taken by his subordinates,[71] and if the machinery was in any way defective he had only to take the matter into his own hands.

The Cabinet had a further function in that ministers, besides deciding policy and conducting administration, were also the leaders of a party. Some Cabinets were coalitions and all Cabinets had fringe members who might drift away, but while there was a Prime Minister and a number of leading colleagues of a given political complexion, they constituted the nearest approach to a party leadership. They had to defend their own actions before Parliament and in public and in so far as national issues played a part in elections, it was their record that was being judged. Peel never wanted to be labelled as a party man but his address to his constituents was bound to have a wider implication, and it was at a Cabinet dinner that the Tamworth Manifesto " was discussed and finally settled." [72] At elections some ministers would usually keep in contact with the Whips and party managers and in 1847 Lord Campbell actually refers to this body as " a committee of the Cabinet to superintend the elections." [73] Facing the critical election of 1868, Disraeli told Stanley that " what we want is to raise £100,000 which, it is believed, will secure the result. It

---

[71] Sir Charles Trevelyan complained of the way in which responsibility to Parliament pervaded the Civil Service. "Everything is sacrificed to Parliament, and the main object to which all others yield is to get well through the session and then after some necessary relaxation, to consider how to get through the next." J. Hart, *art. cit.*, pp. 106–107.

[72] Sir T. Martin, *Life of Lord Lyndhurst*, p. 325.

[73] *Life of Lord Campbell*, Vol. II, p. 223.

can be done if the Cabinet sets a good example." [74]   It was this function of party leadership which the principal members of a Cabinet retained after they left office.   Meetings held to concert tactics were usually referred to in the same way as " Cabinets," or sometimes as " Quasi-cabinets," [75] " Anti-cabinets " [76] or " Cabinet Councils." [77]   The earliest instances of such gatherings specifically composed of ex-Cabinet Ministers and their leading supporters were those held by the Stanleyites after they left the Whig Ministry in 1834. [78]   Faced with possible divisions between conservatives in the Lords and in the Commons over the Irish Municipal Reform Bill in early 1836, Peel decided on " some previous confidential communication with the most intelligent and discreet of our friends " and called together a select number of his former Cabinet. [79]   The Whigs were too dispirited to undertake much co-ordinated opposition during Peel's great ministry, but after 1846 the major parties in Parliament held " cabinets " as the need to discuss party or parliamentary tactics arose.   The predicament of the Peelites revealed the difficulties of any group whose ex-Cabinet members failed or refused to perform their party functions.   Sir Robert supported Lord John Russell from the opposition bench and would not either hold meetings of his former colleagues or give any direction to the rank and file who had voted with him in 1846 [80] and therefore the Peelites were not able to operate as a party even in the terms of the 1840s.   When Peel died, his followers had no machinery available for choosing a leader from among their ex-Cabinet Ministers.   Gladstone suggested that if Aberdeen would not undertake the duties of leadership, the Peelites should meet and elect the Duke of Newcastle.   The latter put the position succinctly in his reply to Sidney Herbert:

> "It has always appeared to me that the idea of *electing* a leader is a mistake, and an inversion of the proper constitutional view of party mechanism. A leader should become

[74] Monypenny and Buckle, *op. cit.*, Vol. V, p. 56.
[75] The Whigs held quasi-cabinets in 1858. Fitzmaurice, *op. cit.*, Vol. I, p. 304.
[76] Panmure refers to an " anti-cabinet " in 1842. *The Panmure Papers*, Vol. I, p. 21.
[77] Malmesbury, *op. cit.*, p. 317.
[78] Parker, *Sir James Graham*, Vol. I, p. 219.
[79] Parker, *Sir Robert Peel*, Vol. II, p. 319.
[80] See J. B. Conacher, " Peel and the Peelites, 1846–50," *E.H.R.* (1958) p. 431.

such either because he is generally recognised as *facile princeps* in position, popularity, talent, discretion, debating power, or other qualifications necessary to balance the differences of opinion to be found in all parties, or by being selected by the Sovereign as her adviser when her ministers have resigned . . . You will at once see that the drift of all this is that Lord Aberdeen may *take* the leadership by consent of all, if he will leave his easy-chair and summon his friends; but as for Gladstone's alternative, it is *impossible*." [81]

In other words, if the former Peelite ministers were prepared to act together and acknowledge a leader, this was satisfactory, but the party did not exist in a form which would permit an election.

These gatherings of ex-Cabinet Ministers to concert action were quite different from the " cabinets " that were often planned when governments seemed likely to fall. The former seldom numbered more than five or six prominent men who met because their speeches and votes gave some guidance to their more regular followers and because divisions between them would be widely publicised, causing disunity and dismay. If office seemed possible in the near future, they might then begin to discuss the distribution of the main posts and to consider which individuals or groups could be drawn in to make a viable Cabinet of thirteen or fourteen, though such a body would not actually assemble until the existing government had resigned.

It was because the Cabinet so clearly took the major decisions and gave political leadership to the whole administration that it tended to stand or fall as a unit. In July 1834 Brougham told the House of Lords that only the Premier (Lord Grey) and Lord Althorp had resigned and the rest of the ministry were still in office.[82] This was true in legal theory and later Lord Salisbury was to make the same point—that he held his office from the Crown and not from the Prime Minister. Were the latter to die overnight, this would not terminate the offices of the other ministers but it was now accepted that their posts were all at the disposal of the new premier, once he was commissioned. If Brougham was merely suggesting that he was an indispensable member of any Whig Cabinet, the point is unimportant,

81 Lord Stanmore, *op. cit.*, Vol. I, p. 145.
82 Lord Broughton, *op. cit.*, Vol. IV, p. 353.

but if there was any suggestion that the resignation of the premier did not open the question of the entire membership of the Cabinet, he was wrong. This error of judgment was not demonstrated in 1834 because the Whigs had not been defeated and Melbourne decided to retain most of his former colleagues. Later, when Peel's government was beaten in June 1846, Brougham outside and Ellenborough inside the Cabinet wanted to let Peel and Graham go while the rest of the ministry reunited with the Protectionists.[83] This time the point was driven home, for the Prime Minister's resignation meant that the Queen commissioned Lord John Russell and the old Cabinet was at an end. During the lifetime of a Cabinet the same factors enforced a united front in face of Parliament. Sir James Graham found he could not agree with a decision of Lord Althorp (taken on the floor of the House of Commons) to accept a Committee of Inquiry into the conduct of an Irish judge and, after voting against his colleagues, offered to resign. Grey urged him not to persist and the proposal to set up a committee was in fact rescinded.[84] The enforcement of collective responsibility in minor cases lay with the Prime Minister and the Cabinet. For example, they considered disciplinary action against Lord Hill for failure to vote in the division on the Local Courts Bill, though discipline was not so rigidly enforced at this time because the large majorities of 1833 permitted some laxity.[85] The Commons could also enforce collective responsibility in the sense that it might not accept the resignation of an erring minister as exculpating the Cabinet.[86]

On the return of Lord John Russell from Vienna in July 1855, his apparent changes of front, on top of a vulnerable record, so

[83] Jones, *op. cit.*, p. 120, and *Letters*, Series I, Vol. II, p. 96.
[84] Parker, *Sir James Graham*, Vol. I, pp. 184–186. This is a rare instance, because disagreement was normally revealed at Cabinet and followed by resignation well before the matter at issue came to a vote in Parliament.
[85] Greville, *op. cit.*, Series I, Vol. III, p. 12.
[86] The Commons also enforced individual responsibility. If a minister (or his department) erred, the premier and Cabinet might decide that they should accept collective responsibility or the minister might be discarded. But the pressure was not just of convention or punctilio. If the minister was defended by the Cabinet, there was a danger of a critical motion being carried either against the government as a whole or against the individual. In 1865 the Chancellor, Lord Westbury, was censured over an appointment by a Select Committee of the Lords, and found wanting in caution over another appointment by a Committee of the Commons. On both occasions, Lord Palmerston refused to accept his resignation and he was removed by the passage of a direct vote of censure in the Commons. Herbert Paul, *op. cit.*, Vol. II, pp. 375–377.

angered the House that the government was saved only by his resignation. Similarly the reaction against Lord Ellenborough's admonitory despatch to the Governor-General of India, Lord Canning, was so strong that the government was only saved by Ellenborough's resignation, though the Opposition did not immediately withdraw their motion of censure.[87]

MEMBERSHIP AND ORGANISATION

It now remains to explain the organisation of the Cabinet itself and the distribution of power between its members. The Cabinets of the period averaged fourteen members, never rising above sixteen or sinking below thirteen.[88] Lord Grey faced the Reformed Parliament with eight peers and six ministers in the House of Commons. The pressure of business in the Lower House increasingly tended to even out the numbers representing each House in the Cabinet. By 1851 Disraeli was remarking that he needed six men on the Treasury bench but eight would be better.[89] Palmerston felt that seven each was the best arrangement [90] and in the 1850s this usually came about, though from 1858 onwards the balance just tilted in favour of the House of Commons. One reason for the surprisingly large number of peers was that being a minister in the Commons entailed much harder work. More political and debating capacity was required in the Lower House, while it was much easier to persuade peers to take the lighter offices. Sidney Herbert went to the Lords when his health declined, Sir John Cam Hobhouse asked for a peerage when he could not bear the brunt of another election and Earl Russell confessed that he could never have endured the Foreign Office between 1861 and 1865 had he remained on the Treasury Bench.

Turning to the Cabinet itself, some historians have tried to assess who was "the first Prime Minister." All that such an

[87] The despatch condemned Canning's apparent severity towards the mutinous landlords of Oudh. The debate was prolonged by Derby's hints of a dissolution, and then the production of further explanations which should have been handed to Ellenborough by the outgoing ministers produced a revulsion of feeling and the motion of censure was withdrawn. Monypenny and Buckle, *op. cit.*, Vol. IV, pp. 140–150.

[88] Disraeli in 1856 produced a scheme of administrative reform which involved cutting the Cabinet to ten but he was not able to achieve this in practice. Blake, *op. cit.*, p. 365.

[89] Monypenny and Buckle, *op. cit.*, Vol. III, p. 288.

[90] *Letters*, Series I, Vol. III, p. 190.

evaluation can show, after 1832, is that the attributes and powers of Prime Ministers have varied, though it is helpful to consider some of the variations. In fact, during this period, the Prime Minister had to work so closely with his senior colleagues that it is difficult to find any differences of category between the leading members of a government. As the discussion above has shown, the position of a Prime Minister did not rest on any clear-cut or assured basis but was the result mainly of the opinions of the leading politicians, in part of standing in Parliament and before the public, and finally of royal appointment. The Prime Minister's choice of his principal colleagues was narrowly circumscribed and major policies had to be determined by the entire Cabinet. He could not, without the support of his Cabinet, safely demand the resignations of ministers or decide how or when the Cabinet was to come to an end.

As a result, the difference of authority between one premier and another and between premiers and their senior colleagues depended on the personalities and habits of the individuals in question. If the Prime Minister was a peer, a distinguished leader of the House of Commons occupied an almost equal position.[91] When Lord John Russell suggested in 1850 that Palmerston might be tempted to leave the Foreign Office by the offer of the leadership in the Commons (Russell going to the Lords), Prince Albert at once objected that "the Leader of the House of Commons in these days has the real power in the country and can dictate absolutely to his colleagues."[92]   Though he exaggerated a little, Albert had spotted where leadership was required and where its skilful exercise could confer power.   Leadership was also needed to keep a Cabinet active and united. Sir James Graham pointed out to Melbourne that Lord Grey's government had disintegrated in part because of "the imperfect control which the Prime Minister had exercised over his colleagues."[93]   Sidney Herbert, Lord Campbell and Lord John Russell all at one time or another complained of Melbourne's apathy or "virtual abdication" while Clarendon declared that "our Cabinet is a complete

[91] Referring to the case of Derby and Disraeli, Argyll in 1852 pointed out that the latter was the effective leader. On the other hand Disraeli, at this stage, could not have done without Derby as premier. Argyll, *op. cit.*, Vol. I, p. 361.
[92] B. Connell, *Regina* v. *Palmerston*, p. 117.
[93] Parker, *Sir James Graham*, Vol. II, p. 209.

republic." [94] However, it was Melbourne's capacity to conciliate all parties that prevented his ministry breaking up during the Near Eastern crisis of 1840.

From these contemporary comments it is evident that the Prime Minister was expected to occupy an especial place as the chairman of the Cabinet, and certainly be one of the most important of the active members. He ought to be consulted on all major points.[95] Yet, once this is said, it becomes evident that no Prime Minister played precisely such a role. Peel was this and much more besides. He drew up an agenda for each Cabinet and discouraged irrelevancies or gossip.[96] As Graham said, Peel " makes himself felt in every department, and is really cognisant of the affairs of each. Lord Grey could not master such an amount of business. Canning could not do it. Now he is an actual minister and is indeed *capax imperii*." [97] But by 1846 Peel was declaring that " he defied the Minister of this country to perform properly the duties of his office " and even thought the task could only be performed from the shelter of the House of Lords.[98] Aberdeen began his period of office, like Peel, as a generally trusted adviser but by 1854 " he was out of humour with the whole thing, took no interest in anything that was done," while " in the Cabinet he takes hardly any part, and when differences of opinion arise he makes no effort to reconcile them." [99] Though Disraeli often had difficulty in galvanising Derby during their long periods in opposition, the latter was quite decisive as Prime Minister. Greville in 1852 noted that " the other members of the Cabinet have appeared as mere dummies, and in the House of Lords Derby has never allowed any of them to speak, taking on himself to answer for every department." [1] In 1866 Disraeli, in difficulties with the First Lord of the Admiralty, appealed to Derby for help.

---

[94] Lord Stanmore, *op. cit.*, Vol. I, p. 58; *Life of Lord Campbell*, Vol. II, p. 204; *Later Correspondence of Lord John Russell*, ed. G. P. Gooch, Vol. II, p 2 and Greville, *op. cit.*, Series II, Vol. I, p. 299.

[95] It was taken as one of the signs of Melbourne's weakness and of Palmerston's decline in his last year or two that ministers raised matters at Cabinet without consulting them first.

[96] Sir Algernon West, *Recollections*, Vol. I, p. 185.

[97] Morley, *op. cit.*, Vol. I, p. 248.

[98] Martin, *op. cit.*, Vol. I, p. 266. See also Peel's own account of the duties of a Prime Minister in the evidence before the Select Committee on Official Salaries, 1850, pp. 40–41.

[99] Greville, *op. cit.*, Series III, Vol. I, p. 184.

[1] Greville, *op. cit.*, Series II, Vol. III, p. 456.

" All extraordinary motion in the great departments should come from you." " The Admiralty is beyond the control of a Chancellor of the Exchequer, or any other subordinate Minister. It is the Prime Minister who alone can deal with that department. . . ." [2] There were many criticisms of Lord John Russell as premier for his lack of business-like method, his dislike of opposition and his tendency to conceal matters from the Cabinet. But with Palmerston as Foreign Secretary it was almost a twin-headed ministry, and Lord John survived the dismissal of Palmerston in 1851 only because he had the unanimous support of the Cabinet. On the other hand when Palmerston became First Lord of the Treasury his colleagues were agreeably surprised at his openness to argument and his fairness to all opinions. When he wanted to go his own way he pressed his point and at times tried to commit the Cabinet in advance, but still there were few complaints.

A Prime Minister could thus be the driving force in a government, or one of a group of able and equally influential men, or he might have been selected as a mild but acceptable figurehead.[3] The office itself carried no distinctive powers other than that of recommending appointments and being the principal channel of communication with the Crown. The role of the Prime Minister becomes clearer after an examination of the working of the Cabinet and the relationships between its members.

Any minister could call the Cabinet together.[4] Meetings were held in the Cabinet Room at the Foreign Office till 1856 when they were transferred to No. 10 Downing Street, though occasionally ministers met in Westminster or at the house of an indisposed member.[5] Normally Cabinets were held on Saturdays during the session to arrange the next week's business with a Cabinet dinner every Wednesday, each member taking it in turn to act as host. The lack of administrative work and the preoccupation with political questions and parliamentary leadership was shown by the way Cabinets ceased to meet every August

---

[2] Blake, *op. cit.*, p. 454.
[3] When Lord Lansdowne was considered as a possible Prime Minister in the negotiations of late 1852, it was intended that he should fulfil this last role.
[4] Though it became customary to mention the matter to the Prime Minister. Evidence of Aberdeen to the Select Committee on the Army before Sebastopol, 1854–55, IX, Part III, p. 290.
[5] Sir Edmund Hertslet, *Recollections of the Old Foreign Office*, p. 23.

when the session ended. A few ministers would remain in town, but collective decisions were postponed till late October or what was often termed "the November Cabinets." Frequent gatherings were then held to prepare for the opening of Parliament in January, regular meetings took place during the session and a successful outcome was celebrated as Parliament dispersed with the annual "fish dinner" at Greenwich.

One of the first problems for a minister was to decide what matters should be brought before the Cabinet. The general policy was to raise all questions that might engage the attention of Parliament or in any way affect the fortunes of the government. With a relatively small amount of business to conduct, the easiest rule was that if any doubt existed the problem could be mentioned. An unusual violation of this rule occurred when Lord Panmure announced that the Army in the Crimea would have its pay doubled without telling his colleagues. Palmerston was furious and told the Queen that not only should Treasury sanction have been obtained but "it is a standing rule that no head of a department should take any important step without first consulting the Cabinet, or, at all events, without the concurrence of the head of the government." [6] Panmure had to apologise and accept a modified pay increase. On the other hand the Cabinet did not like being asked to settle trivial points, and how much a minister put before his colleagues really depended on the personality and judgment of the individual concerned.

A more important reason why major matters did not always come before the Cabinet was that the leader in the House of Commons, and to a minor extent in the Lords, had often to express opinions and make concessions during debates when consultation was impossible. In a debate on reform in 1851, Lord John Russell said he would introduce legislation on that subject next year before obtaining the consent of his colleagues.[7] Disraeli made major amendments to the Cabinet's resolutions on the government of India in 1858 and incurred a heavy rebuke from the Prime Minister.[8] His actions in promising to bring in an immediate Reform Bill in February 1867, and in accepting

---

[6] B. Connell, *op. cit.*, pp. 178–180.
[7] Walpole, *op. cit.*, Vol. II, p. 120.
[8] Monypenny and Buckle, *op. cit.*, Vol. IV, pp. 137–139.

Hodgkinson's amendment (which might have added half a million voters) were both taken on the floor of the House, without Cabinet approval, in the expectation that his colleagues could not but agree.

The Cabinet, like the public, was not very interested in the small change of foreign affairs and much was left to the Foreign Secretary. Labouchere pointed out that departmental ministers could not read all the papers which were circulated and they expected the Prime Minister to keep a general watch over foreign policy.[9] Lord Grey had supervised Palmerston in the early 1830s and Aberdeen held a watching brief over Lord Clarendon in the first two years of his ministry. Lord John Russell was able to control Palmerston only by continual assertions of his rather deficient authority. As early as 1845, Lord John Russell was assuring the Queen " that the Foreign Office is to be a department of the Government, the affairs of which are to be considered in common, and not dealt with according to his (Palmerston's) good will and pleasure." [10] Yet with less controversial Foreign Secretaries much freedom of action was permitted. When he was Prime Minister, Peel watched over foreign affairs, read the despatches and added his notes, but he trusted Aberdeen and the latter's sentiments and tone usually predominated.[11] The Cabinet could call the Foreign Minister to heel, but often this was only after actions had been taken which produced trouble and excited attention. As Clarendon said " I soon became aware how easy it was for a Foreign Secretary to act dishonestly towards his colleagues without being detected," and half the trouble with Palmerston before 1851 was not only that he escaped detection, but that when he was detected he won general applause.[12] All that the Cabinet could do short of demanding his resignation was to force Palmerston to withdraw despatches and to submit all

---

[9] Greville, *op. cit.*, Series II, Vol. III, pp. 311–312.

[10] Greville, *op. cit.*, Series II, Vol. II, p. 322. In fact Russell did not succeed in this and there were constant complaints from Cabinet colleagues. See D. Southgate, *op. cit.*, pp. 243–246.

[11] A. B. Cunningham, " Peel, Aberdeen and the Entente Cordiale," *Bulletin of the Institute of Historical Research*, Vol. 30, pp. 192–197.

[12] Clarendon made this remark in May 1860. Maxwell, *op. cit.*, Vol. II, p. 214. In 1861 he reported an occasion when he and Palmerston agreed that Vera Cruz ought to be blockaded. Palmerston asked him to give the orders— " Surely not without bringing it before the Cabinet?"—" Oh, ah! the Cabinet —very well; call one then if you think it necessary." *Ibid.*, p. 240.

outgoing messages to the Prime Minister. When, as between 1859 and 1865, the Prime Minister and the Foreign Secretary combined to pursue their own policy and both disliked deferring to the Cabinet, the problem of maintaining Cabinet control became even more acute. On two occasions Palmerston and Russell were called to order by their colleagues; though in one case Palmerston announced that he still felt at liberty to state his view unofficially to a foreign Power or, as he put it, " to make a notch off my own bat." [13]

In domestic affairs there was less scope for this kind of behaviour, and though ministers might avoid bringing up too controversial issues this was usually because the reactions of the Cabinet were already well known.[14] The one problem which arose was that of controlling occasional utterances by men who were indispensable and could therefore commit their party. Neither of the declarations known as the Edinburgh and the Durham letters of Lord John Russell was submitted to his colleagues (he was in office in the latter instance), though both profoundly affected Whig policy.

With the emphasis on economy and the fact that private M.P.s could still challenge and carry reductions in the estimates, the personality and ability of the Chancellor of the Exchequer played a considerable part in the success or failure of a Cabinet. The story that Disraeli sought this post in 1852 because " a strong man armed with the power of the purse must necessarily be supreme " [15] has been refuted, yet his career at this office in 1852, 1858 and 1866 and Gladstone's two periods at the Exchequer showed that it did confer both power and prominence. But it also brought conflicts with colleagues. In 1864 Gladstone told Palmerston that he wanted to cut down the estimates by a definite sum. The Prime Minister replied that the correct method was to meet in Cabinet, consider the financial needs of each of the Services and weigh the cost in the light of the interests of the

---

[13] *Later Correspondence of Lord John Russell*, Vol. II, p. 291 and Bell, *op. cit.*, Vol. II, p. 381.

[14] When Lord John Russell intimated that he was giving up the controversial Appropriation Clause in January 1837 Melbourne asked : " Is it necessary to bring that question again before the Cabinet? I rather fear the wrong-headedness of some of them." Walpole, *op. cit.*, Vol. I, p. 276.

[15] Spencer Walpole in *The History of England from 1815*, Vol. V, p. 452, is responsible for the story which is refuted in R. Blake, *Disraeli*, p. 312.

nation. If the Chancellor of the Exchequer was allowed to fix an arbitrary sum which his colleagues had to accept, this would be claiming " a Supreme Control at Home." Gladstone denied that " the usual process of going over the heads of service and the names of stations is one adequate to the occasion. The state of information in a Cabinet never allows this operation to be a searching one." His objective in approaching the Prime Minister was not to impose his will on his colleagues but " to avoid the renewal of struggles in the Cabinet such as might wear that unseemly aspect." [16] On matters of defence, Palmerston was one of the chief " spenders " and it is doubtful, even if he and Gladstone had agreed, whether they could have forced the other ministers to accept an arbitrary sum fixed for them by the Chancellor of the Exchequer. How the latter raised the money was a matter which he could settle, subject to revision by the Cabinet, but the level of expenditure had to be decided by open discussion in the normal manner.

In general then, the Cabinet was consulted on all matters that required preparation or might cause trouble, though it was possible for the Prime Minister, the Leader of the House of Commons (if these were separate positions) and the Foreign Secretary to take many decisions on their own, and in so doing to put their colleagues at a disadvantage if they desired to check or reverse these policies.

Having decided to take a matter to the Cabinet, the normal procedure was for a minister to consult the Prime Minister and then raise the question at the next meeting. But if the Premier was weak or indifferent like Melbourne in his later years or Aberdeen in 1854, ministers might not bother to start in this manner. On difficult questions, such as defence, it was a common practice to write a memorandum and circulate it with the other Cabinet papers. Each member would add his views till there was a bundle of notes and the minister would have a basis on which to frame his proposal. If the matter was controversial, it was often worth while sounding a few of the more forceful characters before the open discussion. This practice could lead to the belief that the place was being set by an inner or " interior

[16] The correspondence is set out in P. Guedalla, *op. cit.*, pp. 292–320.

Cabinet." [17]   As with many informal practices, much depended on the methods and the motives of those involved.   Lord Argyll realised that " in every Cabinet the leading spirits do a good deal by private and personal understandings," [18] and that this was often essential for the efficient conduct of business.   Peel took many decisions on his own or with the advice of Graham and told his Cabinet as much as he thought was necessary.[19]   Disraeli was careful to " square " Lord Derby before he issued his election address in 1852 to guard against the complaints (made by Herries and Henley) that he had not consulted the Cabinet.[20] Later, in preparing his Budget, Disraeli feared criticism from the same quarter and asked for an interview with the Prime Minister : " I should dread going into Cabinet without further discussion." [21] Except on the few foreign issues which excited him, Palmerston was much more open to advice and persuasion from the Cabinet than Lord John Russell.   Besides the Premier, the " working heads " [22] were the Foreign Secretary, Leader of the House of Commons (if the Prime Minister was in the Lords) and perhaps the Home Secretary and the Chancellor of the Exchequer.   (To have no office or one which involved little action reduced the influence of the minister.[23])   If the senior men, who had probably played a leading part in forming the government, merely met to clear the ground and then reopened the whole problem at the Cabinet, they performed a useful service.   Between August and November it was quite normal for the Cabinet to leave decisions to the few departmental ministers who remained in town.   Thus it was well known that the foreign policy of the Aberdeen Coalition was largely determined by the Prime Minister, Lord John Russell, Palmerston and Clarendon.   In March 1853 they were assembling to go over the incoming despatches before

[17] Mrs. Simpson, *op. cit.*, pp. 216–217, and Parker, *Sir Robert Peel*, Vol. III, p. 535.
[18] *Argyll's Memoirs*, Vol. I, p. 383.
[19] *Letters*, Series I, Vol. II, p. 77.
[20] R. Blake, *op. cit.*, p. 319.
[21] *Ibid.*, p. 334.
[22] Phrase used by Gladstone in 1855, *Argyll's Memoirs*, Vol. I, p. 526.
[23] Lord John Russell believed that to be the leader in the House of Commons made him virtually Prime Minister (*Letters*, Series I, Vol. II, p. 504), but when he was a minister without portfolio his influence declined (Greville, *op. cit.*, Series III, Vol. I, p. 64). Stanley said that being Secretary of State for War and the Colonies left him a worthless cypher (Parker, *Sir Robert Peel*, Vol. II, pp. 154–155).

the Cabinet met and they were left in control through the summer months. As Gladstone said " it implied no disparagement to the Cabinet, a machine incapable of being worked by anything like daily, sometimes hourly, consultation, if Lord Clarendon thus became the centre of a distinct set of current communications, the upshot only of which would become known on the more important occasions to the ministers at large." [24]   A definite group of this kind was less common than the tendency of a Prime Minister to rely on one or two more trusted colleagues. Melbourne took up most of his problems with Lord John Russell, rather as the latter came to rely on Lansdowne in the late 1840s and early 1850s. The security for the rest of the Cabinet lay in the ease with which they could detect any attempt to lead them and the pressure they could bring to bear. It was not hard to become influential within a government as Cabinet Ministers had no strong sense of hierarchy, each member could speak as often as he liked and there were no motives for subservience. Threats of resignation from any quarter were serious matters and great efforts were made to obtain a broad measure of unanimity.

Sometimes single ministers tried to persuade or lead the Cabinet. Palmerston fought for his own policy through the Near Eastern crisis of 1839–41 and triumphed probably over a majority of his colleagues. He did so in part because he was always able to commit them to one step and while they were contesting it, the policy was successful and Palmerston had taken the next step, and in part because Melbourne worked hard to hold the Cabinet together. (At the most crucial period Palmerston's position was made easier by the fact that Parliament was not sitting.)   Gladstone had to struggle for his great Budgets of 1853, 1860 and 1861 almost alone, though in the first case he had the valuable support of Aberdeen. When two ministers worked together it might look more sinister, though the position was essentially the same. After 1859 Lord John Russell and Palmerston agreed on all the important issues. Lord John would read a despatch and suggest an answer. After a few contributions, Palmerston would weigh the situation and come down in favour of Lord John's

[24] W. Gladstone, " The History of 1852–60 and Greville's Latest Journals," *E.H.R.* (1887) p. 289. See also Greville, *op. cit.*, Series III, Vol. I, pp. 55 and 84.

proposals.[25]   But this was still only the opinion of two ministers. The others could and did reject their advice and accept alternative suggestions.[26]   In 1855 Gladstone felt that the views of three men would exercise a major influence on the new Cabinet—those of Palmerston, Lansdowne and Clarendon.[27]   At other times, the section in favour of a policy might be four to five or there might be a virtually equal division.   In any attempt to win over the Cabinet, it was an advantage to possess an office which permitted a minister to commit his colleagues a little more than they had anticipated before the matter was raised for decision.   But once the interest of the other members was aroused, they could not be denied full information and free discussion.   Few ministers, however new to office, were inhibited by the fear of damaging their political career or of antagonising the Prime Minister.   The desire to avoid resignations affected the individuals who were trying to lead the Cabinet as well as their critics.   In the last resort what carried the day was the persuasiveness of the argument, the confidence of its exponent, and the evidence of support from Parliament and the public.

The only occasion on which there was a definite accusation that some ministers had attempted to deceive the Cabinet arose over the Conservative Reform Bill of 1867.   Disraeli was not sure of his ground in a difficult situation.   As his ideas evolved, he discussed them with individual ministers and took advantage of each softening in the Cabinet to move a stage further.   Looking back on the process Carnarvon concluded (and Cranborne agreed) "that an interior Cabinet was carrying out a pre-arranged scheme of policy to be kept back for the moment from the majority of the Government for fear of prematurely alarming them." [28]   There is no evidence of this and it is clear that Disraeli was only slowly making up his own mind, though it is possible to see how his almost too clever management could convey such a suspicion. The next year Disraeli, faced with further divisions over the question of a dissolution, did indulge in attempts to set the stage.   He

---

[25] Greville, *op. cit.*, Series III, Vol. II, p. 270.

[26] When, in August 1859 Palmerston and Russell asked for fuller powers to act on behalf of the Cabinet during the recess, they were "met by a general assurance of readiness to come up by night trains." *Letters*, Series I, Vol. III, p. 468, and E. Fitzmaurice, *op. cit.*, Vol. I, p. 358.

[27] Lord Stanmore, *op. cit.*, Vol. I, p. 244.

[28] Sir A. Hardinge, *The Fourth Earl of Carnarvon*, Vol. I, p. 341.

obtained the Queen's support, won over Lord Cairns and Gathorne-Hardy and told the former how he would open the discussion and "appeal to you first, not only because you are my principal colleague, but because there is only one black sheep in the Cabinet, the Duke of M[arlborough] and as he sits far from you he will be governed by the numerous opinions that will precede his own." [29]

The atmosphere in Cabinet was informal and almost unbusinesslike. While meetings were held at the Foreign Office ministers did not sit at a table but spaced out in a room which contained a small table. At Downing Street they sat round a large table and in both cases each minister had his accustomed place. There appeared to be no need to curtail contributions. Gladstone spoke for three hours when he explained his 1853 budget,[30] while two hours were needed for the same purpose in 1861 [31] and forty-five minutes in 1860 on the paper duties.[32] It was possible to talk too much (as Macaulay did) [33] but Gladstone's performances won the admiration even of his critics. As expert knowledge other than that of the ministers was rarely needed, there are references to outsiders attending on only two occasions. The Duke of Wellington and the police commissioners, Sir Richard Rowan and Sir Charles Mayne, were present when the plans to deal with the Chartists in 1848 were settled,[34] and the Attorney-General attended in 1857 to explain the legal aspects of the Arrow incident.[35] Such was the state of relaxation that Kinglake, the historian of the Crimean War, was able to make play with the fact that several ministers (he alleges a majority) were asleep at the Cabinet when it was decided to invade Sebastopol.[36] Lord John Russell retorted that the matter had been well debated beforehand,[37] but this was not an isolated occurrence and Granville said "one half of them seem to be almost always

[29] Monypenny and Buckle, *op. cit.*, Vol. V, p. 28.
[30] *Argyll's Memoirs*, Vol. I, p. 422.
[31] Morley, *op. cit.*, Vol. II, p. 39.
[32] *Ibid.*, p. 31.
[33] Lord Broughton, *op. cit.*, Vol. V, p. 228.
[34] Lord Broughton, *op. cit.*, Vol. VI, p. 214.
[35] *Argyll's Memoirs*, Vol. II, p. 67.
[36] Kinglake, *The Invasion of the Crimea*, Vol. II, pp. 248–250.
[37] Walpole, *op. cit.*, Vol. II, p. 223.

asleep, the first to be off being Lansdowne, closely followed by Palmerston and Charles Wood." [38]

The Cabinet did not like to proceed without a broad measure of agreement and if there were serious divisions it was quite common to adjourn the meeting to give time for adjustment. If divisions persisted but were not of the level which led to resignations it was often easiest to settle the matter by going round the members or simply voting for or against a given proposal. [39] Again this was a symptom of the large measure of equality between Cabinet members. The Prime Minister could not wait till three or four of the " working-heads " had supported him and then sum up in his own favour—three or four opponents, no matter what posts they held, left the situation balanced and anyone could suggest a vote. Lord Althorp disliked prohibiting public meetings in Ireland in 1834 and "divided the Cabinet against the clauses." [40] On at least twenty-two other occasions (including the decision first to execute and then to transport the Chartist, Frost) [41] questions were settled in this manner. It is difficult to generalise about the process of decision taking. Often the opinion of the Cabinet was obvious, on other occasions the discussion had taken place round the drafting of a despatch or a clause. Peel would sum up a discussion while other premiers left it to the minister in question to take the sense of the meeting.

The decisions of the Cabinet on major matters such as Bills and important despatches were conveyed to the Crown by letters from the Prime Minister. The old habit of sending a formal minute had declined since the 1780s, and virtually died away after 1800 as it ceased to be necessary for the King to give orders to make Cabinet decisions effective. [42] More and more, ministers had executed their own decisions and communication with the Crown was simply to let the monarch know what had happened. There was a revival during the Reform Bill crisis (the senior Whig

---

[38] Greville, *op. cit.*, Series III, Vol. II, p. 160. Clarendon described the order in which they succumbed as Palmerston, Lansdowne and then Macaulay. Maxwell, *op. cit.*, Vol. I, p. 181.

[39] Especially if there were many minor points like the choice between a £6 and an £8 franchise in the boroughs or which boroughs were to be disenfranchised. Gladstone records divisions on these issues in 1866 in his Cabinet notes. *Add. MSS.* 44, 636 fo. nos. 21 and 23.

[40] Le Marchant, *op. cit.*, p. 497.

[41] Lord Broughton, *op. cit.*, Vol. V, p. 243.

[42] See above, p. 63 and n. 2.

statesmen remembered the practice from earlier years) as the King's active participation might be required, and William IV wanted to be sure of the unity of the Cabinet and the precise terms of the advice.[43]   After 1832 minutes were only employed on exceptional occasions of considerable importance or when the Cabinet was giving advice on matters concerning the royal family.[44]

Despite the informal nature of the discussions, the only doubts about what had been decided arose when ministers had strong personal inclinations in one direction.   In July 1859 Lord John Russell had suggested a favourable response to a French request for a conference on Italy.   The Cabinet thought that it had decided to reserve freedom of action for Britain till an existing conference at Zurich was over, but Lord John understood them merely to have asked for his reply to be delayed till the Zurich conference was over.   The Duke of Argyll observed that " the decision of the Cabinet in respect to drafts is not given effect to, or it is misunderstood, and that what is said seems to leave the vaguest possible impression on Lord John's mind." [45]   Palmerston and Gladstone had a mild quarrel in 1861 when the former denied that Gladstone had had permission to convert a paper on economy into a Treasury minute and to lay it before Parliament.[46]   In 1864 Lord John Russell was apologetic to Gladstone, but he understood that the Cabinet had approved the embodiment of Palmerston's bellicose remarks on the possibility of an Austrian fleet entering

---

[43] Aspinall, *The Cabinet Council*, pp. 194–199 has counted 18 minutes in the 1830–32 period. In *The Gladstone Papers* (sometimes listed with no author but sometimes attributed to A. Tilney Bassett) there is a long letter from the third Earl Grey to Gladstone explaining his father's practice but he seems to lay too much stress on its regularity as no minutes have been preserved for the period between May 1832 and July 1834.

[44] There was a minute when the Whigs declared their support for the Queen over the Bedchamber Crisis in 1839 with a dissentient by Howick (*Letters*, Series I, Vol. I, p. 210), another on July 8th, 1840, when it was proposed to sign a convention with Austria, Russia and Prussia to expel Mehemet Ali from Syria with Holland and Clarendon dissenting (Maxwell, *op. cit.*, Vol. I, p. 196). Lansdowne wrote a letter explaining his objections to the Irish Poor Rate to the Prime Minister in 1849 because there was no minute to which he could dissent. (*Later Correspondence of Lord John Russell*, Vol. I, p. 234.) On March 11, 1857, Palmerston sent a minute giving the Cabinet's views on the " Act for settling the Rank of the Husband of the reigning Queen " (B. Connell, *op. cit.*, p. 245) and in 1862 there was a final minute on the provision for the Prince and Princesses (P. Guedalla, *op. cit.*, p. 229). See also Appendix 1.

[45] *Argyll's Memoirs*, Vol. II, pp. 143–144.

[46] P. Guedalla, *op. cit.*, p. 180.

the North Sea, in a despatch to Vienna.[47]   In view of the variety of opinions expressed and the extent of the differences, especially between 1859 and 1865, it is surprising that there were not more accusations of ill-faith, but the subject-matter before the Cabinet was relatively simple, the decisions were usually on specific drafts on recommendations and ministers knew that once the sense of the Cabinet had been taken, to flout it was a most serious breach of confidence which had led to the fall of even such a giant as Palmerston in 1851.

This concludes the description of the distribution of power within the Cabinet and the way in which this body worked. It is possible to build up a picture only by a process of analysis and example because the Cabinet fulfilled so many functions and depended for its form not only upon particular individuals and circumstances but also on its relations with such differing agencies as Parliament and public opinion on the one side and the Crown on the other.

---

[47] Lord E. Fitzmaurice, *op. cit.*, Vol. I, p. 462.

Part Four

The Transition to a " Cabinet System "—1868–1914

CHAPTER 6

CHANGES IN THE BALANCE BETWEEN
COMMONS AND CABINET

THE early Victorian Cabinet could be described by examples chosen from any time between 1832 and 1868. This is so because the form and behaviour of the House of Commons remained fairly constant (once the effects of the first Reform Act were assimilated) and these were the chief factors conditioning the life of the Cabinet. It is possible to detect minor changes in the temper of mid-century politics, but significant alterations occurred only after the second Reform Act had been put into practice at the general election of 1868.

Under the Act the electorate was increased from 1,300,000 to 2,500,000, and this expansion introduced some new elements into political life.[1] Its effects not only slowly altered the relations between the Cabinet and the House of Commons, but also gave a new aspect of these two institutions. New tendencies were confirmed when the Reform Act of 1884 again enlarged the electorate and added a sweeping redistribution of seats. Men in public life naturally tended to retain the habits and assumptions of previous years, only slowly sensing the changed conditions and adjusting their conduct. The younger politicians of the 1870s and 1880s more readily accepted the need to put a fairly elaborate case before the enlarged electorate. Yet, by doing so, they gradually altered the balance of the constitution. Previously, Cabinets had been responsible for policy, but they were formed out of elements assembled in the House of Commons (with the addition of some peers) and worked under the informed observation and control of that body.

The newer practice of appealing for votes meant that Cabinets rested, in large part, on the approval of the electorate. The individual M.P. might criticise and press specific points, but it became questionable whether his constituents expected him to

---

[1] D. E. Butler in *The Electoral System in Britain, 1918–1951*, points out that this Reform Bill increased the electorate by 88 per cent., compared with 67 per cent. in 1885 and 49 per cent. in 1832.

vote against the Cabinet if this meant a change of government. Having voted for a party and a programme, both the electors and those M.P.s who were in tune with the times expected that Parliament would enact the programme.   The task of the House of Commons became one of supporting the Cabinet chosen at the polls and passing its legislation.   Procedure in the Commons and the whole position of the House of Lords were adjusted to these ends.   By the 1900s, the Cabinet dominated British government. The House of Commons still exercised a strong influence, but it did so more as an indicator of public opinion, a warning of what the electors might decide at the next election, than as an authority that might dethrone a Cabinet or reverse its policies.[2] These changes, being gradual and self-imposed, often escaped both the practitioners and theorists of politics.   Each generation of M.P.s tended to imagine that, since the external characteristics of the House of Commons had not changed, it occupied the same position as it had under Pitt or Palmerston.   This tendency was reinforced by the fact that the maxims used to characterise the political system were largely drawn from the pre-1868 period and in particular from Walter Bagehot's classic, *The British Constitution*, which describes the practices of these years.

So the period between 1868 and 1914 cannot be treated as an entity, and in this chapter it is necessary to describe the changes by which the older mixture of Cabinet and parliamentary government developed into the " Cabinet system " prevailing by the turn of the century.

THE FIRST EFFECTS OF THE 1867 REFORM ACT

In the years before 1868 the position and functioning of the Cabinet had depended for the most part on its relations with a House of Commons whose members were supporters of certain political principles, rather than members of a party.   A major influence on the attitude of these M.P.s had been their relations with the powerful elements in their constituencies, a situation which required careful handling and consistent conduct but not constant support of given party leaders.   Both relationships were

---

[2] When there was a possibility that a Cabinet might be removed by the House of Commons, as in early 1910, it was because a separate organised party, the Irish, might have decided to turn its voting strength against the government.

affected by the enfranchisement of virtually all male householders
in the boroughs and of occupiers of houses rated at £12 in the
counties.   The increased electorate affected these connections
principally by creating a more uniform constituency, particularly
in the larger towns and in the counties.   Previously, the smaller
number of voters had led to the predominance of local interests,
political, personal or sectional, and matters that swayed one
constituency frequently failed to affect many others.   The 1867
extension not only added more voters but tended to include
whole groups with similar attitudes and needs.   Thus while local
influence was still powerful, particularly in the smaller boroughs,
there was a common element in many constituencies which
reacted similarly to such nation-wide influences as unemployment,
better organisation or political appeals.   As a result, where
national factors tended to benefit the government or its opponents
in general elections, this benefit was registered by some successes
in every type of seat.

Taking the three general elections after the 1867 Reform Act,
the Whig-Liberal-Radical elements had the advantage in 1868
and 1880, and the Conservatives in 1874.   These advantages were
apparent not only in the large boroughs, but also in the small
boroughs and the counties as well as in specific areas such as
Scotland.[3]   Governments in the 1850s and 1860s had seldom had
large majorities and major questions of confidence were often
lost or carried by a handful of votes, but this new situation gave
the Liberal Cabinet of 1868 a majority of 112 and that of 1880 a
lead of forty-one overall (173 if the Home Rulers voted with the

[3] The figures are:

			Liberals	*Conservatives*
English counties	1868		46	124
	1874		27	143
	1880		54	116
Small English boroughs	1868		68	50
(under 20,000 population)	1874		57	57
	1880		73	41
Large English boroughs	1868		108	30
(over 20,000 population)	1874		74	64
	1880		105	33
Scottish seats	1868		54	6
	1874		41	19
	1880		54	6

(These figures are compiled from *Dod's Parliamentary Companion*, doubtful
cases being checked by voting records in a number of crucial divisions.)

government), while Disraeli in 1874 had a majority of fifty. In his 1868 Ministry when party organisation was still undeveloped, Gladstone did have to nurse his followers as Palmerston had done between 1859 and 1865, but to start with such majorities, even if loosely bound and sometimes lukewarm, made the position of the Cabinet easier, at any rate in the early years of each Parliament.

As has been said, the addition of largely similar elements to the various types of constituency meant that the response to political agitation was more uniform. Since the new electorate enjoyed the novel sense of participation in public life and had a definite interest in a number of political issues as well as a lively appreciation of whether " times " had been good or bad, the response was also more positive. Biographical and newspaper accounts of the campaigns describe excited meetings, with the frequent repetition of certain political themes such as in 1868 the Ballot and the disestablishment of the Irish Church. These national themes were supplemented by local issues, and local influence was still of considerable importance, particularly in constituencies which had not received a very large addition to the electorate. It is hard to disentangle the relative effects of bribery, personal prestige and local connection (all still very strong) from the more general attitudes induced by social conflicts and the campaign issues raised by the leading statesmen.[4] For example, English counties tended to return Conservatives, but the most probable reason is that there existed a genuine bond of political and social sympathy between the aristocracy and the richer farmers. This was influence in the sense that one section of the rural community was prepared to accept a certain kind of guidance and leadership

---

[4] When H. J. Hanham in his *Elections and Party Management* is estimating local influence, he uses three criteria (p. 196). One is to look at the seats won against the national trend, and this does provide some evidence. The second is to count as victories for local influence all uncontested seats, but it is clear that many seats were left uncontested not for fear of challenging some local power but because the normal divisions on national political issues made them so hopeless for one side that the parties could not find candidates to put up the money or make the effort. The third criterion he takes is the difference between the polls of candidates of the same party running in the same seat. This is not entirely satisfactory as one Liberal may run ahead of another for reasons of local prestige but the explanation may well be that he is the more radical on national issues (*e.g.*, is right about disestablishment in Scotland or non-sectarian education) in a radical constituency.

from another section. There may have been an element of concealed coercion but it does not follow that the influence could
not have been rejected. In some Scottish counties where the
landowners were regarded as an alien element, political independence was asserted, if after a serious struggle. In many boroughs
there was a similar real unity of outlook between Liberal manufacturers and workmen, but its dependence on a common series
of aspirations and political attitudes was revealed when the workmen did not follow the numbers of Liberal employers who went
Unionist after 1886. Besides these fairly simple political divisions
there were counties containing sufficient Whig landowners, or
urban areas which for economic or regional reasons (political,
nonetheless) contained sufficient Conservative voters, to produce
marginal seats and fierce contests. With the heightened interest in
politics and the efforts of party managers, the number of contested
seats rose from 284 (out of 658) in 1859 to 442 in 1868, 465 in
1874 and 542 in 1880.

Statesmen slowly came to realise that there was an audience
in almost every part of the country eager to hear and support
their views. Some electors may merely have felt that the Liberals
were often nonconformists who shared their principles or that
the Conservatives were men with proper traditions and a sound
outlook. But the politicians were soon prepared to put these feelings into fine words. Before 1868 Disraeli had confined his
speeches to Parliament or his constituency. Now, he found himself a figure known to a wider public, applauded in the streets
and he responded by addressing a mass rally of Conservative
Working Men's Associations in Manchester in April and then
the National Union of Conservative and Constitutional Associations at the Crystal Palace in June 1872. Gladstone, again in
response to the demands of the crowds, had to stop and address
meetings at the major stations on the route from Hawarden to
Midlothian in 1879 and became the first British statesman to
"stump the country." (Lord Salisbury and Sir Stafford Northcote
followed suit in 1880.) Aided by a metropolitan and provincial
Press which printed verbatim reports of all major speeches in
the House, the leaders of both parties put themselves and their
views before the wider electorate and asked for power to carry
out certain definite policies. The elections of 1874 and 1880

repeated the clear-cut decision of 1868; in each case the defeated Cabinet resigned once the results were known so that the old assumption that the House of Commons made and unmade ministries was slipping into the past.[5] It was noted that neither Gladstone nor Disraeli had a strong hold on their followers in Parliament,[6] their strength and the greater stability of their Cabinets coming from their direct appeal to and hold on the electorate.

THE SURVIVAL OF FORMER POLITICAL HABITS

There had been some alarm (especially among certain Conservatives) over the extension of the franchise, but few of the men active in politics expected any definite changes in the conditions of public life after 1867. Members of Parliament tended to assume that their relations with their constituencies on the one side and their control over the executive on the other would remain substantially unaltered. For this reason and because the influence of the mass electorate took time to become apparent and to adapt old or create new institutions, the established patterns of political behaviour continued, though with diminishing force, into the eighteen eighties.

In 1868 many candidates still refused to accept any party label or to acknowledge any leader.[7] To determine the political views of M.P.s, Dod's *Parliamentary Companion* can only quote their record on a few outstanding issues. Men who had voted for Gladstone's resolutions against the Irish Church and for the Ballot in 1853 were clearly strong Liberals. For non-Liberals the situation was more obscure since many had declared in favour of " reasonable reform," and membership of the Carlton Club is a quicker and easier guide than past voting records. Even on one of the newer politico-moral issues such as the Irish Church, a few men who were usually counted as Whigs (such as Roundell

---

[5] Lord Selborne commented that the first Midlothian campaign " was very remarkable; but it was a precedent tending in its results to the degradation of British politics, by bringing in a system of perpetual canvass, and removing the political centre of gravity from Parliament to the platform." Roundell Palmer, Earl of Selborne, *Memorials*, Vol. I, p. 470.

[6] *e.g.*, by Speaker Brand in 1872. The Earl of Oxford and Asquith, *Fifty Years of Parliament*, Vol. I, p. 5.

[7] In his address to the electors of Westminster in 1868, W. H. Smith claimed to be a Liberal-Conservative " unpledged to any particular party." Sir H. Maxwell, *Life and Times of W. H. Smith*, Vol. I, p. 136. By 1874 Smith was standing as " an avowed member of the Conservative Party." *Ibid.*, p. 248.

Palmer) opposed disestablishment while some Conservatives felt that the existing position could not be defended. By 1874, political lines were becoming harder. More men fell easily into the categories of "followers of Mr. Gladstone" (or of Mr. Disraeli) and Dod begins to put "Lib" and "Cons" after the names of candidates. By 1882 [8] W. S. Gilbert can satirise politics by making his sentry think it is comical

> "How Nature always does contrive
> That every boy and every gal,
> That's born into the world alive,
> Is either a little Liberal,
> Or else a little Conservative!"

As most of the Members of the 1868–74 Parliament owed their election not to party ties but to the advocacy of certain principles and the expenditure of a fair sum of money, backed in some instances by local influence, they could and did indulge in cross-voting. On occasions in this Parliament, the Conservatives as an organised force saved the Cabinet from its own back-benchers (*e.g.*, over attempts to delete clause 25 of Forster's Education Act), but the kind of cross-voting that kept some power in the hands of individual M.P.s occurred when men who normally voted Liberal or Conservative decided not to follow their leaders on specific questions. This element of independence gained strength from the government's attempt to push through a large volume of legislation and gave the House of Commons a measure of direct control over the Cabinet and its policies. The opposition, especially in the first two or three years after 1868, was not so much the organised effort of Disraeli and the Conservative Party as the work of such individuals as Colonel Lloyd-Lindsay and the other officers who resisted Cardwell's reforms and of other independent Conservatives who opposed the Ballot. The government also met with a measure of resistance from a group of dissident Liberals sitting below the gangway.[9] As one of their number, Henry James said, "he felt he had a right to speak very freely, for he owed no allegiance to Her Majesty's Government, except when they did

---

[8] The date of the first production of *Iolanthe*.

[9] In 1871 Gladstone complained that "the rank and file only of the opposition come from the other side . . . they were 'led and officered' from the Liberal Party." Earl of Selborne, *op. cit.*, Vol. I, p. 148.

right, and he was disposed to criticise them when they did wrong." [10]   Another, Sir Charles Dilke, adopted from 1870 an attitude " of detachment bordering on hostility " towards the Cabinet, while in the last session of 1874 the Radical, Henry Fawcett, voted 160 times with the government and 180 times against.[11]

A House of Commons prepared to behave in such a manner could enforce changes in even the most important items of policy. Robert Lowe, the Chancellor of the Exchequer, lost two of his proposals for new taxation in 1871, a match tax and a rise in probate and succession duties and had to recast his budget.   Out of more than 130 government Bills introduced in 1871 only one major item, the University Tests Bill, was passed in its original form and two important measures—Bruce's Licensing Bill [12] and Goschen's Local Government Bill—aroused such opposition that they had to be withdrawn.[13]   It was possible, even, to impose alternatives on the government.   W. H. Smith was instrumental in defeating an attempt to put government buildings on the Thames Embankment below Westminster Bridge.   After getting a committee to report in its favour, the Cabinet tried again in 1872 but was beaten on the motion of W. V. Harcourt, the Commons persisting till the land was handed over as a public garden to the Metropolitan Board of Works.[14]   In April 1872 the Cabinet suffered three defeats in one week, the most noteworthy if least damaging being when Sir Massey Lopes as leader of the country squires carried, by a majority of a hundred, a motion to relieve the land of £2,000,000 worth of rating charges.   In June of the same year Henry Bruce just managed to get his Mines Regulation Bill through.   Finally, it was the defection of individual Liberals (such as Horsman, who spoke very effectively) that led to Gladstone's defeat over the Irish Universities Bill in March 1873 and

---

10 Lord Askwith, *Lord James of Hereford*, p. 30.

11 S. Gwynn and G. M. Tuckwell, *Life of Sir Charles W. Dilke*, Vol. I, pp. 165 and 173.

12 This " met with . . . a heavy double-fire of attack from the licensed victuallers on one side and the intemperate ' Temperance ' party on the other " and was lost. *Letters of the Rt. Hon. Henry Austin Bruce, Lord Aberdare*, p. 270.

13 Monypenny and Buckle, *The Life of Benjamin Disraeli*, Vol. V, p. 140.

14 Sir H. Maxwell, *op. cit.*, Vol. I, pp. 184 and 204, and E. Drus, ed., *A Journal of Events during the Gladstone Ministry, 1868–1874, Camden Miscellany*, Vol. XXI, p. 28. (Hereafter cited as *The Kimberley Papers*.)

the resignation of the Cabinet. Disraeli's refusal to form a government forced Gladstone back into office, rather than into power, for a further year.

Just as private Members could defeat proposals, they could push through significant amendments. In May 1872 the Member for Glasgow, E. S. Gordon, succeeded in carrying a resolution retaining provisions for religious instruction in the new Scottish Education Bill.[15] Henry James and W. V. Harcourt defeated the clause in the abortive Ballot Bill of 1871 which had laid payment for returning officers and other official election expenses on the rates. The next year, E. A. Leathem, the Member for Huddersfield, carried an amendment to the new Ballot Bill by one vote, but when Gladstone accepted the principle involved and asked the House to annul the motion, the Prime Minister lost by twenty-eight.[16] The power of the House was strikingly revealed over the Irish Universities Bill. As the Bill encountered rising opposition, Gladstone suggested that certain clauses might be left as open questions to be settled in committee—an expedient which failed to save the measure.[17] Such pressures could affect the careers of ministers as well as of governments and Goschen, for instance, was transferred to the Admiralty largely because his policies at the Poor Law Board had been unacceptable to the landed Members.

Gladstone was in these years leading a composite majority by the strength of his personality within the House and by the great appeal he and his measures had for the informed public outside.[18] His Cabinet, likewise, was not a tight party group. Roundell Palmer was opposed to the disestablishment of the Irish Church and therefore refused the Lord Chancellorship,[19] but Lowe accepted office though he disagreed on this issue, on Irish land reform and the ballot, and had bitterly opposed any extension of the suffrage. He was prepared to join a Cabinet including men like Bright and Goschen because he thought Gladstone's views

15 H.C. Debates, Vol. 211, cols. 288 to 355, 1872.
16 E. A. Leathem's amendment made it illegal for the voter to exhibit his ballot paper so as to show for whom he had voted. H.C. Debates, Vol. 210, cols. 1292 to 1304, 1872. The later debate is cols. 1481 to 1512.
17 Sir H. Maxwell, *op. cit.*, Vol. I, p. 238.
18 J. Morley makes this point in his *Life of Gladstone*, Vol. II, p. 387.
19 Earl of Selborne, *op. cit.*, Vol. I, p. 113.

modified in a conservative direction by Parliament were preferable
to Disraeli in a minority driven to courting the radicals.[20]

With a broadly-based Cabinet leading a House which contained a large majority of men on the whole inclined to a moderate
liberalism, much depended on the measures introduced and the
persuasiveness of the front bench.   Ministers still sat throughout
debates and eloquent speeches could and did swing votes.   The
appointment of Sir Robert Collier to the Judicial Committee of
the Privy Council led to a motion of censure, but speeches by
Roundell Palmer and Gladstone made a good impression and
" many who had announced their intention to go away without
voting, remained to support us," [21] the government emerging with
a majority of twenty-seven.   When the Liberal colliery owners
were organising opposition to the Mines Regulation Bill, Gladstone reported to Glyn that " Bruce has quite changed the opinion
of the House." [22]   The Prime Minister tacitly recognised the
importance of debating talent when he refurbished his government
in late 1873 with the ablest critics from below the gangway—
Playfair, Harcourt, James and Lord Edward Fitzmaurice.

At the same time the Cabinet was in a stronger position than
its predecessors, for behind the loose majority in the House lay the
constituencies and both the Members and the outside public
appreciated that a measure of consistency was required.[23]   Most of
the M.P.s who had declared their support for Gladstone or for
Liberal measures in 1868 were ready for a fair number of reforms
and they knew that without their active co-operation there was
little hope of progress.   The procedure of Parliament still permitted any two Members to hold up business by alternately moving
the adjournment.   To pass major measures like Irish Church and
Land Reform, Education and Ballot Bills, the House had to
enforce a degree of self-imposed discipline—an impatience with
recalcitrant Members and the convention that after the second
reading of a Bill its principle was accepted and attention should

[20] A. Patchett Martin, *Life and Letters of Viscount Sherbrooke*, Vol. II, p. 361.
[21] *Aberdare Papers*, p. 326. (Sir R. Collier, the Attorney-General, had been
made a judge for a few weeks to qualify him for the Judicial Committee and
this appeared to be evading the intention of the Act which specified previous
judicial experience.)
[22] *Ibid.*, p. 347.
[23] Though on some issue like Education (among Liberals) the constituencies
could pull against the policy of the Cabinet.

be turned to details.[24]   The Cabinet could thus assume a considerable degree of support and a real desire to see certain
problems solved.   When 200 amendments, half by Liberals,
seemed to prejudice the passage of the Ballot Bill, Gladstone held
a party meeting at Downing Street and persuaded his followers to
withdraw their amendments and to agree to a " policy of silence "
in order to get the Bill through.[25]   At this time Parliament was
taking less interest in foreign affairs than in the days of Lord
Palmerston and though some Radicals complained that the House
was not consulted, the Cabinet was left fairly free to operate
within the broad limits which it knew the Commons would
tolerate.[26]   Indeed the errors of Gladstone and his colleagues and
their declining influence over the Commons were due not to asking
too much of their following but to their strange failure to appreciate Liberal feelings over such matters as education and Irish
universities—errors which weakened their position outside even
more than inside Parliament.

Yet despite the reasonable record of the Ministry and Gladstone's own great belief in the need for convincing his back-
benchers, he left office with a " keen sense of their disloyalty
during the last three years," [27] and told Bruce " it is absolutely
necessary to party action that they should learn that all the duties
and responsibilities do not rest on the leaders, but that followers
have their obligations too." [28]   This is an excellent example of
how the facts of political life led Gladstone, always conservative
on such matters, to change his attitude to the duty of Members of
Parliament and to relations that should exist between the Cabinet,
the House of Commons and the electorate.   In these years he had
acted according to established conventions and had accepted a
number of defeats, only resigning when he held the honour of the
government to be involved in the rejection of the Irish Universities Bill.   It seemed natural to resign and let his various opponents form a Cabinet.   Disraeli, however, appreciated the recent

---

[24] It was these customs that were abused when small sections of the House and
later the Irish began to obstruct business in the 1870s. See below pp. 193–194,
note 61.
[25] Sir H. Maxwell, *op. cit.*, p. 197.
[26] These are the conclusions of Miss Sheila Lambert in her excellent unpublished
M.A. thesis at London University, *The Influence of Parliament upon the
Foreign Policy of the Gladstone Government, 1868–74.*
[27] Morley, *op. cit.*, Vol. II, p. 497.
[28] *Aberdare Papers*, p. 361.

changes of political emphasis and realised that power must come not from installation by the House of Commons but from the constituencies. He preferred to wait till the change of sentiment in the electorate was decisive and was registered at a general election. But, in defending himself Disraeli skilfully appealed to the older conventions. He characterised Gladstone's argument as saying:

> "whenever a minister is so situated that it is in his power to prevent any other parliamentary leader from forming an administration likely to stand, he acquires thereby the right to call on Parliament to pass whatever measures he and his colleagues think fit, and is entitled to denounce as factious the resistance to such measures. Any such claim is not warranted by usage, or reconcilable with the freedom of the legislature. It comes to this: that he tells the House of Commons, 'unless you are prepared to put someone in my place, your duty is to do as I bid you.' To no House of Commons has language of this kind ever been used; by no House of Commons would it be tolerated." [29]

Gladstone never intended to put the House of Commons in this position and merely felt, with all previous Prime Ministers, that defeats of a certain magnitude permanently impaired the credit of a government. But as the Cabinet became responsible for virtually every major item of business, any defeat began to assume this vital significance and Liberal Members who cross-voted were being put in the position of deciding which was more important—the specific issue on which they were voting, or the maintenance in power of a ministry whose general views they and their constituents shared. A general election was held in early 1874 and as it became apparent that the Conservatives would have a majority of over forty, Gladstone's first reaction was that his Cabinet should meet Parliament. He naturally clung to the existing convention that "it is Parliament not the constituencies that ought to dismiss the government, and the proper function of the House of Commons cannot be taken from it without diminishing somewhat its dignity and authority." [30] This was true, but

---

[29] Morley, *op. cit.*, Vol. II, p. 453.

[30] *Ibid.*, Vol. II, p. 493. The convention had already been broken once when Disraeli resigned without meeting Parliament after his defeat in the General Election of 1868. Gladstone also explained his worries on this point to Queen Victoria in *Letters of Queen Victoria, Series II*, Vol. II, p. 316. When the convention was broken again in 1880 Gladstone wrote to Granville that "it

what was the point in impeding the formation of a new government if defeat was inevitable?   After a considerable discussion, the Cabinet decided to resign before Parliament assembled.

The experience of the 1874–80 Parliament finally altered Gladstone's attitude.   He appealed in the House of Commons against Disraeli's foreign and colonial policy and failed, not only to win over any Conservative M.P.s but also on some occasions to carry all the Opposition with him.   Yet when he turned to the electorate Gladstone obtained the response that he felt his case deserved and it was the constituencies, not the House of Commons, that dismissed Beaconsfield's Cabinet in 1880.[31]   As recently as 1868 Gladstone had protested against Disraeli's " penal dissolution "—the Conservative Cabinet had been defeated and the correct course was to resign and let the House of Commons instal its opponents in office.[32]   But when Gladstone lost his first Home Rule Bill in 1886, he and his Cabinet decided to appeal from the House of Commons to the electorate and this only six months after the previous general election.   The Grand Old Man may have been a little worried about constitutional proprieties since he submitted a thirteen-point memorandum to his colleagues which bears all the traces of being written as much to convince himself as to influence the Cabinet.   The key point was that " we have submitted a great subject to a Parliament chosen when it was (we admit) very partially before the country.   Viewing its nature, the country has a strong claim to elect a Parliament upon it." [33]

has often been on my mind, to say something about the three continuous cases of Resignations in '86, '74 and '80 without any vote of Parliament: not to blame anyone in the slightest degree, *but* to point out that they are only to be justified by their peculiar circumstances and that the normal mode, whenever the public interest permits it, is to take the sense of Parliament as in 1841 and 1859." *Gladstone: Granville Correspondence*, ed. A. Ramm, Vol. I, p. 128.

[31] With great skill, Gladstone appealed to a carefully selected section of the electorate, the Scottish middle class, which was most likely to respond to his message.   Also other factors were probably more important than the Midlothian campaign in swinging votes but none of these points diminish the influence of these years on Gladstone's thinking.

[32] See above, Chap. 3, pp. 93–95.

[33] *Gladstone Papers, Add. MSS.* 44,647 § 121.   Commenting on this in June 1886, Selborne wrote to Sir A. Gordon: " It is almost a revolutionary thing in itself that a Parliament elected only three (*sic*) months ago should be dissolved rather than that there should be a change of Ministry after a large adverse vote upon a question of primary importance," but he went on to point out that " it was the general opinion, that no Ministry which was possible could go on without a dissolution." Selborne, *op. cit.*, Vol. II, p. 227.

The Conservatives adapted themselves to the new political conditions a little more readily because their members were usually less likely to insist on maintaining special individual viewpoints; they had a greater sense of group loyalty and soon came to regard Liberal governments led by Gladstone as a national disaster. Disraeli, for his part, was very conscious after all the moves that had been made against him, of the need for a leadership which had a firm grip on its back-benchers. When a number of Members slipped away for dinner and allowed the Opposition and the Irish to beat the government by two votes on May 2, 1874, those ministers who were absent from the division received a sharp note of reproof from the Prime Minister.[34] Always adept at sensing the atmosphere of the House, Disraeli preferred to withdraw a proposal rather than have it defeated. For example, in July 1874, when it became evident that the Cabinet was likely to lose its Endowed Schools Bill, the Prime Minister assured the Commons that its clauses were so obscure as to be unintelligible to him and it was withdrawn and greatly modified.[35] A year later the government was resisting Lowe's motion for a select committee on the grievances of Indian civil servants, but as Disraeli felt the debate going against his colleagues he offered to act if Lowe would withdraw.[36] On the whole, the Conservative majority was fairly steady. At times the government was hard pressed, as it was over the clumsy and unfortunate circular apparently ending a slave's right of refuge on British ships of war, yet even on this occasion its majority was forty-five. When the ministry suffered a defeat in 1877 over an appointment to a post recently condemned by a select committee of the House, there was no difficulty in getting the vote reversed once Beaconsfield had explained his reasons in the House of Lords.[37]

The Conservative downfall in the General Election of 1880 led to an influx of new Members whose Liberalism was of very varied intensity.[38] Divided Liberal leadership in the late 70s followed by an " each-for-himself " election campaign left many of

---

[34] A. E. Gathorne-Hardy, ed., *A Memoir of Gathorne-Hardy, First Earl of Cranbrook*, Vol. I, p. 338.

[35] Monypenny and Buckle, *op. cit.*, Vol. V.

[36] A. P. Martin, *op. cit.*, Vol. II, p. 426.

[37] Monypenny and Buckle, *op. cit.*, Vol. VI, p. 164.

[38] R. Spence Watson in his book, *The National Liberal Federation*, says that in a number of cases it " was scarcely skin-deep," p. 28.

them free from any strong sense of obligation to the party. It is not surprising that in the first two months of the new Parliament Liberal Members "showed signs of independence that almost broke the spirit of the ministerial Whips." [39] A Cabinet measure on hares and rabbits was met with amendments by Liberals, and a motion for local option was carried against Gladstone and Hartington, while a resolution for a memorial to the Prince Imperial was defeated, though it had been proposed jointly by the government and the Conservative leader, Sir Stafford Northcote.[40] An attempt to create a special post for Sir Henry Layard, the Turcophil ambassador on leave from Constantinople, had to be abandoned, and the whole problem of controlling the House was brought out by the Bradlaugh affair.[41] Nevertheless, these were all relatively minor matters. The first serious question on which an adverse vote might have led to the resignation of the government arose with the Compensation for Disturbance Bill in June 1880. The Conservatives played for Whig support,[42] thus forcing the more moderate Liberal Members to consider whether they were prepared to defeat a Cabinet whose major work in foreign and domestic policy had not even begun. In the event, only sixteen voted against the measure. From then on the problem of Ireland exerted heavy political pressure and Members had to decide to support Gladstone or to oppose him—there could be no middle way. This, along with the increasing interest of the active section of the electorate, which was often expressed in the form of direct appeals to support the Cabinet, served to discipline Liberal Members. On occasion they could still assert themselves over details and when Gladstone sought to delete a clause in the Crimes Bill (brought in after the Phoenix Park murders) permitting searches at night, he "tried the Party too high and they revolted" as Harcourt reported to Spencer.[43] The government's position was in fact fairly secure, though it was still possible for strong interests to obtain some concessions. In 1884 the Cabinet wanted to delete some amendments inserted by the House of Lords in a

[39] Morley, *op. cit.*, Vol. VI, p. 5.

[40] *Ibid.*, pp. 6–10.

[41] Lord E. Fitzmaurice, *The Life of Lord Granville*, Vol. II, p. 200.

[42] Andrew Lang, *Life, Letters and Diaries of Sir Stafford Northcote, First Earl of Iddesleigh*, p. 335.

[43] A. G. Gardiner, *The Life of Sir William Harcourt*, Vol. I, p. 450.

Bill to deal with cattle diseases, but was unable to do so. On another occasion the majority refused a request to grant time for an opposition motion of censure.[44]

After four years, however the ministry found itself facing acute problems in Egypt as well as the prolonged crisis in Ireland, and its credit was evidently declining. Some Liberals were moving away from the main principles of the party. The attacks of men such as Cowen, Forster and Goschen were not cross-voting in the old sense so much as evidence of a general change of political position on their part, while Radicals like Sir Wilfrid Lawson and Henry Richard were totally disenchanted with the Cabinet's overseas policy.[45] These defections together with some Irish opposition reduced the government's majority to twenty-eight in a vote of censure on its handling of Egyptian affairs in May 1884. In February 1885 after the news of the fall of Khartoum, the majority fell to fourteen and only two things saved the government —Hartington's frank admission that errors had been made, and the disinclination for an election in February just before one in November on the reformed register.[46] In April the margin in the debate on the Cabinet's policy in Afghanistan was only thirty and no one was surprised that defeat came in June 1885, seven Liberals opposing and seventy-six abstaining on a motion against part of the Budget.

Thus, for a period after the Reform Act of 1867, the House of Commons continued to watch over and hedge the Cabinet much as it has done since 1832. Lord Robert Cecil was correct when he told the 1914 Select Committee on Procedure that "if you look back to the 'seventies and 'eighties, you will see that there were a relatively large number—I do not say actually large—of cases in which the Government was . . . defeated, not on Second Readings so often, but on Questions in Committee, against their declared wish in the House of Commons." [47]   But in time the larger electorate, the greater intensity of party warfare, and the growth of party organisations, all modified the position of

---

[44] Roy Jenkins, *Sir Charles Dilke*, p. 167.

[45] Herbert Paul, *A History of Modern England*, Vol. IV, p. 268.

[46] Lord George Hamilton, *Parliamentary Reminiscences and Reflections*, 1868–1885, p. 266.

[47] Evidence of Lord R. Cecil, No. 728, before the *Select Committee on House of Commons* (*Procedure*) 1914, Vol. VII, No. 378.

Members of Parliament. As the statesmen appealed to and rested their power more on the decisions of the voters, the duty of the private Member, though still involving criticism and pressure, became primarily one of supporting a given group of leaders. As a corollary, the constituencies became more interested in backing a given party than in the personal views of their own Member.

These changes complicate the task of the historian. It was relatively easy to give some picture of the limitations on the power of the Cabinet when control came primarily from a single institution and was exercised either by open voting or by shifts in Cabinet policy to meet the threat of adverse votes. But after the 1890s the limitations on the Cabinet were less precise and less tangible. The Commons influenced the Cabinet not so much by hostile votes as by passing on its own attitudes. Ministers might adjust their actions if they felt that the House was against them or if they sensed alarm among their own supporters. The Cabinet could be affected by direct reports of hostility among certain sections of the public or by threats to resist certain policies.[48] In these conditions, the Press had a different role. It was now an essential channel of communication informing the electorate of the views of the politicians and, in some degree, warning the latter of changes in the public mind.

The effect of these developments was to leave the Cabinet much greater freedom of action. The mid-century House of Commons had been able to distinguish between the total record of a ministry and its individual proposals. A mass electorate wanted its MP's to be consistently Liberal or Conservative. This was in part because the machinery of a general election put the choice in this form and in part because the public could not be expected to scrutinise too many specific policies. The loyalty of large blocks of voters, once established, was not easily shaken. Cabinets were, of course, aware that unpopular actions might affect their standing at the next general election. But they were also aware that this might be several years off in time and that judgment would be given on the whole period of office.

---

[48] J. A. Spender and C. Asquith, *The Life of Lord Oxford and Asquith.* Asquith says that the decision to prohibit certain aspects of a Catholic procession in 1908 was amply justified by the contents of his letter bag. Vol. I, p. 237.

GROWTH OF NEW POLITICAL PRACTICES UNTIL THE 1880s

So far, this chapter has considered the impact of an expanding electorate and has described the gradual changes in the balance of forces affecting the Cabinet. To appreciate the cumulative effect of these forces, it is necessary to examine the political practices which evolved or altered in these years.

It has often been pointed out that from the late 1860s the party leaders sought to base their election appeals on one or two issues. Gladstone fought the 1868 campaign on the disestablishment of the Irish Church and the old Liberal principle of economy. In 1874 he offered the abolition of the income tax. Beaconsfield tried to raise the danger of Home Rule in 1880, while Gladstone attacked the foreign and colonial policy of the government. Lack of an attractive policy so worried Joseph Chamberlain in 1885 that he produced his " unauthorised programme." On the other side, Lord Salisbury stood on the principles he had enunciated in his "Newport Speech."

But this identification of a party with certain long-term ideas and a number of immediate aims was not just a matter for election time; it was a fairly constant endeavour. As he felt his Cabinet losing vitality in 1873, Gladstone told Bright that " what we want is a *positive* force to carry us onward as a body." [49] The creation of a definite image in the public mind was a major purpose of Disraeli's Ministry, which combined measures of reform for the urban working classes with vigour in foreign affairs. Gladstone could not plan a conscious policy of this kind but achieved the same effect in spasms when he found some major injustice to be remedied. His great power as a Liberal leader arose from the unerring way in which his discovery of evils and his modes of solution fitted the mental processes and excited the moral fervour of an important section of the electorate. Yet both he and his Cabinet colleagues cast about for ways of strengthening their position (as in 1873), and Harcourt wrote to Granville in 1883 that this session " we must have at least one political measure from a Party point of view. I can see none but either Liquor or County Franchise." [50]

The opposition likewise tried to create a picture of the Cabinet

49 Morley, *op. cit.*, Vol. II, p. 479.
50 A. G. Gardiner, *op. cit.*, Vol. I, p. 470.

as a body of men engaged in a few misguided or dangerous policies. Lord Salisbury, reproved for his persistent critical questioning in the House of Lords in May 1885, replied that "our absolute sovereign is the people of this country, and it is they and they alone who can bring a remedy to the mischief that is going on." [51] It was his task, therefore, to lay the errors of the Cabinet clearly before the electorate. When Gladstone began his campaign to arouse the public conscience over the Bulgarian atrocities, his original objective had been to alter the direction of British policy. But, as the Conservative M.P.s stood firm behind the Cabinet, he turned to the alternative of building up a general indictment of Beaconsfield's record. "It seems to me," he wrote, "good policy to join on the proceedings of 1876–79 by a continuous process to the dissolution" [52] and the first Midlothian Campaign in November 1879 was undertaken for this purpose. After Gladstone's decision to take up Home Rule had become public in early 1886, the Salisbury Government was so eager to make its attitude to the Irish problem plain before the inevitable defeat that the suppression of the National League was announced without even the prior approval of the Irish Secretary.[53]

Besides setting out the arguments for or against a government it was natural, in such conditions, to try to ensure that dissolutions would occur when the public reaction was favourable. Disraeli was assured by the firm of solicitors who acted as Conservative agents in 1868 that he would get a working majority, though an election (on the new register) was unavoidable after the defeats inflicted by Gladstone.[54] The Liberal leaders facing the possibility that the Lords would reject the Ballot Bill in 1872, asked the Whips' advice as to the merits of a dissolution in the autumn of 1872 or the spring of 1873.[55]

The first time an early election was contemplated purely as a means of securing a party majority (that is, without the government's being near the end of its term or having suffered any check from its opponents) was after the Congress of Berlin in 1878. On August 10 the Cabinet sat for three hours discussing a dissolution

---

[51] Lady Gwendolen Cecil, *Life of Robert, Marquis of Salisbury*, Vol. III, p. 131.
[52] Morley, *op. cit.*, Vol. II, p. 587.
[53] Winston Churchill, *Lord Randolph Churchill*, Vol. II, p. 46.
[54] H. E. Gorst, *The Earl of Beaconsfield*, p. 111.
[55] The Whips estimated a loss of 25 or 30 seats, leaving a majority of 25. *The Kimberley Papers*, p. 33.

and finally decided not to try to snatch a party victory out of a temporary triumph in foreign policy.[56]   When Beaconsfield did decide to go to the country in 1880, he chose the early spring because the Conservatives had just won by-elections at Liverpool and Southwark, but better information would have shown him that these were misleading pointers.

With political battles fought on these lines, the function of the House of Commons was clearly not quite the same as it had been before. The clearest indication of the relations between the Commons and the Cabinet is in the Standing Orders of the House, as these rules define the amount of criticism and control which is open to M.P.s.[57]   In the eighteenth century, the procedure of the Lower House was still essentially that of a body independent of a royal executive and though the Cabinet was composed of Members of both Houses, ministers had no more rights in the House of Commons (except in matters of taxation) than private M.P.s. This equality of private and official Members began to alter with the Standing Orders of 1833. The old right to raise debates on the presentation of petitions was abandoned by 1839. Government orders were given priority on Mondays and Fridays, so that between 1832 and 1868 private Members still had many powers, but ministers had some distinct advantages in initiating and passing legislation. This arrangement was a true reflection of the relations between the Cabinet and the Commons and of the low priority Palmerston and his followers gave to legislation.

It has often been suggested that obstruction by Parnell and his followers in the 1870s and 80s forced the Commons to alter its procedure, but in fact the Irish only gave the final impetus. The real reason was the new emphasis on Parliament as a legislature. Gladstone's 1868–74 Cabinet found great difficulty, as has been shown, in getting its measures passed and supply voted by August of each year. "Morning sittings" (2 p.m. to 7 p.m.) were instituted, and in 1872 the government obtained the major concession that amendments to the motion to move into Committee of Supply

---

[56] Monypenny and Buckle, *op. cit.*, Vol. VI, p. 369 and Gathorne-Hardy, *op. cit.*, Vol. II, p. 78.

[57] For this whole section, see Joseph Redlich, *The Procedure of the House of Commons*, Vol. I, Part II, and P. Fraser, "The Growth of Ministerial Control in the Nineteenth-Century House of Commons," *E.H.R.* (1960), p. 444.

could be moved only on the first occasion when each section of the estimates (Army, Navy and civil) was discussed. This lapsed under Disraeli but was renewed in 1882.

The Radicals on both sides of the House rapidly became impatient with older forms which prevented the Commons acting as they wished. Joseph Chamberlain declared that " the primary object of a parliamentary assembly is, in my opinion, to carry out the decisions at which the nation has arrived . . . instead of as at present frustrating and postponing the decision of the constituencies." [58] Later in 1882, Harcourt sent a memorandum round the Cabinet in which he insisted that it was "essential to secure to a majority the right to prevail which lies at the bottom of parliamentary institutions." [59] Gladstone's Cabinet considered the reform of procedure on several occasions but major changes were deferred because of absorption with Irish and foreign problems and because of differences between ministers. When Randolph Churchill took over as leader of the House of Commons in 1886, he wanted to give reform of procedure the highest place in the list of the government's objectives. Labouchere, as might be expected, had the most extreme attitude and urged frequent general elections, after which measures could be passed without any elaborate discussion as this would all have taken place in the constituencies. [60] What is more impressive is that in time, the pressure of business (which really gave obstructionists their opportunity) convinced the traditionalists on both sides. [61] Just as Gladstone had been driven to press for more discipline among his party's back-benchers, he was brought round to the need for rules to limit their freedom of debate and to make the task of the Cabinet easier. Sir Stafford Northcote, for the Conservatives, was ready to support him, though Lord Randolph and his associates insisted that on this, as on other matters, the opposition must oppose. [62]

---

[58] J. L. Garvin, *The Life of Joseph Chamberlain*, Vol. I, p. 377.
[59] A. G. Gardiner, *op. cit.*, Vol. I, p. 462.
[60] Quoted by M. Ostrogorski, *Democracy and the Organisation of Political Parties*, Vol. I, p. 214.
[61] The credit for starting obstruction does not go to the Irish. It was begun by James Lowther and his friends in the early 70s "as a legitimate defence against perpetual sittings and wholesale legislation " (Lord G. Hamilton, *op. cit.*, p. 46) and was carried on against the Ballot Bill by G. C. Bentinck (Gwynn and Tuckwell, *op. cit.*, Vol. I, p. 98) and then by " the colonels " against the abolition of purchase in the Army, before it was taken up by Parnell in 1877.   [62] Viscount Esher, *Journals and Letters*, Vol. I, p. 80.

Select Committees on Procedure had sat at intervals of eight or ten years since 1832 and had weighed the advantages of revising the Standing Orders. The Committee of 1861 examined various proposals but came " to the conclusion that the old rules and orders, when carefully considered and narrowly investigated, are found to be the safeguard of freedom of debate, and a sure defence against the oppression of overpowering majorities." [63]   The first change of importance was, as already mentioned, the 1872 extension of the " rule of progress " prohibiting diversionary amendments to the motion to move into Committee of Supply. Gradually the notion gained ground that the day's programme should be arranged by the government and protected from disruption by private Members.   In 1869 a fixed part of the Order Paper and a fixed time were set aside for questions, largely because the old opportunities to intervene at any stage and demand information or raise a debate were being curtailed.   On top of the difficulties created by the increased demand for legislation and the desire of more M.P.s to take part in debates,[64] there now arose the problem of obstruction.   Parnell and his followers merely used the opportunities open to every Member, but used them to bring the machinery to a standstill rather than to influence the government or make a case.

The Select Committee of 1878 made certain suggestions of a defensive nature, but little was done till Speaker Brand was forced to close a forty-one hour sitting on February 2, 1881.   The Speaker was immediately given extra powers under an " Urgency Procedure " and Gladstone introduced a series of new Standing Orders in 1882.   Not all were passed and some were allowed to lapse, but the outcome was that dilatory motions for adjournment were prohibited, speeches had to be relevant and closure of debate could be imposed by a simple majority.[65]   These restrictions were only carried after many heart-searchings.   Conservatives,[66] Irish

---

[63] J. Redlich, *op. cit.*, Vol. I, p. 102.

[64] The constituencies liked to hear that their Members had spoken in the House and more Members were being elected on their merits as speakers and politicians.   In the 1833 session 395 Members spoke and made 5,765 speeches. In the 1883 session 458 Members spoke and made 21,160 speeches.

[65] See the discussion by E. Hughes, " Changes in Parliamentary Procedure, 1880–82," in *Essays presented to Sir Lewis Namier*.

[66] The Conservatives were genuinely worried when the government abandoned the old practice of giving itself a majority of one on all committees in favour of numbers proportionate to party strengths in the House.   A Committee of

and a few Radicals had opposed them, yet after a few years of " relevant obstruction " and regular failure to pass many measures, most agreed with Gladstone on " the absolute and daily-growing necessity of what I will describe as a great internal reform of the House of Commons." [67] The task was taken up and carried through by W. H. Smith between 1887 and 1891 and A. J. Balfour between 1895 and 1902.

A further development which affected the position of the Cabinet was the growth of new forms of party organisation. The local committees founded to support particular candidates in particular constituencies (described in the previous chapter) had continued after 1867. But with a wider electorate and the possibility of winning a decisive majority, the leaders in Parliament began taking more interest in elections and in the individual constituencies. The first to make a positive move was Disraeli. In the 1860s organisation at the centre had been left to a firm of lawyers. After 1868 the task was given to John Gorst who set out to find a Conservative candidate for each constituency. With the aid of Major Keith-Falconer, an efficient Conservative Central Office was established and the National Union of Conservative and Constitutional Associations was revived.[68]

But such developments did not mean that the organisation could impose on the constituencies. In practice the Central Office could only offer advice, contacts and the promise of honours to come later. The extension of the franchise had increased the expenditure at elections, the average county contest costing around £3,000 and the average borough contest around £1,000,[69] so that the small sums collected in London made little difference. Men with safe seats were most reluctant to find extra money and risk losing it in a marginal contest. Disraeli had to appoint a special committee in 1873 to try to persuade the wealthier elements in the

23 instead of 12 Liberals and 11 Conservatives, from June 1880 had 12 Liberals, nine Conservatives and two Home Rulers—a much weaker position for the Opposition. A. Lang, *op. cit.*, p. 322.

[67] J. Morley, *op. cit.*, Vol. III, p. 123.

[68] The state of the Conservative organisation is discussed in H. E. Gorst, *op. cit.*, and E. J. Feuchtwanger, " J. E. Gorst and the Central Organisation of the Conservative Party, 1870–1882," *Bulletin of the Institute for Historical Research*, November 1959. R. Blake, *Disraeli*, points out that it was Disraeli himself who had the words " Working Men's " dropped from the title of the organisation as he wished no emphasis on class conflict, p. 536.

[69] There are precise figures for the general elections in 1868, 1874 and 1880 in H. J. Hanham, *op. cit.*, pp. 249–251.

party to take a few chances.[70]   The Conservative Central Office concentrated on the larger boroughs (as they held the key to victory) and on areas where the party was particularly weak such as Scotland.   Essentially this was a method of mobilising local influence, emphasising the need for money, preparation and an effective local candidate.

On the Liberal side, the Whips' Office was the only central organisation and it had to struggle in 1868 to raise £10,000 to £15,000 to help candidates.   A few pamphlets were issued (emphasising Gladstone's views and leadership) but otherwise all organisation was left to the localities.[71]   Liberal strength was greatest where there was similarity of social outlook and of political aspiration between the middle class and the newly enfranchised sections of the working class.[72]   A number of local Liberal associations gave proof to this unity by including some representatives of the Liberal electors, chosen at public meetings in each ward.   But on national issues, the tendency was still to set up special associations to agitate for each particular objective— temperance, land or educational reform.   Liberal and Whig statesmen regarded these associations, quite rightly, as attempts to put pressure on the Cabinet by influencing the public and Parliament and, on the whole, disapproved.   When Forster's Education Act roused the antagonism of nonconformists in the boroughs, the National Education League began an open campaign to change the Cabinet's policy.   Pledges to repeal the 25th clause of the Act were exacted from 300 out of 425 Liberal candidates in England and Wales and the League intervened at a by-election in Bath when the Liberal refused to give such a pledge.   Such activities were both a symptom and a cause of disillusionment over the record of the government and played a considerable part in the Liberal defeat of 1874.

Not all these critics, however, had expected or wanted to see a Conservative Ministry in office.   To punish a Liberal Cabinet so severely that the Conservatives were returned might only make matters worse.   It would be far better to have Gladstone and his

[70] Marchioness of Londonderry, *Henry Chaplin, A Memoir*, p. 150.

[71] See A. F. Thomson, " Gladstone's Whips and the General Election of 1868," *E.H.R.* (1948).

[72] See Trygve R. Tholfsen, " The Origins of the Birmingham Caucus," *The Historical Journal*, Vol. 2, 1959.

associates in office providing there was some means of influencing their actions. The leaders of Birmingham Liberalism (the home of the National Education League) decided to change their form of organisation so that they could seek a Liberal victory and at the same time make sure that as many of the victors as possible would be radicals who could press for radical policies from the Cabinet. In May 1877 a Conference of Liberal Associations held in Birmingham decided to set up the National Liberal Federation.[73] A similar development took place at Manchester where Liberals wanted to revive the National Reform Union and Bright, still thinking along the old lines of the Anti-Corn Law League, suggested that they should campaign for a single issue such as the reform of the land laws.[74] But the Manchester Liberals appreciated that since they had the vote, the task was not to exert external pressure on a Cabinet chosen by other people but to return the kind of Cabinet they wanted by their own exertions. Lord Hartington, who had been chosen as the Liberal leader in the Commons when Gladstone retired in 1875, refused to deal with the National Liberal Federation or with any other body designed to put pressure on the leaders of the Party. Gladstone, however, was acting in a private capacity and from deep revulsion against Beaconsfield's Balkan policy. He was glad to urge his views upon the founding conference of the Federation, the Grand Old Man and the N.L.F. moving hand-in-hand into the campaign that culminated in the Liberal victory of 1880. Thereafter the N.L.F. gradually entered into a fuller co-operation with the Liberal Whips' office and absorbed the other unions of local Liberal associations, the process becoming complete after the headquarters of the Federation moved to London in 1886.

Thus by the 1880s both parties had organisations connecting the party associations in a fair number of more important constituencies. These local associations and the office-bearers they elected for the national union or federation could exercise some

---

[73] The origins of the N.L.F. were traced by Ostrogorski, *op. cit.*, to the Minority Clause in the 1867 Reform Act. F. H. Herrick, "The Origins of the N.L.F." *Journal of Modern History*, 1945, has shown that while the local association in Birmingham had to put out an extra effort to meet the minority clause, the contacts with other associations and the impulse to found the N.L.F. came from the experience of the National Education League. There is also a background account by Tholfsen, *art. cit.*, and a political account by R. Spence Watson, *op. cit.*

[74] Ostrogorski, *op. cit.*, p. 218.

influence on Members of Parliament and thus, on rare occasions, on the Cabinet. In the case of the N.L.F. this had been part of its original purpose, the motive force being that the N.C.O.s and amateur strategists of the Liberal army were often more eager for headlong attacks than the generals. But with the deepening party conflict, the same zeal was spreading among Conservatives. When a minority of the Cabinet was struggling against a definite commitment to the Turks in 1877, Carnarvon noted that " the wire pullers of the Carlton . . . impatient of what they called the irresolution of the government, got up meetings and addressed protests and remonstrances." [75]   The feeling that the rank and file wanted action was exploited by " the Fourth Party " and by its leading member, Lord Randolph Churchill. He had founded the Primrose League to press for the more vigorous and popular Conservatism, with which he rapidly became associated. When the League hung fire, Lord Randolph turned to capture the National Union of Conservative Associations and to demand that it should play a positive role in the counsels of the Party. In this campaign (and especially when he resigned the chairmanship of the Association) Lord Randolph did have a measure of direct support from the local associations leading to his re-election as chairman by the 1884 annual conference.[76]   A compromise was reached in July of that year the effect of which was to admit Lord Randolph to the inner circle of the Party but to put the special claims made for the National Union on one side. This whole episode reveals that the organisation had little life of its own and no capacity to formulate views and press them on the Party. Lord Randolph was capitalising on a feeling of frustration that was widespread (G. C. T. Bartley, the chief Conservative agent, resigned in March 1885 on the grounds that opposition was too mild) [77] but even this feeling was only a factor to be used by men who were already prominent politicians. The associations were in general too eager for Conservative success to sustain pressure on the leadership. Some sections of the Party did express the opinion in June 1885 that Lord Salisbury should take advantage

---

75 Sir A. Hardinge, *The Fourth Earl of Carnarvon*, Vol. II, p. 358.

76 The chairmen of seven associations met in London to urge Lord Randolph to withdraw his resignation and they also saw Lord Salisbury. See R. R. James, *Lord Randolph Churchill*, p. 149.

77 Sir H. Maxwell, *op. cit.*, Vol. II, p. 144.

of Gladstone's resignation and form a government.[78] Once, however, the Party won the election of 1886, the National Union
reverted to an implicit loyalty. This attitude did not waver in
1887 on the resignation of Lord Randolph as Chancellor of the
Exchequer and the groundswell of frustration which Churchill
had used disappeared so long as the Party remained united and
powerful.[79]

　The National Liberal Federation, though possessing an independent origin and much greater powers of initiative, was heartily
Gladstonian. After the 1880 victory, it was so concerned to
support the Party that it had no time and no desire to try to
influence the Cabinet. On one or two occasions it did not pull
behind the leaders, for example, when some constituencies pressed
their Members to exclude Bradlaugh,[80] but in crises such as the
fall of Khartoum it refused to protest " in order not to embarrass
Mr. Gladstone." [81]

So the views and activities of the party organisations had
virtually no immediate effect on the policy of either Cabinets or
shadow cabinets in these years.[82] Their influence on the life of
a ministry arose in two ways. The most obvious was their direct
contribution to winning or losing elections. Of more long-term
significance was their tendency to encourage loyalty among M.P.s.

The desire to exhibit a degree of independence of judgment
was a pronounced characteristic among some Liberals and the
Party organisation naturally found that these Members—
especially with a majority like that of 1880—posed the most
serious problem. Ostrogorski, in his pioneer work on party
organisation, drew a picture of this new and alien monster devour-
ing such sturdy old Radicals as Joseph Cowen and W. E. Forster
and suppressing C. Marriott as a man who stood for freedom of
debate. In its early stages, the N.L.F. combined only a hundred
local associations (1879) but it gradually spread as rivals were

---

[78] Sir Winston Churchill, *op. cit.*, Vol. I, p. 410.
[79] The view of Randolph Churchill's motives taken in this paragraph is accepted
by A. J. Balfour in his *Chapters of Autobiography* and by both Lord
Randolph's biographers.
[80] Joseph Chamberlain, *A Political Memoir*, ed. C. H. D. Howard, p. 5.
[81] Quoted by Ostrogorski, *op. cit.*, Vol. I, p. 217.
[82] Though Buckle comments on the help leaders of both parties got from
stronger organisations. Monypenny and Buckle, *op. cit.*, Vol. V, p. 186.

absorbed and more constituencies set up organisations. The men in these local bodies and the officials they elected to the N.L.F. were the most ardent and sincere local Liberals, exemplified by Robert Spence Watson, the national chairman from 1890 to 1902. They could and did, on occasion, differ from the policy of Liberal Cabinets but their differences did not go the length of wanting to see the Conservatives in office.[83] They were men of conscience prepared for their representatives to have doubts and voice them but it was a different matter when (as in the case of Cowen, Forster and Marriott) specific differences gave way to a general or persistent opposition. The older school of commentators, particularly Ostrogorski, argued that M.P.s were supposed to represent the whole constituency, not a small band of party militants. It was true that both Joseph Cowen in Newcastle and W. E. Forster in Bradford were returned in 1885 despite the opposition of the local Liberal associations. But the explanation was that they were returned with the aid of Conservative votes. The Liberal associations had no objection to them being elected in this fashion—the objection was to them standing as " Liberals." It was quite open to these M.P.s to run under any other banner but they should have recognised that voters who wanted to see a Liberal Cabinet in power were entitled to a candidate of similar convictions.

The difference really arose out of the changing conditions of politics. Till the 1860s, a Member stood on his principles and if they varied, the nature of his support might alter, but his position was in no way compromised. After 1867 many electors became Liberal or Conservative by inclination, later confirmed by habit. When a candidate clearly stood on his personal reputation, voters had no right to complain, but in most cases candidates declared party affiliations and received at least part of their support because they were Liberals or Conservatives rather than for any of their personal viewpoints. If a man came forward as a Liberal but in fact intended to oppose a Liberal Cabinet, it could fairly be said that he was gaining some votes on false pretences.

To ensure loyalty, two methods were adopted. The primary

---

[83] For example, R. S. Watson would have preferred an immediate withdrawal from the Transvaal and no military action in the Sudan. P. Corder, *Robert Spence Watson*, p. 240.

one was to insist that candidates carrying the party label must
have been selected by the local association rather than merely
stand with the aid of a few individual supporters as had recently
been the custom. It followed that Members who failed to act as
the association wanted might not be readopted at the next election. Between elections the associations prodded by the national
organisation, reminded Members of the consequences of deviation
by holding meetings, sending up petitions, letters and direct resolutions, all urging support for the Cabinet. In 1880 sixteen
Liberals had opposed the Compensation for Disturbance Bill and
when the Irish Land Bill seemed to be threatened " the Executive
Committee of the Federation found it necessary, in June 1881, to
issue a circular to the Federated Associations calling their attention to the existence of this disloyalty, and asking them to take
such action as might appear desirable." [84]   The same type of
action was taken at crucial moments over the Transvaal, Afghanistan, the land laws and the revision of the Standing Orders.[85]
The N.L.F. was quite open about such actions as its paramount
objective was to keep Mr. Gladstone in power. Trouble only
arose in those cases where Members had begun their parliamentary careers more or less on their own initiative and resented
both recent trends in the Liberal Party and these new conditions
in the constituencies. In time candidates went forward fully
appreciating the implications of the party label and cross-voting
declined as much because the new Members had no desire to
exercise this older form of independence as from any subservience
to party dictation.

NEW PRACTICES CONFIRMED AFTER THE 1880s

All these developments were intensified and became established
features of British politics during and after the mid-1880s. The
third Reform Act of 1884 raised the electorate to about five
million and this, combined with a thorough-going redistribution
of seats, greatly weakened local influences. Elections were fought

[84] R. Spence Watson, *op. cit.*, p. 29.
[85] On this issue, Ostrogorski says 100 Liberals had indicated their approval of
Marriott's resistance to closure by simple majority. The associations pressed
and only five supported Marriott and 16 abstained. It is almost impossible
to estimate how many of the 100 had actually intended to vote against the
Cabinet, but clearly the flood of letters from the associations was a powerful
factor. Ostrogorski, *op. cit.*, p. 214.

much more explicitly by a few party leaders asking the electorate to give them power to carry out certain specific policies. At the same time, the demand for Home Rule for Ireland touched a deeper level of political emotion. From 1886, those interested in politics had to subordinate all other matters to the simple question of whether they wished to see a Home Rule or a Unionist Government in office. Lord Salisbury told the Queen in 1889 that " there are *no* Moderate Liberals in the present day. The old judicial type of Member, who sat rather loose to his Party and could be trusted to be fair . . . has disappeared. They are all partisans . . ." [86] As Salisbury observed to W. H. Smith, " we are in a state of bloodless civil war " [87] and the conduct of the Unionists over such matters as the Parnell Commission showed how deeply they were imbued with partisan feeling. [88]

Naturally, such feeling led to a general tightening of party organisation. The party label now became of major importance since the first question for many electors was whether the candidate was a Unionist or a Gladstonian. The local associations' powers over the Members increased because they alone could confer the label. There was now little hope for an independent candidate, however definite his views on Ireland, if an " official " Home Ruler or Unionist was in the field. On the other hand, men entering politics appreciated that to win a contest involving a mass electorate, an organisation was essential. So the practice of joining a party and standing only if one was adopted as the official candidate became regular. Joseph Chamberlain's appeal to local Liberal committees to desert Mr. Gladstone made it clear that those associations which remained faithful (the vast majority) were the only repository of true Liberalism. At the same time, the National Liberal Federation, with its headquarters in London, settled down as the agent of the party in the localities. Among Conservatives, the need to subordinate local interests to the overall cause had to be emphasised in order to persuade constituency associations not to run candidates in seats held by Liberal

---

[86] *Letters*, Series III, Vol. I, p. 510.

[87] Sir H. Maxwell, *op. cit.*, Vol. II, p. 240.

[88] Lord Salisbury's own conduct was affected in many ways. When his strong desire not to abandon a number of Bills in 1890 was rejected by the Cabinet, Salisbury told the Queen that he would normally have preferred to resign but a dissolution at this moment might endanger the Union. *Letters*, Series III, Vol. I, p. 619.

Unionists. In addition to these factors, Sir Henry James' Corrupt Practices Act of 1883 had imposed a real restriction on the amount of money that could be spent at an election. As a result, contributions from the central party chest assumed a greater significance and much larger fighting funds were raised.[89]

Party discipline within Parliament became more rigid as the battles grew keener and the issues tended to resolve themselves into holding or gaining power. For the government there was the hard and delicate task of keeping the Liberal Unionists and the Conservatives together and of maintaining a constant majority in the face of Irish and Radical M.P.s who never left the House. This was largely the work of the Conservative Chief Whip, Aretas Akers-Douglas. A paper reported that he had " adopted a very faultless and comprehensive system of book-keeping. He knows to a nicety how often every one of his men have attended the House, and how often they have voted. Those who are slack are brought severely to task." [90] Yet the necessary degree of discipline could not have been imposed without the M.P.s' overall willingness which rested in turn on the pressure of a convinced and trusting electorate and the leadership of a united front bench. Gladstone's narrow majority in 1892 had likewise to be carefully marshalled and J. A. Spender records that " never in subsequent years can I remember such discipline as was imposed on and cheerfully accepted by the rank and file of M.P.s at this period." [91] If differences arose within parties, every effort was made to resolve the dispute without affecting division lists in the House. Although the Conservative Free Traders definitely disliked Balfour and Joseph Chamberlain's views after 1903, the majority of them

---

[89] Herbert Gladstone, the Liberal Chief Whip, spent £60,000 on 397 candidates in 1900 and £100,000 on 518 candidates in 1906. See Sir Charles Mallet, *Herbert Gladstone, A Memoir*, pp. 192–193. Steel-Maitland, as Unionist organiser in 1912, aimed at an annual income of £120,000 for the party. Robert Blake, *The Unknown Prime Minister, The Life and Times of Andrew Bonar Law*, p. 100.

[90] Viscount Chilston, *Chief Whip, The Political Life and Times of Aretas Akers-Douglas, First Viscount Chilston*, p. 121.

[91] J. A. Spender, *Life, Journalism and Politics*, Vol. I, p. 53. The Liberal Chief Whip was Edward Marjoribanks whose " one aim was to give the party a majority of forty in every division." Hearing that two Liberals had left for a short holiday on the Continent unpaired and finding that appeals failed, he wired the news of their departure to every paper in their constituencies. The local associations reacted and the two Members were back in the House the next day. E. Marjoribanks, Lord Tweedmouth, 1849–1909, *Notes and Recollections*, p. 51.

continued to prefer a Conservative Cabinet that was doubtful on this issue, to a Liberal victory. Austen Chamberlain, for the protectionists, found that he could make little progress if he asked members to disobey the Whip, even when the party was in opposition.[92]   Describing the situation in 1910, Lord Templewood has recorded that " the Conservative Whips' room was run like the orderly room of a Guards regiment. Acland Hood, the Chief Whip . . . was determined that his men should parade in full strength and that there should be no talking in the ranks. The new Members were there to vote and not to speak . . ." [93]   There was a similar discipline among the Liberals though no Liberal M.P. ever had the Whip withdrawn nor was one ever formally reported to his constituency. There was no need for such direct and external pressures. Members contributed to and felt the party spirit of the era and responded to the need to support their government. If there was any weakening, reprimands from the local party associations did not have to be solicited from London.

With the opposition in Parliament eager to resist the government in an organised manner over long periods, passing major items of legislation under the existing procedure grew more and more difficult. In the 1886 session, Lord Randolph Churchill decided to oppose all private Bills and motions in an attempt to get the Cabinet's business finished. Despite the introduction of the closure by a bare majority in early 1887 and of the first " guillotine " resolution in June of that year, there was little improvement and most of the government measures brought forward in 1890 had to be abandoned at the end of the session.[94] There was a further failure over Balfour's Education Bill in 1896 despite his decision to take the entire time of the House. In that year, Balfour changed the rules of procedure and allotted a fixed number of days to the Committee on Supply. Debates on supply, offering a wide scope for amendment, had been the best opportunity for the private Member but now each day tended to be given to a party topic and the votes went through " on the nod."

---

[92] Sir Austen Chamberlain, *Politics from Inside*, p. 50.
[93] Viscount Templewood, " Were those the Days?" in *The Listener*, January 29, 1959.
[94] Viscount Chilston, *W. H. Smith*, pp. 244 and 253. The difficulty even with closure and guillotine led Redlich to observe that " these events clearly proved that no form of closure, however violent, could ensure expeditious despatch of Bills opposed by a party." *Op. cit.*, Vol. I, p. 180.

The last major alteration came in 1902 when Balfour carried his "parliamentary railway time-table" on a party vote. By these rules (not far removed from those operating now) private Members were left only Friday afternoons and the government was able to arrange virtually all the business of the House and fix the time by which motions were to be carried. Had it not been for these rules, the 1902 Education Act would never have reached the Statute Book. The new Standing Orders marked the end of a process which had definitely changed the functions of the Commons. In earlier years the House had been able, on occasion, to take a different view from that of the Cabinet and to act as a positive check on its actions. Now the Commons became an instrument in the hands of the Cabinet, with the opposition and private Members retaining facilities for making their views known rather than any actual power.

In politics, power and access to information usually go hand in hand. Men or institutions with power will demand information and without it, the capacity to influence decisions declines. The attention of the House was chiefly concentrated on home affairs and though committees of inquiry could no longer be forced through against the government, there was still adequate information on most questions. It was over foreign policy that some complaints were made. L. L. Dillwyn in May 1879 argued that the purchase of the Suez Canal shares, the Anglo-Turkish Convention and other matters, were undertaken without telling the House. Yet his motion received negligible support, though it was true that Beaconsfield had presented Parliament with *faits accompli* on a number of occasions, such as the settlement at the Berlin Congress and the decision to bring Indian troops to Malta. After 1885, the general lines of foreign policy were accepted by most of the leaders on both sides so that the House had little motive for extracting information even if it had possessed the power to do so. Lord Salisbury, Lord Rosebery, A. J. Balfour and Sir Edward Grey all were disinclined to tell Parliament more than was necessary and the Blue Books they published avoided the major issues between the great powers.[95] There was no positive intention to deceive the House and when questions

---

[95] Temperley and Penson describe the decline in information by studying the Blue Book policy of each Foreign Secretary. See their *Century of Diplomatic Blue Books*.

were asked, the explanations were usually full and frank.[96] (Question time was developed in these years as a means of obtaining information which also permitted M.P.s to harry particular ministers.)   The Cabinet could probably have prevented any inquiry into the weaknesses of the War Office which were revealed by the Boer War but in this case the Prime Minister and his colleagues shared the general feeling among Conservative M.P.s that they were bound both in honour and by the national interest to grant an inquiry (though only after the war was over).[97]   Some ministers on both sides did think that the less public attention was drawn to aspects of British policy the better, yet this was achieved more by discretion or silence than by deliberate concealment and Parliament had no conscious feeling that it was being starved of information or opportunities.   Stronger party divisions meant that information could not be forced out of the government but it also meant that Members tended to restrict themselves to controversies (which largely excluded foreign affairs) where the main lines of argument were well known.   The old desires to scrutinise each estimate, to re-write particular clauses of Bills and to gather information for private legislation, had declined. It was the government's task to govern and to legislate while the opposition endeavoured to win over sections of the public by attacking on a small number of fairly straightforward issues.

It follows that under these conditions cross-voting, which had declined markedly by the early 1880s, virtually ceased.   Now, if party members did vote against the Whips, it was a much more serious matter.   Sometimes groups objecting strongly to Cabinet policy might abstain or cross-vote, but only after a careful calculation that this would register a protest without endangering the position of the government.   For instance, Joseph Chamberlain and one or two of his followers voted against the proscription of the Irish National League in August 1887 and for Welsh disestablishment in 1891, but it is almost certain that they would not have done so if there had been any chance of Lord Salisbury resigning.   Another occasional motive for such calculated minor shows of resistance on the part of back-benchers was the desire

---

[96] Grey held that Parliament was entitled to know about any binding agreements " but it cannot be told of military and naval measures to meet possible contingencies "—or of any hypothetical or precautionary policies.   Viscount Grey of Fallodon, *Twenty-Five Years*, Vol. I, p. 290.

[97] Lord Salisbury to King Edward VII, June 14, 1902, *Salisbury Papers*.

to influence debates known to be going on within the Cabinet. This occurred during the dispute on Uganda in 1894 and in several of the struggles over Naval Estimates in the Liberal Ministries after 1906. When governments did face an element of abstention for other than tactical reasons, as over the publication of the Spion Kop despatches in 1900 or in February 1904 when there was cross-voting in the debate on the Address, it was a sign of definite trouble in the party. On this latter occasion, twenty-seven Conservatives voted with the Liberals, a defection which seriously impaired morale on the government side for the rest of the ministry's period in office.[98] But even when a Cabinet was evidently weak and divided, with declining credit in the country, its position really depended on its own resolution. After 1886, Members never in fact voted in decisive numbers against their party in a division which was likely to bring down the government. The chances of defeat rested on the remote hope of by-election results changing the balance in the Commons or on the possibility of a split in the governing party. In the case of Lord Rosebery's Government, the majority was always narrow [99] but there was no need to have resigned after the unexpected defeat on June 20, 1895, over the supply of cordite for the Army. The whole episode was part of a careful plot by the Conservative and Liberal Unionist Whips who had observed that attendance on Friday evenings was growing thin.[1] The object was to harry and tire the government as even if the stratagem succeeded, the vote could have been reversed when all the Members were in attendance on the following Monday.[2] As it happened, the episode found Rosebery with an intense desire to give up office and after two long meetings and much difference of opinion, the Cabinet agreed to resign.[3] By this time defeat was so rare that any lapse was a serious matter. When A. J. Balfour's ministry was beaten over a minor point in the Irish estimates on July 2, 1905, his

---

[98] Blanche E. C. Dugdale, *Arthur James Balfour*, Vol. I, p. 411.
[99] There had been a defeat in early 1894 on a propagandist amendment to the Address moved by Labouchere.
[1] Sir Austen Chamberlain, *Down the Years*, p. 89.
[2] Queen Victoria, when she first heard of the defeat " did not quite see that this would cause a crisis." *Letters*, Series III, Vol. II, p. 521. Asquith pointed out in *Fifty Years of Parliament*, Vol. I, p. 232, that the government could easily have remained in office but was sick of living from hand to mouth.
[3] *Letters*, Series III, Vol. II, p. 522.

colleagues, though divided and despondent, decided simply to apply the Whips and get their majority to reverse the decision.[4] Similarly on November 11, 1912, the Liberal Cabinet considered their defeat of the previous evening, rated it as accidental and asked the House to reconsider its opinion.[5]

Since maintaining the support of the Commons had now become a matter of party leadership and management, a Cabinet's future was ultimately determined by its appeals to the electorate. The older view that dissolutions should take place only near the end of the span of a particular Parliament, or after the government had suffered a serious reverse, had been questioned in 1878.[6] It had long been normal practice to try to choose a suitable time of year when a dissolution was due. In May 1892, when that Parliament had run for six years, the leaders of the Liberal Unionist and Conservative parties and their Whips met at Devonshire House to fix the date. Joseph Chamberlain preferred the autumn, but the Whips, the local agents (by report) and the other leaders settled for June.[7] Both Rosebery in 1895 and Balfour in 1905 preferred to resign rather than dissolve, as they realised that popular feeling was not in their favour. Rosebery seems to have been moved chiefly by a desire to leave office but his ministry was not in a position to make a united appeal as an existing government to the country. Balfour hoped that the Liberals would have difficulties in forming a Cabinet and that any signs of division or delay could only aid the Conservatives. It was in 1900 that the 1878 situation was repeated. The Unionists were in office and high in public favour for their conduct of the South African War, with their opponents evidently divided. Parliament had two full years of life ahead but the Cabinet decided to seize this favourable opportunity. As Lord Salisbury told the Queen, the election " would then only be on the settlement of South Africa, whereas if it took place later on there might be all sorts of

---

4 It is interesting that both Redmond and Campbell-Bannerman tried to claim that Balfour was acting unconstitutionally—a claim which showed how exceptional even a casual defeat had become. Sir S. Lee, *op. cit.*, Vol. II, p. 187.

5 Cabinet Letter to the King, November 11, 1912, *Asquith Papers*, Dep. 6, f. 177.

6 See above, p. 179. Sir William Hart Dyke, the Whip, had advised against dissolution then as " it would be like throwing up a rubber at whist, whilst holding nothing but good cards." Monypenny and Buckle, *op. cit.*, Vol. VI, p. 369.

7 J. L. Garvin, *op. cit.*, Vol. II, p. 537.

difficulties and other questions." [8]   The Duke of Devonshire put the Cabinet's view in the form of a simple analogy: " We all know very well that the captain of a cricketing eleven, when he wins the toss, puts his own side in, or his adversaries, as he thinks most favourable to his prospects of winning." [9]   It became the normal practice that, unless there were exceptional situations (for instance with three fairly evenly balanced parties in the House), a ministry could ask for and be granted a dissolution at any time it chose.

INFLUENCE EXERCISED BY THE COMMONS ON THE CABINET

The degree of control or influence exercised by the Commons over the Cabinet must be estimated, taking these changes in political outlook and conduct into consideration. It is evident that the old, fairly tangible powers of the private M.P. to object, to force explanations and perhaps to alter measures had, after the 1880s, passed to bodies of Members working together, or to the opposition in particular. The system of closure adopted in 1881 required a majority of three to one with at least 300 M.P.s voting so that it could be used against the Irish Nationalists but not the regular opposition. Hartington pointed out to Gladstone in October 1882 that a strong and resolute opposition could defeat by delaying any items to which it strongly objected.[10]   Even after the closure by bare majority in 1887, an organised opposition could cause major delays, so that through the 1890s Cabinets had to give constant consideration to the views of the opposition. Time was a major factor and ministers accepted the fact that if a measure aroused real resistance, it might not only fail, but all the other proposals of the government might have to be abandoned unfinished, as happened in the sessional failure of 1890. If the Unionists were in office, they knew that certain issues would arouse the passions of the Irish and the Liberals—issues such as coercion, any educational proposals which favoured the Church of England, or support for the drink trade—and that they must either leave them alone, or attempt only bi-partisan solutions.

---

[8] *Letters*, Series III, Vol. III, p. 578. Balfour did feel that they could not ask for a dissolution "*unless* some definite incident marking the conclusion of the purely military stage in S.A. affairs gives us a legitimate occasion for asking the verdict of the country on its future settlement." Balfour to Salisbury, July 5, 1900, *Salisbury Papers*.

[9] B. Holland, *op. cit.*, Vol. II, p. 278.

[10] *Ibid.*, Vol. I, pp. 371–376.

Even these were liable to break down after irritating the more ardent elements on both sides. In 1890 the Chancellor of the Exchequer, Goschen, proposed a tax on drink to buy up licences and though it was quietly received, opposition from the temperance elements, from the trade and from Liberals in general grew and finally forced him to withdraw.[11] When Liberals formed a government, the Unionists did not have to press so hard, as they always had the veto of the House of Lords in reserve. Yet Liberal ministers still had to spend each sitting in the House and defend any controversial measures clause by clause. H. H. Fowler, in charge of the Parish Council Bill in 1893, faced 1,025 amendments by the opposition, of which 402 were moved. The government wanted to see the Bill through and was prepared to concede on a number of points, but Fowler had to speak 800 times in fifty-seven sittings before the Bill passed the Commons in 1894.[12] Perhaps the most striking instance of the power of the opposition occurred in 1896. The Liberals had just been badly beaten in a general election and were facing a Unionist majority of 152 with their own leadership weak and divided. But when A. J. Balfour brought in a Bill to give state aid to voluntary schools with some concessions to nonconformists in the shape of separate religious instruction, he was attacked from all sides and 1,200 amendments were put down before he abandoned the attempt.

Pressure declined in the late 1890s in part because the opposition was divided over the Boer War and in part because the government was too busy with the War to take any interest in major items of domestic legislation. Before attention had fully reverted to home affairs, Balfour in 1902 revised the Standing Orders and opposition of the kind that has just been described was no longer possible. It is doubtful, as has been said, whether the 1902 Education Bill, the 1904 Licensing Bill or several of the measures introduced by the Liberals after 1906 could have been passed under the old procedure. But it is also important to appreciate that the role of the opposition and the way in which it attempted to influence the Cabinet now altered. After 1868 the opposition leaders had spoken to the Members of Parliament whom they hoped to win over, to any who were doubtful on

[11] Hon. Arthur D. Elliot, *The Life of Lord Goschen*, Vol. II, p. 166.
[12] Edith H. Fowler, *The Life of Lord Wolverhampton*, p. 274.

their own side and, indirectly, to the electorate. As the chances of defeating the Cabinet declined and all but disappeared, the tendency to speak to the outside audience, as the ultimate arbiters, increased. In the period from the 1880s to 1902, the opposition worked to influence the situation both within and without Parliament, but once the power to delay and thus indefinitely postpone a measure had gone, the real task of the shadow Cabinet was to score points and build up public opinion on its side. When private M.P.s told the Select Committee on Procedure in 1914 that their power and that of the opposition had declined seriously in the last twenty years, Balfour replied with a masterly summary of the opportunities for criticism open to the House in general and to the opposition in particular.[13] This was valuable but quite missed the point, as the complaints were not over lack of any chance to speak but over lack of any positive power to alter government policy.

Whether the opposition was attempting to amend measures before the House or whether it was placing more emphasis on convincing the electorate, its strength clearly depended in large part on its prospects of success at the next election. If the politicians and the public were convinced that the opposition was going to lose the next election the Cabinet could afford to ignore criticisms and resistance to partisan measures would, in time, have been worn down. In theory, this was quite possible. A party which had won a majority for a given programme could carry out its promises, play on the weaknesses of its opponents, and offer to meet the needs of new voters. Men of ability might prefer to enter a party which was in a position to act and each victory would confirm the voting habits of the electorate. Yet from 1868 to 1895 it appeared to be more common for governments to decline in vitality and lose support, so that statesmen and political writers began to assume that it was natural in a two-party system for floating voters to transfer their allegiance from the government to the opposition. H. H. Asquith, whose views were formed in this period, considered that "at the successive general elections, which substituted a new for an old House of Commons, the law of the 'swing of the pendulum' operated almost automatically."[14] The fact that oppositions did gain

[13] Select Committee on Procedure, 1914, p. 86, question 1258.
[14] H. H. Asquith, *Fifty Years of Parliament*, Vol. II, p. 161.

strength and win elections and the popular belief that this was likely to happen did a great deal to help the Commons retain a measure of control over the Cabinet. The government's capacity to order the time of the House and to stop debates, and its freedom to carry on despite growing public criticisms, all became more tolerable and the Cabinet more open to argument with the expectation that the opposition might well be exercising these powers before very long.

It does not weaken this argument to point out that the " swing " was never analysed, that it only occurred in any regular form between 1868 and 1880 and that there were other more important long-term shifts in voters' allegiances.[15] In fact the theory strictly ceased to apply when the Liberals won the election of 1885. But they split and were defeated in the next year so that the Conservatives had their turn, only to be defeated or, rather, replaced by the Liberals (dependent on Irish votes) in 1892. The Conservatives won the next general election in 1895, the first obvious departure from the theory being in 1900 (which was also the first premature election held to capitalise on a wave of pro-government feeling) and then politicians were surprised. Lord Salisbury, while protesting that his victory was entirely fair, remarked " that the love of justice should have overborne the great law of the pendulum I confess puzzles and bewilders me." [16]

As in many other aspects of thinking and writing about British politics, the maxims used even till the 1950s [17] were drawn from the experience of this limited but vivid period from the 1860s to the 1890s and so long as politicians considered that a " swing of the pendulum " was likely at the next election, they were both more moderate in their use of executive power and more buoyant when in opposition. But while this meant that a Cabinet might have more respect for the reactions and position of the House of Commons, it also encouraged a tendency to look beyond it to the new sovereign, the electorate. By-elections were of increased importance, as was the tone of the Press, the reports of party agents

---

[15] See J. P. D. Dunbabin, " Parliamentary Elections in Great Britain, 1868–1900: A Psychological Note," *E.H.R.*, Vol. 81 (1966); G. N. Sanderson, " The 'Swing of the Pendulum' in British General Elections, 1832–1966," *Political Studies*, Vol. XIV (1966).

[16] A. E. Gathorne-Hardy, *op. cit.*, Vol. II, p. 374.

[17] See above, pp. 573–578.

on the state of the constituencies and the impressions of ministers themselves. What mattered was not so much the outcome of the next big clash in the House but how the policies would affect reactions outside.

The same change of emphasis can be seen in the different implications when a minister advised against a certain course of action on the grounds that the House "won't take it." In its original usage, the meaning was literal. Lord Salisbury, negotiating at Constantinople in December 1876, urged that Elliot, the Ambassador, should be moved. Unfortunately, Ignatieff, the Russian representative, had made the same suggestion and Salisbury was told that if Elliot was disturbed "we should be turned out on the first day of session by our own men." [18] This may be doubted, but the government would not want to strain the loyalty of its followers too much on such a question. In 1880, Childers told the Queen that the Cabinet had to fall in with the strong Liberal desire to abolish flogging in the Army.[19] When Gordon at Khartoum asked the Cabinet to send up the Soudanese slave-trader, Zebehr, to help him, Gladstone favoured the idea but was convinced that whether the Cabinet agreed or not, the Commons would throw it out.[20]

By the latter years of the decade, there was less fear that the government would have its requests rejected. It was assumed that the opposition would oppose and that the Cabinet's supporters would vote; the real problem was to see that they did so without the kind of straining or muttering which would bode ill for the unity and vigour of the party. Indeed, once the need to persuade some independent or doubtful M.P.s was a thing of the past, the Cabinet's chief concern became the temper of its own regular adherents. Liberal Ministers decided to grant extra money to the Navy in 1885 because so many Liberal back-benchers felt that this was essential. Lord Salisbury's Cabinet, after 1886, set its teeth against any concessions to the Gladstonians and when it gave way over a downward review of Irish rents in 1888 and over resistance to Greek action in Crete in 1889, it was for fear of reactions among Liberal Unionists and liberal

---

[18] Lady G. Cecil, *op. cit.*, Vol. II, p. 120.
[19] Lt.-Col. S. C. Childers, *Life and Correspondence of Hugh C. E. Childers*, Vol. I, p. 274.
[20] Morley, *op. cit.*, Vol. III, p. 159 and Lord E. Fitzmaurice, *op. cit.*, Vol. II, p. 387.

elements in the Conservative Party.[21] Salisbury was very angry
in 1891 when House of Commons ministers made some concessions (over moneys for the Queen's grandchildren) to "'the feeling of the House,' which means, *not* the votes of a majority, but
the outcry of a small number who are generally almost entirely
our opponents." A major offender was Sir William Hart Dyke,
who was "penetrated with the fallacy through and through. He
is not thinking of the ultimate effect of the measure, or of his
chances of obtaining a majority—but of what the people on the
other side will say—which is a matter of no importance
whatever."[22]

In the 1890s, the phrase was not that "the House won't stand
it," but, as Morley told Lord Rendel "our fellows won't stand
it." [23] Over Naval matters the Liberal Cabinet had again to move
with a tide of feeling in their own party as conveyed to them
by Marjoribanks, the Chief Whip,[24] though in this, as in other
instances, the sentiment was as strong or stronger on the other
side of the House. When Balfour was rebutting Bigge's suggestion
that the Cabinet should ignore a widespread desire for an inquiry
into the conduct of the Boer War, he pointed out that "a majority
is not an inanimate machine and those who use it must be prepared to honour it." [25] The government was often sensitive if a
positive group among its adherents showed signs of united resistance. Conservative Cabinets wanting to reform the Army had
to take account of the military men among their own back-
benchers. Balfour almost gave way over sending the Guards on
overseas duty in 1897 [26] and Arnold-Forster's various proposals
came to a standstill in 1904–05 because the M.P.s connected with
the Militia were hostile and the Cabinet did not think the scheme
was worth a showdown.[27]

After 1906, the Liberals had renewed difficulties with Radicals
opposed to the level of expenditure on defence. Whiteley, the

---

[21] Lady G. Cecil, *op. cit.*, Vol. IV, pp. 131 and 150. The Liberal Unionists and
Chamberlain had a special degree of influence over Cabinet policy. See
Garvin, *op. cit.*, Vol. II, pp. 305–306, 411–414, 417–421 and 432.
[22] *Ibid.*, pp. 151–152.
[23] *Personal Papers of Lord Rendel*, p. 183.
[24] *Private Diaries of the Rt. Hon. Sir Algernon West*, ed. H. G. Hutchinson,
p. 214.
[25] Balfour to Bigge, January 5, 1901, *Salisbury Papers*.
[26] The Earl of Midleton, *Records and Reactions, 1856–1939*, pp. 96–97.
[27] Mary Arnold-Forster, *Memoir of H. O. Arnold-Forster*, pp. 261–280 and
Viscount Esher's *Journals*, Vol. II, p. 58.

Chief Whip, reported that a motion put down in February 1908 by a Liberal, J. A. M. Murray Macdonald, calling for reduced expenditure in the Navy, was likely to be carried by 100. The interest of this crisis was that rank and file pressure was only an element and a minor element. The real problem was a division in the Cabinet with the Sea Lords threatening to resign if there was any reduction. Ultimately Sir Henry Campbell-Bannerman settled almost entirely in favour of the Sea Lords. Then ministers were able to use their control of the business of the House to postpone Macdonald's motion till they had made their case. When it came up, Members knew that the opposition were supporting the Cabinet, yet only seventy-three (mostly Labour and Irish) voted with Macdonald.[28] Sometimes back-benchers went even further and tried to suggest positive action. In the spring of 1910, as the Liberal Cabinet was evidently struggling to decide on its next step, the more Radical M.P.s urged a royal guarantee to create peers if the Lords again rejected the Budget. They pressed the Whips, and those representing Scottish and Northern constituencies held meetings and passed resolutions to the same effect.[29]

Thus pressure from the Cabinet's supporters could play an important part, especially when the Cabinet was divided but it is significant that little of this process had to be overt or to take place in the House of Commons. The debates remained lively but were chiefly confined to an exposition of the party viewpoints. Members of the party in power did not try to influence the Cabinet by explaining their doubts on the floor of the House— they spoke to the Whips, the private secretaries and, if possible, to ministers. The opposition slowly came to realise that, on major matters of dispute, they were speaking not to the House but to the outside public. Austen Chamberlain noted in May 1907 that since after-dinner speeches were hardly ever reported in the Press, attendance became very slack unless Members had to stay to vote.[30] For Conservatives, this situation was made tolerable up till 1911 by the existence of the veto of the House of Lords. They knew they could delay the actions of a majority in the Commons at least until another general election had been held. A large part of the explanation of Conservative behaviour

[28] Esher, *op. cit.*, Vol. II, pp. 280–284.
[29] Lucy Masterman, *C. F. G. Masterman*, p. 159, and Spender and Asquith, *op. cit.*, Vol. I, p. 272.
[30] Rt. Hon. Sir Austen Chamberlain, *Politics from Inside*, p. 86.

between 1911 and 1914 is that they never were fully reconciled to the position of an opposition without a reserve power—that is an opposition which on major issues simply had to wait till the next general election. It was all very well to sit in the House and make speeches for next morning's papers but the knowledge that however eloquent they were and whatever the response of the public, certain detested measures were bound to become law, drove them to desperation. They resorted to such reckless courses as urging the King to revive his power of veto, threatening to hold up the annual Army Bill and talk of armed resistance to the government.

By the 1910s the decline in the Commons' capacity to control the Cabinet and the tendency for influence to be exerted more along private channels in the governing party than overtly in debates and divisions in the House, had led to a slight diminution of interest in Parliament. Thirty or forty years earlier, there had been elements in the political battles which had concentrated the attention of most literate sections of the community on Parliament. Part of the explanation for this interest in the 1860s and 1880s was the recent grant of the franchise, but the main attraction was that the battles in the House of Commons were real. A number of simple yet vital issues were settled in the House after brilliant debates by divisions whose results were not certain till the last M.P. had been counted. Such contests attracted the ablest men in public life and were singularly satisfying for all. It is true that in these years government played a much smaller role in the life of the community, but the matters left to political decision were important and of a kind which could be settled one way or another. If certain men were elected or changed their minds, there would be Home Rule for Ireland, no truck with bloodstained Turks, elective county councils, the disestablishment of the Welsh Church, and so on. Recent writers have emphasised the limited nature of nineteenth-century government but these limits were self-imposed. There was a great belief in the power of Parliament. No modern commentator would say that " Parliament can do anything except make a man into a woman " and the section on " the sovereignty of Parliament " has been omitted from the more recent editions of the old textbooks. At the same time, each side appealed to a recognised and reasonable series of beliefs (national interests, the constitution and orderly progress or freedom to vote, worship, act and be ruled as one wanted) and could feel that, by general standards, there was substantial justice in the decisions of the electorate. So there was a strong belief not only in the power but in the value of popular government—all sentiments which helped to emphasise the right of the House of Commons to check the Cabinet.

Yet, despite the prestige of Parliament and its apparently commanding position,[31] some of the older Members appreciated that there had been changes. Lord George Hamilton, looking back to 1868, remarked that then " an influential M.P. was . . . in the world at large, a person of real importance " but now in 1916 " independence of thought and action are on the wane, the repute of the House is declining and there is little to do but loaf and vote." [32] The Earl of Midleton (first elected in 1879) came to the same conclusion [33] and the senior back-benchers explained their doubts before the 1914 Select Committee on Procedure. To the newer Members, however, watching Lloyd George put through the 1911 Insurance Bill, there seemed little wrong. Now Parliament was capable of passing the complex and lengthy measures desired by the electorate. They saw a consummate politician moulding a Bill, offering changes to deputations, giving the House a free vote on one clause and finally emerging triumphant. In the debate on the Third Reading, Bonar Law said that

> " as a matter of fact, the House of Commons during this Autumn Session has really had no more to do with the real difficulties of this Bill than the House of Lords. All the difficulties have been arranged in hole-and-corner meetings of some of which we have heard and lots of which we did not hear at all. And when under pressure of those different interests the right hon. Gentleman made up his mind he came down here and we registered his decrees. That is what we have done in the House of Commons." [34]

---

[31] There was, for the first time since the 1860s, some scepticism about and even a little ridicule of Parliament in the years just before 1914. Hilaire Belloc and G. K. Chesterton made various criticisms, some officials doubted the power of Parliament (see Sir Almeric Fitzroy, *Memoirs*, Vol. I, p. 49) and George Lansbury headed his *Daily Herald* column on Westminster, " The House of Pretence." R. Postgate, *George Lansbury*, p. 139.

[32] Lord George Hamilton, *op. cit.*, Vol. I, pp. 17, 213.

[33] The Earl of Midleton, *op. cit.*, p. 53.

[34] H.C. Debates, Vol. 32, col. 1513, 1911.

Lloyd George had been working out the details with and making concessions to powerful outside agencies whose failure to co-operate would wreck his whole scheme.   To the House, this part of Bonar Law's criticisms was of little interest—Members were concerned with the points of substance that could be taken up in the battle for power in the Press and on the platforms before the public.   The Liberals were in power and it seemed natural that the Bill had been prepared by the civil servants and that, once the Cabinet had given its approval, it should go through.   In the House there was excitement as each side took up its position. Able speeches won headlines and perhaps office or promotion for the successful Member. It was old-fashioned and impracticable to expect the House to understand, debate and have the power to enforce alterations.   There would have been little point in pursuing Bonar Law's criticisms of the way in which the measure was drafted and passed as the public wanted such legislation and saw nothing wrong with this form of government.   The Cabinet now had a greater freedom of action but it was open to question and argument in the House, and to pressure from specific groups, while its general record in office had to be acceptable to the public. Otherwise the abstention of supporters, renewed energy among opponents and changes of mind among a small section of the electorate could, at set intervals, put an alternative Cabinet in power.

CHAPTER 7

THE DECLINE OF THE HOUSE OF LORDS

As Cabinets became dependent on the decisions of the electorate expressed in terms of majorities in the House of Commons, the real importance of the Lords declined. The views of the peers played no constructive part in the formation of Cabinets or of their long-term policies. It was fundamentally a sign of weakness that the Lords were able to assert themselves only by exercising their powers to amend or veto the Cabinet's legislative proposals. These powers were used almost entirely against Liberal Governments and the actual place of the Upper House in the political system was best revealed not when the Lords were engaged in a bout of resistance to radicalism but when the Conservatives were in office or in quiet periods of a Liberal administration.

In this situation, the Lords had a negligible influence over the Cabinet. It was advisable to have some competent peers in high office as governments lost face if their front bench in the Lords was not able to make a reasonable case.[1] The Upper Chamber could, at times, do some useful work tidying up legislation on minor or non-controversial points often with the agreement of the government. The Lords reflected the opinions of a section of the community which, though numerically small, had influence, especially in the Conservative Party. In the earlier years of the period when there was still a possibility of cross-voting in the Commons, Conservative Cabinets were unhappy if the Lords showed signs of wavering. Disraeli felt that their strong endorsement of his Afghanistan policy in December 1878 should steady the ranks in the Lower House.[2] When some peers indicated alarm over the Royal Titles Bill or later over the proposal to create elective county councils, this had to be taken into consideration, though in both cases the governments decided to carry on. Liberal leaders had paid some attention to the views of the aristocracy when the Whig element was still powerful in the party, but after

---

[1] Granville told the Queen that the loss of Lansdowne in July 1880, over the Compensation for Disturbance Bill, would make his position as chief government spokesman in the Lords very difficult: *Letters*, Series II, Vol. III, p. 117.
[2] Monypenny and Buckle, *op. cit.*, Vol. VI, p. 399.

1886 the Lords were so entirely opposed to the major items of Liberal policy that there was no point in attempting conciliation.

The role of the Lords only aroused attention if they decided to exercise their powers to amend and reject Bills. Most peers were prepared to take such action only in exceptional circumstances and agreed with Lord Salisbury that their task was to estimate whether the Commons " does or does not represent the full, the deliberate, the sustained convictions of the body of the nation." [3] Moreover, the Lords could not afford to make such a calculation, reject measures and be proved wrong on more than a very few occasions. If there had been a series of Liberal victories, the powers of the Lords would either have lain dormant and decayed or there would have been a clash and the kind of redefinition which took place in 1911.

So the capacity of the Lords to resist Liberal measures rested on the evidence that a Liberal government was likely, before long, to be replaced by the Conservatives. At first, after Gladstone's great victory in 1868, many wondered if Conservatism could ever reassert itself under the new electoral conditions. The Lords felt the force of a Commons majority of 113 in the debates on the Irish Church and their opposition, though whole-hearted in many individual cases, really only amounted to an attempt to get better financial terms.[4] The Irish Land Bill of 1870 was reluctantly accepted and the Ballot Bill, rejected in 1871, was taken in 1872 because some of the Conservative leadership felt that this was not the time nor the issue on which to fight. But as the vitality of the ministry declined, the political atmosphere altered; there were no more major Bills and so no clashes with the Lords. The evidence that Conservatism could revive and, in 1874, win an election, reassured the peers. If a swing of the political pendulum was to be expected, the Upper House could exercise its powers against a Liberal Cabinet and be vindicated at the next election. In this situation, there were several possible courses of action. One was to introduce moderate amendments in the hope both of appealing to the public and of obtaining concessions from the government. A more drastic course, when a ministry had been in office for a period and appeared to be losing support, was to delay major

---

[3] Lady G. Cecil, *op. cit.*, Vol. II, p. 25.
[4] Monypenny and Buckle, *op. cit.*, Vol. V, p. 105.

items of legislation on the grounds that they should be resubmitted to the electorate. Such delaying actions both embarrassed the government and gave time for a swing to develop. In 1893 when the Queen asked Unionist leaders whether she should try to force Gladstone to dissolve, Lord Salisbury told her that " a dissolution now . . . would arrest a change of opinion which is still incomplete " and that the Lords could, in the meantime, block any unpleasant legislation.[5] Even more extreme, if the Conservative leaders were confident that the political climate had changed, the Lords could flatly reject Liberal measures in the hope, not of altering or delaying them, but of forcing a dissolution. Lord Salisbury first suggested such action at the time of the Arrears Bill of 1882 as he and the leading Conservatives in the Commons agreed that " a dissolution would have been a welcome issue." [6] In late 1884 Lord Salisbury, Lord John Manners and Rowland Wynn wanted to reject the third Reform Bill with the knowledge that Gladstone would reintroduce it in an Autumn Session. If it was once again rejected, they felt the government would be forced to dissolve.[7] This suggestion was not adopted and the election of 1885 did not provide a clear verdict on the wisdom of the Lords' actions during the previous five years.

The next Liberal Government, installed in 1892, faced much more consistent opposition from the Lords. Not only the second Home Rule Bill but most of the major items which had appeared in the Liberal election programme were mutilated or destroyed. The peers grew in confidence as the government was evidently weak, divided and reluctant to accept their challenge, the whole record of the Lords being triumphantly vindicated by the swing to the Conservatives in the general election of 1895.

The Lords were thus in the curious position of not being an important part of the normal constitutional machine and of having virtually no regular influence on the Cabinet, but of playing a major part in the political battles of the period. The large Conservative majority among the peers since the late 1850s had

---

[5] *Letters*, Series III, Vol. II, p. 298.

[6] *Letters*, Series II, Vol. III, p. 329.

[7] Sir A. Hardinge, *op. cit.*, Vol. III, p. 117. A majority of the Shadow Cabinet preferred a compromise and discussions continued till the third Reform Bill included electoral redistribution and was, in this form, accepted. See also C. M. Weston, " The Royal Mediation in 1884," *The Historical Journal*, Vol. 82 (1967), pp. 296–322.

responded to the leadership of the 14th Earl of Derby but after his death it had by no means always obeyed the orders of the Conservative Cabinet.[8]   Disraeli's arrival put an end to this and thereafter Conservative control and use of the Lords was normal. When the Liberals won the election of 1880, Beaconsfield told Salisbury that "much would depend on the management of the House of Lords. . . ."[9]   Despite the dual leadership after Beaconsfield's death, tactics were settled at meetings of the former Conservative Cabinet members from both Houses. Balfour put the position most clearly in a speech at Nottingham after the defeat of 1906 when he said that with the aid of the Lords, "the great Unionist Party should still control, whether in power or whether in opposition, the destinies of this great Empire."[10]   In March 1906, Lord Lansdowne wrote to Balfour that "it is essential that the two wings of the Army should work together."[11] Unity was so well accomplished that the Lords destroyed the Education Bill, the Licensing Bill, Plural Voting, Scottish Small Holdings and Land Valuation Bills but passed the Trades Disputes Bill which they disliked even more, as this accorded with the strategy of the Conservative Shadow Cabinet.

The kind of issue on which management was required by Conservative leaders and where there could be independent action came up in the Arrears Bill of 1882. In this case the peers rejected Lord Salisbury's advice and passed the Bill in part because the Irish landlords feared that their influence would decline even further if there was a dissolution and in part because Conservative Members in the Commons were unhappy both about the outcome and the cost of an election.[12] However, the responsibility for the cardinal blunder of rejecting the 1909 Budget lay with the Shadow Cabinet, Balfour himself having helped to draft the

[8] R. Blake, *Disraeli*, p. 568.
[9] A. J. Balfour, *op. cit.*, p. 123.
[10] Quoted by H. H. Asquith in *Fifty Years of Parliament*, Vol. II, p. 39.
[11] Lansdowne to Balfour, March 5, 1906, *Add. MSS.* 49,729 (*The Balfour Papers*), f. 226.   Kenneth Young in his *Arthur James Balfour*, p. 265, suggests that Balfour was "tactful" and quotes his letter to Lansdowne: "I incline to advise that we should fight all points of difference very stiffly in the Commons, and should make the House of Lords the theatre of compromise." The record shows that there was little compromise over the central items in the Liberal programme of legislation.
[12] See Lady G. Cecil, *op. cit.*, Vol. II, pp. 42–54; Sir A. Hardinge, *op. cit.*, Vol. III, p. 84; A. E. Gathorne-Hardy, *op. cit.*, Vol. II, p. 182 and *Letters*, Series II, Vol. III, pp. 328–329.

resolution which declared "this House is not justified in giving its consent to the Bill until it has been submitted to the judgment of the country." [13] By 1910, the die-hard peers were taking matters into their own hands. A majority of the Conservative leadership was in favour of abandoning further resistance, but old divisions were exacerbated by adversity and Balfour's authority was fading.[14]

In fact in 1910 the Lords had run into the one situation which had always threatened if they made a provocative use of their rights—a run of Liberal victories. If, fulfilling no essential function in the machinery of government, the Lords used their powers on purely party lines and were not vindicated at the next election, the Liberals were bound to retaliate. The Parliament Act of 1911 only prevented the Lords blocking the major policy proposals on which a non-Conservative Government had won an election. The whole experience of this struggle forced the Lords to appreciate and be content with the position to which they had been relegated when Cabinets became dependent first on the House of Commons and then on the electorate. Between 1868 and 1911, governments found the House of Lords useful for certain routine purposes, but otherwise the peers exercised influence only when Liberal Cabinets had to consider them as a powerful addition to the forces which the Conservative opposition could bring to bear.

---

[13] B. E. C. Dugdale, *op. cit.*, Vol. II, p. 58. The object in 1909 was to use the power to reject the Budget to force a dissolution as the Conservatives were convinced that they could win an election.

[14] *Ibid.*, p. 68.

CHAPTER 8

THE ROLE OF THE PRESS

ONCE the politicians began to look beyond the confines of Parliament and to concentrate on the reactions of the electorate, they faced the problem of communication. It was important to follow the movements of public opinion. The most obvious and still very sound method was to listen to the reports of the Whips who collected the views of Members and the news from local agents and party enthusiasts. In addition, ministers received letters and had their own contacts, often relying on a few personal impressions and a hunch as to which were valid. The danger in such parliamentary and personal reactions was that too much emphasis might be placed on London opinion and on the situation as viewed from Westminster. Some indications could be gleaned from the Press.

Most methods of contact worked both ways but the Press differed in that its function of conveying political information to the electorate became much more important than its own views or its capacity to reflect popular attitudes. In the 1850s and 1860s there was a relatively large number of papers in London and a few, notably *The Times*, had stimulated and even started lines of argument in governing circles. An expanded electorate invited a wider spread of political news and party propaganda and the Press became an essential link between the men in public life and voters. After the telegraph came into general use in the 1870s there was a rapid growth in the provincial Press, most big cities having one or more morning papers of reasonable quality usually supplemented by working men's evening *news*papers.

In these years, the pattern of journalistic behaviour was clear-cut. Most papers had a definite party allegiance, but they provided full reports of all speeches by men of any prominence and M.P.s received at least a column in their local paper.[1] Men of great

---

[1] J. A. Spender, editor of the *Eastern Morning News* in Hull in the 1880s said: " It never occurred to us as possible that speeches by Gladstone, Salisbury, Joseph Chamberlain or Harcourt should receive less than the full honours of a verbatim report." *Life, Journalism and Politics*, Vol. I, p. 34.

ability worked on an anonymous basis for such papers as *The Times,* the *Daily Telegraph,* the *Daily News,* and the *Standard.* Their leading articles were vigorously written and helped to build up the assumption that government was a matter of argument until the correct solutions were reached. It was because the Press concentrated on providing political news and had avowed party ties, that it had almost no direct influence on political fortunes or on the Cabinet. What could be done, on occasion, was to concentrate attention on one or two issues or individuals and, by providing new information, make the politicians take up a position, or by exciting informed public opinion, force the politicians to react. For instance, in 1870 when Russia decided to abrogate the sections of the Treaty of Paris governing the neutrality of the Black Sea, the Press whipped up public feeling and Queen Victoria asked Granville: " Could any hint be given to the leading journals to refrain from rousing the war spirit?" Gladstone procrastinated till there was more calm.[2] With more effect, W. T. Stead, editor of the *Pall Mall Gazette* (who had been primed by Arnold Forster and some Naval officers) produced a series of articles in 1884 entitled " The Truth about the Navy." In these years public men were beginning to have an uneasy feeling that the world was not such a safe place for Britain. Stead's articles roused this sentiment and focused attention on one evident source of danger. There was a marked reaction from most of those interested in British policy, including M.Ps. and Liberal ministers. The Cabinet decided to introduce a supplementary Naval estimate of £3 million without waiting for the First Lord of the Admiralty to return from a visit to Egypt.[3] In a similar way, when anxiety about the Irish problem was acute in 1886, Stead brought the ruthless evictions on Lord Clanricarde's estate before English newspaper readers and, though nothing could change Unionist policy, the need to prevent such examples of landlordism was widely felt.

A natural part of political criticism in the Press was to attack the record of any minister or opposition leader who seemed to be particularly vulnerable. This had little effect if the ministers, as

---

[2] W. E. Mosse, " Public Opinion and Foreign Policy: The British Public and the War-Scare of November, 1870," *The Historical Journal,* Vol. VI (1963), p. 50, and the same author's " The End of the Crimean System: England, Russia and the Neutrality of the Black Sea, 1870–71," *ibid.,* Vol. IV (1961), pp. 164–190.

[3] B. Mallet, *Earl of Northbrook, A Memoir,* pp. 205–215.

in the case of Henry Bruce in 1870 or of Cardwell in 1871, were pursuing Cabinet policy. But when feeling in the party and the Cabinet was divided, the Press (especially if it was normally friendly) could provide extra ammunition for one side. W. E. Forster resigned in 1881 because he was not satisfied about the conditions exacted from Parnell before the latter's release from prison. It would be hard to estimate how far the campaign against Forster's policy conducted by John Morley in the *Pall Mall Gazette* contributed to this result. Forster was definitely worried by the criticisms which culminated in a call for his resignation, but probably the most that can be said is that Morley strengthened the feeling among Liberals that a new departure in Ireland was needed and thus made it easier for the Cabinet to face the loss of Forster.[4] The Liberal Press likewise probably helped Gladstone to pass over the ageing Lord Granville when forming his Cabinet in 1886.[5]

For their part, most politicians did not trouble about the Press as a whole but both parties wanted, at any rate in the 1860s and 1870s, to win the approval of *The Times* when they came to form a government. In 1868 Disraeli wrote to Delane, the Editor, " I can't resist sending you a line of congratulation on the successful manner in which our Chancellor of the Exchequer has been received " and later in the same year Delane notes that Gladstone not only wrote to give him a full list of the new Liberal Cabinet but was " most attentive " when they met at dinner.[6] During this ministry, Granville corresponded almost daily with Delane but *The Times*' support for the government declined sooner even than that of the electorate and was transferred at once to Disraeli's new Cabinet in 1874. Despite the attention Delane (till he retired in 1877) and then John Walter received from the leading politicians, the correspondence of such men as Gladstone and Granville, while covering the entire decision-making process, gives no indication that they changed the form or content of their policies to conciliate the Press.[7] The prestige and pre-

---

4 F. W. Hirst in *The Early Life and Letters of John Morley*, Vol. II, pp. 96 and 114, certainly overestimates the power of the Press when he says, " It was Mr. Morley whose rapier thrust gave the *coup de grâce* to his [Forster's] ministerial career."

5 Lord E. Fitzmaurice, *op. cit.*, Vol. II, pp. 480–481.

6 A. I. Dasent, *John Delane, 1817–1879*, pp. 222, 229.

7 See *Political Correspondence of Mr. Gladstone and Lord Granville, 1876–1886*, ed. A. Ramm.

eminence of *The Times* declined after its blunders in using the forged Pigott letters in 1887 and its too close association with partisan Unionist politics.[8]

A rather different use was made of the Press when there were differences within a government. For instance, the 1880–85 Liberal Ministry contained several factions, some ministers entering into close relations with journalists so that they could prepare the ground for an argument in Cabinet and provide their followers in the party with ammunition. W. E. Forster had connections with Chenery of *The Times* and Mudford of the *Standard*, while Dilke usually turned to Hill of the *Daily News*. Joseph Chamberlain's close co-operation with Morley on the *Pall Mall Gazette* (and sometimes with Escott on the *Standard*) was conducted with an air of statesmanship, though it had elements of the later type of Press-and-politician alliance. These contacts caused some stir in political circles but did little to affect the formation of policy and the position of individuals, though they did serve to bring down Gladstone's severe displeasure on the persons involved.[9]

In general, then, the influence of the Press was small, though favourable treatment always heartened politicians and, on a few specific points, newspapers could increase interest that was already stirring so that action came more rapidly. The papers did, by their news and stories, stimulate the concern with Empire and helped to create a climate of opinion in which it was possible to lay down a major programme of Naval expansion in the Navy Act of 1889. But they were not reliable as a guide to public feeling. Lord Derby observed in October 1876 that, " we are fairly well supported in the Press, which I suspect is a better test than provincial meetings. *Pall Mall, Telegraph, Post* and *Standard*—for; *Times* uncertain and trimming; only *D. News* and *Echo* against us." [10] How far this was true in 1876 cannot be judged, but in 1880 the Conservatives still had the vast majority of the metropolitan papers behind them and lost the election. After the

---

[8] Viscount Chilston, "The Tories and Parnell, 1885–1891," *Parliamentary Affairs*, Vol. XIV (1960–61), pp. 55–71.

[9] This is discussed by J. A. Spender in *The Public Life*, Vol. II, pp. 96–97.

[10] Monypenny and Buckle, *op. cit.*, Vol. VI, p. 76. Even as the results of the 1880 election came in, Queen Victoria clung to the thought that "the newspapers, except the really violent ones, are all so strong in support of Lord Beaconsfield that the Queen feels sure that there will be the very greatest difficulty in forming a Government." *Ibid.*, p. 526.

Home Rule split, the two leading Scottish papers, the *Scotsman* and the *Glasgow Herald*, both went Unionist and yet the Liberals normally still won two-thirds of the seats in Scotland. The most striking evidence that the Press neither reflected nor moulded public opinion came in 1906 when the Conservatives suffered their overwhelming defeat after six years in which the papers had pilloried Sir Henry Campbell-Bannerman and given solid support to the government. Most of the leading statesmen, as has been said, knew the uses of the papers but disregarded them as serious political factors. J. S. Sandars, Balfour's faithful private secretary, noted that when the Esher Committee Report on War Office Reform came out, " I think . . . I should manipulate the Press, not an agreeable task, but I think a necessary one." [11] Yet Balfour himself never bothered to read any papers and both Grey and Bonar Law were indifferent to their comments. Rosebery was hypersensitive, but his longing for approval was such that he abandoned public life rather than face the inevitable buffets.

In the 1890s the techniques and conduct of the newspaper industry underwent a series of changes. The introduction of the rotary press made mass production possible and the need for advertising revenue led more papers to seek a large circulation. In trying to please a wider public journalists discovered that politics was only part, and not even a major part, of the average man's interests. As circulations rose, the number of papers declined and Fleet Street was stratified into the old (and shrinking) " heavies " and the newer penny Press modelled on the *Daily Mail*. At the same time splits in the Liberal Party over imperialism and later among Conservatives over protection produced repeated attempts to capture the traditional party organs. In part these efforts were made because internal warfare is often more intense than the struggle between the parties, in part because the faithful might be swayed by the attitude of the paper they trusted. H. W. Massingham, the leading radical opponent of Liberal Imperialism, was evicted from the *Daily Chronicle* in 1899. In return, the pro-Boers captured the *Daily News* in 1900 and replaced its editor, E. T. Cook, by an anti-imperialist, R. C. Lehmann. These transactions, followed by open attempts to obtain political influence through the ownership of papers, all drew attention to the public-

[11] *Balfour Papers, Add. MSS.* 49,762, f. 49

relations aspect of politics and exaggerated the importance of the Press. It is curious that such men as Harmsworth and Max Aitken, who realised that the interests and attitudes of the public were slow in forming and largely habitual (and allowed for these conditions in the news and entertainment sides of their papers), still thought they could easily influence political loyalties.

They could, with some truth, have countered that they did not think that Liberals could be changed into Conservatives, but that ardent partisans were open to argument about tactics or the application of particular principles. In the internal dispute over tariff reform, Conservative papers such as *The Observer* had some influence. When *The Times, Daily Mail, Manchester Courier* and *Yorkshire Post* all advised Bonar Law to give up food taxes and concentrate only on defeating Home Rule, they revealed the feeling of Conservative voters and gave it weight and precision. Austen Chamberlain said that ". . . the loss of *The Times* is serious and I do not underrate it." [12] Bonar Law wanted to retain at least imperial preference in his programme, but the defection of Lord Derby and the open revolt of the Lancashire Unionists, supported by the Conservative Press, all helped to convince him that party sentiment was otherwise. The result was that he bowed to the general feeling that he should remain as leader but with a modified policy.[13] It was certainly easier to influence the Shadow Cabinet, though members of the Liberal Government also used their contacts in Fleet Street. Haldane was undoubtedly helped in gaining acceptance for his Army reforms and recruits for the Territorials by the support of *The Times* and later of the *Daily Mail*.[14] In the recurrent battle over Naval estimates, J. L. Garvin in *The Observer* was able to put the case of the Sea Lords [15] while the economists, Lloyd George and Winston Churchill, were buoyed up by the backing of the Liberal Press.[16] Looking back on the outcome of these disputes in 1908, 1909 and 1914, the important factors seem to have been the stand of the Sea Lords and their Cabinet spokesmen, the march of events (above all, the level of German shipbuilding) and finally the views of the Prime Minister. The newspapers, despite all the claims made for them, were useful

---

[12] Austen Chamberlain, *Politics from Inside*, p. 500.
[13] See R. Blake, *op. cit.*, pp. 112–114.
[14] Sir F. Maurice, *Lord Haldane*, Vol. I, pp. 228 and 240.
[15] A. M. Gollin, *J. L. Garvin and the Observer*, pp. 52–55.
[16] Lucy Masterman, *op. cit.*, p. 124.

in providing outlets for information and in exemplifying aspects of public opinion, but it is impossible to find a single major decision taken primarily because of journalistic pressure.[17]

While most papers had simply to meet the needs of their customers and therefore had to provide the kind of news that was wanted, they could use their role as intermediaries to try to damage individuals or whip up particular interests. The entire Northcliffe Press turned on the Insurance Act of 1911 and sought to arouse middle class ladies, doctors and domestic servants against it. The campaign failed, but it gave the ministers involved a much heavier task. J. A. Spender quotes a newspaper magnate as saying "the power of the Press is to suppress " [18] and when a chain began a vendetta against a politician, as Northcliffe did against C. F. G. Masterman, it could be damaging and unnerving. It was little comfort to reflect that such tactics would not work against the first flight of party leaders, whose performances had a news value that could not be ignored and whose personalities were too well known to permit of gross distortion.

The Press, then, had a vital task in acting as the link between public men and the electorate. So long as it concentrated on this function it exercised very little influence. Later, when ambitious men and politicians sought to use the Press for particular political ends, they encountered serious obstacles. The cheaper journals with a mass circulation found that the reactions of their readers were formed by long-term and inarticulate processes that were not readily affected by leading articles, while too obvious attempts at propaganda only aroused suspicion and even ridicule.[19] Serious and informed comment in the columns of *The Times,* the *Westminster Gazette* or *The Observer* reached only a small circle of those concerned about public affairs and though new ideas and information could be brought forward, they were only effective if the body of the electorate was ready to move in the given direction. Cabinets wanted a favourable Press and political leaders in both parties could benefit from discriminatory support, but all this was within the context of existing political disputes. General

[17] A case could be made out that some minor attitudes or actions (such as the hostility towards King Leopold's policy in the Congo) were largely determined by Press revelations and campaigns.

[18] J. A. Spender, *The Public Life,* Vol. II, p. 111.

[19] Such as the *Daily Mail* had earned by its twists and turns between 1903 and 1905. Gollin, *op. cit.,* p. 14.

elections were fought at intervals of several years with a choice between the overall record of one party or the promises of the other, a situation which gave political leaders a solid foundation to work on and one which was not fundamentally affected by blasts from Fleet Street.

But in a less evident manner, the conduct of newspapers could affect the atmosphere in which various parts of the constitution worked. When papers in the 1870s and 1880s had printed so much of what was said in Parliament or on the platform, they helped to keep issues before the public and to encourage politicians to explain their views. All this maintained the prestige of Members of Parliament and emphasised the importance of *how* decisions were taken, as well as making people aware of the reasons for these decisions. The later trend to pay more attention to sport, personalities and sensational events was a genuine reflection of the interests of a much wider reading public, but it also tended to demote Parliament. Attention slowly shifted from the arguments as to whether a policy was right or wrong to the feelings of well-being or adversity produced by a policy. At the same time, papers and public both came to realise that, in the conditions of politics after the turn of the century, the views of private Members and of minor politicians had little effect on events and were therefore not worth noticing. The total effect was a subtle change which emphasised the decisions of the Cabinet, the views of opposition leaders and the reactions (on a broad level) of the electorate—all of which tended to reduce interest in Parliament and in the formation of policy and thus gave the Cabinet greater scope, provided the general taste left in people's mouths was acceptable.

CHAPTER 9

POLITICS AND THE CROWN

IN a previous chapter, the degree of influence open to Queen Victoria was estimated. As the Queen had to be consulted and could comment on any matter that attracted her attention, she helped to create the atmosphere in which the senior ministers worked and her views had always to be noted, if not considered. When statesmen or Cabinets had definite policies and secure positions, the Crown was merely offering another opinion, there being no power to enforce royal suggestions. But where the situation was indeterminate, when great men hesitated to accept the burdens of office, or the Prime Minister had no definite candidate for a post, respect for the Crown and the cogency of the Queen's arguments might tilt the balance. Naturally Queen Victoria preferred mid-century politics when so much was indeterminate or dependent on the relations between a small number of men whom she knew personally.

After 1868, the Queen came to dislike the changed conditions of public life because new factors were introduced—the electorate, strong partisan feelings, problems requiring legislation—which she did not fully comprehend and because clear-cut decisions at general elections narrowed the field in which her advice and personal influence could have any effect. A certain result at the polls meant that the Queen had to accept certain men as her ministers and endorse their policies without any of the conversations and negotiations which had allowed her to feel she played a real part in the 1840s and 1850s. As she protested " She *won't* be a *machine*. But the Liberals always wish to make her *feel* THAT, and she *won't accept it*." [1] On only one occasion in the rest of her reign was there any doubt about which party would take office. When Gladstone was defeated in June 1885 Lord Salisbury hesitated in case a minority Conservative Government would give the Liberals time to recover before the general election. Gathorne-Hardy noted that Salisbury's " feeling for the Queen, who cannot

[1] *Letters*, Series II, Vol. III, p. 594–595.

retire or resign—like Richmond's, John Manners', and mine—
was such as to overbear all other considerations, and to this Beach
came fully round." [2] At an earlier meeting of the ex-Cabinet on this
question, only Hicks Beach and Lord George Hamilton had been
in favour of remaining in opposition and the party had strongly
urged the leadership to take office, but the Queen's feelings provided an added and satisfying motive for acceptance. In every
other instance, the Queen's views had no effect whatever on the
kind of government that was formed, for while she strove hard
to get Liberal Unionist support for Lord Salisbury in 1886, the
decision to back a Unionist Government was never in doubt.

For the same reasons, ministries lasted till they suffered defeat
at the polls or chose to resign. On one or two occasions the Queen
wrote to " her ministers " in such strong terms that the recipients
said further denunciations might lead them to resign. In May
1882 Lord Granville felt that " some sentences in her letter (on
the Phoenix Park murders) are such as would almost require our
resignation if I were to show the letter to my colleagues." [3] When
Gladstone received the famous telegram *en clair* saying that the
death of Gordon might have been prevented by earlier action, he
took the matter up with Sir Henry Ponsonby " as a question of
whether he could remain in office if publicly condemned by the
Queen." [4] Even Disraeli, stung by the comment that his policy
of neutrality in the Near East was " a painful humiliation," replied
that while the Cabinet could not in honour resign, " Your Majesty
has the clear constitutional right to dismiss them." [5] Yet in none of
these cases was there any serious possibility of the Cabinet giving
up office on the Queen's account. In each instance, the government was subject to fierce attacks by the opposition and their own
party would never have considered surrender. Also, to resign
in such situations because of lack of royal confidence would have
branded the Queen as a partisan and have meant that subsequent
battles would have turned on her intervention rather than on
the merits of the case. Neither Gladstone, Granville nor Disraeli

[2] E. A. Gathorne-Hardy, *op. cit.*, Vol. II, p. 220.
[3] Arthur Ponsonby, *Henry Ponsonby, his Life from his Letters*, p. 191.
[4] *Letters*, Series II, Vol. III, p. 603.
[5] Monypenny and Buckle, *op. cit.*, Vol. VI, p. 246. R. Blake's comment on this remark is that it " was nonsense and both Disraeli and the Queen must have known it." *Disraeli*, p. 548.

would ever have put the Queen in this position and their comments were really serving notice that such extreme or open criticism must cease.

Had either King Edward VII or King George V refused the advice of their ministers in the crisis of 1910–11, this would have been tantamount to a dismissal. It is hard to say what Edward VII's ultimate reactions might have been, or how much should be read into such remarks as " this government may not last " (made in February 1910).[6] His statements that he would not accept advice all deal with specific situations such as a refusal to create peers without a second appeal to the country. George V muddled through chiefly on the advice of Knollys but he does not appear to have realised that, had he refused the promise to create peers and had Asquith then resigned, Balfour taking over and dissolving, the King would have been drawn into the political controversy.[7] It was always open (as it is today) for the monarch to dismiss a government in the sense that such an action has never been forbidden, but to do so would have been contrary to the working principles of the constitution and would have led to an immediate controversy and probably a tacit or explicit prohibition.[8]

Just as the decisions of the electorate and the reactions of the politicians presented the Crown with certain governments, the same forces removed any element of choice in the appointment of a Prime Minister in all but a few exceptional situations. In February 1868, when Derby resigned, Disraeli was the natural choice, though the Queen could possibly have turned to Stanley or to Richmond. No Conservative leader then had the clear backing of the whole party or a strong hold on the electorate. Indeed, dissatisfaction among Conservatives in Parliament increased so

---

[6] Dudley Sommer, *Haldane of Cloan*, p. 230. The King may simply have been thinking of the frequent reports that the Irish might abandon Asquith if he proceeded with the Budget before tackling the problem of the House of Lords.

[7] This emerges from his remark in 1913 that had he known that Balfour was prepared to form a government (a fact suppressed by Knollys), he might have refused to give a guarantee. Roy Jenkins, *Asquith*, p. 220, says this would have been " an act of constitutional folly which might well have affected not only his personal position but the whole future of the British monarchy." See also Philip Magnus, *King Edward VII*, p. 460.

[8] This is why I cannot accept F. Hardie's argument that this possibility constituted part of the influence of the Crown. To be " possible " an action must be capable of repetition or at any rate not lead in the near future to further restrictions on the Crown. See *The Political Influence of Queen Victoria*, pp. 84–85.

much after the defeat in late 1868 that there was talk of replacing Disraeli. The malcontents assumed that if the party clearly appointed a spokesman and rallied to him, the Crown would endorse their choice after an election had been won. Gathorne-Hardy noted that there was no machinery for ensuring this result, but if the Queen nominated an individual whom they had all agreed to repudiate as leader, no one would join his Cabinet and the task would be handed on to a more acceptable person.[9] In the years after 1871, however, Disraeli completely restored his position and by 1874 there was no question of commissioning any-one else. During Disraeli's ministry, the struggle over Near Eastern policy destroyed any confidence that had remained between the Queen and Gladstone. When it became evident that the Liberals were winning the election of 1880, Queen Victoria declared " she will sooner *abdicate* than send for or have any *communication* with that *half-mad fire-brand* who would soon ruin everything and be a *Dictator*." [10] She summoned Hartington and then Granville, who both explained that only Gladstone with his great popular following could lead the party, and so the Queen was left with no alternative. When the Gladstone ministry resigned, there were two Conservative leaders, Sir Stafford Northcote in the Commons and Lord Salisbury in the Upper House. It was well known, however, that several prominent members of the opposition would not consider serving under Northcote, so that Salisbury's position rested on the fairly evident preference of the Conservative element in the electorate and of the Conservative Members of both the House of Commons and the House of Lords. A year later the Liberal split led to some discussion as to whether the Liberal Unionist Hartington or the Conservative Salisbury should lead the anti-Home Rule government, but the negotiations were carried on directly between the two statesmen with Queen Victoria making appeals for unity in the background. Any prospect of a Liberal revival filled the Queen with alarm and she carefully considered alternatives to Gladstone as a dissolution approached in 1892. The most suitable person from her point of view was Lord Rosebery and she had intended summoning him till an attack by Rosebery on Lord Salisbury made her abandon

9 A. E. Gathorne-Hardy, *op. cit.*, Vol. I, p. 305.
10 A. Ponsonby, *op. cit.*, p. 184.

the project.[11] Harcourt was mentioned, but ultimately the Queen " supposes she will have that dangerous old fanatic thrust down her throat," though it will only be because " her hand is forced." [12]

The occasion when Queen Victoria's intervention is most commonly held to have been decisive was in the selection of Lord Rosebery to succeed Gladstone as premier in 1894.[13] It was evident early in the '90s that the Grand Old Man, though apparently inexhaustible, could not go on for many years. Morley and Harcourt had agreed not to support a peer as Liberal Prime Minister in 1891, but since then Harcourt's ill-temper had alienated his ally and most of his colleagues. When, on January 9, 1894, Gladstone was left in a minority over the Naval estimates and was clearly on the verge of retirement (or ejection, as he regarded it), negotiations became almost continuous.[14] The key was Harcourt's unpleasantness and Morley's reluctant adhesion to " the leading junta inside the Cabinet " consisting of Rosebery, Spencer, Acland and Asquith.[15] Harcourt had no followers, and if those just mentioned refused to join, a Cabinet under his leadership was impossible. The chief intriguer was Harcourt's son, Lou Lou Harcourt, who tried to entice Morley with the offer of the Exchequer or the Foreign Office under Harcourt, but Morley was indecisive and " Rosebery at last definitely accepted the obligation, and agreed that he would under any circumstances undertake to go on with the task if the Queen sent for him." [16] Harcourt, aware of the feeling against him and sensing the drift to Rosebery, merely tried to insist on certain conditions before he would join a Cabinet led by a peer. On March 3, Gladstone resigned and the Queen sent for Rosebery.[17]

Whether the royal action was decisive depends on the answer

---

[11] Queen Victoria to Sir Henry Ponsonby, May 30, 1892; *Letters*, Series III, Vol. II, p. 120 and A. Ponsonby, *op. cit.*, 215.

[12] *Ibid.*, p. 216.

[13] The best accounts are Rosebery's Diary printed in *History To-Day*, January 1952; Morley, *Recollections*, Vol. II, pp. 1–22 and A. G. Gardiner, *The Life of Sir William Harcourt*, Vol. II, pp. 252–270.

[14] Harcourt gave Gladstone partial support, but said he could find the money for the increased Naval estimates and Gladstone turned his back on Harcourt while the latter was speaking. Sir Edward Hamilton reported Rosebery as saying, " Mr. G. had apparently carried with him not one of his colleagues, unless it was Shaw Lefevre." R. R. James, *Rosebery*, p. 296.

[15] Morley, *op. cit.*, Vol. II, p. 11.

[16] *Ibid.*, pp. 15–16.

[17] The best account is in R. R. James, *op. cit.*, Chapter 9.

to one question. If the Queen had summoned Harcourt, would
the Rosebery group have carried through their plan to refuse to
serve? A failure by Harcourt, or the summoning of Spencer or
Kimberley, would all alike have led to the only other alternative,
a Cabinet formed by Rosebery.[18] The answer will never be
known, but Morley, Rosebery, Asquith,[19] Harcourt's biographer,
A. G. Gardiner and the authoritative biography of Rosebery by
R. R. James all accept that by this stage the matter was settled in
Rosebery's favour.[20] The one close observer who thought otherwise was J. A. Spender, editor of the *Westminster Gazette*. He
argued that though " the vows (not to serve) were certainly loud
and deep as regards Harcourt," none of the reasons for refusing
could have been put in public and that the other ministers would
have fallen in with him rather than reveal personal dissensions.[21]
There is something in this, but the objections to Harcourt were
deep-seated and there would have been no need for public
explanations by those reluctant to serve. It would merely have
been announced that, after discussions, Sir William Harcourt had
failed to form a Cabinet and the Queen had sent for Lord Rosebery. The whole episode is instructive because it shows that even
in an area where the Crown had traditionally some freedom of
choice, it was not a matter simply of pulling names out of a hat.
An element of choice could arise only in very special circumstances
when the normal process for selecting a leader had not had time
to operate or had reached deadlock and even then the choice was
likely to be restricted to two possibilities, with strong indications
that one was more likely to succeed.

King Edward VII was never faced with a situation involving
a similar degree of choice. In 1906, the Liberal Party looked,
almost without exception, to Sir Henry Campbell-Bannerman
and to have passed him over would have led to an outcry. This

---

[18] Spencer, though preferred by Gladstone, had been a constant member of the
group which had urged Rosebery to accept the premiership. Kimberley was
the official leader in the Lords but was " a Rosebery man " also.
[19] H. H. Asquith, *Memories and Reflections*, p. 135.
[20] Gardiner says " the decision rested with Harcourt's colleagues in the Government and sensible as they were of his title they were equally sensible of the
difficulties of his temper " . . . " and Lord Rosebery was clearly emerging
as the choice of the Cabinet ": *op. cit.*, Vol. II, pp. 261–262. There can be
no doubt that Rosebery would have refused to serve under Harcourt and
this alone would probably have been enough to prevent the formation of
a Cabinet.
[21] J. A. Spender, *Life, Journalism and Politics*, Vol. I, pp. 55–56.

was recognised by the former Liberal Imperialists, Grey, Asquith
and Haldane. They decided to accept Campbell-Bannerman
but to refuse office unless he went to the Lords. Haldane records
that " to place this on a sure foundation it was felt that we needed
the sympathy and possible co-operation of King Edward." [22]
Knollys, the King's Secretary, asked them whether they would
not be better to join the Cabinet in any case.[23] When the time
came, the King did mention a peerage to Campbell-Bannerman
but there was no question of any pressure. The new Prime
Minister decided to stay in the Commons and the Liberal
Imperialists ultimately agreed to accept office under him. As
Campbell-Bannerman's health declined in late 1907, Morley talked
of preferring Grey as his successor and Esher insisted that the
King " would exercise his prerogative unaided." [24] In practice,
this meant that the King, after soundings by Knollys, turned to
H. H. Asquith as by far the most acceptable candidate both to
the Cabinet and to the party.

It had, then, been evident since the 1830s that the Crown could
not impose ministers on the Commons or policies on the Cabinet,
but there had been scope for some influence. Once parties
hardened and Cabinets came to power with definite programmes
backed by reliable majorities in the House, the area open to royal
influence narrowed. Whether the Crown had any influence at
all really depended on how far the Prime Minister was prepared to
accept royal suggestions on matters where neither the party nor
the Cabinet had any strong convictions. Historians have, in this
context, spent far too much time on the fascinating subject of
the Queen's attitude to her ministers when such effect as the
Crown could exert depended on the ministers' attitude to her and
therefore to her advice. Gladstone, for example, had the greatest
deference for the Crown but believed that it should never intervene
in political decisions. In his 1868–74 ministry, Queen Victoria
was barely consulted over even the most important matters.
Ponsonby noted in 1873 that her ministers " seem to care less and
less what they submit to her." [25] After Disraeli had revived

[22] Haldane, *Autobiography*, p. 159.
[23] D. Sommer, *op. cit.*, p. 147–148.
[24] Esher, *op. cit.*, Vol. II, p. 256.
[25] A. Ponsonby, *op. cit.*, p. 76. Goschen had remarked that " the best form
of government was a Queen who always lived in Scotland and never troubled
her ministers." *Ibid.*, p. 71.

the practice of constant consultation, the Queen wanted to know what was happening in Gladstone's second Cabinet but was only told about appointments and decisions. She lamented " the utter disregard of all my opinions which after forty-five years of experience ought to be considered " and Granville, the only minister she trusted, " never *even answers* my remarks ! ! !" [26] Disraeli brilliantly developed a relationship which permitted him to confide whatever he wanted to the Queen (giving him great personal pleasure) and to have the royal influence, for what it was worth, ranged behind him. At some points the Queen's support, built up by Disraeli, outran the possibilities of the situation, but the only occasions on which he had to change his plans to meet royal enthusiasm were over the Public Worship Regulation Bill of 1874 and the Royal Titles Bill of 1876 and over some minor points of ecclesiastical patronage. Some of Disraeli's colleagues were worried by the pleasure he got out of cultivating this relationship. In 1874 Derby asked " is there not just a risk of encouraging her in too large ideas of her personal power?" [27]

For Lord Salisbury, the monarchy was an essential institution and he had a great respect for the Queen, yet Mary Ponsonby noted his " utter lack of sentimentalism about the Crown." [28] When Queen Victoria objected to Brodrick's appointment as Under-Secretary at the War Office, Lord Salisbury remained adamant till she gave in. [29] His usual argument in such circumstances was that " for Lord Salisbury to ' put his foot down ' on a question when the great majority of his Cabinet . . . are against him, would mean breaking up the government " and H.M. would not want this. [30] Salisbury was completely impervious to outside criticism once his mind was made up and this included the Crown. Edward VII urged him " not to consent to . . . an inquiry " over the South African War and was told that

> " he has *no* power to interpose such a veto against a decision of the Cabinet. His colleagues would have the right to refuse to be overruled by the Prime Minister; and in a matter which they regard as a question of honourable adherence to a pledge they would doubtless do so." [31]

[26] *Letters*, Series II, Vol. III, pp. 298–300.
[27] R. Blake, *op. cit.*, p. 548.   [28] Mary Ponsonby, *A Memoir*, p. 69.
[29] The Earl of Midleton, *op. cit.*, p. 93.
[30] *Letters*, Series III, Vol. III, p. 485. Midleton, *op. cit.*, p. 159.
[31] Lord Salisbury to King Edward, June 14, 1902, *Salisbury Papers*.

King Edward sent this letter on to Lord Knollys with a covering note saying that he accepted the situation but that Lord Salisbury "ought to have let me know sooner the decision of the Cabinet. The latter is apparently so powerful a body neither I or (*sic*) the Prime Minister can gainsay them." [32]

A. J. Balfour seldom invoked the authority of the Cabinet and simply assumed that political decisions were taken by the politicians. He regarded the Prime Minister's task as being purely a matter of operating the governmental machine and earned the dislike of the Court for being too explicit on this point.[33] It was not surprising that King Edward preferred the genial Campbell-Bannerman and "found his new ministers readier than their predecessors to consult his wishes in ceremonial and other matters which touched his *amour propre*." [34] By the time George V came to the throne it was fully appreciated by both sides that the Crown only had the rights to be consulted, to encourage, and to warn.[35] When the King was faced with the advice of his ministers, though distasteful to him (as over the guarantee to create peers), he accepted and they went about their political business, only considering his views if it was a matter concerning the royal family or if the King had some special interest or contribution to make. The Prime Minister most open to royal influence was Lord Rosebery, not so much because his position was weak, but because of his intense desire to be appreciated, above all by the Queen. When she attacked Home Rule and other features of the Liberal programme Rosebery was profoundly miserable, attributed them to the legacy of Gladstone (which, as the Queen retorted, he could now cast aside) and finally seemed almost to apologise for any connection with the party he was leading.

While the condition of politics in the 1850s had meant that ministers sometimes talked over issues with the Crown before they were settled in Cabinet and Prime Ministers did, at times, recount divergent views, such practices declined after 1868. Though

---

[32] *Royal Archives*, Vol. R 22, f. 98.

[33] See the criticisms of Sir Sidney Lee, *King Edward VII*, Vol. II, pp. 43–44 and 188. Balfour told the King little and Edward could probably have found out more about the Cabinet crisis over tariff reform in 1903 from the newspapers than he could have learnt from Balfour's Cabinet letters.

[34] *Ibid.*, pp. 445–446.

[35] As a young man he had summarised and learnt Bagehot's famous precepts. Sir Harold Nicolson, *King George V*, p. 61.

Gladstone was prepared to explain problems to Queen Victoria, often at wearying length, he did not enumerate the views of his colleagues, reporting only what the Cabinet decided. This contributed to Disraeli's success. His entertaining accounts delighted the Queen, who was reported as saying " that she had never had such letters in her life . . . she never before knew *everything.*" [36] Yet the motive was partly pleasure derived by the Prime Minister and partly that her lectures delivered at the right time to wavering Cabinet colleagues might be helpful; there was no intention of listening to royal advice. So when Gladstone resumed in 1880 he received complaints that he was informing the Queen of decisions rather than putting before her the advice of her ministers. Gladstone tried to argue that he did not use the word " decide " in such questions, but whatever the form of words, the effect was the same.[37] Although the Queen sent minatory letters to Lord Rosebery, he conducted foreign policy (which was about all his government could do) on his own.

Balfour was more explicit on this matter and was determined that the King would not see confidential Cabinet papers " as of right." The policies being matured in Cabinet were none of his business. " It is impossible for us to yield on matters of this kind " and the King was only told of decisions, even in areas of special interest to him, such as the working of the Committee of Imperial Defence.[38] Asquith wrote a two- or three-page letter after each Cabinet meeting " biased, not to mislead the King, but to interest him. Foreign and military discussions were described at greater length . . . and any matters of specifically royal concern were given extra stress." There was also " Asquith's bland economy of style and his natural desire to give the King an impression of a united and decisive Cabinet. 'After much discussion the Estimates were in substance approved,' he wrote, . . . after a particularly difficult and indecisive meeting on the naval building programme." [39]

Excluded in this way from the formation of policy, royal influence depended on the attitude of leading ministers and how

[36] R. Blake, *op. cit.*, p. 492.
[37] *Political Correspondence of Mr. Gladstone and Lord Granville, 1876–1886,* ed. A. Ramm, Vol. I, pp. 246–247.
[38] K. Young, *op. cit.*, pp. 201–202, and Sir P. Magnus, *op. cit.*, pp. 280–281.
[39] R. Jenkins, *op. cit.*, pp. 185–186.

far they were willing to listen to royal arguments. These could have some effect in two fields; in minor political or patronage appointments and in special aspects of policy. The same situation held in both cases. When the Prime Minister insisted, as over the appointment of Clarendon to the Foreign Office in 1868, he got his way. Queen Victoria complained to the Prince of Wales in 1880 that " *all* the *worst men* who had no respect for Kings and Princes or any of the *landmarks* of the Constitution *were put into this Government in spite of me*." [40] In 1870 she pressed Gladstone to remove Ayrton without success.[41] Later, in 1882, she objected strongly to both Derby and Dilke entering the Cabinet but, after minor adjustments, they did so.[42] At times Gladstone's patience wore thin and after the Queen had tried to block two appointments at the Parliamentary Under-Secretary level, he exploded to Granville, " I think this is intolerable. It is by courtesy only that these appointments are made known to Her Majesty." [43] On the other hand, when she had objected to the suggestion of the Duke of Somerset as Chancellor of the Duchy of Lancaster in 1872, Gladstone told Granville that " as there is no great matter of duty or principle involved in making the offer, I am disposed to think we should give way to the Queen's wish." [44] Similarly Gladstone agreed to reconsider his nomination of Childers for the War Office in 1886 and appointed Campbell-Bannerman as the Queen had asked.[45] At the same time, he agreed with her that Granville was not really up to the Foreign Office. The Queen believed that she had been responsible for suggesting Rosebery as Granville's successor, but in fact this had been part of plans for a new administration set out by Gladstone, Morley and Rosebery in earlier discussions at Dalmeny.[46]

Disraeli, for all his different handling of the Queen, behaved in much the same manner. He had no objection to a veto on the

[40] *Letters*, Series II, Vol. III, p. 299.
[41] P. Guedalla, *The Queen and Mr. Gladstone*, Vol. I, p. 229.
[42] *Letters*, Series II, Vol. III, p. 371–382, and P. Guedalla, *op. cit.*, Vol. II, p. 212.
[43] *Ibid.*, p. 166.
[44] *Gladstone-Granville Correspondence*, Vol. II, p. 328. Also ministers were more disposed to consider royal wishes in appointing the posts like the Chancellorship of the Duchy where some personal contacts between the Crown and the minister were involved.
[45] *Letters*, Series III, Vol. I, pp. 40–42.
[46] Compare *ibid.*, 58 with Lord Crewe, *Lord Rosebery*, Vol. II, pp. 397–399.

Duke of Beaufort for a household appointment in 1874,[47] but when Queen Victoria wanted to move Layard from his ambassadorial post at Madrid [48] and to accept Derby's resignation in January 1878, Disraeli refused.[49] Lord Salisbury, as has been said, insisted on his nominations, if there was political or administrative reason behind them. In 1885, however, he offered alternatives when the Queen said she did not want Stanley at the War Office.[50] Lord Cross probably remained in the Cabinet longer than many expected because the Queen urged his retention and it was not a matter of much importance.[51] In 1900, Salisbury discussed his appointments with the Queen and though he stuck to Brodrick for the War Office, her views and those of Balfour led him to reconsider his early notions that Balfour of Burleigh might go to the Admiralty and Hicks Beach to the Home Office.[52]

On honours, military and clerical appointments the Queen had also to be consulted, her views usually being considered in all routine decisions. Yet when the ministry did lay some store on a given case, it was forced through. Disraeli's Cabinet wanted to send Sir Garnet Wolseley to South Africa as High Commissioner and the Queen sanctioned the appointment " but she would *not approve* it." [53] Her distrust of Wolseley (as an Army reformer and critic of her cousin the Duke of Cambridge) led to a fruitless opposition to his nomination as Adjutant-General in 1881,[54] though she managed to withstand the attempt to raise him to the peerage from March 1881 to September 1882.[55] In 1885 Lord Randolph Churchill and the Cabinet prevented the Queen, partially aided by Salisbury, from edging the Duke of Connaught into the position of Commander-in-Chief in Bombay.[56]

In ecclesiastical appointments, the Queen had definite views and Disraeli gave way over the appointment first of the Bishop

47 *Letters*, Series II, Vol. II, p. 323.
48 Monypenny and Buckle, *op. cit*., Vol. V, p. 418.
49 R. W. Seton-Watson, *Disraeli, Gladstone, and the Eastern Question*, p. 301.
50 *Letters*, Series II, Vol. III, p. 664.
51 *Letters*, Series III, Vol. I, p. 247.
52 There is an extensive discussion between Salisbury and Balfour of the persons suitable for these posts in the *Salisbury Papers* for October 1900.
53 Monypenny and Buckle, *op. cit*., Vol. VI, p. 429.
54 *Letters*, Series II, Vol. III, p. 244.
55 P. Guedalla, *op. cit*., Vol. II, p. 134, No. 210.
56 Sir Winston Churchill, *op. cit*., Vol. I, pp. 504–511.

of Peterborough and then over Dr. Tait as Archbishop of Canterbury. On these issues Disraeli was both ill-informed and lacked any political incentive for adhering to his original preferences.[57]

Edward VII was convalescing in 1902 when Balfour's Government was formed and took no part in the consultations. The divisions over Protection in 1903 led to a reshuffle and the King telegraphed—" With regard to appointments I conclude they will naturally not be offered until after full consultation with me." Balfour proceeded to discuss changes in London though a second and stronger telegram of protest led him to visit Balmoral. After some consideration the Prime Minister decided to move Brodrick to the India Office and make Arnold-Forster Secretary of State for War. King Edward reminded Balfour of " the reasons why he does not approve of Mr. Arnold-Forster's appointment " and he saw " no reason why he should change his mind now." Balfour replied that he was dismayed at the royal attitude and repeated his arguments. The King, being reassured by Selborne, gave way about Arnold-Forster while Balfour accepted his suggestion that Londonderry should become Lord President and Sir William Anson President of the Board of Education.[58] When the Liberals came to power, the King only intervened in the Court appointments and even then Campbell-Bannerman refused to make Lord Farquhar, a Liberal Unionist, Lord Steward.[59] On the military side, royal support helped Sir T. Kelly-Kenny to become Adjutant-General [60] but when King Edward urged that Kitchener be made Viceroy of India, Morley, the Secretary of State, would not hear of it.[61] On the other hand, Edward VII's interventions twice prevented Sir John Fisher resigning his post as First Sea Lord and his suggestion of Lord Esher as Chairman of a Committee on the Reorganisation of the War Office was accepted by Balfour. George V offered no major objections or counter-suggestions to the various Cabinet appointments Asquith had to make between 1910 and 1914.

---

[57] R. Blake, *op. cit.*, pp. 507–511.
[58] *Royal Archives*, Vol. R 24, ff. 89–103 and R 24, ff. 1 and 2. Balfour had intended to make Salisbury Lord President but the King pointed out that this might revive the old cry of the " Hotel Cecil " and so he made Salisbury Lord Privy Seal—a post with no emoluments and no rival claimants.
[59] Sir S. Lee, *op. cit.*, Vol. II, pp. 445–446 and 469.
[60] *Ibid.*, p. 86.
[61] *Ibid.*, p. 711.

Royal views might also influence some aspects of policy. On all controversial issues, the Cabinet was unlikely to consider anything but the attitude of the electorate and of its party in the House and outside. Queen Victoria often disliked Liberal measures but she did not consider it was her duty to press for changes. Her main concern was with foreign and colonial policy.[62] When Germany and Austria asked Britain to protest about Turkish atrocities in August 1877, the Queen agreed only if a similar protest was made to Russia. Disraeli wondered whether there was any evidence of Russian atrocities, though he was not unwilling to remonstrate. The Queen's tenacious memory recalled a hearsay report of Russian artillery firing on ambulances and a protest was duly sent.[63] She was strongly opposed to any reversal of Disraeli's policy and resisted the evacuation of Kandahar. This involved objecting to telegrams of instructions, asking for the opinions of the local military authorities and remonstrating about a reference in the Queen's Speech at the start of the 1881 session.[64] But the decision was taken by the Cabinet and carried through, if with a little delay and embarrassment. Esher observed that " she knows she stands no chance against a united Cabinet, she prefers to avoid going through the form of yielding by tacitly ignoring the difference, after it has been once stated." [65] Over Egypt, the Queen wanted Britain to intervene single-handed and later, in 1884, urged that Gordon be supported. When Sir Evelyn Baring advised an advance to Berber and the Cabinet turned it down the Queen was not able to alter the content of the telegram, but she had the wording made less peremptory.[66]

These attempts to influence policy were usually made by writing to the Prime Minister or the Foreign Secretary and in extreme cases by refusing to sanction despatches till they had been reconsidered. If the Queen felt the Cabinet as a whole was behaving badly (or if she merely wanted to make a suggestion, say about preventing railway accidents) she asked the minister most in favour to take a letter to the next meeting. Gladstone dutifully began by reading the letter from the Queen and then the Cabinet

---

[62] Naturally the Queen yielded to no one in her concern for all matters affecting the position of the Royal Family and its upkeep.
[63] A. Ponsonby, *op. cit.*, pp. 165–166.
[64] *Letters*, Series II, Vol. III, pp. 140, 155, 178–180.
[65] Esher, *op. cit.*, Vol. I, pp. 74–77.
[66] *Letters*, Series II, Vol. III, p. 489.

turned to consider its business. In the early 1860s when Palmerston and Russell sometimes acted on their own, this had been a good method of bringing the matter to the attention of their colleagues, but when the situation was normal, it had little effect. As Rosebery told Ponsonby "I have great doubts of the wisdom of her sending rescripts to be read at the Cabinet. Such is the jealous temper of Britons that these utterances are more likely to produce reaction than compliance!" [67]

King Edward had a more limited interest in public policy and confined himself almost entirely to following foreign affairs and watching over defence.[68] He occasionally wrote asking the Cabinet to consider questions affecting the Crown (such as the civil list, its liability to income tax, the Declaration to be read at the Coronation Service, etc.) but he never sent letters on political questions directly to the Cabinet. (Though irritation over Lloyd George's Limehouse speech made him threaten to send a reprimand unless Asquith could give adequate assurances.) He did, on rare occasions, write directly to the Prime Minister. Difficulties over Venezuela in 1903 drew a three-page letter of comment from the King. He also sent Balfour his views on relations with Tibet, on the merits of General Butler and a suggestion that the Tariff Reform Controversy be put before a Royal Commission. Knollys, on his behalf, told Campbell-Bannerman that it would be unfortunate if the 1906 Trade Disputes Bill legalised " peaceful picketing." But apart from such isolated instances, his suggestions were confined to requests for more information (especially over Liberal intentions towards the House of Lords).[69]

Occasionally, Edward VII made some useful points on the subjects in which he was well informed. His comments on certain aspects of the South African War were valuable and when it was agreed to reform the War Office, he proposed a committee of three under Lord Esher to make recommendations. The King expressed himself strongly on such matters as starting an Army journal and readjustments of pay, though in both cases the plans

[67] A. Ponsonby, *op. cit.*, pp. 276–277.
[68] The King himself emphasised that he "takes such a deep interest in the welfare of his country, and especially in all matters connected with its defence." *Royal Archives*, Vol. R 23, f. 47.
[69] All these examples are in the *Royal Archives*, Vols. R 22, 23, 27 and 28.

of the Secretary of State for War were carried through.[70] One of the few occasions when Edward VII did try to resist his ministers was over the grant of the Garter to the Shah of Persia. The King objected that it was a Christian Order and generally felt the Shah was an unworthy recipient, only giving way when Balfour took a very firm stand. Later, in 1907, he maintained his refusal to make this award to the King of Siam.[71] Foreign policy interested King Edward but it is generally agreed that he played a supporting rather than a formative role. The only real protest he registered was against the Morley-Minto reforms of 1909 and specifically over the appointment of an Indian to the Viceroy's Council. Morley was told that " the King regrets that he cannot change his views. . . . The reasons are well known to the Secretary of State . . . but as the latter apparently is putting great pressure on the subject, and at the last meeting of the Cabinet Council, the Government were unanimous . . . the King has no other alternative but to give way much against his will." [72] Edward VII in fact encountered a fairly steady degree of firmness on the part of all his ministers and the readiness to consider royal views had clearly declined since the time of the old Queen.[73]

In the four years before the war George V did not press his opinions but where they were called for, he showed some judgment. The pledge to create peers was only extracted by threat of resignation, but he persuaded the Cabinet to send the veto resolutions up to the Lords in November 1910 and to introduce the Parliament Bill before dissolving, so that it and the Conservative counter-proposals would be well understood during the campaign.[74] After the election, he made the important and sensible suggestion that Asquith should send the Bill back to the Lords with their amendments rejected so that every constitutional step was taken before the question of creating peers came up.[75] The King's only other

---

[70] Sir S. Lee, *op. cit.*, Vol. II, p. 81.
[71] Lord Newton, *The Life of Lord Lansdowne*, pp. 237–238 and Sir P. Magnus, *op. cit.*, pp. 301–305 and 392–393.
[72] Sir S. Lee, *op. cit.*, Vol. II, p. 385. See also Morley, *Recollections*, Vol. II, p. 301.
[73] Sir S. Lee makes the same point in Vol. II, p. 383. It was well illustrated as early as 1901 when Balfour insisted in the name of a united Cabinet that the King and the C-in-C give way to the decision of the Secretary of State for War over the appeal of an officer cashiered in South Africa. See F. Ponsonby, *Recollections of Three Reigns*, p. 126.
[74] H. Nicolson, *op. cit.*, pp. 133 and 150.
[75] *Ibid.*, p. 153.

personal intervention was the idea that he should go to India and crown himself at a Durbar in Delhi—a project that met with hesitant acquiescence from the Cabinet.[76]

With such a limited field of influence and only one or two highly circumscribed powers open to it, the position of the Crown on the broadest level was not open to much doubt. All the policies of the country were to be formed and regulated by the Cabinet dependent on the electorate and its representatives in the Commons. The monarch had a valuable formal part to play and, in certain situations, provided a mechanism for ensuring a smooth transition to a new executive. It followed that the Crown could urge its opinions on ministers but was not expected to take part in politics or to try actively to pursue its own personal policies. Despite this, Queen Victoria still retained the conviction that in some sense she actually governed the country and found it hard not to trespass on politics. In part it may simply have been that her convictions ran away with her, for she realised, in most cases, that any campaign against her ministers had to be conducted in secret and that she could not openly seek advice from other sources. Also there were methods by which she could attempt to influence decisions, methods which, though out of date and contrary to the spirit of the late nineteenth-century constitution, were not positively prohibited.

For instance, when Disraeli had told the Queen of the differences of opinion in the Cabinet, she helped him by giving recalcitrant ministers " wiggings "[77] and sent the Foreign Secretary, Lord Derby, a very severe snub which had actually been drafted by Disraeli.[78] King Edward could, at times, help men like Sir John Fisher or R. B. Haldane by open support of their policies, but interventions of this kind never prevented a policy on which the Cabinet was agreed.

A more dangerous line of action, because it was not under any ministerial control, was to engage in discussions with the

---

[76] *Ibid.*, p. 168 and Pope-Hennessy, *Life of Lord Crewe*, p. 90.

[77] November 5, 1877, Disraeli wrote that " it is of the utmost importance that your Majesty should use yr. M's influence and prepare the minds of those of yr. M's ministers whom yr. M. may see in the interval." *Letters*, Series II, Vol. II, p. 570. As a result Carnarvon reported that " Cabinet Ministers have been sent for to receive ' wiggings '—which it is their affair and fault if they allow to impair their independence." H. Gladstone, *After Thirty Years*, p. 141.

[78] R. W. Seton Watson, *op. cit.*, p. 221.

opposition. There was no harm in the Queen sending messages to the opposition during elections to warn them she would not hear of certain proposals. In April 1880, before a government was installed, Ponsonby was to tell the Liberal leaders "there must be no democratic leaning, no attempt to change the foreign policy." [79] Similarly her views were passed on in May 1892, though no incoming Cabinet took such royal messages very seriously. But definite objections would have been raised had it been known that Disraeli continued, at the Queen's request, to write to her and comment on public affairs after his defeat in 1880, the correspondence ending only with his death a year later. [80] Equally serious were messages from the Queen to Wolseley, both directly and through Lady Wolseley, urging him to use strong language in objecting to instructions from this " incorrigible " government and even to threaten resignation if there was no change. [81] In the Home Rule crisis, the Queen wrote frequently to Goschen and to Hartington and Forster urging them to abandon Gladstone and the Liberals and later to enter Lord Salisbury's government. [82]

These departures from accepted practice reached their most extreme form when the Queen secretly asked Salisbury in 1886 whether it would suit the Unionists to grant or refuse Gladstone's request for a dissolution. It is evidence of Salisbury's intense partisanship in domestic politics that he was in no way worried by or saw anything improper in this communication and replied that granting Gladstone his dissolution was both in the interests of the opposition and would cause no controversy. [83] In July 1893 there were further discussions with Argyll, Salisbury and Devonshire about the wisdom of insisting on a dissolution if Gladstone tried to reintroduce the Home Rule Bill. [84] The Queen raised the matter again in secret letters to Leader of the Opposition in March and in October 1894. On the second occasion Devonshire, Chamberlain, Sir Henry James and Argyll were also consulted. The first three thought that any such move was not only

[79] *Letters*, Series II, Vol. III, p. 75.
[80] *Letters*, Series II, Vol. III, pp. 125 and 143.
[81] *Ibid.*, pp. 620, 631, 634.
[82] *Ibid.*, pp. 704, 710, 712 and Series III, Vol. I, pp. 17, 23, 33, 57, 98, 100–125 and 130 and A. Ponsonby, *op. cit.*, p. 201.
[83] *Letters*, Series III, Vol. I, p. 128.
[84] *Letters*, Series III, Vol. II, pp. 279, 280, 297.

unnecessary but would "raise the propriety of the Queen's action."[85] Salisbury merely considered it inexpedient as time was on the side of the Conservatives. As, on each of these occasions, the interests of the opposition coincided with normal constitutional practice, no damage was done.

The attitude of the Unionist leaders requires some explanation. In part it reflects the bitter party warfare of the period. It might just have been possible in 1886 for Unionists to convince themselves that they were within the letter of the constitution. The Queen still could, under exceptional circumstances, refuse a dissolution and had the Liberal Unionists preferred to combine forces with the Conservatives and form a government, there would have been no need for an appeal to the country. Yet the consultation was not to find out whether a strong government could be formed without an election but to concert plans for defeating the Liberals. It is hard to make any excuse for the later discussions as to whether the Queen should insist on a dissolution; that is, dismiss her Liberal ministers. Such an action had not been attempted since William IV's ill-fated experiment in 1834–35. Moreover, all these consultations violated the older maxim that the Crown only takes advice from its accredited servants. Part of the explanation for the co-operation of the opposition leaders was the conviction that the Crown was their natural ally in saving the country from a temporary Radical aberration and that what they did could not be wrong. (A similar arrogant assumption governed their use of the House of Lords after 1905 and ended in disaster.) In the case of Queen Victoria the initiative had come from her though any row would probably have been hushed up, as neither party would have wished to damage the monarchy. It was, however, fortunate that when Bonar Law and other Conservative leaders kept stressing in their speeches between 1912 and 1914 that George V had the right to dissolve, that is to dismiss the Liberals, they met with no definite response. George V adhered to the normal working of the constitution and accepted the advice and proposals of his Cabinet.

Apart from any influence the Crown might have by the exercise of its normal rights to comment, the monarch could be both a help and a hindrance to ministers in carrying out their plans. For

[85] *Ibid.*, pp. 370, 374 and 430–452. See also Lord Askwith *Lord James of Hereford*, p. 232.

example, the Crown could urge the House of Lords to come to terms with a Liberal Cabinet. As party warfare grew stronger the desire to meet royal wishes became a less powerful motive but Queen Victoria could always ask both sides to reopen negotiations without loss of face. In 1868, she wrote to Derby deprecating a clash between the two Houses over the disestablishment of the Irish Church. After the second reading was passed, the Archbishop of Canterbury considered postponement but found the Queen pressing him to come to terms. A final settlement was reached by Granville and Cairns, with the encouragement of Disraeli. The Queen played no important part, but she did act as a kind of Master of Ceremonies to the statesmen conducting the negotiation.[86] In the prolonged deadlock between the two Houses over the 1884 Reform Bill Lord Salisbury was trying to force a dissolution on the existing franchise. The Queen wished to avoid an election on the conduct and position of the House of Lords. Gladstone knew that Conservative M.P.s did not want an election on this issue, and offered reasonable terms; and the Queen's letters to Richmond and Cairns encouraged them to overturn Salisbury at a meeting of Conservative peers and later at a meeting of the whole party. It was quite proper for Gladstone to pay tribute to the Queen's " wise, gracious and steady exercise of influence . . . which has so powerfully contributed to bring about this accommodation." [87] When conflict between the two Houses arose again after 1906, King Edward tried to mediate but found the pressures too strong. As Sir Sidney Lee says, " the blank refusal of the Conservative leaders to entertain his warnings was unwelcome to his *amour propre*, and his inability to qualify the course of events was a great disappointment to him." [88]

One of the helping functions the Crown had performed in previous years had been to persuade men of rank and wealth to

[86] Cairns and Granville are given credit for the settlement in *The Kimberley Papers*, p. 6; Sir H. Maxwell, *Life of Clarendon*, Vol. II, p. 361; Morley, *op. cit.*, Vol. II, pp. 269–278; Monypenny and Buckle, *op. cit.*, Vol. V, p. 108; Sir Algernon West, *Recollections*, Vol. I, p. 343 and *Letters*, Series II, Vol. I, p. 604–Vol. II, p. 22.

[87] The best accounts are in Morley, *op. cit.*, Vol. III, pp. 130–138; A. Lang, *Diaries of Sir S. Northcote*, pp. 353–354; A West, *op. cit.*, Vol. II, pp. 214–219; Lady G. Cecil, *op. cit.*, Vol. III, pp. 104–122. Corinne C. Weston in " The Royal Mediation in 1884," *E.H.R.*, Vol. 82 (1967), pp. 296–322 starts by arguing that the Queen's actions " may well have been decisive " and ends by saying that this proposition cannot be established.

[88] Sir S. Lee, *op. cit.*, Vol. II, p. 568.

undertake the labours of government. As the two-party system became the accepted form in politics, a leadership developed which had every intention of winning and, if possible, holding on to office. Nevertheless the attitude of the Crown could make a big difference to the atmosphere in the upper reaches of the Cabinet. For Disraeli, " the Court is a department in itself," [89] while Gladstone told Rosebery that " the Queen alone is enough to kill any man." [90] In a moment of exasperation in 1886, Salisbury said he could manage two departments but he considered that at that moment he had four, " the Prime Ministership, the Foreign Office, the Queen and Randolph Churchill—and the burden of them increases in that order." [91] When Disraeli contemplated handing on the premiership to Derby in 1876, the latter " utterly scouted the idea " for, among other reasons, " he could never manage H.M." [92] Ministries could and did last their full political life on the worst possible terms with the Queen and, in some ways, this involved less burden than the constant demands imposed on Disraeli by close collaboration. Nevertheless he did enjoy the relationship and was buoyed up by marks of favour, such as the royal visit to Hughenden in the midst of the Near Eastern dispute. Rosebery, similarly, liked to think that he was pleasing the Queen. Both Edward VII and George V took far less of their respective Prime Ministers' time for they did not have the Queen's absorption in the detail of all aspects of public affairs. They received regular information and made further inquiries as the need arose. The friendship and backing of Edward VII was of value to some ministers, such as Haldane, but lack of royal favour was no handicap to such men as Balfour, Lansdowne or Lloyd George.

There were some more specific aspects of policy where the Crown's attitude might make matters easier. The problem of War Office reform and senior appointments in the Army always involved the Queen, as she trusted her cousin the Duke of Cambridge (Commander-in-Chief since 1857) who was totally opposed to any changes. Nevertheless, all that was needed was a combination of tact and firmness. Cardwell was able to carry through his proposals, albeit after careful explanations. The Duke of

---

89 Monypenny and Buckle, *op. cit.*, Vol. V, p. 355.
90 Crewe, *op. cit.*, Vol. I, p. 165.
91 Lady G. Cecil, *op. cit.*, Vol. III, p. 180.
92 E. A. Gathorne-Hardy, *op. cit.*, Vol. II, p. 3.

Cambridge was ultimately retired with the aid of the Queen (due to Campbell-Bannerman's tact) and first Wolseley and then Roberts were made Commander-in-Chief despite royal opposition.[93]

On imperial questions the Queen favoured a forward policy, and so her support usually went to the men on the spot as they tended to be convinced imperialists. After the severe criticism of the Conservative record in South Africa, there was some surprise when Gladstone decided to retain Sir Bartle Frere as High Commissioner. The Cabinet had come round to the view that he was best able to carry through a policy of federation. " A less substantial, but still not wholly inoperative reason, was the strong feeling of the Queen for the High Commissioner." [94] Similarly she backed Sir Evelyn Baring in the 1880s, her technique being to delay approval of telegrams till there had been further consultations with the local agent, in the hope that the Cabinet would change its mind. This had little effect in practice but did encourage her representatives. Baring told Ponsonby in 1892 that " I can never cease to remember with the utmost gratitude the personal support I received from Her Majesty in the dark Gladstonian days when pretty well everyone's hand was against me." [95]

Finally, the Queen had some useful sources of information from abroad, especially in difficult areas like Bulgaria in the 1880s. Her wide network of relationships allowed the Foreign Secretary to address remarks to foreign potentates through the Queen which could not have been made by normal diplomatic exchanges.

Edward VII's chief interest, after matters of ceremonial, was the Army and Navy, though even here he concentrated on appointments, promotions, uniforms and honours. The King had few definite ideas, but a reforming Secretary of State encountered heavy opposition from back-benchers in the House of Commons, often stimulated by senior officers. If the King made it clear that he agreed with the despised politicians,[96] this dampened some of the

---

[93] On both occasions, the Queen wanted her son, the Duke of Connaught, but " as my ministers think otherwise, I suppose I cannot object." Lord Newton, *op. cit.*, pp. 135 and 187.

[94] These are Morley's words. *Op. cit.*, Vol. III, p. 23. The Conservatives would have recalled Frere had it not been for the strong support of the Queen and the Colonial Secretary. A. J. Balfour, *op. cit.*, p. 114.

[95] A. Ponsonby, *op. cit.*, p. 236.

[96] " Those dirty swine " as General Gough called them in early 1914; H. Nicolson, *op. cit.*, p. 238.

critics. Royal support helped Brodrick to reform the Army Medical Corps and to get medical officers treated in a better manner.[97] Despite this help, ministers were careful to see that the King did not encroach, and when Knollys asked for regular reports of the proceedings of the Army Council, he met with a flat refusal.[98] Haldane, who was not for all his ability a strong or forceful minister, was happy to have King Edward's support for his plans. The type of situation in which royal aid could be effective occurred when it came to launching the Territorial Army, as the King consented to call together all the Lords Lieutenant and to ask for their co-operation. Later, the King wavered in his support for the Territorials and subscribed to many of Lord Roberts' criticisms, especially of their artillery, but by July 1908 Haldane had answered his doubts.[99]

It is over the development of Britain's foreign relations that most misconceptions about the role of Edward VII have arisen. His spectacular visits to foreign capitals were taken by some (and especially by Germans) to have definite diplomatic objectives. Yet all the leading statesmen of the period have been unanimous on this point. Balfour, writing to Lansdowne about Holland Rose's book on the *Origins of the War,* says " he quite confidently attributes the policy of the Entente to Edward VII, *thus embodying* in a serious historical work a foolish piece of gossip . . . As far as I remember, during the years which you and I were his Ministers, he never made an important suggestion of any sort on large questions of policy." [1] Sir Edward Grey confirms that " the visits were not made the object of important strokes or developments in foreign policy " and on despatches " comment of any sort was rare, and I do not remember criticism or suggestion." [2] Two of his close friends, Lord Esher and Sir Frederick Ponsonby, appreciated that the King's role was to help and cement the policies decided on by his ministers.[3] Such aid could, however, have a positive aspect. When the Conservatives were losing the election in December 1905, the French Government was doubtful about the

[97] Midleton, *op. cit.*, pp. 159–166.
[98] *Balfour Papers, Add. MSS.* 49,722, f. 233.
[99] Sir P. Magnus, *op. cit.*, pp. 382–387.
[1] Lord Newton, *op. cit.*, p. 292.
[2] Viscount Grey, *op. cit.*, Vol. I, pp. 151 and 204–205.
[3] Viscount Esher, *The Influence of King Edward*, pp. 50–57 and F. Ponsonby, *op. cit.*, p. 172.

attitude of Campbell-Bannerman and his colleagues. Cambon was sent to see King Edward and tell him of various anti-French moves being made by Germany, on the grounds that some of them centred round remarks by his fellow monarch, Alphonse of Spain. The real object was to put out feelers through the King as to whether the Liberal Cabinet was prepared to maintain the close relations which had developed under the previous government and the response did much to reassure the French Government.[4] Edward VII was more than just a skilful public relations officer. He was able "as a popular and accessible monarch to smooth away difficulties and create an atmosphere favourable to friendly discussion." [5]

George V was less interested in foreign affairs, but he was always ready to offer his services as a mediator. In the disputes over the House of Lords and over Home Rule, passions were too high to permit the King to alter any of the basic positions but, on Asquith's advice, he was prepared to ask the two sides to meet and confer. Bonar Law only attended the Buckingham Palace Conference (on the exclusion of Ulster) in deference to the King's wishes. Even this measure of compliance was helpful, though the Conference produced no results.

The analysis in this section has tried to produce an estimate of how far the Crown affected the Cabinet in the latter's task of governing the country and retaining popular confidence. The conclusion has been that apart from one or two well-defined situations the Crown had no power and little influence, though it could both help and take up the time of statesmen. There has been a tendency to exaggerate royal influence for several reasons. One is the habit of looking at the monarch's activities in isolation, without asking how far royal views or actions definitely changed the pattern of events. Time and again the argument is put forward: "Queen Victoria suggested A; A was done; therefore the Queen carried through a personal policy." [6] Such an argument would only follow

---

[4] *Documents Diplomatiques Français*, Second Series, Vol. VIII, No. 262.
[5] This is the conclusion of Sir S. Lee, *op. cit.*, Vol. II, p. 727.
[6] The classic case of this kind of argument is F. Hardie's *Political Influence of Queen Victoria*, the bulk of which details the attitude of the Queen to her ministries and their policies. This is interesting but proves nothing about royal influence, as little attempt is made to see whether the royal attitude had any effect. Particularly in the case of appointments, it is essential to ask whether the Prime Minister intended to appoint anyone other than the obvious person suggested by the Queen.

if there was evidence that the politicians wished to do B, and if no factors other than the Queen's desires intervened before the decision was taken. Secondly, the conduct of the Crown has a certain fascination, especially when coupled with the personality of Queen Victoria. Thirdly, an unrivalled source of information in the volumes of her letters and in the many memoirs of individual statesmen, all of which contain detailed accounts of any dealings with the Queen, has given the subject more prominence than the facts warrant. (This section on the monarchy is itself out of proportion to the importance of the topic but must be so to cover all its facets.) If bulk of information is thought to have some relation to importance, one should imagine for a true comparison a collection of letters covering all the principal interventions in politics not merely of one Premier but of all the Queen's Prime Ministers. Or the effect of the Queen on a single Cabinet can be assessed by studying the slight part she plays in the correspondence of Mr. Gladstone and his chief aide, Lord Granville, throughout the 1880–85 ministry.[7] Or again, the impact of the Court on Liberal Cabinets could be contrasted with the total effect of a single problem like the government of Ireland or of a single institution like the House of Lords. There is less to say about either of these topics, but they loomed larger in the life of Liberal Ministries than the attitude of the Crown. There is no desire here to write down the influence of the monarchy and there has been no attempt to estimate its moral or social value; its relations with the Cabinet have been the only matter under examination.

---

[7] M. R. D. Foot in his review of *The Political Correspondence of Mr. Gladstone and Lord Granville, 1876–1886*, ed. A. Ramm in *Victorian Studies*, Vol. V, 1962, p. 340, says "these letters let us see Queen Victoria herself as she appeared to ministers whose politics and personalities she distrusted. The small extent of her interference in day to day business, and its unpredictability, and the often trumpery nature of the things she chose to interfere about, come out here."

CHAPTER 10

THE FUNCTIONS OF THE CABINET

The Cabinet's chief tasks were still to decide on policy and to provide leadership; these functions were the source of its authority. Ministers assembled to consider all the principal questions coming before the government and their decision was final. When Kimberley decided to refuse the post of Viceroy of India in 1872 he reflected that " the office of a Cabinet Minister is really higher. It sounds grandly to be Viceroy over 180 millions of men, but it is in truth a much greater thing to be a member of the governing committee of the whole Empire, India included." [1] Only a few formal matters were outside the competence of the Cabinet. When Queen Victoria doubted whether ministers could refuse the retiring Viceroy, Lord Lytton, a step in the peerage and the Garter, Gladstone quoted precedents showing that " in the public mind, and in ordinary practice, the Cabinet is viewed as the seat of ultimate responsibility " and it must be free to decide.[2] Exercising this power meant that there was a gulf between ministers in the Cabinet and other office holders. The contrast comes out most clearly in the relative positions of the Lord Lieutenant and Chief Secretary for Ireland. In mid-century Cabinets the Lord Lieutenant had normally been a member and therefore dominated the Chief Secretary, who was not. After 1868, the Secretary tended to move up as he had to defend the Irish Administration in Parliament and Gladstone put C. S. Fortescue in his first Cabinet. When Cowper and Forster resigned in the crisis of 1882, Gladstone told the Queen that Irish Administration " had to be conducted at this time with the utmost degree of authority . . . the authority of a Cabinet Minister." [3] So the new Lord Lieutenant, Spencer, became a member, and both the Secretaries who served with him (Trevelyan and Campbell-Bannerman) realised

---

[1] *The Kimberley Papers*, p. 27.
[2] *Letters*, Series III, Vol. II, p. 351.
[3] *Letters*, Series II, Vol. III, p. 270.

that they were expected to play subordinate parts.[4] As violence subsided and the centre of attention returned to the Commons, the Chief Secretary had to have greater weight and thereafter only one Lord Lieutenant, Earl Cadogan, was in the Cabinet.[5] By the time Walter Long became Chief Secretary in 1905, the Lord Lieutenant was not even consulted on all points and when he (Dudley) protested, A. J. Balfour replied that modern conditions " have now transferred the real leadership of the Irish Government to the Minister who happens both to be in the Cabinet and in the House of Commons." [6] It was the conviction that outside the Cabinet little could be achieved that led Chamberlain and Dilke to combine to try to force an entry in 1880. Lord Rosebery likewise felt that " I could not be an efficient minister for Scotland without a direct voice in the Cabinet " [7] and Henry Chaplin refused the Presidency of the Board of Agriculture in 1886 for the same reason.

On a few occasions (noted in the next chapter) the Prime Minister and other senior ministers tried to avoid calling Cabinets or acted in the name of the Cabinet either because they wished to avoid control or simply because their colleagues were dispersed on holiday. Yet such instances were rare and it was accepted that the Cabinet was the body which governed the country, provided party leadership and put business through Parliament.

It was because the Cabinet was the centre of policy-making that there was such concern over its composition (discussed in detail in the next chapter). All the major controversies of the period were decided in Cabinet; the shape of each series of policies to meet the Irish problem, reactions to Russian and Turkish activities in the Balkans, the degree of enthusiasm to be shown over imperial expansion, the kind of social reform, the level of expenditure on armaments and the decision to go to war in 1914.

---

[4] Trevelyan after 15 months implored Gladstone to put him in the Cabinet. " To enable him to conduct Irish business with any semblance of authority, he had to be a Cabinet minister." Quoted by R. B. McDowell, " The Irish Executive in the 19th Century," *Irish Historical Studies*, Vol. 9.

[5] George Wyndham, the Secretary, said that addressing the Cabinet through Cadogan was " like speaking through a megaphone with a pudding in the orifice." J. W. Mackail and G. Wyndham, *Life and Letters of George Wyndham*, Vol. II, p. 425.

[6] C. Petrie, *Walter Long and his Times*, p. 96.

[7] Crewe, *op. cit.*, p. 173.

There is less evidence of party considerations and less time was spent on this but the Cabinet framed each Queen's speech and expected to be consulted on the leader's address to his constituents.[8] It settled whether there should be a collective resignation or a dissolution. There is also little information about parliamentary management and much was settled on the front bench or in the Premier's room at the House. But during sessions, there was a regular meeting every Saturday, a major item on the agenda being business for the coming week. When questions raised difficult issues of policy the answers were discussed and drafted in Cabinet.[9] The arrangement of the Autumn and January Cabinets was designed to enable legislation to be prepared in good time for each forthcoming session.

This task of deciding policy, providing leadership and, to a lesser extent, of planning tactics in Parliament also had to be performed by the opposition. As the parties became more organised and the struggle for power more intense, ex-Cabinets or as they were termed by some in the 1880s Shadow Cabinets met more regularly. By March 1868 Gladstone was emerging from his mood of aggrieved defeatism and Argyll, Granville, Fortescue, Cardwell, Brand and Glynn met at his house to consider the terms of his resolutions on the Irish Church.[10] Similar meetings of up to seven ex-ministers and two Whips took place regularly in May to discuss tactics, though more frequent informal contact was kept up with a smaller group. In 1875 the Liberal ex-Cabinet met to determine such matters as its attitude to the government's refusal to allow slaves to take refuge on British warships, though there was no great unity or vigour.[11] The machinery was just strong enough to prevent a serious split over Gladstone's resolutions condemning the government's Near Eastern policy in 1877. One was modified, three were dropped, and pressure from Hartington persuaded most of the Liberal rank and file to support their leaders in the division.[12] Indeed, if the ex-Cabinet was not operating, this was a sign of serious divisions

[8] Morley, *op. cit.*, Vol. II, p. 486.
[9] There are clippings of questions from the Order Paper and draft answers scattered through the *Gladstone Cabinet Papers, Add. MSS.*, 44,636–44,648.
[10] A. J. Walling, ed., *The Diaries of John Bright*, pp. 316, 320–326.
[11] T. Wemyss Reid, *Life of Forster*, Vol. II, p. 105.
[12] *Ibid.*, pp. 172–175.

in the party and no very effective opposition could be maintained in the House. Gladstone was determined to keep a free hand after he left office in 1885 and refused to call his ex-colleagues together despite requests from Harcourt. He appreciated that a meeting was not likely to produce agreement or even a measure of unity. This situation was a reflection of divisions in the recent Liberal Cabinet and foreshadowed the cleavage that was to occur when his decision to take up Home Rule became known. In fact the former Cabinet was falling into several groups, soon to consolidate and form the Liberal and Liberal Unionist front benches. Gladstone had been consulting Spencer and Granville, and a radical group met to prosecute " the Unauthorised Programme," while Selborne, Northbrook, Hartington, Derby, Carlingford and Lord Monk-Bretton agreed that they would oppose any move towards Home Rule.[13] Similarly, the divisions of 1894–1896 made it hard for Rosebery and then Harcourt to convene the ex-Cabinet, and yet failure to do so prevented any concerted opposition.

Conservative and Unionist Shadow Cabinets had worked fairly smoothly in the early 1880s and between 1892 and 1895, but after 1906 there were difficulties. Middleton records that " constant meetings were held of the ex-Cabinet, in which the divisions of opinion as to throwing out the Budget were only less acrimonious than those which ensued on the Parliament Act." [14] Balfour pointed out one difficulty: " Had it been a real Cabinet, one of two things would have followed. Either the dissentient minority would have resigned, or they would have silently acquiesced in the decision of the majority. There could, of course, be no question in the case of a Shadow Cabinet of resignation. There certainly has been no silent acquiescence." [15] The former point was not strictly true. Rosebery, Harcourt and Morley had all ceased attendance at Liberal Shadow Cabinets at various points in the late 1890s while Long had threatened to resign from the Conservative front bench in 1907. But it was also true that elements often remained or tried to gain entry in the hope that they might capture the Shadow Cabinet before the next ministry was formed. Thus Harcourt and his radical allies had tried to force their way

13 Selborne, *Memorials*, Vol. II, p. 202, and Fitzmaurice, *op. cit.*, Vol. II, pp. 462–465.
14 Midleton, *op. cit.*, p. 270.
15 Sir C. Petrie, *The Life and Letters of Sir Austen Chamberlain*, Vol. I, p. 285.

into Liberal meetings in the 1870s, the Liberal Imperialists refused to leave in the 1890s and after 1906, under Balfour, neither the Protectionists nor their opponents would abandon the field. Obtaining agreement among the Shadow Cabinet was so difficult that Balfour acted on his own in giving the Albert Hall pledge in late 1910, meetings being virtually suspended during the crisis over the leadership in 1911. After his selection, Bonar Law, taking Balcarres' advice, tried to call meetings as rarely as possible, only doing so when controversial issues came up and some authoritative party pronouncement had become imperative.[16]

Modern writers have sometimes suggested that the tactics of opposition in this period were to attack the government from every angle simply aiming to discredit it, there being no attempt to present a coherent series of alternatives.[17] Nothing could be further from the case. At a time when the opposition expected to be in office with the next electoral swing and political memories were longer than they are today, great care was taken to advocate only what could be put into practice.[18] Gladstone may have failed to alter all the policies he had condemned in his Midlothian campaigns, but he had spoken in good faith. Pledges were held to be binding, and Gladstone assumed that front bench support for a motion by Trevelyan (in the late 1870s) for household suffrage in the counties committed the next Liberal Cabinet to such a measure. Queen Victoria urged Forster " when out of office . . . to be very cautious *not* to *pledge* himself *strongly* to *any particular* cause, and to particular measures for they invariably hamper a statesman who takes office." [19] The whole point of the struggles over imperialism in the Liberal Shadow Cabinet and over protection among Conservatives arose from the Opposition's need to present a viable and consistent alternative to the policy of the existing Cabinet.

[16] R. Blake, *op. cit.*, pp. 102–108.
[17] This attitude is implicit in the articles urging Labour in the early 1960s and the Conservatives in the late 1960s not to behave as alternative governments but just to oppose. See B. Crick, " Two Theories of Opposition," *The New Statesman*, June 18, 1960, and the argument between Mr. Iain Macleod and Mr. Edward Heath on this point in 1967.
[18] In 1915 Bonar Law told Carson " that in normal times the functions of an Opposition were twofold, that is to say, to be a vigilant critic of ministers and to provide an alternative administration when necessity arose.' Sir C. Petrie, *The Life and Letters of Sir Austen Chamberlain*, Vol. II, p. 25.
[19] *Letters*, Series II, Vol. II, p. 315. She made the same point to Gladstone; *ibid.*, p. 319.

The next major task of the Cabinet was to govern the country, and this aspect developed to a considerable extent between 1868 and 1914. In its simplest form government was just administration, but the Cabinet had the task of considering defects in the current system and of legislating to solve them or to embody changes of policy. In preparing Bills, increasing use was made of Cabinet Committees to do work which was too much for individual ministers but which it was not thought proper to devolve on civil servants. The bases of the Bill disestablishing the Irish Church were settled in two sittings of the Cabinet and the rest of the work was left to a Committee including the Law Officers for Ireland and two draftsmen.[20]

It was always open to a minister with exceptional knowledge and energy to tackle the problem himself. For example, Gladstone framed most of the clauses of the Irish Church Bill. Dilke was given a Committee to help with the 1884 Redistribution Bill, but he preferred to put it aside and work out the details with the aid of an official. In this case, the draft was accepted by Lord Salisbury and then put before the Liberal Cabinet, some of whom disliked it, but their lack of expert knowledge reduced them to what Dilke described as " swearing at large." [21] On other occasions a Cabinet Committee had to come to the rescue, as over Bruce's Licensing Bill in 1872 when Kimberley, Cardwell, Lowe, Goschen and Hartington found only an outline which required alterations and drafting.[22] There were other motives for passing Bills to Committees. When tackling the Irish land problem, Gladstone wrote that " this is a question arduous and critical within as well as without the Cabinet. . . . A Committee keeps a Cabinet quiet." [23] With such insight, it was surprising that the Grand Old Man laid himself open to the charge that the first Home Rule Bill was concocted between the Irish Secretary and himself and that the Cabinet had had no voice in the matter. He did not make the same mistake in 1893, the second Home Rule Bill being carefully worked through a Committee which contained all interested parties.

20 *Kimberley Papers*, p. 3.
21 Gwynn and Tuckwell, *op. cit.*, Vol. II, pp. 68–74. Dilke did much the same with a Committee on London Government in 1882; Vol. I, p. 421.
22 *Kimberley Papers*, p. 30.
23 *Gladstone-Granville Correspondence*, Vol. I, pp. 58–60.

In the 1868–74 Liberal Ministry, a series of Cabinet meetings in the Autumn worked out legislative proposals ready for the Queen's speech and the assembly of the House in January. This " system " was revived after the Liberal victory of 1880 but only worked well in that year and in 1883, the difficulty being disagreements within the Cabinet and the complexity of the measures. When the party recovered office in 1892, a refinement was adopted. The Cabinet drew up a list of measures and all the more intricate ones were handed over to Committees. (In that year Bills on Local Government, the London County Council, Local Veto, the Single Vote, Welsh Land and Irish Government were treated in this way.[24] Sir Courtney Ilbert in his book on *Legislative Forms and Methods,* published in 1901, describes the reference to a Cabinet Committee as part of the regular procedure.[25] The process was outlined by Morley in 1909. " The Cabinet . . . settles the principles of the Bill, then refers it to a committee of that body; the committee threshes out details in consultation with all the experts concerned and at command; the draft Bill comes to the Cabinet, and it is discussed both on the merits and in relation to parliamentary forces and parliamentary opinion." [26] Morley does well to emphasise a feature which was much more marked in these later years, the increased use of experts and civil servants. In theory they could not be members of Cabinet Committees, but in practice some had to give such constant attendance that the distinction between members and officials at this stage was not marked; it was a joint effort to draft the clauses. Braithwaite, the Assistant Secretary to the Board of Inland Revenue, moralising about the early history of the 1911 Insurance Bill, said, " it is quite certain that the English Government machine could not, working in the normal way, have produced this Bill in three years, and it would probably have choked it to death if it had done so! I don't say that this Bill was properly prepared; I only know that I worked night and day preparing it." [27]

Besides preparing Bills, the Cabinet had to bring together the various sectors of government, think ahead, and provide the motive

---

[24] *Gladstone Papers, Add. MSS.,* 44,648, folios II, 35 and 84. Altogether 24 Bills were on the list for the 1893 session.
[25] pp. 227–228.
[26] Morley, *Recollections,* Vol. II, p. 321.
[27] W. J Braithwaite, *Lloyd George's Ambulance Wagon,* p. 154.

power behind the whole administration. As a machine for co-ordinating and planning, it was poor. With no system for pre-paring information, registering decisions and ensuring that they were carried out, the Cabinet's weaknesses were revealed when a number of complex problems had to be solved at much the same time. Beach wrote to Frere in 1879 that " the question of future policy in South Africa is so large and so difficult, and we have at this time so much else demanding the attention of the Cabinet that I have not been able to get from my colleagues any final decision." [28] Hartington's complaint " that there is no chance of the Cabinet, or of getting Mr. Gladstone to pay attention to Egypt while the Arrears Bill is going on " [29] is usually accepted as evidence of Gladstone's tendency to be obsessed with a single problem. It is true that Gordon might have been saved had the Prime Minister not been absorbed in Egyptian finances and the Reform Bill of 1884, but the Cabinet was to blame also. To some extent the disaster was due to dislike of an expedition on the part of other ministers, but it was also evidence of the difficulty of get-ting attention and action if the Prime Minister was not interested.[30] Once the Cabinet did turn to the Sudan problem, it still remained incapable of keeping several lines of activity going simultaneously. In late 1884, towards the end of a Cabinet meeting, a minister asked if there were any further points. " No, we have done our Egyptian business, and we are an Egyptian government," Glad-stone replied.[31]

In the 1890s and 1900s the papers left by Cabinet Ministers show a steady increase in the work and preparation for Cabinets. Printed memoranda take the place of scraps of notepaper. Glad-stone had always drawn up a rough agenda of items which grew

---

[28] Lady V. Hicks Beach, *op. cit.*, Vol. I, p. 142.

[29] B. Holland, *op. cit.*, Vol. I, p. 365.

[30] Lord George Hamilton thought that " as an executive and administrative body the Cabinet must necessarily, from its composition and numbers, be a failure, unless the Prime Minister is a man of determination and strength and he constitutes himself the Cabinet and its mouthpiece." Lord G. Hamilton, *op. cit.*, Vol. I, p. 301. It was the importance of getting the Prime Minister's ear and interest that put some influence, in secondary matters, into the hands of the Prime Minister's Private Secretary. Men like Montagu Corry, Algernon West and Jack Sandars arranged the Premier's timetable and cor-respondence and while all important matters were at once sent up for attention, less significant items or persons could get a better chance if they were favoured by the Private Secretary.

[31] Morley, *op. cit.*, Vol. III, p. 49.

longer and more complex, sometimes decisions being jotted down beside the points. Cabinet Committees were used for digging out facts about misappropriation of Post Office money in 1873, corrupt practices at elections, the state of London government, possible bases in the East Mediterranean, the condition of secondary education and the smuggling of arms into Northern Ireland.[32] Even with these changes some ministers felt that matters were handled in a rather amateur fashion. In December 1901 Balfour told Lansdowne that some of their difficulties arose

> " out of the perhaps rather hasty decision come to at the first of our Autumn Cabinets with regard to Japan. No papers were circulated to me on this subject before the Cabinet: nor was there any warning that it was likely to be discussed. I was a few minutes late and found the brief debate already in full swing, and the Cabinet not very anxious to hear any views on the general aspects of a problem, which they were treating in the main as one confined to the Far East." [33]

Esher summed up the problem when expressing his fears that attempts to reform the service departments and to get them to work together might break down if special machinery was not maintained. " Nor are these questions in their constructive stages, matter which can be treated adequately by the Cabinet . . . The Cabinet, composed of men absorbed in administrative and parliamentary duties, growing heavier year by year, cannot undertake to inquire into, nor to construct elaborate schemes involving much technical consideration. The special function of the Cabinet is to arrive at decisions upon facts or theories carefully presented in concrete form." [34] The effect of these weaknesses was that the government tended to remain merely a collection of departments with the Prime Minister as the only connecting link. Gladstone thought that this was inevitable (" The Government must in this country be a Government of Departments ") and he objected to Salisbury combining the posts of premier and Foreign Secretary because it meant that " there is no one either to assist or at all check the Foreign Minister," [35] Lord Salisbury, commenting on

---

[32] The first three of these examples are taken from the Gladstone Cabinet Papers, the others from Monypenny and Buckle, *op. cit.*, Vol. VI, p. 254, Sir A. Fitzroy, *Memoirs*, Vol. I, p. 67, and Spender and Asquith, *op. cit.*, Vol. II.

[33] Balfour to Lansdowne, December 12, 1901, *Balfour Papers, Add. MSS.*, 49,727, f. 159.   [34] Esher, *op. cit.*, Vol. II, p. 114.

[35] Sir A. West, *op. cit.*, Vol. II, p. 287.

Disraeli, said that " as the head of a Cabinet his fault was want of firmness. The chiefs of departments got their own way too much. The Cabinet as a whole got it too little . . ." [36] The more a Cabinet had to do, the more true this became and many ministers have commented on the way in which Liberal Cabinets between 1906 and 1911 were absorbed in departmental affairs, an absorption which weakened Cabinet control over policy of each individual department.[37]

In forming and carrying out policy, Cabinets encountered certain other obstacles or imperfections in the machinery at their disposal. At this time the Civil Service was undergoing rapid reorganisation and expansion. A number of able, dedicated men such as Robert Morant, Alfred Milner, Sir Francis Bertie or, for all the controversy around him, Sir Alexander Macdonnell, entered the service and helped build up departmental independence and self-confidence. Their efforts improved and galvanised the administration but did not always make Cabinet control easier. Some of the older departments had the tradition and assurance without any of the reforming elements and of these, the most difficult were the Admiralty and the War Office. Referring to the situation in the late 1880s, Sir George Clarke wrote that " both at the Admiralty and the War Office the permanent officials at this time were too powerful, and fleeting Naval Lords were rarely able to leave an impress upon the Administration." [38] Most of the political leaders were aware of the problem. Disraeli thought that " the Horse Guards will ruin this country, unless there is a Prime Minister who will have his way," [39] while Salisbury confessed " I am really puzzled to know what to do with the Admiralty. I see that it is given up to pedantry of the worst sort." [40] Once again the difficulty was that, if departments lacked the capacity to generate their own reforms, the Cabinet lacked the persistence and the time to do so. When Cardwell

---

[36] A. J. Balfour, *op. cit.*, p. 113.

[37] The increasing need for special knowledge of departmental work led to the practice of asking Shadow Cabinet members to watch over certain subjects. In 1893 Long " was charged by Mr. Balfour with the duty of following all the questions which might be raised affecting my old Department." Long, *op. cit.*, p. 109.

[38] Col. Lord Sydenham of Combe, *My Working Life*, p. 100.

[39] Monypenny and Buckle, *op. cit.*, Vol. VI, pp. 473–474.

[40] Lady G. Cecil, *op. cit.*, Vol. IV, p. 189,

determined to make some alterations in the War Office and was backed by his colleagues, he achieved his ends. The report of the Hartington Commission was carried out in as far as Campbell-Bannerman agreed with its conclusions (which meant retiring the Duke of Cambridge). Lansdowne could do little more because he was not a strong minister and the Cabinet showed no great concern. At the Admiralty, Lord George Hamilton found " a state of chaos " in 1886, replaced the whole Board and if no further progress was made, it was because he felt that all was well.[41] The South African War led to investigations and reports, but the same situation held good. If the departments decided to act or if a united Cabinet or strong minister wanted changes they could be achieved. Arnold-Forster failed because the Army Council opposed his scheme and he could not convince the Cabinet of its merits. Haldane succeeded because the generals accepted most of his ideas and the Cabinet was prepared ultimately, to agree. The Admiralty was to some extent revived by Fisher, but owed little to its First Lords. Only a showdown at the Committee of Imperial Defence in 1911 and the appointment of Winston Churchill brought naval war plans into line with those accepted by the War Office, the Defence Committee and the Cabinet. Even then, Churchill was unable to create a Naval Staff, though whether he preferred not to fight on this issue or whether he became convinced that a Staff was unnecessary, is hard to say.

Thus the generals and admirals with the Court, Society, groups of M.P.s and often sections of the Press behind them, were formidable. A united Cabinet or a strong minister could carry through policies, but when there were many other questions clamouring for attention it was hard to keep a Cabinet up to the mark on such a (politically) unprofitable issue long enough to make an impact, unless the departments were also prepared for a change.

The Foreign Office in the 1870s and 1880s was still largely a group of clerks transmitting the orders of the Foreign Secretary. It did little in the way of collecting information. Disraeli complained that he was not told all the essential facts in 1876 (he mentioned this to Derby on several occasions) while Salisbury lamented the lack of talent in senior posts. Under Lansdowne the pressure

---

[41] Lord G. Hamilton, *op. cit.*, Vol. II, p. 278. It is interesting that Salisbury's comments quoted above were made six years after Hamilton had gone to the Admiralty and when he, as First Lord, clearly felt all was well.

of business, the greater activity in foreign affairs, the complexity of African and Asian rivalries all forced increased professionalism and the acceptance of a hierarchy in the office; one which could sift the incoming business and offer actual advice. After 1906 Sir Francis Bertie and Sir Louis Mallet took part in the formation of policy, they helped Sir Edward Grey transform the Anglo-French Entente into an alliance and they built up the records and research sections of the Office. Compared with the 1880s its atmosphere had been transformed from that of a " cozy, if sometimes rather tedious family party to that of a great and efficient Department of State." [42]

After the Mutiny, little interest was taken in Indian affairs. The chief control over the Secretary of State for India came from the very able men on the Council of India.[43] The civil servants in the Office were recruited by competitive examination from the Order in Council in 1870 and were of a high quality and far superior to those in the Colonial Office which, despite the active period under Joseph Chamberlain, was not noted for its efficiency or even for its knowledge of overseas conditions.

The Cabinet's chief problem in executing its colonial and Indian policies was that of controlling the governors and high commissioners in the field. Part of the difficulty had been slowness of communication. India could be reached by cable but telegraph messages to South Africa only went as far as Madeira, the rest of the distance having to be covered by ship.[44] Even when direct lines were established, pro-consuls with considerable backing at home could act to meet situations and so place the Cabinet in the awkward dilemma of having to endorse their actions or disavow and recall them. The first two examples of this occurred under Gladstone's Ministry. In 1873 Sir Garnet Wolseley backed by Cardwell and Kimberley jockeyed the Prime Minister and the Government into the Ashanti expedition while Bartle Frere took action to suppress the slave trade of Zanzibar relying

---

[42] Zara Steiner, " The Last Years of the Old Foreign Office," *The Historical Journal*, Vol. VI (1963), p. 87.

[43] Donovan Williams, " The Council of India and the Relationship between the Home and Supreme Governments, 1858–1870," *E.H.R.* (1966), pp. 56–73.

[44] Referring to Bartle Frere in South Africa in 1878, Beach said " I cannot really control him without a telegraph (I don't know that I could with one)— I feel it is as likely as not that he is at war with the Zulus at the present moment."—Lady V. Hicks Beach, *op. cit.*, Vol. I, p. 103.

on " the weaknesses of the government and the strength of the public agitation he had set up to carry him through." [45]

Over India, Lord Salisbury " followed the accepted constitutional tradition and left the initiative with the Government in India " [46] but when Lord Northbrook, the Viceroy, brought in Cotton Duties without telling him, he had to disallow the Bill. Lord Lytton took over as Viceroy in 1876 and though relations began by being easy, he too became difficult to control. Lytton pushed ahead with pressure on Afghanistan, twice disobeyed orders from London, and invited snubs from Kabul till the Cabinet was forced to sanction an invasion. [47] At the same time, Sir Bartle Frere who had arrived in South Africa as High Commissioner went beyond his instructions, [48] and became involved in a Zulu war which was only won after initial disasters and serious embarrassment to the Government at home.

The difficulties Gladstone and his colleagues faced in Egypt and the Sudan between 1882 and 1885 was largely their own fault but Gordon's conduct shows how a local agent could force a Cabinet into policies it disliked or involve it in serious criticism. In most cases the official in the colonies (or the private agent such as Rhodes in the 1890s) had supporters in the Cabinet, and the argument that the man on the spot should be trusted always carried force. Yet when the Colonial Secretary, the Prime Minister or the Cabinet had definite policies, obedience was not hard to enforce. The famous dispute between Curzon and Kitchener, which led to the former's resignation, was only the culmination of a series of clashes between the Viceroy and the Cabinet over a remission of Indian taxes and over relations with Tibet and Afghanistan. Midleton considered that Curzon " did not in the slightest respect the feelings of the Cabinet, and was inclined to

---

[45] W. O. McIntyre, " British Policy in West Africa: The Ashanti Expedition of 1873–74," *Historical Journal*, Vol. V (1962), pp. 19–46 and R. J. Gavin, " The Bartle Frere Mission to Zanzibar, 1873," *Historical Journal*, Vol. V (1962), pp. 122–148.

[46] Lady G. Cecil, *op. cit.*, Vol. II, p. 66.

[47] M. Cowling, " Lytton, the Cabinet and the Russians, August to November, 1878," *E.H.R.* (1961) pp. 59–79.

[48] Frere was in fact censured by the publication of a despatch in which the Cabinet said he had taken " without their full knowledge and sanction a course almost certain to result in a war which, as they had previously impressed upon him, every effort should have been used to avoid."—*Ibid.*, p. 127.

challenge their right to interfere." He was, as Balfour said, making claims which "would raise India to the position of an independent and not always friendly power." [49] Morley declared that he "would not have stood from Curzon for two months what (the previous Cabinet) . . . have stood for two years [50] and made it quite clear to Minto that "the Government of India is no absolute or independent branch of the Imperial Government." Definite on this issue and backed by his colleagues, he was able to insist that the Viceroy was "in every respect answerable to the Cabinet." [51]

In examining how far the machinery at the disposal of the Cabinet weakened or impeded its action, the position of the Treasury must be considered. Economy was a matter of passionate belief for Victorians (for Lord Randolph Churchill as much as for Gladstone), while the principles of free trade and nondiscriminatory taxation kept revenue down. So for both ideological and practical reasons public expenditure was cut to a minimum and the Treasury was built up until it had a central role in the government. In 1869,

> "The Cabinet desire notice to be taken by all members of the Government or others who may either have to take proceedings in Parliament, or prepare bills on the part of the Government that whenever it is proposed to repeal, or alter, or to grant exemption from any tax or duty . . . or to impose any charge upon the Exchequer, much inconvenience will be avoided if the person or persons concerned communicate with the Treasury before making any declaration, or taking any public proceedings, of a nature to commit themselves and the Government, so that the matter may be considered, and a common conclusion arrived at. And the Cabinet accordingly, direct that such communication shall be made in all cases without fail. . . ." [52]

Entrenched behind this power, the Treasury built up two functions. One was the business of estimating revenue, planning taxation and negotiating the three major estimates, in which every Chancellor of the Exchequer took the fullest interest. The

---

[49] Midleton, *op. cit.*, pp. 190–200.
[50] *Ibid.*, p. 208.
[51] Morley, *Recollections*, Vol. II, p. 308.
[52] *Gladstone Papers, Add.Mss.*, 66,637, f. 73, June 21, 1869. The Treasury had been gaining power within the administration since the 1850s (when Sir Charles Trevelyan, the Assistant Secretary, had said it should become "really a *supervising* office ").

second aspect was that of going over and authorising or objecting to each item of expenditure as it arose during the year. Such a revision might well impinge on the policy of a department, yet this was the part of Treasury business which Chancellors often left to officials. Sir Reginald Welby, the permanent Under-Secretary, hoped Childers would be " more visibly *head of the Treasury."* How much was referred to the Chancellor was up to him. Lowe had seen a good deal; Sir Stafford Northcote began similarly but soon passed much on to his Parliamentary Under-Secretary, while " Lord Beaconsfield, as you may imagine, never cared for Treasury business." [53]

In the hands of officials this power of review sometimes became a kind of double-check, so that matters which the Cabinet had accepted in principle had to be fought out again when it came to paying for them. The result was delay and sometimes the frustration of the policy. Cardwell found his attempts to clean up Army administration made much harder when the Treasury tried to refuse compensation for redundant civil servants and he was forced, ultimately, to curtail his programme of reforms. At the Board of Education, Lord George Hamilton found that the Treasury asked for a routine reduction of £10,000 a year without considering whether this might cripple the Cabinet's policy in education. Treasury authorisations were so slow that one-third of the service life of warships was lost in the time taken over their construction. There is no doubt that Treasury control helped to weld the Civil Service into a unified body and produced some admirable habits of mind, but it did make the execution of policy harder and sometimes stopped promising developments.

Lord Salisbury was the Treasury's chief critic. He had encountered its resistance to grants from the Secret Service Fund, and when the Cabinet agreed to lend some art treasures to Denmark only to be refused £100 for packing and transport, he exploded: " Has the Cabinet *no* authority? " On a later occasion he said " these Treasury officials are enough to drive one mad . . . It is quite intolerable that they should be allowed to thwart a policy which has been adopted at so much trouble and with so much deliberation." [54] There was some foundation for the view that

---

[53] Lt.-Col. S. C. Childers, *op. cit.*, Vol. II, p. 146.
[54] Lady G. Cecil, *op. cit.*, Vol. IV, pp. 113–116.

the Treasury was economising by sweating the public service, though it was unjust of Salisbury to appear to blame the Treasury for the weaknesses revealed by the South African War.[55] Hicks Beach was right to point out that " all the expenditure proposed by the War Office in order to carry out the (Cabinet's) decisions has been accepted." [56]

Hicks Beach was among the last of the Victorian Chancellors of the Exchequer whose budgetary policy reinforced the revisions and economies imposed by the Treasury.[57] The South African War, expanding armaments programmes and the start of social services all created a desperate shortage of money. It became impossible to maintain that enough could be raised on the old Gladstonian principles of taxation buttressed by constant economy. It may be true that after wars expenditure has risen to use up the available revenue, but between the 1890's and 1914 revenue lagged and ministers were driven to advocate protection or differential rates of taxation, which involved an element of soaking the rich. In this situation, the important struggles were over new ways of raising money, and expenditure of five- or six-figure sums to build so many battleships or start old age pensions. The Treasury could still make life difficult (as when it refused to provide a staff for the National Insurance Commission), but once the Cabinet had decided on a naval programme or on setting up a series of Labour Exchanges, the Treasury had to fall in to line.

So the old weaknesses of the Cabinet as an executive body and the inadequacy of some of its agencies were emphasised and intensified by a growing volume of business of increasing complexity. As a method of reaching decisions on matters of policy the concept of a group of men sitting round a table and discussing till they reached a solution was still adequate. Such a gathering also sufficed to handle parliamentary tactics. But with departments establishing a tradition and developing expertise, with Britain requiring elaborate government and the colonies wanting protection, the Cabinet had to do more than just take decisions. The

---

55 H.L. Debates, Vol. 78, cols. *30–32*, 1900.

56 Lady V. Hicks Beach, *op. cit.*, Vol. II, p. 116.

57 Beach killed one of Chamberlain's schemes to put Suez Canal profits in a special fund for colonial development. If the money was earmarked in this way, Beach said he would have to impose fresh taxation. Garvin, *op. cit.*, Vol. III, pp. 175–177.

work of the various departments had to be co-ordinated and plans made for future eventualities. Policies now required continuity over a period of time and the Cabinet had to be capable of keeping several lines of activity going simultaneously.

All these problems combined and were therefore most evident in the field of defence. The War Office and Admiralty both required overhaul, yet the Cabinet was not a suitable body for making long and intricate inquiries, hearing evidence and writing reports. Besides the internal difficulties of these departments, they had to be persuaded to co-operate with each other and with the Colonial, India and Foreign Offices, while some of their decisions would require Treasury sanction. In addition, a record was of obvious value since situations were likely to recur. Once the defence of a port, a method of supplying troops on the North-West frontier of India, or the advantages of a new field gun had been worked out, the information was worth keeping and bringing up to date in case this problem recurred.

These points were only slowly appreciated after considerable experience and various experiments. The first reaction, as with internal problems, was to employ Cabinet Committees when specific questions arose. In 1870 Gladstone's Cabinet appointed five ministers to decide whether the Suez Canal route was to be considered available in time of war.[58] The Near Eastern crisis of 1876–1878 with rumours of war led both the colonies and the Colonial Office to examine their defences, and an inter-departmental Committee reported in June 1878 on the installations at ports in Africa, the West Indies, Australia and Canada. The Committee brought the War Office, the Admiralty and the Colonial Office together over one specific issue, but its work did not involve the Cabinet. Later in 1879, Carnarvon was appointed chairman of a Royal Commission on the Defence of British Possessions and Commerce Abroad which studied the problem for three years but no further practical steps were taken till Russian movements near Penjdeh in Afghanistan brought renewed tension in 1885. Then further requests for advice from the colonies led to the revival of the inter-departmental committee (now known as the Colonial Defence Committee) with the same Secretary, Captain Jekyll.[59]

---

[58] *Gladstone Papers, Add. MSS.*, 44,638, ff. 76–77.
[59] He had also acted as Secretary to the Royal Commission.

The reports of the Committee show that it was really a series of conferences between representatives of the three departments who examined schemes for the defence of colonial ports, the annual reports on colonial forces, and colonial acts and ordinances on defence.[60]

The Cabinet itself was not particularly concerned until the late 1880s when there were various war scares in Europe and, in May 1888, Lord Wolseley announced that the country was open to invasion from across the Channel. Next month, the Government appointed a Royal Commission under Hartington to " enquire into the Civil and Professional Administration of the Naval and Military Departments and the Relation of those Departments to each other and to the Treasury." At the same time, Lord Salisbury set up a Cabinet Committee of National Defence and took the chair himself. The Duke of Cambridge and Sir Garnet Wolseley both gave evidence and Salisbury circulated a minute arguing that " it is one's duty to see that the subject has been carefully considered in all its details, and that plans for resisting invasion have been thoroughly worked out by the two departments." If an attack comes " there will be no time then to work out the necessary dispositions." An investigation during the winter revealed serious deficiencies at the Admiralty and led to the Naval Defence Act of 1889. Lord Salisbury was alarmed by his discoveries, and one of the remedies he considered was " setting up a tribunal of three or five Cabinet Ministers to determine all questions at issue between the (Service) Departments," [61] Ministers continued to discuss the problem from 1888 till 1892 and Harcourt reported that " in the late Government . . . they had a standing Committee of the Cabinet sitting *en permanence* on naval affairs." [62] A further product of all these discussions was an inter-departmental body known as the Joint Naval and Military Committee. Started in 1891, it was really a War Office Committee to consider aspects of coastal defence in which the Admiralty were also interested.

The Hartington Commission had reported in 1890, recommending the creation of a Naval and Military Council presided

---

[60] There is a short history of the Committee between 1885 and 1904, when it was converted into a Sub-committee of the Committee of Imperial Defence, in the Committee of Imperial Defence Papers for November 1904.

[61] Lady G. Cecil, *op. cit.*, Vol. IV, pp. 186–190.

[62] A. G. Gardiner, *op. cit.*, Vol. II, p. 342. A meeting of the Committee on November 9, 1888, is described by Gathorne-Hardy, *op. cit.*, Vol. II, p. 299.

over by the Prime Minister, including the ministers in charge of the two services and their chief professional advisers. They also advised that the proceedings and decisions of the Council should be recorded. Naval administration was regarded as largely satisfactory, since the First Lord had ample expert advice, but the Commissioners concluded that a General Staff was needed for the Army, that the Secretary of State should be advised by an Army Council and that the post of Commander-in-Chief should be abolished. Speaking in the Commons, the Secretary of State for War, Edward Stanhope, said that the proposed co-ordinating Council did no go far enough. The government wanted a Naval and Military Council formed from within the Cabinet and including the Secretaries of State for the Colonies, India and Foreign Affairs, under the presidency of the Prime Minister.[63] Why this was not carried through has never been explained, as Salisbury and Stanhope were both in favour of it. The failure is probably further evidence that even when a Cabinet approved of proposals, some resistance from the departments, lack of drive on the part of the Secretary of State and the First Lord and a full programme of immediate tasks made any large-scale reorganisation very hard.

Neither Gladstone nor Rosebery's Cabinets had the energy or the inclination to reconsider these questions, but when Lord Salisbury returned in 1895 a Standing Defence Committee of the Cabinet was constituted under the Lord President of the Council, the Duke of Devonshire. Between August and December a series of minutes were compiled in which the ministers concerned set out their views of the nature and tasks of the Committee. Balfour wanted it to deal with Imperial Defence—strategy, co-ordination of the departments, controversies over estimates, distribution of ships, coaling stations, pattern and character of guns, and so on. Salisbury put the matter simply as determining " the work for which the Army and Navy have to be fitted, and how they are to be fitted for it," and Devonshire agreed. Goschen as First Lord argued that this was far too much. The Committee should tackle only those matters in Imperial defence which were not the sole responsibility of the War Office or the Admiralty, such as the bases at Hong Kong and Gibraltar, and it might undertake a preliminary examination of the Estimates. He supported Balfour's views

[63] H.C. Debates, Vol. 346, cols. 764–767, 1890.

without any appreciation of the wider implications of strategic planning which Balfour had included. Lansdowne generally sided with Goschen.[64] As the Committee could only work with the support of the Service Ministries, and again because the Cabinet was absorbed in the regular work of government, Goschen's approach prevailed.

In the late 1890s both the Queen and Lord Salisbury were worried about the War Office, Her Majesty describing it as being in "a state of confusion and want of proper efficiency," [65] while the Prime Minister said, "most of his colleagues were in despair about it." [66] Yet Lansdowne complained that the Cabinet showed little interest in his attempts at reform, which involved reducing the powers of the Commander-in-Chief and creating a Military Board and a Consultative Council. He was continually harried by Hicks Beach's demands for economy (and had, for instance, to enlist Salisbury's help before Hicks Beach would part with money for practice manoeuvres). In February 1898 Lansdowne offered to resign and let a Royal Commission or the Defence Committee try to produce an acceptable reorganisation. Salisbury replied that as each member of the Cabinet seemed to have his own ideas no new departure was possible, but this was no reason for resignation. Lansdowne then stood by his proposals for reform and the Cabinet gave way, but war intervened.[67]

The disasters in South Africa revived the whole issue. Salisbury told the Lords that the British Constitution was not adequate as a war machine [68] and Balfour created a storm by saying that "the man in the street knew as much as the man in the Cabinet." [69] The first reaction within the Government came when Devonshire raised the question of the Defence Committee in November 1900. He said it had not worked as intended, having "met rarely without any definite agenda . . . No minutes have been kept, and in general there have been no definite decisions to record." Goschen replied that the Committee had done excellent work. It had dealt with docks at Bermuda, Jamaica and Singapore, whether the Army

[64] P.R.O. Cab. 1, box 2, No. 55.
[65] *Letters*, Series III, Vol. III, p. 318. This was after the Nile expedition of 1898.
[66] *Ibid.*, p. 403.
[67] Lord Newton, *op. cit.*, pp. 137–139 and 148–151.
[68] H.L. Debates, Vol. 78, col. 30, 1900.
[69] Dugdale, *op. cit.*, Vol. I, p. 303.

or the Navy should control Wei-hai-Wei and had arranged programmes for building coal depots and barracks. He was opposed to regular meetings, a permanent secretary or a wider field of action, as these would " be the beginning of a Court of Revision, a surveillance by other Cabinet Ministers " of the work of the War Office and Admiralty. Hicks Beach likewise had " never thought it possible that the Committee of Defence could undertake either the work which was suggested for it by the Prime Minister's minute of 1895, or that which the Lord President states the Royal Commission, of which he was Chairman, had in view." All the Committee could do was discuss points in dispute between the departments and between these and the Treasury. Both thought that a Committee of the Cabinet could not have outsiders as members and Beach was opposed to a secretary or minutes.[70] Only Lansdowne supported Devonshire's desire for an expansion of the Committee's duties, and no changes were made.[71]

The impression of the Committee that emerges from this exchange is substantially correct. It had only considered a few minor matters which involved both service departments and were referred to it from time to time by the Cabinet, though it had done some work on the Estimates.[72] During the war, the Committee's only contribution was to sanction the supersession of Sir Redvers Buller by Sir Frederick Roberts. This decision was, in fact, taken by Lord Lansdowne and Balfour who fortified themselves with the approval of the Committee as all the Cabinet were not available.[73]

Once hostilities were over, a Royal Commission was appointed to inquire into the preparations for and conduct of the war.

---

[70] The view that only ministers could be members of the Cabinet or a Cabinet Committee was generally accepted, but the attempt to prevent any outsiders attending had in practice been breaking down. Experts had been called to give evidence on a number of occasions. Dilke attended in 1882, though only Under-Secretary for Foreign Affairs, pro-consuls like Baring and Milner came to report on local conditions, while military men (Wolseley and Roberts) and the law officers gave special advice. After 1900 officials like Morant and Braithwaite worked in conjunction with Cabinet Committees and were regularly present at their meetings, though the practice of excluding non-ministers from membership was maintained till after 1914.

[71] P.R.O. Cab. I, box 3, No. 53.

[72] See Balfour's speech in the Commons on March 5, 1903. H.C. Debates, Vol. 68, cols. 1578–1586 and the *Report of the Royal Commission on the War in South Africa*, 1904 (Cd. 1789) XL, pp. 135–137. Disputes over the Army Estimates were referred, in the first instance, to the Committee in 1896 and 1899. Lady V. Hicks Beach, *op. cit.*, Vol. II, pp. 57 and 84.

[73] Dugdale, *op. cit.*, Vol. I, pp. 294–296.

St. John Brodrick and his successor as Secretary of State, Arnold-Foster, each came forward with plans for setting the Army on a new basis but neither won the support of the generals or of the Cabinet. There had been some moves in the direction suggested by the Hartington Commission (an Army Council had been set up to advise the Secretary of State in 1895 and in 1904 the post of Commander-in-Chief was abolished), but with no apparent effect. The Service Ministers did, however, win one round. Selborne, the First Lord, had told Balfour in March 1902 that he would not go on fighting for money in annual portions. A decision had to be taken about the size of Navy the country wanted, and then he would be able to ask for a reasonable amount over a series of years.[74] He and Brodrick followed this up with a Memorandum on November 10, 1902, in which they demanded an authoritative committee (not specifically a *Cabinet* Committee, so that experts could be members) to think ahead and plan the strategy of defence, the size of forces needed, and their cost. Balfour was reluctant at first but then agreed.[75]

On December 18, 1902, the Defence Committee was reconstituted with the Duke of Devonshire as Chairman. After Devonshire left the Cabinet in October 1903 the Prime Minister took over the chairmanship. The Committee was a consultative and not an executive body, designed to " survey as a whole the strategical military needs of the Empire." [76] It would not be bound by the conventions which applied to Cabinet Committees since it was to be a committee responsible to the Lord President, and after 1903 to the Prime Minister. There was to be a fixed nucleus consisting of the Prime Minister, the Lord President, the Service Ministers, the First Sea Lord, the Senior Army Officer and the heads of Naval and Military Intelligence. Also agenda, minutes and records of decisions were to be kept. At the second meeting on February 18, 1903, the title of Committee of Imperial Defence was adopted. The old inter-departmental Colonial Defence and Joint Military and Naval Committees became sub-committees of the Committee of Imperial Defence.

---

[74] *Balfour Papers, Add. MSS.*, 49,707, f. 105.
[75] The Memorandum is in the Committee of Imperial Defence Papers, November 10, 1902, and the background in Midleton, *op. cit.*, pp. 140–145.
[76] Balfour's speech on March 5, 1903.

Even at this stage, there were reservations. Minutes were being kept by a member of the Committee, and when the report of the Esher Committee in January 1904 suggested a civilian secretary and full-time staff, Balfour wrote " I confess . . . I am a little afraid of it." [77] However, he accepted the argument shortly after. By February 1904 he had decided that the Prime Minister would be the only permanent member—the others would all come by invitation, and in May 1904 a Treasury minute agreed to pay for a secretary, two assistant secretaries and clerical help.[78]

Historians have taken a considerable interest in these developments up till 1904. There has been little information about the actual work of the Committee between 1904 and 1914 and it has, perhaps, been natural to assume that the Committee handled all the preparations for a possible war, including staff talks with the French Army. For students of British government this may lead on to the assumption that the problems of ensuring effective Cabinet supervision, departmental co-operation and long-term planning were well on the way to solution. The question of Cabinet control is discussed in the next chapter (pp. 334–342 below), but in considering the problems of co-ordination and the capacity to think ahead, it is more accurate to regard the establishment of the Committee as simply a stage in a long-drawn-out process. Broadly speaking, by 1914 departmental isolation had not been broken down and it became evident that though some officers had attended meetings at the Committee of Imperial Defence, neither the War Office nor the Admiralty had accepted the need for close co-operation when the serious business of fighting began.[79]

In preparing the Army and Navy for the exigencies of a European war, progress was made, but not through the efforts of the Committee of Imperial Defence. The Esher Committee on the Reconstruction of the War Office had made useful suggestions in 1904, but the real reorganisation of the Army was carried out by

[77] *Balfour Papers, Add. MSS.*, 49,722, f. 118.

[78] All the details are in the First Minute Book, Committee of Imperial Defence Papers, and the Treasury Minute is in *Parliamentary Papers*, 1904, LXXXIX, p. 111.

[79] See N. H. Gibbs, *The Origins of Imperial Defence*, J. Ehrman, *Cabinet Government and War*, F. A. Johnson, *Defence by Committee*, J. P. Mackintosh, " The Role of the Committee of Imperial Defence before 1914," *E.H.R.*, Vol. 77 (1962), pp. 490–503, and Lord Hankey, *The Supreme Command*, Vol. I, pp. 11–150.

Haldane and the Army Council after 1906.[80] They planned the Expeditionary Force and conducted the military conversations with France. Naval policy was largely under the control of Fisher and there is no clear indication of how much he confided in his First Lords, Tweedmouth and McKenna.

The tasks left to the Committee of Imperial Defence were the discussion of those points which were not clearly the business of either the Admiralty or the War Office, or involved scientific or theoretical speculations which did not play a major part in the thinking of either department. The minutes of the Committee record eighty-two meetings during the Conservative Ministry, fifteen under Campbell-Bannerman and thirty-one with Asquith presiding.[81] In its early stages the Committee examined the general question of invasion and studied some recurring problems such as the defence of the North-West frontier of India, of Southern Persia and the Gulf and of Egypt. Later it turned more to specific difficulties, and a random selection of the subjects under discussion between 1910 and 1914 shows the defence of St. Helena, insurance of merchant ships in wartime, the frontiers of India again, the uses of wireless telegraphy, defence of the Shetlands, the implications of a Channel Tunnel, naval strength in the North Sea, and the charging of customs duties in wartime. At three meetings in 1911, members of the Imperial Conference were present. Sir Edward Grey gave a survey of international relations and of British commitments, and then military and naval preparations by the various parts of the Empire were outlined and problems of co-ordination discussed. But crucial questions of the composition, numbers and deployment of the British Army, the strength and tactics of the Navy, and co-operation between them in the event of war with Germany were not dealt with by the Committee.[82]

The staff talks with the French Army began in December 1905 and there are records of four small conferences between then and

---

[80] See A. Tucker, " The Issue of Army Reform in the Unionist Government, 1903–05," *Historical Journal*, Vol. IX (1966), pp. 90–100.

[81] The minutes are in the Papers of the Committee of Imperial Defence open under the Fifty-Year Rule (at the time of writing) to 1910. The minutes for 1910–1914 can be read in the *Asquith Papers*, Box 6.

[82] This is why, as will be argued later, it was quite possible for ministers like Morley to attend meetings without ever hearing that it had been arranged for the B.E.F. to go to France in the event of war.

January 1906 in the C.I.D. records.[83] Thereafter the talks continued in secret. The British side of the plan to send a force to France was revised in July 1907 and put before a sub-committee of the C.I.D. set up in 1908 to consider the military needs of the Empire. An account of Britain's Treaty obligations had been submitted by the Foreign Office, and the sub-committee then considered sending a force to France, Belgium, Holland or Denmark, which were possible targets for German attack. There were three meetings (December 3 and 17, 1908, and March 23, 1909) at which the General Staff argued that the best policy was to send five of the six divisions of the British Expeditionary Force to reinforce the left wing of the French Armies. Only at the last meeting were the staff talks mentioned, though their existence was not referred to in the minute, which recorded simply that the General Staff's plan was accepted. This was reported to a full meeting of the C.I.D. on July 24, 1909. Then Sir John Fisher exploded and after his denunciation of the Army's scheme the matter was not pressed to a conclusion.[84] Clearly major strategy was being worked out inside the War Office and the Admiralty, and when plans were brought to the Committee of Defence, it was not acting as a final tribunal or policy-making body but just as a conference chamber where the two sides could meet.[85] And when sharp disagreement was revealed, the Committee of Imperial Defence did not enforce a settlement or reconciliation. Esher, commenting on the situation, noted that " the Admiralty is very obstructive . . . We come to decisions, and they are treated as the amiable observations of a few well-meaning but harmless amateur strategists." [86]

---

[83] Lord Hankey was not attached to the C.I.D. at this time and it is not surprising, therefore, that he repeats the error that Grey initiated the talks in January 1906 and he is also wrong in saying that the Cabinet did not learn of the talks till 1912: *op. cit.*, pp. 62–63.

[84] J. E. Tyler, *The British Army and the Continent*, 1904–1914, pp. 92–93, and Admiral Sir R. H. Bacon, *Lord Fisher*, Vol. II, pp. 182–183. Two indeterminate resolutions were passed leaving matters as they stood. Lord Hankey, *op. cit.*, p. 70.

[85] Lord Hankey says that in 1908 " naval and military plans were as yet being worked out in complete isolation. . . . No central body was privy to both plans and able to give a guiding hand," *op. cit.*, p. 64.

[86] Esher, *op. cit.*, Vol. II, p. 430. F. A. Johnson in his *Defence by Committee* has provided a very detailed history of the Committee of Imperial Defence in this period. He was writing too early, however, to be allowed to see the minutes. As a result he does not examine the efficacy of the Committee of

The major issues came up a second time at the Committee of Imperial Defence, when Haldane asked for a meeting to consider what action was to be taken if the Agadir crisis led to a war between France and Germany. At the meeting on August 23, 1911, Sir Arthur Wilson, Fisher's successor, revealed even more precise objections to the Army's plan and refused to transport the B.E.F. to France. The General Staff then wanted to send all six divisions. Asquith was not happy about stripping the country of regular soldiers directly war broke out but he agreed, under pressure from Haldane, that such discrepancies between naval and military planning could not be allowed to continue.[87] The Navy was brought into line in the following year after Admiral Sir Arthur Wilson had retired and Winston Churchill had been appointed First Lord.

After the 1911 meeting, the Committee met five times in 1912, four times in 1913 and again four times before the outbreak of war in 1914. On these occasions it continued to examine the difficult but rather peripheral problems which involved both naval and military elements. When the French asked for a naval agreement and talks in 1912, the matter was settled in principle in the Cabinet while the Admiralty handled all details. The Committee of Imperial Defence was not informed of the French proposals but was consulted about the most desirable disposition of the Navy. It replied that the main fleet should be kept in home waters and a squadron maintained in the Mediterranean equal to the strength of the largest naval force there, excluding the French.[88] The Committee made one other contribution in this field. A permanent sub-committee set up in late 1911 compiled a War Book of detailed

Imperial Defence and accepts the usual claims that between 1906 and 1911 it was " the centre of strategic planning." And this despite the known fact that by 1911 the plans of the War Office and the Admiralty had not been reconciled either by the Committee of Imperial Defence or by any other body.

[87] Asquith wrote to Haldane on August 31, 1911: " Sir A. Wilson's ' plan ' can only be described as puerile, and I have dismissed it at once as wholly impracticable." He accepted the General Staff's plan in principle but " it should be limited in the first instance to the despatch of four divisions. Grey agrees with me, and so (I think) does Winston . . ." *Haldane Papers, MSS.,* 5,909, f. 140.

[88] *Asquith Papers,* Dep. 6. Cabinet letter for July 5, and Box 6, Minute of the Committee of Imperial Defence for July 4, 1912.

instructions for all departments concerned in the movement of the B.E.F. to France.[89]

Further evidence of the indeterminate position occupied by the Committee of Imperial Defence was that its role in the event of war had not been thought out. Haldane had hoped that it could be transformed from an advisory body into the centre of executive control.[90] Esher, on the other hand, considered that " in war, its doors should be closed: yes, at the very first shot." [91] In fact, a somewhat different body called the War Council met irregularly in a part-executive, part-advisory capacity after November 1914. All that remained of the Committee of Imperial Defence was a series of sub-committees considering minor problems which required research or co-ordination of departments.[92]

Looking back to the foundation of the Committee, there is no absolutely clear statement of the functions Selborne, Brodrick and Balfour had originally expected it to fulfil. The various requests and memoranda from 1895 to 1904 suggest that they expected it to work out the size, type and deployment of British forces in any conflict that could be foreseen and to estimate the peacetime bases, training and equipment that such forces would need. But they also insisted that the Committee was purely advisory and not executive. In this case its chances of becoming the centre of strategic planning depended on two possibilities. If the service departments had been convinced of its value, they could have submitted their problems and their plans and then acted on the recommendations of the Committee. Instead, they kept all the most important matters to themselves and only explained their views when summoned to what were really occasional conferences held under the auspices of the Committee.

The other possibility was that powerful ministers, and of these much the most likely was the Prime Minister, would decide to use

---

[89] There were three other permanent sub-committees: the Oversea Defence Committee, which was the former Colonial Defence Committee dating from 1885, the Home Ports Defence Committee which was the former Joint Naval and Military Committee of 1891, and an Aerial Navigation Committee. There is a paper on the constitution and functions of the Committee of Imperial Defence dated August 27, 1912, in the *Asquith Papers*, Box 15.

[90] Haldane, *op. cit.*, p. 235. The Secretary, Sir Maurice Hankey, also took this view. See Lord Hankey, *Government Control in War*, p. 32.

[91] Esher, *op. cit.*, Vol. II, p. 250.

[92] There is a list of 23 of them in the *Asquith Papers*, dated September 1914, Box 6. The War Council is discussed below, in Chap. 12.

the Committee and insist that it should go over all plans, and then have its suggestions adopted. But this would have turned the Committee into an executive body. Nevertheless it might have happened had the Prime Ministers of the period been of a different disposition. As it was, Balfour rapidly became fascinated by the intellectual problems involved in the hypothetical situations and semi-scientific problems that were raised. Under his chairmanship, the Committee met on average once a fortnight and considered many minor questions, but also some that could have been important. It debated alternative plans for defending the Indian frontier (and produced more than thirty-six memoranda on the subject) and considered the value of ports in North Africa. The premier also presided over a sub-committee on the possibility of an invasion of Britain and submitted his own views in a lengthy paper. The trouble was that Balfour, though intellectually acute and interested, was not a hard-headed administrator who watched his decisions go down the chain of command till the right result emerged.[93] Despite the view of Balfour's Committee that invasion was not a serious danger, the matter was re-examined (with the same conclusion) under Asquith in 1907–08 and yet the War Office's old fears all revived after 1914. Nor was there any attempt to see that the Navy adapted its preparations to fit in with these conclusions.

Campbell-Bannerman accepted the Committee but called it together on average only every second month. He had never believed that Britain needed a General Staff to make plans for possible wars between the Powers, and his experiences on the Committee of Imperial Defence were not such as to worry him on that account.[94] The activity of the Committee declined a little further under Asquith. He was a brilliant moderator, an advocate who spoke to his brief with the maximum of effect, but he was not a man of action capable of seeing the need for new machinery or of starting and establishing new patterns of administration.

[93] This was clearly revealed in his period as First Lord of the Admiralty during the war.

[94] It was Campbell-Bannerman who had objected to the Hartington Commission's recommendation that a General Staff be established. His minute argued that " in this country there is no room for ' general military policy ' in this larger and more ambitious sense of the phrase." All that was needed was a tightening up of the defence of our depots and coaling stations. His letter to Sir George Clarke saying that he had been " sceptical as to the

There was a great improvement in the state of both the Army and the Navy in the years before 1914 but the credit must go to Haldane and the generals in the one case, and to the admirals, later aided by Churchill, in the other. The one really successful combined operation of the War, getting the B.E.F. to its station in France, was the work of these two departments after the Cabinet had forced them to co-ordinate their plans in 1911.[95]

Many writers have hailed the Committee of Imperial Defence as the germ of the later War Cabinets and of the Ministry of Defence. It is natural to predicate such a connection, as the composition of the Committee of Imperial Defence was very similar to that of the War Council called together on August 5, 1914, and it in turn is supposed to have developed into Lloyd George's War Cabinet. There was some overlapping of personnel and the Secretariat of the Committee passed on to the War Cabinet but the roles of these two bodies were totally different. The Committee, as Balfour had always insisted, was purely advisory and had not played a continuing or decisive part in the formation of war plans before 1914. The War Council (not set up till November 1914) was an indeterminate body existing alongside the full Cabinet its advice being sought on new departures and combined operations. Lloyd George's War Cabinet differed entirely in that it was purely executive and derived from the Cabinet itself.[96]

use and working of the Committee " but was now " completely converted " suggests (as do the minutes of the Committee of Imperial Defence) that this was because the Committee tackled depots and coaling stations rather than that Campbell-Bannerman had discovered a new interest in strategy and co-ordination of the armed forces. (*Report of the Hartington Commission,* 1890 (Cd. 5979) XIX, p. XXIX, and Lord Sydenham of Combe, *op. cit.,* p. 209.)

[95] Haldane told his mother on October 24, 1911, that with the change at the Admiralty " I hope now, in conjunction with Churchill, to have the chance of bringing the two Services more closely together." *Haldane Papers, MSS.,* 5,986, f. 167. Looking back on this period in 1925, Haldane reflected that " If our plans had been made, not in the War Office and in the Admiralty, but in the Committee of Imperial Defence, and had been presented to France from that body . . . I believe that . . . our influence would have been correspondingly greater." D. Sommer, *op. cit.,* p. 396.

[96] The view that the Committee of Imperial Defence was the true ancestor of the War Council of 1914 and later of the War Cabinet comes largely from the writings of Lord Hankey (see his Lee Knowles lecture, *Government Control in War,* published in 1945, which relies mainly on his own evidence before the Dardanelles Commission of 1917). This is largely a matter of pride of parentage, for there are evident connections—the main one being the Secretariat under Hankey—but for the purposes of the historian the important point is that before 1914 the Committee of Imperial Defence met

It was, in fact, unrealistic of Balfour to expect the Committee of Imperial Defence to occupy an important place at the highest levels of government while remaining advisory. If the Prime Minister had regularly sought and enforced the opinions of the Committee of Imperial Defence, it would have become an executive body, a kind of sub-Cabinet or a super-ministry. With no place in the chain of command and no right to have questions referred to it, the Committee gradually fell back to studying selected items of technical difficulty or collecting information on interdepartmental matters.[97] The corollary of such an advisory function (and the Committee of Imperial Defence was better equipped to provide informed advice than any previous body) was that the Cabinet should hear its views and give clear decisions on the big issues. Yet most of the major questions went direct from the departments to the Cabinet and were either settled or left open on political grounds. The sort of advice which the Committee of Imperial Defence could give was seldom requested except on rare occasions such as the naval redistribution of 1912. After 1914 this function was handed on to the War Council but the Cabinet was still left with the problems of overall control and co-ordination of military effort which had not been elucidated by the practice of the previous decade.

These difficulties and the attempt to adapt the machinery of government were most evident, as has been said, in the field of defence. But they were not different in kind from the adjustments which had to be made to meet the changing conditions of administration at home and in the colonial areas. There was the same tendency for the older departments with established practices to resist new developments. The Treasury, once described by Lord Randolph Churchill as " a knot of damned Gladstonians," had the strongest of traditions. Salisbury often commented on their influence on the otherwise irreproachable Hicks Beach. When

occasionally and played a minor advisory role, while Lloyd George's War Cabinet was the executive body meeting every day and running the war. The latter took over the powers and outlook of the peacetime Cabinet and added some of the practices of the old Committee of Imperial Defence. The developments during the war are examined more fully below, in Part 5.

[97] As Haldane summed up the situation writing to Spender on October 30, 1911, " . . . The Committee of Imperial Defence never touches policy. It ascertains facts and supplies technical information," *Haldane Papers, MSS.*, 5,909, f. 168. Asquith also confirms that " no large question of policy was settled by the conclusions of the Committee of Imperial Defence," *The Genesis of the War*, p. 114.

Ritchie went out of his way to condemn protection while repealing the Corn Tax, Balfour said " it can only be explained by the fact that he was completely under the control of Mowatt and Edward Hamilton." [98] This was probably true since Mowatt's dislike of protection led him to resign in 1903. The Liberal ministers who were interested in social reform after 1906 had to battle with the Local Government Board's total opposition to any positive policies.

There was also a need for departments to work together or to produce new offshoots. When unemployment insurance was contemplated, it clearly cut across the interests of the Treasury, the Board of Trade and the Local Government Board. If, as in 1912, national strikes threatened, they might be police matters for the Home Office or trade disputes for the Board of Trade. In fact new sub-departments were created to run the Insurance Act and the Trade Boards Act.

Cabinet Ministers were no longer in the old, relatively simple position of being able to master the whole work of their departments and, if necessary, devise their own policies and write their own letters. In some cases the departments might fail to provide the necessary information or expertise, while in others they might actually be pressing for action and guiding the minister's hand. Sir Robert Morant, the Permanent Under-Secretary (with the aid of Sidney Webb), played a large part in devising the 1902 Education Bill and steering it through the Cabinet Committee. While Chairman of the Board of Inland Revenue, Milner was the chief architect of Harcourt's Death Duties Bill of 1894.[99] When Winston Churchill was at the Home Office he led the attack on the demands of Reginald McKenna, the First Lord of the Admiralty, for more battleships. By 1913 they had exchanged departments and advisers and each was thoroughly convinced that the case he had been making was absolutely wrong, so McKenna now pled for economy while Churchill demanded more battleships.

When problems of co-ordination or the need for information

---

[98] Dugdale, *op. cit.*, Vol. I, p. 245. Sir Francis Mowatt was the Permanent Under-Secretary. After he resigned two Permanent Secretaries were appointed, Sir Edward Hamilton in charge of the financial side and Sir George Murray with control of the Civil Service and the administrative side.

[99] J. E. Wrench in *Alfred, Lord Milner*, records that an associate considered that the duties were wholly the work of Milner's ingenuity. Harcourt " used to fluster about his own claims to authorship; but Milner more than once whispered in my ear that Harcourt never understood them and never would," p. 149.

arose at a ministerial level, the solution which had been developed was to employ a Cabinet Committee. This was most evident in overseas matters where the situation might be obscure, several interests might be (and usually were) involved and mistakes might have serious consequences. At various times there were Cabinet Committees on such subjects as Somaliland, the Cameroons, Swaziland, Madagascar, Central Asia, the Transvaal, the Heligoland–Zanzibar agreement with Germany and on terms of ending the war in South Africa. On domestic matters where some examination of the facts and draft proposals were required, the Cabinet also set up Committees. Groups of ministers were asked to consider Joseph Chamberlain's scheme for Irish regional councils, Edward VII's Civil List, methods of reforming the House of Lords, the Irish crisis in early 1914 and so on. A further use for Cabinet Committees was to solve disputes between ministers. Arguments between Hicks Beach and Chamberlain over sugar duties, the merits of Arnold-Forster's Army plans, the 1908 naval estimates, the cost of Haldane's proposals and the dispute between Kitchener and Curzon were all handled in this way. None of these Committees sat for any length of time as most of the questions submitted to them were solved one way or another in a matter of months, though some of the colonial questions lasted for the better part of a session.

Along with the other changes there were occasional suggestions that the Cabinet should adopt a more formal system of recording its decisions. The Hartington Commission recommended that its proposed Naval and Military Council should put its resolutions in writing because " instances had occurred in which Cabinet decisions have been differently understood by the two departments, and have become virtually a dead letter." [1] When Lord Lansdowne thought he had had Cabinet authorisation to publish the Spion Kop despatches, while Salisbury and other Ministers believed they had objected to any such action, the Prime Minister wondered whether " our traditional practice of not recording Cabinet decisions is a wise one." [2] There had been a number of

---

[1] 1890 (Cd. 5979) XIX, p. VIII.

[2] Lord Newton, *op. cit.*, p. 184. When Granville " who besides being deaf has a slipshod way of doing business . . . left it to Argyll to take down in writing the words agreed to in the Cabinet " (on the Alabama Treaty negotiations) and the latter made a mistake, Kimberley commented, " What a mode

misunderstandings but, as might be expected, they usually occurred when ministers were divided and each took away a different impression. Gladstone disliked any wasting of time or general conversation at Cabinets and always drew up an agenda. If the Prime Minister summed up a discussion in definite words, there was little room for doubt. On the occasions when no such clear conclusion was apparent, this was either because the Premier preferred to leave a tender point vague or because he thought the sense of the discussion was quite evident. Thus there were complaints in 1876 that Derby had sent off instructions when some ministers thought they were to be reconsidered at the next Cabinet. In late 1877 a group thought they had agreed to stronger terms in a Note to Russia and insisted on redrafting it. There was an extensive dispute over the causes of Derby's resignation, as he included among them the decision to acquire Cyprus and a Syrian port. Salisbury and Disraeli denied that there had been any such decision—at most they had had a conversation leading to further inquiries.[3]

In Gladstone's second ministry Hartington twice formed a slightly different impression from that of his colleagues, and Gladstone believed that Chamberlain had agreed to the introduction of a Land Purchase Bill in 1885.[4] There were similar disagreements between Harcourt and Kimberley after the Cabinet had considered an inquiry into the Mombasa railway in 1895.[5] Balfour and Chamberlain thought that the Cabinet had decided in November 1902 to maintain the corn tax and give the colonies a preferential remission. Devonshire and the Free Trade members of the Cabinet were convinced that the matter had been left open till the following spring.[6]

Over a period of forty years, this was a small number of disagreements. None of them diminished the efficiency of the

of transacting business!" *The Kimberley Papers*, p. 31. See also Appendix I, p. 628.

[3] Monypenny and Buckle, *op. cit.*, Vol. VI, pp. 95, 198 and 273. For Derby's resignation see also A. Lang, *op. cit.*, p. 290; Lady G. Cecil, *op. cit.*, Vol. II, p. 220; Gathorne-Hardy, *op. cit.*, Vol. II, pp. 74–76.

[4] In 1882 Hartington believed that the Cabinet had agreed to have no further communications with Parnell during the debates on the Prevention of Crimes Bill and he was not convinced in 1883 that the Cabinet had committed itself to a further Reform Bill: B. Holland, *op. cit.*, Vol. I, pp. 351 and 388.

[5] Gardiner, *op. cit.*, Vol. II, p. 334.

[6] Dugdale, *op. cit.*, Vol. I, p. 339 and Holland, *op. cit.*, Vol. II, p. 298.

Cabinet, as in each case there was a genuine division of opinion which would not have been removed by the production of a written minute. If ministers were in doubt about the precise terms of a decision they could write down their recollection of the terms and send them round the Cabinet. There are examples of such notes, initialled by all the ministers, in the Gladstone Cabinet papers. The only instances where the conduct of business was impaired were when ministers forgot to carry out decisions or where much turned on the precise wording of instructions. After a Cabinet Committee had decided to annex the Cameroons no action was taken for many months so that five days before a British mission arrived, the Germans had hoisted their flag. There was some suggestion that Derby forgot to implement the decision, but as a mission was sent it seems more likely that the delay was due to the old problem of getting the Colonial Office, the Admiralty and the Treasury to agree and to take action.[7] Gladstone apparently did not remember a decision in 1881 to give a charter to the North Borneo Company, but the Cabinet reminded him of it.[8] It is still not clear whether the paragraphs added to the memorandum insisting on absolute obedience in the Army in 1914 were intended to modify the Cabinet's decision or to expand and add to it. The paragraphs were added by Morley (who had been at the Cabinet) and by Seely (who had not) but the result was a modification which would have been impossible had there been a proper record.[9] But apart from such rare instances, and provided ministers were not, as Devonshire confessed to being, "rather deaf . . . and sometimes inattentive," [10] the Cabinet worked well enough as a machine for taking decisions, and no system of minutes could make for vigorous action if the minister responsible was reluctant or lethargic. On the whole, the Cabinet adapted itself to the increased volume and complexity of business quite well by taking more time for preparation, making greater use of expert advice, circulating many printed memoranda and having frequent recourse to Cabinet Committtees.

---

[7] Garvin, *op. cit.*, Vol. I, p. 490 and Gwynn and Tuckwell, *op. cit.*, Vol. I, p. 535.

[8] *Ibid.*, Vol. I, p. 400.

[9] Blake, *op. cit.*, pp. 197–200. These were the "peccant paragraphs" saying the government would not use the Army "to crush political opposition to the policy or principles of the Home Rule Bill." See also R. Jenkins, *Asquith*, p. 312.   [10] Holland, *op. cit.*, Vol. II, p. 357.

Once the Cabinet had agreed on a policy and had drafted
the necessary legislation, and once the Civil Service was ready
to administer it, there remained the question of reactions
from interested bodies. As government began to touch the
community at a larger number of points, the attitude of Parliament
and of the electorate depended in part on the publicity
given to a policy and on the impression created by it. The
groups affected were bound to put their case to the government,
to Parliament or to the public at large. There had long been
deputations to the Chancellor of the Exchequer on the eve of
the Budget but there is no evidence that much was achieved in
this way. Other ministers had had interviews with interested
elements though such contacts played little part in government
in the 1870s and 1880s.[11] Joseph Chamberlain found that when
he went to the Board of Trade in 1880, it was just an office for
dealing with correspondence. An official noted that " it had been
quite unusual for us to visit Chambers of Commerce or even to
interview commercial people, who were supposed to make their
views known to the Board by writing." [12]

With the belief in the sovereignty of Parliament supported by
evidence that the House of Commons would amend Bills, pressure
groups in these years tended to work on or through Members
of Parliament. Bruce found the opposition to his Mines Regulation
Bill led by colliery owners in the House, while Army
officers objecting to Cardwell's reforms were well represented in
both parties. The Temperance Societies and the Licensed Victuallers
became equally adept at putting pressure on Members of
Parliament and through them on the Cabinet, thus together securing
the withdrawal of Bruce's first Licensing Bill.[13] Sometimes this
pressure was exercised in ingenious ways. When Lowe proposed
a tax on matches, Members were moved by a procession of unfortunate
girls who claimed to have been thrown out of employment.
Bryant and May and other manufacturers had in fact dismissed
them for the day and sent them up in vans to Westminster to
make their appeal.[14] The shipping interest also was powerful

---

[11] Though Lowe did himself some damage by his tendency to be rude and
abrupt to deputations: A. P. Martin, *op. cit.*, Vol. II, p. 373.
[12] Garvin, *op. cit.*, Vol. I, p. 412.
[13] *Aberdare Papers*, pp. 269–270.
[14] Sir A. West, *Recollections*, Vol. II, p. 3.

and had connections on all sides of the House, so that both Conservatives and Liberals found this a difficult matter to handle.
The Lancashire cotton interests, both employers and workers, put
great pressure on their M.P.s and on the Government to remove
the 5 per cent. import duty established by the Indian administration. The Liberals agreed to a modification in early 1895 and the
Conservatives coming in a month or two later cut the duty to a
token level.[15] It is important not to assume that M.P.s who were
directors of companies or had strong ties with particular interests
were dominated by economic or personal motives. In some cases
a Member might have several conflicting interests and his own
political views and those of his constituents might well be the
determining factor.[16]   Also pressure groups tried, and at times
succeeded, in appealing to Members simply on the grounds that
they had a good case or that they could swing some votes. In 1894
Harcourt found that his Budget had a favourable reception, but
then the Irish, the Drink Trade and the landed interest all began
to press information and warnings on Members, so that Harcourt
had to put on the Whips and struggle for every clause.   Thus
the normal procedure up to the turn of the century was to assume
that Parliament framed legislation, to wait till proposals had
been put before the House, and then try to persuade M.P.s to
amend them or resist them as might appear necessary.[17]

   A second method of bringing the claims of particular sections
before the Cabinet was to operate directly on the electorate.
" The Trade " was especially well suited for such activities because
of the number of public houses and the alleged influences of pub-
licans, though it is doubtful whether they made a significant
impact on the election of 1874. What mattered, however, was the
politicians' impression of their strength rather than the actual
fact. By 1885, Gladstone and Childers were prepared to enter into
direct negotiations with pressure groups. On the suggestion of

[15] P. Harnetty, " The Indian Cotton Duties Controversy, 1894–96," *E.H.R.*,
Vol. 77 (1962), pp. 684–702.
[16] The best illustration of the errors produced by this kind of over-emphasis on
economic self-interest is seen in W. H. G. Armytage, " The Railway Rates
Question and the Fall of the Third Gladstone Ministry," *E.H.R.* (1950) p. 18,
and is fully corrected by P. M. Williams, " Public opinion and the Railway
Rates Question in 1886," *E.H.R.* (1952) p. 37.
[17] Sir C. Ilbert in his *Legislative Methods and Forms* (1901) assumes that this
is the normal and proper procedure: p. 230.

Algernon West, they approved a memorandum which West " produced to Sir Arthur Bass, and Messrs. Whitbread, Allsop, Grindling and Gretton, Watney and Bonsor agreeing, this tided over the difficulty of the increased beer duty," [18] though it did not prevent the government being defeated. The Irish Land League, although it had other more direct objectives, did create an atmosphere and a demand without which the 1881 Land Act would neither have been contemplated nor passed. Walter Long, at the Board of Agriculture, determined to suppress rabies by muzzling dogs in the vicinity of outbreaks and imposing quarantine on animals coming into the country. The response was a Canine Defence League run largely by upper class ladies, which produced a petition with 80,000 signatures asking for Long's removal and ran a candidate at a by-election in a Conservative seat. Some Conservatives were alarmed but Salisbury was merely amused and Long's campaign succeeded.[19] A sabre which the opponents of the 1911 Insurance Bill did not hesitate to rattle was the companies' force of 80,000 agents calling at a majority of the houses in the country once a week.[20]

As the party system tightened and cross-voting stopped, the pressure groups were left with three avenues of attack. One was to influence the electorate, but before the days of mass advertising campaigns this could only be done by powerful agencies with many local strongholds. Organisations in this category were " The Trade," the Temperance Societies, the nonconformists churches, the Catholics in Ireland, the insurance companies, and the trade unions. Even then, it was appreciated that voting habits were slowly formed and this kind of pressure was costly, hard to organise and long-term, when what was wanted was usually the amendment of an immediate proposal. Another method by which interest groups with a strong hold on sections of the community could get round the two-party system was to run their own candidates. The chief reason for putting Irish Nationalist and Independent Labour M.P.s into Parliament was that these sections were not getting what they wanted out of either party.[21] The limitation

---

[18] Sir A. West, *Recollections*, Vol. II, p. 238.
[19] Viscount Long, *op. cit.*, pp. 114–124.
[20] W. J. Braithwaite, *op. cit.*, p. 168.
[21] At the 1899 Trades Union Congress the Parliamentary Committee reported " that with the present mode of procedure of the House of Commons it is almost impossible to get any useful Bill through the House, unless the

on this kind of pressure was that only a very few groups were sufficiently strong and localised to be able to run candidates with any chance of success.

If pressure groups could not hope to create an impression of power by virtue of their influence on the electorate, or to return M.P.s, the next best possibility was to interest a number of Liberal or Conservative M.P.s and keep them informed. Successful campaigns of this kind would, it was hoped, lead these M.P.s to contact Ministers and speak in the House in a manner which would make the Cabinet consider their views in framing any legislation.[22] The weakness of this policy was that Cabinets were not influenced by elements that were traditionally hostile. " The Trade " knew it could hope for nothing from the Liberals and nonconformist organisations did not bother with the Conservatives. Nevertheless, bands of active, well briefed M.P.s served to keep Ministers on their toes by asking questions and leading deputations. The Armed Services group, set up after the defeat of the Liberals, on the cordite motion of 1895, was always strong and fed by appropriate leaks from the War Office and the Admiralty. Morley as Secretary of State found the ex-India M.P.s were no danger but could be a nuisance, while the Irish Unionist group worked chiefly to keep opposition to Home Rule the main point in the Conservative programme.

Once groups had established themselves either by proving their power over the electorate, their capacity to return M.P.s, or their influence with important elements in the party, they found that the most satisfactory mode of operation was direct negotiations with the government. It is surprising to realise that Gladstone made no attempt to consult the Irish M.P.s, landowners, or any other element over the Irish Land Bill of 1870, nor did he sound the Catholic hierarchy before bringing in the Irish Universities Bill of 1873. But by the time of the Home Rule Bills his attitude had changed and there was " free and constant

Government allow it to pass by withdrawing its opposition, and in their opinion, if any remedy is to be effected, it must be done by the working class at the polls." Later the resolution calling the conference which set up the Labour Representative Committee was passed. *Report of the 34th Annual Trades Union Congress*, September 1899.

22 An excellent example is the way in which F. J. D. Lugard and Sir John Kirk coached M.P.s in order to arouse their interest and obtain their support in the crucial debates over the retention of Uganda in 1894. See M. Perham, *Lugard, The Years of Adventure*, pp. 457–463.

communication " with the Irish leadership.[23] " The Trade " had reached a similar relationship with the Conservative hierarchy by the turn of the century and in 1904 J. S. Sanders (Balfour's Secretary) attended a meeting of " the more sensible members . . . to see what is the minimum of their insistence." [24] In 1908 they made it clear that unless the Lords rejected the Liberal Licensing Bill they would reconsider their longstanding support for the Conservative Party.[25]

The difficulty of influencing a Cabinet which regarded the group in question as among its regular opponents could lead to moods of extreme frustration. It was not comforting to reflect that retribution might come at the next election four or five years off. Such frustrations account for the readiness to threaten resistance, or a refusal to co-operate should the government touch a few very tender spots. After the government had applied the closure and forced through the 1902 Education Bill, nonconformists in some areas refused to pay the educational rate. When Beach put a shilling a ton export on coal, the mine-owners protested and the miners threatened a strike.[26] Over the 1911 Insurance Act, there was a possibility that some sections of the community might refuse to pay their contributions and a much more serious danger that the doctors, led by the British Medical Association, would refuse to participate. In fact all the doctors did was raise their price and when it became high enough they deserted the militants of the B.M.A. and joined in the insurance scheme.[27] A slightly different form of pressure was attempted by the Women's Social and Political Union, for they were not resisting but inviting government action. It was hoped that violent action would lead to attention and sympathy and the concession of votes for women. Cabinets may have wanted to avoid being involved in disputes between the two sides of industry. But with the possibility, after the trade union amalgamations of the 1900s, that industrial disturbances in certain industries would be nation wide, it could be forced to intervene and even to take sides. The most serious challenge of the period came from the

[23] Morley, *Life of Gladstone*, Vol. III, pp. 202–203.
[24] *Balfour Papers, Add MSS.*, 49, 762, f. 45.
[25] Lord Newton, *op. cit.*, p. 367.
[26] Lady V. Hicks Beach, *op. cit.*, Vol. II, p. 145.
[27] There are excellent accounts of this dispute in the books by Lucy Masterman, W. J. Braithwaite, and B. M. Allen's *Sir Robert Morant*.

Ulster Unionists when they said that they were "justified in taking or supporting any action that may be effective to prevent (the Home Rule Bill) being put into operation, and more particularly to prevent the armed forces of the Crown being used to deprive the people of Ulster of their rights as citizens of the U.K." [28] This pledge was backed by the well armed Ulster Volunteers and open disaffection in parts of the British Army. Also a part of the Liberal Cabinet sympathised with the Ulster case. Together these forces were sufficient to extract the promise of separate treatment for an area of Northern Ireland. The effect of the whole dispute was to postpone a settlement of the Irish question till after the War when it was, in fact, too late for the British Cabinet to exercise any control over the situation.

Surveying these pressure groups and their impact on the Cabinet, it must be remembered that provided there was no threat to break the law, there was nothing intrinsically improper about their activities. They merely brought the case of a particular section of the community before the government, Parliament and the public with special force. Such activity was only reprehensible if the broader interests of the community were overlooked or ignored.

The tighter organisation of politics and the reliance on fixed majorities returned at general elections had steadily strengthened the Cabinet. After the 1880s it could afford to ignore such pressures unless a fair number of its own voters might be offended and driven to abstain at the next election. Thus Cabinets were able to apply the test of the well-being of at least their own political adherents to the demands of the pressure groups. The Cockerton judgment of 1901 made an Education Bill essential, and a Liberal Cabinet would have been influenced by the strong nonconformist element that normally voted Liberal just as the Conservatives in fact paid considerable attention to Anglican views. Yet neither of these groups could have insisted that their interests were catered for in a manner which prevented the development of state-aided secondary education. The Irish were able to wring several major measures and the promise of Home Rule out of the Liberals, but only because Gladstone and the bulk of the party accepted the justice of their case. The Labour

[28] These were the words of the Ulster Covenant.

Party likewise succeeded with its Trade Disputes Bill in 1906 after Campbell-Bannerman had come to appreciate the force of the Labour case and most Liberal M.P.s had indicated their agreement. The Licensing Trade did well out of the Conservatives not just because of the funds it contributed but because the party believed it embodied a form of property that ought to be protected. Only over Ulster was a pressure group able to force the Cabinet to change its policy. Even in this case a resolute and united Cabinet could probably have prevented the situation deteriorating and have carried through its proposals. Asquith vacillated and most of his colleagues were prepared, and some were even eager, to give way. This was in fact a case of rival pressure groups, and the Ulster Unionists won because all the influential circles in Britain and, in the last resort, the Cabinet itself sympathised with their case more than with that of the Irish Nationalists.

CHAPTER 11

THE CONDUCT OF AND DISTRIBUTION OF
POWER WITHIN THE CABINET

IN this period the formation of a Cabinet was a much simpler process than it had been in the 1850s. There was usually no doubt as to which side was to form a government, and the Crown had simply to start the sequence of events by commissioning the party leader. The occasions when the leadership was in doubt have been discussed in the section on the monarchy, and it is only necessary to consider the steps taken after a given person had kissed hands as Prime Minister. The task became easier as political sentiment and organisation developed, since the parties were now eager to seize any chance of taking office. While great noble men such as Lord Rosebery or the Duke of Devonshire could still hang back and men of talent such as Randolph Churchill or W. V. Harcourt could still try to make conditions, most leading politicians regarded office as their objective and were more willing to fall into line.

When a party was in opposition ex-ministers considered they had a right to attend Shadow Cabinets. The leader could summon new men who had not been in previous Cabinets and the Whips and Law Officers might be called, but it gave serious offence if former colleagues were excluded.[1] Despite this no one could claim a title to be included in a new Cabinet when the party came to power.[2] In 1873 when there was some doubt as to whether the Conservatives should take office as a minority government, the ex-Cabinet was consulted. In this case they (like Disraeli's closer advisers, Hardy, Richmond and Cairns) counselled refusal, but when the same situation arose in 1885 all but one of the Shadow Cabinet were for acceptance. This time their decision

---

[1] Chaplin attended after 1906 though he had not been a member of the 1900–1905 Cabinets. Balcarres told Bonar Law that "there is no particular qualification and no definite membership," but all those who had been in former Cabinets came. Blake, *op. cit.*, pp. 102–103 and Dugdale, *op. cit.*, Vol. II, p. 68.

[2] Gladstone did, however, think that ministers in former Cabinets should be considered first and for the same offices, when a new one was being formed.

allowed Lord Salisbury to go ahead and form a government, but it in no way restricted his choice for a new Cabinet. His problems were the usual ones (given his position as a peer) of finding a suitable Foreign Secretary and Leader of the Commons, and of reconciling his ageing colleague Northcote with young Randolph Churchill.[3] The accession of Lord Rosebery in 1894 was out of the usual because of the divisions in the Liberal Cabinet, and though Rosebery emerged with most support, Harcourt and Morley were still strong enough to impose some conditions. They tried to hold out for a Foreign Secretary in the House of Commons, but Rosebery insisted on a free choice (he took a peer, Kimberley). Harcourt accepted the Leadership of the Commons provided he saw all Foreign Office despatches and was given a certain freedom of manoeuvre in debates, while Morley agreed to remain as Irish Secretary provided no other work was expected from him. Rosebery acquiesced, though " deeply pained." Harcourt's points were, however, quite reasonable with a peer as Premier, and Morley was just exhibiting his tendency to crotchets. Sir Stafford Northcote had asked for the same signs of confidence when he considered serving as Salisbury's Leader in the Commons in 1885, and a similar relationship was later developed between Salisbury and his First Lords of the Treasury, W. H. Smith and A. J. Balfour. Had Rosebery shown drive in the leadership and a capacity to manage men, his position would have been the same as that of any other Prime Minister in the Lords with a troublesome lieutenant in the Commons.[4] The one other occasion when there was an attempt to restrict the freedom of choice of a new Prime Minister was in December 1905. Haldane, Sir Edward Grey and Asquith had earlier agreed that they would all refuse office in any new Liberal Cabinet unless Campbell-Bannerman went to the Lords and left Asquith to lead the Commons. They also wanted the Foreign Office for Grey and the Lord Chancellorship for Haldane.[5] Campbell-Bannerman made it clear that he intended to form a Cabinet with or without them and then, on his wife's advice, determined to remain as

---

[3] The best account of the formation of the Cabinet is in an Appendix to Charles Whibley's *Lord John Manners and his friends*, pp. 307–313.

[4] All the details are set out in Lord Rosebery's own record printed as " Mr. Gladstone's Last Cabinet," *History To-day*, January 1952.

[5] This was known as the Relugas Compact after the shooting lodge where it was made.

Leader in the Commons. At this stage, the three had to consider whether they would insist on standing aside. For the good of the party, Asquith decided to accept the Exchequer and Haldane then persuaded Grey to accept office.[6]

Thus Prime Ministers entering office had on their side the ardent support of the party and of a large section of the electorate. As the aristocratic element in politics declined and men entered Parliament with a desire for positive achievement, there was less diffidence among those suitable for high office. Plans were usually formed in the period before a general election in consultation with the three or four men who were trusted by the Leader of the Opposition and were likely to occupy the senior posts. As the results of the 1874 election came in, Disraeli arranged the shape of his Ministry with Derby, Cairns, Northcote and Hardy.[7] In 1880, Gladstone could not be denied the leadership and he chose his Cabinet, relying only on the advice of Granville and Bright.[8] Home Rule was such a menace and Lord Salisbury's position was so strong in 1886, that he formed his ministry virtually single-handed, dealing directly with each individual in turn. In 1892, Campbell-Bannerman observed that " the government is being formed for the special purpose of enabling Mr. Gladstone to carry out his ideas: it is in an unusual degree *his* government. Is not the first thing necessary that he should be comfortable in it? " [9] The process of formation, was, however, the same as before. At Dalmeny in May, Gladstone had talked over the framework with John Morley and Rosebery. In London three months later, the group was expanded to include Harcourt, Kimberley, Arnold Morley, Spencer and Marjoribanks (the Chief Whip) and the minor posts were distributed.[10] Lord Salisbury asked Devonshire, Balfour and Chamberlain to consult with him in 1895, but Balfour in 1902, Campbell-Bannerman in 1905, and Asquith in 1908 all acted without the aid of any inner ring of advisers.

---

6 D. Sommer, *op. cit.*, pp. 144–151.

7 Monypenny and Buckle, *op. cit.*, Vol. I, p. 285.

8 *Bright's Diaries*, p. 439. Glyn, the former Chief Whip, later Lord Wolverton, had some part in these conversations and plans.

9 J. A. Spender, *Sir Henry Campbell-Bannerman*, *op. cit.*, Vol. I, p. 124.

10 Sir A. West, *Private Diaries*, p. 50, and Lord Crewe, *op. cit.*, Vol. II, pp. 391–392.

In the 1870s and 1880s one or two politicians made conditions before they would accept Cabinet office. Salisbury was still very suspicious of Disraeli in 1874. He asked Derby for full details of the new ministry and then obtained a pledge from the Prime Minister that no legislation against ritualism would be either introduced or supported. Gladstone was shocked to find when he offered Dilke a post in the 1880 government that the latter had an agreement with Chamberlain. Both must have office (one of them in the Cabinet) or they would take nothing. Such attitudes became less tenable and less frequent. When Balfour took over the Premiership in 1902, Hicks Beach asked for an assurance of support on the issues which had arisen between him and Chamberlain, but he knew that this was unlikely and that he was, in fact, taking the preliminary steps towards resignation. The only occasion on which a Prime Minister had to explain his policy and persuade men to join in the old-fashioned manner was when the Liberals were falling apart in January 1886. Gladstone's own position was not fully known, and his former colleagues had to consider making what might become a permanent break with Liberalism or accepting an Irish policy which many of them had, till then, flatly rejected. Gladstone drew up a short memorandum saying that he proposed to consider the possibility of setting up a legislature at Dublin under certain conditions. This was then read to each person invited to join the Cabinet. Hartington, Goschen, Derby, Northbrook and Bright refused. Trevelyan and Chamberlain entered with evident reluctance and misgivings, but after much help from Harcourt, Gladstone assembled a government.[11]

When selecting a Cabinet, the Prime Minister worked along a few simple lines. Until 1892 the average number of places to fill was fourteen, though Disraeli managed to keep his Cabinet down to twelve. A small group had a less formal atmosphere and, on the whole, made it easier to reach agreement. Gladstone lamented that he had to go back to fourteen in 1880. The pressure to enlarge arose from the increasing number of departments whose chiefs all wanted a place in the Cabinet. In these years a new post of Secretary for Scotland was created, and a Board of Agriculture was set up, while the Board of Education (under the

11 Morley, *op. cit.*, Vol. III, pp. 290–296.

Vice-President of the Council till 1905), the Local Government Board, and the Post Office were all of sufficient importance to claim membership.[12] In 1912 when Rufus Isaacs, the Attorney-General, complained at being passed over for the Lord Chancellorship, he was let into the Cabinet as a solatium. His successor as Attorney-General, Sir John Simon, was also admitted.[13] Thus membership rose and averaged nineteen in the five Cabinets before the war. Some said that this led to a decline in quality or gave undue advantage to the loud-voiced and pugnacious members, though Asquith felt that " in practice I have rarely experienced any inconvenience from its size." [14]

Whatever the final number, the character of the government was largely determined by the Prime Minister together with the five Secretaries of State,[15] the Lord President and the Chancellor of the Exchequer. Gladstone considered that after he had taken the Exchequer in addition to the Premiership in 1880, the next most important posts were the Foreign and India Offices.[16] While Chamberlain was evidently of Cabinet rank, Gladstone was taken aback in 1885 at his request to be Secretary of State for the Colonies.

Some of these portfolios had to go to peers, and Disraeli aimed at the equal division which had been customary in the

---

[12] In November 1886 Lord Salisbury submitted " that in view of the fact that Scotland is not represented in the Cabinet and that in the impending legislation there are many important Scotch questions to be dealt with, it is expedient that Mr. Arthur Balfour, Secretary for Scotland, should be a member of the Cabinet " and five months later he told the Queen that " in view of . . . the Irish Land Law Bill it is very desirable to have Lord Cadogan as Lord Privy Seal in the Cabinet. . . . At the same time it may be desirable to put Mr. Ritchie in, who holds a very important office " (he was President of the Local Government Board): *Royal Archives,* Vol. A 65, ff. 17 and 73.

[13] Both came to deprecate Law Officers sitting in the Cabinet. (It had not happened since 1806.) Isaacs felt that the Attorney-General might find a conflict between policy-making and advising on questions of law, while Simon held that it was " an undesirable combination of offices," for the same reason. The Marquess of Reading, *Rufus Isaacs,* Vol. I, p. 225, and Viscount Simon, *Retrospect,* p. 89.

[14] H. H. Asquith, *The Genesis of the War,* p. 3. Esher talked about larger Cabinets having a lower average calibre (*op. cit.,* Vol. II, p. 308) and Haldane, who was notably ineffective in Cabinet, complained " that two or three had the gift of engrossing its attention for their own business." *Autobiography,* p. 217.

[15] At the Foreign, Home, Colonial, India and War Offices.

[16] P. Guedalla, *op. cit.,* Vol. II, p. 85.

1850s and 1860s.[17] Liberal Cabinets, however, had fewer peers and this became a debated point. Whig Lords had held a controlling position in the Liberal Party up till 1868 and Gladstone had given them enough power to play a moderating role in his 1880 Cabinet. Their tendency to a common political attitude was revealed on a number of occasions when the Cabinet divided so that peers and Hartington were opposed to commoners and Granville, and their alarms made it evident that there was less and less room for the Whig aristocracy in a Gladstonian party.[18] In 1885 Hartington said, " there is one thing in which I agree with Harcourt, which is that the Peers . . . cannot expect half the places in another Liberal Cabinet." [19] Salisbury and Balfour still kept nine peers to ten and eleven commoners, but in the three Liberal Cabinets after 1892 the proportion was under a third. Indeed, after 1906, not only did the representatives of the peerage fall away but middle-class men predominated in the leadership of both parties.

Usually most of the senior posts chose themselves though sometimes there was difficulty in finding a suitable Foreign Secretary.[20] Among the portfolios of medium rank, the War Office was always regarded as a bed of thorns and Campbell-Bannerman, who had learned to distrust Haldane, chuckled at the thought of " Schopenhauer in the Kailyard." [21] Grey held that a

---

[17] Disraeli, like most Prime Ministers, preferred to have the Secretary of State for War and the First Lord of the Admiralty in the Commons, as the Army and Navy Estimates constituted such a large part of public expenditure and were so liable to attack. Asquith told Lord Haldane that the deciding factor in appointing Churchill to the Admiralty (rather than Haldane) was " the absolute necessity of keeping the First Lord in the House of Commons. We shall have to encounter there our own little navy men, the experts, such as they are, of the official opposition and, as our plans develop, the spokesmen of the discontented admirals and the old class of naval specialists." *Haldane Papers*, October 10, 1911, MSS 5909, f. 146.

[18] The Cabinet divided in this way over the prosecution of Parnell, Chamberlain's scheme for Irish Councils and Northbrook's proposals for Egyptian finance.

[19] Gardiner, *op. cit.,* Vol. I, p. 539.

[20] It was held to be a disadvantage not to be able to speak French and the post required a statesman of almost bi-partisan breadth of mind.

[21] During the discussion about a suitable Secretary of State for War in 1903, Balfour observed to King Edward that " it would be a very unfortunate thing, in the public interest, if it became obvious that to go to the War Office meant seriously damaging a promising political career. There appears to be some danger of this becoming a rule without exception—especially if the unfortunate Secretary of State endeavours to be a reformer! " *Royal Archives,* Vol. R 24, f. 10.

good Cabinet minister had to have three qualities. He should be able "to work sincerely in matters of difference of opinion and difficulty for a Cabinet decision," "accept full responsibility for Cabinet decisions, when once agreed to" and never threaten resignation unless he meant it.[22] Unfortunately, few Prime Ministers were free to choose on such qualities alone, though men like Crewe were valued for just these reasons. A Cabinet had to contain the leading protagonists of the party, yet they might make poor administrators, as in the case of John Bright. On the other hand, Northcote, Cross and W. H. Smith were all able heads of departments, but only the last named emerged as a capable House of Commons man. When there were divisions or shades of opinion in a party it might be desirable to include some from each wing. Gladstone told the Queen in 1880 that Chamberlain "was selected as a representative of particular views" [23] and later, the admission of Dilke was held to require the entry of a Whig to maintain a balance. Even in 1908, Morley was still thinking of the Liberal Cabinet in terms of Pro-Boers and Liberal Imperialists and felt it was desirable to keep the two sections on an equality.[24] Disraeli, who was always very conscious of short-term dangers, told the Queen in 1874 that "I have contrived, in the minor and working places, to include every 'representative' man, that is to say everyone who might be troublesome." [25] He was also glad to have two representatives of that new Conservative centre of strength, Lancashire, in the persons of Derby and Cross. In 1877 when he was proposing W. H. Smith as First Lord of the Admiralty, Disraeli gave as his reasons that Smith "is purely a man of the middle class" and later that it was most important for the Conservatives to have "a City or Borough member in the Cabinet." [26] On the other hand, when Carnarvon resigned in 1878, he appointed Northumberland, the only reason being Disraeli's desire to keep up the number drawn from the ancient noble families.[27]

When a Cabinet had taken office, it usually met once a week during the parliamentary session to consider policy and settle

[22] Grey, *op. cit.*, Vol. I, p. 67.
[23] *Letters*, Series II, Vol. III, p. 88.
[24] Morley, *Recollections*, Vol. II, p. 248.
[25] Monypenny and Buckle, *op. cit.*, Vol. V, p. 295.
[26] Viscount Chilston, *W. H. Smith*, p. 94.
[27] R. Blake, *Disraeli*, p. 657.

the order of business.[28] In the 1880s the normal day was Saturday but with the growth of the " country-house weekend," Wednesday became more favoured, with a possible extra meeting on a Monday. After Parliament rose in August, ministers dispersed for their holidays, though the political crisis of 1909 and 1910 was such that some Cabinets were held in September. In late October or early November work was resumed with a spate of meetings to prepare for the coming session. Cabinets were held in No. 10 Downing Street with the Prime Minister sitting in the centre of one side of a long rectangular table, facing the fireplace.[29] In Gladstone's last ministry his deafness made it hard for him to catch what was said around the table and the Cabinet moved upstairs to the " Picture Room " where the Prime Minister sat on a chair in the centre so that each contributor could make himself heard.[30] When Rosebery took over, they returned to the usual room and table.[31] There was no order of precedence, but ministers always occupied the same place. When Derby withdrew his resignation in early 1878, he indicated his qualified return by leaving his old seat beside Disraeli and sitting apart in the one vacated by Carnarvon. After the resignations of October 1903, Sandars wrote to Balfour:

" I planned last night the sitting of the cabinet at the cabinet table, and I propose to send you a plan which Bob Douglas and I have sketched for your consideration. It is drawn upon ideas of the usefulness of certain contiguities. I happen to know that Lord Salisbury was always careful to make such an arrangement when he started with new colleagues." [32]

28 There are some references in the *Gladstone* and the *Dilke Papers* to informal or " quasi-cabinets " in 1873 and during the 1880–1885 ministry, the explanation for the title being that they were held at the House of Commons and not in the normal Cabinet room. *Add. MSS.,* 44,641, f. 81; 44,645, ff. 54, 75, 126 and 132; 44,644, f. 49; 44,646, f. 155.
29 There is a drawing of the seating plan by Gladstone with the changes that took place when his third Cabinet took office in February 1886. *Gladstone Papers, Add. MSS.,* 44,647, f. 5.
30 *Gladstone Papers, Add. MSS.,* 44,648, f. 2. Ministers sat about the room on chairs. When most of them were deep in the Second Home Rule Bill " Rosebery and W. V. H[arcourt] sat on a sofa behind and away from the others. . . . Their ostentatious position apart from the rest seemed to make J. Morley and Spencer nervous and uneasy. Spencer at one time came and sat down between them but W. V. H. said, ' Go away, you have no right here, this is the English bench ' " Gardiner, *op. cit.,* Vol. II, p. 218.
31 In Salisbury's last ministry, Cabinet meetings were held on a number of occasions in the Foreign Office. See *Royal Archives, R* 22.
32 *Balfour Papers,* J. S. Sandars to Balfour, October 14, 1903. *Add. MSS.,* 49,761, f. 108.

In the earlier years of this period Cabinets were very informal. Dinners were still given in the 1870s and Disraeli revived the end of session outing to Greenwich. Bruce regularly wrote to his wife while at the Cabinet, and Smith and Hardy also caught up on their correspondence, while Dilke and Chamberlain exchanged rhymes to pass the time. Speeches could be long, Gladstone addressing his colleagues for an hour on militarism and Harcourt was as long in explaining his death duties budget. In time, however, the atmosphere became more business-like and it was not assumed that members all knew each other on dining or close terms. Prime Ministers exercised more control over the discussions and when Crewe spoke for twenty minutes, many of Asquith's Cabinet regarded it as an intolerable imposition.

H. H. Asquith in his *Fifty Years of Parliament* says that the question of a dissolution (or a resignation) was always put to the Cabinet.[33] This is true though there were usually preliminary discussions between the Prime Minister, a few senior colleagues and the Whips. For instance in 1874, when Gladstone wanted to revive his party by proposing the abolition of the income tax he ran into conflict with the Service ministers, Cardwell and Goschen. At a meeting of five senior ministers on January 19 this could not be resolved and they decided it would be better to go to the country without mentioning the disagreement.[34] This was put to the full Cabinet on January 23, 1874, and accepted.[35] By 1880 another general election was due and Disraeli, on the advice of his election experts, thought that the best time was in March just after two by-election victories. He went round the Cabinet giving Members of the Commons priority, as they would

[33] Vol. II, p. 196.
[34] Gladstone never denied that the real reason was the unresolved conflict over service estimates (Lord E. Fitzmaurice, *op. cit.*, Vol. II, p. 143) but Selborne, Childers and James thought the explanation lay in his worries as to whether he should have vacated his Greenwich seat and been re-elected on becoming Chancellor of the Exchequer. This view is put in R. R. James, "Gladstone and the Greenwich Seat," *History Today*, Vol. IX (1959), but W. H. Maehl, "Gladstone, the Liberals and the Election of 1874" in the *Bulletin of the Institute of Historical Research*, Vol. 36 (1963), pp. 53–69 establishes that it was the estimates problem. The Cabinet was told that the adverse by-elections and weakness of the government could best be cleared up by a general election. But there was some validity in Bright's view (expressed in 1875) of Gladstone's personal role that "the late sudden dissolution was so much his own act."
[35] *Gladstone Papers, Add. MSS.*, 44,641, f. 245.

have to bear the brunt of the battle.[36] Only Beach and Lord
John Manners dissented.[37] Mr. Gladstone's second ministry was
never very cohesive and when, in February 1885, the Liberal
majority fell to fourteen the Cabinet discussed resignation, opinion
being equally divided till Gladstone spoke in favour of carrying
on.[38] There was no argument in the Cabinet after the defeat
on a fiscal issue in June 1885. When the Home Rule Bill was
rejected in the next year, three members of the Cabinet favoured
resignation but Gladstone produced his memorandum putting
twelve reasons for dissolution and won them over.[39] By temperament, Gladstone was readily inclined to elections as the campaigns gave him new strength and, he confidently expected,
increased political power. Thus the 1874 dissolution had been,
as he said, " an escape from a difficulty " [40] and in a similar vein
he threw out the suggestion of an appeal to the country in February 1894, ostensibly on the conduct of the Lords, but in fact
to try to solve the deadlock between himself and the rest of the
Cabinet. It was the clearest evidence of his declining hold on his
colleagues when they refused to consider the idea. The Liberal
defeat in June 1895 was, as has been argued, on a minor matter
and it was clearly open to the Cabinet to stay or go. Rosebery,
Harcourt, Ripon and Tweedmouth were for resignation and, after a
four-hour discussion, this unusual combination carried their
point.[41]

Conservative or Unionist Cabinets operated in the same way.
When the life of the Parliament elected in 1886 was running out, Salisbury attended a small meeting with Devonshire,
Chamberlain, Balfour and the Conservative and Liberal Unionist
Whips to select a suitable time for a dissolution, their decision
being accepted by the Cabinet.[42] After their victory in 1895,
no election was needed till 1902 but with successes in the
Boer War, the time seemed ripe. Joseph Chamberlain was eager
for an appeal to the country and " his definiteness soon began

---

[36] Until 1910 it was a convention that peers should not take part in election
campaigns.
[37] *Letters*, Series II, Vol. III, p. 71.
[38] Morley, *Life of Gladstone*, Vol. III, p. 177.
[39] Morley, *op. cit.*, Vol. III, p. 340, and *Gladstone Papers, Add. MSS.*, 44,647,
f. 121.
[40] Morley, *op. cit.*, Vol. II, p. 485.
[41] Crewe, *op. cit.*, Vol. II, p. 504.
[42] *Letters*, Series III, Vol. II, p. 118.

to prevail in the Cabinet as a body, against the inclination of the Prime Minister and some other ministers," [43] so that the decision to dissolve was taken in late July 1900.

The first exception to the practice of submitting this decision to the Cabinet occurred in 1905. In November of that year, Balfour had wanted to resign but some of his colleagues were opposed. He raised the question a second time on November 24 and reported that " the Cabinet were greatly divided in their opinions—but Mr. Balfour did not think it necessary or desirable to estimate the comparative strength of the compelling views. He may bring up the question again: or he may decide it on his own responsibility. . . ." [44] The other ministers appreciated this and one of those who favoured remaining in office, Acland Hood, noted that " he will resign and I don't see what further can be done to influence him the other way." Balfour then drew up a memorandum giving his reasons for preferring resignation and put it before the Cabinet on December 2. Again there was resistance and Long urged him to delay while " realising fully that it rests with you and with you alone to decide what course you will adopt." [45] The Cabinet was not asked for a decision, since Balfour had, in fact, made up his mind and concluded his letter to the King—" So ends the last Cabinet in the present Administration." [46] His official resignation was handed in on December 4.

This change was typical of the somewhat highhanded way in which Balfour had managed his Cabinet, particularly during the crisis over protection in mid-1903. Now his behaviour became a precedent and he recalled this episode in 1918 when he told Bonar Law that " the responsibility of a dissolution must rest with the Prime Minister. It always does so rest in fact; and on some previous occasions the Prime Minister of the day has not even gone through the form of consulting his colleagues." [47]

Turning to the position of the various ministers within the Cabinet, the most noticeable change was the increase in the power of the Prime Minister. Many factors tended to produce this effect.

[43] J. L. Garvin, *op. cit.*, Vol III, p. 583.
[44] Balfour to King Edward, *Royal Archives*, Vol. R 26, f. 95.
[45] Sir C. Petrie, *Walter Long and his Times*, prints the letters from Acland Hood and from Long, pp. 98–104.
[46] *Royal Archives*, Vol. R 26, f. 99. The King's opposition to any notion that Balfour should resign also had no effect.
[47] R. Blake, *op. cit.*, p. 385.

The primary factor was that the electorate came to know the party leaders well and to give them the steady support which was built up around the popular impression of conservatism and liberalism. Salisbury, though at the time a bitter critic of Disraeli, stressed that " for all practical purposes Mr. Disraeli . . . is the Conservative Party." [48] On the other side, as *The Times* truly said of Gladstone " in the eyes of the Opposition, as indeed of the country, he is the government and he is the Liberal Party." Some commentators thought that the personalities of the day helped to popularise the notion of party government. It was apparent that Disraeli's brilliant sallies and Lord Salisbury's tough partisan speeches strengthened their side, but neither of these statesmen would have counted for much had they been individual prophets crying in the wilderness. Their power came because they led the Conservative Party and were able, each in his own way, to epitomise and intensify Conservative sentiments.

With the two-party system at its zenith in these years, neither governments nor oppositions could do well without effective leadership. In earlier decades much of the work of criticism had been left to private Members but the new conditions required someone to plan strategy and lead the attack. The Liberals were in a poor state for a year after 1874 when Gladstone neither attended the House with regularity nor handed the task on to anyone else. Hartington did something to restore their position after 1875 while the Grand Old Man's attack on Disraeli's Near Eastern policy enthused the radicals and his Midlothian campaigns made him the personification of his party and the only possible choice as Premier. Facing Gladstone's towering prestige, Randolph Churchill and " the Fourth Party " gained much of their credit by providing the Conservatives with some badly needed leadership. Members of Parliament soon came to realise that while their party might make capital out of the mistakes of the government or benefit by certain social developments, opportunities could be lost and their opponents encouraged by clumsy or dispirited direction. A successful leader was rewarded with intense loyalty while failure produced doubts, murmurs and in the last resort, dismissal. Balfour was replaced because he was associated with three defeats. Campbell-Bannerman was able to hold off the Liberal Imperialist

[48] R. Blake, *Disraeli*, pp. 499–500.

challenge by calling a party meeting where the rank and file's deep desire for a united and strong leadership confirmed his position.

The Prime Minister, as leader of his party, normally had the support of the party organisation. This enabled him to exercise some influence in the constituencies and his powers in this respect and in Parliament were enhanced by his control of patronage. The distribution of honours played a large part in any Prime Minister's affairs. Sometimes the object was to repay electoral support (" such men must be rewarded " Disraeli wrote to the Queen [49]) sometimes to bolster the position of the party in the Commons by the award of baronetcies and sometimes in the Lords by bringing in new recruits. In Gladstone's first ministry he created thirty-seven peers, Disraeli twenty-two and in his second administration Gladstone ennobled twenty-eight Liberals.[50] Disraeli used such Civil Service patronage as still existed but was more cautious about ecclesiastical appointments.[51] The plight of Liberal Party funds led Gladstone in 1891 to promise two peerages in return for financial contributions. This practice and the award of honours to men who had made their mark in commerce, industry and finance increased steadily from the 1890's.[52] In all, the use of patronage as Disraeli said when the Queen accepted his 1875 list " will greatly strengthen Your Majesty's Ministers and inspirit their friends.[53] "

To increase the Prime Minister's authority in the country, in Parliament and in the party clearly affected his relations with his colleagues in the Cabinet. They, likewise, desired and respected effective leadership. In previous years, it has been possible for the Cabinet to provide this on a collective basis but conditions were changing in a way that distinguished the Premier from his colleagues even when the latter included such vivid personalities as Lloyd George and Winston Churchill and such able ministers as Grey, Morley, Haldane and Crewe.

There were several ways in which this difference of kind slowly emerged. It was in these last decades of the Victorian era that

---

[49] R. Blake, *Disraeli*, p. 690.
[50] *Ibid.*, p. 687.
[51] H. J. Hanham, " Political Patronage at the Treasury 1870–1912," *The Historical Journal*, Vol. III (1960), pp. 75–84.
[52] H. J. Hanham, " The Sale of Honours in Late Victorian England," *Victorian Studies*, Vol. 3 (1959–60), pp. 277–289.
[53] R. Blake, *Disraeli*, p. 688,

political life had its greatest glamour and as the element of aristocratic detachment declined, the desire for office increased. Gladstone thought that by the 1890s there had been " a change in the style of men of Cabinet rank. The old stamp of Cabinet Minister was above all a good man to row with. All pulled together for the benefit of the boat. But now each man seemed to have his own axe to grind. Men looked out for themselves, first and foremost." [54] Yet this meant that the Prime Minister who alone could satisfy such ambitions found his position enhanced. When the Liberal Ministry was being formed in 1892, Fowler saw Morley who had taken part in the discussions. " Is it the Cabinet? " " Of course, but——! " and Morley found it hard to break the news that Fowler was to get only the Local Government Board.[55] Bryce was disappointed in 1905 at not being offered a post of greater status in the official hierarchy than that of Chief Secretary for Ireland. Earlier, while the Conservative Ministry was still in power, Walter Long quoted the Prime Minister as saying " that as on one or two occasions I had consented to be ' passed over,' in his judgment the time had come when I must be transferred to a ' higher ' post in the government or there might be a misunderstanding as to my position." [56] Morley in 1908 said he was prepared to waive his claims, based on seniority, for Asquith's place at the Exchequer. It was as well, for Lloyd George had entered his application by the more direct method of threatening resignation if he were not promoted.[57] Men like John Bright, Lord Rosebery and Sir Edward Grey still had to be coaxed to serve but Prime Ministers no longer had any difficulty in filling their Cabinets and the increased desire for office did strengthen their hand.

As a corollary of appointing and promoting, the power to dismiss began to be more evident. Since the end of royal control over Cabinets, Prime Ministers had planned and carried out changes but with the delicate balance of early and mid-nineteenth-century ministries, this could often be done only if there was general agreement. It was normally assumed that a minister remained in his office until he wanted to resign or the government collectively

---

[54] *Personal Papers of Lord Rendel*, p. 138.
[55] Edith H. Fowler, *op. cit.*, p. 254. She says that this was " one of the hardest blows " her father had ever received.
[56] Viscount Long, *op. cit.*, p. 140.
[57] Esher, *op. cit.*, Vol. III, p. 303, and Lee, *op. cit.*, Vol. II, p. 651

left office unless he had committed some error or failed in the
eyes of the House of Commons. In 1878 Salisbury pressed this
view on Carnarvon who was contemplating resignation. Ministers
were members of a Cabinet, not servants of the Premier and should
not resign unless they disagreed with the Cabinet as a whole.[58]
But he felt that Derby, who was clearly out of sympathy with the
majority of his colleagues after January 1878, was in such a position and should be called on to resign and he strongly censured
Disraeli for not doing so.[59] In practice, Prime Ministers were
reluctant to ask men to go even when a new leader took over and
it was accepted that all Cabinet posts were at his disposal. On
becoming Premier in February 1868 Disraeli in fact dismissed
Lord Chelmsford to the latter's great indignation. There was still
some notion that once a Cabinet was formed it had some collective rights to be consulted about such changes and in 1882
Gladstone found that he had to explain to a colleague that " the
notion of a title in the Cabinet to be consulted on the succession
to a Cabinet office is absurd." [60] Later, when he was hesitating
about the removal of Carlingford (C. S. Fortescue) from his
post as Lord Privy Seal, Harcourt reassured him on the same point.
" I confess I have never doubted that Cabinet offices were held
durante bene placito of the Prime Minister." [61] This was becoming
the accepted doctrine in the more rigorous form that the Prime
Minister might have reasons for reshuffling other than the personal
capacity of the ministers concerned. As in so many of the changes
of this period, the pressure of acute party conflict played a large
part. Lord Salisbury was so anxious to complete the rearrange-
ment of his Cabinet after Randolph Churchill's resignation that
the first intimation Northcote, by then the Earl of Iddesleigh,
had that he was no longer Foreign Secretary was when he saw the
announcement in the morning papers.[62] After the 1900 general
election in the reconstruction of Salisbury's government Chaplin
and Ridley were dropped in what appeared to many to be a rather
unceremonious fashion. Some of Chaplin's friends urged him to

---

58 Lady G. Cecil, *op. cit.*, Vol III, p. 170.
59 *Ibid.*, Vol. II, p. 211.
60 Morley, *op. cit.*, Vol. III, p. 101, n. 1.
61 A. G. Gardiner, *op. cit.*, Vol. I, p. 508.
62 *Ibid.*, Vol. III, p. 342.

resist but he preferred to go with dignity.[63] In 1903 when there had been months of serious recriminations over financial policy, Balfour evidently thought he would be better without the extreme free traders in his Cabinet and Devonshire recorded that " I have never heard anything more summary and decisive than the dismissal of the two ministers." [64] This was, in fact, the first time that a Prime Minister decided to cast aside a section of his Cabinet on a policy issue though Balfour still thought it better to provoke them into resigning than merely to ask for their resignation. Asquith was a different personality and managed his changes (which were on grounds of personal capacity) smoothly though both Elgin and Tweedmouth resented their displacement in 1908.

While discussing the increased power of the Premier to make and unmake his Cabinets, it is important to note the limitations that still existed. Salisbury was right when he told Carnarvon that Disraeli could not have survived their departure in 1877 as easily as he had done in 1867. After all his difficulties in forming a government in 1886, Gladstone realised that there was a limit to the number of resignations he could face, and he was ready to compromise to keep Childers. Similarly the Unionist coalition after 1886 lacked front bench talent and with the opposition in full cry, Salisbury worked hard to avoid any signs of weakness.[65] It was this that led Randolph Churchill to over-estimate his strength and though he was not intending to force his way back into the Cabinet when he resigned in late 1886, Lord Salisbury had great difficulty in constructing an adequate front bench. The Conservative Party was much stronger after the 1890s but Balfour felt that the convulsions of 1903 had made it important to avoid further reshuffles and so Arnold-Foster was kept at the War Office although it was obvious that he was a failure.

The greater strength of the Cabinet, especially after the 1880s,

---

[63] Marchioness of Londonderry, *op. cit.*, p. 173. Goschen, writing to Balfour, reminded him of " my idea that all the Cabinet should have notified Salisbury *before* the election that they were prepared to resign "—a precaution that would have prevented all their heart-burning. *Balfour Papers, Add. MSS.*, 49,706, f. 267.

[64] Holland, *op. cit.*, Vol. II, p. 340, and A. Gollin, *Mr. Balfour's Burden*, p. 132.

[65] Salisbury asked Lord Halsbury to urge Henry Matthews not to resign. " The loss of him at this time would very seriously imperil the government, and I think I am not rating our value too high when I say that the fall of the government at this moment would probably be fatal to union." A. Wilson-Fox, *The Earl of Halsbury*, p. 129.

and the loyalty on which the Prime Minister could usually rely made it easier for him to face resignations, though there was a great reluctance to lose men of weight in the party or the country. In earlier years one or two leading fighters going over to the opposition could imperil a ministry, but Disraeli did not feel the loss of Carnarvon and Derby in 1878.[66] Gladstone, commenting on the way in which his Cabinet had kept its strength after the secessions of Argyll, Forster and Bright in 1882, said that " the Duke being a peer had not much weight, that Forster's obstinacy was most extraordinary . . .; Bright's resignation . . . had he shown anything but the loyalty with which he had acted, would have been very serious." [67] In general, the importance of individual politicians, whatever their standing, was declining as compared with that of the government. Lord Randolph Churchill did not, as the old story had it, " forget Goschen " but he did commit the grave error of trying to win his case in the Cabinet by an expedient which endangered Unionist resistance to Home Rule. Whatever issues he had chosen, it is doubtful whether rank and file Unionists would have considered them worth another dose of Gladstonian remedies.[68]

It greatly strengthened a dissentient if he had reliable allies. Chamberlain's threats of resignation were much more serious when Gladstone knew that Dilke would go with him, and that this would be taken as a definite rejection of radical policies by the Cabinet. When he next took office in 1895, Chamberlain was an influential member of a united Cabinet. He " discarded altogether his old resort, the threat of resignation, and never once made the mistake of underestimating those resources of Hatfield House which had been fatal to Randolph Churchill." [69] The most clear-cut demonstration of self-confidence on the part of a Prime Minister was when Balfour decided it was better to shed the free traders, Balfour of Burleigh, Lord Hamilton and Ritchie, faced them in

---

[66] Disraeli had long appreciated that Carnarvon could be dropped overboard without any splash, but Sir Stafford Northcote emphasised that Derby's resignation " would shake our Lancashire members to the centre, and would greatly discourage the moderate men on both sides." *Letters*, Series, Vol. II, p. 599.

[67] West, *Recollections*, Vol. II, p. 168.

[68] The best description of the fall of Lord Randolph Churchill is in R. R. James's biography, Chap. 10.

[69] Garvin, *op. cit.*, Vol. III, p. 5.

Cabinet, and accepted their resignations without disclosing that he had Joseph Chamberlain's resignation in his pocket. He had not intended to drive out the Duke of Devonshire (" that silly old Duke ") though this, too, was weathered. It is significant that among all the reasons for Conservative defeat in 1906, Cabinet weaknesses did not feature. The real problem was Balfour's inability to provide a clear and convincing lead for all sections of his party. Had he been able to do so, the fact that he was captaining a rather scratch eleven would have made little difference. Indeed, as Selborne had observed over Forster's resignation, the government was led by the Premier and there was little point in an individual minister remaining in office if confidence between him and the Prime Minister had ceased to exist.[70]

Besides the development of a special relationship with his colleagues, the Prime Minister also acquired a measure of control over the working of the Cabinet itself. Formerly any member could call a meeting, but it became accepted that this was done through the Prime Minister. Also it became established that only the Premier could summon the Cabinet. In December 1870, Gladstone told Granville that "the Cabinet appears not to have been called in the usual manner through me," and the proper form was observed for the rest of the ministry.[71] Disraeli went one step further when a Cabinet asked for by Carnarvon over the annexation of Fiji was postponed indefinitely, and a request to call a Cabinet on the uproar over the Bulgarian atrocities was simply refused.[72] Members who were worried about the Prime Minister's policies sometimes felt that Cabinets might not be called till the decisions had been taken. Harcourt feared that there would be no time to revise the second Home Rule Bill before Parliament met and he asked for some Cabinets in December 1892 but got no support. Later Morley and Asquith wanted a meeting and West noted in his Diary "Trying to get a Cabinet—but it is wonderful how Mr. G. is able to push off what he does not like."[73] In his last crisis, when Gladstone went to Biarritz, he forbade any meetings in his absence. Normally Cabinets were held with

70 Selborne, *op. cit.*, Vol. II, p. 52.
71 *Gladstone-Granville Correspondence*, Vol. I, p. 186 and Vol. II, pp. 312, 324 and 335.
72 Sir A. Hardinge, *op. cit.*, Vol. II, pp. 74 and 336.
73 West, *Diaries*, p. 149.

sufficient regularity to make requests for special meetings unnecessary, and any desire for extra gatherings was granted, though these instances reveal the Prime Minister becoming the central and essential element in the system.

Once a meeting was called, the Prime Minister controlled the discussion and items that seemed of small importance to him came near the end or were postponed till another day. Gordon was left in Khartoum because Gladstone was absorbed in the Reform Bill and disliked the whole subject, while Hartington had not the personality or determination to force the matter on the Cabinet. Northbrook likewise could not get his scheme for Egyptian finances discussed. This problem was less serious with men like Asquith and Balfour who saw themselves as chairman of a meeting where all points could be raised.

It must not be imagined that the other members in any way resented these developments for they arose out of the necessities of contemporary government. Most ministers found that they were fully occupied by departmental work and wanted someone who could control the Cabinet, obtain decisions and watch over the general progress of the government. Several of Gladstone's colleagues complained that he showed too much deference to the various opinions in his Cabinets. Stansfeld thought he " should have said ' This is my policy. What do you think of it? ' and then have fought it out until they came to an agreement." [74] Balfour reports Salisbury as saying of Disraeli that—

> " As the head of a Cabinet his fault was want of firmness. The chiefs of departments got their own way too much. The Cabinet as a whole got it too little, and this necessarily followed from having at the head of affairs a statesman whose only final political principle was that the Party must on no account be broken up, and who shrank therefore from exercising coercion on any of his subordinates." [75]

Lord Salisbury himself realised that a lead was necessary and he skilfully let matters take their course in the autumn of 1886. As Randolph Churchill attempted to set the pace and intervened in foreign affairs, Salisbury held back till his colleagues were urging

---

[74] J. Stansfeld, *Review of Reviews*, Vol. XI for 1895. Argyll took the same view. Morley, *op. cit.*, Vol. III, p. 4.
[75] A. J. Balfour, *op. cit.*, p. 113.

him to give more guidance to the members of the Cabinet. Gathorne-Hardy wrote that, " Interrogated separately, each expresses an opinion; but all would be prepared to make concessions. . . . If you were to make a statement on a review of what has passed defining your opinion, and asking our assent to a plan . . . I am confident you would obtain almost if not quite unanimous support." Salisbury replied that his reticence was due to special circumstances and to the need to detach the Liberal Unionists from Randolph Churchill.[76] By the time the latter resigned, the whole Cabinet was eager for a firm lead. The senior members of Campbell-Bannerman's Cabinet found it was very difficult to carry on while the chief was an invalid in early 1908 and the Premiership virtually in commission. Lord George Hamilton summed up his experience by saying that " as an executive and administrative body the Cabinet must necessarily from its composition and numbers, be a failure unless the Prime Minister is a man of determination and strength and constitutes himself the Cabinet and its mouthpiece." [77]

The old notion of the equality of ministers had meant that much the same weight was attached to each voice and decisions could therefore be reached, when every opinion had been given, by counting those for and against. Now that gradations in the ministerial hierarchy were becoming more marked, such practices declined in favour of a summary of the sense of the meeting by the Prime Minister. Gladstone's first two Cabinets had worked on the earlier assumptions and his jottings contain a number of division lists. In several cases it is evident that no actual division was taken but as each member spoke, Gladstone put a tick under the headings " Ayes " and " Noes." Voting or the recording of voices was adopted on major as well as on minor matters, the decision to arrest Dillon being taken on Gladstone's casting vote.[78] The future of the Duke of Wellington's statue led to a stiff battle and three divisions were taken before a final solution was reached.[79] On issues which concerned Gladstone deeply, he would postpone a decision if he was losing the argument and on other occasions

[76] Gathorne-Hardy, *op. cit.*, Vol. II, p. 265.
[77] Lord George Hamilton, *op. cit.*, Vol. I, p. 307.
[78] *Gladstone Papers, Add. MSS.*, 44,642, f. 177.
[79] *Ibid., Add. MSS.*, 44,644, f. 98.

his strength of feeling gave a minority victory.[80] In time the practice of taking division lists declined and there are none in the Gladstone Papers after he left office in 1885. Early in the next ministry, Granville passed a note (he sat beside Gladstone) saying "the majority is with you about Dongola—But I hope when the time comes, you will try to avoid a counting of noses—It perhaps occurred too much last year." [81] Salisbury still used this device; a Cabinet letter to the King in January 1902 records that "at the close the Cabinet determined by a small majority of eleven to eight to accept the proposals of Mr. Brodrick *en bloc*" and there are three references in the same year to decisions being reached on a majority vote.[82] After Salisbury retired, divisions were only taken on trivial issues such as the time of the next meeting, a show of hands being requested simply as a convenient and quick way of settling the matter.

Asquith, who first entered the Cabinet in 1892, could confidently assert that it was not the custom to count heads, but that it was left to the Prime Minister to collect and interpret the general sense of colleagues.[83] Sometimes he simply gave a decision. Campbell-Bannerman was ill during the struggle over the 1908 Naval Estimates when the Board of Admiralty was refusing to budge and five Cabinet Ministers threatened to resign. The Prime Minister heard Fisher's case and sent for Asquith. " I have decided that the Naval Estimates are to stand. Haldane will take £300,000 off his instead. Nothing need be said at present to any other member of the Cabinet." [84] It was only by Asquith's support that Lloyd George managed to get his 1909 Budget through the Cabinet. The land taxes "were saved . . . by the action of Mr. Asquith when a vote in the Cabinet would have rejected them by an overwhelming majority." On another occasion, Lloyd George told Masterman: "Take the section about the children. They were all

---

[80] On July 5, 1884, Dilke noted after a Cabinet that "the matter was adjourned, as matters always are adjourned when the P.M. is against the Cabinet." Earlier that year Gladstone had twice triumphed when the figures were 6:8 and 8:9 against him. Gwynn and Tuckwell, *op. cit.*, Vol. II, pp. 60–87.

[81] *Gladstone Papers, Add. MSS.*, 44,647, f. 21.

[82] *Salisbury Papers*, Cabinet letters to the King dated January 24, March 18, May 27, and June 12, 1902. On the issue that came up on March 18 (the scale of payments for Irish land purchase) it was by a majority of only one.

[83] Earl of Oxford and Asquith, *Fifty Years of Parliament*, Vol. II, p. 196.

[84] Esher, *op. cit.*, Vol. II, pp. 280–284.

against it and they all said so, and then Asquith rubbed his chin and said: ' I think the balance of argument is in favour,' and put it through. He did that lots of times." [85] When the staff talks between the British and French armies came up in the Cabinet in 1911, the majority were hostile but Asquith's authority smoothed the matter over. On other occasions, such as the 1909 and 1913–1914 disputes over Naval Estimates, the Prime Minister was able by a mixture of postponement, compromise and firmness, to settle dangerous disputes.

In attempting to describe the Prime Minister's rise to a position with some powers and considerable influence not enjoyed by other senior ministers, continued explanations may have led to too definite and strong an impression. Premiers were bound to their Cabinets by the doctrine of collective responsibility, which meant in practice that members could object to actions or statements which had not been sanctioned by the Cabinet. Usually the offenders were ministers who wished either to take up a position which would then commit the Cabinet or wanted to keep themselves clear with their followers in the party. Chamberlain and Bright had abstained in a division involving Cabinet policy in the Transvaal in 1880 and Dilke refused to vote against women's suffrage in 1884. Chamberlain also was guilty of speaking on Irish and other matters in a manner which scarcely represented the Cabinet's views. Gladstone took a strong line over such behaviour but was not prepared for a showdown on these (carefully selected) points. Prime Ministers likewise had to remain within the bounds set by the Cabinet. There are a few exceptions, as when Campbell-Bannerman accepted a Trade Disputes Bill put forward by a Labour Member in 1906 which embodied principles explicitly rejected by the Cabinet. His action caused some irritation and it was safer to win the battle in the Cabinet than to try to upset a decision after it had been taken.

Within the Cabinet, the Prime Minister could well be on the losing side in an argument. He might even find himself isolated and defeated though in this case it was not the same as any other minister losing a point, since if the Premier chose to resign it

[85] Lucy Masterman, *op. cit.*, pp. 133 and 173. In December 1916 Asquith ruefully recalled that "he had saved him (Lloyd George) over the Budget of 1909, when everyone else in the Cabinet had turned against him." Lord Beaverbrook, *Politicians and the War, 1914–1916*, Vol. II, p. 271.

would mean the end of the government. Gladstone and his supporters failed to secure an immediate release of Fenian prisoners
and a remonstrance to Germany over the annexation of Alsace-
Lorraine in 1870. Later, the majority of the Cabinet insisted
on a stiffer tone in the Alabama negotiations. In the 1880 ministry
his side lost over sending Zebehr to help Gordon and had to agree
to an autumn expedition to the Sudan. The Peace Preservation
Bill was introduced and Chamberlain's scheme for Irish Councils
was turned down against Gladstone's advice. It was one thing to
find a majority of his colleagues disagreeing, but when his desire to
cut the 1894 Naval Estimates was flatly rejected by the whole
Cabinet, Gladstone decided to resign. Salisbury likewise was
occasionally overruled. His Cabinet postponed the question of
free passage of the Suez Canal in time of war against his advice,[86]
and refused to threaten action against the Greeks in Crete in 1889.
When the House of Commons ministers insisted on abandoning the
reform of procedure and most of the 1890 programme of legislation, Salisbury told the Queen that, had it not been for the dangers
associated with Gladstonian Government, he would have resigned
after so serious a difference with his colleagues. Lord Rosebery
did not like Harcourt's 1894 Budget but had to give way. Campbell-Bannerman and Asquith managed their Cabinets very well, but
it was not done either by exercising an overriding authority or by
acting always as an impartial chairman.

While a Prime Minister might be overruled in these cases, it was
a sign of weakness if the Cabinet could not come to a decision
despite the efforts of the Prime Minister. The symptoms of such
periods of conflict and deadlock were repeated threats by members
to resign (Rosebery at one stage threatened to go himself in early
1895) and a tendency to take stands outside the Cabinet on issues
that had not yet been decided. The departure of some members, a
change in the course of events or determined leadership could
restore the situation, as happened for the Conservatives in 1876–78.
Alternatively, further policy failures, more ministers trying to
rally outside support, deadlocks in which the Prime Minister
could not resolve the conflicts, all presaged the defeat or collapse

---

[86] Both Salisbury and Iddesleigh thought that the Gladstone Government had
committed us so far to the French on this point that it was impossible to
withdraw " but the Cabinet took an opposite view generally." *Royal
Archives*, Vol. A 65, f. 14.

of the ministry, as occurred to the Liberals in 1884–85 and in 1894–95 and in part to the Conservatives in 1905. Asquith's Government faltered in this way in the winter of 1910, but the Prime Minister pulled himself and then his followers together. Under these conditions more positive leadership was necessary than had been the case in the 1850s and 1860s and only the Prime Minister was in a position to give it. King Edward VII was merely recognising the facts when in 1906, in Viscount Esher's words, he " settled the precedence of the Prime Minister, in accordance with a constitutional development that has taken place during the past thirty years with the result that the holder of that great office is now Primus among his colleagues, and no longer *primus inter pares.*" [87]

The minister who worked most closely with the Prime Minister was the Foreign Secretary. Gladstone had easy relations with Clarendon, whom he described as " excellent, communicating more freely with the Cabinet and carrying out their policy more faithfully, than any Foreign Secretary I have known." [88] Granville followed in this pattern and the success of Gladstone's first and most harmonious Cabinet was built on the working partnership between them. When difficulties arose in 1870, Granville asked " for an understanding between ourselves that when, amid the many and complex movements of the wheels, any one goes wrong, we two shall first talk it over together." [89] Disraeli maintained equally close contact with Derby in the early years of his ministry when there was full confidence between them, and a similar relationship was set up after Salisbury came to the Foreign Office. Fully aware of his own aptitude and finesse in foreign affairs, Salisbury could not bear to watch other men handle this work. As Prime Minister in 1886, he spent a few unhappy months with Lord Iddesleigh in the Foreign Office and then solved the problem by taking over the task himself. Balfour left Lansdowne a considerable margin of freedom but it was based on mutual confidence, as were the relations between Sir Edward Grey and his

---

[87] Esher, *op. cit.*, Vol. II, pp. 347–348. What King Edward did was to give the office of Prime Minister formal recognition for the first time and place it fourth on the list of precedence after the Archbishop of Canterbury, the Lord Chancellor and the Archbishop of York. Sir P. Magnus, *King Edward VII*, p. 281.

[88] Morley, *op. cit.*, Vol. II, p. 417.

[89] *Gladstone-Granville Correspondence*, Vol. I, p. 115.

two Prime Ministers. Apart from Disraeli's total disagreement
with Derby in 1877, the only instance of friction was between
Gladstone and Rosebery. On the two major issues that came up
in 1892 and 1893—the future of Uganda and of the Upper Nile—
they disagreed and Gladstone reflected that

> " ... It is the first time, during a Cabinet experience of twenty-
> two or twenty-three years, that I have known the Foreign
> Minister and the Prime Minister to go before a Cabinet on a
> present question with diverging views. It is the union of these
> two authorities by which foreign policy is ordinarily worked
> in a Cabinet." [90]

Rosebery got his own way in both cases by a mixture of postponement, obtaining favourable reports from agents or simply
threatening resignation. Looking back on this relationship, Gladstone thought Rosebery's error " was his total and gross miscon-
ception of the relative position of the two offices we respectively
held, and secondly his really outrageous assumption of power
apart from both the First Minister and the Cabinet." [91]

This second problem, that of Cabinet control, could be even
greater when the Prime Minister and Foreign Secretary agreed.
If they brought all major questions to the Cabinet and executed
policy in keeping with its sentiments, there was no difficulty.
Gladstone and Granville were, as has been mentioned, kept up to
the mark by their colleagues over the Alabama question. In the
1850s and 1860s the danger had been that Palmerston would
commit the country beyond the intentions of his fellow ministers,
but in the last third of the century it was as often a question of
ensuring sufficient action. When Derby disagreed with the policy
developed by Disraeli, Salisbury, and the Cabinet in late 1877,
he dragged his feet and failed to convey their meaning in his
despatches. He went further than could be imagined possible
by telling the Russian ambassador Shuvalov of Cabinet discussions in order to frustrate the Prime Minister's policy. After
being persuaded to withdraw his resignation in January 1878,
Derby " relapsed into a state of paralysed apathy " [92] and foreign

[90] R. R. James, *Rosebery*, p. 265.
[91] *Ibid.*, p. 270.
[92] R. Blake, *Disraeli*, pp. 623 and 638.

policy was actually conducted by a committee consisting of
Disraeli, Salisbury and Lord Cairns. They saw all incoming messages, drafted replies, took them to the Cabinet, and then made
sure they were sent. By 1900 most of the leading members of Lord
Salisbury's Cabinet had become critical of the lack of precision and
intention in his foreign policy; when the Germans offered to
discuss joint action in the Yangtse valley, they pushed him into
making an agreement.[93] On the other hand, Rosebery, who wanted
a forward policy and had been urged by the Queen " to bring as
little before the Cabinet as possible," [94] did consult and extract
consent for all his major steps while he was Foreign Secretary.
He was less scrupulous when, as Prime Minister with Kimberley
as Foreign Secretary, he tended simply to ignore the Cabinet.
Salisbury complained about " Joe's war " in 1899 but Chamberlain
could claim that all his major steps had the approval of his fellow
ministers though sometimes he had anticipated their sanction
for particular despatches.

There were some doubts on both sides at Salisbury's combination of the post of Foreign Secretary with the Prime Ministership.
Gathorne-Hardy thought that " in such cases all home work gives
way to foreign," but Salisbury did not deluge the Cabinet with
the details of foreign policy.[95] Gladstone objected because

> " The Foreign Office, though necessarily not so much under a
> Parliamentary check as other departments, was, within the
> Cabinet, under a kind of dual control, since the Secretary
> for Foreign Affairs never failed to consult the Prime Minister
> on any question of any importance. . . . But with the Prime
> Minister as Foreign Secretary a kind of autocracy was set
> up. The Prime Minister became absolute master of the situa-
> tion. The most serious questions might all be kept locked in
> his own breast." [96]

His fears were not realised in this instance because Salisbury
had no desire and no motive to withhold the principles on which
he was acting from his colleagues. But Gladstone's argument
did not apply solely to the case of a combined Prime Minister

[93] See J. D. Hargreaves, " Lord Salisbury, British Isolation and the Yangtse
Valley," *Bulletin of the Institute of Historical Research*, Vol. 30, 1957.
[94] *Letters*, Series II, Vol. I, p. 45, note.
[95] Gathorne-Hardy, *op. cit.*, Vol. II, p. 251.
[96] *Personal Papers of Lord Rendel*, pp. 119–120.

and Foreign Secretary. If the only insurance against deception or unsanctioned actions was the constant supervision of the Premier, these dangers were just as great if the posts were separately held by men who wished to conceal matters from the Cabinet. The question how far Sir Edward Grey and his Prime Ministers agreed to keep certain matters from their colleagues will be considered in the section on inner Cabinets.

Discussing the position of Chancellor of the Exchequer, Gladstone told Lowe that " no man wants so much sympathy . . . , no man gets so little." [97] The Chancellor's relations with the rest of the Cabinet had several facets. As head of the Treasury, he was involved in inter-departmental disputes about particular items of expenditure, but though this duty caused some friction, it led to no major disputes. Then there was the task of raising the revenue. In the past when each tax had had separate treatment, the Cabinet had reviewed them as they came up. During Gladstone's period as Chancellor after 1859, all taxation had been consolidated in a single Budget and explained to the Cabinet only a few days before the announcement in the House. Kimberley thought that " the practice of laying the Budget proposals so late before the Cabinet that there is practically no opportunity to discuss them arose when Gladstone was Chancellor of the Exchequer under Palmerston. They were always quarrelling, and Gladstone kept his Budgets back to the last moment in order to prevent Palmerston from . . . getting the Cabinet to object to them." [98] Certainly Chancellors liked to give the impression that the matter was settled and that they were simply informing their colleagues, but the Cabinet never gave up its right to review. Chancellors differed in the extent to which they invited the aid of the Cabinet. Hicks Beach was always ready to submit his proposals to scrutiny. In March 1900, considering his Budget, the Cabinet resolved not to introduce an export duty on coal, but by the next year a majority favoured the project. In 1902 Hicks Beach told his colleagues that he had to raise between five and six million pounds by direct taxation and gave them the choice—a penny on the income tax and a corn duty or various stamp and house duties.[99] This was an unusually open attitude and Kimberley observed that if Lowe had given more time

[97] Morley, *op. cit.*, Vol. II, p. 372.
[98] *The Kimberley Papers*, p. 22.
[99] *Royal Archives*, Vols. A 76, f. 50, and R 22, ff. 8 and 75.

for discussion, some of the faults of his 1871 Budget would have been removed. The Cabinet asked Childers to postpone his statement in 1885 so that they could alter some of his duties on drink. When Harcourt produced his " death duties Budget " in 1894 there was an exchange of memoranda with Rosebery before Harcourt agreed in Cabinet to a reduction of the maximum rate from 10 per cent. to 8 per cent. Ritchie managed to repeal the Corn Tax in 1903 because there was no time to fight out the whole question of protection, but the prolonged discussion of this topic, and of Lloyd George's 1909 Budget, showed that the Cabinet still had full control of all major departures in taxation.

The real difficulties of the Chancellor arose over the estimates, those for the Army and Navy tending to rise steadily during the period. While the House of Commons and many Cabinet Ministers were imbued with Manchester School principles, it was slowly appreciated that the new electorate did not respond to the cry for economy and that there was general support for an expansion of the armed forces. Chancellors found that when the estimates had risen, it was almost impossible to go through them and point out economies, as the Admiralty and the War Office had long operated on a tight margin. It was scarcely the business of the Treasury (though they did try at times) to go further and suggest that units be disbanded or ships remain uncommissioned, since this would affect policy. Thus battles usually took the form of the Chancellor trying to fix a ceiling (determined by the general financial position) and the service minister inviting him to come and explain how the country could be defended for less than the requested sum. Gladstone wanted to revive the flagging fortunes of his ministry by cutting taxation in 1873 and 1874. Cardwell gave way in the first instance and the deadlock in the second was only solved by the loss of the general election. In 1886 Harcourt tried to insist on no increases, while Campbell-Bannerman and Childers wanted a total of £4 million more. Meetings took place between them with Gladstone in the chair. Harcourt refused to go into the estimates in detail as he knew his case would then be lost. Reductions of £1·5 million were made by several stages, and then Harcourt agreed to the estimates.

In the celebrated battle which marked the end of Randolph Churchill's career, much more was at stake than finance, but any

other Chancellor would still have had to face rising estimates and
a growing feeling that too much economy could be dangerous.
In the debate in the House, Churchill again laid down the proposition that the only way in which the Treasury could check expen-
diture was by cutting aggregates without going into details.
Gladstone was in difficulties because in his heart he agreed and
he had adopted the identical stand in his earlier years at the
Exchequer. Yet he saw that the Cabinet could not be denied
final authority. The result was the somewhat involved point that
Churchill was "entirely wrong in supposing that the Finance
Minister has any ruling authority on the great estimates of defence.
If he had, he would be the master of the country. But although
he has no right to demand the concurrence of his colleagues in his
view of the estimates, he has a rather special right . . . to indicate
his own views by resignation." [1] Faithful to this, the Grand Old
Man, though deserted by his Chancellor, resigned when his ceiling
on the estimates was not accepted in 1894. These disputes began
between the ministers concerned, drew in the Premier, perhaps
went to a committee of ministers to have some detailed points
examined, and if there had been no settlement, then came to the
Cabinet. Randolph Churchill knew that he would lose at a full
meeting of the Cabinet and resigned before one was called. Beach
likewise realised that the current was running against him in 1901.
He sent round a memorandum pointing out that expenditure had
gone up 40 per cent. in six years and calling for a halt. Salisbury
doubted if this was possible and Beach said he was simply giving
him notice and time to find a successor. In the regular disputes
on defence estimates after 1906, the situation was slightly altered
by the exploitation of new sources of revenue. It was now more
a matter of competition between ways of spending the money
than whether it should be spent at all and the Chancellor found
allies among the home departments when he was tackling the Services. Resignations were bandied about (especially in 1907), but
the Prime Minister and Cabinet were able to meet most of the
demands and thus take the edge off the disputes.

The only other situation which might affect relations within
the Cabinet occurred when the Premier was a peer. This meant
that special powers accrued to the Minister who led the House and

---

[1] Morley, *op. cit.*, Vol. III, p. 365.

made any concessions or answers to unexpected questions. In so doing he might well commit his colleagues to a form of words or a strength of expression which was not exactly what the Cabinet had in mind. Disraeli had sometimes done this when Derby was Prime Minister but he himself was well served by Sir Stafford Northcote after he went to the Lords. The one case of extreme friction was when Harcourt became Leader of the House after being passed over as Premier. He tried to exact conditions which would have made him at least joint Premier with Rosebery and when these were not granted communications between them deteriorated till this became a factor in the collapse of the Ministry.[2] But a united Cabinet with a will to live had few problems on this score. Salisbury was on excellent terms with W. H. Smith and Balfour, seeing them every day during the session. On one occasion in 1891 he wrote to Goschen, " It has seemed to me several times that the Cabinet does not quite get fair play from the leaders of the Government in the House of Commons, . . . The course on which the Cabinet resolved is sometimes . . . manifestly departed from. . . ."[3] Examining the events, it is hard to find any evidence, apart from one matter of provision for the Queen's grandchildren, to justify the complaint. Salisbury could be irritable over small matters if his plans were disturbed.

It is a rather different point to say that a Premier in the Lords was at a disadvantage within his own Cabinet. Certainly both Salisbury and Rosebery had on occasion to bow before the argument that, however desirable a proposal might be, the party in the House of Commons would not stand for it. The point could not be made often as peers, especially in the Conservative Party, had ample means of ascertaining rank and file opinion, and control became easier as the Cabinet tightened its hold on the procedure of the House. The Leader in the Commons had had good reason for asking to see all despatches and for maintaining as close contact with the Prime Minister as did the Foreign Secretary. Provided there was confidence between the senior members of the Cabinet, this situation did not need to cause any special difficulties. The Cabinet remained the source of all major

---

[2] On some occasions Harcourt's complaints either that Cabinet decisions were not followed or that he was kept in the dark were justified. R. R. James, *Rosebery*, pp. 349, 351, 377.

[3] Lady G. Cecil, *op. cit.*, Vol. IV, p. 151.

decisions, with day-to-day tactics arranged in conferences between the leaders of the two Houses.

In describing the formation and dissolution of Cabinets and the relations of the principal members, much has been said about the conduct of business and the ways in which decisions were reached. Some points, however, remain. The theory of Cabinet responsibility held that all major political decisions had to be put before that body. The sanction underlying the practice was that failure to do so might lead to complaints and ultimately to the disruption of the Ministry. Yet all business could not go before the Cabinet and many day-to-day decisions were left to the Prime Minister (or the Leader of the Commons, if this was a different person) and the Foreign Secretary. Besides these, some more important matters were not within the normal province of the Cabinet. The Home Secretary's duty to advise on reprieves and remissions of sentence was exercised on his own responsibility and neither the Cabinet nor the Crown could intervene in his decisions.[4] The Colonial Secretary and the Secretary of State for India had a similar duty in their areas of responsibility.

There were some other issues which were normally settled by particular ministers but which might be reviewed collectively in special circumstances. Queen Victoria held that "the Prime Minister may privately consult the Secretaries for Foreign and Colonial Affairs, etc.: but the distribution of Honours is not a question for the Cabinet."[5] Gladstone pointed out that in the case of Honours distributed as a reward for political services, it was not usual to consult the Cabinet, but they had the right to review any action for which they were collectively responsible. Appointments at a senior level in the Army and Navy, to Governor-Generalships and to the office of Viceroy of India came in the same category. Viceroys were normally nominated after consultations between the Prime Minister and the Secretary of State,

---

[4] The precedents relating to the Crown were of long standing. Peel and Wellington insisted that George IV should abandon an attempt to reprieve an Irishman found guilty of arson in April 1830 (Parker, *Sir Robert Peel*, Vol. II, pp. 147–150). Harcourt had some correspondence with Queen Victoria who was worried about the number of remissions of sentence and of reprieves in cases of infanticide. Harcourt would explain his reasons but not consider any revisions (Gardiner, *op. cit.*, Vol. I, pp. 394–403). The Cabinet never considered any intervention.

[5] *Letters*, Series III, Vol. II, p. 350.

but if there was controversy over the policy of the existing incumbent, as in the cases of Ellenborough, Lytton or Curzon, the matter came before the Cabinet and they could recall the man
concerned. If the next appointment was of great importance or
involved special personal difficulties, it might also be discussed.
Both the Budget and the Queen's Speech at the opening of Parliament were composed without the aid of the Cabinet, but alterations could be made in either if there was a widespread objection
in the Cabinet.

On all other subjects the Cabinet was consulted regularly,
the only question being whether it was worth raising a particular
issue or, if no meeting was due, having a special one called. As
a general rule, any changes of policy or actions that might lead
to political controversy had to be mentioned. Gladstone was
extremely careful about this and to Forster's suggestion that the
ministers in town could go ahead and recognise the French
Republic, he replied that this " ought to be the work of the
Cabinet." [6] He similarly insisted that the arrest of Parnell was
too novel an application of the Coercion Laws to be undertaken
without Cabinet sanction. The public gauged the importance of
events in part by the number and length of Cabinet meetings,
and at least one newspaper kept a man with a stop-watch in
Downing Street. When Gathorne-Hardy wondered whether a
Cabinet should be called to sanction an advance to Kabul in 1879,
Disraeli felt " it is not necessary but perhaps the country expects
it." [7] The problem of calling a special gathering declined as the
holiday recess shrank and was punctuated by occasional meetings,
though the increasing volume of work made it more and more
necessary to bring only questions of policy to the Cabinet.

Matters to be raised were mentioned to the Prime Minister,
talked over with colleagues, and explained in printed memoranda which were circulated before the appropriate meeting.[8]
Most departmental ministers were deeply embedded in their own
work and found, as issues became more complicated, that they

[6] *Gladstone-Granville Correspondence*, Vol. I, p. 130.
[7] Gathorne-Hardy, *op. cit.*, Vol. II, p. 119.
[8] In 1880, Childers (Chancellor of the Exchequer) observed that " it is
very interesting to get daily telegrams from the India Office : one reads much
more as a member of the Cabinet than I did in '69–'70, everything of
importance being now circulated in print." S. C. Childers, *op. cit.*, Vol. I,
p. 272.

had little time to acquire the information necessary for proper comment on other topics. Provided a scheme accorded with the general spirit of party policy and was not going to cause dangerous controversies or cost large sums, the advantage was with the proposer. Even when there were doubts this remained true, especially in foreign and colonial affairs where each question had a complex history. Carnarvon told Salisbury that his efforts to reach agreement at the Constantinople Conference in late 1876 were little appreciated. " It is not easy to fight these questions in Cabinet, for I have but little information, no real support, and do not know till I get into the room the exact point which is for discussion." [9] Henry James described the procedure in the 1890s:

> " In a Cabinet of nineteen members business could not be carried on if everybody talked much. So a tacit understanding seems to exist that on most subjects those only who have a special knowledge of it should express any detailed opinion. For instance, when dealing with Indian affairs, George Hamilton and Lord Lansdowne guide the Cabinet. On matters affecting the proceedings in the House of Commons, Balfour and Chamberlain are the chief advisers. Some of the members of the Cabinet seldom express an opinion even on the most general of subjects." [10]

The tendency to be absorbed in departmental work was most marked in the Liberal Cabinets between 1906 and 1914, when a mass of involved domestic legislation and administrative reform was carried through. Haldane observed that

> " looking back, I think I ought to have taken a more active part in the general business of the Cabinet. But my hands were full with military affairs, and, while I was ready to suggest fresh ideas, I could only prevail in counsel when the conditions existed for which I was best fitted, those of working with two or three colleagues who knew me . . . we lived as a Government too much from hand to mouth, dependent for our achievements on the initiative not of the body as a whole but of individual members." [11]

In these circumstances it was of the greatest value, as has been argued, to have the backing of the Prime Minister. But it was also

9 Hardinge, *op. cit.*, Vol. II, p. 348.
10 Lord Askwith, *op. cit.*, pp. 255–256.
11 Haldane, *op. cit.*, pp. 216–217.

helpful to have the support of one or two other members, particularly of those senior men who carried weight on general topics. Bright had such a position because of his moral stature and his standing with the older radical elements. Granville and Spencer were both respected as moderate, sound men while Crewe was influential both for this reason and for his experience of business in a range of departments. If a dispute arose, the attitude of one or two ministers could affect the whole balance of opinion in the Cabinet. Disraeli knew that Salisbury's adhesion would restore his control over his colleagues in 1877. Sometimes a minister's views were important because of his reputation with the party or the public. Salisbury's strength in the 1870s was largely due to his reliable and traditional conservatism. In 1911 and 1914 Lloyd George held a key position, since his radicalism and reputed leanings towards pacifism made strong words on his part so much more significant and decisively weakened the section opposed to active support for France.

All these points, the attitude of the Premier, support from the holders of the principal offices, the need for information and the tendency of ministers to concentrate on departmental affairs, affected the handling of foreign policy by the Cabinet. The first occasion on which foreign affairs became of major importance after the Crimean War was in Disraeli's 1874–80 Ministry. In its earliest days, the Prime Minister pointed out to Salisbury (then Secretary of State for India) that while official despatches were printed and went round all the Cabinet, letters from the Viceroy, like letters from ambassadors to the Foreign Secretary, should be sent only to the Prime Minister and not circulated. It was essential that these two Secretaries of State and the Premier should meet and talk over all important matters.[12] This practice of sending the more informative and valuable papers only to a group within the Cabinet continued under Gladstone, and Dilke protested in 1884 that his inclusion involved him in too much work.[13] Salisbury marked the names of those who were to see the more important papers on the cover. After A. J. Balfour became Leader of the House, he saw them all, and Chamberlain received those which touched on colonial affairs. When Milner wrote in February

---

[12] Monypenny and Buckle, *op. cit.*, Vol. V, p. 411.
[13] Gwynn and Tuckwell, *op. cit.*, Vol. II, p. 80,

1898 saying there must be reform in the Transvaal or else war was likely, the letter went to Balfour, Goschen, Beach, Devonshire and Lansdowne. (Salisbury was absent through ill-health.[14]) A despatch from H. G. Macdonell at Lisbon was marked by Salisbury to go round Balfour, Chamberlain, Devonshire and Goschen.[15] When the Foreign Office picked up some information from a German official, Richthofen, Lansdowne sent it to Balfour with a note saying, " unless you wish it I am not inclined to circulate these documents to the Cabinet, or to send them to the King. Richthofen may favour us with further indiscretions, and it is not desirable that the fact of his being communicative should get about." [16]   In 1906 when the Liberals came to power Ripon told Grey " that he knew there were always some Foreign Office papers that were sent to the Prime Minister, and not circulated to the Cabinet, at any rate in the first instance; he asked that these should also be sent to him, as he would have to speak on Foreign Affairs in the House of Lords." [17]   In April 1911, the British Military Attaché in Paris sent in a report that General Foch wanted staff talks so that the British and French armies could act together at once in face of a German attack. Grey minuted that it should go to the Prime Minister, Morley and Haldane.[18] Thus, there were some grounds for Lloyd George's complaint that the lack of information on foreign affairs made it hard for rank and file members of the Cabinet to follow or criticise policy.[19]

With some essential information being kept for a few ministers who consulted first, and were, in any case, usually among the most influential members, it is not surprising that at times there was talk of an inner Cabinet. The precise meaning of the phrase is not always clear. Disraeli had a few men in whom he placed considerable trust—Cairns, Derby,[20] Hardy and Northcote—and he preferred to reach general agreement with those that were involved before the Cabinet met. Yet his critics never attacked him on these

14 Garvin, *op. cit.*, Vol. III, p. 365.
15 *Balfour Papers, Add. MSS.*, 49,717, f. 16.
16 *Balfour Papers, Add. MSS.*, 49,729, f. 4.
17 Grey, *Twenty-Five Years*, Vol. I, p. 74.
18 Gooch and Temperley, *British Documents on the Origins of the War*, Vol. VI, p. 620.
19 David Lloyd George, *War Memoirs* (1938 ed.), Vol. I, pp. 26–30.
20 Later Salisbury replaced Derby in what Blake describes as " the inner Cabinet." *Disraeli*, p. 544.

grounds, and the lack of any control or predetermination of policy by an inner Cabinet was evident when disagreement over near-Eastern policy paralysed his government for over a year. On the Liberal side, Gladstone worked closely with Granville and valued Bright's advice, but there were no complaints until his last ministry. Then there is an entry in West's *Diary* for August 3, 1892: "an inner Cabinet" and both Fowler and Rosebery protested "against a ring in the Cabinet" composed of Gladstone, Harcourt and Morley.[21] There is, however, no evidence of any conscious attempt to pre-digest policy. The group mentioned did meet in the early weeks but only to discuss the distribution of offices. Not long after, Gladstone was deep in the Home Rule Bill about which Harcourt had grave doubts (chiefly on the financial clauses); meantime Morley rapidly turned against Harcourt and by June 1893 was wondering "whether there was a precedent for sending a round-robin to the P.M., asking him to dismiss a colleague."[22]

The most persistent talk of an inner Cabinet occurred during Salisbury's 1895–1902 ministry. At the start, the Premier, Balfour, Devonshire and Chamberlain had discussed the allocation of post. By 1897, Chamberlain was calling Lansdowne, Balfour, Goschen and Hicks Beach to meet him (Salisbury was abroad) and, after discussing the situation in South Africa, he wrote to the Prime Minister "to ask your assent to what we may determine on these lines."[23] Letters from Milner were sent round the same group with the addition of Devonshire, though Chamberlain, convinced that he knew the mind of the whole government, often replied without consultation. Later, in 1901, papers on the negotiations with Germany were seen by Salisbury, Lansdowne, Balfour, Devonshire and Beach.[24] Even in this case, there was no definite attempt to lead or manipulate the rest of the Cabinet. The only complaint came from one of the so-called "inner group," Beach, who told Salisbury that "the telegram No. 1 of August 28 [1899] was of sufficient importance to have been considered by the Cabinet, and I hope that if the Boer reply is unfavourable, we shall have a Cabinet before any decision is taken on it." The Prime Minister agreed that lack of consultation on this despatch was

---

[21] Sir A. West, *Diaries*, pp. 43, 73 and 78.
[22] *Ibid.*, p. 155.
[23] Garvin, *op. cit.*, Vol. III, p. 141.
[24] Gooch and Temperley, *op. cit.*, Vol. II, p. 64.

" a grave mistake." His further remark that " there were members of the Cabinet with longer memories of South African affairs who were uneasy over the trend of official correspondence and would have preferred an attitude of more patient forbearance," [25] shows that disagreements among these senior ministers were as strong as any that occurred between them as a body and the rest of the Cabinet. At times most of the Cabinet were worried about Milner's uncompromising attitude and therefore about the support the Colonial Secretary gave him, though none of them had any criticisms of substance, but only of the pace which Chamberlain set. Thus an inner ring existed only in the practical sense that Salisbury was declining in vigour and that a group of six ministers, which comprised all the alternative leadership and talent in the Cabinet was shown most of the important despatches (though Chamberlain was shown only those that concerned him while Balfour saw all). It did not exist in the form of a group united in policy and with the object of leading the rest of the Cabinet in a given direction.

There were no contemporary accusations that Campbell-Bannerman had an inner set of confidants.[26] Grey observed that he worked as well with old opponents such as himself and Haldane as with his former allies. It was, however, true that only Campbell-Bannerman, Grey, Ripon and the Under-Secretary, Lord Edward Fitzmaurice, took a continued interest in foreign affairs.[27] Asquith, likewise, used his influence with all sections of his Cabinet, supporting Lloyd George over his budget yet backing the Admiralty over naval estimates, and taking the radical line over the House of Lords while supporting Grey's foreign policy. The only suggestion that he had an inner circle comes from Sir Harold Nicolson who remarks that Asquith showed Lloyd George's scheme for a Coalition Government " to the five members of his own inner Cabinet." [28] Yet there is no other reference to this group

25 Lady V. Hicks Beach, *op. cit.*, Vol. II, p. 105.
26 Sir S. Lee says that in 1906 " the new Cabinet was large, though not beyond recent precedent, and it was recognised that there must necessarily be an inner and an outer Cabinet, the main course of policy being determined by the former." But he brings no evidence either of events or of comments to support this statement. *Op. cit.*, Vol. II, pp. 445–446.
27 L. Wolff, *Life of Lord Ripon*, Vol. II, p. 298.
28 H. Nicolson, *op. cit.*, p. 131. Nicolson may be thinking of a group set up in 1911 and referred to by Sir A. Nicolson as " the Cabinet Committee." It consisted of the Prime Minister, Grey, Lloyd George, Morley, Crewe

(one can only guess at its composition—Grey, Lloyd George, Morley, Crewe, Haldane?) and no sign of its existence in any of the Cabinet crises in these years. But it is against these two Prime Ministers, Campbell-Bannerman and Asquith, that the most serious charge has been laid of concealing major policy decisions from their colleagues in the Cabinet. It is alleged that the contacts between members of the British and French military authorities, which began in December 1905,[29] converted the Entente into something resembling an alliance or at any rate committed Britain to an extent which would have been repudiated by the Cabinet, had they been kept fully informed.

There has been some doubt about the actual course of events and the importance that should be attached to these military conversations. When Grey came to the Foreign Office, he heard that the General Staff had been considering military help for France in case of a German attack and that there had already been some personal contacts with the French military authorities. In the papers of the Committee of Imperial Defence there are minutes of two conferences between Viscount Esher, Sir John French, Captain Ottley and Sir George Clarke on possible plans for mobilising a force and taking it to France. The first conference was on December 19, 1905, and the second on January 6, 1906. On January 10, Cambon asked Grey whether France could count on British support in the event of a German attack and suggested that unofficial communications between the War Office, the Admiralty and the French Attachés should continue. Grey agreed on the latter point, and at the next two conferences on January 12 and 19, General Grierson, the Director of Military Operations, took part and on January 16 he began his official talks with Huguet. At the conference on the 19th a general scheme for shipping British

and Runciman and was to consider relations with Germany. There is no evidence that it played any major role and indeed the only explicit reference is in *British Documents on the Origins of the War*, Vol. VI, No. 440.

[29] There is little new evidence in the Committee of Imperial Defence Papers, but the minutes mentioned in the next paragraph are all consistent with J. D. Hargreaves' argument in *History*, October 1951, that the unofficial contacts between General Grierson and the French Military Attaché in London, General Huguet, began in December 1905 after Balfour had, in fact, resigned.

troops to France was outlined and it was agreed that no further meetings were necessary.[30]

Meanwhile Grey sent the record of the conversations to Campbell-Bannerman and Ripon and obtained Haldane's consent to military talks, but the episode was not mentioned to the Cabinet. Thereafter the military talks continued in an entirely secret fashion. The British plan was revised by the War Office in July 1907 and approved by Grey.[31] Sir George Clarke, Secretary of the Committee of Imperial Defence till 1907, was quite correct in stating that " the ' conversations ' with the French . . . were never dealt with by the Secretariat " [32] and that they were never mentioned at the Committee of Imperial Defence in his period of office. Asquith referred the revised War Office scheme to a sub-committee of the Committee of Imperial Defence on the Military Needs of the Empire. This met three times (December 3 and 17, 1908, and March 23, 1909), the Cabinet Ministers present besides the Prime Minister being Crewe, McKenna and Haldane. The discussions were connected with British proposals to aid various countries, notably France, if they were invaded by the Germans. At the last meeting Sir Charles Hardinge did mention the talks when he said that " the only grounds upon which the French could base any hopes of military assistance were the semi-official conversations which had taken place between the French Military Attaché and our General Staff." [33] In its final report, the Committee simply recommended that the plan drawn up by the General Staff (making no mention of any co-ordination with the French) be accepted. The report went to the Committee of Imperial Defence on July 24, 1909, with only the same four Cabinet Ministers present. Fisher made a vigorous attack on the whole concept of an immediate expeditionary force, but the minute records that the plan was adopted.[34]

How much impression this brief reference made on Asquith is not certain. When the British Military Attaché in Paris reported

---

[30] These conferences all discussed British procedure in certain eventualities and never mentioned any talks with the French Army, nor were French plans ever outlined. P.R.O., Cab. 18, No. 24.

[31] As this was purely a British scheme, it can just be squared with Grey's letter to Asquith on April 16, 1911, in which, referring to the talks, he says " What they settled I never knew." Grey, *op. cit.*, Vol. I, p. 94.

[32] Lord Sydenham of Combe, *op. cit.*, p. 196.

[33] Report in the papers of the Committee of Imperial Defence.

[34] See above, pp. 279–286.

* Foch's desire for military liaison in April 1911 (knowledge of the talks appears to have been almost as limited on the French side), Grey felt it necessary to tell Asquith that talks had been authorised in 1906.[35] The despatch then went to Morley and Haldane, but the former received no similar covering note. In the summer, the Agadir crisis revived both the issue and the dispute between the Admiralty and the War Office, the conflict coming out at a special meeting of the Committee of Imperial Defence on August 23, 1911. On this occasion the Cabinet Ministers present in addition to the Premier were Grey, McKenna, Winston Churchill and Lloyd George.[36] When the generals found that the Navy's attitude had hardened into a positive refusal to convey the Expeditionary Force to France they naturally pointed out that, after the conversations, the French expected British troops to be there at the scheduled time. News of the talks spread back, probably from Lloyd George and Churchill, to the rest of the Cabinet.[37]

Something in the nature of a ministerial crisis arose in September and October. Morley led the group that felt it had been shamefully treated and wanted assurances that this would not happen again. Asquith was disturbed and wrote to Grey that

> "conversations such as that between General Joffre and Col. Fairholme seem to me rather dangerous; especially the part which refers to possible British assistance. The French ought not to be encouraged in present circumstances to make their plans on any assumptions of this kind." [38]

The Foreign Secretary replied that to stop the talks now would cause consternation among the French, and Asquith made an effort to smooth matters over. Esher, who had recorded " a very Secret Defence Meeting (not a very wise proceeding) " at the time the Committee of Imperial Defence was held, noted " a Cabinet cabal against the Entente with France and the Defence Committee. The original fault lay with that imprudent summoning of a packed Defence Committee in August . . ." The mistake was to leave out Morley and Harcourt, and now it was " fifteen members of

---

[35] Grey, *op. cit.*, Vol. I, p. 94.

[36] Minutes of the 1911 meeting are in Box 15 of the *Asquith Papers.*

[37] Asquith wrote to Haldane on September 9, 1911, that " J[ohn] M[orley] has evidently been told of the meeting of the sub-committee : I wonder by whom? He is quite the most impossible colleague that ever entered a Cabinet." *Haldane Papers, MSS.*, 5,909, f. 146.

[38] Grey, *op. cit.*, Vol. I, p. 95.

the Cabinet against five." [39] Describing the Cabinet meeting held on November 1, 1911, Asquith told the King that

" Lord Morley raised the question of the inexpediency of communications being held or allowed between the General Staff at the War Office and the General Staff of foreign states, such as France in regard to possible military and naval co-operation, without the previous knowledge and direction of the Cabinet. Lord Haldane explained what had actually been done, the communications in question having been initiated as far back as 1906 with Sir Henry Campbell-Bannerman's sanction, and resumed in the Spring and Summer of the present year. The Prime Minister pointed out that all questions of policy have been and must be reserved for the decision of the Cabinet, and that it is quite outside the function of military or naval officers to prejudge such questions. He added that he believed (and Sir Edward Grey concurred) that this was fully recognised by the French Government. Considerable discussion ensued, and no conclusion was come to, the matter being adjourned. . . ." [40]

On November 15, the Cabinet returned to the question and Asquith reported:

" a prolonged and animated discussion. Sir E. Grey made it clear that at no stage of our intercourse with France since January 1906 had we either by diplomatic or military engagements compromised our freedom of decision or action in the event of a war between France and Germany. On the other hand there was a prevailing feeling in the Cabinet that there was a danger that communications of the kind referred to might give rise to expectations, and that they should not, if they related to the possibility of concerted action, be entered into or carried on without the sanction of the Cabinet. In the result, at the suggestion of the Prime Minister, unanimous approval was given to the two following propositions:
1. That no communications should take place between the

[39] Esher, *op. cit.*, Vol. III, pp. 58 and 74. It seems to be true that the members of the meeting on August 23 were carefully selected. Sir Henry Wilson noted in his Diary that " Asquith arranged for a small special meeting of the C.I.D. for tomorrow week." (Perhaps this is why Asquith refers to it in a letter to Haldane as a sub-committee meeting. See note 37, above.) Later in October Wilson recorded that there was a row in the Cabinet over the military talks—" Morley, Crewe, Harcourt, and some of the small fry were mad that they were not present on August 23." Sir C. E. Calwell, *Field-Marshal Sir Henry Wilson*, Vol. I, pp. 99 and 106.
[40] Asquith and other Prime Ministers frequently adjourned or postponed difficult questions so that, in Disraeli's words, " they might be better understood." On November 14, 1911, Haldane told his sister that " J[ohn] M[orley] is getting up the old row again for tomorrow's Cabinet. H. H. A[squith] came in here late last night and we concerted plans," *Haldane Papers, MSS.*, 6,011, f. 162.

General Staff here and the Staffs of other countries which can, directly or indirectly, commit this country to military or naval intervention.

2. That such communications, if they relate to concerted action by land or sea, should not be entered into without the previous approval of the Cabinet."

On a loose leaf with a draft of these two resolutions, there is a note by Sir Edward Grey: "I think the last paragraph is a little tight." [41]

In May 1912 Cambon asked about naval co-operation in the event of war and by July the Cabinet had agreed to permit conversations and alter the disposition of the British fleet, but it was decided to reiterate "that such communications were not to be taken as prejudicing the freedom of decision of either government . . . in the event of war." [42] The matter was adjourned over the summer recess and resumed in October and November, when Cambon produced a formula designed to express the character and purpose of the Anglo-French Entente. After a long discussion on November 20 and 21, the Cabinet agreed to a letter to Cambon explaining that "consultation between experts is not, and ought not to be, regarded as an engagement that commits either Government to act in a contingency that has not arisen and may not arise." Cambon accepted this definition and so matters stood at the outbreak of war in 1914.[43] It is apparent that the Cabinet members who thought they had been excluded up to 1911 were determined that there should be no further concealment and, since the revelations occurred at a meeting of the Committee of Imperial Defence, their suspicions fastened on that body. The number of Cabinet Ministers in attendance at the Committee up to August 1911 had been about four, but thereafter it averaged nine and at times rose to ten and eleven.

According to Grey himself, he had no intention of conducting

---

[41] *Asquith Papers*, Cabinet Letters to the King for November 1, November 15, 1911, in Dep. Asquith 6, ff. 76 and 79–80. Haldane, on the other hand, reported that it had not been a pleasant experience, but "I emerge unhampered in any material point." *Haldane Papers, MSS.*, 6,011, f. 162.

[42] Letter for July 15, 1912, f. 155.

[43] These letters are printed in Grey, *op. cit.*, pp. 97–98. Both he and Lloyd George said in their books that the existence of the talks became known to the whole Cabinet at this point in 1912 when the question had, in fact, been thrashed out in November 1911. This may have been a slip of memory or they may have preferred to pin it on the known facts of the Cambon Letters rather than reveal all the details of the earlier dispute and of the Cabinet's resolutions.

a secret policy and he said that the failure to ask for Cabinet
sanction in 1906 arose from the inexpediency of the moment (in
a general election), his own inexperience and the fact that both
Ripon and Campbell-Bannerman were in agreement. Grey had
assumed that those ministers, such as Morley, who had attended
the Defence Committee had heard of the conversations, but in
any case he emphasised that the talks were completely non-
committal. All these lines of argument are somewhat disingenuous.
The Foreign Secretary had explained his reasons quite clearly to
Cambon in January 1906. The latter reported that Grey and
Campbell-Bannerman

> " ont reconnu l'identité des intérêts de l'Angleterre et de la
> France dans le cas d'une offensive de l'Allemagne, mais on
> est tombé d'accord sur ce point qu'une extension de nos accords
> devrait donner lieu à une discussion au sein du Cabinet et
> qu'à l'heure actuelle cette consultation aurait des inconvénients
> car certain Ministres s'étonneraient de l'ouverture de pour-
> parlers officieux entre les administrations militaires des deux
> pays et des études auxquelles elles se livrent en commun.
> On a donc pensé qu'il valait mieux garder le silence et con-
> tinuer discrètement des préparatifs qui mettraient les deux
> Gouvernements en état de se concerter de d'agir rapidement
> au besoin." [44]

Moreover, Grey's point that Morley ought to have known because
he had attended meetings of the Committee of Imperial Defence,
is untenable. Morley was invited on the numerous occasions when
Indian defence problems were considered, but was not asked to
the two meetings when the Army's plans to send an expeditionary
force to France came up.

The most valid line of defence for Grey was that he had been
making preparations in order that, should the Cabinet desire to
take certain actions when a crisis arose, the technical means for
doing so would be available. In international relations, however,
to take precautions in case of a given eventuality may make that
eventuality more likely. To authorise such talks was a source of
comfort to the French—as Grey pointed out when he stressed the
effect of countermanding them in 1911. While appreciating Grey's

---

[44] Cambon to Rouvier, *Documents Diplomatiques Francais*, Second Series, Vol.
IX, No. 106 for January 31, 1906. When Lord Sanderson, the Chief Under-
Secretary, used the same argument with Cambon on February 2, 1906, Grey
noted " I am glad this point was so well pointed out to M. Cambon."
Gooch and Temperley, *op. cit.*, Vol. III, p. 184.

motives and even applauding the results, there is no escaping the conclusion that he and Campbell-Bannerman deliberately gave a slant or emphasis to British policy which they concealed from the Cabinet. Asquith inherited this situation and was not very clear about the precise implications until late in 1911. He was undoubtedly right when he said " I must repeat that no large question of policy was settled by the conclusions of the Committee of Imperial Defence." [45] His broader defence of the whole conduct of foreign policy has its merits: " The heavy and always increasing pressure of departmental duties makes it impossible for the majority of Ministers to follow from the study of telegrams and despatches the vast variety of complicated matters which are being handled day by day at the Foreign Office. By frequent meetings of the Cabinet they are able to keep in touch with all the developments of our external relations. . . ." This is the other side of the picture presented by Lloyd George, who recalled that there was an air of hush-hush about every allusion to relations with France, Germany and Russia. Only the senior statesmen tended to contribute to these discussions, he said, the rest feeling uninformed and inexperienced.[46] In large part this reticence must have been due to lack of interest, for it is hard to imagine Winston Churchill or Lloyd George faltering nervously and declining to speak, had they really wanted to take part. It confirms Asquith's general description of the Cabinet as a body which helped ministers in charge of active departments to keep in contact, and authorised major steps in policy. But a Cabinet working in this way had little control if a minister's intentions did not have to be made public and he chose to conceal them from his colleagues.

In describing the process by which decisions were reached, it has been shown how developments tended to strengthen the position of the Prime Minister, and made it easier for those who were well-informed and who held the senior offices to carry the Cabinet. Other members could still play a large part and push their way up by extra ability or force of personality, and there remained always

---

[45] H. H. Asquith, *The Genesis of the War*, p. 114.

[46] Lloyd George, *op. cit.*, Vol. I, pp. 28–30. Even on the question of information, much depended on the degree of interest taken. Spender said most foreign correspondents knew more than the " domestic group " in the Cabinet simply because they did read and study the foreign news. *Life, Journalism and Politics*, Vol. I, p. 241.

the weapon of resignation. Its value had declined as party loyalties and the desire to remain in office became stronger, but it could still be effective. The history of the military conversations with France shows that to the development of levels of power within the Cabinet must be added the further possibility of withholding information or the early stages of policy-making from the Cabinet. Indeed, the two are inter-connected, for the only sanction behind the convention that the Cabinet must be consulted on all import- ant questions was fear of the consequences—a crisis and the dis- integration of the ministry. All the factors which gave the Pre- mier a stronger position and increased the politician's desire for office also made ministers less likely to force showdowns or resign in large numbers on the grounds that they had not been fully informed, albeit on some very important issues.

The final crisis over Britain's reaction to the outbreak of war is a perfect example of many of these points. The Cabinet was immersed in the Ulster problem when, on July 24, Grey read out the Austrian ultimatum to Serbia. Discussion showed that mem- bers were divided, with Grey, Haldane and Churchill insisting on the need to support France while Morley, Harcourt and some of the less influential members of the Cabinet were for neutrality. Asquith moderated, kept the issue open and leant in the direction of intervention. Past decisions now had their effect as the French asked whether Britain would honour the division of naval duties agreed to by the Cabinet in 1912. Being forced to pronounce on this point, the Cabinet agreed, John Burns resigned and Morley said he must go. The position of Lloyd George was crucial, as he was the one influential minister whose attitude was in doubt. By Monday, August 3, the issue of Belgian neutrality had brought him over to the action party. That morning Asquith said that he had received four resignations. " I understand further that many others in the Cabinet, perhaps a majority, share their views, though not at present following the same course." [47] Asquith kept the matter open, waiting for news of German movements, and later asked the four men to reconsider. Burns and Morley on August 4 definitely resigned, and Grey sent the ultimatum to

[47] Morley, *Memorandum on Resignation*, p. 25. See also R. Jenkins *Asquith*, pp. 324–331 for an account from the other side of the Cabinet.

Germany to keep out of Belgium. Events and the influence of the leading members had slowly changed the atmosphere. The Cabinet never actually authorised the ultimatum or the declaration of war on Germany. These actions rested on the authority of the Prime Minister interpreting the wishes of his colleagues.

Part Five

The War and the Post-War Coalition—1914–1922

RELATIONS within the Cabinet, and between it and the other public institutions, continued in much the same form for the decade before 1914. The Prime Minister chose and led a Cabinet which made most of the decisions or gave formal approval to proposals prepared by committees or groups of ministers. In performing this task ministers had the services of an able and sometimes opinionated Civil Service—a Civil Service which was just beginning to govern on a scale involving steady contact with large numbers of private persons and interests. Cabinets were supported by a well-organised body of M.P.s, backed by an eager following in the country. All these people wanted results which could be guaranteed after 1902 in that the government controlled the business and timetable of the House of Commons, a guarantee which was complete when the Parliament Act laid down a procedure for overriding the veto of the Lords.

The pressures of war have always tended to force on the pace of social and institutional change. A conflict which required massive efforts by the whole nation, as between 1914 and 1918, meant cutting corners, recognising weaknesses and adopting methods that might otherwise have waited for a generation. The country cried out for political leadership so that the growing emphasis on the position of the Prime Minister was likely to be carried even further. Government expenditure shot up, departments grew in numbers and strength, the Cabinet having to evolve methods of watching over or directing business and manpower at home as well as foreign and military affairs. In view of this it might seem that the account of the Cabinet during the war could be included merely as a part, albeit an intensified part, of the developments that took place between 1914 and the present.

There is, however, one abnormal feature of the period. The power of Cabinets had grown because once the electorate had returned a certain party with a majority, the leaders of that party had a large measure of freedom in trying to carry out their policies.

There was a continual process of fine adjustments by which Cabinets, their followers in the House of Commons and the party stalwarts in the country kept in touch. Provided that the usual measure of harmony was maintained, the Prime Minister and his colleagues could rely at any moment on a loyal and disciplined majority in the Commons, a propaganda network putting their case in every constituency, and the implicit support of large numbers of the voters.

But after May 1915 the war was conducted by a Coalition with no single party machine or fixed loyalties on which it could rely. Normal allegiances to individuals as Liberal or Conservative leaders might well be subordinated to the feeling that certain men were or were not acting with vigour; that they had or had not the will to win. As doubts about the ability and efficiency of some soldiers, politicians and civil servants could not be readily debated in Parliament, the public had to judge by results and by what they read in the papers. Bad news, rumours of mistakes in high places and newspaper criticisms were not combated by the political agencies which backed any normal party government. Thus the Coalition Cabinets, though wielding great powers and having all-party support, rested on an unsure foundation in the House of Commons. Success brought great dividends and if it could be suggested that any opposition was factious or unpatriotic, the government rose to a stronger position than a peacetime party ministry. Failures or doubts, however, could lead to an equally sharp swing towards insecurity. M.P.s who turned against an incompetent or lethargic ministry with evident justification would earn the gratitude of their constituents but mistaken criticism could lead to a charge of putting party or personal feelings before country. In such a situation much depended on the hold party leaders in the Coalition had over their followers in the House. For a while the usual appeals put out by the Whips and the accredited spokesman kept the members in line. But both Conservatives and Liberals had a deeper loyalty to national survival, and continued doubts could produce appeals to the leaders to leave or alter the Coalition. Able speakers capable of voicing these doubts became a menace and the leaders themselves felt more and more uneasy.

Thus, though in most respects the war tended to accelerate constitutional development, the relations of the Cabinet with the

Commons and with the public (and therefore the part played by the Press) did not quite follow the previous pattern. This was not a return to the sort of control the House had had over the executive in the mid-nineteenth century but was a special situation which merits separate treatment. Some of the conditions just outlined continued, after 1918, so long as the wartime coalition under Lloyd George lasted. This government had all but some ninety of the House of Commons returned as supporters in the General Election of 1918, but the vast majority were Conservatives and the Prime Minister did not have control of the party machine. So long as the Coalition was successful the Premier remained on the pinnacle of power he had reached just after the election. But most Conservative M.P.s did not identify their future or their party's with the person of Lloyd George so that when support for the Coalition declined many began to put their loyalty to their party first. For a while, Conservative leaders in the Coalition Cabinet were able to hold the rank and file in check. Increasing worries, however, led back-benchers to listen to alternative spokesmen and when the Conservatives met and decided to withdraw their support, the Coalition collapsed in October 1922.

Since this relationship was different in several features from the kind of government based on party conflict which existed before 1914 and which continued to develop after 1922, the history of the Cabinet in these eight years is being treated separately in this section. Also since there was a series of complicated changes in the Cabinet machinery with many other bodies devised for providing direction, one succeeding another as circumstances, individual reputations or the balance of political forces fluctuated, this period is treated chronologically rather than in the analytic form adopted in the other sections of the book.

CHAPTER 12

THE MACHINERY OF GOVERNMENT UNDER ASQUITH, AUGUST 1914 TO DECEMBER 1916

AFTER the ultimatum had been sent to Germany, Asquith asked Haldane to call a Council of War and to select those who should attend. The next day (August 5) Asquith, Grey, Haldane and Churchill assembled with all the leading soldiers and sailors, including Lord Roberts and Lord Kitchener. They went over the plans to send the B.E.F. to France, reopening the whole question of the size and destination of the force. It was agreed to recommend the despatch of four divisions. Haldane and Churchill wanted to send all six but there were some doubts on this point.[1] On the 6th the full Cabinet met and agreed that four divisions should go at once and that a fifth should follow. By this time Lord Kitchener had been appointed Secretary of State for War and came in his new capacity to the second meeting of the Council of War, which was held after the Cabinet on the 6th.[2] The Council arranged the details of the movement to France.[3]

Haldane's list for the two meetings of the Council included more soldiers and sailors than the old Committee of Imperial Defence, which now ceased to meet as such. However, some of its subcommittees continued to operate for various periods, examples being committees on home defence and on the insurance of British shipping, while an "offensive committee" planned operations against the German colonies.[4]

---

[1] Lord Beaverbrook in *Politicians and the War*, Vol. I, p. 43, says that Haldane wanted to keep the B.E.F. in Britain but all the other records confirm Haldane's own assertion that he wanted to send the full force at once.

[2] Kitchener's special status in the Cabinet was symbolised by the fact that he sat on the Prime Minister's right hand and was allowed to draw three salaries. R. Jenkins, *Asquith*, p. 342.

[3] The minutes of the two Councils and a letter to the King describing the Cabinet are in the *Asquith Papers*, Box 6 and Dep. 7. The soldiers have been very scathing about both the inadequacy of the plans and the British Government's reluctance to act without reopening the question. Sir W. Robertson, *Soldiers and Statesmen, 1914–1918*, Vol. I, pp. 47–49. Sir George Arthur, *Life of Lord Kitchener*, Vol. III, pp. 4–5.

[4] See note 92, p. 283, above.

In effect, the immediate direction of the war passed into the hands of Kitchener at the War Office and Churchill at the Admiralty, acting under the aegis of the Prime Minister. Asquith was anxious to maintain the responsibility and control of the full Cabinet. It met almost every day from August 10 till September 3 and thereafter at least twice a week. Letters from the Prime Minister to the King indicate that Kitchener and Churchill gave reports on the action they had taken. The Cabinet would then go on to consider foreign policy questions, the dislocation of trade, industrial and financial problems, which led them to appoint committees on such subjects as food supplies for Holland, separation allowances for the wives of new recruits and price rises. The atmosphere was one of implicit trust in Kitchener, and Asquith did not press him for details, put ideas before him, or encourage any member of the Cabinet to do so. The Prime Minister himself took a very detached view of the whole proceedings, being content to make an interested note when Kitchener told the Cabinet on September 14 that we had 213,000 men in France and to record that, over the defence of Ostend, " Winston . . . takes the whole adventure . . . very seriously." [5] In early October Kitchener complained of War Office obstruction in the matter of munitions and so a Cabinet Committee was set up on the 14th with Kitchener in the chair. It had only six meetings before the end of the year and then lapsed as Kitchener said he was too busy to attend.[6]

The Secretary of State for War had indeed a fantastic burden. He had been left the supreme direction of British strategy, the recruitment of a million men and the supply of all materials for the entire Army. He came to the War Office with a contempt for the Committee of Imperial Defence and its various preparations as well as for the Territorial Army. Meetings with Churchill took place, of necessity almost every day, but there was no real mutual trust.[7] Asquith and Kitchener were much closer. The Prime

---

[5] The Earl of Oxford and Asquith, *Memories and Reflections*, Vol. II, pp. 29 and 32. Jenkins observes that " the pattern of Asquith's life during these first nine months of the war did not undergo any great change," pp. 343 and 346. On one of his weekends at Walmer, he was out for a drive with Lady Tree, who asked him, " Mr. Asquith, do you take an interest in the War?" *Ibid.*, p. 348.

[6] Philip Magnus, *Kitchener*, p. 333.

[7] For example, Kitchener vetoed Churchill's scheme for joint operations on the Belgian coast and ordered him to hand over his mobile unit (the " Dunkirk circus ") to the Army. *Ibid.*, p. 308.

Minister had really abdicated his rights of guidance and final decision to the soldier, while Kitchener appreciated Asquith's trust and his habit of preventing the Cabinet pressing for information or discussing war policy. In these early stages, British policy was dominated by the long-foreseen need to aid the French and fit in with their plans. The one intervention by Kitchener in the actual conduct of the fighting came when, after a hasty conference with Asquith, Churchill, McKenna Pease and Lloyd George, he went over to France and insisted that General French keep the B.E.F. in its station on the left of Joffre's armies.[8] But the extension of the conflict to the Near East (war was declared on Turkey in early November), where British interests were predominant, raised new issues and required fresh plans.

On November 25, the War Council was called again, Asquith, Lloyd George, Churchill, Grey, Balfour,[9] Kitchener, the First Sea Lord and the Chief of Imperial General Staff being invited. The intention was to start a series of regular meetings which would consider " serious questions involving new departures in policy or joint strategic operations." [10] Altogether, the War Council held eighteen meetings (two of them on the same day) before it was superseded by the Dardanelles Committee on June 7, 1915. At no time were the powers of the War Council or its relations with the Cabinet or the Departments clearly defined.[11]

At the opening meeting in November the discussion had ranged over home defence, coastal positions, Egypt, and Churchill's idea of forcing the Dardanelles. No decisions were reached and at the next two meetings (on December 1 and 16) the topics were coastal defence again, the finances of allied powers, and Fisher's project of seizing an island off the German coast. At the end of the year Lloyd George was complaining about the lack of plans, and at the fourth meeting on January 7 he asked where Kitchener's new

---

[8] On August 30, French had telegraphed that he intended to break off contact with Joffre and withdraw the B.E.F. behind the Seine. There was no particular significance about these five names—they were simply the five who could be gathered most quickly for an emergency meeting.

[9] Asked because of his previous interest and experience—he was not an official representative of the Conservatives. Crewe was added in December 1914, Haldane and Arthur Wilson in January 1915 and McKenna and Harcourt in March.

[10] Quoted by Lord Hankey in *Government Control in War*, p. 36.

[11] The working of the Council is described in Lord Hankey, *The Supreme Command*, Vol. I, Chapter XXII.

armies were to be employed. The reply was that Kitchener wanted to keep 870,000 men for home defence and otherwise British policy was to co-operate with Joffre. Nonetheless the Admiralty was allowed to prepare plans to take an island on the north shore of Germany. The next day there was another meeting and Kitchener took up one of Churchill's earlier ideas, that of forcing the Dardanelles (the First Lord was more interested in the North Sea proposals at this point). At three meetings on January 7, 8 and 13 wide-ranging discussions took place in the Council, which concluded by authorising plans for a naval attack on the Dardanelles.[12]

It is clear that during these months the War Council operated, as intended, as a group discussing the merits of various lines of strategy. Meanwhile Churchill and Kitchener (accepting Joffre's general policies) were in effective control, backed but not directed by Asquith who " never thought it his duty to impose strategic decisions upon the service chiefs." [13] The Cabinet met eleven times in this period to consider financial matters, to try to work a way through the intricacies of Balkan politics, to hear reports on the fighting in France and at sea, and finally to approve the Dardanelles project.

This imaginative scheme became possible because both Kitchener and Churchill liked it; but the direction of the attack was never put in the hands of one person or one body. The War Council continued to meet irregularly and to consider other matters, such as sending troops to Salonika and to Zeebrugge, so that it never turned into an executive council. (Yet the few conclusions it reached were the only orders that were given, since the Cabinet never did more than endorse its decisions.) Nor can the Council be regarded as an inner Cabinet. The most powerful ministers—Asquith, Kitchener, Churchill, Lloyd George, Grey and perhaps Crewe—attended, but so did the service chiefs and only new strategic plans were put before it. Asquith, replying to criticisms of the Dardanelles Commission that there was no meeting of the

---

[12] This account is taken from the printed minutes in the *Asquith Papers*, Box 6. The last words are intentionally vague, as it later emerged that Asquith thought they had authorised plans only in the sense of permitting the preparation of a scheme, while Churchill thought that to approve plans was to accept the principles: see *Report of the Dardanelles Commission*, 1917, Cd. 8490, p. 21.

[13] Jenkins, *op. cit.*, p. 350. He says Asquith " would no more have thought it right to issue a directive which ran counter to their united voices than to tell the Lord Chief Justice what judgments he should deliver," *ibid.*, p. 351.

War Council between March 19 and May 14, argued that there were no new policies to consider and that in any case the Cabinet met twelve times between these dates.[14] The conduct of the expedition really depended on Churchill and Kitchener, with the latter having the last word. On January 28 the naval attack was settled, but Kitchener began to say that he could collect troops for the Balkan theatre. At some time between this date and February 16 it became accepted that these troops would be used at the Dardanelles, though no explicit decision to change the character of the attack is recorded in the minutes of the War Council or in Asquith's Cabinet letters to the King. There followed that extraordinary series of delays in which Kitchener held back the 29th Division, the core of the force, till March 10 and thus destroyed any real chance of success. The missing factor in the whole story is leadership from the Prime Minister. Had Asquith pressed for information and examined proposals, had he drawn his colleagues together and insisted on harmonising the plans of the War Office and the Admiralty, the position would have been transformed. If he had acted in this way in the full Cabinet, in the War Council, or in smaller meetings with the ministers concerned, whichever body he chose would at once have become the effective centre of government. As it was Asquith simply endorsed Kitchener's views and when the latter wavered he followed suit, so that the eventual decisions came in part from the War Council and in part from the War Office, but in both cases from Kitchener.

It was Asquith's failure to find out the views and harness the energies of the War Council which destroyed his government. The resignation of Sir John Fisher, who had sat in brooding opposition to Churchill's plans, finally brought Conservative dissatisfaction to a head and the Prime Minister had to agree to form a Coalition on May 18, 1915. After a week the new Cabinet, twenty-two in number, decided to appoint a smaller body called the Dardanelles Committee, though again its precise powers and duties were not laid down. The Committee began with eleven members, rising later to fourteen, but it met more regularly than the old War Council and was more willing to take decisions affecting the conduct of the war as a whole. The formation of the Coalition

---

[14] J. A. Spender and C. Asquith, *The Life of Lord Oxford and Asquith*, Vol. II, p. 140.

revealed a lack of confidence in the direction of the war, and any reconstitution of the government inevitably damaged the position of those who had been primarily responsible. Churchill was only able to survive as Chancellor of the Duchy of Lancaster (but keeping a seat on the Dardanelles Committee) and though both Kitchener and Asquith were considered to be indispensable, their prestige was seriously weakened. On the other hand, the Cabinet now contained a number of men accustomed to criticising the Liberal leaders who came into the new government full of doubts and ready to object.

As a result, the relations between the Cabinet and the Committee underwent a change. When the smaller body recommended reinforcing the Army at Gallipoli with three divisions, several members of the Cabinet resisted strongly before the proposal was accepted. By the early autumn Bonar Law and Lloyd George had serious misgivings about the expedition, although Kitchener and Churchill remained faithful. Meanwhile Joffre was insisting on the Loos offensive and Kitchener, who was not optimistic about it himself, could only meet the objections of several of the Cabinet by pointing to the need to stand by our ally. The French, after constant emphasis on the priority of the Western Front, now suddenly pressed for an expedition to Salonika, a project which emerged as an alternative to Gallipoli. Caught between these various policies, and with no firm lead from the Prime Minister, both the Dardanelles Committee and the Cabinet sank into a state of paralysis.

Throughout October and November the triangular conflict between the advocates of the Western Front, Gallipoli and Salonika, continued in both bodies. In the hope of bringing in new factors to break the deadlock, the Dardanelles Committee referred the whole issue to the staffs in the War Office and the Admiralty. Their report, in line with Kitchener's views, urged concentration on the Western Front but also perseverance at Gallipoli. Asquith tried to keep all groups contented with the suggestion that 150,000 troops be sent to Egypt, to go either to Salonika or Gallipoli depending on the report of a senior officer. Bonar Law and Lloyd George were both dissatisfied with this compromise and Sir Edward Carson, the Attorney-General, resigned in despair at the endless indecisions. In September Asquith had suggested the creation of a new, smaller and more effective War Council. This was killed by Balfour's criticisms and Lloyd George's belief that nothing would work while Kitchener remained at the War Office. The latter's abilities were clearly flagging and on November 1st Asquith came forward with the suggestion that he should take over the War Office for a period, a proposal which Bonar Law vetoed.[15] The Prime Minister now persuaded the Cabinet to send Kitchener to the Dardanelles to make a further report, in the hope that this would alter the balance of opinion and also permit him to make changes at the War Office and in the High Command while Kitchener was away. Bonar Law on reflection concluded that this further postponement achieved nothing and threatened to resign unless an immediate decision was taken on the future of the Gallipoli operations. Under this pressure Asquith, on November 11, 1915, set up a new small War Council of five members and agreed to support evacuation irrespective of what Kitchener might ultimately report.

The Cabinet itself had played a part in bringing about these changes. On September 22 it had " expressed a strong opinion that the time had come for a reconstruction and reinforcement of the General Staff here at home," [16] so that there should be adequate information for ministers. The Prime Minister suggested two new Cabinet committees, one to deal with the conduct of the war and the other to plan finances. The proposal was carried the length of actually appointing the committees on October 4, but a " fusillade of cross-criticism " [17] ultimately killed the scheme. In mid-October Asquith became ill and Crewe took the chair at two rather acrimonious meetings on the 19th and the 21st. " It was the unanimous view of the Cabinet that the present system is the opposite of effective, if only owing to the undue size of the Council [*i.e.*, the Dardanelles Committee]." Crewe was instructed to report " the unanimous conviction of the Cabinet that a drastic change is imperatively necessary." " All were agreed that the body should be quite small and, so far as can be, non-departmental." [18] Carson had resigned for much the same reasons on

---

[15] Bonar Law in his letter said " The criticism which is directed against the government and against yourself is chiefly based on this—that as Prime Minister you have not devoted yourself absolutely to co-ordinating all the moves of the war because so much of your time and energy has been devoted to control of the political machine." Jenkins, *op. cit.*, p. 380.

[16] Asquith's Cabinet letter to the King for that date, *Asquith Papers*, Dep. 8.

[17] Asquith, *op. cit.*, Vol. II, p. 23.

[18] Crewe to King George V, *Asquith Papers*, Dep. 8.

October 12, and on November 2 he gave his explanations after Asquith had announced changes in the House. The Prime Minister, faced by the point-blank demand of the entire Cabinet, announced the creation of the new small War Council to replace the Dardanelles Committee. It was evidently to take many more decisions but would still report to the full Cabinet, whose responsibility Asquith did not want to diminish. Carson effectively pointed to the weakness of the two complementary bodies that had operated since May 1915 and said the scheme would only work if the small Council assumed all the powers of the Cabinet and became the sole executive authority.[19]

Three weeks later Kitchener telegraphed recommending the evacuation of Suvla and Anzac but the retention of the Helles bridgehead. The War Council was in favour of total evacuation but the full Cabinet reversed this decision. Meanwhile Kitchener's absence was used by Asquith to carry out some changes which had, by common agreement, become essential. French was replaced by Haig as C.-in-C. on the Western Front. On his return in December Kitchener felt his position had been so undermined that he resigned. Asquith, however, refused to accept the resignation though it was made clear that the new C.I.G.S., Sir William Robertson, would be the government's chief adviser on strategy. Robertson, who was a skilful politician, only accepted the post after an Order in Council had defined his position and given him direct access to the Cabinet. The new War Council or Committee consisted of Asquith, Kitchener, Balfour, Lloyd George, Bonar Law and McKenna and its creation represented the final defeat of the strategic plans of Churchill (who resigned from the government) and of Kitchener, though the latter still possessed considerable influence on such matters as conscription.

On the whole, the War Committee acted in a more decided fashion, but it was bedevilled by the Premier's desire to leave final responsibility with " the plenum of the Cabinet " as he called it. As has been said this conflict of authority gave immediate trouble over the question of evacuating Gallipoli, the War Council's recommendation being resisted by Curzon and other Cabinet ministers at a series of meetings till Bonar Law circulated a

---

[19] He then somewhat marred his case by linking it with his own support for the Salonika expedition. H. C. Debates, Vol. 75, cols. 529–537, 1915.

memorandum of protest on December 4 concluding that " the war cannot be carried to a successful issue by methods such as these." [20] A little later, in January 1916, Robertson told Haig that Balfour had reopened the matter at the Cabinet. " Not being able to talk the War Committee round to his point of view he has now written a long memo to the Cabinet arguing quite contrary to the War Committee's conclusions. He has several supporters, as every other member of the Cabinet always has, no matter what the question may be." [21] In June the larger body vetoed any offensive at Salonika, and later wobbled over conscription, so that on major issues the Cabinet remained the final court of appeal. There conflicts were not helped by the fact that the original notion of a small Council of non-departmental ministers had not been followed, most of the members having departments while the non-departmental ministers had little to do but sit in the full Cabinet and reopen the decisions of the War Council.

The War Committee itself grew in size, rising from five to six to eleven members, with the First Sea Lord and the C.I.G.S. making thirteen. Robertson complained that it talked too much and Crewe concluded " that the meetings . . . tended to become far too large and to produce general discussions similar to those that had clogged the action of the earlier War Council." [22] On the military side there was an improvement, in that memoranda and appreciations were regularly provided by the General Staffs of the Admiralty and the War Office. Both bodies, under the chairmanship of Asquith, lacked the bite to take hold of the main lines of policy and the result, as the Prime Minister intended, was to leave strategy to Robertson and Haig. Throughout 1916 these two generals had virtually a free hand to try to reach a conclusion on the Western Front. Lloyd George at first was busy at the Ministry of Munitions. Later, in the War Office after Kitchener's death, he was hamstrung by the Order in Council which left military policy to the C.I.G.S. Bonar Law accepted the generals' views and felt that politicians should not impose their opinions on experts. So the only two political leaders who had the capacity or interest to take control stood aside and Asquith, with the

[20] *Asquith Papers*, Box 16.
[21] R. Blake ed., *The Private Papers of Douglas Haig*, p. 119.
[22] Crewe's Memorandum printed in Asquith, *op. cit.*, Vol. II, p. 128.

acquiescence of Grey, Crewe and McKenna, was able to leave the war to the soldiers.

By the autumn of 1916, however, Lloyd George and Bonar Law were becoming restive. Their views differed as Lloyd George was chiefly moved by the catastrophes in France, while Bonar Law was impressed by the general aimlessness, the failure to reach decisions about such proposals as the establishment of an Air Board, the appointment of a Food Controller and the recommendations of the Manpower Board.[23] Both concluded that " a paralysis of will seemed to have seized the government. Whatever the subject, it was impossible to get a move on. . . . The government was getting into that nervous condition where they could neither wage war nor negotiate peace." [24] In December 1916 they came together to oust Asquith and instal Lloyd George as Prime Minister.

So for the first two years and four months of the war, there was a series of attempts to devise appropriate methods of direction within the normal framework of Cabinet government. Although improvements took place and routine work was fairly well done for most of 1916, it cannot be said that any of the systems tried was really satisfactory. It is worth considering why.

The greatest mistakes of 1914 and 1915 were over munitions and the Dardanelles and both arose because there was no adequate General Staff in the War Office to collect information, forecast future needs and prepare plans.[25] Here the immediate errors sprang from Kitchener who permitted the Staff to dissolve as its members took up field duties in France and who regarded later requests for more staff work and information as a reflection on himself. But it was, in the last resort, the duty of the Prime Minister to see that the Secretary of State for War was not overburdened and that he understood the previous plans. Yet Asquith allowed Kitchener to abandon Haldane's careful scheme of using the Territorial Army to reinforce the B.E.F. He accepted the target of a million soldiers without ever asking what such numbers would require in the way of guns and ammunition and he sympathised with Kitchener's

23 Rt. Hon. Christopher Addison, *Four and a Half Years*, Vol. I, pp. 256–269.
24 Lloyd George, *Memoirs* (1938 edition), Vol. I, p. 580.
25 Lord Hankey, *The Supreme Command, 1914–18*, says " the Secretary of State virtually became C.I.G.S. himself and for nearly a year, to the great misfortune of . . . the nation, the General Staff ceased to function . . .", p. 179.

reluctance to give any information to the Cabinet.[26] The Secretary of State for War insisted that all telegrams and reports from the various fronts came to him and the Cabinet was told only such facts as he cared to disclose. As a result, letters from Sir John French appealing for more shells were never seen by the Cabinet, and even the Cabinet Committee on munitions set up in October 1914 was reduced to impotence for lack of information. (One of the few occasions when Asquith intervened was in backing Lloyd George's demand for the reconstruction of a munitions committee with adequate powers in March 1915.) The War Council had to discuss the possibility of expeditions to the Baltic and to the Near East without being told in detail the numbers of British, Allied or enemy troops in the various theatres, the reserves of men and supplies, or the rate of replacement. One civil servant in the new Ministry of Munitions reported that " Cabinet ministers . . . appear . . . to be nearly as ignorant of the essentials of the situation as an intelligent man in the street." [27]

The failure to insist on adequate staff work and information had several causes. Kitchener was both awe-inspiring and inarticulate while the Cabinet had a strange feeling of inadequacy in this field. The record of the War Office and of British generals in the Crimean and Boer wars was so poor that military reform had been a constant topic. Directly the idea of a major continental army was launched, it should have been evident that this raised problems which no British officer had ever encountered and that in matters of strategy, supply, manpower and transport, many politicians and administrators had had far more experience than the average general. Had Asquith appointed a civilian Secretary of State and insisted on overall control by political leaders after they had heard the advice of the generals and seen reports from a competent General Staff, the dichotomy between soldiers and politicians might never have arisen. As it was, in 1914 Kitchener had enormous prestige as an expert and traded on it. It was not likely that his reports would be questioned by the junior members of the Cabinet and the seniors, for various reasons, held back. Haldane, the civilian expert, was poor in cabinet and

---

[26] Kitchener said it was " repugnant to him to have to reveal military secrets to twenty-three gentlemen with whom he was barely acquainted." Spender and Asquith, *op. cit.*, Vol. II, p. 123.
[27] Addison, *Four and a Half Years*, Vol. I, p. 119.

weakened by popular abuse, Churchill had more information but found his energies occupied at the Admiralty, while Lloyd George had not yet developed his interest in the war. The traditional Liberals such as Crewe, Harcourt and McKenna felt that fighting was outside their terms of reference while Grey, whose advice on matters like Balkan policy ought to have been of such value, rapidly lost his physical and mental resilience. In such a situation, when Asquith, the one man with a special and overriding responsibility, clearly left all that concerned the war to Kitchener, the rest of the Cabinet followed suit. The Secretary of State was never challenged or overruled on any issue till May 1915, when the Ministry of Munitions was set up, and never on any military issue till his return from Gallipoli in November 1915.

All then turned, in the first nine months, on Kitchener's capacity to conduct the war single-handed. His greatest asset was his capacity to inspire the public with confidence and his appeal was invaluable in recruiting. Within the War Office, however, he failed to appreciate the need for planning or delegation though he did leave the fighting to G.H.Q. in France. Kitchener's weakness was his inability to think ahead and form a clear picture of the war as a whole and thus establish an order of priorities. He clung to the French High Command's Western policy and yet favoured the Dardanelles, so that when both sides exerted pressure, he vacillated badly. The worst case was over the 29th Division whose departure for Gallipoli he held up for six weeks when, as Churchill pointed out, to keep it in reserve in France could not be decisive whereas to send it to the Straits might well change the whole situation.[28] Later in the autumn he again showed a painful indecision, acquiescing in a French offensive despite an earlier agreement to stand on " active defence." He then failed to reinforce the Dardanelles at the right time though he could not bring himself to abandon the attempt. It is only fair to add that no amount of clear thinking would have won the war for the Allies by mid-1915. But it would certainly have been possible to carry out Britain's share with a degree of skill which would have achieved

---

[28] On this Asquith made one of his rare interventions and " appealed most strongly to Lord Kitchener (on February 26) not to allow the force available in the East to be deprived of the one Regular Division so necessary to its effective composition." But Kitchener still refused to release it till March 10. (These are Churchill's words, *The World Crisis*, p. 373.)

certain limited objectives, kept casualties down, and have maintained Kitchener's high prestige and overall authority.[29]

As it was, his failings became evident to the leading politicians between May and December 1915. And it was Kitchener's failure that finally dragged Asquith down. The Prime Minister had made his Secretary of State for War the second figure in the Cabinet, denied him no powers and imposed no restraints so that the subsequent series of blunders diminished the stature of both men. Even in the autumn of 1915, Asquith could have restored his own position if he had resumed the powers which Kitchener was incapable of wielding. All the machinery was there to his hand in the form of the Dardanelles and War Committees and his new and old colleagues alike were impatient for a change. Yet the Prime Minister did not act and his inability to fill the vacuum at the top led to a dispersion of power. The only man who could have dismissed Kitchener was Asquith but he feared political repercussions and had no clear idea of an alternative. So he tried to solve the problem by peeling off Kitchener's duties and handing them to other people. Lloyd George was given munitions in May 1915, strategy was passed to the C.I.G.S. in December, the Secretary of State for War being left only recruitment and establishment matters to handle. This did remedy the shortage of munitions but it did nothing to improve the central direction of the war and left a series of major obstacles to be removed when a capable War or Prime Minister eventually came into office. On the home front, Asquith's lack of any definite policy about the nature or personnel of the government and about matters like conscription meant that he balanced between rival forces, gave hostages to both sides and often only acted under a threat of resignation. The Conservatives forced their way into his Cabinet in May 1915 and drove Churchill out of the Admiralty. Once the formation of a Coalition was conceded, the Prime Minister was even more open to threats from the Conservative leader, Bonar Law. Such pressure forced the

[29] Lord Hankey, *op. cit.*, provides (*e.g.*, Vol. I, pp. 209–210, 224–226, 320–329) a number of analyses of the failures of direction of the war, concluding that the Prime Minister and his colleagues had as much to learn in the art of conducting a war as the generals. The point he fails to grasp is that the generals contended that they were already experts in all aspects of war and its organisation and that the Prime Minister not only accepted this view but constructed machinery which made it very hard for anyone else to check on this claim or to share in control once it was found to be false.

evacuation of the Dardanelles. Lloyd George used the same device to ensure some progress on conscription, while Bonar Law pushed Lloyd George into the War Office in June 1916. Asquith's biographers assert that he could not have exercised plenary authority in the late summer of 1915, but all the evidence suggests that a clear lead would have been welcomed. This was in effect what the Cabinet were wanting when they demanded a smaller, more efficient War Committee that November. Power was steadily dispersed in late 1915 and 1916 only because Asquith would not fulfil the functions of a wartime Premier. Lloyd George, starting from a much weaker political position, was able, in slow stages, to gather the reins back into his hands in 1917–18.[30]

There is no escaping the conclusion that all these weaknesses in the central direction stemmed from Asquith. He had always had brilliant parliamentary gifts and been able to state a case with the maximum effect. In 1909 he had steered Lloyd George's Budget through a largely unsympathetic Cabinet but, as the years went by, Asquith's very intellectual ability led to a kind of aloof disdain for enthusiasm or actual involvement in business. He had solved the 1910–11 Parliament Bill crisis and the entry into the war most satisfactorily by the technique of keeping the Cabinet together, never forcing the issue and waiting on events. These tactics solve problems where the other side—the House of Lords or the Germans—make such mistakes that only one outcome is possible. But it does not work where an opening has to be seized before a situation changes for the worse. Asquith had failed in peacetime politics when quick and firm action was required in the Irish crisis of 1913–14 and it was just these qualities that were needed in the war. Immersed in his private social circle and friendships, writing long personal letters even during meetings of the War Cabinet, he still managed to preside and moderate with skill particularly over such domestic issues as conscription. Yet his whole concern was how to get round or combine the views actually put before him, when in war what is needed is a grasp of the actual situation and a determination to get results. As time went on, Asquith deteriorated choosing men in order to bolster his position and to

---

[30] Lord Hankey, *op. cit.*, Vol. I, p. 323, says that Asquith could not have induced his colleagues to adopt the type of War Cabinet set up by Lloyd George but he not only produces no evidence for this but immediately admits that Asquith would never have contemplated such a concentration of power.

prevent the kind of activity he disliked. McKenna was brought into the War Cabinet to balance Lloyd George, Bonar Law was confronted by his rival Curzon and the Order in Council giving wide powers to the C.I.G.S. was kept so that Lloyd George could not really take action even when he had moved to the War Office.

The experience of these years confirms two points about the history of the Cabinet. The first is that the position of the Prime Minister had become so definitely a special one above the rest of the Cabinet and no other person or arrangement could suffice as a substitute. A Prime Minister infused his own qualities and atmosphere into the upper reaches of the government. A man with a desire for action need not have great ideas or capacities provided he lent the weight of his office to those of his ministers who were capable of action. To wait on events, to appoint men who preferred to delay decisions, soon slowed down the whole machine. While such a Prime Minister might be successful in time of peace in that he might reflect the mood of the nation, these attributes were disastrous in war. In fact, there was nothing wrong as a war machine with a structure consisting of Prime Minister, War Committee, Cabinet Ministers and Departments. In November 1915 Asquith could have had (and very nearly did have) an organisation identical with that set up by Lloyd George. So the second point that emerges is that at the very senior levels of administration, machinery however suitable and efficient, will not work unless there are men with proper abilities to operate it. Facing the stresses imposed by a world war under modern conditions the Prime Minister has to become the effective directing head of the government.

CHAPTER 13

THE INFLUENCE OF PARLIAMENT
AND PUBLIC OPINION, 1914–16

AT first Asquith continued with the same Liberal Government that had been in office since the General Election of December 1910. But it soon became evident that in face of a national emergency no government could lead the nation on a party basis. There had to be a general acceptance that policies and personnel were satisfactory or the capacity to lead might simply crumble. Ministers, aided by the Whips, by personal contacts and the Press, had to try to still any doubts or criticisms before they reached serious proportions. Similarly, M.P.s were reluctant to make open attacks in the House for fear of damaging public morale or, if carried too far, of being branded as unpatriotic. The government told the House very little, partly for reasons of secrecy and partly because it was easier not to confide in Parliament.[1] As a result, when worries arose among M.P.s they were often based on news brought back from the Front by individuals or on reports in the Press. Such doubts would be discussed in private and might spread and reach serious proportions before they were made public. Members preferred to speak to their leaders at party meetings or through the " normal channels " rather than raise debates in the House. On the opposition side, the Unionist Business Committee (which later called itself the War Committee) was formed in January 1915, its membership expanding to take in almost all the back-benchers. Sub-committees were set up to collect information and, in time, after the Conservative leaders had joined the government, it came to speak for what had been the opposition. When feeling among M.P.s became too strong and representations to ministers no longer sufficed, tension tended to be revealed in debates on secondary matters or on domestic issues rather than in any direct challenge on the conduct of the war.

---

[1] Winston Churchill lamented this tendency to ignore the House of Commons whenever possible; *The World Crisis*, p. 471.

In the spring and early summer of 1915 the opposition was becoming both alarmed and restless. Bonar Law and his colleagues were refraining from criticism, or from any demands for information, and yet had no share in directing policy. The resignation of Fisher brought matters to a head, because a debate might be forced on the government which would involve revealing internal divisions. The Commons would be invited to judge the merits of the Dardanelles campaign and of a series of persons and individual decisions connected with it. Almost at the same time Lloyd George was encouraging leaks from the Front about shell shortage, so that Press revelations would help him force his munitions policy on the War Office. Bonar Law might have held his followers in check on this issue, but it was preceded by Fisher's resignation, and here restraint was impossible since the old Admiral was a firm favourite among the Conservatives. The Leader of the Opposition wrote to the Prime Minister saying that " things cannot go on as they are," and Asquith agreed to a Coalition at once and without consulting any of his colleagues.[2] The newcomers were able to insist on the exclusion of Haldane and the removal of Churchill from the Admiralty.

After May 1915, pressure could be exercised in several ways. Ministers could threaten to resign on issues which, though unknown to the House, might be expected to cause serious trouble if explanations had to be made. In the case of Bonar Law, resignation would have had the even more serious consequence of breaking up the Coalition. It was on this basis that the Conservative leader forced the evacuation of the Dardanelles and the appointment of Lloyd George to the War Office. Lloyd George talked of resignation a little too often, but he made genuine use of this threat in the struggle over conscription. On the same issue Grey, Runciman, McKenna and Simon declared that they might leave the government if Lloyd George's side won, but in the event only Simon did so, and he found no response from the Liberal rank and file. Lack of confidence in the direction of the war led to constant mutterings among the senior ministers, but their threats had meaning only in as much as an open rift would lead to serious consequences in the Commons.

[2] R. Blake, *The Unknown Prime Minister*, p. 246, and J. Pope-Hennessy, *Lord Crewe*, p. 148.

A second method was back-bench pressure on the leaders of the respective parties. The Liberals were, on the whole, docile, and on the one occasion when there was strong feeling—over the failure to consult them before the Coalition was formed—Asquith restored order at a party meeting. Among the Conservatives there were more doubts, in part because the government was driven to try to end such old difficulties as Home Rule and in part because the Conservatives tended to want a more relentless prosecution of the war. When the Irish Question became urgent both Bonar Law and Balfour supported the proposals put before the Cabinet (Home Rule with the provisional exclusion of the six counties) but they could not go on without the backing of their party. At a meeting in the Carlton Club back-bench feeling was clearly hostile and Bonar Law closed the proceedings without even asking for a vote.

Sometimes during these years M.P.s grew restive on general issues which did not fall along party lines and ministers were never happy at the thought of such orators as Carson or Churchill on the loose when awkward debates were coming up. The House resented the way it had been relegated to a mere forum for government announcements and believed there was nothing unpatriotic in demanding information. So when motions were put down for Royal Commissions of inquiry into the Dardanelles and Mesopotamian campaigns in mid-1916, the Whips counselled acquiescence. Carson, at about the same time, had led the Commons in condemning a compromise on conscription and Asquith withdrew the Bill. When the Home Secretary tried to leave the vexed matter of soldiers' votes to a committee of the House, Carson again had the sympathy of Members in his criticisms and this proposal was also withdrawn. After one of these attacks in October 1916 Lord Robert Cecil told the Prime Minister that " I take the gravest view of the situation last night. It seemed to me that the House of Commons was entirely out of hand. . . ." [3]

In retaliation, Asquith could try and cut off potential resigners by putting them on Cabinet Committees to investigate such questions as competing economic and military claims for manpower, hoping that by the time the committee had reported there

---

[3] Spender and Asquith, *op. cit.*, Vol. II, p. 240.

would be less room for objection. Another recourse was a secret session of the House, such a meeting on April 19, 1916, being told by Asquith that he intended to resign unless Cabinet differences were composed. The result was a demonstration of Liberal support for the Prime Minister but no long-term strengthening of his position.

Besides Parliament, the government did consider other forms of public opinion. On the outbreak of war there was a general outcry in favour of giving Kitchener a senior post. No one had any doubt that he would be offered suitable employment, but it was Asquith and Haldane who favoured making him Secretary of State for War. In May 1915, when Bonar Law, Balfour, Lloyd George and Asquith all considered moving Kitchener to some such post as C.-in-C., the *Daily Mail* attacked him and the result was a demonstration of popular support. The *Mail* was burnt at the Stock Exchange, the rest of the Press reacted strongly so it seemed easier to leave him where he was. Later when the same men wanted Kitchener to stay in Egypt as C.-in-C. for the Middle East, a premature disclosure in the *Globe* led to angry questions in the House and the government decided to repudiate the suggestion. The Press played a diverse role in such mixtures of parliamentary and public pressure. As is often the case when relations between ministers become strained, Cabinet security was bad and newspaper magnates such as Beaverbrook and Northcliffe could be used to plant stories in order to create a crisis atmosphere or to undermine opponents. The Press could also be used by critics such as Carson urging a more vigorous prosecution of the war. The generals in France soon realised its value, and Press support could easily be won by offering prior or special information. The effect of revelations in the news columns or of direct criticism by the Press depended on a number of factors. Reports had to feed existing doubts if there was to be any reaction, a strong or successful government having little to fear. Unfortunately in these years there were only too many grounds for alarm about the conduct of public policy. While normally the Press played only an ancillary role in political combinations *The Times*' leading article of December 4, 1916, was of major importance in that it drove Asquith to reject Lloyd George and Bonar Law's proposals for a small War

Committee thus provoking their resignation and Asquith's final downfall.[4]

In this period, it has been necessary to distinguish between the Prime Minister, the government and the Cabinet. The reason is that the Cabinet was now only one among a series of policy-making bodies in the government, and different groups or individuals in the Cabinet were often driving in different directions. To change the policy of the government might mean persuading Bonar Law (or, with less effect, Lloyd George) to exercise his influence. More often it involved pressure on Asquith, since a decision by him would usually tilt the Cabinet one way or another, but sometimes the only solution was to threaten to debate or examine the policy of the government as a whole. In resisting such demands both the Prime Minister and the government had very considerable resources.

On the side of the ministry, there were all the loyalties conjured up by the war. In the interests of secrecy the government controlled the dissemination of all immediate news and of all discussion—at any rate till a certain period after the events. Members of Parliament had to be chary lest their conduct could be labelled as factious. This was one of the few periods since the hardening of the party system when a dissolution could be used as a threat to discipline Members. It was most unlikely under normal conditions that any party Cabinet would ever go to the country when its rank and file were rebellious and ask for the electorate's help in defeating some of its own supporters. During the war, however, the Coalition did not need a party majority and might well have said the House was unmanageable—would the country please return Members who were equal to the occasion? Bonar Law, in the autumn of 1916, considered that events were leading to a choice between a new government and a dissolution.[5] The King and all the senior men who gathered at Buckingham Palace in the political crisis of December 1916 realised that the new Prime Minister

---

[4] It is still not absolutely clear whether this story was deliberately leaked by Lloyd George, though it appears to be the most likely explanation. Jenkins, *op. cit.*, pp. 444–448. In the last negotiations which excluded Asquith, his only bitterness was over the Press and " he urged that whatever government might come into office, measures should be taken to prevent the continuance of their Press tyranny." Stamfordham's memorandum quoted by Jenkins, *op. cit.*, p. 457.

[5] Beaverbrook, *Politicians and the War*, Vol. II, p. 104.

would possess this very effective weapon. In his discussions with Conservative ministers Lloyd George said he would use it if the House did not support him.[6]

In meeting ministerial threats of resignation, the Prime Minister had the great asset that no one, above all in wartime, was indispensable. For every man who resigned there were a score ready to step into office. Politicians had to be very careful, for resignation at such a time had to be justified by motives of the highest patriotism and had to receive rapid public endorsement. To miscalculate these factors, as Simon did over conscription, cost him (by his own reckoning) a fifteen-year setback in his political career. Curiously enough, Asquith underestimated these points when he both challenged Lloyd George to form a government at the end of 1916 and refused to serve in it himself. Balfour accepted office with the plea that Lloyd George had " put a pistol at my head," but many ex-ministers discovered that "there were not enough pistols to go round." [7]

The final crisis of December 1916 saw a combination of all the methods of parliamentary and popular pressure that have been described. The House of Commons had had no regular control over the personnel or actions of the government but doubts, especially among Conservative M.P.s, had been increasing steadily. As usual, they reached Bonar Law through the Whips and in time broke out over such an apparently unimportant issue as enemy properties in Nigeria, when Carson took sixty-five Conservatives into the anti-government lobby against the seventy-three who followed their Leader. Bonar Law then realised that there would have to be changes and reached an agreement with Lloyd George. Asquith and his supporters were faced with the threatened resignations of the only two men who had real backing among the rank and file M.P.s and all the Cabinet knew that this challenge could not be accepted on the floor of the House. Lloyd George and his henchmen swung the Press into line but, though this warned the country of what was happening, it did not alter the essential balance of forces. Asquith decided the only way out was to let his

---

[6] *Ibid.*, pp. 305–327. The possibility of a dissolution formed one of Lloyd George's motives in pressing soldiers' registration on the Cabinet, in case an election was ever needed to destroy those who were lukewarm about the war. Addison, *Four and a Half Years*, Vol. I, p. 220.

[7] Spender and Asquith, *op. cit.*, Vol. II, p. 278.

opponents try to form a government. Once Lloyd George and Bonar Law announced that they had taken office, all the forces of patriotic desire to get on with the war, of ambition to serve and fear of annihilation in any election came to their aid and a new Coalition was formed.[8]

---

[8] The accepted and brilliant account of this crisis is in Lord Beaverbrook's *Politicians and the War*, Vol. II. The only possible reservations are over the motives and objectives of the group of Conservative ministers, Chamberlain, Cecil, Curzon and Long. In a detailed examination of relations between ministers, the background of discontent in the House of Commons, which was the cause of and underlay the whole crisis, must not be overlooked.

CHAPTER 14

LLOYD GEORGE'S WAR CABINET

THE new Prime Minister, working in the closest collaboration with Bonar Law, set up a small War Cabinet of five members, the other three being Curzon, Milner and Arthur Henderson.[1] Lloyd George's most important change was to give this body final responsibility, and the old Cabinet of twenty-two members disappeared. Yet there was nothing new about Lloyd George's scheme. It had been urged by Carson in November 1915, and would have come about then if Asquith had made it clear that the War Committee formed in that month should take decisions and issue orders without recourse to the full Cabinet. The idea of a small War Cabinet was sometimes contrasted with the notion of two committees, one dealing with the war and the other with domestic affairs. Asquith had made such a proposal in October 1915 and it was revived by some Conservative ministers and the *Morning Post* in the crisis of December 1916. Though apparently very different, the result would have been much the same since war needs so clearly took priority that the home committee would have become a body of secondary importance.[2]

Under Lloyd George, the War Cabinet assembled virtually every day and held over 500 meetings between its formation and the armistice in November 1918. Only Bonar Law had a department, the other members being available for continuous supervisory work and decision-taking. The War Cabinet should at once have taken control of the major lines of policy, but the dispersion of power in the past two years was not so readily undone. The Prime Minister's political position was weak, since the Leader of the

[1] Needless to say Lloyd George did not select this group simply for their administrative ability. He had also to think of consolidating the maximum political support. See P. A. Lockwood, "Milner's entry into the War Cabinet, December, 1916," *The Historical Journal*, Vol. VII (1964), pp. 120–134 and A. M. Gollin, *Proconsul in Politics*, Chapter XIV, both of which argue "that Milner was included . . . because of the political benefits that would follow upon his selection." Gollin, p. 374.

[2] One reason for such a proposal was that men whose views were disliked by Asquith or by the generals could have been relegated to the home policy committee.

371

Liberal Party and all its official machinery was in opposition, while Conservative support depended on Bonar Law's capacity to keep in line a number of men who had little confidence in Lloyd George. At the start, the Prime Minister had to accept limitations. A group of Conservative ex-ministers only joined the government on condition that Haig was to be left in command in France, that they were not committed to Home Rule, and that neither Churchill nor Northcliffe was to be considered for office. He was further circumscribed in his choice of ministers since Conservative support had to be cemented by giving Curzon a place in the War Cabinet and the Labour Party had to be promised a similar place, three junior posts, and a number of points of policy. The generals had developed close contacts with the Press and various politicians ranging from Lord Derby at the War Office to former Liberal Cabinet Ministers. Sir William Robertson still had the Order in Council which made him the only source of military advice and information for the Cabinet. Careful propaganda had convinced the public that the soldiers were in danger of being overruled by ill-informed civilians whose motives might well be mixed. The Navy, though buttressed by nothing as precise as an Order in Council, could still rally a great deal of support if the Admirals felt that their opinions were being overruled. Finally the British Government still had to work alongside its Allies, co-operating closely with the French G.H.Q.

Lloyd George made his first attempt to take control of strategy in January 1917, when he tried to persuade an Allied Conference at Rome to declare in favour of an offensive in Italy, but the British and French military staffs turned down the proposal. In this case his objective was to break away from the exclusive concentration on the fighting in France with which Robertson and Haig were identified. But Lloyd George distrusted these generals so much that strategic questions came second to his desire to reduce their freedom of action. One way of doing so was to plead the excellent case for a unified command on the Western Front and subordinate them to a French commander. The newly promoted General Nivelle attracted Lloyd George and he persuaded the War Cabinet (when both Robertson and the Secretary of State for War, Lord Derby, were absent) to put the British armies under the operational control of the French for the duration of the forthcoming offensive planned by Nivelle. This decision was then sprung on Haig and Robertson at a conference in Calais in February (ostensibly on transport problems) and though the generals submitted, their position was fully restored when the offensive ended with defeat, demoralisation in the French armies, and the demotion of Nivelle.[3]

Meanwhile the submarine menace threatened disaster and the Cabinet found that it could not effectively break through the chain of command and force such experiments as the use of convoys on the Admiralty. As so often in 1917, " the Cabinet " initially meant Lloyd George alone, since Milner was busy in administration, Bonar Law had his hands full leading the House, and Henderson, the Labour Party member, was relatively light weight. Carson, as First Sea Lord, gave the Sea Lords under Jellicoe his complete backing and the Prime Minister, aided by Curzon and Milner, had literally to take over the Admiralty for an afternoon and insist that the convoy system be given a trial.[4] The next step was to gather the support of Bonar Law and Milner and to bring in Haig, who was thoroughly alarmed by the rate of sinkings. Lloyd George went on to offer Carson a place in the War Cabinet (where he could both be kept quiet and overruled) and, when he reluctantly agreed, put Sir Eric Geddes in the Admiralty. Even then, the Prime Minister and the new First Lord did not feel strong enough to dismiss Jellicoe till December 1917.

Having failed to gain control of strategy at Rome and being left with the same men in charge after the collapse of Nivelle, Lloyd George had to turn to the problem of policy-making for the summer and autumn of 1917. His chief difficulty was that Robertson and Haig were the sole source of expert advice. Information could only come from G.H.Q. in France and planning could only be done there and by Robertson's Staff at the War Office. The Cabinet was presented with one carefully documented proposal and had to take it or face resignations from men who had considerable public standing as well as the strong case that they, the experts, were

---

[3] The generals were backed at this time by Lord Derby who had become Secretary of State for War and who regularly wrote to Haig and Robertson assuring them of his support. Derby also had direct access to the King. Randolph Churchill, *op. cit.*, pp. 450–452.

[4] Carson in March 1917 said " as long as I am at the Admiralty, the sailors will have full scope. They will not be interfered with by me, and I will allow no one else to interfere with them." A. M. Gollin, *op. cit.*, pp. 421 and 431–442.

being overruled by amateurs. Lloyd George twisted and turned in an attempt to get advice from other sources. He had hoped that the series of Imperial War Cabinets in the spring would give him grounds for urging alternatives on the War Office, but the only Premier capable of helping at this level was Smuts. Lloyd George asked him to stay and serve as a member of the War Cabinet though it later transpired that Smuts's view was that in the last resort the generals' advice should be accepted. Between June 8 and July 20 a special War Policy Committee of the Cabinet considered Robertson's and Haig's proposals for an offensive in Flanders. In his private letters to Haig, Robertson had expressed doubts about French co-operation and wondered whether it would not be better to send artillery to help the Italians. Haig confuted these notions and not a word of them reached the Cabinet. Nor did Haig report his own views about the weakness of the French armies, while Robertson never mentioned to the Cabinet that he considered G.H.Q. estimates about the low level of German reserves to be far too optimistic. On June 13, Robertson noted that the War Policy Committee " have started, quite among themselves . . . to review the whole policy and strategy of the war, and to ' get at facts.' They are interviewing people singly, and sending out to Departments various specific questions to be answered." [5] Such attempts to get information from sources other than the C.I.G.S. achieved little and the Committee had to make up its mind whether to accept or reject the generals' scheme. Smuts favoured the offensive, since Haig said he could break through the German lines and clear the coast.[6] Curzon on the whole agreed but Lloyd George, Milner and Bonar Law were sceptical, although the last two felt that unanimous military advice could not be ignored. On June 21, the Prime Minister read a lengthy paper giving six reasons for " real misgivings " about the offensive. Two days later Robertson replied to Lloyd George point by point and reaffirmed his confidence in Haig's plans.[7] The Cabinet reluctantly gave its approval.

[5] These letters are printed in the *Haig Papers*, pp. 236–239.
[6] W. K. Hancock, *Smuts, The Sanguine Years, 1870–1919*, p. 453 says Smuts had two reservations about French activity and an early stop if casualties were high but neither made any impression compared with his coming down on the generals' side.
[7] The minutes of the two meetings are in the *Milner Papers*, New College, Oxford, Box AE 1.

Even when the offensive was evidently failing neither the Prime Minister nor the War Cabinet were prepared to insist on a halt. On September 5, Milner still thought the Cabinet must endorse the unanimous view of the soldiers though by the 18th Bonar Law wanted to stop further action. A month later Lloyd George had won over Milner, who wrote that " almost all high military opinion is against us, and the majority of the Cabinet bow—not always with conviction—to the unanimity of military opinion. I hope you and I are wrong." [8] Lloyd George let the offensive sink slowly into the mud of Passchendaele, but continued meanwhile to seek alternative authorities on military matters. On October 11, he summoned Sir John French and Sir Henry Wilson to the Cabinet and asked for their advice. Both sent in memoranda adverse to Robertson and recommended a War Cabinet or authoritative council of the Allies to co-ordinate military policy. Pushed along by the disaster at Caporetto and the need to aid the Italians, the Cabinet accepted the proposal as did the Allies at a Conference in Rapallo on November 7. At last Lloyd George had weakened Robertson, for whether the latter stayed as C.I.G.S. or went to the Supreme Council at Paris there was now alternative advice to lean on. Asquith and his supporters challenged the Cabinet, but were brushed aside. The next step was to gain control of military operations in the West. Lord Derby, the Secretary of State for War was asked to replace Haig and Robertson in December 1917. He refused. Lloyd George then offered Derby the post of Ambassador in Paris. He refused to desert the generals. Lloyd George then decided to approach the problem by creating a single-inter-allied reserve as a step towards a unified command. When Robertson objected that this would transfer power to such a command at Versailles, he was offered the choice between his post as C.I.G.S. and that of British representative at Versailles. Whichever he chose he was to be quietly relegated, so he resigned. Neither Haig nor Derby went with him. As a result the attack launched by the Liberals, Conservative dissidents and the Press (all briefed by Robertson) failed. But the Prime Minister fully appreciated Haig's strength and did not try to order him to carry on with the project of an inter-allied reserve.[9] When such a force was finally created and Foch given the Supreme Command, it was because Haig decided that this was the only way of combating Pétain's defeatism in the face of Ludendorff's offensive. The war ended with Lloyd George and his Cabinet still some way short of complete authority over the Army and over strategy.

Throughout these two tense years, the War Cabinet worked fairly smoothly. The frequent meetings were attended by the five members (six after Smuts joined) aided by a constant flow of non-Cabinet ministers and experts. Some of them were regular though not constant attenders and saw all papers (such as Addison at Munitions, Balfour at the Admiralty, or Cave at the Home Office) while others might come only once or twice to contribute their special knowledge. Matters on which several departments disagreed or where new, co-ordinated plans had to be prepared, were normally handed to an *ad hoc* sub-committee presided over by one of the non-departmental members of the Cabinet—usually Milner or Smuts. The system enabled a more rapid and efficient flow of business, though a great deal depended on the Prime Minister. A number of those close to the Cabinet thought it was overworked. Treasury control was virtually abandoned because it took too much time and in any case finance had become a secondary consideration. There was a tendency to shirk major decisions if Lloyd George was not there to lend his authority, but he could not always get his way. He claimed that he did not stop the Passchendaele offensive because he could not rely on Cabinet support nor would the Cabinet have acquiesced in any attempt during 1917 to dismiss Robertson and Haig.[10]

To aid in preparing, recording and enforcing all Cabinet decisions, the Prime Minister had set up a Secretariat under Colonel Hankey. It is important to distinguish between the various rings of secretaries and advisers. Lloyd George had some trusted friends with whom he liked to talk matters over. At this time he saw Christopher Addison, Lord Riddell (of the *News of the World*), Robertson Nicoll, and Sir Frederick Guest fairly frequently but made no attempt to formulate policy with them. These meetings

---

[9] Lloyd George's failure to establish control over Haig was best revealed by his attempt to prevent another offensive in France not by direct instructions but by denying Haig adequate reinforcements.

[10] Lloyd George, *War Memoirs*, Vol. II, p. 1315.

were semi-social occasions where Lloyd George tried out his ideas, listened to and gossiped with men of similar interests. Then there was his own secretariat under Professor W. G. S. Adams aided by four assistant secretaries who divided up the field between them. Philip Kerr looked after foreign and colonial matters, Waldorf Astor and David Davies [11] covered the House of Commons, and Joseph Davies collected information on the crucial areas of scarcity —raw materials and shipping. The real task of these men (often known as the Garden Suburb because they worked in a series of huts erected in the garden of No. 10 Downing Street) was to devil for Lloyd George, and while Kerr was trusted and became an adviser, Joseph Davies remained simply a statistician assembling useful facts.[12] Hankey's office in theory was entirely different. It had grown out of the Secretariat of the Committee of Imperial Defence and was defended in 1922 as a department concerned purely with recording the proceedings of the Cabinet and its committees and communicating the decisions to appropriate bodies. It is clear, however, that Hankey and his assistants did slip in helpful suggestions from time to time, press a point on the Prime Minister or on a committee, and even sharpen up a minute if the decision had been a little woolly. These tendencies were abruptly checked by the debate on the Cabinet secretariat in June 1922 and by the criticisms that continued to be made during the election of that year.[13]

In addition to the official meetings of the War Cabinet, it became the custom for all ministers to assemble on Monday mornings to hear a general report on the military and naval situation so that they appreciated the full picture. Addison occasionally refers to further meetings of the " full Cabinet "—that is of all ministers of Cabinet rank—in order that such a briefing might take place. To keep in touch with his own Liberal and Labour colleagues, Lloyd George held gatherings every Wednesday morning over breakfast.

Below the War Cabinet there were the series of committees appointed to solve disputes, prepare plans, and deal with particular commodities, areas or subjects. Some came to an end after one

[11] Later replaced by Cecil B. Harmsworth.
[12] See Sir Joseph Davies, *The Prime Minister's Secretariat.*
[13] H. C. Debates, Vol. 155, cols. 213–275, June 13, 1922.

meeting, others lasted for months and two were put on a permanent basis. These committees helped to co-ordinate the departments and obtain decisions, but there were complaints that Lloyd George liked to try to keep his hands on too many levers and that he refused to delegate enough work to committees.[14] Nevertheless, when the Cabinet was so busy, much preliminary work and many minor decisions were taken by committees. When Austen Chamberlain rejoined the Cabinet in April 1918 he made certain conditions about the contents of any Home Rule Bill. Lloyd George assuaged Chamberlain's doubts not only by granting him these points but by assuring him that he would be on the Cabinet Committee that drew up any Bill—a promise that Chamberlain was careful to confirm in his letter of acceptance.

Despite the great increase in Cabinet business, the war had enforced a fairly clear order of priorities. Military matters and the organisation of industry and manpower took the whole attention of the Cabinet, foreign policy and normal domestic issues arising only in so far as they impinged on the conduct of the war. But as the fighting turned in favour of the Allies in the summer of 1918, problems of reconstruction, demobilisation and relations with friendly and defeated powers crowded the agenda. In 1917 there had been an Economic Offensive Committee under Carson to study economic questions in both the war and the immediate post-war settings. It did little and was passed on first to Milner and then to Austen Chamberlain. On June 4, 1918, the Committee persuaded the Cabinet to turn it into a standing Committee on Economic Defence and Development. Its new features were a regular weekly meeting and the instruction that all suitable matters should be sent at once to the Committee by the Secretariat (instead of awaiting reference by the War Cabinet). Only major questions, important changes of policy or disputed issues were to be referred to the Cabinet.

Almost at the same time (on June 5), Addison wrote to Lloyd George protesting at the constant delay in reaching decisions on domestic affairs. The Bill setting up a Ministry of Health had just been postponed for the fourth time—on this occasion, after being the second item on the agenda of a Cabinet called specifically to clear up the backlog of business. On June 10, the Prime Minister

14 Addison, *Politics From Within*, Vol. II, pp. 252 and 261.

agreed to the formation of a second standing committee, the Home Affairs Committee. It also automatically considered all matters within its province before they went to the Cabinet, though care was taken that the parent body reviewed all decisions of importance. These two standing committees, together with the Post-War Priority Committee set up in October, prevented the War Cabinet and the Prime Minister from being swamped by details in the last months before the armistice.[15]

[15] The purposes and powers of the two standing committees as originally proposed by Addison are set out in *Four and a Half Years*, Vol. II, pp. 535–538 and 542.

CHAPTER 15

THE COALITION CABINET, 1918-22

FOUR years of total war had confirmed and emphasised the role which the Prime Minister had to play. The office had become the directing centre of the government. If the occupant failed to fulfil his function, no other person or agency could adequately replace him, power became diffused and the machinery ill co-ordinated. A Prime Minister still had to carry his colleagues and operate within limits imposed by his need for political support, but success led to a steady accession of strength. As the Allied armies pushed the Germans back, Lloyd George's stock rose, and as fighting came to an end the power of G.H.Q. in France declined in importance and then faded away. At the General Election of December 1918 the Coalition won 484 seats, and there were forty-eight further Conservative M.P.s whose support, at this stage, was assured. Altogether, only 101 M.P.s were likely to oppose Lloyd George's administration [1] and he now reached a pinnacle of power, marred only by the reflection that he still lacked the support of an organised party and had to convince Conservative leaders and back-benchers that the Coalition was the best method of governing the country.

One immediate problem was whether to continue with the small War Cabinet. Nine days after the Armistice, sufficient representatives of the Dominions had gathered in London to constitute an Imperial War Cabinet which met almost daily till the end of the year. At its first meeting Curzon raised the possibility of bringing the Kaiser to trial, and at a later meeting F. E. Smith convinced the Cabinet of the need to do so after a forty-five minute oration. The members went on to consider all Imperial interests in the impending peace settlement. Most of the Dominion leaders then accompanied Lloyd George and the British delegation to Versailles. When difficult points arose, the Prime Minister consulted one or two selected colleagues, but on the crucial matter

---

[1] There were also 73 Sinn Fein members, but they refused to come to Westminster.

of Germany's request for a modification of the peace terms, Lloyd George invited nine British Ministers and the Dominion Premiers to his flat in Paris. There, after a debate lasting nearly two days, they agreed to accept some of the German requests.

Meanwhile the situation at home was not very clear. When the new government was formed in December 1918, Austen Chamberlain had been incensed at being offered the Chancellorship of the Exchequer without a place in the Cabinet. Lloyd George's explanation was that the former War Cabinet had not included departmental ministers, but he was evidently wishing to delay any decision about the composition of the Cabinet till he had had time to consider various possibilities. He mentioned the idea of having two Cabinets, one for Imperial and the other for British affairs.[2] To keep the matter open, the Premier then suggested that while he, Balfour and Bonar Law were in Paris, it would be scarcely satisfactory to hold Cabinets and it might be easier simply to leave individual ministers to administer their departments without appointing a Cabinet. Bonar Law agreed to delay, as he thought the old type of Cabinet of fifteen or more members would talk so much that it could never cope with the greatly increased volume of business. A compromise was found in the re-appointment of the old War Cabinet, of which Austen Chamberlain had been a member, so that he could be re-admitted without raising the thorny question of which departmental ministers were entitled to membership.

So the War Cabinet was continued, lasting in theory till the autumn of 1919. In practice, till the end of the Peace Conference Lloyd George dealt with all important matters on the advice of the senior ministers who were available in Paris and such other advisers as seemed suitable. In London there were meetings of the War Cabinet to which further ministers were invited as the business required. In January 1919 housing and land problems were passed to the Home Affairs Committee under the chairmanship of H. A. L. Fisher. On February 10, when the King's Speech had to be authorised, twenty-five ministers were called to what Lloyd George's assistants dubbed as " the Duma." Usually most of those who would normally have been included in the Cabinet attended the meetings, but only the War Cabinet saw important papers, its members being more powerful as well as formally responsible for

2 Sir Austen Chamberlain, *Down the Years*, p. 143.

all decisions. The strongest personality excluded by this system was Winston Churchill (Secretary of State for War), and by May he was protesting hotly against the existing system of government with its inner ring of ministers. He said the Prime Minister had promised him that normal Cabinets would be restored after the election.[3] Bonar Law curtly replied that if he did not like the arrangements he could always resign, but Churchill preferred to stay and fulminate.[4] By July, Worthington-Evans (Minister of Pensions) and Edwin Montagu (Secretary of State for India) were becoming restive about their status. On major questions Lloyd George's opinion was usually obtained while memoranda on the reorganisation of the Cabinet were being sent to Paris by Hankey, Churchill and others. None of these schemes was able to cut the numbers below eighteen, and the final solution when the Cabinet was reconstituted in October 1919 was a return to the normal pre-war size of twenty.

In considering the relations of Lloyd George and his Cabinet, the most striking fact is that it was *his* in a more marked fashion than had been the case even with such self-assured Premiers as Balfour or Campbell-Bannerman. When Lloyd George was considering a dissolution in late 1918, there was no question of consulting the body of the Cabinet. Bonar Law was inclined to leave it to Lloyd George, and Balfour agreed that " the responsibility of a dissolution must rest with the Prime Minister." [5] In 1922 the situation was more complex, as many Conservative M.P.s and the party organisation did not want to go to the country as a Coalition. On October 10 Austen Chamberlain raised the question of a dissolution in the Cabinet and the idea was accepted. The final decision however lay with Lloyd George and those who were then his closest advisers, Churchill, F. E. Smith, Balfour and Chamberlain. At first they favoured an immediate election but on October 16 Lloyd George decided to wait till after the Carlton Club meeting on the 19th, with disastrous results.

[3] W. S. Churchill, *The World Crisis—the Aftermath*, p. 52.
[4] Beaverbrook reports Churchill's reply to Bonar Law: " That is a question you have no right to ask. Only the P.M. is entitled to question his subordinates in such terms." Beaverbrook, *Men and Power, 1917–18*, p. 127.
[5] Blake, *op. cit.*, p. 385. Before 1914 there had only been one occasion on which the Cabinet had not been consulted about a dissolution. See above, pp. 306–308.

Membership, promotion and dismissal also lay with the Prime Minister, though he usually acted after consultation with his chief ally, Bonar Law. As early as July 1917 he was telling Lord Derby of " the prerogative of the Prime Minister to appoint those whom he thought likely to help him." [6] This was a generally accepted view but by 1918 he could take an even stronger line. When Churchill said he would like to know the names of the rest of the Cabinet before accepting office, Lloyd George replied: " Surely that is an unprecedented demand. The choice of the Members of the Government must be left to the Prime Minister, and anyone who does not trust his leadership has but one course, and that is to seek leaders whom he can trust." [7] In October 1918 it came to light that W. Hayes Fisher, the President of the Local Government Board, had mismanaged the preparation of the electoral register and Lloyd George wrote informing him of his immediate dismissal. Bonar Law saw the letter and urged milder treatment. Asked whether he was denying the Premier's right to demand a resignation he said " I did not make that claim, which would be intolerable," but he thought he had a right as Conservative leader to ask for considerate treatment of Conservative ministers. Lloyd George did not care how it was done provided that Hayes Fisher was " a dead chicken by tonight." [8] Addison, who was one of Lloyd George's strongest supporters and confidants, found that when he lost favour his days were numbered. He was eased out of the Ministry of Health but kept in the Cabinet without portfolio for a few months till his position was so unsatisfactory that he resigned. Milner, who had been a tower of strength to Lloyd George in 1917 and early 1918, was told to pull himself together in no uncertain terms when he showed signs of fatigue and indecision after the war. Not only in numbers and membership, but also in its place of meeting, the Cabinet waited on Lloyd George. During the negotiations with Sinn Fein an important stage was reached while the Prime Minister was on holiday in the Highlands, and so to the intense irritation of his colleagues he

[6] Randolph Churchill, *op. cit.*, p. 281.

[7] Frank Owen, *Tempestuous Journey*, p. 495. If anything was unprecedented, it was the refusal to discuss the complexion of a Cabinet with a potential member being offered a place.

[8] Blake, *op. cit.*, p. 383. The matter was solved by giving Fisher a peerage and a directorship of the Suez Canal Company.

called a Cabinet meeting in Inverness Town Hall. In addition to these powers, Lloyd George insisted on building up a personal Political Fund by the sale of honours and other methods, though the greater share of offices and awards which went to the Coalition Liberals was " a continual and exasperating cause of dispute." [9]

To appreciate Lloyd George's dealings with his Cabinet it is important to remember that, besides being the man who had won the war and the election of 1918, he was also the only member of the Versailles " Big Four " who continued to hold political power. The Prime Minister attended nine international conferences in 1920, seven in 1921 and seven in 1922, and at most of these he was the central and dominating figure. In such circumstances there was little point in having a leading personality as Foreign Secretary and Lloyd George was fairly confident of carrying the Cabinet. Curzon, who was left in charge of the Foreign Office during the Versailles Conference, complained that there were not enough meetings of the War Cabinet and that he did not receive sufficient information.[10] Usually, however, Lloyd George worked along lines accepted by his colleagues and, when he acted on his own, returned to put his case before them. The offer of a general guarantee of France was made to Poincaré in January 1922 without previous Cabinet sanction, yet both sides knew that it would be valueless unless accepted by the Premier's colleagues. Before going to the Genoa Conference Lloyd George promised the Cabinet that he would give the Russians no credits. Once there he proceeded to offer them loans but when a junior member of the delegation threatened to dissociate himself, Lloyd George said: " Don't you know I can break your political career? " and " Surely you want to become a Cabinet minister? " The Genoa agreement collapsed and Lloyd George never had to honour his offers of aid to Russia but his conduct during this conference contributed to the doubts and feelings of insecurity which were spreading among some of his colleagues.

In dealing with his two Foreign Secretaries, Balfour and Curzon, the Prime Minister made it clear that he intended to handle the major European questions himself. The Foreign Secretary by not being a member of the War Cabinet was in fact demoted, but

[9] Lord Beaverbrook, *The Decline and Fall of Lloyd George*, p. 25.
[10] Lord Ronaldshay, *Life of Lord Curzon*, Vol. III, p. 251.

there is no evidence that Balfour felt matters were being managed in any improper fashion and he was quite satisfied with his own attendance at over 300 of the 500 meetings of the War Cabinet. Lloyd George used his secretary, Philip Kerr, to keep him in touch with the Foreign Office. On one occasion in Paris Balfour asked Kerr if the Prime Minister had read one of his memoranda. " I don't think so," was the answer, " but I have." " Not quite the same thing is it, Philip—yet? ".[11] But Balfour considered that the Premier and the Foreign Secretary should work in the closest harmony and he accepted Lloyd George's leadership. Curzon, who took over in October 1919, was much less happy in this relationship though his interests were concentrated on Near Eastern questions, which Lloyd George left to him except in the case of Turkey and the Straits. Curzon was twice overruled, in the first instance over his desire to expel the Turks from Constantinople and in the second, over his proposal that the Milner Memorandum should be accepted as the basis of British policy towards Egypt. On each occasion, however, it was the full Cabinet that turned him down. The real source of friction lay in Lloyd George's almost contemptuous treatment of Curzon [12] and in the vague feeling that the Prime Minister's entourage was working for friendship with Russia and a pro-Greek policy which the Cabinet (rather than Curzon) had in each case rejected. In the late summer of 1922, when the government's policy had brought Britain to the verge of war with Turkey, Curzon was humiliated by finding himself excluded from the small circle who directed affairs. He protested against Lloyd George's private interviews with ambassadors and on October 4 prepared a strong letter:

" There has grown up a system under which there are in reality two Foreign Offices " . . . but . . . " whereas I report not only to you but to all my colleagues everything that I say or do, . . . it is often only by accident that I hear what is being done by the other F.O." Curzon said he had " no desire to question the prerogative or the paramount influence of the Prime Minister in general or of yourself in particular. These

---

11 B. E. C. Dugdale, *Arthur James Balfour*, Vol. II, p. 272.
12 At one point in 1921 Curzon wrote that " I am getting very tired of working or trying to work with that man. He wants his Foreign Secretary to be a valet almost a drudge." Beaverbrook, *The Decline and Fall of Lloyd George*, p. 40.

are undisputed and indisputable, and, with due co-ordination, can be wielded as effectively in the domain of Foreign Affairs as in every other Department of Government." [13]

Curzon was always afraid that he might find himself with no alternative but resignation and perhaps he realised that the Cabinet would not have supported him in any showdown over his relations with the Prime Minister. This letter exaggerates the influence of the Garden Suburb (Kerr had resigned in May 1921 and his place had been taken by Sir Edward Grigg) though it fairly reflects the growing antagonism to Lloyd George among the solid Conservatives. Curzon asked Balfour for his comments before sending the letter and he was still considering it when the Carlton Club meeting put an end to the Coalition.

Despite the rumours and suspicions which accumulated in 1921 and 1922, Lloyd George realised that his senior colleagues in the Cabinet could not be by-passed or ignored. He was prepared to use all sorts of devices like committees or conferences of ministers, individual talks or inner groups, to try to win adherents and to get quick action, but there was never any attempt to deceive the Cabinet (though, as has been mentioned, he sometimes acted beyond instructions during negotiations with foreign powers). Moreover, ministers agreed that these committees and conferences were all necessary as the machinery of government was fully stretched by the pressures of post-war reconstruction.

Devices that had been found useful in the rush of business at the end of the war, such as the Home Affairs Committee, continued to operate. On July 5, 1922, Winston Churchill asked if it was true that Bills were passed by the Home Affairs Committee and then sent direct to the House of Commons. If so, he said, it was a complete departure from Cabinet practice, which had long been that every Bill must come to the Cabinet before being presented to Parliament. The answer was that Bills which involved changes of policy went direct to the Cabinet, but otherwise measures went to the Home Affairs Committee first and if agreement was reached, the measure was circulated to Cabinet members, a formal note of approval being inserted in the minutes. Austen Chamberlain, as Leader of the House, found it useful to read the minutes of the

---

[13] Ronaldshay, *op. cit.*, Vol. III, pp. 316-317.

Home Affairs Committee "which is almost a Cabinet within a Cabinet " in preparing to introduce the various measures.

Some committees which were not listed as " standing " still met regularly over long periods. After the Armistice an Eastern Committee was set up to try to reconcile the position of Palestine and Mesopotamia with the various secret agreements made during the war. Having presided over more than 150 meetings, Curzon threw the whole thing up in January 1921 when Lloyd George transferred responsibility for these areas from the Foreign to the Colonial Office. A Cabinet Committee struggled with the Irish problem from October 1919 and handled the complex negotiations with the Sinn Fein leaders between June and November 1921 without any reference to the already overburdened Cabinet. The group of ministers which met in April of the same year to deal with industrial unrest was usually called a conference, because so many civil servants and outside experts attended.[14] Lloyd George was in the chair and explained that while the conference could negotiate, prepare the Territorial Forces and even order the arrest of ringleaders in Fife, large questions of policy such as calling up reservists would have to go before the Cabinet.

In September 1922, as Mustapha Kemal advanced towards Constantinople and the small British force at Chanak, Curzon was unwilling to take any strong stand and policy-making fell into the hands of Lloyd George, Winston Churchill and F. E. Smith. The Foreign Secretary attended the meetings of this inner ring (except for one crucial week-end when he was at his country house, which had no telephone) and was able to appeal to the Cabinet against their proposed ultimatum calling for a Turkish withdrawal. On this issue Curzon was overruled, as only Baldwin and Griffith-Boscawen supported him. Lloyd George, Churchill and F. E. Smith, who had come together in the concluding stages of the Irish negotiations, were able to lead over Chanak because they had the backing of other ministers such as Balfour, Austen Chamberlain and Worthington-Evans. Thus supported they were able to carry a majority of the Cabinet.

In dealing with his colleagues, Lloyd George did not hesitate

---

14 Conferences were called on many subjects. On July 27, 1920, Edwin Montagu came to No. 10 Downing Street because he had heard there was to be a Cabinet. " On seeing it was not a Cabinet but a Conference, to which I had not been summoned, I withdrew."

to employ all the advantages open to a Prime Minister. The more important Foreign Office telegrams were sent only to a small inner circle of the Cabinet, as had been the practice since the 1870s. Churchill observed that " Mr. Lloyd George . . . had a habit of picking his colleagues for any preliminary discussions so as to have a working majority of those who were favourable to his view." [15] Ministers who might oppose could be seen individually and charmed, threatened or cajoled, as seemed most suitable. The Committee system allowed the Prime Minister to guide or restrict a colleague. When Chamberlain was appointed to the Exchequer in December 1918, Lloyd George suggested a committee of himself, Chamberlain, Bonar Law and Milner to look at all disputes between the Treasury and other departments before they reached the Cabinet. Later, when the emphasis had swung heavily over to economy and he suspected that Chamberlain was not being tough enough, Lloyd George appointed the Geddes Committee to push both the Chancellor of the Exchequer and the Cabinet in the direction he wanted. Ministers, experts and deputations responded to this situation by trying to put their case directly to the Prime Minister.[16] So the whole trend of Lloyd George's premiership was to emphasise the drift away from the old concept of the Cabinet as the sole decision-making body in which the Prime Minister shared power with his colleagues. In these years, the pattern was more that of a cone with the Premier at the apex, depending on and supported by widening rings of advisers. Nevertheless, it remained the case that the most important of these rings was the Cabinet since it was the only one which had a definite, publicly announced membership and the right to complain if it was not consulted.

These developments received some unfavourable publicity in March 1922 when E. S. Montagu, the Secretary of State for India, published a telegram from the Viceroy of India recommending that the Allies should evacuate Constantinople and leave the Sultan in full sovereignty. When it appeared there was a storm, Chamberlain dissociated the Cabinet from an action taken by the

---

[15] Churchill, *op. cit.*, p. 374.
[16] When Addison found his Bill for a Ministry of Health hanging fire, and later when he wanted a grant of Home Rule to come at the same time as conscription in Ireland, the only solution was to try to catch and convince Lloyd George. Addison, *Politics from Within*, Vol. II, pp. 228–230 and 244.

Secretary of State on his own responsibility and Montagu resigned. He then defended himself by declaring that while Lloyd George was a genius, the price had been "the total, complete, absolute disappearance of the doctrine of Cabinet responsibility ever since he formed his government." [17]   Montagu was on weak ground in this instance as the telegram was clearly published in an attempt to commit the Cabinet to a policy which it had accepted two years earlier but now wished or felt it had to discard.   On March 15 there was a frank discussion of the episode in the Cabinet. Members agreed that there was more committee work and pre-digestion than previously but none voiced any grievances.   Balfour observed that "all Prime Ministers in my time have been charged either with being figureheads run by abler men or tyrants.   There is no middle position."   Chamberlain concluded that everyone knew the Prime Minister had been very careful to have members of divergent views on committees.   It is significant that even in 1922 when the end came, all the Cabinet except Baldwin and Griffith-Boscawen wished to keep the Coalition in being, while Curzon was waiting to see how the situation developed.   There was considerable disloyalty to Lloyd George in early 1922 but this was more a function of the declining political fortunes of the Coalition than of any changes in the machinery of government. The Prime Minister knew that if he could score a real success at the Genoa Conference bringing relaxation in world affairs, revived trade and full employment, all criticism would vanish.   Equally, failure was likely to worsen relations between ministers and to prevent this Austen Chamberlain was anxious that all the Cabinet understood and assented to the instructions given to the Prime Minister.   "If there are any differences of opinion among our colleagues, we should be in a very weak position if we dealt with so large a question in a mere Committee of Ministers" [18]; his chief fear was that Winston Churchill would dissociate himself from the Genoa policy and condemn any rapprochement with Russia.

Lloyd George reacted strongly to any question of dictation by Churchill and proceeded in his normal fashion.   He held a series of private conferences with small groups of ministers, so that by the time the whole Cabinet met he had thought out his position in

[17] *The Times*, March 13, 1922.
[18] Owen, *op. cit.*, p. 611.

discussions with his selected colleagues and had reached an accommodation, in which he had given considerable ground, with Churchill. The conclusions were accepted by the Cabinet and put before the House of Commons in the form of a motion of confidence.

As has been said, the position of the Cabinet rested on the fact that Lloyd George had to maintain his Coalition. Cabinet ministers expected to be and could insist on being consulted about all major government policies, inasmuch as the resignations of men who could lead back-bench discontent might prove serious. It might be worth risking trouble by assuming agreement at one or two conferences with the Irish, with trade unions or foreign Powers, in the hope that success would still any objections. But actions which were not liked by the Cabinet or episodes which left members feeling tricked or aggrieved could only weaken and perhaps destroy the ministry, as Lloyd George fully realised. And though junior ministers usually contributed little, there was no point in overlooking or brushing aside any considerable body of opinion in the Cabinet.

Indeed, Lloyd George was overruled on a number of occasions and on others a genuine division of opinion postponed definite action. In the spring of 1921 the Cabinet was divided over the question of Ireland. Churchill wanted a dual policy of total repression of Sinn Fein together with the offer of self-government within the Empire. Others doubted the possibility of putting down Sinn Fein by force but were not yet ready to grant the Irish complete Dominion status. The Prime Minister's position was based on no fixed points. He preferred to combine sterner police measures with further negotiations and this proved to be the only way out, but it was clear that the Cabinet would have to be carried at every stage. In the original discussions of a settlement in the Near East, both Curzon and Lloyd George wanted to expel the Turks from Constantinople. When their proposals reached the Cabinet on January 6, 1920, a majority definitely declared in favour of leaving the Turks in possession and this was included in the Treaty of Sèvres.[19] Later, as described above, Lloyd George's desire to accord recognition to Russia at the Genoa Conference was carefully circumscribed by the Cabinet.

[19] Curzon wrote a memorandum of protest against the Cabinet decision. See H. Nicolson, *Curzon, The Last Phase*, pp. 113–114.

So the Cabinet remained the body which could and did ask to review all major decisions. It met twice a week from 11 a.m. to 1.30 p.m., often carrying on with unfinished business in Austen Chamberlain's room in the House of Commons in the afternoon.[20] The agenda was drawn up by the secretariat but Lloyd George took the items in the order he preferred. Information was circulated with the Cabinet papers and discussions could not be raised till all the departments concerned had expressed their views— which meant that the Treasury could sometimes delay proposals it did not like. The atmosphere was informal and some members began smoking at meetings.[21] Lloyd George managed the proceedings well, did not intervene too much and usually chose the right moment to stop discussion and sum up. Contributions were brief and only the senior men spoke regularly. Addison weakened his position by talking far too often, though Churchill was able to indulge in frequent long speeches without losing the respect of his colleagues. The Cabinet as a whole made varying impressions on individual members. H. A. L. Fisher thought it was excellently conducted, at any rate until the last few months and A. J. Balfour observed that he never remembered a Cabinet which had worked

---

[20] Before the war there had been about 40 Cabinets a year. In 1920 there were 82 and in 1921, 93. Including conferences and standing (but not sub-) committees, there were 332 meetings in 1920 and 339 in 1921.

[21] There is a story of the War Cabinet which serves as a reminder that Cabinets had their cross-talk and lighter moments. Lloyd George used to sit at the Cabinet table arranging letters and giving instructions over his shoulder to one of his secretaries while the other members assembled. The few who had taken their seats on this occasion began to converse: "What about waste?" said Bonar Law. "I was on a train to Newcastle full of service-men reading cheap papers—there must be a terrible waste of newsprint." Carson replied that "after all, men have minds, and are disposed to think about things, and when these thoughts come to fruition they may well turn to writing books or serial stories." Barnes intervened to say that "it would be wrong to deny service-men good books—but not the sort of stuff that is printed in France." Curzon had come in and felt he should put the problem in its proper perspective. "Of course there are cycles in history when people enjoy scandal, and sensation—take the time of Titus Oates . . ." "Oats," said Lloyd George, who had just finished his letters and caught a couple of words, "there's waste! Cavalry eating oats, wheeling about behind the lines wasting time, then men making trouble with the wives of French soldiers who are at the Front—oats indeed! 500,000 horses—" ("50,000, Mr. Prime Minister," said Hankey)—"Yes, thousands and thousands of horses wasting oats when this is a war of machines, tanks and big guns."

The minute of this Cabinet discussion read—"it was agreed that with the current emphasis on supply on the Western Front, it was important to preserve a clear grasp of priorities."

together in greater harmony.[22]   Baldwin, on the other hand, often spoke of his feeling of revulsion. " You can't imagine the impression the meetings of the Cabinet made on me . . . watching each of its members under a microscope—I felt I was in a thieves' kitchen. Nobody seemed to have any principles. There was the most awful cynicism." Part of Baldwin's dislike was probably due to the restless desire to act and solve problems which possessed the leading members—Lloyd George, Churchill and F. E. Smith— though the Prime Minister, encouraged by the admiring smiles of Sir Robert Horne and Sir Edward Grigg, had perhaps become a little too adept at reconciling disputes and " finding a formula." After the meetings the Secretariat had been in the habit of circulating the minutes including not only the conclusions, but also a list of those who had spoken and a brief report of their views. In 1921 they stopped naming ministers and from early 1922 onward minutes were sent only to the Prime Minister and the King. The other ministers received a letter of reminder containing the conclusions reached on their particular items of business.

[22] H. A. L. Fisher, *An Unfinished Autobiography*, pp. 134–139. Sir A. Griffith-Boscawen agrees with Balfour's view. See *Memories*, pp. 230–232.

CHAPTER 16

THE INFLUENCE OF PARLIAMENT AND PUBLIC OPINION, 1916–22

LLOYD GEORGE'S great weakness was that he never had control of a party machine either in the Commons or in the country. After the change of government the Liberal organisation was still managed by Gulland, Asquith's Chief Whip, so that " practically every Liberal Association in the Kingdom is today the servant of an anti-Lloyd George bloc." [1] To try to create a unified body of support, the Prime Minister had long talks with Bonar Law during the winter of 1919–20 about a fusion of Coalition Liberals, Lloyd George supporters, and Conservatives. All such proposals were difficult because, as Bonar Law said, the slower-moving members of his party would not " agree to scrap their . . . organisation and give up their powers of defence and offence." [2] In March 1920 ninety-five M.P.s signed a letter in favour of " a single United Party " but on this occasion the Liberal Coalition ministers objected to any loss of their special identity and Bonar Law was not sorry about a postponement which in effect ended the possibility. There were also discussions about possible reunion of the Coalition and Asquithian Liberals which came to nothing. So Lloyd George was dependent on the trust and confidence of the House in a way which a normal party Premier was not. In the years before victory was in sight, Lloyd George faced the resentment of Asquith's Liberals and the suspicion of diehard Conservatives. A serious military reverse or accusations that he was thwarting trusted generals might well have undermined Bonar Law's capacity (or, in the last resort, his desire) to maintain the Coalition. Even after victory and the electoral landslide of December 1918 Lloyd George's great strength rested almost entirely on the success of his ministry and on fears of what might happen without him. Once the Coalition's fortunes waned, it was

---

[1] Sir Joseph Davies, *op. cit.*, p. 34. Davies was rejected as prospective candidate for a Liberal seat at Derby when the local association's preference for him was overruled by the Executive, on the Whips' recommendation, because he was " an Ll.G. man."

[2] Lord Riddell's *Intimate Diary of the Peace Conference and After*, p. 126.

bound to occur to Conservatives that they might save their Party and their principles by withdrawing from this association. So there had to be a thread of confidence connecting the public, the Conservative Party and M.P.s, their leaders in the Cabinet and the Prime Minister. Any strains which were not immediately felt by ministers were soon registered by the lower ranks of the Party and the real difficulty was in assessing the intensity of feeling on any issue. One point was clear. Doubts about the reality of discontent could not be allowed to go too far as once the thread had snapped, the Coalition was at an end. It was hard to assess the situation at any point since criticism was not revealed by adverse votes in the House of Commons. So long as the parties in the Coalition backed Lloyd George, a majority was assured [3] and the problem was to put a proper value on smoke-room grumbling, lack of enthusiasm in the Chamber or at party conferences and complaints in certain parts of the Press. Bonar Law was adept at this and, while he remained, he was the Premier's mainstay. After he retired in May 1921 his successor, Austen Chamberlain, was less capable of sensing the situation, the degree of miscalculation being revealed when the Party rejected Chamberlain's advice at the Carlton Club on October 19, 1922.

If it was hard for contemporary politicians to estimate the earnestness of the government's back-bench critics, it is no easier for the historian. Austen Chamberlain thought that Lloyd George was too frightened of the House and that he should never have consented to a Court of Inquiry on the findings of the Mesopotamian Commission.[4] Some of the Prime Minister's advisers, such as Sir Frederick Guest and Christopher Addison, kept telling him he underestimated his strength in 1917 and 1918, saying that the generals had no great popular backing and that Conservative sentiment was behind him.[5] W. Ormsby-Gore, one of the Whips, reported that the House gave a false impression because it was

---

[3] The Coalition was defeated twice. The first time was in October 1919 in a minor amendment to the Aliens Bill, but " it required all Bonar Law's tact as leader to induce the House to reverse this decision." (Blake, *The Unknown Prime Minister*, p. 413.) The second occasion was over the Teachers' Superannuation Bill on May 16, 1932, when the Cabinet set up a committee to consider the points made in the Commons.

[4] Sir Charles Petrie, *Life and Letters of Austen Chamberlain*, Vol. II, p. 87.

[5] See Beaverbrook, *Men and Power, 1917–18*, p. 128, and Addison, *Four and a Half Years*, Vol. II, pp. 483 and 533.

largely empty. The most reliable Members were in the Administration or at the Front and the atmosphere created by the oddments who stayed to complain soon altered when the House filled.[6] But it is hard not to sympathise with Lloyd George when he confided to Lord Riddell in March 1918 that " my position is at the present time very difficult. I am not sure of the House of Commons." [7] Yet when the challenge came in the Maurice debate on May 8, he scored a decisive victory both in the argument and in the division, with a vote of 293 to 106.

Conversely, after 1918 and especially after Bonar Law had retired, Lloyd George tended to over-rate his strength in the House. He seldom attended, and his first appearance at Question Time after the formation of the Coalition was on November 13, 1919. When he did appear, the Prime Minister swept aside all objections and few ventured into the anti-government lobby. Once again, debates and division lists were no real guide to members' feelings. It is significant that the decision which ended the government was not taken in the House but at a private meeting in the Carlton Club.

Within this general framework, pressure could be brought to bear in several ways. The most obvious and direct influence was that of Cabinet Ministers when they felt and voiced the views of their followers. There is little doubt that the exclusion of Beaverbrook, Churchill and Northcliffe in December 1916 was based on suspicions that had spread throughout the Conservative Party and Lloyd George had the greatest difficulty in giving the two former men office later on in the war. If the leaders did not share the views of the body of the party, restlessness in the House served as a warning. No Cabinet relished the prospect of such men as Churchill and Carson, unattached to the Government, giving impetus to the tides of doubt that sometimes moved the Commons. Backbench opinion was also voiced by the Unionist War Committee. This body tended to support the generals, though dislike of Asquith kept it loyal to Lloyd George during the Maurice debate.[8] Even

6 *Milner Papers*, Letters, Vol. 6, Report submitted on November 1, 1917.
7 Lord Riddell's *War Diary*, p. 317.
8 This was a debate in the House of Commons on charges by General Sir Frederick Maurice that Lloyd George and Bonar Law had made inaccurate statements in Parliament on military matters. The debate, on May 8, 1918, became a major test for the Government.

if unwilling to vote against the government, members might sign letters of protest in the hope that a long list of signatures would move the Cabinet. One hundred Conservatives put their names to a resolution of protest when Churchill was readmitted to the Cabinet and in April 1919 370 M.P.s signed a letter to Lloyd George in Paris urging him " to present the Bill in full " to the Germans. Later, in June 1921, 180 Conservatives supported a request that Addison be dismissed from the Ministry of Health, while 300 signed a motion for a select Committee on the award of honours in 1922. Lastly, the National Union of Conservative Associations could reveal the sentiments that were prevalent among the hard core of party enthusiasts. When the Annual Conference of the National Union passed a resolution in favour of Tariff Reform in June 1919, it was a declaration against fusion with the Coalition Liberals.[9] In late 1921 there were fears that the Conservative Annual Conference at Liverpool might condemn the negotiations with Sinn Fein and thus undermine the whole position of the Government. F. E. Smith (by then Lord Birkenhead) travelled to Liverpool and persuaded the most influential local Conservative figure, Alderman Stanley Salvidge, that negotiations should be allowed to continue—a view which the conference later accepted with reluctance. In October 1922 the monthly meeting of the Executive of the National Union had a motion aimed against the Coalition on its agenda but allowed it to be withdrawn. Austen Chamberlain refused to put the question of an election and of maintaining the Coalition to the Annual Conference. He could not, however, avoid a party meeting, once the National Executive decided to call an emergency conference on these issues.[10]

In resisting such pressures, the Prime Minister had a variety of weapons. During the War, Lloyd George could count on the backing of individuals of repute such as Milner and Smuts because he looked the best man to lead the country to victory. He could even use the generals against the admirals.[11] But this kind of support faded after hostilities ceased and Lloyd George, as leader of a mixed and increasingly restive Coalition, was driven back on his capacity to appeal to the people in terms of his own

[9] Lord Birkenhead, *Frederick Edwin, Earl of Birkenhead* (1935 edition), Vol. II, p. 129.
[10] A party meeting consisted of all M.P.s and endorsed candidates.
[11] A. N. Gollin, *op. cit.*, pp. 431–432.

choosing and to win an election. Most Conservative leaders had grave doubts about their party's capacity to secure a majority single-handed—a feat which it had not achieved since 1900. If Lloyd George was able to further Conservative policies, stave off the Labour Party and Asquith's Liberals and give his allies a preponderant share in political power, Conservative statesmen had every reason for persuading their followers to accept the adjustments and concessions imposed by life in a Coalition. But the motive for accepting the strains of Coalition life declined once the Prime Minister's stock in the country fell and he looked less powerful as an election winner. After Bonar Law retired in 1921, friction between Lloyd George and a series of his ministers— Churchill, F. E. Smith, Montagu and Curzon—all endangered the Prime Minister's position.

So long as the official Conservative leaders supported Lloyd George, back-benchers and the party conferences could be managed. The normal threats of withdrawal of the Party Whip or official ostracism had much less effect if the local association joined its Member in disliking the Coalition, but neither M.P.s nor party stalwarts liked opposing their leaders, especially if the latter were evidently to continue in power. In the last resort, Lloyd George could always use the weapon which no party Premier likes (or usually needs) to use against his own followers, the threat of a general election. Bonar Law had considered a dissolution to defeat Asquith and his supporters in early 1918. Later, when 370 members questioned the Prime Minister's policy in April 1919, Lloyd George told them that if their objections continued, he would ask the constituencies to settle the matter. In June 1921 he was again contemplating a general election to restore his authority. Conservative M.P.s who talked of running on an independent or non-coalition basis before the Carlton Club decision in 1922 had to face the danger that if the Coalition decided to fight as a unit, they might well be wiped out by official candidates.

There was much discussion at this time of the Press entering the political arena as a separate force which could affect political decisions and influence governments. Leading newspapers no longer, as in the 1880s and 1890s, attached themselves to particular parties or policies and acted merely as mouthpieces of the politicians. Newspaper owners like Beaverbrook, Northcliffe, Rothermere and Riddell had their own views and might press for single points, attack individuals, or offer their support on certain conditions. In October 1918 Northcliffe told Riddell (to tell Lloyd George) that he could not back " a new government . . . unless he knows definitely in writing, and can approve, the personal constitution of that Government."[12] Later Northcliffe asked if he could be a member of the British delegation at Versailles and then if he could manage official propaganda for the government—all these requests being refused. Beaverbrook used his *Daily Express* to support Lloyd George in 1918, but he attacked Churchill's intervention in Russia, pressed for heavy taxation of fortunes made in the war, urged a settlement with Sinn Fein, and finally advocated the breakup of the Coalition.

In all such campaigns the Press could only have influence if it affected the conduct of ministers or of M.P.s, or if it changed the public's voting habits but none of these were easy achievements. In wartime the Press had extra power in that it might make accusations or revelations which the government were wishing to prevent or could not contradict. The generals knew the value of such backing and kept most of the Press on their side, but it was hard to stampede the politicians or the voters unless there was considerable evidence to support any charges. Northcliffe's charge that Lloyd George was capitulating to the Germans in early 1919 was worked up inside and outside the Commons but collapsed when the Prime Minister counter-attacked on both fronts. A good example of successful pressure was Beaverbrook's campaign for an end to the embargo on the admission of Canadian cattle to Britain. The minister concerned, Sir A. Griffith-Boscawen, had to be returned at a difficult by-election with the tide running against him. The *Daily Express* attacked on this single point and he was defeated. Whether the paper's opposition was instrumental or not is difficult to say, but Griffith-Boscawen thought so. He agreed with the *Daily Express* that a Royal Commission should be appointed to review the Canadian cattle question and was left alone by the paper at his next by-election. When the Commission reported in favour,

12 Lord Riddell's *War Diary*, p. 366.

the House was given a free vote and the Canadian cattle were consequently admitted.[13]

In these years the Press often brought issues before the public in a more challenging manner than the Parliamentary Opposition. But papers could also be persuaded to put the ministers' case. Lloyd George had had a Press section under Sir William Sutherland in his entourage at 10 Downing Street, from May 1917. It was most successful in projecting the Prime Minister's personality and was so assiduous that sometimes other ministers felt credit was being transferred from them to Lloyd George.[14] In late 1918, Lloyd George asked Beaverbrook to recruit general support among the Press for the forthcoming election. While such careful use of connections with Fleet Street had obvious advantages it could also be damaging and in early 1918 the Commons were restive about the number of newspaper owners who were in or connected with the government. Austen Chamberlain, then out of office, won widespread applause for a speech deprecating these connections.

Although there was much excitement and some genuine fear over the power of the Press in these years, most politicians appreciated that once a leader had news value he could not be ignored and that the Press could raise questions only if there was a public ready to be interested in them. The full battery of Northcliffe's *Times*, *Daily Mail*, *Evening News* and *Weekly Dispatch* was turned against the Coalition during the 1918 election, yet this in no way diminished Lloyd George's victory. If the Cabinet or a Party was divided, Press criticism that brought out real public feeling might help tilt the balance, but in doing so the Press was only fulfilling its proper function as a medium of communication between the public and the politicians.

All the forms of pressure that could be exercised for or against the government came into play in the last throes of the Coalition.[15] In 1921 Lloyd George faced the hostility of many Cabinet colleagues and open resentment among some Conservative backbenchers. Attempts were made to bring back Bonar Law or to canvass alternative leaders. In June the Prime Minister fought off an attack over Dr. Addison's salary as Minister without Portfolio

[13] See Beaverbrook, *Politicians and the Press*, pp. 23–34.
[14] Addison, *Politics from Within*, Vol. II, p. 147.
[15] See the account in Beaverbrook, *The Decline and Fall of Lloyd George*.

by making a large concession. Each group was manipulating the Press. In the autumn the Irish question increased tension though Lloyd George established an alliance with F. E. Smith and Churchill in the Cabinet and Beaverbrook outside. The Prime Minister and this inner group contemplated going to the country as a Coalition in December, 1921, but the Chairman of the Conservative Party, Sir George Younger, not only objected but told the Press. The result was a series of declarations by 184 local associations and by individual M.P.s that they would not support or run as Coalition candidates. The temper of government backbenchers in the House deteriorated and the party organisation, reinforced by Sir Leslie Wilson, the Chief Whip, indicated that the strain on loyalty to the leadership was becoming unbearable. The Conservative Press, joined by Beaverbrook's *Daily Express* (which had formerly backed Lloyd George), now gave point to these feelings. In retaliation Conservative ministers in the Cabinet including their Leader, Austen Chamberlain, worked hard to maintain unity. The effect was to undermine Lloyd George's authority over his colleagues. Beaverbrook said that " thereafter the Prime Minister was not even ' first among equals ' " [16] but, over the Genoa Conference, the Cabinet held together as it did in the Chanak crisis. Yet rank-and-file discontent was increasing and Bonar Law had indicated his return to politics with a letter to *The Times*. If Lloyd George could have held an election with his leadership endorsed by the official Conservative leaders, the dangers and dilemmas that would have faced those who disliked the Coalition would have been intolerable. So the entire effort of the critics was aimed at preventing such an election, while Lloyd George, for his part, could not act without the agreement of such men as Chamberlain, Balfour, F. E. Smith, Sir Robert Horne and Churchill. Chamberlain and his associates decided to call a party meeting and quell the rebels before holding the election. At this point, however, Bonar Law confirmed his return to politics by announcing that he preferred to abandon the Coalition. The arrival of a trusted alternative leader rallied and reassured all those who were discontented, and at the Carlton Club meeting the Coalition was rejected by 187 votes to eighty-seven.

[16] *Ibid.*, p. 141.

CHAPTER 17

THE PLACE OF THE CROWN

IT might be thought that the diffusion of political power in the early years of the war—a situation which was not fully remedied till late in 1918—would have left greater scope for royal initiative. Yet this was not so. Intense party warfare between 1910 and 1914 had required the most careful neutrality from George V but had also emphasised the position of the Crown as a non-political centre of loyalty. During the war, leaders, coalitions or parties might fail but the nation remained united in purpose and the King no longer felt isolated as the sole symbol of national unity.

Up till December 1916 King George had received a regular letter from the Prime Minister describing the opinions and decisions of each Cabinet. After the Cabinet secretariat began work he was sent a copy of the minutes. The Prime Minister had regular audiences and the Secretaries of State for Foreign Affairs or for War called when any special matters arose which they felt they ought to convey in person. Normally the King never wrote to the Cabinet and there are only records of two letters from him. In July 1915 Stamfordham wrote explaining the King's anxieties about a Welsh coal strike and in 1921 he sent a letter to Hankey saying that " His Majesty is very much troubled by the unemployment question. . . . As the King hopes that the question will come before the Cabinet at an early date, he would ask you to lay before them . . . this letter. . . . He does most earnestly trust that the Government will agree to some scheme by which work and not doles, will be supplied. . . . It is impossible to expect people to subsist on the unemployment benefit of 15s." [1] On August 24, 1915, Asquith, Grey, Kitchener and Balfour went to Buckingham Palace to explain the problems of manpower and the royal proclamation that would be needed even for a limited form of conscription. This audience became a round table discussion with the King, but it was noted by the participants just because it was so unusual.[2] Apart from

---

[1] H. Nicolson, *King George V*, p. 342.
[2] Asquith, *op. cit.*, Vol. II, p. 108.

401

these contacts with his ministers, the King was entitled to reports from the commanders in the field, from the Viceroy of India and from Governors General and ministers at foreign capitals.

King George was quite clear about his own position. He was entitled to full information and could, if he felt it was necessary, express his views bluntly and strongly, but there was never any question of denying the politicians' right to make the ultimate decisions. All the experience of his early difficult years on the throne and the advice of Stamfordham confirmed this standpoint.

So the only influence which the King could have was by warning, advising and encouraging certain individuals, since he had virtually no dealings with the Cabinet and none with politicians outside the government. The chief line of influence open to the King was through conversation with the Prime Minister. King George told Asquith in May 1915 that he hoped the new Cabinet would include a Minister of Munitions in the person of Lloyd George and in September 1919 he indicated grave alarm over the policy of reprisals in Ireland and the conduct of the Black and Tans. He could also offer help or moral support. When Asquith's Cabinet was divided over conscription, the King told Asquith that " he would stand by him and support him, even if all his colleagues were to leave," in the attempt to prevent any compulsion.[3] Lloyd George threatened to resign a few months later if there were more delays over conscription and Lord Reading, on Asquith's behalf, suggested to the King that direct royal pressure would be unwise but that Stamfordham might try to dissuade Lloyd George. The appeal failed and conscription was announced.

The King was entitled to consider any request for a dissolution and might, in certain very special situations, refuse.[4] In December 1916 the capacity to threaten a dissolution was a major asset for the prospective Prime Minister, but King George announced " that he would refuse, if asked, to accord . . . a dissolution," [5] because it would cause too much upheaval and mutual recrimination when all should be united in prosecuting the war. Bonar Law was worried by this remark, but the King's words were a little ambiguous. He had first put the question to Lord Haldane. " If

---

[3] Nicolson, *op. cit.*, p. 272.
[4] See above, Chapter 1, pp. 16–17.
[5] Nicolson, *op. cit.*, p. 289.

the King were asked to dissolve Parl. as a condition of anyone undertaking to form a Government, could His Majesty constitutionally refuse to do so? " [6] Haldane's reply was rather pedantic. He said the King could not bargain about a dissolution with a potential Prime Minister but that once the man had kissed hands as Prime Minister, the only alternative to accepting his advice was dismissing him and this was a very dangerous step. It seems that when the King said he would refuse to grant a dissolution, he meant only that he would not promise it to a potential Prime Minister.[7] It would certainly have been both unlikely and unwise to him to have refused a request from Lloyd George once the latter had been announced as Premier. In fact, Lloyd George told Conservative ex-ministers a few days later that he would, if necessary, adopt this expedient. In November 1918 the King still did not like the idea of a dissolution, preferring to wait till the country had settled down a little, but when Lloyd George was evidently intent on an election he gave way.

The one difficulty in these years was that the King, quite rightly, kept in close contact with his generals and when they resisted political control, he was in the awkward position of getting views, if not advice, from rival camps. King George was on good terms with Kitchener and when the latter refused Asquith's suggestion that he might become Commander-in-Chief (May 1915), the King agreed with his decision. " You have acted very rightly about the question of C.-in-C. It is important that whatever happens you remain Secretary of State." [8] One should not be misled by the King's blunt style. If Asquith and his Cabinet had insisted, Kitchener would have had to obey, but when much turned on Kitchener consenting to move the King's views definitely stiffened his inclination to refuse. By the time Lloyd George became Prime Minister, the King was a partisan and urged " that the politicians should leave the war to experts." [9] Sir William Robertson had been pressing such views on King George since he had become C.I.G.S., while Haig was a personal friend who visited Buckingham

---

[6] Nicolson, *op. cit.*, pp. 288–289.

[7] It is interesting that the King did not take this view in 1931. Then he not only discussed the possibility of a dissolution but promised to grant one to Ramsay MacDonald if and when he became the Prime Minister in a National Government. Nicolson, *op. cit.*, p. 465.

[8] Sir Philip Magnus, *op. cit.*, p. 341.

[9] Nicolson, *op. cit.*, p. 288.

Palace whenever he came to London. For most of the time Lord Derby was at the War Office he both backed up the generals and was a method of conveying their views and information about Cabinet discussions to the King. George V appears to have felt uneasy about the tone of his correspondence with the generals for he told Haig " that no one but he and Wigram (his Assistant Private Secretary) would know what I had written." " He would treat my letters as secret, and would not reply. . . . " [10] There was a constant flow of semi-political opinions from Haig and Robertson to the King, but it stopped at the Palace. There is no evidence that the King used this information or passed it on in any way that prejudiced the position of his ministers. All that happened was that his evident sympathy encouraged the generals, though neither Haig nor Robertson would have flinched in pressing their case whatever the King's attitude. When, in early 1918, Robertson did not want to remain as C.I.G.S. with restricted powers and royal influence was brought to bear on him to stay, he said he would not do so " even for the King." [11] The furthest King George ever went in encouragement of the generals was to tell Haig that if he had heard at the time of the Cabinet decision to put the British armies under Nivelle,[12] he " would have unquestionably demanded further explanation before giving his consent to the proposal." " You are not to worry: you may be certain that he [King George] will do his utmost to protect your interests." [13] Here again all that the King meant was that he would press Haig's views on the Prime Minister. In February 1918, when Stamfordham stated that the King " strongly deprecated the idea of Robertson being removed from the post of C.I.G.S.," Lloyd George simply said that if this was the case " the Government could not carry on and His Majesty must find other Ministers." Stamfordham at once retracted and assured Lloyd George that the King " had no idea of making any such insistence." [14]

King George was also entitled to discuss appointments and he

[10] *Haig's Papers*, pp. 97–98.
[11] Nicolson, *op. cit.*, p. 321.
[12] The minute of the War Cabinet at which this decision was reached was not sent to the King till after the Calais Conference had met and the arrangement announced to the British generals.
[13] *Haig's Papers*, pp. 205–206.
[14] Owen, *op. cit.*, p. 461.

could voice objections or help persuade the reluctant to take office. He had " grave misgivings " about the recall of Fisher as First Sea Lord in 1914 (Fisher was 74 years old), and when Churchill insisted he recorded his objections in a formal letter.[15] Through his contacts in the Army and on his visits to the Front the King became aware that Sir John French had lost the confidence of many officers by the autumn of 1915. Haig, in his diaries, gives the King some credit for the change in command when Haig replaced French as Commander-in-Chief. This is understandable as the generals had always overrated royal influence. French had had a heart attack on November 6, was distrusted in the Army and ignored in Whitehall. Asquith was, no doubt, encouraged by the King's approval, but he hesitated in making the changes (announced on December 10) solely because the senior ministers wished to reduce Kitchener's powers at the same time and Asquith preferred to wait till the Secretary of State was safely despatched on a tour of the Near East. In February 1918 the King objected to the appointment of Lord Beaverbrook as Chancellor of the Duchy of Lancaster and did not like the idea of F. E. Smith as Lord Chancellor in December of that year, but Lloyd George was not deflected in either case.

On certain occasions, the King offered his services in making public pronouncements. He took a pledge to consume no alcohol for the duration of hostilities as drinking was hampering the war effort in certain areas. This gesture had little effect. In June 1921 King George told Smuts how much he deplored the situation in Ireland. Smuts suggested that he should take advantage of an engagement to open the Northern Irish Parliament and make an appeal for conciliation. The Prime Minister agreed and a suitable speech was drafted. The result was a resumption of negotiations. At a later stage, when fresh difficulties arose, the King moderated the language used by Lloyd George. His advice and position as a respected figure above the battle therefore contributed materially both in starting and in continuing the final series of discussions.

King George had always taken a special interest in honours and decorations, but the Prime Minister was able to insist on all his nominations. The King objected strongly to the award of a peerage to Lord Beaverbrook when the Coalition Government was formed. Northcliffe was granted a higher title in 1917 and Sir Edward

---

[15] Blake, *The Unknown Prime Minister*, p. 236, and Nicolson, *op. cit.*, p. 251.

Russell and Sir Henry Dalziel, among others, were ennobled despite objections from the Palace. Similar resistance delayed an advance in the peerage for Lord Rothermere for a year and kept Sir Edward Hulton to a baronetcy. Sir George Riddell was not only the tenth newspaperman to receive an honour from Lloyd George but was also divorced and yet Lloyd George forced his name on to the list of peers. That the King had been justified in making certain objections came out when questions in the Commons and a Royal Commission revealed that there had been some trafficking in honours.

So the King discharged his duties and made the maximum use of the limited opportunities open to him for advising his chief minister. Differences occasionally arose (as over the question of Lord Hardinge's resignation [16]) and both King George and Lloyd George were given to blunt statements, but there was never any serious departure from the rule which the King and Lord Stamfordham had evolved, of leaving government and politics to the politicians.[17]

CONCLUSION

Thus the war and Coalition confirmed and advanced earlier developments. In some cases, such as the disbandment of the Garden Suburb, the reaction to wartime conditions and Lloyd George's dominance produced definite attempts to turn the clock back. But the major changes in practice and emphasis that had come about by 1922 remained. The House of Commons, despite the special weaknesses of the Coalition leadership, declined as an agency of effective criticism and containment of the executive. Attendance at debates was thin, few front-benchers bothered to sit

[16] Lord Hardinge was criticised by the Commission on Mesopotamia and Lloyd George suggested he should resign before the debate in the Commons. The King regretted that Hardinge should be asked to go and the Prime Minister said such interventions were undesirable. Ultimately Balfour (Hardinge's chief) refused to accept his resignation and he remained as Permanent Under Secretary at the Foreign Office.

[17] The only authority for this period who talks as if the King did possess some real power is Lord Beaverbrook. Of several hints and suggestions to this effect, the most definite is his remark that if, in early 1918, Haig, Robertson and several Conservative politicians had resigned, the King " might decide to refuse a dissolution, and dismiss his Prime Minister, setting up a new administration." There is no evidence for this and it would have been totally out of keeping with the King's practices and principles. See *Men and Power, 1917–18*, pp. 205–208.

and listen to private Members' views and ministers were chosen for their administrative capacity or for their political weight, but debating skill now mattered less. The machinery of government had expanded far beyond the limits of what had been thought possible or desirable a generation earlier. Amid the complex of decision-taking bodies, the Cabinet had receded in prominence and the Prime Minister had added to his authority. Lloyd George had shown that an able Premier who had the backing of the country (even without the support of a party machine) might well dominate an entire administration. In this case, so long as the Prime Minister had the confidence of his colleagues, government consisted not just of the Cabinet but of a series of ministers, committees, conferences and departments radiating downwards from the Prime Minister. Of these bodies, the Cabinet was far and away the most important, not because it necessarily took the major decisions (though most of them passed through the Cabinet), but because if the Prime Minister or his senior colleagues blundered, or if disputes arose, it was the Cabinet alone that had the right to complain, and it was there that unresolved disagreements or restored harmony would finally be registered.

Part Six

The Cabinet in Modern Conditions

CHAPTER 18

THE MODERN CABINET

SINCE the 1920's there have been changes in the practice of British government and the tone of British politics, but the relations between the Prime Minister, the Cabinet, the Civil Service, Parliament and the public have remained sufficiently similar to permit analytic rather than chronological treatment. Lloyd George for a time established an ascendancy which few later Premiers could have exceeded without altering the nature of British government. The House of Commons has had periods of greater and of less activity but its essential powers have remained at the level permitted by the Standing Orders of 1902, though a better appreciation of its position by the public has tended to diminish its prestige. The administration has grown and become further involved with industry, public services and individual welfare and has developed increased self-confidence and momentum. Yet the balance of forces within the constitution has not altered to any marked extent, though the working of the system has been adapted for quiet negative government, for emergency reactions in war and for various styles of leadership in the post-war period.

One development that has become more marked is that the ministry has become a much larger and more complex hierarchy: it is no longer merely the Cabinet. Whereas in 1923 there were only 59 ministers (including the Cabinet), under Mr. Wilson the number has risen to 100. Thus in modern conditions a distinction can arise between the duties of the government with its many decision-taking committees and the functions of the most senior committee, the Cabinet. In terms of the actual agenda of the Cabinet, there have been fewer changes. Throughout the history of the Cabinet, the management of Parliament and of the government's supporters has always come second to the major task of administration and this is still the case. Each week forthcoming parliamentary business is discussed, the Leader of the House (since 1940 a task no longer undertaken by the Prime Minister) and the Chief Whip being mainly concerned. (The Chief Whip attends all Cabinets but is not officially listed as a member.) [1] In such discussions there is little concern over the attitude of the opposition and government measures are expected to pass by the normal majority. Reactions among the government's own supporters in the House, the party at large, and among the public are considered much more carefully but are usually subsumed in the planning and discussion of all proposals. Twice since 1951 Conservative Cabinets have included the chairman of the party organisation in a non-departmental post, to help interpret the views of the Cabinet and the party to each other. On most occasions there is no need to devote special time or trouble to this aspect as the Cabinet members are themselves the foremost products of the party, but they will react at once if there is any hint of abstentions on the part of government back-benchers. Though such demonstrations are likely to be toned down to a level which will not be a serious threat, even a few abstentions will delight the newspapers and lead to damaging talk of a " split." It is, therefore, important to carry all the Parliamentary Party with the government and, on the occasions when this is in doubt, the problem will come before the Cabinet.

The Cabinet also see the major policy decisions, but a body with an average number of twenty regularly facing a heavy agenda is not very suitable for thrashing out problems and making long-term plans. In recent years parties have tended to work out quite elaborate series of proposals when in opposition and to carry these with them into office. Once in office, policy is formed by the application of party principles to the problems raised by the departments. Decisions are made in the departments, in Cabinet Committees, in private talks between the Prime Minister and the ministers mainly concerned, the differences that remain being settled in the Cabinet itself. Governments are usually too busy to have much time for framing plans for the next quinquennium and this job is sometimes given to a Cabinet Committee. In 1929 and again in October 1935 the Conservative Cabinets set up committees of ministers to prepare an election programme. Normally, however, this task is discharged by some of the leading members of the

---

[1] It is difficult to establish which government began the practice of having the Chief Whip in constant attendance but it appears to have operated at least since the time of James Stuart, now Lord Findhorn, in the Second World War.

party organisation in consultation with the Premier and a few senior ministers.

The main task of the Cabinet is to co-ordinate the work of the various departments and committees and thus ensure that the activity of the government has a certain coherence. The Cabinet performs this function in that almost all the main decisions are reported to it. Ministers outside the Cabinet who are taking any important steps are called in to announce and explain them. If the work of one department is lagging behind, as when the Labour Minister of Transport (Mr. Alfred Barnes) was showing no evidence of preparations for the nationalisation of the railways, the Cabinet may simply order the work to be done. In dealing with Bills proposed by the various departments and the fixing of estimates, the Cabinet acts as a court of appeal when agreement cannot be reached either at inter-departmental talks or at a Cabinet Committee.

The Prime Minister and Foreign Secretary may take many steps on their own initiative but their policies have to be outlined to the Cabinet.[2] Even the strongest Foreign Secretary has to make his weekly statements to his colleagues. Some matters are, by convention, outside the normal purview of the Cabinet. The Chancellor of the Exchequer is expected merely to submit his Budget proposals, changes in the Bank Rate or in the rate of exchange. Neville Chamberlain did not inform his colleagues of his plans to convert £2,000 million of 5 per cent. War Loan to $3\frac{1}{2}$ per cent. in June 1932 till the last moment. Yet in all these cases, as in the series of measures to combat inflation taken by Mr. Thorneycroft in 1957,[3] the financial proposals are part of a general economic policy which has come before the Cabinet in many segments and been approved. In 1967 the decision to devalue was taken by the Prime Minister and the Chancellor of the Exchequer but was reported to the Cabinet which sat some time later (for a total period of thirty-two hours) to work out the complementary economic measures. Despite the convention that the Cabinet is merely informed of the Budget, a clear consensus of opinion against a given proposal can produce a change, the

---

[2] It is true that policies may simply be reported to and barely noticed by the Cabinet, as happened over the decision of the 1945–50 Labour Government to manufacture an A Bomb.

[3] See above, Chapter 1, pp. 26–28.

Labour Cabinet of 1945–51 on one occasion refusing to accept an alteration in the tax on fuel oils and on another Hugh Dalton made marginal changes after the Cabinet meeting.[4] Similarly the Home Secretary is solely responsible for deciding whether to grant a reprieve, and the Colonial Secretary had the same right in cases arising in the colonies. But when, for example, the death sentence was passed on young Cypriots for offences during the struggles for independence in the late 1950s, the Cabinet might well have broken through the convention to consider the effect of executions on world opinion or on negotiations about the future of the island. An earlier example of the way political implications force Cabinet consideration of a matter normally reserved to a specific minister arose over the capture of the Irish nationalist Roger Casement in 1916, when it took four Cabinet meetings to decide on execution.[5] The Colonial Secretary, likewise, had a free hand in the selection of governorships, as had the Secretary of State for India in his sphere before 1947, though both operated within the framework of a policy known to and approved by the Cabinet.

So the major task of the Cabinet is not to lead the party, to manage Parliament or to think out policy; it is to take or review the major decisions, to consider (though not necessarily at the formative stage) any proposals that might affect the future of the government and to ensure that no departmental interests are overlooked, thus giving the work of the government a measure of unity.

The limitations on the scope of Cabinets before the 1880s were far-reaching and complex but they came principally from the power of the House of Commons. Once Parliament had been persuaded to grant money or pass a Bill (regulating factory hours, granting votes or setting up county councils), the matter was settled. It was appropriate, therefore, in the sections of this book dealing with the nineteenth century to look at these limitations on the Cabinet before examining the institution itself. Since the introduction of universal suffrage (for men 1918, for women 1928), the party system has become much stronger. Once a general election is won, the victors remain in power, barring a total collapse, till the legal period of the Parliament nears its end or the Prime Minister chooses to go to the country. While there

---

4 Hugh Dalton, *High Tide and After*, p. 25.
5 R. Jenkins, *op. cit.*, pp. 403–404.

is now a degree of stability and certainty on the political side, the pitfalls and problems lie more in the intractable nature of the tasks a government faces—balance of payments deficits, colour conflicts, traffic congestion. Failure to solve these problems has little immediate effect on the strength of a government as there may be some time before the verdict of the polls though gross unpopularity can weaken a government.

The changes mentioned have tipped the balance of power in favour of the executive and in so doing have strengthened and confirmed the special position of the Prime Minister. Once a party has selected its leader and he has presided over an electoral victory (or inherits a majority) the Prime Minister can then choose his colleagues. He can promote or dismiss ministers, he sets the tone of the government, guides its policies and determines the date of the next dissolution. In certain circumstances, which will be examined below, these powers can be circumscribed and the Prime Minister can prefer or be made to share them with other leading figures in his party but, barring quite exceptional situations, it is impossible to remove a Prime Minister.

From such a position of power he and his colleagues rule through the House of Commons and the Civil Service; they deal with the pressure groups and the other central, intermediate and local agencies necessary for modern administration. It is therefore more appropriate in this period to reverse the order of treatment. The Prime Minister is discussed first, then his relations with his colleagues and the place of the Cabinet within the government as a whole. Having examined the centre of executive direction, it is logical to look at the influences which might divert, retard or accelerate action. The first is the effect of Parliament and of forms of public pressure such as the Press, interest groups, opinion polls and by-elections. The second is the way a complex administrative machine can condition its operators.

But since the keystone of the arch is the Prime Minister, it is best to start with his appointment. Till 1965 it could be argued that one of the few remaining situations where royal influence could have a marginal effect was if the Conservatives were in doubt as to which of several candidates should be their leader. To set this part of the process in its proper perspective, the first chapter deals with the Crown.

CHAPTER 19

THE CROWN

As Sir Harold Nicolson has said, King George the Fifth had " an unfailing desire to observe the strict proprieties of constitutional theory " [1] which meant that he could express his views in the most forthright manner, but all decisions were left entirely in the hands of the politicians. When he was asked how he was getting on with his first Labour Government, the King replied: " Very well. My grandmother would have hated it; my father would have tolerated it; but I move with the times." [2]

Information reached the King in the form of Cabinet minutes, regular interviews with the Prime Minister and Foreign Secretary and letters from the Viceroy of India and Colonial Governors. There was still a daily letter during the parliamentary session describing the situation in the House, but though of interest and of help in conveying atmosphere and the relations of individuals, these reports could cast little light on government policy and were written by a junior Whip.

King George never hesitated in making his opinions known. He told Ramsay MacDonald at their first interview that he objected to some of Lansbury's remarks, he thought the combination of the Foreign Office and Premiership was too much for one man, he hoped he would not have to meet any ambassador from Russia, and could the Labour Party give up its practice of singing the " Red Flag "? Later he urged Stanley Baldwin to come " to really close and powerful grips with such questions as housing, unemployment, the cost of food and education." [3] In 1926 he warned the government of the dangers of undue provocation during the General Strike and especially of any attempt to stop the banks paying out money to strikers.

On the matter of appointments, the King sometimes expressed a view but he never went any further. In 1924 he told Baldwin

---

[1] *King George V, His Life and Reign*, p. 427.
[2] Lord Riddell's *Intimate Diary of the Peace Conference and After*, p. 413.
[3] Nicolson, *op. cit.*, p. 403.

that he would be glad to see Austen Chamberlain as Foreign
Secretary. When a successor was required for Lord Reading as
Viceroy, King George suggested Haig but the Cabinet wanted
a civilian. He then put forward the name of Edward Wood (later
Lord Halifax) and this was welcomed on all sides. One of Arthur
Henderson's first actions after becoming Foreign Secretary in 1929
was to call for the resignation of Lord Lloyd as High Commissioner for Egypt. The King was unhappy about this decision but
his only comment was that Lloyd had a right to a full account of
the government's reasons. King George also thought that the proposed Anglo-Egyptian Treaty of that year was unsatisfactory but
here his doubts were encouraged by hints that the Prime Minister
shared his views. When the Ministry was being formed in 1929, the
King had actually suggested that J. H. Thomas should go to the
Foreign Office but this question was settled entirely by Henderson,
Thomas and MacDonald. In 1931 Baldwin rejected King George's
notion that he might go to the Exchequer and leave Neville
Chamberlain to the Ministry of Health.

Only once after 1922 is there any record of the King's views
being mentioned in the Cabinet. This was when he took the
strongest exception to the way in which Allenby, dressed in civilian
clothes and backed by cavalry, had demanded reparation from the
King of Egypt after the murder of Lee Stack. In 1926 and 1929,
Stamfordham asked for sections of the King's speech to be rewritten
to give " a more direct, personal and stirring appeal " and this
was done. King George did press his objection to receiving any
ambassador from the régime which had murdered his cousins, the
Tsar, the Tsarina and their children. Arthur Henderson reported
that " I didn't argue or interrupt. I just let him run on. And then
I said: ' Well, your Majesty, that's the Cabinet decision, to
exchange Ambassadors, but perhaps the Prince of Wales could
receive him for you? ' " [4] And this solution was adopted.

The two situations in which it was possible that there might
have been an element of discretion open to the Crown were the
selection of a Prime Minister when no party had a clear majority
or the Conservatives had not selected a leader, and the decision
to grant a dissolution. King George took the quite proper view

[4] H. Dalton, *Call Back Yesterday*, p. 233.

that his task was to encourage stable government and to avoid frequent and unnecessary elections. But he also realised that he could not reject the advice of a Prime Minister in any other than exceptional circumstances.[5] So he tried to dissuade Stanley Baldwin from going to the country in November 1923 when the Parliament was barely a year old, though this had no effect.[6] In October 1924 he was reluctant to grant MacDonald's request but the Labour Government had a proper claim to put its case to the electorate and the other parties were also eager for an election. The King contented himself with a minute in which he explained his regret at the Prime Minister's request. He considered that an election caused dislocation, that the Campbell case was not a vital issue on which to go to the country and that there was a possibility that the parties would be returned in roughly their existing numbers. In fact, no other decision was feasible once the Liberals and Conservatives had decided not to take office and the election did produce a definite result.

The one occasion on which King George had been accused of intervening in an unconstitutional manner was during the collapse of the second Labour Ministry and the creation of a national government in 1931. The criticisms have variations of emphasis but the essence is that the King should have accepted MacDonald's resignation and called on the Leader of the Conservatives, Stanley Baldwin, to form a government. Instead, he took advice from all the party leaders and then asked MacDonald to become Prime Minister in a national government. The suggestion is that MacDonald was asked to take this post on a personal basis rather than as the Leader of the Labour Party and that the King ought to have realised that the effect would be to paralyse any further opposition from the Left. It is argued that leaders only have standing because they command a following in Parliament, and to act in a manner which leads to a disruption of this relationship is to

---

[5] See above, pp. 16–17. These are, briefly, that an election would be unlikely to give any definite result and that an alternative combination with a definite majority in the House of Commons is ready and willing to take office.

[6] He also urged Baldwin to meet Parliament rather than resign after hearing the results of the election. Baldwin wished to put the onus of installing a Labour Government on the Liberals and had already decided on this course of action.

intervene in politics and may be very dangerous for the Crown.[7] The same situation might have arisen, for instance, had divisions in the Conservative Cabinet over the attack on Suez become so acute as to have led the Prime Minister to resign. Then Mr. Gaitskell announced that he would support a temporary national government under the leading anti-Suez Conservative. The Crown might well have welcomed such a solution and pressed it upon the appropriate politicians. In this case the sort of doubts raised by the 1931 situation would certainly have recurred.

Yet in such circumstances, there is only one line of action open to the Crown. If some or, as in 1931, all the party leaders advise a national government, the King must accept. The only alternatives are to insist that the leaders consult their Cabinets or Shadow Cabinets, or for the Crown to sound senior Privy Councillors on each side. In the first case, such a consultation would be pointless, since it is Cabinet divisions that have caused the crisis and for the Crown to go behind leaders' backs to other Privy Councillors would invite endless charges of intrigue. If it is accepted that the party is the basis of parliamentary strength and that its unity must be respected, the Crown has no alternative but to deal with the accredited leader so long as he retains this title. There can be no doubt that, faced with the task of obtaining the strongest government possible and with the advice put before him in 1931, George the Fifth not only acted correctly but had no other choice open to him.

Apart from these two situations where an element of discretion may exist in very rare cases, the King's advice has influence only on the most minor matters or on individuals for whom royal wishes may make a difference. In 1926 Austen Chamberlain wanted King George to pay a state visit to Madrid, but accepted his reply that such occasions had ceased to have any political importance. After the National Government was formed, MacDonald came under heavy and bitter attack. Hoare observed that his " temperament needed a friend's encouragement. In the King, he found an adviser who was ready to give him a definite and straightforward answer to the questions that were worrying his over-sensitive

---

[7] The argument is put most cogently by G. C. Moddie, in " The Monarch and the Selection of a Prime Minister," *Political Studies*, February 1957. I am also grateful to J. D. Hargreaves for letting me see his unpublished reply.

mind." [8] Similarly a word from the King prevented Lord Burnham resigning from the Simon Commission before it had reported.[9]

Thus King George played precisely the role cast for a constitutional sovereign, standing aside from the government of the country, expressing his views on the issues put before him and very occasionally exercising a marginal influence on matters which were not of major political importance.

The abdication of Edward the Eighth reveals much about British government. When the Crown had definite power in the period before 1832, monarchs could behave as they liked, but once this authority disappeared and the chief value of the Crown was as a figurehead above controversy, no monarch could afford to violate accepted standards of belief or practice. Neville Chamberlain had prepared a memorandum of censure on the King six months before the abdication and before the question of Mrs. Simpson had been raised. It must, therefore, have dealt with Edward's failure to "settle down," his unconventional dress, his visits to areas of heavy unemployment and his attempts to interest Conservative Ministers in slum clearance. The memorandum " was discussed by an inner group of ministers, and Stanley Baldwin dissuaded them from sending it to the King." [10] Once the divorce case and the King's relations with Mrs. Simpson could be concealed no longer, Baldwin put the situation in simple, straightforward terms. The King must take his advice or it might mean the resignation of the government—and the Prime Minister had ascertained from the leaders of the Labour and Liberal Parties that they would not take advantage of such a situation and accept office. The advice was clear-cut. A morganatic marriage was rejected by the Cabinet and by the Dominions. Edward could give up the idea or abdicate. The King's ministers refused to permit him to broadcast his case

[8] Lord Templewood, *Nine Troubled Years*, p. 39.
[9] When Stanley Baldwin prepared to go for his annual holiday in Aix in August 1926, with the national coal strike still in full swing, " the King had plainly been shocked and Wigram said so as politely as possible." Baldwin was most upset but thought " that the King's view amounted to prohibition." The Prime Minister's *aides* felt that the only solution was to get him a medical certificate saying a holiday was essential. The trouble was that most of the leading doctors were on holiday, but a certificate was eventually produced, neither the King nor Baldwin being aware that it had been furnished by an eminent gynaecologist, and the Prime Minister departed to join Mrs. Baldwin at Aix.
[10] Tom Jones, *Diary with Letters*, p. 37.

to the people and insisted on a rapid decision. Edward had just the one choice before him and when he decided to leave, he agreed to Baldwin's request that a paragraph should be inserted in the abdication speech saying that the Prime Minister had always shown him every possible consideration. Not only does the episode underline the position of the Crown, but all the political decisions were taken by Baldwin and a few of his senior colleagues.[11] The rest of the Cabinet were merely informed of the position and asked to turn down the morganatic scheme. Parliament was told nothing until the whole question was settled.

George the Sixth determined to return to his father's emphasis on a quiet and normal family life, though he himself was politically naive and much less positive than George the Fifth. As a result, he was told less and contributed little of value in the way of comment. Edward VIII had stopped the nightly letter on parliamentary affairs, its place being taken by a short note of some 600 words on what had happened at Question Time, any ministerial statements and the tone of the opening speeches. It was felt that what happened after 6 p.m. in the House was more predictable and could wait till the next morning's papers. During the war, Mr. Churchill formed the habit of lunching with the King every Tuesday and a weekly meeting has been normal since 1945. The chief source of information other than these meetings was the Cabinet minutes, but in 1938 King George heard of Mr. Anthony Eden's resignation from the Press before the minutes had reached him. (It was agreed in future to speed matters by sending the King a draft copy.) Similarly, the King knew there had been friction between Hore-Belisha and some senior officers but he thought Neville Chamberlain was going to smooth it over. When news came that Hore-Belisha had been dismissed, "the King was as much surprised as anyone."[12] While King George was kept informed of most developments until August 1939, he could be told little during the war and often felt frustrated. In October 1943 General Smuts explained that Britain should concentrate on victory in Italy and invading the Balkans. King George was so

---

[11] King Edward saw Sir Samuel Hoare in the hope of winning him as a spokesman in the Cabinet, but "Mr. Baldwin, he warned me, was in command of the situation; the senior ministers were solidly with him on this issue." Lord Templewood, *op. cit.*, p. 220.

[12] J. W. Wheeler-Bennett, *King George VI, His Life and Reign*, p. 433.

impressed that he decided to use his constitutional right to suggest
the idea to Mr. Churchill. The King, General Smuts and the
Prime Minister dined together and Mr. Churchill explained why
his plans fitted all the Allies' requirements. When the time came
for the D-Day landings, Mr. Churchill and the King both wished
to watch them from a cruiser. Sir Alan Lascelles dissuaded his
master and the latter then urged Mr. Churchill to stay at home.
The Prime Minister said that in any case he would have advised
the Cabinet to refuse permission for the King. Lascelles then
asked if the Premier could leave the country without royal consent.
Mr. Churchill said he was going. Later he changed his mind but
argued that while the Cabinet could advise the sovereign not to go
" I do not admit that the Cabinet have any right to put restrictions
on my freedom of movement." [13]

King George's opinions were those of the moderate and politically uninterested London clubman. He had complete confidence
in Neville Chamberlain and the policy of appeasement and included
references to " the magnificent efforts of the Prime Minister " and
the need to " place entire confidence in . . . [our] leaders " in his
public messages.[14] During the " phoney war " period the King
suggested he should have a talk with the Labour and T.U.C.
leaders and urge them to give Chamberlain more whole-hearted
backing. Chamberlain agreed to this and told the King that he
found the opposition leaders in " a chastened mood " as a result.[15]
When the Prime Minister had suffered his serious loss of support
at the end of the Norwegian debate but was still hoping to carry on
as leader of a national government, the King again offered his
services. " I said to the P.M. would it help him if I spoke to Attlee
about the national standpoint of the Labour Party, and say that
I hoped that they would realise that they must pull their weight
and join the National Government." [16] This time Chamberlain
declined the offer, but King George still resented the way the
Premier " was always subject to a stab in the back from both the
House of Commons and the Press." [17] After it was definite that

13 Wheeler-Bennett, *op. cit.*, p. 606.
14 *Ibid.*, pp. 355 and 352.
15 Quoted from the King's Diary by Wheeler-Bennett, p. 431.
16 *Ibid.*, p. 439.
17 *Ibid.*, p. 440. He also thought that " the Conservative rebels like Duff Cooper
ought to be ashamed of themselves for deserting him at this moment."

Chamberlain could not remain, the King preferred Lord Halifax to Mr. Churchill but it was decided at a meeting between Chamberlain, Churchill and Halifax that the latter would be unsuitable and Chamberlain formally advised the King to send for Churchill. When the war was over, the Labour Government never experienced any difficulty with King George, though he had no understanding of its aims. In August 1947 he became alarmed by opposition criticism of the Supplies and Services (Extended Purposes) Bill and asked Mr. Attlee for an explanation. He was told politely that it was just a Conservative stunt. Yet there can be no doubt that the King felt a certain relief when Mr. Churchill returned to power in 1951.

With such few opportunities and having so little insight into the complexities of politics, King George had virtually no impact on public policy. He often offered to help his ministers and suggested that he might write to Hitler in 1938 " as one ex-serviceman to another." The ideas of writing to the Emperor of Japan and to King Victor Emmanuel were turned down, but he was asked to send messages to Boris of Bulgaria, President Lebrun, Marshal Pétain, King Farouk and finally President Roosevelt. The Conservative leaders in 1938 obtained the approval of the other parties for a royal broadcast appealing for voluntary national service but abandoned the idea when the Governor of the Bank of England and the Chief Press Liaison Officer of the Government said it would cause too much alarm and might lead to a slump on the Stock Exchange.[18] King George's name was used, however, in individual cases and when Lord Woolton was reluctant to move to the Ministry of Reconstruction during the war, a hint that it would please the King settled the matter.

The one occasion on which it has been alleged that the King's advice made a difference was when Mr. Attlee recommended Ernest Bevin rather than Mr. Dalton for the Foreign Office. Mr. Attlee at first intended to put Mr. Dalton at the Foreign Office but he has been quite explicit that he changed his mind because he wanted Bevin's extra weight in external affairs and because he wanted to keep Bevin well away from Mr. Morrison (who was on home affairs) as their relations were not always amicable. The dates completely support Mr. Attlee's account.

[18] J. W. Wheeler-Bennett, *John Anderson, Viscount Waverley*, pp. 219–220.

He visited the Palace on July 26 and heard the King's point of view. Next morning just before lunch Mr. Attlee saw Mr. Dalton and told him it was " almost certainly the Foreign Office." [19] At 4 p.m. that evening he told Mr. Dalton that it would be the Exchequer. So the Prime Minister changed his mind on the afternoon of July 27 after seeing a number of his colleagues and talking to the Chief Whip. There was no contact with the Palace on that day. There was, however, one rather curious proposal made during the war over which King George may have had some influence. Mr. Churchill considered sending Mr. Anthony Eden to succeed Linlithgow as Viceroy of India but the King said he wanted Mr. Eden in Britain during Mr. Churchill's absences. The Prime Minister then had some idea that Eden might be Viceroy but retain his seat in the Cabinet, an idea which was very properly scouted by the King, and Wavell was appointed.[20]

Little is known of the attitudes or practices of Queen Elizabeth the Second. However on two occasions she has had to face the problem of appointing a Prime Minister from within the Conservative Party following on the resignation of the existing leader. The first of these was when Sir Anthony Eden resigned in January 1957. There were two possible candidates for the leadership of the Conservative Party, Mr. Butler and Mr. Macmillan. The Queen's Secretaries proceeded to sound feeling as had been done when Bonar Law resigned in 1923. Many Conservative M.P.s and local dignitaries poured in letters and telegrams to the Chief Whip objecting to Mr. Butler and this information was passed on. The Queen consulted two of the senior statesmen of the Party, Sir Winston Churchill and Lord Salisbury, and they both recommended Mr. Macmillan. On the other hand there was a core of liberal Conservatives who included " the Rule of Law group " of the time of Suez, and those favouring the abolition of the death penalty, who were strongly opposed to Mr. Macmillan. Had there been a suitable third candidate (had Sir David Maxwell Fyfe still been in the House of Commons) he would have been nominated. To resolve the deadlock, Lord Salisbury and Lord Kilmuir, who

[19] See H. Dalton, *The Fateful Years*, p. 468, and the fuller account in *High Tide and After* (Vol. III of Dalton's Memoirs), Chapter I. This account is also supported by Francis Williams in *Triple Challenge*, p. 65 and in *A Prime Minister Remembers*, pp. 4–6.

[20] J. W. Wheeler-Bennett, *John Anderson, Viscount Waverly*, p. 275.

considered themselves excluded by virtue of their peerages, took a straw poll of the former Cabinet. Each member went in in turn and stated his preference, only Mr. Patrick Buchan-Hepburn (now Lord Hailes) declaring in favour of Mr. Butler. This information was conveyed to the Queen who then sent for Mr. Macmillan and asked him to form a government.[21]

Six years later in October 1963 Mr. Macmillan resigned because an operation was required on his prostate and he had already contemplated retirement. His decision to do so was reported to the Conservative Party during its annual conference in Blackpool. At once canvassing began on behalf of several claimants, Mr. Butler, Lord Hailsham, Lord Home,[22] Mr. Maudling and to a lesser degree for Mr. Heath and Mr. Macleod. From his sick-bed, Mr. Macmillan prepared to give advice to the Queen at the time of his resignation. He instructed the Lord Chancellor to poll the Cabinet, the Chief Whip to sound M.P.s, the Chief Whip in the Lords to do likewise and leading members of the National Union to try and contact the constituency parties. There have been arguments over aspects of this procedure (considered in the next chapter) but Macmillan is said to have received reports that the Cabinet was strong for Lord Home, the M.P.s narrowly in favour and the peers overwhelmingly in support. When the Prime Minister sent his letter of resignation, the Queen visited him in hospital, asked for his advice and invited Lord Home to form an administration.[23]

The only criticism of the part played by the Queen came from Mr. Paul Johnson, the Editor of the *New Statesman*.[24] He argued that the Queen's power to choose was " unqualified," that she must have known that there were disagreements within the Conservative

---

[21] Sir Ivor Jennings in his *Cabinet Government* (3rd ed., p. 28) says the Conservative " Party was prepared to follow either Mr. Butler or Mr. Macmillan and was ready to accept the Queen's choice." This is incorrect and gives a misleading impression of both the attitude of the Queen and of the Conservative Party.

[22] It was possible to consider both Lord Hailsham and Lord Home because of the Peerage Act of 1963 which allowed peers to disclaim their titles and stand for election to the House of Commons.

[23] The accounts of this contest are Randolph Churchill, *The Fight for the Tory Leadership*, Iain Macleod in *The Spectator* for January 17, 1964, M. Redmayne, *The Listener*, December 19, 1963, Quintin Hogg, *The Sunday Times*, March 8 and 15, 1964, and D. Wood in *The Times*, March 14, 1964. (This last is the Maudling version.)

[24] Paul Johnson, " Was the Palace to Blame?," *The New Statesman*, January 24, 1964.

Party and she should have undertaken inquiries to find out whether Mr. Macmillan's advice was soundly based. The weaknesses in this case are first, that if the retiring Prime Minister gives advice and the Crown refuses either to hear it or accept it, this would open the Crown to the gravest charges of meddling in politics. The Queen would have been rejecting advice from the most qualified person, the leader of the Conservative Party. Secondly, to try and check on the accuracy of Mr. Macmillan's soundings would have opened the Queen to further accusations of intrigue. Indeed it would scarcely have been possible as further advice could only come from the same sources—the Whips. The point Mr. Johnson is groping towards is that further delay might have given a " stop Home " group time to consolidate, but it was not the Queen's duty to facilitate this. The Crown's choice is not unqualified; every effort must be made to go through the established channels in seeking advice and in this case it had to involve asking for and accepting the advice of Mr. Macmillan.

After the experience of this public competition for the leadership and the loss of the 1964 general election, the Conservatives decided to adopt a procedure which would formalise the process of " soundings in the party " and produce one definite nominee. In February 1965 Sir Alec Douglas-Home explained the system. A candidate could be elected on a first ballot of all Conservative M.P.s if he had an absolute majority and 15 per cent. more votes than the nearest rival. If not, a second ballot could be held with new names added, an absolute majority being the sole requirement. If this failed, a third ballot with the top three names on the second ballot and a second preference system would ensure an absolute majority for one candidate.[25] The first leader to be elected on this system was Mr. Heath, five months later, but the effect is that now no possible element of influence or discretion exists for the monarch in the selection of a Prime Minister.

The Crown has many functions in the social life of Britain and of parts of the Commonwealth which are not considered here. It might be suggested in certain quarters that these functions have political repercussions but any benefit that is to be obtained from the aura cast by the Crown is available for whatever government is

---

[25] The system is set out in Anthony King ed., *British Politics*, Documentary Appendix.

in power.[26] Similarly the politicians, having complete control, can alter the role of the monarchy should they think it desirable. All the evidence suggests that a sovereign playing no political part but providing a figurehead who performs many duties and gives much pleasure, is acceptable to virtually the whole community.

[26] See K. Martin, *The Crown and the Establishment* and A. Sampson, *The Anatomy of Britain*, Chapter Three.

CHAPTER 20

THE PRIME MINISTER

THE position and power of the Prime Minister has been the focal point of modern Cabinets. This has not been due to the personality of any particular Premier or to the triumph of personal desires to arrogate power. The explanation lies in several aspects of the British political system. The Prime Minister has a leading place in the eyes of the public and has increased his control of appointments and promotions within the Government. Modern politicians are anxious for office and an element of hierarchy and dependence on the favour of the Prime Minister has arisen. In addition a body of the size of the Cabinet, loaded with business, will simply fail to operate unless it is subordinated to a chairman who can guide, summarise and close the discussions. All the forces of party loyalty and organisation naturally tend to support the individual who is most closely identified with the success of the party, and this sentiment is at its strongest while the party is in power and its leader is Prime Minister. None of these points is meant to suggest that the Premier is the master of his Cabinet and there is evidence that in modern ministries policies advocated by the Premier have, on occasion, been modified or rejected. But it does mean that his position is a special one with powers differing in kind from those of the other senior ministers. A Premier soon imparts his own tone to his government and if he fails to bind his ministers together, to tackle contemporary problems, or to ensure action, then there is no one who can, so to speak, steer the bus from a back seat.

The strength of the Prime Minister rests not only on his powers but on his security in his office. The process of selection, once the Conservative Party had established an elective system, is relatively simple. The deciding body is the Parliamentary Party in each case. The Labour Party holds a series of ballots, the candidate with the lowest votes being eliminated till one has an absolute majority. According to the constitution, there is an annual election but this only operates in opposition and contests only occur if there is a major battle going on inside the Party.

Thus when the Labour Party suddenly increased its strength and its pre-war leaders returned to the House in 1922, there was a contest between Ramsay MacDonald, the pre-1914 leader and Clynes, who had spoken for the Party since 1920. There were no further contests till Ramsay MacDonald became Prime Minister in a National Government in 1931. Arthur Henderson then succeeded as leader for two months till the general election after which Lansbury was chosen. Lansbury led the opposition till 1935 when he resigned. After the 1935 general election, the leadership was contested by Attlee, Morrison and Greenwood, Attlee being elected on the second ballot. There were no challenges in the form of demands that there should be another election until December 1955 when Attlee went to the Lords. Mr. Attlee did face attempts by Laski to have him replaced in 1945 (which were utterly feeble) and some muttering among senior members of the Cabinet in 1947. In this case, the loyalty of Ernest Bevin put paid to any plots and the situation did not recur. When Attlee left the Commons, Gaitskell, Bevan and Morrison were the candidates, the first being elected. Gaitskell was the first Labour leader to face an open challenge to his position. In November 1960 Harold Wilson contested Gaitskell's re-election and lost by 166 to 81 votes. When Gaitskell died in January 1963, George Brown, James Callaghan and Harold Wilson sought election, the last winning on the second ballot.

Thus it can be seen that despite the federal elements in the Labour Party and a tendency to internal divisions, the leaders have been remarkably secure. Only one has ever been challenged and that was while the Party was in opposition.

Among Conservatives, the situation has been more complex, in part because the idea of " evolving " a leader (up to 1965) left an element of uncertainty, in part because the Party assumes that it is normal for it to form the Government, so that failure is resented and more readily punished. In 1922, when doubts about continuing as members of Lloyd George's Coalition had spread among a majority of Conservative M.P.s, they reacted against Austen Chamberlain's attempt to lead them into an election as a Coalition. At the Carlton Club meeting of October 19, 1922, not only was a policy rejected but with it Austen Chamberlain as leader of the Party. The King asked Bonar Law to become Prime Minister as he had been the leader till he had retired on health grounds eighteen months earlier and he clearly had the support of the anti-Coalition elements of the Party.

Bonar Law retired in 1923 again because of his health and was succeeded by Baldwin,[1] who faced a series of challenges to his leadership. In December 1923, only a year after the last general election, he asked for a dissolution, the result of which was a loss of 107 seats and a period of Labour government. Criticism of these tactics came from the Coalitionist Conservatives, Austen Chamberlain and F. E. Smith, and from Lord Derby, yet there was no rebellion. " The instinct of self-preservation alone compelled the body of the party to range themselves under the only leader who could restore them to office." [2] Though there was criticism of Baldwin's tenderness towards the Labour Government, the rapid Conservative return to power in October 1924 restored his position. The main factor which caused Baldwin difficulty was the failure of his government to restore prosperity in industry and agriculture. He told the 1925 Conservative Conference that " when the Party wants to change its Leader I will step down," [3] but he faced no real threat till he had led the Party to defeat in the 1929 general election and was no longer Prime Minister. Lord Beaverbrook backed by Lord Rothermere and W. R. Hearst attacked Baldwin's leadership in a way which would have been scarcely possible had he still been in office. What was more serious was restiveness in the Conservative Party in the Commons about his attitude to Indian self-government and to imperial preference. Churchill joined his opponents but the economic crisis and impending collapse of the Labour Government dampened down these divisions. Back in office in 1931 first as the power behind Ramsay MacDonald and then as Prime Minister, Baldwin's position was secure.

Neville Chamberlain faced no serious challenge as a peacetime Premier. He decided to resign after the debate on the conduct of the Norwegian campaign (May 8, 1940) when his majority fell to 81, 33 Conservatives voting against and some 60 abstaining. Even then, he might have tried to continue and Churchill urged him to

---

[1] See p. 20 above for the circumstances of his selection by the King.
[2] G. N. Young, *Stanley Baldwin*, p. 73.
[3] R. T. Mackenzie, *British Political Parties* (2nd ed.), p. 124.

do so as he still had " a good majority," [4] but Chamberlain felt that he needed to introduce Labour Ministers and form a Coalition. When he heard that the Labour Party would not serve under him he decided to relinquish the Premiership. It is doubtful whether he could have remained as Prime Minister in view of the degree of resentment over his methods of conducting the war and the setbacks that had been suffered.

After 1940 there were some rumblings over Churchill's leadership till the tide turned in 1943 but none thereafter.[5] Nor did Churchill face any challenges in his post-war ministry, though as his health declined in 1954 and early 1955, there were those who wished that he would be quicker about his departure.[6] The two really interesting cases where it has been suggested that a Conservative Premier might have been forced out of office by his party are those of Sir Anthony Eden and Harold Macmillan.

Just as Neville Chamberlain had been regarded as Baldwin's obvious successor, Eden was the heir apparent to Churchill.[7] Yet soon after he took over, hostile articles began to appear in such Conservative papers as the *Daily Telegraph*. There was discussion about his future and predictions about resignation which Eden met with a formal disclaimer. There followed the disastrous events of the Suez War and Eden, a very sick man, had to leave for recuperation in the Carribbean. He returned in December 1956 and in January he resigned. The question is whether he was forced out of office, the answer of those most closely involved being unanimous. Lord Kilmuir " was anxious that Anthony should try to go on, and believed that we could rely on the inherent loyalty of the Conservative Party." [8] Six ministers met Eden at lunch on December 26, 1956, and all urged him to stay, not so much because of confidence in him but because they felt it was essential for unity and that this was not the time for a change. Then on January 7, 1957, Eden's doctors told him he could not

[4] Sir Winston Churchill, *The Second World War*, Vol. I, p. 522.
[5] Ernest Bevin believed that Beaverbrook was trying to organise a plot in June 1942. Alan Bullock, *The Life and Times of Ernest Bevin*, Vol. II, pp. 177–178.
[6] Lord Moran, *Winston Churchill, The Struggle for Survival, 1940/65*, pp. 627–628.
[7] He had been nominated as early as January 1945 when King George VI asked Churchill whom he should appoint if the Prime Minister was killed. J. W. Wheeler-Bennett, *John Anderson, Viscount Waverley*, pp. 315–317.
[8] Lord Kilmuir, *Political Adventure*, p. 282.

carry on and he resigned on the 9th. It is impossible, therefore, to say that Eden was edged out of office—he went on grounds of health despite appeals to stay, though some of those pressing him to remain felt that he might be better to go later when the political climate had improved for the Conservatives.

The process by which Mr. Macmillan was chosen as Prime Minister has been described above (pp. 424–5) and the quite new feature was the part played by the Cabinet. Hitherto the method of selection had been that either someone was generally recognised in Conservative circles as the next Prime Minister or, when there were doubts—candidates with much the same claims—the Crown consulted the retiring Prime Minister or senior Conservative Privy Councillors. On this occasion, the Whips not only sounded members but Lords Kilmuir and Salisbury took a straw poll of the Cabinet. Much the same took place when Macmillan resigned in 1963 but then the Cabinet played a smaller part as members were " sounded " rather than polled on the instructions of Mr. Macmillan and he and the sounder, Lord Dilhorne, were left free to interpret the results. In fact the process of selection in 1963 was a step towards the electoral system for discovering the consensus of the Parliamentary Party which was adopted in 1965.

The second time when it has been argued that a Prime Minister was edged out was Macmillan's departure in 1963. Professor Robert Mackenzie has argued that this " is perhaps a marginal case, but he is nonetheless a serious candidate for the list of Conservative leaders who have, in effect, been forced out of office." [9] The case rests on the fact that Macmillan's credit, and therefore that of the Government, slumped in 1962; in April 1963 he tried to tell a meeting of the 1922 Committee that he did not intend to retire and then in October he took advantage of a minor operation to resign. Yet this account overstates the pressures on the Prime Minister. In June twenty-seven Conservative M.P.s had abstained in what was, in effect, a vote of confidence over Macmillan's handling of the Profumo affair. But the majority was still sixty-nine, there was no campaign or group pressing for a change and no alternative leader. At the Cabinet meeting on October 7, just before the Party Conference, the Prime Minister had asked his colleagues if they thought it would be in the interests of the

[9] R. T. Mackenzie, *op. cit.*, p. 594n.

Party to have a change before the next election. Mr. Macmillan even left the room so that members could discuss this without the inhibiting presence of " the Head." Yet not a voice was raised to suggest a change and all but one of the Cabinet left assuming that Macmillan would remain. The exception considered that the Prime Minister wanted to stay but saw signs of the forthcoming illness in Macmillan's face and assumed that a change was unavoidable.[10] Randolph Churchill records that Macmillan had contemplated retirement in August or September but by the eve of the Conference he had decided that there was no suitable alternative and that he should lead the Party into the next election.[11] This certainly was the impression he gave to his colleagues.

Then Macmillan was struck with a very painful illness, his doctors at first fearing that the obstruction might be malignant. This tilted the balance in his mind in favour of resignation. All the evidence supports this thesis—that given proper health Macmillan could have retained the Premiership as long as he liked. There was no sign of pressures on him which forced his hand or would have done so had he gone on as Prime Minister.[12]

The strength of a Prime Minister is well revealed by the case of Mr. Wilson. His great achievements were to make the Labour Opposition look like an alternative government and to convince the electorate that he would be a competent Premier before the 1964 election. Then he managed his Party, his Government and Parliament brilliantly for 18 months on a majority of 4. After his victory at the General Election of March 1966, few Prime Ministers have stood higher in the estimation of their followers or the electorate. Yet only four months later, there was a rumour of a plot against Mr. Wilson. In one form spread in the City, talk was of a coalition government led by Mr. Callaghan. Of this there was not a trace in Westminster. In the other form (not widely discussed

[10] This is the result of interviews the author has had with 18 of the 21 Cabinet Ministers present at that time. All thought he was secure as long as he wanted to remain Prime Minister provided his health did not fail.

[11] Randolph Churchill, *op. cit.*, p. 94.

[12] A remark by Mr. Iain Macleod (in the *Spectator* article cited above) has caused confusion. He wrote " I was, I think, at the end perhaps the only member of Macmillan's Cabinet to hold steadily to the view that the Tory Party would do better under Macmillan's leadership at the polls than they would under any of the possible alternatives." By this he did not mean that he was the only person who thought Mr. Macmillan *could* or *would* stay: he felt he was the only consistent and active proponent of the view that Macmillan was the Party's best electoral asset.

till the Conference of the Labour Party that October at Brighton), it was an attempt at a Cabinet coup. It was said that while Mr. Wilson was in Moscow over the weekend, July 16–17, 1966, senior ministers who preferred devaluation to deflation agreed to insist on such a policy and that they thought that if Mr. Wilson refused, he could be replaced by Mr. Callaghan. These changes were to be forced on the Premier by a threat of simultaneous resignation by the five senior members of the Cabinet, an event which, in the middle of a sterling crisis, would have been so disastrous that the Prime Minister would have had to agree.

It is highly unlikely that any such plot ever existed or could have existed or could ever have had any chance of success. It assumed agreement on a successor to Mr. Wilson when such unanimity not only did not exist in this case but would be rare among the senior members of any Cabinet. It assumed no capacity on the part of the Prime Minister to sense a situation and win over individuals or make concessions. It assumed that a Prime Minister as strong as Mr. Wilson in July 1966 with a second and third eleven waiting impatiently in the pavilion could not have made any necessary replacements.

The second time Mr. Wilson's leadership was called in question was in January 1968 when his stock was much lower as a result of economic difficulties, a forced devaluation, failure to enter Europe and to quell the Rhodesian rebellion and a series of disastrous by-elections. Then the Press made much of twenty-five abstentions by Labour back-benchers in a vote of confidence in the Government on January 18 and asked how long the Prime Minister could last. But again action in the Parliamentary Labour Party could only take place if there was a generally accepted alternative and even then, an adverse vote might simply lead to a general election, the defeat of many of the M.P.s concerned and the destruction of the Labour Movement for years to come. No Party, especially when it is divided and electorally unpopular will throw away over three years of office in which it might recover its confidence and electoral popularity.

And these are the only two ways a Prime Minister can be removed, provided he has a majority and retains his health. One is a Cabinet coup, the other is overthrow at a back-bench meeting of his Party. Both are so unlikely as to be almost impossible.[13] There have been only three such rejections of a Prime Minister this century. One was engineered from within the Cabinet when Lloyd George ousted Asquith in 1916 but this was during a war when a Coalition was essential and Lloyd George had the firm backing of the leader of the Conservative Party. Two came about because of back-bench revolts, though in each case there were exceptional circumstances. Lloyd George was rejected at the 1922 Carlton Club meeting but he was leading a Coalition based on a majority of members drawn from another party. In 1940 Chamberlain suffered not defeat but a slump in his support because Conservative M.P.s back from the forces, men of unimpeachable loyalty in all normal situations, thought that the Prime Minister was leading the country to total defeat.[14] No Prime Minister has been rejected or edged out while in office under normal conditions of party conflict in peace time in this century.

Turning to the powers of a Prime Minister, the first is his right (Lloyd George called it a " prerogative ") to choose the other ministers. In practice this is subject to some restrictions. In 1922 Bonar Law could not draw on the Conservatives who had taken their stand with Lloyd George and his Cabinet consisted largely of the Under-Secretaries who had opposed the continuance of the Coalition. Stanley Baldwin faced the same problem in forming his first ministry a year later, while the membership of the National Governments of 1931 and 1940 was naturally a subject for negotiation between the leaders of the various parties. Normally, however, the Prime Minister has a free hand, except that he is likely in his own interests and in those of his government to consult some of his senior colleagues.[15] Labour politicians in the 1920s were a little self-conscious about the process of forming a government as they were new to the task and had, in the past, been critical of the established practices. In

---

[13] This view is cogently argued in Anthony King's chapter in *European Politics*, I, ed. W. G. Andrews.

[14] A good example of such feeling was Sir William Anstruther Gray who returned from his unit to the House convinced that Chamberlain must be replaced. Sir William was, in party terms, a complete loyalist who later became Chairman of the 1922 Committee.

[15] Lord Woolton concludes that " whilst it is probable that he [the Prime Minister] may confidentially consult some of his potential colleagues as to the choice of the ministers he should submit to the Crown, the decision is his, and his alone." *Memoirs*, p. 363.

December 1923 six of the most prominent Labour front-benchers agreed to take office and to leave their leader, Ramsay MacDonald the customary freedom in selecting his colleagues.[16] The new Premier laid his plans while on holiday in Lossiemouth and talked over some of his ideas with Lord Haldane and J. H. Thomas before issuing the invitations. In 1929 Mr. Dalton and his friends were anxious as to whether " J. R. M. [shall] make his Cabinet unaided, or rather unofficially aided by a few intriguers and lick-spittles, or shall he have something in the nature of an official advisory committee? " [17] Snowden feared questions on the same subject from the National Executive Committee, but when it came to the issue MacDonald again consulted and appointed as he pleased.

There might be some difficulty if a senior party member refused an offer or tried to insist on a given post though the effect would just be to hand the problem back to the Prime Minister. Various attempts were made to circumscribe Mr. Attlee's freedom of action before he formed a government in August 1945. But once the summons came to take office, his new position as Prime Minister scattered all the restrictions and he had the same scope as Stanley Baldwin (after 1923) and Neville Chamberlain had enjoyed. Post-war Premiers have had complete freedom unless their parties have recently suffered internal splits so that some offices have had to be offered to different sections. Mr. Macmillan made virtually a clean sweep when he took over in 1957, fifty-two offices changing hands, whereas in 1963 Sir Alec Douglas-Home was faced with the refusal of Mr. Iain Macleod and Mr. Enoch Powell to serve and so he had to collect every other Conservative of note into his Cabinet. Mr. Wilson in 1964 had to placate the Gaitskellites as well as his own followers in order to get a harmonious government. When he won his decisive majority in 1966 he could have made whatever changes he liked but he preferred to continue with substantially the same team.

There is no obligation on a Prime Minister to select members of his Shadow Cabinet when he attains office or to give them the departments they have watched over. In the case of a Conservative leader, automatic promotion for Shadow Cabinet members is more likely as he has selected these men in the first instance

---

[16] R. W. Lyman, *The First Labour Government*, 1924, p. 99.
[17] H. Dalton, *Call Back Yesterday*, p. 207.

while the Labour Party in opposition elects its Shadow Cabinet
or Parliamentary Committee as it is called. Mr. Attlee's decision
to switch Bevin and Dalton has already been mentioned and in
1964 Mr. Wilson suddenly switched Mr. Crossman who had been
Shadow Minister of Education with Mr. Stewart who had spoken
on housing.

In addition to his powers on the formation of a ministry, the
Prime Minister also promotes, reshuffles or dismisses ministers.
When, as in the 1960s, this means he has the disposal of some
seventy-five places for his side of the House of Commons, it will
be seen that this gives a very considerable hold over M.P.s.
Moreover the decline in the influence of the private M.P. has
meant that most of those men of ability who intend to spend a
portion of their life in politics want office. They want office
perhaps because of a desire for success and fame but many
want office because this is the only way they can achieve the
purposes for which they entered politics, this is the only way they
can have any effect. Similarly when a party appears to be condemned to opposition for an indefinite period, some of its men of
talent tend to leave for other occupations because they see no
hope of achieving anything in the House of Commons.

The power of appointment is therefore one of the chief ways a
Prime Minister keeps his control over his party and while there
are some restrictions on a Premier taking office for the first time,
he has much greater freedom when it comes to later rearrangements. This power applies not only at first appointment but at
every stage up the hierarchy and can be used with great subtlety.
A man whom the Prime Minister does not care for may be given
a tough assignment so that if he fails, he is destroyed, but if he
succeeds the government as a whole and its leader can take the
credit. Observing the political scene Lord Woolton concluded
that " Prime Ministers are apt to be autocratic in the disposal of
their ministers, and I can see no other way by which the practice
could operate." [18] In his draft Introduction to the new Edition of
Bagehot's classic, *The English Constitution*,[19] Mr. Crossman, after
eighteen years in politics, included a sentence that the British
Prime Minister can liquidate the political career of one of his

[18] Woolton, *op. cit.*, p. 260.
[19] Published by Fontana in 1963.

colleagues as effectively as any of the leaders of the Soviet Union can remove rivals. His publishers protested and he removed the observation. In 1967 after three years in the Cabinet, the only thing he regretted about his Introduction was the omission of this sentence.[20]

The way in which these powers are operated naturally differ from one Prime Minister to another. Stanley Baldwin shrank from episodes involving personal tension and had no strong views on policy which might have made him contemplate changes. His chief desire was to keep the Conservative Party strong and give no chances to Labour or Lloyd George. Thus he left Austen Chamberlain and F. E. Smith out of his Cabinet in May 1923 when it became clear that their appointment would cause more disruption than their exclusion. Although he had fought the 1923 election under the banner of protection, Baldwin appointed the turbulent free-trader, Churchill, as his Chancellor of the Exchequer in 1924 and endured him for five years. Baldwin did not, however, disguise his relief when the landslide of 1931 and the reduced number of posts available in the National Government allowed him to relegate all those whom he had found restless or uneasy colleagues. Neville Chamberlain, in contrast, had no such hesitations. When he appointed Lord Maugham (a complete stranger) as Lord Chancellor, he told Maugham that the office might have to be surrendered if he, the Prime Minister, needed it in a reshuffle.[21] In May 1938 Chamberlain dismissed the Secretary of State for Air, Lord Swinton, although the latter had the confidence of the Cabinet and was evidently a successful administrator.[22] Hore-Belisha, who had been active and efficient at the War Office and had had Neville Chamberlain's confidence till late in 1939, was asked, without any warning, to resign on

[20] Mr. Crossman has given his permission for the use of this information.
[21] The Rt. Hon. Viscount Maugham, *At the End of the Day*, p. 341.
[22] There is an element of mystery about this episode. The official explanation was that there had been trouble in the House of Commons and Swinton was asked to resign so that a Secretary of State could be found who was able to defend the Air Ministry in that House. Yet the government's very large majority was absolutely secure and nothing could be more out of character than the suggestion that Neville Chamberlain would abandon a man he wanted to keep, and who was doing good work, just because of a single row in the Commons. There is evidence that Swinton had crossed some powerful industrialists by being tough in his handling of aircraft contracts and that those men, who had close connections with the Conservative Party, approached the Prime Minister directly and asked for the removal of Swinton.

January 4, 1940. The Prime Minister had been to France, found
there was acute resentment against Hore-Belisha among the senior
British officers and decided to change his Secretary of State for
War. At various times in 1938 and 1939 senior ministers had
urged Chamberlain to broaden the membership of his Cabinet,
but he flatly refused to take in men like Churchill or Eden who
had disagreed with him. " I won't have anyone who will rock the
boat." [23]

Lord Attlee has said that an important quality in a Premier
is the capacity to dismiss inadequate ministers.[24] When one such
person was summouned and told to resign he is reported to have
hesitated, hoping for some words of condolence from Attlee, and
as none were forthcoming, to have asked why he was being
removed. " Because I don't think you measure up to the job " was
the answer.[25] Senior ministers might, on occasion, press their
views on Mr. Attlee. Sir Stafford Cripps and others urged that
Mr. Shinwell should be removed from the Ministry of Fuel and
Power in 1947 (this was done) and the Prime Minister discussed
the question of Bevin's successor at the Foreign Office with Mr.
Morrison and with Bevin himself but in every case the final
decision was made by Mr. Attlee. Mr. Churchill was not above
repaying old scores and in 1951 he was reluctant to give places
to those who had, from his point of view, let him down in the
appeasement period. The most dramatic display of Prime Ministerial power occurred in July 1962. Then Mr. Macmillan, with
no warning summoned and dismissed seven members of a Cabinet
of twenty. He had heard alarming reports about the probable
result in a by-election (after a series of reverses) and felt that
unless the government presented a more youthful and vigorous
image it would decline even further. In addition to this unprecedented action, he also made some spectacular promotions,

[23] R. J. Minney, ed., *The Hore-Belisha Papers*, p. 130.
[24] Mr. Attlee on " The Art of Being a Prime Minister," *The Times*, June 15,
1958.
[25] Francis Williams, the Prime Minister's Press Secretary reports that " when he
came to the conclusion that certain ministers were not adequate he dismissed
or demoted them without any attempt to soften the blow." *Triple Challenge*,
p. 48. It is interesting to compare these examples with Lord Salisbury's
remarks in 1890 that though he had long wanted rid of Matthews from the
Home Office, there was no precedent and no justification " except on some
open and palpable error " for a Prime Minister dismissing a colleague.
Queen Victoria's Letters, Series III, Vol. I, p. 661.

such as that of Mr. Michael Noble to be Secretary of State for Scotland after being in the House only four years and making only a single speech. [He had served as a junior Whip.] Mr. Wilson, perhaps because of the unhappy repercussions of Macmillan's action in 1962 but more because of his dislike of hurting people, has had annual minor rearrangements. Indeed a feature of his policy has been a reluctance to remove ministers, preferring to find them other posts rather than replace them on the back-benches. Yet he brought Mr. Shore into the Cabinet very rapidly to act as his assistant at the D.E.A. Later in April 1968 he reconstructed his Cabinet so as to ensure a majority of his personal supporters in the top ten posts.

In addition to the original power to appoint, other factors affecting relations are the Prime Minister's capacity to determine the scope of the various offices or to take over a department either in practice or by actually adding it to his own responsibilities. There can be a variety of motives for such an action. Baldwin remained Chancellor of the Exchequer after he had become the head of the government in order to keep a place open for McKenna when the latter could be found a seat in the House. In 1924 MacDonald decided to be Foreign Secretary as well as Prime Minister, and Winston Churchill assumed the additional title of Minister of Defence in 1940. (He also took over the Ministry of Defence for four months at the beginning of his 1951–55 government.) When MacDonald let Arthur Henderson go to the Foreign Office in 1929, he made it quite clear that he was keeping Anglo-American relations in his own hands. Cabinet Committees can be used to keep a check on a minister whose orthodoxy is not absolutely certain. Mr. R. A. Butler was given the important post of Chancellor of the Exchequer in 1951 but was also to be aided by a committee of four ministers including Lord Woolton and Lord Swinton.[26] When new drive was needed at the Ministry of Fuel and Power after Mr. Shinwell left, the young and untried Mr. Gaitskell was watched over and encouraged by an Emergency Fuel and Power Committee of the Cabinet under the chairmanship of Mr. Attlee.[27] It is not, of course, necessary

---

[26] Woolton, *op. cit.*, p. 371, and Francis Boyd, *R. A. Butler*, p. 106.
[27] "Earl Attlee Remembers," *The Sunday Times*, November 27, 1960.

for a Prime Minister to create a new office or assume a title himself in order to watch over a specific department. Mr. Macmillan could move in on foreign policy if a summit conference was in the offing and he could virtually become Minister of Labour if a National Railway strike threatened. Mr. Wilson has used all these methods. He created the Department of Economic Affairs and the Ministry of Technology. When he has felt it necessary, he has assumed control of foreign policy and of negotiations with Rhodesia, he has personally handled a seamen's strike and a threatened national railway stoppage. In September 1967 he rearranged the responsibilities of the Department of Economic Affairs so that he could take personal charge of economic policy.

In shaping the institutions and making the appointments in the higher reaches of government, the Prime Minister and the competing politicians are highly aware of just how much power and standing attaches to each office. Lord Woolton observes that "there is in government a sort of hierarchy, and Ministers look forward to promotion in it. I remember the Prime Minister sending for me one day, and in a most kindly interview, trusting that I was not disappointed at the fact that I had not received any promotion." [28] The two posts most likely to carry succession to the Premiership are those of the Chancellor of the Exchequer and the Secretary of State for Foreign Affairs. Since the Second World War, powerful figures have also been appointed Lord President of the Council. There is no constant order within the three or four senior positions though it is sometimes said that they rank in the order in which they are printed in the lists of ministers. Such a hierarchy is largely the creation of the Premier of the day so that if he resigns, the choice of a successor reverts in the case of the Labour Party to the Labour M.P.s, and for the Conservatives up to 1965 to the form of "soundings" that have been described. The short-lived custom of naming a Deputy Prime Minister did not ensure that, when soundings

---

[28] Woolton, *op. cit.*, pp. 259–260. Duff Cooper has laid it down that "office is the ambition of every M.P., competition for it is eager." *Old Men Forget*, p. 160. The only instance of politicians refusing Cabinet office since 1918 was when Lord Derby and the Duke of Devonshire each declined Montagu's place as Secretary of State for India in the last year of Lloyd George's Coalition.

were taken or a ballot held, that person would be chosen.[29] But in as much as it gave extra prestige and a chance to claim the reversion, the post was coveted. For some, the request to preside at the Cabinet in the absence of the Prime Minister seemed a sure pointer. Curzon, in early 1923, felt that it " was more than a mere formality: it was an indication: it was a promise." [30] Neville Chamberlain found that all was going well in mid-1931:

> " I have, I believe, recovered the second position in the party, Winston having separated himself from his colleagues, while Hailsham has, perhaps unjustly, somewhat lost credit for his handling of the Lords, and Horne has receded into the background." [31]

One of the questions which crossed Chamberlain's mind when Churchill was suggested for the new Ministry of Defence in February 1936 was whether this might not raise doubts about the succession on Baldwin's retirement.[32] After 1945, the ranking in the Conservative Party was Churchill, Eden and then Oliver Stanley, and when the latter died, there was much discussion as to whether Mr. Butler had succeeded to third place.[33] When Mr. Macmillan moved from the Foreign Office to the Treasury in December 1955, he " accepted the Treasury on the strict understanding that this was to be regarded as a step towards, and not away from, the Premiership." [34] Each member of the Cabinet has a regular place at the table in No. 10 Downing Street and Lord Morrison was undoubtedly right in saying that there is " some relationship to ministerial status." [35] The senior men sit beside the Prime Minister or opposite to him where they can easily and frequently contribute. At each reshuffle ministers move in towards the centre of power or out. When Mr. Cousins was Minister of Technology he was No. 7 but on the appointment of Mr. Wedgwood

---

[29] It was King George VI who pointed out to Sir Winston Churchill that in naming Sir Anthony Eden as Deputy Prime Minister (as well as Foreign Secretary) in 1951, he was filling a non-existent office. Mr. Attlee had been referred to in this way during the war-time Coalition and Mr. Morrison had the title from 1945 to 1951. See J. W. Wheeler-Bennett, *King George VI*, p. 797.

[30] This is how Harold Nicolson expresses Curzon's feelings in *Curzon, The Last Phase*, p. 353.

[31] K. Feiling, *Life of Neville Chamberlain*, p. 188.

[32] *Ibid.*, p. 278.

[33] F. Boyd, *op. cit.*, p. 89.

[34] Lord Kilmuir, *op. cit.*, p. 256.

[35] Morrison, *Government and Parliament*, 2nd ed., p. 4.

Benn, he dropped to the foot of the table. When Michael Stewart was moved from the Foreign Office to the D.E.A. he claimed he had been promoted as he had become No. 3. Later, on being transferred to the post of co-ordinator of the Social Services, he was allowed to keep his title of First Secretary of State. For these reasons ministers have sought to avoid offices which carry little weight or where there is no chance of enhancing their reputations. Between the wars the Presidency of the Board of Education was low on the list as was the Board of Trade. Ramsay MacDonald was surprised to find his colleagues shunning the Ministry of Labour as the "cinderella of the government offices," [36] while the Secretaryship of State for Scotland has never been regarded as a stepping-stone to higher places.[37]

There is a great desire for office. In 1929 Snowden wondered if the National Executive would ask questions about the process of Cabinet-making but "everybody there who was an M.P. evidently hoped that he would be in the new Government, and was afraid to speak." [38] After the government had been formed, Ramsay MacDonald confessed that he had had some unpleasant interviews in Downing Street. "It has been terrible. I have had people in here weeping and even fainting." [39] Two years later Baldwin told the Conservative Shadow Cabinet that he had agreed to join a National Government (rather than insist on a purely Conservative administration) and not a voice was raised against him; "They were thinking of their offices." [40] Malcolm MacDonald wrote saying that he admired Duff Cooper's courage in disputing with Neville Chamberlain over the naval estimates just before the latter succeeded to the Premiership. "Some people would have done anything rather than quarrel with Neville Chamberlain then! ".[41]

In such an atmosphere politicians become very conscious of what Mr. Dalton had called their "place . . . in the ever-shifting

---

[36] B. Webb, *Diaries, 1912–24*, p. 262.

[37] Willie Graham, an obvious choice for the Secretaryship of State for Scotland in 1929, "had always regarded it as a dead end and almost as much a political grave as the Ministry of Agriculture." T. N. Graham, *Willie Graham*, p. 174.

[38] Snowden, *Autobiography*, Vol. II, p. 762.

[39] Dalton, *Call Back Yesterday*, p. 217.

[40] G. M. Young, *op. cit.*, p. 167.

[41] Duff Cooper, *op. cit.*, p. 249.

Parliamentary queue "[42] and of the need to maintain their credit with senior ministers and above all, with the Premier. Mr. Churchill made it evident from the middle of the war that he regarded Sir Anthony Eden as his successor.[43] At one point during the " Bevanite " dispute in the Labour Party, Aneurin Bevan was proclaiming that he had been promised the reversion to the Chancellorship of the Exchequer by his old mentor, Sir Stafford Cripps. The effect of this atmosphere has been to make ministers more and more wary of carrying differences the length of resignation.

Resignation in any case has many difficulties.[44] The minister who is leaving has to explain his reasons for objecting to his colleagues' policy. He will want to win his party and the Cabinet over to his point of view without damaging its electoral prospects. The stalwarts in his constituency association may well make his position very difficult. Also it is hard to choose the right moment to resign. Most ministers naturally prefer to remain in office so that they can try to modify a policy they dislike. But if there is no sign that this will be possible and they have already accepted steps A, B and C, a resignation after C, or after the further stages D or E, can always be made to look niggling or inconsistent. Aneurin Bevan accepted a large-scale rearmament programme and even spoke on its behalf from the Front Bench before he stuck on a cut of £13 million for that year (1951) in the Health Service. Mr. Thorneycroft accepted several increases in estimates but jibbed at a final £50 million and Mr. Macmillan was able to say that the resignation had raised no issue of principle. Those who resign either have to regard the action as clearing their consciences and then lie low hoping to work their passage back into office, or they must fight. If the latter course is adopted, it is hard not to widen the breach retrospectively by questioning the earlier decisions

---

42 Dalton, *The Fateful Years*, p. 20. Mr. Dalton believes that if he had not been defeated by 755 votes in 1931, he might well have been elected leader in 1935 and thus have become Prime Minister in 1945 but he had lost his " place in the queue."

43 In June 1942 Churchill had advised George VI that if he was killed the King should send for Eden. Later, in early 1945, when both Eden and he were off to Yalta he added as a second alternative Sir John Anderson. Wheeler-Bennett, *op. cit.*, pp. 544–545.

44 The two comprehensive discussions of this subject are in P. J. Madgwick " Resignations," *Parliamentary Affairs*, Vol. XX, 1966–67, pp. 59–76 and R. K. Alderman and J. A. Cross, *The Tactics of Resignation*.

which were swallowed with reluctance. So the Bevanites rapidly moved from the £13 million cut in the Health Service to an attack on the level of armament and then to an alleged lack of new leftward policies and vigour in the Attlee Cabinet. The same problem beset the Labour ministers who went into opposition in 1931. They could either stand by all the proposals they had accepted up to the moment of resignation and thus have no clear grounds for objecting to a small further step in the same direction, or they could object to this whole line of policy and be accused of inconsistency or even of deceit.

Prime Ministers have realised their strength in dealing with threats of resignation, though naturally they have always preferred to keep a united and harmonious Cabinet. When Neville Chamberlain told Hore-Belisha that he was to leave the War Office and offered him the Board of Trade, Hore-Belisha hesitated. Chamberlain was surprised. " You are an ambitious man. You surely do not want to go out into the wilderness." [45] Curzon endured all Lloyd George's interventions in foreign policy because he knew that any complaints were likely to lead to his replacement and " he would often cite . . . [this] as a complete justification of his unwillingness to resign." [46] L. S. Amery chafed under the Free Trade policies of Baldwin's second ministry and was writing letters which hinted at resignation in late 1927. When he returned from a Commonwealth tour in February 1928 he found he had lost ground both inside and outside the Cabinet and decided it was best to remain in office. Some ministers could still use the threat, especially if they were disputing with another minister rather than with the Premier. In 1925 Winston Churchill was refusing to pay for the Navy's minimum demands for cruisers. William Bridgeman, the First Lord of the Admiralty, insisted on his programme, and Baldwin asked Churchill if he would resign. The latter said it was an important issue on which he felt very strongly, but hardly a resigning matter. Baldwin then turned to Bridgeman: would he resign? Certainly; and so the cruisers were built. Later, in the final stages of the policy of appeasement Mr. Anthony Eden (now

---

[45] *Hore-Belisha Papers*, p. 270. When Hore-Belisha did decide to resign, the Prime Minister asked him to add a word or two to his letter saying there had been no difference on matters of policy and Hore-Belisha did so.
[46] H. Nicolson, *Curzon, The Last Phase*, p. 23.

Lord Avon), Duff Cooper and Lord Cranborne (now Lord Salisbury) resigned but it is interesting that they did not concert action either among themselves or with the other Conservative critics of Neville Chamberlain. Walter Elliot considered resigning over Munich but was dissuaded by those closest to him on the grounds that such an act would destroy his standing in the party.[47] Recent evidence suggests that the position of the Prime Minister is stronger than ever and Mr. Macmillan was able to characterise such episodes as the resignation of Lord Salisbury (Lord President of the Council) or of Mr. Thorneycroft (Chancellor of the Exchequer) as " little local difficulties " and that is all they appeared to be. Indeed, in the decade since these resignations in 1958, there have been only four resignations (Mr. Mayhew, Mr. Cousins, Miss Herbison and Lord Longford) on grounds of policy despite all the strains and reversals that have been imposed on successive Conservative and Labour Governments.* Of these, the first Cabinet Minister to resign was Mr. Cousins and the interesting feature of his case is that he never regarded himself as a politician, he was essentially part of another career structure. Mr. Macleod and Mr. Powell refused to join Sir Alec Douglas-Home's ministry in 1963 but at the time they may have doubted whether he could form one. Since Labour entered office in 1964, Mr. George Brown threatened to resign in July 1966 but was dissuaded and, apart from Mr. Cousins, the only case has been the little-known Lord Longford. The disinclination to leave office even when Cabinets adopt policies bitterly disliked by individual members (such as Mr. Jay's dislike of the Common Market application shown after he was dismissed) or when sharp reversals are forced on ministers (as in the decision not to buy the F111 aeroplane and to leave East of Suez by 1970–71), this disinclination has become a feature of modern politics. Conversely it tends to be assumed that to give a critic office effectively silences him as a refusal of office or a subsequent resignation is so seldom contemplated as a serious possibility.

In assessing the relations of the Premier and his colleagues, the former's control over the machinery of the Cabinet must be

---

[47] Over Elliot's hesitation, Duff Cooper felt that " it would be easier for me to go alone, as I have no wish to injure the Government, which I should not do if my resignation was the only one." Duff Cooper, *op. cit.*, p. 242.

* Since this was written Mr. George Brown has left office (March 1968) but it is not fully clear whether he really intended to go or had a tantrum accepted at its face value by the Prime Minister.

taken into consideration. Meetings of the Cabinet are held twice a week during the parliamentary session but the Prime Minister arranges the order of business and can keep any item off the agenda indefinitely.[48] It is regarded as quite improper for a minister to raise any matter which has not previously been accepted for the agenda by the Prime Minister. For instance, on June 29, 1927, Neville Chamberlain wanted to discuss the dispute over the reform of the House of Lords. It was not on the agenda and though he did try to bring it up at the end of the listed business, Baldwin rose and walked out of the room, thus ending the Cabinet. The more important foreign despatches are only sent to those members of the Cabinet who must have the information and the Prime Minister has to give his consent before there are any departures from the rule. In March 1938 Duff Cooper wrote a paper advocating the end of the system whereby the Service departments' finances were rationed out but the Chancellor of the Exchequer and Chamberlain stopped it going any further.[49] Hore-Belisha wanted to circulate memoranda advocating partial mobilisation and conscription on April 15, 1939. Neville Chamberlain refused, though he later permitted Hore-Belisha to raise the matter verbally.[50] Mr. Wilson's insistence that disputes on matters of fact must never come before the Cabinet can have the same result. A series of papers on the effects of Britain entering the Common Market put before a Cabinet Committee end up as a single memorandum for the full Cabinet and if one of the papers (for instance from Mr. Jay at the Board of Trade) was hostile and three others were in favour, these would carry the day and Mr. Jay's paper would never reach the Cabinet. While Mr. Wilson and Mr. Macmillan both wished to bring entry to the Common Market before the Cabinet in the most favourable light, Sir Anthony Eden used all the same techniques to prevent a subject he disliked being raised at all.[51] When discussion begins at the Cabinet, the Prime Minister has the advantage

---

48 A good example is the way Mr. Attlee told the Cabinet nothing about British work in the field of nuclear weapons until the public were informed that successful tests had taken place.
49 Duff Cooper, *op. cit.*, pp. 218–220.
50 *Hore-Belisha Papers*, pp. 190–198.
51 Sir Philip de Zulueta in "The Power of the Prime Minister" in *Swinton Journal*, Autumn 1966 lists three sources of the Prime Minister's power: appointments, "unique position to initiate policy" and the power to "obstruct ideas of which he disapproves." In the third case it was Eden's ability to prevent Europe being raised which was one of his examples.

of having gone over most matters beforehand with the senior ministers concerned. As Lord Attlee has explained: "A Prime Minister has to know when to ask for an opinion—he can't always stop some ministers offering theirs, but he can make sure to extract the opinion of those he wants when he needs them." [52] Mr. Macmillan was a past-master at holding prior discussions and then knowing when to declare his hand. If the discussion seems to be going the wrong way, there are all the devices of adjournment or passing the matter to a Cabinet Committee for further elucidation. Junior members are usually absorbed in the work of their departments and seldom contribute unless the subject concerns them. A minister outside the senior group who wants to object is in a very weak position. He knows that there has been a long process of inter-departmental discussion and agreement first and that he will have to speak after the sense of the meeting has been set by the introductory statement of the minister who is responsible. Without a brief or expert knowledge, he must try to sway a number of men whose attitudes have been worked out over a considerable period. Too many such interventions ending in failure will destroy a minister's reputation and no-one will put forward a major change of policy (such as devaluation or withdrawal from East of Suez) unless the ministers concerned are open to the idea or if a change seems likely to be carried. Otherwise the discussion is left to the appropriate departmental heads and when one or two more ministers have been asked to contribute, the Prime Minister will sum up and declare the sense of the meeting. This is the point at which the card of collective responsibility is played and members of the Cabinet must either accept the decision or resign. [53]

The final power at the disposal of the Prime Minister is that he decides how and when the government shall be terminated,

---

[52] "Earl Attlee Remembers," *The Sunday Times*, November 27, 1960.

[53] On one or two occasions during the 1945–51 Labour Cabinets, ministers claim to have indicated their dissent after the Prime Minister had summed up. This, however, made no difference and they still had to accept responsibility before the public or resign. There is no voting in modern Cabinets, the last word always remaining with the Prime Minister. On one or two occasions when trivial points like the time of a special meeting has to be settled, it may be by show of hands. Other references to votes at times of great importance (*e.g.*, Bassett, *op. cit.*, pp. 76 and 82) mean that the Premier has gone round the table and the number of those for and against has become obvious.

unless he is defeated in the House or loses a general election.[54] In 1924 Baldwin resigned when he had been defeated by the combined Liberal and Labour forces on a motion of confidence. After the election of 1929, no party had an absolute majority though it was certain that the Liberal and Labour members would again combine to oust the government. Austen Chamberlain urged Baldwin to meet Parliament but " the Prime Minister thought otherwise, and when the Conservative Cabinet met for the last time on June 3 he informed his colleagues of his determination to resign at once." [55] Neville Chamberlain's resignation in 1940 was decided by the news that the Labour Party would not join a Coalition under his leadership.

The important choice for a Prime Minister is when his government is in power and he has to decide the best moment to hold an election since a further period of office or defeat may hang on his calculations. Since the First World War it has been accepted that this power lies with the Prime Minister. If there was any occasion on which the Cabinet might have revived its former practice of considering the merits of a dissolution it was in the autumn of 1923. Baldwin was as yet an unimpressive and inexperienced leader, the Parliament was only a year old and some members of the Cabinet were alarmed at the Prime Minister's desire to announce a policy of protection. However, once he had said that he personally favoured tariffs to combat unemployment, public interest was aroused and an election became likely.[56] Four ministers whom Baldwin consulted (Devonshire, Cecil, Wood and Novar) advised delay, " all . . . in great deference, recognising that fixing these matters is your special perquisite." [57] The Cabinet was still divided at its meeting on November 9 but the Prime

---

[54] Mr. Geoffrey Marshall in an article " Advice to Dissolve " in *The Guardian*, March 8, 1966, said there was no constitutional or political reason why this decision should lie with the Prime Minister rather than the Cabinet. This ignores the simple growth in the power of the Prime Minister and in his capacity to withdraw decisions from the Cabinet. The first Premier to do this was Lloyd George and no Cabinet has had the strength to insist on consultation, reiteration of past practice now being taken as an established convention.

[55] Sir Charles Petrie, *Life and Letters of Austen Chamberlain*, Vol. II, p. 370.

[56] During the 1922 general election Bonar Law had promised that the Conservatives would not adopt tariffs without a further appeal to the electorate. It was clear that Baldwin fell heir to this promise and when he began to talk about protection, it was assumed that an election was not far away.

[57] G. M. Young, *Stanley Baldwin*, pp. 66–67.

Minister did not show his hand and announced a dissolution four days later. On the two subsequent occasions when Baldwin had to make the same decision (in 1929 and 1935) he was well established and everyone accepted that it was his task to pick the most suitable moment for going to the country.

There was a slightly unusual case in 1931 since the Prime Minister, Ramsay MacDonald, was entirely dependent on Conservative support. He had undertaken that there would be no immediate appeal to the electorate by the National Government but Conservative pressure was intense and MacDonald gave way.[58] The one occasion on which the Cabinet did settle the manner and occasion of a government's demise was over the Campbell case in October 1924. The Liberal Party had announced that directly the recent treaty with Russia was debated, they would join the Conservatives to defeat the Labour Ministry. Before this matter arose, the Liberals moved for a Committee of Inquiry on the withdrawal of a charge against Campbell, the editor of the *Workers' Weekly*, while the Conservatives put down a motion of censure. The Cabinet agreed to treat both motions as matters of confidence and when the Liberal motion was carried, an emergency meeting was held. " After a stormy talk, we decided to go to the country." [59]

More recently, in 1950 and 1951, Mr. Attlee consulted a few senior colleagues but clearly made up his own mind about the dissolutions which terminated his two administrations.[60] When it became evident that an election was needed after the end of the war in Europe, Mr. Churchill took a straw poll of leading Conservatives as to whether the date should be June or October, but observed

---

[58] In his passionate defence of MacDonald, Mr. Bassett suggests that the election was precipitated by the unexpected tenacity of Labour opposition which produced further uncertainty and financial alarms. He says the Labour Party's " vigorous and increasingly virulent opposition to the National Government was the major cause of the election" (*1931 Political Crisis*, p. 293). A further flight from the pound did take place in September but this was due more to Conservative rumours of an impending election and of talk of going off the gold standard than to Labour opposition. Indeed when the financial position deteriorated, MacDonald told Samuel on September 20 that " obviously there is not even a theoretical justification for an election now " (the government had a firm majority of seventy). Yet by October 5 MacDonald had agreed to an election in face of the absolute determination of the Conservative leadership and of the 1922 Committee.

[59] The Rt. Hon. J. R. Clynes, *Memoirs*, Vol. II, p. 63.

[60] Lord Morrison, though Deputy Premier, evidently disagreed with the timing of both elections. See his *An Autobiography*, pp. 268 and 283.

that "this of course did not govern. The right of recommending a dissolution to the Crown rests solely with the Prime Minister." [61] This has been regular Conservative practice. The Prime Minister in 1955 and 1959 consulted the party Chairman, the Chief Whip and one or two close colleagues before making up his mind. The discussion was wider in the case of Sir Alec Douglas-Home as clearly the party stood in danger of defeat. It appears to have been the advice of the Central Office (resisted by Mr. Maudling, the Chancellor of the Exchequer) to postpone the election from June to October 1964. Mr. Wilson had a similar plethora of counsel over the timing of his dissolution but he was finally moved not so much by arguments from Mr. Crossman (who was in many ways his party manager) as by the Labour victory in the North Hull by-election in February 1966.

The power to advise a dissolution includes the power to use this as a weapon against recalcitrant Members on the Government back-benches. Though this is mentioned in many books (and examined below, pp. 591–2) and was included in a party speech by Harold Wilson on January 17, 1968, it is no longer an effective weapon. No back-bencher seriously imagines that a Prime Minister will court his own defeat by having a general election at a time when his party's morale is low and its backing in the country weak.

Having considered the security of a Prime Minister's position and his sources of strength, the picture has to be balanced by examining how far these powers are circumscribed when a Prime Minister is weak and under political pressure. These circumstances occur when the policies of a government fail and its political fortunes decline, situations which have occurred only too frequently since 1945.

Prime Ministers have been in such exposed positions in 1947 as a result of the fuel crisis and post-war austerity, in 1957 after the failure of the Suez invasion combined with economic difficulties, in 1962–63 with a recession and the Profumo scandal and in 1967–68 when devaluation succeeded deflation and setbacks in foreign affairs. In each case the political future of the government seemed uncertain, there was unrest among back-benchers and criticism of the Prime Minister. In assessing the strength of an institution it is perhaps best to consider it at a moment of

[61] Winston Churchill, *The Second World War*, Vol. VI, p. 511.

maximum weakness rather than when the circumstances are most favourable.

As has been argued above, a feature of all these situations is that, though the Prime Minister has been held mainly responsible, there has never been any serious possibility of edging him out, given health and a desire to hold on. In the case of Attlee in 1947 or of Eden in 1957 certain combinations of Cabinet Ministers could have made a difference but either the difficulty of getting agreement among possible successors or the difficulties of the political situation prevented any steps being taken. But though it is virtually impossible to remove a Prime Minister, some of the powers of the office do decline when the holder is under fire. For instance, the power to dismiss can be used drastically in a time of difficulty as Macmillan did in July 1962 but the reception of his action and the continued political misfortunes of the government meant that Macmillan could scarcely have made a similar purge again. Mr. Wilson was strong enough to have reshuffled his Cabinet in any way he liked up till the end of 1967. But after the devaluation in November and the appointment of Mr. Jenkins as Chancellor of the Exchequer, it is doubtful whether Mr. Jenkins could have been removed. The Prime Minister was, at least for a time, dependent on him.

Although during these stresses, the parties inside and outside Parliament remained preponderantly loyal, Prime Ministers could be faced with trouble in the form of abstentions, some personal attacks and tricky debates in the party annual conferences. Though none of these pressures need deflect a Prime Minister until the policies of the government have more success and the political standing of the government improves, such attacks weaken the leader and make it harder to retain control and self-confidence. It is possible that in these circumstances the Prime Minister's position in the Cabinet may decline and he may have to accept policies proposed by some senior colleagues when, in times when his stock was higher, he could have intervened at an earlier stage or given a more definite lead. But it is at such times that the leading members of a party realise the need for unity, that if the Prime Minister fails, it will affect the whole ministry and the desire for self-preservation becomes evident.

In all the periods of weakness mentioned, it has not proved

possible to find or provide a substitute for the leadership of the Prime Minister. There are only two possibilities which can save the government, either the government scores some successes and the Prime Minister recovers his élan or he decides to retire and a new Premier presides over the recovery. Mr. Attlee remained after 1947–48 but, though the government pulled back considerably, it was not sufficient and a combination of inactivity and gloom allowed the Conservatives to win. The Conservative recoveries after the slumps of 1957–58 and 1962–63 were both managed by new Prime Ministers (it is not often realised that the significance of Sir Alec Douglas-Home's year as Premier is not that he lost the 1964 election but that, faced by so many handicaps, he almost won). It will be left to Mr. Wilson between 1968 and 1970 to demonstrate whether recovery can be managed by a resourceful, optimistic and relatively young Prime Minister once the economic tide turns in favour of his government.

But the lesson for students of British Government is that even at times when the record and capacities of a Prime Minister are under the maximum criticism and therefore the office is at its weakest, overall direction can come from no other source, no junta can take command, powers that are circumscribed are not taken up by others but merely fall into abeyance and the only way out of the impasse is a recovery of the authority of the Prime Minister.

CHAPTER 21

THE CABINET: COMPOSITION AND CONDUCT

AROUND the Prime Minister, across the table and beside him sit the senior ministers who play the chief part in shaping the policy of the government, who chair the major Cabinet committees and who contribute most at Cabinet meetings. Of these, one of the leading figures is the Foreign Secretary.

THE FOREIGN SECRETARY

The conduct of foreign policy involves a rather special relationship between the Foreign Secretary, the Prime Minister and the rest of the Cabinet. With the Cabinet, the position is fairly constant. The Foreign Secretary is expected to conduct day-to-day business on his own (or with the aid of the Prime Minister) keeping the Cabinet informed of the general lines of policy. Once a week ministers are given a *tour d'horizon* with, perhaps, a request for a decision. The Foreign Secretary does not often send minutes or memoranda round the Cabinet and, when this does happen, it is usually to outline the background to some new problem which may have a rather obscure history. If a particular area or question requires constant detailed attention, the Foreign Secretary may ask for a Cabinet Committee to be set up. Sir Anthony Eden found that relations with Iran were " so complicated that I felt I could not handle it effectively by frequent references to the Cabinet " and he asked Sir Winston Churchill to form a committee. " I would report the results of our work to him and to the Cabinet from time to time." [1] Similarly a committee was set up in late July 1956 to prepare the diplomatic and military reactions to the nationalisation of the Suez Canal by the Egyptians.

Relations with the Prime Minister have always been close but have varied in form and emphasis. A. J. Balfour considered that

" It's the rarest thing when the Prime Minister and the Foreign Minister don't clash. . . . But you can't expect the P.M. *not* to

[1] Sir Anthony Eden, *Full Circle*, p. 199.

454

interfere with Foreign Office business. It's only when you get a combination of two men who see absolutely eye to eye and work in perfect harmony that you can avoid it. Lansdowne and myself were one of the rare cases—but I could give you any number of instances of the other. The fact is that the Foreign Office cannot be in a watertight compartment." [2]

On the other hand, Gladstone told Rosebery in 1893 that this was " the *first* time, during a Cabinet experience of twenty-two or twenty-three years, that I have known the Foreign Minister and the Prime Minister to go before a Cabinet on a present question with diverging views. It is the union of these two authorities by which foreign policy is ordinarily worked in a Cabinet." [3]

Both these views were in a sense correct in that if the Foreign Secretary and the Prime Minister had both strong and divergent views, there was bound to be a clash and the government could not be carried on if such disagreements were frequent or took place in full Cabinet. In order to resolve this problem, some accommodation was usually reached, falling into one of three patterns: a Prime Minister conducting external affairs with the aid of a compliant Foreign Secretary, complete harmony between the two men, or a strong Secretary of State who was trusted and given his head by the Premier.

Friction has arisen on four occasions since the First World War. Bonar Law was at the head of a frail and inexpert Cabinet whose supporters had strongly objected to Lloyd George's adventurous policy in the Near East. He therefore had to tell Curzon in clear-cut terms that he would not consider an open breach with the Turks over the question of Mosul and Curzon's petulant replies went far to convince Bonar Law that he was not a suitable successor as Prime Minister. [4] Having been Foreign Secretary as well as

---

[2] B. E. C. Dugdale, *Arthur James Balfour*, Vol. II, p. 292–293.

[3] R. R. James, *Rosebery*, p. 265.

[4] There is an example both of this petulance and the sort of support Curzon expected in a letter to Stanley Baldwin after the latter had become Prime Minister: " I must confess I am almost in despair as to the way in which Foreign Policy is carried on in this Cabinet. Any member may make any suggestion he pleases and the discussion wanders off into helpless irrelevancies. No decision is arrived at and no policy prepared. Do please let us revert to the time-honoured procedure. I am at any time at your disposal for discussion. I have no fear we shall not achieve harmony. But we must act together and the P.M. must see his F.S. through." G. M. Young, *op. cit.*, p. 50.

Prime Minister in 1924 and being both fascinated by and convinced of his own capacity for foreign affairs, Ramsay MacDonald could not bring himself to trust Arthur Henderson. The latter had plenty of self-confidence and did not need to lean on MacDonald who retaliated by saying (to King George V among others) that the negotiations for a treaty with Egypt had been badly conducted and by trying to circumscribe Henderson's activities.[5] These were, however, minor instances of friction compared with the breach that arose between Eden and Neville Chamberlain. The former believed that " it is essential that the Prime Minister and the Foreign Secretary should have a similar outlook and wish to pursue similar methods." [6] Yet Chamberlain's views were so definite that any underlying divergence of outlook between him and Eden soon became evident.[7] The Prime Minister began to act on his own, rejecting Franklin D. Roosevelt's offer of a conference on the maintenance of treaties without consulting anyone. He also by-passed Eden in dealings with the Italian ambassador and opened a direct line to Mussolini. Ultimately the Foreign Secretary found his position untenable and told the Cabinet he must resign. Neville Chamberlain noted that " I thought it necessary to say clearly that I could not accept any decision in the opposite sense." [8] Eden was replaced by Lord Halifax and he and Chamberlain had " absolute confidence in one another and a complete identity of purpose." [9] Halifax carried weight in the Cabinet and was a man of integrity and ability, his views happening to coincide almost directly with those of the Prime Minister. They disagreed only once when Chamberlain told the Press on March 10, 1939, that a disarmament conference might well be in session by the end of the

[5] H. Dalton, *Call Back Yesterday*, pp. 228 and 246, and Nicolson, *King George V*, p. 443. One result was that Henderson was not able to get his Heads of a Treaty with Egypt through the Cabinet.

[6] Quoted from Mr. Eden's resignation speech by Randolph Churchill in *The Rise and Fall of Anthony Eden*, p. 130.

[7] Iain Macleod denies that " Chamberlain interfered more with Foreign Office business than is natural for a Prime Minister at a time when foreign affairs are the dominant issue " but he realises that for this interference to be tolerable real harmony had to exist and this meant a Foreign Secretary who agreed in time and content with Chamberlain. See *Neville Chamberlain*, pp. 217, 220.

[8] K. Feiling, *op. cit.*, p. 338.

[9] This is Halifax's description of the relations that ought to obtain between the Prime Minister and Foreign Secretary and did so in his case. *Fullness of Days*, p. 195. See also The Earl of Birkenhead, *Halifax*, pp. 362, 364, 422, 425.

year. The Foreign Secretary protested that he had not been consulted, Chamberlain apologised, and Halifax for his part said that " nobody recognises more readily than I do that the *ultimate* responsibility must be yours." [10] Under Mr. Churchill, Eden sometimes complained that he was ordered about and overruled and given the minor but distasteful tasks, but he acquiesced.[11] When Eden became Prime Minister, he had Macmillan for a short period as Foreign Secretary. There was considerable friction and they disagreed over policy towards Russia, but in general Macmillan resented the rather querulous and constant interference of the Prime Minister in the work of the Foreign Office.[12]

Austen Chamberlain and Ernest Bevin were both examples of strong Foreign Secretaries given a free hand by their Prime Ministers. In the first instance, Stanley Baldwin took little interest in external policy and Austen Chamberlain laid all major matters before the Cabinet. His colleagues rejected the Geneva Protocol on his advice and agreed to try to reach a rapprochement with Germany which gave some security to France. After Chamberlain had gone to Geneva, Churchill, F. E. Smith and Amery had doubts about this " Locarno policy " but the Foreign Secretary replied that " I . . . will not consent to hold the post if the policy of the Cabinet is to be changed every few days." [13] Chamberlain persuaded his colleagues to accept his agreement with Egypt in November 1927, but on several occasions the High Commissioner, Lord Lloyd, was able to swing the Cabinet against the views of the Foreign Secretary by means of skilfully worded despatches.[14]

While Austen Chamberlain encountered something like the older notion of Cabinet control, Ernest Bevin settled most matters himself, usually after he had explained the position to Mr. Attlee. The latter carefully avoided personal intervention but supported Bevin when such questions as the Canal Base and relations in the Near East came before the Cabinet.

The final pattern is that of a Foreign Secretary acting as the

10 Feiling, *op. cit.*, p. 397.
11 Lord Moran reports Harold Macmillan as saying " for fifteen years . . . Winston has harried Anthony unmercifully, lectured him and butted in on his work, until poor Anthony is afraid to make a decision on his own." *Churchill, The Struggle for Survival, 1940–65*, p. 627.
12 A. Sampson, *Macmillan*, pp. 101–102.
13 Sir C. Petrie, *Life and Letters of Austen Chamberlain*, Vol. II, p. 264.
14 L. S. Amery, *My Political Life*, Vol. II, p. 306.

adviser and agent of the Prime Minister. Anthony Eden was a little more than this during the war and between 1951 and 1955, yet all major decisions went across the road to No. 10 Downing Street.[15] (In his first tenure of the office, Eden was often tried by Baldwin's reluctance to help him and to shoulder responsibility.[16]) When Macmillan left the Foreign Office and Mr. Selwyn Lloyd was appointed, Eden had an able and hard-working executor of his policies. Mr. Selwyn Lloyd continued in this post after Suez and the change of government as he also suited Macmillan, who developed that passion for foreign affairs which has gripped so many Premiers. The relationship changed a little during Sir Alec Douglas-Home's period in the office as he, though quiet, had great self-confidence and clarity of vision. Also he did not entirely agree with the Prime Minister's "wind of change" views on African affairs and preferred a return to an older concept of the primacy of British interests.

When Mr. Wilson became Prime Minister he intended to establish the kind of relations with Mr. Gordon-Walker which Attlee had had with Bevin. The two men met frequently for talks and certainly before every Cabinet, yet even in the three months that this relationship lasted (Mr. Gordon-Walker was unable to find a seat in Parliament, losing the Leyton by-election in December 1964) the Foreign Secretary found Mr. Wilson sending for foreign ambassadors and issuing statements on his own. Mr. Michael Stewart, who then took the office, was appointed on the assumption that Mr. Wilson handled the major themes of foreign policy and there was an easy co-operation. In the summer of 1966 Mr. George Brown moved to the Foreign Office, saying that he was an admirer of Ernest Bevin and clearly intended to be his own master. But by this time Mr. Wilson's personal interest and control were too clearly established and though Mr. Brown added a special impetus, particularly in European affairs, it was as second in command. This became evident when he accompanied the Prime Minister on a tour of the European capitals to test reactions to any British application to join the Common Market.

---

[15] Bevin "liked Eden, whom he thought well intentioned and able but weak in his relations with Churchill." F. Williams, *Ernest Bevin*, p. 230.
[16] Halifax, *op. cit.*, p. 193.

THE CHANCELLOR OF THE EXCHEQUER

The position of the Chancellor of the Exchequer is complex be-cause of his several functions. Economic and financial policy is so important that the occupant naturally tends to be one of the few who are in regular consultation with the Prime Minister. Austen Chamberlain had urged Bonar Law to take the post in 1915. " That office gives its holder great authority and power. There is none other except the Prime Ministership which gives such influence, or such a starting point for influence in the whole field of policy. It is second in the Government when in the right hands." [17] In framing his Budget, the Chancellor of the Exchequer deals only with the Prime Minister. On broader issues of economic policy, he acts as a senior minister in the Cabinet but he may, like Mr. Thorneycroft in January 1958, find himself deserted by the Premier and earning the old title of " the loneliest man in the Cabinet." The further task of supervising expenditure involves the Chancellor in intricate negotiations with individual departments.

The process of preparing a Budget follows a fairly regular pattern. The Chancellor may confine himself to his Treasury experts or he may sniff the air outside in the City, in industry, or even in certain academic circles. Meanwhile deputations come in and their views are noted. A Conservative may consider the sug-gestions of the Financial Committee of his Party, though Labour Chancellors have shown little respect for the financial views of their back-benchers. Then proposals are framed and the Chancellor will have a word with the Prime Minister, though this will not usually extend beyond three or four talks. Finally, the Cabinet is given a brief résumé before the Budget is put to the House. The original motives for leaving as short a time as possible between the explanations in Cabinet and the public announcement have been discussed [18] but in recent years the need for secrecy has been an additional reason. In 1930 the Budget Day was a Monday and MacDonald said the week-end allowed too much time for leaks. Snowden should tell the Cabinet on the Monday at 10.30 a.m. rather than on the Friday before. There are some grounds for this caution. In 1936 the proposals were disclosed ten days before

---

[17] Blake, *The Unknown Prime Minister*, p. 249.
[18] pp. 324–325, above.

Budget Day so as to avoid calling a special Cabinet during the Easter holidays. Rumours of leakage arose and finally led to charges against the Secretary of State for the Colonies, J. H. Thomas, who had to resign.[19] However, examples can be found of a Cabinet altering items in a Budget.[20] This is usually confined to the kind of political or administrative snags which would otherwise have to be withdrawn or amended in passage through the House. For instance elements in the Conservative Party and the City persuaded Mr. Heathcoat Amory to withdraw a retrospective tax on dividend stripping in 1959, and in 1966 Mr. Callaghan had to allow exemptions from the Selective Employment Tax for charities and alter its method of collection in agriculture. Nevertheless it remains true that the Cabinet exercises control over budget-making only inasmuch as the Chancellor is made aware of the general views of his fellow ministers and has to fit in with certain agreed lines of economic policy. Lord Woolton felt that over taxation " the Cabinet has all too little influence on one of its major responsibilities " and that since " the Cabinet has little to say . . . the Chancellor of the Exchequer is called upon to carry a responsibility much too heavy for any one man." [21] Mr. Enoch Powell agreed and also wanted budgetary policy to be made for several years at a time. Yet he recoiled from " the spectre of a budget-making Cabinet . . . with its terrors " and would prefer greater supervision by the Prime Minister instead.[22] Sir Anthony Eden agreed with this and said that " a Chancellor of the Exchequer is wise if he shares his burdens to some extent with the Prime Minister; clearly he cannot share them with the whole Cabinet." [23] This has, in fact, happened since Mr. Wilson took office. In 1966 the Chancellor proposed certain increases in taxation but the Prime Minister thought that they were too traditional and did not help economic change, the result being that the Selective Employment Tax was devised. This relationship may alter if the Prime Minister is not interested in or informed about economics but the political consequences of taxation and

[19] Viscount Simon, *Retrospect*, p. 224.

[20] p. 413–414, above.

[21] Woolton, *op. cit.*, pp. 373–375.

[22] J. Enoch Powell, " Treasury Control in the Age of Inflation," *The Banker*, 1958.

[23] *Full Circle*, p. 269.

of economic policy in general are so important that there will always be an element of supervision. It was disagreement on such broad economic matters that drove a wedge between Mr. Macmillan and Mr. Selwyn Lloyd leading in the end to the dismissal of the Chancellor of the Exchequer in July 1962.

The Chancellor's role as a supervising minister has arisen slowly over a considerable period of time. Long before 1914 all departments wishing to spend money had to win Treasury approval or take the dispute to the Cabinet. In the 1920s the Chancellor was supported by certain broad lines of policy, such as the economy proposals of the Geddes Committee and the working rule that the armed services would not be involved in any major conflict for ten years. Mr. Churchill in this office, imposed the Treasury's free trade views on a Cabinet which included such convinced protectionists as Austen and Neville Chamberlain and Leopold Amery. The first two Labour Governments had their domestic policy controlled by Philip Snowden, who was delighted when the Press began to refer to him as " the Iron Chancellor." Ministers, such as Lansbury, would bring schemes for relieving unemployment or aiding industry to the Cabinet. As they began to explain the project Snowden would break in with his harsh voice and emphatic manner. " It may shorten discussion on this matter Mr. Prime Minister, if I say that there is no money for it." " But we made a pledge in our election campaign on this point and . . ." " I made no such pledge," Snowden would retort. " It certainly featured in all my election speeches and was in my election address." " More fool you," was the crushing rejoinder. When Amery heard that J. H. Thomas was to be Lord Privy Seal with the task of combating unemployment he sent a letter of warning: " Jimmy, you are starting a job with a noose round your neck and the other end of the rope in Snowden's hands." [24] Under Neville Chamberlain as Chancellor and later when he lent his support as Prime Minister to his successor, Sir John Simon, the Treasury's grip on policy was in some ways even stronger. The rule that papers should be circulated only after they had been seen by all the departments concerned became a bulwark of Treasury policy. A proposal by Duff Cooper for expanding recruitment was delayed from October

[24] Amery, *op. cit.*, Vol. II, p. 502.

1936 till early 1937 primarily because the Chancellor, Chamberlain, did not like it.[25]

To this practice of having general lines of policy urged by strong Chancellors of the Exchequer, there was added, during the Second World War, a general responsibility for watching over the economic health of the country, the level of investment, employment, and prices and the balance of payments. An Economic Planning Section was set up which moved with Sir Stafford Cripps into the Treasury where it stayed till 1964. The planners forecast the desirable level of public expenditure and, thus armed, the Chancellor turned to the departmental ministers and told them to tailor their demands to fit the available material. At first sight it seems inevitable that the planners should be working in the Treasury and that overall responsibility for economic policy should lie with the Chancellor of the Exchequer. Such a situation must emphasise his position as a supervising minister, and yet it is by no means certain that " economic necessity " is not in fact his political policy dressed up in economic jargon. Aneurin Bevan took this view and felt that planning should be taken away from the Treasury and given to a separate Ministry of Planning whose proposals could be discussed on their political as well as financial merits by the Cabinet. He objected when a political decision to create a Health Service which did not inflict charges on the sick was undermined by budgetary decisions to create charges which, he was told, were economically essential and were in any case the business of the Chancellor of the Exchequer.[26] In 1958 Mr. Thorneycroft and his supporters prophesied financial ruin if deflationary policies were not enforced when, to many people the problem was one of lack of investment rather than too much. In this case the Prime Minister did not support his Chancellor and all the departmental ministers wished to continue their spending programmes, so that Mr. Thorneycroft

---

25 Duff Cooper, *op. cit.*, p. 199.
26 Aneurin Bevan also felt that financial planning tended to be unreal. He would vividly re-enact his disputes with the planners. " Sir Edwin Plowden came to me and said we must cut imports and to do this we must increase agricultural production. ' We need 35,000 more men on the land and I'm afraid the only answer is to cut your house-building programme.' So I replied: ' I know of no crucible which will take an unemployed plasterer in London and turn him into a cowhand in Kent in three months '." (This was told to the author in an interview on July 1, 1958.)

was overruled.[27] In the late 1950s, the Plowden Committee examined the whole question of financial co-ordination and control and reported in 1961, one of its recommendations being that there should be more careful vetting of departmental demands at Cabinet level. As a result, the Conservatives set up a special committee of the Cabinet serviced by a parallel committee of officials. The Labour Government in 1964 broadened the base of economic planning by establishing the Department of Economic Affairs. It consisted of the economic planning section of the Treasury, the regional development section of the Board of Trade and the officials attached to the National Economic Development Council. The Cabinet committee known as the Public Expenditure Scrutiny Committee (P.E.S.C.) was continued, its main purpose being to help the Chancellor in his task of controlling the spending departments. With three ministries concerned with trade, finance and economic planning, it was possible to agree that if the committee reported in favour of a cut, the department concerned would not reopen the matter in the Cabinet. But on broader issues, such as the choice between deflation or devaluation or the adoption of a prices and incomes policy, the Prime Minister has remained in control. The methods by which this control has been exercised have varied. At first in 1964 and 1965 the major decisions were taken by Mr. Wilson, Mr. Callaghan and Mr. Brown. After the sterling crisis of July 1966 the Prime Minister took a more active part by becoming chairman of a new economic policy committee and he personally announced the deflationary measures introduced in that month. The following summer Mr. Wilson decided to take personal charge of economic policy by becoming head of the D.E.A. with the new Cabinet Minister, Mr. Peter Shore, supervising the day-to-day work of the department. Three months later, in November 1967, Mr. Wilson and Mr. Callaghan as Chancellor agreed that devaluation could not be avoided and drew up a list of supporting economic measures. When a further " package " of cuts was needed to free resources for export, the Prime Minister was so determined that this unpleasant series of decisions could not be said to be the work of a narrow group and that no minister could

---

[27] When the dispute over the Health Service charges led to Bevan's resignation, Mr. Morrison was presiding over the Cabinet while the Prime Minister was in hospital. Mr. Attlee felt that Morrison came down too rapidly on Mr. Gaitskell's side and that " he lost me three ministers."

complain of lack of consultation, that he made the entire Cabinet and ministers of Cabinet rank meet for a total of thirty-two hours (some were only allowed to speak for a few minutes) while the Chancellor's proposals were put through.

Since the nineteenth century, the number of spending departments has increased, but the Treasury's relations with the Defence ministries still offer the best example of the difficulties of retaining financial control. Snowden summed the problem up succinctly. "It is useless for a Chancellor to argue with the Sea Lords on the technicalities of the Naval strength. The only effective policy that he can pursue is to say to the Admiralty: ' I can only afford to give you so much money ' . . ." [28] In 1938 Simon showed his power by imposing a ceiling on defence expenditure and leaving the three Services to work out their shares of the total. The relegation of the Chancellor of the Exchequer (that is the recognition that defence was more important than the desire to pursue orthodox economic policies) occurred when the Services were told to order all they needed irrespective of cost. After the war, Mr. Dalton and then Sir Stafford Cripps reimposed a maximum figure and it took the difficulties in Palestine in 1947 and Ernest Bevin's massive weight to get the total raised.[29] When rearmament was given top priority in 1950–51, the Services again were asked to say what they wanted and the finance would be found. After the Conservative victory in 1951, the pressures of the Korean War emergency declined and defence was again made to fit, with other items, into the overall total the government was prepared to spend. Under the Labour Government returned in 1964, a ceiling was fixed of £2,000 million at 1964 prices and the Defence Ministry asked to arrange its expenditure accordingly. Mr. Christopher Mayhew resigned on the grounds that for this sum the existing defence commitments could not be maintained: it had to be more money or fewer commitments.[30] Ultimately he was proved right when the Government was forced to withdraw from East of Suez by 1970–71, a decision which had to follow from financial cuts imposed by the full Cabinet on the Ministry of Defence. This only served to

[28] Snowden, *op. cit.*, Vol. II, p. 623.
[29] E. Shinwell, *Conflict Without Malice*, p. 198.
[30] He explains the arguments and the circumstances of his resignation in *Britain's Role Tomorrow* (Hutchinson, 1967).

emphasise that financial control is part of general policy and the Treasury can only act within the broader framework of government policy.

OTHER MINISTERS

The Minister of Defence is a relatively new appointment but his position in the Cabinet has been among the senior half dozen since the Second World War. In 1936, for a mixture of political and practical considerations, a Minister (Sir Thomas Inskip) was appointed, but he had no staff and few powers. As a result Inskip's chief task was to act as a kind of buffer between the armed forces and the Treasury, helping to share the funds allocated by the Chancellor between the three Services.[31] Lord Ismay has summed up the situation before 1940: " The root of the matter was that no living man . . . could have made a success of the appointment, unless he had been given not only a clear mandate that the rearmament programme was to have the highest priority . . . but also an assurance that he would have the whole-hearted support of the Prime Minister and his colleagues in the Cabinet in any steps which he thought necessary." [32] Mr. Churchill took the additional title of Minister of Defence during the war though his staff, in this capacity, consisted only of the Secretariat of the Committee of Imperial Defence. As the war came to an end, Mr. Attlee did not restore the Committee of Imperial Defence, but used a Defence Committee of the Cabinet under his chairmanship to provide the main directions.

In 1946 the Minister of Defence Act created a post whose function was " formulating and applying a unified policy " for the Services.[33] The first incumbent, Mr. A. V. Alexander, was content to meet the Chancellor of the Exchequer and fix the amount of money to be spent on defence. He then worked out its allocation

---

[31] Lord Chatfield, Inskip's successor in 1939, says that " the Treasury hope was that the Ministry of Co-ordination of Defence, would act as a kind of supporter of that department in its financial difficulties, and tone down the demands of the fight in departments." *It Might Happen Again*, p. 170. Both Hore-Belisha (*Papers*, pp. 34–35) and Duff Cooper (*Old Men Forget*, p. 216) confirm this judgment.

[32] Lord Ismay, *Memoirs*, p. 75.

[33] Mr. Duncan Sandys's words quoting from the Act in the debate on Defence on July 28, 1958.

among the forces with the aid of the Service Ministers.[34] Meanwhile the Prime Minister, working through the Defence Committee of the Cabinet, kept a special watch over the whole field. The authority of the Minister of Defence has slowly been increased, the chief steps being in January 1957, July 1958 and July 1963 when he was first given definite powers of decision over all important questions of policy and then the control of a single Ministry of Defence. In the debate on the 1958 White Paper (Cmnd. 476), Mr. Antony Head, a previous occupant of the post, said that the minister had always had adequate powers since he controlled the allocation of money. But the exercise of these powers required a minister who had been in office long enough to know what he wanted and who enjoyed the backing of the Premier. A feature of the post in the 1950s has been the rapid turnover of its occupants. There were seven Ministers of Defence in the six years between 1953 and 1959. The subject is a mystery to the ablest amateur, and it is very hard to acquire in a short time the competence necessary for effective control by means of financial and planning powers. Probably the explicit grant in 1957 and 1958 of powers that had hitherto been latent in the position was in response to the desire of new ministers to have all their authority conferred on them at once. In 1963 a further White paper (Cmnd. 2097) stated that these " arrangements . . . have not in practice secured the degree of central control . . . necessary in the national interest." A unified ministry was established and while defence policy was assigned to the Defence and Oversea Policy Committee of the Cabinet under the chairmanship of the Prime Minister, command and administration of the Services was placed in the hands of a Defence Council presided over by the Secretary of State for Defence.

Mr. Sandys was a powerful occupant of the post under the older arrangements, though his position was due in large part to Mr. Macmillan's support at that time for the policies Mr. Sandys was pursuing. Under the new dispensation, Mr. Healey by 1968 had held the office for three years and though he had established an unequalled grasp of its technicalities, his period in

---

[34] It was this policy of siding with the Chancellor that so infuriated Lord Montgomery and led him to ask the other members of the Chiefs of Staff Committee to join him in an appeal to Mr. Attlee to dismiss Mr. Alexander. The other Chiefs of Staff thought better of the idea.

office was marked by a continuous series of readjustments and reductions, those of January 1968 marking a turning point in the scale down of Britain as a military power.

Finally, among the major departments, the Home Office involves a series of duties in the field of law, order and internal regulation which, though not conferring any special power or preferment, have attracted some of the more senior men and considerable attention with the increasing concern over matters such as police powers and civil liberties.

In addition to these important offices, Lord President of the Council and Lord Privy Seal are ancient and dignified appointments which carry no departmental duties. Usually at least one of them is occupied by a major figure in the Cabinet. In recent years these posts have been combined with such functions as leading the House of Commons, a task which was performed by the Prime Minister—with the exception of Lloyd George—till 1940, but has since been left to a senior colleague. Other incumbents have led the House of Lords or have had special duties as chairmen of Cabinet committees or in the party organisation. Just as the Prime Minister has shed his task of leading the House of Commons to a senior minister, so the task of handling M.P.s and keeping contact with the party in the House has been delegated to the Chief Whip. For this reason, the Whip is now a constant attender at Cabinets and, in times of difficulty, can become a major figure. It is often said that Mr. Heath held the Conservative Party together as Chief Whip and paved the way for his election to the party leadership. Experience as varied as that of James Stuart (Chief Conservative Whip, 1941–51) and Mr. Silkin (Chief Labour Whip, 1966–68) shows that the job requires the highest abilities and can lead to senior ministerial appointments. The Whip should be and usually is consulted on appointments and promotions, the able discharge of his duties relieves the Premier of many worries and so the Whip, as in the case of Martin Redmayne, may become one of the most powerful members of the government.

Among the rank and file of Cabinet Ministers power varies, in part with the personality of the individual or his standing in the party, but more with the role of his department in the overall work of the government. Fuel and Power and Transport had added importance in the early years of Mr. Attlee's Government when major changes were taking place in these industries and again in the 1960s with the run down of the mining industry and the constant increase in traffic congestion. The Colonial Secretary was prominent in the period when the remaining African colonies were travelling rapidly along the road to self-government. It is unlikely that the Secretary of State for Scotland, the Ministers of Labour, of Housing and Local Government or of Education will ever be omitted from the Cabinet but none of these posts have offered much scope for the kind of work that attracts public attention or confers special powers on their occupants.

In the nineteenth century virtually all ministers were included in the Cabinet and the two posts which rated next in importance under the Cabinet were the Under-Secretaryships at the Foreign Office and the Treasury. Since 1945 between thirteen and sixteen departments have been left out of the Cabinet while the full number of political offices at the disposal of a government now totals a hundred. It cannot be said that this increase in the number of posts has been entirely due to administrative necessity as some junior ministers do not, nor were they appointed in the expectation that they would, fulfil essential government functions. These posts constitute one of the main methods by which a Prime Minister retains his control over his parliamentary followers.

PRIME MINISTERS AND THEIR CABINETS, 1922–40

Having considered the power and position of individual ministers, the next stage is to look at their relations in the particular Cabinets in which they served. As so much of the conduct and atmosphere of a government depends on the Prime Minister, it is both easiest and most suitable to group Cabinets under the names of the various Premiers.

Bonar Law's ministry was a " more or less conscious return to the traditional system, after Lloyd George's experiments in various kinds and degrees of overlordship." [35] In his election programme, the Premier promised to reorganise the Cabinet Secretariat and return the conduct of League of Nations and Foreign Affairs to the Foreign Office. He tried to leave departmental matters to the ministers concerned and when a delegation of the unemployed

[35] Lord Eustace Percy, *Some Memories*, p. 124.

called at No. 10 Downing Street, they were sent to see the Minister of Labour. In practice, this meant that the Garden Suburb was dispersed. Mr. (later Lord) Hankey was alarmed and wanted an inquiry into the work of the Cabinet Secretariat, which proved to be unnecessary as Bonar Law appreciated both the need for a secretariat and the value of Mr. Hankey's work; the latter now becoming Clerk to the Privy Council as well as Secretary to the Cabinet.[36] Despite this desire to shed some of his authority, Bonar Law found that his colleagues were inexperienced and he had to keep a careful watch on them, especially Curzon, who was revelling in his release from the dominance of Lloyd George. The one serious difference that occurred in this Cabinet was when Stanley Baldwin accepted a settlement of the British debt to the United States and then announced the terms as he stepped off the liner at Southampton, although the Prime Minister was strongly opposed. In the Cabinet only Novar and Lloyd-Greame (now Lord Swinton) supported Bonar Law and he contemplated resignation but finally agreed to accept the terms and stay rather than divide the Party again. Without his leadership the government could scarcely have survived and the other Cabinet Ministers sent Devonshire, Baldwin and Cave to implore him to remain. There was no inner Cabinet in any sense but the Premier had a small circle of men whom he liked and trusted—Lloyd-Greame, Beaverbrook and McKenna (the last two both outside the ministry). They all advised him to stay, and he decided to do so. Whatever his original intentions, L. S. Amery records that

> " Bonar Law, under his diffident manner, was really much more of an autocrat than Lloyd George, and much more set in his views. He was a businessman for whom an agenda was something on which decisions were to be got as quickly as possible, not a series of starting points for general discussion. Sooner than let discussion roam afield, or controversy be raised, he would cut things short by suggesting a committee." [37]

He had a clear mind and was a precise chairman in that his

---

[36] Warren Fisher, the Permanent Under-Secretary at the Treasury did, however, remind Mr. Hankey that he was a Secretary and pointed to the danger of being tempted to slip in occasional items of advice on foreign policy or to give precision in the minutes to vague and ragged Cabinet discussions.

[37] L. S. Amery, *op. cit.*, Vol. II, p. 246.

summary of a Cabinet discussion was always taken down verbatim by the secretary as the best possible record.[38]

Ramsay MacDonald was chiefly engaged by foreign problems and in his first Cabinet he also took charge of the Foreign Office.[39] Haldane considered that MacDonald was able but secretive about his departmental work. " Where he failed with his Ministry was in this that he did not care about other matters. He left them to us with the result that they seemed not to have the attention of the Prime Minister." [40] In his second ministry, foreign affairs were in the hands of Arthur Henderson and it is noteworthy that this was the only department in which MacDonald interfered. He grew alarmed over the decision to sign the Optional Clause (by which disputes were to be submitted to the Court of International Justice) and Henderson had to send MacDonald the minute of instructions for the Geneva delegates with his tick of approval in the margin. When Philip Snowden represented Britain at a reparations conference at The Hague, MacDonald first telegraphed asking Snowden to take a milder line and then retracted when the Chancellor turned on him.

Both Labour Cabinets were harmonious (though not friendly) and the chief complaint was that MacDonald was aloof and inaccessible. Haldane said that " it was almost impracticable to get hold of him for a quarter of an hour," [41] though a few very new adherents like Lord Parmoor could obtain an audience on certain matters such as those concerning the League of Nations. Willie Graham " considered it intolerable that a member of the Cabinet should have to go through a sifting process before meeting his leader." [42] Yet the remoteness of the Prime Minister did not give the rest of the Cabinet greater scope. After careful observation, Beatrice Webb recorded (April 1924) that at the

---

[38] Tom Jones, *Diary with Letters*, 1931–50, p. xxvi. The Earl of Swinton thought that " of all the Prime Ministers of this century Bonar Law had the clearest mind ": *Sixty Years of Power*, p. 56.

[39] MacDonald lightened his burden by being the only Prime Minister to delegate the task of chairing the Defence Committee of the Cabinet, in this case to Haldane.

[40] General Sir Frederick Maurice, *Haldane*, Vol. II, p. 180.

[41] R. B. Haldane, *Autobiography*, p. 332. Harold Nicolson has attributed this tendency in 1924 to a " cloud of overwork " hiding him from his colleagues and supporters (*King George V*, p. 388), but the same trait was apparent in his second government when MacDonald had no extra departmental burdens.

[42] T. N. Graham, *op. cit.*, p. 184.

" meetings only routine daily business is transacted—very few big questions of policy are discussed. The Prime Minister carries on his foreign policy without discussion. Meanwhile each of his Ministers goes his own way in his own department without consulting his Chief. I could not have imagined a body which has less *corporate* responsibility than MacDonald's Cabinet. Are all Cabinets congeries of little autocrats with a super-autocrat presiding over them? ".[43]

Brought up on the older notions of Cabinet government, Beatrice Webb still expected the major policies of the government to be thrashed out in free debate around the table in No. 10 Downing Street. Yet the conduct of this Cabinet, though it may have surprised her, was not so very different from that of its Conservative counterparts between the wars. There was only a difference of practice in that MacDonald did not insist on or give regular reports, especially over foreign affairs, so that the Cabinet was not adequately informed of the decisions that were being taken. Haldane complained that " the P.M., Snowden, Thomas, run the show so far as Allied Conference, Russia, and Ireland are concerned, without consulting anyone else." Sidney Webb did not sympathise as he thought these matters were largely the concern of the Prime Minister, the Foreign Secretary and the Chancellor of the Exchequer, and they should be allowed to handle them.[44] Judging by other governments, Haldane's objection should have been met by the three senior ministers coming to the Cabinet and, at intervals, explaining and talking about the steps they were taking, so that the other members knew what was happening and felt that they had been consulted or at least informed.

This failure to communicate explains the controversy about the Russian Treaty. Haldane in his *Autobiography* asserts that the Cabinet had neither accepted nor even heard that a Treaty had been agreed upon when the news appeared in the Press.[45] Putting together the various accounts, the salient facts emerge. In the spring of 1924, MacDonald called a conference to try to restore relations with

43 B. Webb, *Diaries*, 1924–1932, p. 20. See also *ibid.*, pp. 13, 31 and 38. Later in June, she concluded that " it is one-man government, undiluted in so far as the Prime Minister's work is concerned; and one-man government in each department until the department gets into a mess."
44 *Ibid.*, p. 40.
45 R. B. Haldane, *Autobiography*, p. 239.

Russia. On April 15 the agenda of the conference was circulated to Cabinet members and on July 22 there was a progress report. The various departments gave their views and the Under-Secretary at the Foreign Office, Arthur Ponsonby, was present when the question was discussed on July 30. The Cabinet authorised a loan provided the Russians accepted various terms on compensation, trade, etc. (Wedgwood dissented), and provided the Dominions did not object. The Cabinet then heard nothing till Snowden reported on August 5 that the talks had broken down over compensation for British property nationalised since the Revolution. That day a few Labour M.P.s saw Ponsonby and offered to act as intermediaries, with the positive idea of concluding an agreement which left the two matters of the loan and compensation to be settled later. Ponsonby obtained the consent of MacDonald and Snowden, the Russian and British delegates rapidly drew up a statement of the points on which they had agreed, and this was announced as a settlement in the Commons by Ponsonby on August 6. Thus Haldane's account is substantially correct and when Curzon asked for his comments in the Lords on August 6, he and other Cabinet Ministers had to confess ignorance as the last they had heard was Snowden's report of a breakdown on August 5. The Cabinet meeting on the 6th heard nothing of the Russian Treaty (it was primarily concerned with the Campbell case) and authority for the resumption of talks and the publication of the agreement came only from the Prime Minister and the Chancellor of the Exchequer.[46]

There was some talk of an inner ring in the first Labour Cabinet. Six leading front-benchers had met to decide whether to form a government, but apart from this, few decisions can be traced to any specific group. Beatrice Webb has a number of references to meetings of "the six"—MacDonald, Henderson, Clynes, Snowden, Thomas, and Sidney Webb—though she aptly concludes that they were "more the inner circle of the *Party Caucus* than the inner circle of the Cabinet." [47] The reason for this was that MacDonald did not discuss or concert governmental policy with "the six" or with any group of men. His closest confidant

---

[46] The best single account is in R. W. Lyman, *The First Labour Government*, pp. 192–196.

[47] B. Webb, *op. cit.*, p. 38.

was J. H. Thomas, but even this relationship did not count for much. MacDonald did not reveal his mind or his dealings with France, the League or America to the other pillar of the ministry, Snowden, and the latter kept his financial problems within the Treasury. " The six " met at Monday lunches specifically to consider party tactics in the House, relations with the Liberals and the lines of Labour propaganda in view of the constant possibility of a general election.

In the second Labour Government, five senior ministers discussed the distribution of posts—MacDonald, Henderson, Thomas, Snowden and Clynes—and Snowden reports that in 1931 " the ' Big Five ' of the Labour Party . . . were in the habit of meeting once a week in the Prime Minister's room for a general conversation about the parliamentary situation and the state of the Labour Party generally." [48] Thus the situation that existed in 1924 was reproduced almost exactly, since MacDonald had not altered his habits or his attitude towards any of his colleagues. Snowden remained the most powerful figure on domestic policy while Henderson, whom MacDonald definitely disliked, conducted foreign affairs more or less on his own. The Prime Minister still preferred J. H. Thomas but his confidences extended no further and the meetings of the " Big Five " did not take place to pre-digest matters going to the Cabinet or to plan policy but were concerned with the tactics imposed on a minority government.

The one occasion when some senior ministers did combine forces for certain political purposes was in the final crisis in August 1931. After the May Committee had reported, a Cabinet Economy Committee of five was set up (of the original " Big Five " Clynes was omitted and Willie Graham promoted) to go over the recommendations and put preliminary proposals before the Cabinet. The Economy Committee suggested reductions in expenditure amounting to £78½ million and at its meeting on August 19, the Cabinet provisionally agreed to cuts of a little over £56 million. The Cabinet also " empowered the Prime Minister and the Chancellor of the Exchequer to tell the Liberal and Conservative leaders what was going on from day to day, and keep them fully informed of the facts." [49] (There is no precise account of the

[48] Snowden, *op. cit.*, Vol. II, pp. 924–925.
[49] J. H. Thomas, *My Story*, p. 196.

instructions given to MacDonald other than general phrases such as this one just quoted from J. H. Thomas.) These conferences were intended to keep the other party leaders informed of the development of the financial crisis and of the Labour Government's proposals to combat it. MacDonald and Snowden, however, chose to interpret their task as telling the leaders of the other parties (who held the fate of the government in their hands) of the preliminary suggestions of the Cabinet Economy Committee and of the lower level of cuts so far agreed on by the Cabinet. Chamberlain, for the Conservatives, indicated that these proposals were totally inadequate and " in effect the Prime Minister and Snowden gave us to understand that they quite agreed." [50]

By this stage, the Cabinet Economy Committee had broken up. Henderson and, to a lesser extent, Graham were ranging themselves against some aspects of the economies. Now a genuine inner trio existed, in as much as MacDonald, Snowden and Thomas were trying to win the rest of the Cabinet over to the total sum of economies suggested by the committee. In this process, the decisive event was when the two emissaries to the conference with the leaders of the other two parties indicated that they had proposed cuts of £78$\frac{1}{2}$ million. Directly a figure was named, it became certain that the Conservative and Liberal leaders would not accept a lower amount and the position of any members of the Labour Cabinet who wanted fewer cuts was hopelessly prejudiced.[51]

---

[50] K. Feiling, *op. cit.*, p. 192.
[51] R. Bassett in his *1931 Political Crisis* sees that this is the main criticism of MacDonald's actions before the break-up of the Labour Government. He tries to defend MacDonald and Snowden by the very curious argument that it was correct to reveal the Cabinet Committee's " preliminary survey for the guidance of the Cabinet " (*i.e.*, the proposals for economies up to £78$\frac{1}{2}$ million) but it would not have been right to reveal the sum on which the Cabinet had, at that stage, reached agreement (£56 million). To have disclosed this latter figure would have been open to " legitimate criticism " as showing " the precise state of the Cabinet's unfinished deliberations." The position, in fact, is exactly the reverse. To reveal proposals put forward by a Cabinet Committee and to indicate that the Prime Minister and the Chancellor of the Exchequer agreed with these proposals was to reveal " unfinished deliberations " and to set a target of economies so that if any final conclusion was reached that fell short of £78 million, the other party leaders must know that the Premier and Chancellor had been overruled. To have outlined the £56 million of agreed cuts would have maintained a united front for the Cabinet, left the Liberal and Conservative leaders to take their independent stands, and would certainly not have precluded further economies being put forward by the Labour Cabinet as they continued their examination of the crisis. Sir Ivor Jennings is making the

The three Labour leaders failed in that they were unable to obtain substantial agreement on the figure that they and the Conservative and Liberal leaders considered adequate, and the Labour Cabinet tendered its resignation.

The importance of the Prime Minister comes out in many aspects of these two Labour Governments but never more than in the manner in which each of them came to an end. The success of the 1924 ministry lay in MacDonald's conduct of foreign policy and in the atmosphere of moderate, reformist idealism which he created. Its loss of face and of seats after its quite creditable record was due to skilful tactics on the part of its opponents but MacDonald had allowed himself to be out-manoeuvred. He should never have asked the Cabinet to make his mishandling of the Campbell case a question of confidence, and his own excessive sensitivity and exhaustion led to serious errors of judgment both before and during the election campaign.[52] In 1931 the Labour Party had to leave office and face an election hopelessly handicapped by MacDonald's disagreement with his colleagues and his decision to take the leadership of a National Government. Neither the loss of Snowden nor of any other Cabinet Minister (or their assumption of office in an anti-Labour government) would have raised anything like the difficulties caused by the departure of the Prime Minister and Leader of the Party. The whole question of the formation of a National Government and the participation of the various parties was settled by MacDonald and the other leaders without any consultation of the Cabinet which was still in existence, of the

same point when he says he doubts whether MacDonald and Snowden " represented the Government " in their discussions with the opposition leaders. Bassett's retort that " it is difficult to understand how a government can be more effectively represented than by the Prime Minister and (in circumstances of financial crisis) by the Chancellor of the Exchequer," shows a simple misunderstanding of the word " represent." By it, Jennings was not impugning the propriety of selecting them as delegates. He was questioning, quite rightly, their indication of their own views on policy instead of confining themselves to an explanation (=representation) of the views of the Cabinet as a whole. This could only have been done properly by putting forward the points on which the Cabinet had reached agreement.

[52] Snowden, who agreed with MacDonald on all issues of policy, bewailed " the great opportunities we have wantonly and recklessly thrown away by the most incompetent leadership which ever brought a Government to ruin." Quoted in F. Brockway, *Socialism over Sixty Years*, p. 215.

Conservative or Liberal Shadow Cabinets, of Parliament, or of the parliamentary parties.[53]

After 1931, MacDonald revealed much the same qualities as Prime Minister in the National Government. He was able and adroit in managing Cabinet discussions, largely because he had no fixed views on policy. He had no objection to going off the Gold Standard or to a gradual move in the direction of protection. A Committee of the Cabinet was appointed under Neville Chamberlain to examine the balance of trade and MacDonald, realising that it was bound to recommend a tariff, simply tried to keep the Liberal and Labour Free Traders in the Cabinet. He was not particularly concerned about the merits of either a protectionist or a free trade policy.[54] By 1932, the Prime Minister's chief National Labour colleague, Philip Snowden, was complaining that, " I have not had three minutes' private talk with you this year " [55] and when he and the Liberals resigned, MacDonald remained the tactful and conciliatory but largely powerless chairman of a Conservative Cabinet.

Stanley Baldwin's leadership has provoked much controversy, but his relations with his ministers are not hard to place. " In the full Cabinet he was content to act as an indulgent chairman, letting its members have their head but rarely giving them a lead " but " nevertheless, it was from first to last unmistakably a Baldwin Cabinet." [56] Swinton says that " as Prime Minister he was in command, always quietly but definitely in control. He handled his varied team of ministers with firmness and understanding, and directed the Cabinet's affairs with competence." [57] In one respect his capacity has never been denied. It was put best by Mr. Churchill in his comment that Baldwin was " the greatest party

---

[53] Lord Parmoor observes that he had always accepted Bagehot's account of the central place of the Cabinet in British government " but if this position is to be held by the Cabinet, it is not consistent with the treatment of the Cabinet in August 1931 by the Prime Minister." *A Retrospect*, p. 319.

[54] He told King George that if he could postpone the tariff question, the resignations of the Free Traders, coming at a later date, would not prove so serious. H. Nicolson, *op. cit.*, p. 495.

[55] Snowden, *op. cit.*, Vol. II, p. 1020. Snowden was excluded from a body again known as " the Six " which met to discuss the position of the National Government from time to time. It consisted of MacDonald and Thomas, Simon and Runciman, Baldwin and Neville Chamberlain. The only references to it are in Feiling, *op. cit.*, pp. 199 and 2 41.

[56] E. Percy, *op. cit.*, pp. 127–128.

[57] Swinton, *op. cit.*, p. 79.

manager the Conservatives ever had." [58] Yet there is an element of deprecation in this remark and the criticisms of Baldwin have been of his lack of understanding of world affairs and even of his willingness to subordinate national interests to short-run party considerations. To this he would certainly have replied that it was in the general interest as well as sensible Conservatism " to take all the heat and a great deal of the light out of affairs." [59]

Baldwin had no group of specially-favoured ministers, though he always listened with respect to William Bridgeman's views. For the most part, he relied on his own judgment and G. M. Young noted this as " a theme to which Baldwin constantly recurred. The Prime Minister is a person apart. He has no colleague of equal rank: no one to share his responsibilities: all his decisions are his own." [60] When he was new to the leadership with a strong majority and a recently-elected Parliament, Baldwin took a surprising but astute decision to raise the issue of protection in order to reunite the Conservatives and isolate Lloyd George. His Cabinet was taken aback and Salisbury, Derby, Devonshire and Cecil were opposed. Eventually they accepted Cave's suggestion that " in announcing his policy the Prime Minister should endeavour to avoid committing the Cabinet as a whole." This gave Baldwin all he wanted as he appreciated that the country would draw no distinction between his views and those of the government.[61] On the few occasions when he had an object in mind, Baldwin's leadership was quite definite. As Leader of the Opposition, he committed the Conservative Party to Dominion Status for India in October 1929 without consulting his colleagues and clung to this position through all the storms over the Round Table Conferences and the Government of India Bill. Austen Chamberlain said he had only known Baldwin influence a Cabinet decision on one occasion and that was when a fair number, perhaps even a majority, favoured the MacQuisten Bill (to substitute contracting in for contracting out of the trade union political levy) in 1925. Having asked for each minister's opinion in turn, Baldwin gave his view. After a pause, F. E. Smith declared that " if the Prime Minister could say to the

[58] Quoted by G. M. Young, *op. cit.*, p. 55.
[59] P. J. Grigg, *Prejudice and Judgment*, p. 174.
[60] G. M. Young, *op. cit.*, p. 53.
[61] Baldwin had consulted Neville Chamberlain, Lloyd-Greame and L. S. Amery at some of the stages in this process. L. S. Amery, *op. cit.*, Vol. II, p. 282.

House tomorrow just what he had now said to the Cabinet, he thought that the speech would be made with the unanimous support of the Cabinet, and would carry conviction to the House."[62] In the National Government, Samuel noticed that " Baldwin, rarely, if ever, initiated a proposal; but often, when a discussion was taking an awkward turn, he would intervene at the end with some brief observation, full of common sense, that helped to an agreement." [63] When the Abdication Crisis arose in his last year of office, he saw his way clearly and acted with precision and determination. Though Baldwin did not normally give a lead, ministers soon came to realise that if a measure was to make any progress it was essential to buttonhole the Prime Minister. Neville Chamberlain struggled to get a conference with him to clear the ground for his Poor Law Reforms while Sir Samuel Hoare thought that it was only necessary to have the Prime Minister's consent for his scheme of partitioning Abyssinia.[64]

Thus if Baldwin let the Cabinet drift on most occasions it was because he, his party and the country wanted to drift. Sometimes however, he was unhappy about the turn taken by events. The decision to have a showdown when the T.U.C. threatened a general strike was not typical and was the work of a majority in the Cabinet which did not include Baldwin.[65] As a result he did not attend the Cabinet Committee formed to watch over affairs during the emergency and remained singularly detached from its decisions. To some, it appeared as if he had lost control of the Cabinet in late 1926 and 1927, for he could scarcely have welcomed the Trades Disputes Act (embodying the principle he had resisted in the MacQuisten Bill) and there was a proposal for a reform of the House of Lords which seemed to have been imposed on Baldwin but which was later abandoned.[66]

[62] Halifax, *op. cit.*, p. 102.
[63] Samuel, *op. cit.*, p. 215.
[64] He was not wrong in this so far as the reactions of the Cabinet were concerned. The other ministers were quite prepared to accept the Hoare-Laval proposals and only changed their mind when the public reaction was so hostile.
[65] On Sunday, May 2, with the strike called for the next morning, the T.U.C. decided to press the miners to accept a compromise formula drafted by a Cabinet Committee consisting of Baldwin, F. E. Smith and Worthington-Evans. Before this could be done the Cabinet called off the negotiations on the pretext that a threat by the printers on the *Daily Mail* was an " overt act." See C. L. Mowat, *Between the Wars*, pp. 304–308.
[66] G. M. Young, *op. cit.*, p. 124.

These temporary lapses of control over the government were due to the Premier's lassitude and indolence (bemoaned by his closest supporters) [67] which on occasion undermined both his desire and his capacity to restrain the more active and, in some cases, the more right-wing elements in his ministry. Baldwin was not interested in administration and the only Cabinet committees over which he presided were the Committee of Imperial Defence and a Committee on Unemployment. The effect of the Prime Minister's negative attitude, except where political tactics were concerned, was to dampen down the ardent spirits in his 1924–29 Cabinet and to keep the 1935–37 ministry coherent but quiet.

In the Cabinet itself, Baldwin sat back and let discussion proceed freely. Amery made his civil servants miserable by speaking so much that his proposals lost ground. Churchill, though loquacious, was to the point. Neither Simon nor Hoare were popular but both were effective round a table. Lord Eustace Percy describes the " practice of full and rounded oral dissertations by the Foreign Secretary and the Chancellor of the Exchequer. That practice sometimes irked me, for these dissertations occupied almost the first half of every regular Cabinet meeting; but they had the immense advantage of acquainting the full Cabinet well in advance of proposals for action, with the trend of the minister's mind." He also noted that all significant questions were pre-digested by the senior ministers. " In the years 1924–29 I remember, of course, many occasions when a policy thus worked out was discussed and accepted by the full Cabinet; but none where the discussion taken by itself could be regarded as adequate, and only one when the Cabinet rejected a strong recommendation of a responsible minister." Lord Eustace Percy concluded from his experience of Baldwin's governments that when proposals had been worked out by committees or by individual ministers, and the Cabinet's mind had been prepared in advance, the machinery worked well, but that " no Cabinet large or small can originate policy." [68]

In contrast to Baldwin, Neville Chamberlain " was always ready to take the lead . . . his ideas were positive and clear-cut; he

[67] Tom Jones had been Assistant Secretary to the Cabinet in the 1920s. He was a close friend of Baldwin's and wrote many of the Premier's speeches. Jones' *Diary with Letters, 1931–50* abounds with such remarks as: " His continued silence and passivity greatly weaken his influence and it is very difficult to bring him to the point of positive action ": p. 69.

[68] Lord Eustace Percy, *op. cit.*, pp. 125–126.

was tenacious in pursuit of them, whether in the Cabinet itself, or
its committees, or in the conversations that, as in all governments,
were continually proceeding among its members." [69] Ernest Brown,
his Minister of Labour, recalled "the comfort it had been to
hard-pressed departmental Ministers to know that, when their
subjects have to be discussed, whoever else had not read their
papers and digested them, one man had—the Prime Minister." [70]
This change was quite conscious, for Neville Chamberlain observed
that "in the past, I have often felt a sense of helpless exasperation
at the way things have been allowed to drift in foreign affairs; but
now I am in a position to keep them on the move, and while I
am Prime Minister I don't mean to go to sleep." [71] Swinton
observed that "as Chairman of Cabinet he was incisive rather
than autocratic on home affairs. . . . It was when he ventured
into foreign affairs for the first time in his life that he became
autocratic and intolerant of criticism." [72] On the Committee of
Imperial Defence he was "persistent, single-minded and very self-
confident." [73] His policy was not to remain unconcerned as Stanley
Baldwin had done but to encourage all ministers to come and work
out their problems in personal discussions with the Prime
Minister.[74] Chamberlain also kept a tight hold on the party
machine and on his followers in the House of Commons.[75]

As a result of this definite leadership, "Chamberlain seemed
at once to crystallise all the fluid forces in the Cabinet" [76] and such
men as Mr. Eden and Duff Cooper, whose reactions were slightly
different, soon found their divergencies underlined. There was a
tendency for those whose minds ran on similar lines to find themselves drawn into closer co-operation with the Prime Minister,
while those who had reservations fell back. The same attractions
operated on the Civil Service, so that Horace Wilson became the

[69] Samuel, *op. cit.*, p. 215.
[70] Iain Macleod, *Neville Chamberlain*, p. 201.
[71] Feiling, *op. cit.*, p. 389. Tom Jones records that "he told Nancy [Astor] last
week that he meant to be his own foreign minister and also to take an active
hand in co-ordinating ministerial policy generally, in contrast with S. B.
[Baldwin]." *Op. cit.*, p. 350.
[72] Swinton, *op. cit.*, pp. 110–111.
[73] Ismay, *op. cit.*, p. 93.
[74] *Hore-Belisha Papers*, p. 16.
[75] The Whips went so far as to say that "no Conservative Prime Minister had
ever had so strong a hold on his Party in the House of Commons." Viscount
Templewood, *Nine Troubled Years*, p. 386.
[76] *Ibid.*, p. 257.

Premier's chief assistant in London.[77] A section of the Foreign Office sympathised with Mr. Eden at the time of his resignation, but Chamberlain was able to obtain the advice and information he wanted. Nevile Henderson, who passionately believed in the Premier's policies, was sent as Ambassador to Berlin. At certain crucial periods while Mr. Eden was still Foreign Secretary, Chamberlain established private contacts with the Italian Ambassador in London and with Mussolini through Austen Chamberlain's widow in Rome.

Chamberlain's Cabinet was formed in May 1937 and next month he announced that it would be " the very midsummer of madness " to continue with sanctions against Italy. In his diary he noted: " I did not consult Anthony Eden, because he would have been bound to beg me not to say what I proposed." [78] Mr. Eden, though Foreign Secretary, did not carry great weight, largely because the Prime Minister wanted to direct foreign affairs and did not trust him. Control was exercised through a Foreign Affairs Committee of the Cabinet which had met once or twice under Baldwin but had not been put to regular use. There was no objective reason why Sir Samuel Hoare, who was actively disliked by many Conservatives and had just come through the catastrophe of the Hoare-Laval Pact, should have had more influence than the popular and successful Foreign Secretary. Yet there Hoare was with Simon, Halifax, Oliver Stanley, Malcolm MacDonald and others on the Foreign Affairs Committee to watch over Mr. Eden. Hoare considers this question and concludes that " I suppose it was the sense of agreement both in outlook and method that made him [Chamberlain] take me into his confidence on foreign questions." [79] In early 1938, the Prime Minister rejected Roosevelt's proposal for a Conference on safeguarding existing frontiers,

---

[77] Horace Wilson agreed wholeheartedly with both Chamberlain's domestic and foreign policies. He " more than any Minister or civil servant . . . developed the new technique . . . under which the heads of the principal departments jointly sorted out the data of the more important problems before they went to the Cabinet." Wilson was originally at the Ministry of Labour, but Chamberlain " insisted upon taking him into the new field of foreign affairs." The Permanent Under-Secretary at the Foreign Office, Sir Robert Vansittart, was not in full harmony with the Prime Minister and was moved out of the main line of business to the post of Chief Diplomatic Adviser. *Ibid.*, p. 261.

[78] Feiling, *op. cit.*, p. 296.

[79] Templewood, *op. cit.*, p. 260.

without consulting Mr. Eden or the Cabinet.[80] When the Foreign Secretary objected, his complaint was heard by the Foreign Affairs Committee, and " the Cabinet as a whole learnt of the President's message only when the whole matter was past history, nor were we told that there had been any divergence of opinion between the Prime Minister and the Foreign Secretary." [81] When a further disagreement arose over the resumption of negotiations with Italy, Mr. Eden said he would resign. The matter was taken to the full Cabinet and Chamberlain " thought it necessary to say clearly that I could not accept any decision in the opposite sense." [82]

During the spring and early summer of 1938, the Foreign Policy Committee met regularly. Halifax, the new Foreign Secretary, would explain the latest problem " and Chamberlain would almost invariably be ready with suggestions for dealing with it." Simon, Hoare and Halifax were the Prime Minister's chief supporters and, on occasion, the Committee would even proceed to draft despatches. (The Chiefs of Staff attended to give advice.) The only criticism which Hoare could accept was that these meetings " tended to short-circuit the full Cabinet," but he added that decisions were always reported to the Cabinet and its approval obtained.[83] Chamberlain did not, however, always consult the committee. Over the German seizure of Austria in April 1938 he and Halifax determined the British response, and these two also agreed to naval staff talks with the French.[84] On September 10, the Prime Minister told Hoare of his private plan to fly to see Hitler. Halifax and Simon then called, and the four conferred repeatedly over the next three weeks. They endorsed the idea of a visit to Germany and the Cabinet was told after the telegram had been sent. Throughout the crisis and the three flights to Germany, the " Big Four " discussed and settled British policy and then met the Cabinet. They were better informed, carefully prepared, and were urging a policy which had the support of the majority of the Conservative Party and which was well received in the country. At several points other members of the Cabinet tried to break in. When the French leaders came over to discuss

---

[80] Earl of Avon, *The Eden Memoirs*, Vol. II, pp. 554–555.
[81] Duff Cooper, *op. cit.*, p. 210.
[82] Feiling, *op. cit.*, p. 338.
[83] Templewood, *op. cit.*, p. 290.
[84] Duff Cooper says the staff talks were agreed by Chamberlain and Halifax " disregarding the views of many of their colleagues." *Op. cit.*, p. 220.

the situation created by Hitler's ultimatum at Godesberg, Hore-Belisha passed a note across the table: " Why should not the French Ministers meet the whole Cabinet ? " " Perhaps at the second meeting, but not at the first," was Chamberlain's reply, though even this was not conceded.[85] The " Big Four " saw Daladier and his colleagues, subjecting them to an intense and hostile cross-examination. The last stages of the crisis moved so rapidly that two of the four tended to fall out and Halifax and Chamberlain were left in effective charge. The final agreement at Munich was the work of the Prime Minister and was submitted by him to the Cabinet for ratification.

Sir Samuel Hoare concludes that " whilst the prime mover," Chamberlain " was never the dictator of the Government's policy." [86] This is true in as much as none of the Cabinet objected to the main lines of appeasement. Chamberlain's policy was welcomed by his Party and by the public until April 1939, and even then there were few doubts. The only ministerial critic of his earlier actions had been Mr. Eden, and he did nothing to rally dissidents or build up a different attitude to the assumptions on which the government's policy was based. At the time of Munich, Duff Cooper, Walter Elliot and Oliver Stanley accepted the idea of ceding the Sudetenland to Germany and were unhappy merely over the methods that had been adopted and the guarantees and compensations offered to Czechoslovakia. In the end only Duff Cooper resigned, and he found little response to his arguments.

So it cannot be argued that Chamberlain dictated to his Cabinet in the sense that he imposed a policy on them which they definitely disliked. The significance of these years in the history of the Cabinet is that it adds to the evidence that the Cabinet does not make policy. Decisions are taken at various levels and if the Prime Minister is inactive little is done and most of the plans come from ministers, departments or Cabinet committees. But a successful, strong and opinionated Prime Minister can put his impress on a whole government. His ideas will be worked out either by himself or with a few colleagues. If there is an " inner ring," the qualification for entry is not seniority, office or ability but possession of the Prime Minister's confidence. It is easiest for such a Premier to conduct affairs with the aid of the departmental ministers concerned,

[85] *Hore-Belisha Papers*, p. 147.
[86] Templewood, *op. cit.*, p. 375.

and the Cabinet falls into place as a forum for informing his colleagues of decisions that have been taken. In these circumstances it is very hard for a minister who begins to have doubts to intervene with effect. He has insufficient knowledge, he is always too late, and is contending with the Prime Minister and the men whom the latter has elevated to a position of trust. Also, when decisions have been taken, there is little that can be done other than protest in the secrecy of the Cabinet or resign. Normally such divergencies are avoided because policies take time to mature, and the views of the Prime Minister, if he is a positive leader, either permeate his colleagues or the latter react and leave office. On the other hand the Premier will make adjustments to meet changes of attitude among those who normally agree with him, so that if trouble does arise it will usually be confined to one or two men at the bottom of the table. The interesting fact about the policy of appeasement is not the odd objection it encountered but that Chamberlain could induce such fervent support for it among both the ranks and the leadership of the Conservative Party.

THE SECOND WORLD WAR

On the outbreak of war, Neville Chamberlain formed a small War Cabinet composed of the " Big Four " of the previous year, Lord Chatfield as Minister for Co-ordination of Defence, the three Service Ministers, and Lord Hankey as Minister without Portfolio. The Committee of Imperial Defence was abandoned and the War Cabinet met every day at 11.30 a.m. After the Chiefs of Staff and Service Ministers had reported, members usually faced a long agenda and the Prime Minister only invited those directly concerned to speak.[87]   In October, a Military Co-ordination Committee was constituted with Chatfield and the Service Ministers as members, the Chiefs of Staff always being present as advisers.   So there were three stages in the preparation of war plans.[88]   First, the Chiefs of Staff met and discussed problems which then went to the Military Co-ordination Committee. It would re-examine the question and frame an agreed recommendation, or its view

---

[87] Lord Chatfield, *op. cit.*, p. 180.
[88] Mr. Churchill refers to a Defence Committee of the Cabinet at this stage; *The Second World War*, Vol. I, p. 464. But Lord Ismay is quite explicit that it only played a significant role after Mr. Churchill became Prime Minister, and his definite assertion must carry more weight than a casual, and perhaps misplaced, reference by Mr. Churchill. Ismay, *Memoirs*, pp. 109 and 159–165.

and the reports of the Chiefs of Staff would be sent up to the Cabinet to be re-examined and a final decision reached. As Mr. Churchill puts it: " everything is settled for the greatest good of the greatest number by the common sense of most after the consultation of all." [89]

As might be imagined, such a system did not work well. In September 1939 Mr. Churchill as First Lord of the Admiralty had asked for permission to mine the passages along the Norwegian coast used by ships taking essential iron ore to Germany. The proposal went back and forth between departments, the Joint Planning Committee, the Chiefs of Staff, the Cabinet, the United States and Dominions governments so that a decision was delayed till April 1940. [90] When it was evident that Italy was about to declare war, Mr. Dalton as Minister for Economic Warfare asked for authority to stop ships with valuable war material on their way to Italy. The Cabinet agreed on June 2 but departmental objections and requests for clarification prevented action for eight days till, in fact, Italy had declared war. [91] The Norwegian campaign finally exposed the government's weaknesses both at ministerial level and in the machinery of control. It was found that the leaders of the three Services had not consulted each other over appointments or directives and that there was little grasp of the war as a whole. The Prime Minister was not in sufficiently close contact to enforce co-operation and when the Chiefs of Staff changed their minds, as over the attack on Trondheim, the Cabinet could do little but accept the advice of the experts.

Chatfield had felt for some time that his position as Minister for the Co-ordination of Defence was anomalous since the three Service Ministers were members both of the Military Co-ordination Committee and the War Cabinet. So, on April 3, 1940, he resigned and Chamberlain asked one of these ministers, Mr. Churchill, to take the chair at meetings of the Committee. The latter realised at once that he had " an exceptional measure of responsibility but no power of effective direction " and " soon perceived that only the authority of the Prime Minister could reign over the Military

[89] W. S. Churchill, *The Second World War*, Vol. I, p. 464.

[90] Mr. Churchill's comment is that " one can hardly find a more perfect example of the impotence and fatuity of waging war by committee or rather by groups of committees." *Ibid.*, p. 458.

[91] Hugh Dalton, *The Fateful Years*, pp. 340–344.

Co-ordination Committee." [92] He was also aware of Chamberlain's great hold over the Conservative Party and did not wish to jeopardise his existing opportunity to serve the nation as First Lord of the Admiralty. From the first Mr. Churchill had taken care to give no appearance of challenging Chamberlain or of arguing with him at Cabinet. All his suggestions were put to the Premier privately or by letter. In this way, he urged Chamberlain to come to the Military Co-ordination Committee and the latter presided over most of the meetings concerned with the Norwegian campaign. At this stage, Mr. Churchill went a step further and said the Prime Minister must remain in active control. If not " you will have to delegate your powers to a Deputy who can concert and direct the general movement of our war action, and who will enjoy your support and that of the War Cabinet unless very good reason is shown to the contrary." [93] Chamberlain considered this bid for powers to run the war and on May 1 he authorised Mr. Churchill not only to chair the Military Co-ordination Committee in his absence but to give directions to the Chiefs of Staff, though they and the Service Ministers could still put matters to the Committee or to the Cabinet. This scarcely satisfactory compromise lasted for only a week before the debate on the Norwegian campaign led to the resignation of Neville Chamberlain.

When Mr. Churchill became Prime Minister, he had to work at a desperate pace and it was not till 1941 that his system of control settled into a fairly definite form. At the centre was the War Cabinet of eight to eleven members, most of whom had departmental duties.[94] On the military side, the Prime Minister took the title of Minister of Defence and presided over the Defence Committee of the Cabinet [95] and the Chiefs of Staff Committee. (The Military Co-ordination Committee was abolished.) The Service Ministers were not in the Cabinet or on the Chiefs of Staff Committee and they soon ceased to play any large part in framing

---

[92] Churchill, *op. cit.*, Vol. I, pp. 463–465. Sir Anthony Eden made the same point. See Earl of Avon, *The Reckoning*, p. 90.

[93] *Ibid.*, pp. 505–507.

[94] Mr. Churchill decided that non-departmental ministers " tend . . . to become more and more theoretical supervisors and commentators, reading an immense amount of material every day, but doubtful how to use their knowledge without doing more harm than good." *Op. cit.*, Vol. I, p. 327.

[95] The Defence Committee consisted of the Deputy Prime Minister, the Foreign Secretary, the Minister of Production, the three Service Ministers, the three Chiefs of Staff and the Chief of Combined Operations.

military plans or in the conduct of operations.[96] At first the Defence Committee of the Cabinet met fairly often (forty times in the rest of 1940 and seventy-six times in 1941) but as confidence grew, it became less necessary and only twenty meetings were held in 1942, dropping to ten in 1944. There was a " Cabinet Parade " on Monday mornings when the War Cabinet, Service Ministers, Chiefs of Staff and most departmental Ministers met to report on the week's events. Then the War Cabinet sat alone on the other days to deal with all major questions though, as the war continued, they left military operations increasingly to Mr. Churchill and the Chiefs of Staff.

The Joint Planning Committee (described by Mr. Churchill, on an earlier occasion, as " the machinery of negation ") had worked under the Chiefs of Staff but in August 1940 it was made part of the Secretariat attached to Mr. Churchill as Minister of Defence. (This was the Secretariat of the former Committee of Imperial Defence under General Ismay.) So the Joint Planning Committee was available to provide information and work out ideas coming from the Prime Minister or from the Chiefs of Staff.

In addition, Mr. Churchill took the major lines of foreign policy into his own hands and dealt with the President of the United States and, to a much lesser extent, with Joseph Stalin, by direct correspondence. Some 950 messages went from the Prime Minister to Franklin D. Roosevelt during the war. To maintain constant collaboration on all military plans, a Combined Chiefs of Staff Committee was set up in Washington in December 1941. " Thus the President and Prime Minister, with the Combined Chiefs of Staff as their military advisers, constituted in fact, though not in name, a supreme war council which directed the war efforts, not only of their own countries, but of *all* the nations engaged in war against the Axis, with the exception of Russia." [97]

With a world-wide war, there was a danger that disputes in the

[96] P. J. Grigg, who became Secretary of State for War in February 1942 records that " the share of the Secretary of State for War in major operational policy from 1940 to 1945 was a subordinate one." *Op. cit.*, p. 356. It had been a little more between May and December 1940 under Eden. See Earl of Avon, *The Reckoning*, pp. 129, 134, 138, 144–146.

[97] Ismay, *op. cit.*, p. 245. Mr. Churchill also built up a small personal staff under Professor Lindemann (later Lord Cherwell) which provided him with information, suggested ideas, and chased up the decisions of the War Cabinet. It undoubtedly contributed to the Prime Minister's pervasive influence over all aspects of the government.

various theatres would all be referred back to London. To prevent such delays, a Standing Ministerial Committee under Mr. Anthony Eden was set up in London to watch over Middle Eastern questions.[98] It achieved little and the ultimate solution was the appointment of a Cabinet Minister resident in the area. At first sight, it was impossible for a minister in Cairo, Singapore, West Africa or Algiers to have any precise idea of the views of the Cabinet in Britain but this was not really necessary. The real requirement was that the minister should appreciate the general direction of Allied policy and then simply instil a degree of awe into the local commanders so that his solutions of disputes would be accepted as final. When Mr. Churchill sent Swinton out to West Africa in 1942 he said " You will have absolute power out there, you will be a Cabinet of one, you will get things done, and I will always back you." [99] Mr. Oliver Lyttelton (now Lord Chandos) was very successful as Minister Resident in the Middle East and relieved the generals of so many of their supply and priority problems that, on his recall, there was an immediate request for a replacement.[1]

On home affairs, the War Cabinet was the final authority but most matters were handled by the Lord President's Committee under Sir John Anderson [2] and later Mr. Attlee. It was similar to the old Home Affairs Committee under Lloyd George and became a kind of sub-Cabinet acting for the parent body over a wide field. Much of the success of the machinery of government was due to the delegation of issues such as manpower, food, materials to committees chaired by members of the War Cabinet.

In these ways, Mr. Churchill took the post of Prime Minister with all the powers of appointment, dismissal and direction which had accrued to it since the turn of the century, and refashioned

---

[98] It was appointed on July 10, 1940, and consisted of the Secretaries of State for War, India and the Colonies.

[99] Swinton, *op. cit.*, p. 134. Macmillan, who was sent to watch over an area where the Americans were in chief control (as opposed to the Middle East and West Africa) had a slightly different role. See Harold Macmillan, *The Blast of War*, pp. 215–218.

[1] In addition to Mr. Lyttelton at Cairo, Duff Cooper was sent to Singapore as Minister of State for the Far East (this did not last long as a Supreme Commander was appointed with American agreement) and Lord Swinton to West Africa. Swinton, *I Remember*, p. 158.

[2] Smuts told Attlee (when there was a need for a Viceroy of India) " Don't let Churchill send Anderson away. Every War Cabinet needs a man to run the machine. Milner did it in the First World War, and Anderson does it in this." J. W. Wheeler-Bennett, *John Anderson, Viscount Waverley*, p. 276.

the war machine around it. Increasingly Premiers had found that they could deploy the various offices, and alter the arrangement of Cabinet committees to fit in with their own interests and with the personnel and problems that faced them. Thus Lloyd George had kept a tighter hold than some Prime Ministers on foreign policy and supplemented the Cabinet with conferences of ministers and powerful committees. Bonar Law and Baldwin had ended these arrangements in favour of their own methods of supervising policy while MacDonald in 1924 and Neville Chamberlain had used different devices to ensure that they controlled foreign policy. Mr. Churchill came to this task with many advantages. His exclusion from office in the 1930s meant that he bore no responsibility for the errors of that period, he owed no political debts, had great support in the country, and was liked by the Labour Party as much as, or in the earlier stages more than, by the Conservatives. While Neville Chamberlain had been in office there had been none of the dispersion of power that had taken place between 1914 and 1916 and the new Prime Minister had himself elected Leader of a compact and docile party when his predecessor died in late 1940. Finally he came to power in the gravest possible national emergency, with the widest field of discretion open to him and unrivalled experience on which to draw.[3]

The great virtue of Mr. Churchill's system was that he was able to initiate and watch over the preparation of military plans from the earliest stages. There was no possibility of depriving the Prime Minister of information or of alternative advice. As a result, disputes were kept within the circle of the Prime Minister and the Chiefs of Staff, each protagonist obtaining the facts and arguments he needed from the Joint Planning Committee. Proposals were argued on their merits and not on a politician versus soldier basis, so that Mr. Churchill was never faced with a single cut and dried strategic scheme and no alternative. At the same time he controlled foreign policy and knew that home affairs would be conducted in the manner which gave most support to his war effort. Only a Prime Minister can make final and overruling decisions and Mr. Churchill was able to bring this capacity to bear in so many

---

[3] Oliver Stanley in September 1939, " remarked apropos of Winston that he regretted his expenditure on *The World Crisis*, as Winston in his speeches to the Cabinet recited his own chapters verbatim." *Hore-Belisha Papers*, p. 235.

fields of governmental activity that his "personal, direct, ubiquitous and continuous supervision"[4] gave unity and vigour to the whole conduct of the war from the level of particular military operations to that of world strategy.

Some contact with this system led Harry Hopkins to say that "I have learnt that the provisions of the British Constitution and the powers of the War Cabinet are just whatever Winston Churchill wants them to be at any given moment."[5] Mr. Churchill denies this suggestion and said that while he was seldom challenged on major issues, he always had to carry his colleagues with him. This was true on several fronts. In his constant collaboration with the Chiefs of Staff, the Prime Minister would have plans prepared, constantly scrutinise the proposals put to him, and press his views. But in the last resort he never overruled his military advisers on military questions.[6] When the Admiralty considered the risk of shipping an armoured brigade through the Mediterranean was too high (in August 1940) Mr. Churchill records that "my relations with the Admiralty were too good to be imperilled by a formal appeal to the Cabinet against them."[7] After a disastrous Russian convoy, the Prime Minister wanted to send a large part of the fleet and risk an action with the Tirpitz, but the Admiralty refused. Another answer to the losses on these convoys was to seize northern Norway (operation Jupiter), a typically Churchillian project which was rejected by the Chiefs of Staff. The most serious difference occurred over strategy in the Pacific. At the Cairo Conference the Combined Chiefs of Staff produced a report according to which the quickest way to win the war in the East was a direct naval and airborne attack on Japan itself and Britain was to contribute the left wing of the advance. Mr. Churchill refused to agree on the grounds that Britain, to re-establish herself, must reconquer South-East Asia and the first point was the western tip of Sumatra. Then Singapore would fall. Mr. Churchill had the support of Mr. Anthony Eden, Mr. Oliver Lyttelton, Mr. Attlee,

---

4 Ismay, *op. cit.*, p. 159.
5 Churchill, *op. cit.*, Vol. V, p. 340. Earlier he says "I never wielded autocratic powers, and always had to move with and focus political and professional opinion"; Vol. III, p. 309.
6 Attlee agreed that Churchill did not exercise too much control. "He always accepted the verdict of the Chiefs of Staff when it came to it, and it was a great advantage for him to be there driving them all the time." *A Prime Minister Remembers*, p. 45.
7 *Ibid.*, Vol. II, p. 397.

Lord Mountbattten and his command, the Foreign Office and the Cabinet, but the Chiefs of Staff were adamant and there was an occasional word about resignations. The Prime Minister used every form of pressure, tackling Sir Alan Brooke when he was fresh and the C.I.G.S. was exhausted, writing to the other Chiefs individually, and inducing the Americans to say they would not need our fleet in the Pacific till mid-1945. Next he gave a ruling in favour of his " Bay of Bengal Strategy " on March 20, 1944, only to find a further memorandum of objection from the Chiefs of Staff Committee. The result was a postponement and by May, the Chiefs of Staff thought they had won. When Mr. Churchill reopened the question in July, the other ministers were not sure, Mr. Eden and Mr. Attlee opposed his view and a further postpone-ment finally killed the idea.

In addition to accepting the views of the Service experts in London. Mr. Churchill tended to trust the man on the spot. In early 1941 he and the Chiefs of Staff accepted, though with some misgivings, Mr. Anthony Eden and Sir John Dill's report in favour of sending troops to Greece. Once the home authorities came to a definite conclusion, Mr. Churchill was ready to insist on action. He ordered the reluctant Wavell to send troops to the aerodrome at Habbaniya and to put down the insurgents in Iraq. It was not long before the Prime Minister came to think that Auchinleck was hanging back in the Western Desert and sent him orders to atttack—though again this was only done with the unanimous support of the Chiefs of Staff.

In his respect for the practices of Cabinet government and for the dignity of the House of Commons, Mr. Churchill was an old-fashioned statesman. He carefully asked the Cabinet for its views on all policy questions. As France fell, the Prime Minister wanted to send ten squadrons of fighters instead of the four authorised by the Cabinet. He telegraphed from France and the War Cabinet met and accepted the changed number.[8] In August 1941 the President of the United States met Mr. Churchill for the first time. On a warship off the coast of Newfoundland they drew up the Atlantic Charter which was submitted by telegram to the War Cabinet. It suggested a change in wording (rejected by Roosevelt)

---

[8] Ismay says " it was never his habit throughout the war to take any major decision without the express approval of his ministerial colleagues." *Op. cit.*, p. 128.

and a further paragraph on social security which was accepted. A series of attempts was made to bring Turkey into the war on the Allied side. At the close of the Casablanca Conference, Mr. Churchill decided to go to Cairo and, if possible, see President Inönü of Turkey. The War Cabinet urged the Prime Minister to return and thought that advances to Turkey would probably be rebuffed or end in failure. Mr. Churchill pressed his point only to find that his colleagues reaffirmed their objections. " I got quite upset by the obstruction of the Cabinet," [9] and the next message was a direct request for a telegram to President Inönü explaining the object of the visit. The Cabinet gave way. Later the Prime Minister took strong action against anti-royalist agitation among Greek soldiers in Egypt (" I circulated all my telegrams to the War Cabinet as they were sent, and my colleagues in no way hampered my freedom of action ").[10] As the Germans withdrew from Greece in late 1944, civil war broke out and Mr. Churchill did not have time to call a Cabinet before he sent in British troops. These actions caused some criticism, though none of the Cabinet objected and the Prime Minister won a vote of confidence on the issue by 300 to 30.

Major differences which could not be settled by the joint Chiefs of Staff were directly negotiated between the President and the Prime Minister. Both sides appreciated that the war could only be conducted on a basis of trust and mutual respect, though within this framework there were some hard-hitting arguments. The American Chiefs of Staff did not want landings in North Africa inside the Strait of Gibraltar. The strategic priorities for 1943, Britain's share in defeating Japan, the value of a " diversion " to take bases in the Aegean, the emphasis to be placed on the Italian campaign and the merits of subsidiary attacks on the French coast, all had to be settled in this way. Neither side dominated though President Roosevelt's refusal to spare landing craft put a veto on the idea of taking and holding Cos, Leros and Rhodes.

While Mr. Churchill always tried to obtain the consent of the relevant parties, he made it clear that all dealings were to be with him. Though he could, in special cases like the dispute over " the Bay of Bengal strategy," bring in the Defence Committee of the Cabinet on his side, there was no question of the Chiefs of Staff

---

[9] Churchill, *op. cit.*, Vol. IV, p. 628.
[10] *Ibid.*, p. 488.

appealing to the Cabinet against the Prime Minister. Conversely he would not allow the Cabinet to criticise the Chiefs of Staff.[11] For the same reasons, Mr. Churchill was on the alert against any Anglo-American combination. Sir Alan Brooke noted that "he always feared we should 'frame up' with the American Chiefs of Staff against him. He knew the Americans could carry the President with them and he feared being opposed by a combined Anglo-American bloc of Chiefs of Staff plus President."[12] This never in fact happened and Mr. Churchill retained his freedom of manoeuvre and power till the end of the war.

A typical week during 1942 would begin on a Monday with the parade of Cabinet Ministers and "constant attenders" to hear reports. On Tuesday the Pacific Council would be held, followed by a War Cabinet on the Wednesday. This body assembled again on Thursday after a session of the Defence Committee and there might be further Cabinet meetings on the Wednesday and Thursday evenings. At these gatherings, Mr. Churchill presided in an easy yet authoritative fashion. Sir Anthony Eden has recorded that "a Cabinet as conducted by Mr. Churchill could be a splendid and unique experience. It might be a monologue, it was never a dictatorship. The disadvantage, to those with specific duties to perform or departments to run, was the time consumed."[13] More precise men like Sir Alan Brooke groaned as, after an hour of review and argument, they had not reached the second item on the agenda. Yet such methods had their purpose and, as Mr. Churchill put it: "all I wanted was compliance with my wishes after reasonable discussion."[14] It was one of his great gifts as a statesman that he usually did get compliance, while leaving his colleagues feeling that the processes had indeed been reasonable.

PRIME MINISTERS AND THEIR CABINETS SINCE 1945

Mr. Attlee, in contrast to Mr. Churchill, was brief and kept his colleagues up to the mark. After the first meeting of the Labour Government Sir Alan Brooke was "very impressed by the efficiency with which Attlee ran his Cabinet. There was not the same

[11] A. Bryant, *The Turn of the Tide*, p. 320.
[12] *Ibid.*, p. 627.
[13] The Earl of Avon, *The Reckoning*, p. 497.
[14] Churchill, *op. cit.*, Vol. IV, p. 78.

touch of genius as with Winston, but there were more business-like methods. We kept to the agenda and he maintained complete order with a somewhat difficult crowd. Our work was quickly and efficiently completed." [15] The record of the Labour Governments after 1945 shows that Prime Ministers do not have to be exceptional individuals in order to dominate their ministries. Mr. Attlee had self-confidence and a certain toughness and used the powers by then inherent in the Prime Minister's post to arrange the machinery of government and manage the Cabinet. In 1937 he had given some attention to this question in his book *The Labour Party in Perspective*. Mr. Attlee then considered the old idea of a Cabinet of twenty-two men trying both to think out policy and administer the country, was unworkable. The Cabinet should contain a few ministers " who have the faculty of directing broad issues of policy. . . . Each should, in his own sphere, be . . . the representative of the Prime Minister in relation to a particular group of services, and should preside over a committee of the ministers charged with administration." [16] As the Labour Government encountered its early difficulties with food shortages in 1946 and the fuel crisis of 1947, Mr. Attlee moved in the direction he had contemplated with a few differences of emphasis. By the end of 1947 power was divided among his colleagues in a fashion that once again suggests the image of a cone. The Prime Minister was at the apex overseeing the whole administration and taking the chair at the most important committees—the Economic Policy Committee, Defence, and India and Burma Committees. Below him there were three powerful ministers. Ernest Bevin as Foreign Secretary was closest to Mr. Attlee and many matters were settled in private discussion between the two men. Bevin would then go ahead and, in due course, report his actions to the Cabinet. Next in importance was Sir Stafford Cripps and he, Bevin and Mr. Attlee met to consider economic policy. Lastly, at this level, there was Mr. Herbert Morrison who led the House of Commons and kept watch over social security as Chairman of the Lord President's Committee. These men were powerful partly because of their departments and committees and partly because each had

---

[15] A. Bryant, *Triumph in the West*, p. 483. Sir Alan Brooke had noted these qualities before when Mr. Attlee had deputised for Mr. Churchill. See pp. 251, 428 and 489.

[16] C. R. Attlee, *The Labour Party in Perspective*, p. 174.

some independent standing with the party or the public. The departure of any one of them would have been a severe loss while others, like Mr. Dalton, could be shed without danger.

On the next ring or tier, there were Mr. Alexander, Lord Addison, Mr. Chuter Ede, Lord Jowitt and Mr. Dalton, all with important tasks or definite abilities. Beneath them came the eight departmental ministers who were members of the Cabinet and then a step further down were the twelve heads of departments who were of Cabinet status but were not admitted to the Cabinet.[17] Surveying the position in 1949, Mr. Francis Williams, the Prime Minister's Public Relations Adviser, wrote (with Mr. Attlee's advice and approval) that

> " This change in the pattern of the machine of government has been carried through without the supersession of the Cabinet by an Inner Cabinet and without upsetting the well-established and, indeed, essential principle of Cabinet responsibility . . . [Bevin, Cripps, Morrison] although they are naturally in the closest touch with each other and with the Prime Minister, do not sit as an Inner Cabinet with overriding authority. All major matters of policy are still brought before the full Cabinet for discussion and approval. But the establishment of this system of a small group of functional ministers responsible for directing broad issues of policy in their particular spheres has greatly increased the efficiency and speed of government and very much reduced the size of the agenda which has to be brought before the full Cabinet at its regular meetings. Very many matters which would previously have come to the Cabinet are now settled by one or other of the functional committees over which these ministers preside." [18]

This pattern lasted till ill-health forced the resignation of Bevin and Cripps. Their successors were not men of equal experience or

---

[17] Francis Williams in *Triple Challenge*, p. 41, gives the clearest picture of this development and his account has been supplemented by Lord Attlee's writings in the Press, Mr. Shinwell's *Conflict Without Malice*, and by interviews.
[18] F. Williams' Foreword in *The Labour Party in Perspective and Twelve Years Later* by C. R. Attlee, p. 23. The only reservation necessary is that Mr. Williams over-estimates the extent of the changes introduced by Mr. Attlee. As has been argued, each Prime Minister imposed a slightly different shape on his machinery of control and the methods adopted after 1945 are similar, in some respects, to those evolved by Lloyd George, Neville Chamberlain and Mr. Winston Churchill.

standing and in the last year of Labour rule, the top ring probably consisted of Mr. Morrison, Mr. Chuter Ede and Mr. Griffiths, though it was less clearly on a plane above that of the senior departmental ministers.

In the conduct of his Cabinets, Mr. Attlee was firm. He controlled the agenda and if he so desired, kept matters to himself or discussed them with one or two others. All questions connected with the manufacture of atomic and hydrogen bombs by Britain he considered unsuitable for the full Cabinet. This matter was discussed in the Defence Committee and though its decision was circulated to the Cabinet, the references to such a momentous conclusion were studiously kept minimal and technical and no attempt was made to draw the Cabinet's attention to these items. This was quite deliberate on Mr. Attlee's part as he thought that the fewer people who were aware of what was happening, the better.[19] It is not surprising, therefore, that after the existence of a British H-bomb was announced, several members of the Cabinet said they had no knowledge that work of this kind was being done. Had the matter not been discussed formally in the Defence Committee of the Cabinet or had it decided to record no minutes, there would not even have been the saving clause of an inadvertent acquiescence by the Cabinet.[20] Generally, Mr. Attlee's view was that if the Cabinet approved of a line of policy, the execution could be left to the minister or to a Cabinet Committee. In foreign affairs, a weekly report by Ernest Bevin was sufficient. Labour policy was to extend self-government to India and Burma as rapidly as possible so the conduct of the complex and important negotiations could be left almost entirely to the Prime Minister and the India and Burma Committee. At Cabinet, Mr. Attlee's great objective was to stop talk. There is evidence that two ministers simply talked themselves out of the Cabinet. Discussion was limited by the Premier's habit of putting his questions in the negative. A non-Cabinet Minister with an item on the agenda

---

[19] Mr. (then Lord) Attlee was quite definite about this in an interview with the author on July 15, 1958. I recorded him as saying "I thought some of them were not fit to be trusted with secrets of this kind." It is therefore quite wrong of Mr. G. W. Jones in "The Prime Minister's Power," *Parliamentary Affairs*, Vol. xxviii (1965), p. 182, to say this happened inadvertently as the decision was simply listed among "agreed items."

[20] See the correspondence on this subject between R. H. S. Crossman and G. R. Strauss in the *New Statesman*, May 10, 17, 24, 31 and June 7, 1963, and in *Encounter*, June 1963, August 1963.

would be called in at the appropriate point, simply bursting to
make a speech. Mr. Attlee would begin: " Mr. X, your memo
says all that could be said—I don't suppose you have anything to
add to it? " It was hard to say anything but " No." Then, " does
any member of the Cabinet oppose this? " Someone would indicate a desire to contribute and say: " An interesting case occurred
in 1929 which was very similar to this, and I remember that then
we . . ." " Do you oppose this? " " Er . . . No." " Very good
—that is settled." As Mr. Attlee himself explained " a Prime
Minister has to know when to ask for an opinion. He can't always
stop some Ministers offering theirs . . . but he can make sure to
extract the opinion of those he wants when he needs them." [21]
Once or twice a minister would indicate dissent at this stage but
no notice was taken. The elements of diversity in the Labour
Cabinets were countered by the unifying forces of office with all its
responsibilities and by one " constant attender," the ghost of the
1931 split. It is significant that the quarrel which led to the
resignations of Aneurin Bevan and Mr. Harold Wilson occurred
when Mr. Attlee was ill and Mr. Morrison was presiding over the
Cabinet.

Mr. Churchill retained in peace-time most of the characteristics
he had revealed in the war, except that the objective was not as
simple and obvious and he therefore found it much less easy to
find the precise direction in which to drive. In forming his Government, Mr. Churchill took the Ministry of Defence himself and
named certain ministers as Co-ordinators or Overlords.[22] His
idea was that it would help the political fortunes of the ministry
if he could select men whom the public knew and would trust to
get on with the job. A great deal of ink was spilt over his experiment since Members of Parliament like to know who is responsible
in the sense of which minister must answer questions. In practical
terms, ministers can supervise other ministers either by being
made chairmen of Cabinet Committees dealing with the given
subject or by having explicit powers conferred on them, as in the
case of the Minister of Defence. Mr. Churchill's scheme had the

---

[21] F. Williams, *A Prime Minister Remembers*, p. 81.
[22] The " Overlords " were Lord Woolton (Lord President of the Council) to
watch over food and agriculture, Lord Leathers as Secretary of State for the
Co-ordination of Transport, Fuel and Power, and Lord Cherwell (Paymaster-
General) to take care of research and development.

defect of being neither secret nor explicit and was given up when Lord Woolton (in an answer to Lord Listowel in the Upper House) said that the ministers he was supposed to co-ordinate still had complete responsibility to Parliament for the actions of their departments.

For all the normal purposes of government, the Prime Minister could maintain a general oversight by the use of Cabinet Committees and personal interviews with senior ministers. Mr. Churchill had always believed that the Foreign Secretary should work under his supervision and that there should be unity of outlook and even harmony of temperament.[23] This relationship was happily achieved with Mr. Anthony Eden who had the ability to conceive and execute policy but liked a firm and confident leader on whom to lean. On the other hand, Mr. Churchill at times felt a little guilty about blocking Sir Anthony's path to the Premiership for so long and he did give way to him on such points as granting independence to the Sudan and withdrawing from the Suez base. For different reasons, R. A. Butler had considerable influence in home affairs.

Generalising on such relationships, some of the political columnists accused Mr. Churchill of conducting a system of " Government by Crony." Lord Woolton has said that these accusations arose for two reasons. In the first place the Prime Minister " rarely sent for ministers of Cabinet rank who were not in the War Cabinet or, in post-war days, the inner Cabinet, for a general conversation about what they were doing." [24] Secondly, Mr. Churchill felt the loneliness of the top post (as Baldwin and others had done before him) and liked to try out his ideas late at night on old friends whose judgment he trusted. It is interesting that there were different groups of cronies for different purposes. In these late night sessions, the most regular attenders were Brendan Bracken, Lord Beaverbrook and Lord Cherwell (who caused annoyance by providing facts about other ministers' departments). As with Lloyd George's private circle, these men did not attempt to talk over policy with the Prime Minister so as to form quasi-decisions but acted as a foil and stimulus for his imagination and Mr. Churchill often argued the opposite view later in the

23 Churchill, *op. cit.*, Vol. I, p. 187.
24 Lord Woolton, *op. cit.*, p. 377.

Cabinet. In addition there were a number of ministers, mostly those without heavy departmental duties, whom the Prime Minister regularly consulted, sometimes bringing them in on the nocturnal arguments. Lord Salisbury (Lord Privy Seal) and Lord Swinton (Secretary for Commonwealth Relations) were in the group, but it is clear that these discussions were to help the Prime Minister think things out rather than to undermine executive ministers such as Sir Anthony Eden or Mr. Butler—who were sometimes asked to join in these sessions.

Despite these rings of friends, Mr. Churchill was always punctilious about consulting the Cabinet and carefully went around the table giving every minister a chance to contribute. Departmental ministers who were not among the " cronies " had no feeling that they were being left out. In his care that all ministers should participate, the Prime Minister was harking back to the habits of his earliest years in office. Lord Woolton says that " the Cabinet under Mr. Churchill was often reminiscent of bygone times." He tended to raise large ideas and to talk of " setting the people free " irrespective of all the complex systems of licensing and statutory regulations built up over the last few decades. " Not infrequently the entire time of the meeting had gone before he arrived at the first item on the agenda." [25] The effect of Mr. Churchill bringing his ideas to the Cabinet at such an early stage, and before they had hardened into definite proposals, was to restore some if its control over the formulation of government policy. When Sir Anthony Eden wanted to try to expand the Brussels Treaty Organisation as an alternative to the defunct European Defence Community, the key was an offer not to withdraw any of the four British divisions from the Continent against the wishes of a majority of the Brussels Treaty Powers. Sir Anthony " thought that Cabinet discussion of the position was unnecessary at this juncture; it could come later at the appropriate moment," but Mr. Churchill decided that matters of such magnitude merited " formal Cabinet consideration and decision." [26] In the same way, the Prime Minister enlarged on his views before his colleagues and found himself resisted on several occasions. Later, in 1952, Egypt gave up her claim to the Sudan and Sir Anthony Eden persuaded the Cabinet to offer immediate self-government though it is evident

[25] *Ibid.*, p. 375.
[26] Sir Anthony Eden, *op. cit.*, pp. 162–167.

that Mr. Churchill was among the minority who disapproved.[27] No doubt the other members of the Cabinet would have agreed with Mr. Attlee's comment on the wartime Coalition: " I think that Churchill does need men around him who, while ready to support a good idea, however novel, are prepared on occasions to take an emphatic line against a bad one." [28]

Normally, however, when the Prime Minister sensed any serious doubts, or expected argument, he let an item slip down the agenda till lunchtime was approaching and it had not been reached. The Cabinet would then shelve the question till the next meeting and Mr. Churchill was able to go over all the ground and rehearse the arguments late in the evening with his cronies. After such treatment and further discussion in Cabinet, Mr. Churchill was usually very apt in summarising the general feeling of his colleagues.

Sir Anthony Eden was a very different type of Prime Minister. Nervous and tense, he was always poking into the departmental affairs of his colleagues and could not brook opposition. The most powerful men in his Cabinet were Mr. Butler, Mr. Macmillan and Lord Salisbury. When President Nasser took control of the Suez Canal on July 26, 1956, a Cabinet Committee was formed the next day to prepare counter-measures. It consisted of Mr. Butler, Mr. Macmillan, Mr. Selwyn Lloyd, Mr. Head, Mr. Lennox-Boyd and Lord Salisbury, and its task was " to work out plans day by day to put our policy into effect." [29] A detailed account of this episode has been given in Chapter One (pp. 25–7 above) as it provides an excellent example of British central government in time of stress. The Prime Minister was, in fact, pursuing a personal policy contrary to the advice of the Foreign Office. He withdrew the main decisions to a Cabinet Committee not to override the full Cabinet or for fear of contradiction but simply for convenience. A majority of the Cabinet were told most of the facts and all but three agreed with the actions taken. Sir Anthony

---

[27] *Ibid.*, p. 247. There is no definite evidence (*i.e.*, corroboration from several independent sources) as to the other occasions when Mr. Churchill was overruled but one was probably in March 1953 when the Prime Minister wanted to open direct negotiations with Russia to try to break the deadlock in relations between East and West. The Cabinet demurred and almost at once Mr. Churchill had a serious stroke. Other instances were Sir Anthony Eden's policy of withdrawal from the Canal Zone and the final agreement to leave the base in the hands of civilian technicians in October 1954.

[28] C. R. Attlee, *As it Happened*, p. 140.

[29] Sir Anthony Eden, *op. cit.*, p. 432.

Eden summed it up well when he said that "the Cabinet were kept in touch with our work." [30] Despite the attention it has received, this episode differs little (except in the concealment of the collusion with Israel) from the way in which Neville Chamberlain pursued the Munich policy. It also was intensely personal, the day to day conduct fell first to a Cabinet Committee, then to the Prime Minister and three like-minded senior colleagues and, on critical occasions, to the Premier alone. Once again, when informed of what had been done, a majority of the Cabinet agreed. In the former case Duff Cooper resigned while over Suez Sir Walter Monckton moved to what was called in the eighteenth century "an office of advice but not of execution." The differences were largely in external factors such as the greater public division at the time of the Suez invasion and the collapse of Sir Anthony Eden's health which forced him to resign.

When Mr. Macmillan took over in January 1957, he made a very sweeping reconstruction of the government. The Conservative Party was at a low ebb after the failure of the Suez invasion but though this was a danger to the political future of the Party and the Government, it was a source of strength to the Prime Minister as all realised they must rally behind him. Mr. Macmillan's gifts were primarily those of intellect and political perception. He began by establishing his position in the House of Commons and though this did not reach the general public, it comforted his back-benchers. It also helped him to dismiss the resignation of Lord Salisbury in March 1957 and of the three Treasury Ministers, Mr. Thorneycroft, Mr. Powell and Mr. Birch in January 1955 as matters of no consequence.

Outside the government and the House of Commons, Mr. Macmillan was the first Premier to make full use of television. By 1958 70 per cent. of homes had TV. sets and with rapid jet travel, Macmillan could go on visits to Bermuda to see Eisenhower, on Commonwealth tours and have direct talks in Moscow with his departures, arrivals and short speeches on British interests relayed into every living room. These techniques together with growing economic prosperity meant that by mid-1958 the Conservatives, for the first time since 1955, led Labour

[30] *Idem.*

In the Gallup poll. Mr. Macmillan realised that television conveyed his personality to the electorate and this suited his theatrical temperament. His opponents dubbed him " Supermac " and called him " unflappable," all of which was turned to his advantage. (The latter adjective was singularly unsuitable as he could and did " flap " badly, as he did when he thought the trip to Russia had collapsed or when the summit conference failed or when he sacked the seven members of his Cabinet in July 1962.)

Within the Cabinet, Macmillan had no inner group, though he paid special attention to the views of Mr. Thorneycroft, the Earl of Home, Mr. Heath and Mr. Maudling. In his first two years, his mastery of the Cabinet was complete. He would start discussions but often did not show his own hand for some time, or he might wait, summing up at the end. A vote was never taken but Macmillan did use the techniques of adjourning the meeting or setting up a committee if he did not like the trend of a discussion. Members differ as to whether he was ever overruled. Dr. Charles Hill (now Lord Hill) clearly thought this could occur:

> " I thought Harold Macmillan's chairmanship of the Cabinet to be superb by any standards. If he dominated it (he usually did), he did not do it by *ex cathedra* pronouncements or by laying down the law or by expressing his views too early in a discussion. . . . It was done by sheer superiority of mind and of judgment. He encouraged genuine discussion, provided it kept to the point. If he found himself in a minority he accepted the fact with grace and humour. If I have a criticism it is that, now and again, the Cabinet was consulted at too late a stage in the evolution of some important line of policy: he seemed to forget that many of us had not been present at the Cabinet committee concerned with the topic." [31]

Other members of the Cabinet and some of the officials present do not recall Mr. Macmillan ever being turned down by his colleagues though it is probably true that he was slowed down in his desire to apply to join the Common Market and in the start of regional economic development by the need to carry or swamp some doubters. Mr. Macmillan may have wanted to give up the defence of the " green belts " around some cities, he may

---

[31] Lord Hill of Luton, *Both Sides of the Hill*, p. 235.

have wanted to abolish resale price maintenance, he may have disliked the Trade Treaty with Japan, but while the ministers intimately concerned probably realised he had given way on a point, the Cabinet as a whole may not have appreciated that there had been a concession. Although somewhat aloof in manner, Mr. Macmillan kept his eye on most of the critical areas of policy. He became virtually his own Foreign Minister till Lord Home was appointed in 1960, he made excursions into Commonwealth relations and all serious industrial disputes ended at No. 10 Downing Street.

In the organisation at the top of the government, some changes were made. Mr. Macmillan realised the burden of work at the main ministries and the need for co-ordination. He gave both the Foreign Office and the Treasury two ministers in the Cabinet. In the first case, Mr. Heath was responsible for relations with the Common Market as Lord Privy Seal while Mr. (now Lord) Brooke and later Mr. John Boyd-Carpenter were admitted as Chief Secretary to the Treasury. Cabinet Committees were increasingly used to reduce the burden on the Cabinet and were chaired by the Prime Minister or senior non-departmental ministers. For instance the standing committee on agricultural policy which settled the annual price review was taken out of the hands of the Chancellor of the Exchequer and given to Mr. Selwyn Lloyd who was then Lord Privy Seal. This meant that there was an impartial chairman to mediate in the disputes between the Treasury and the Minister of Agriculture. After the Plowden Committee reported in 1961, a Management of Public Expenditure Committee [32] was set up to aid the Chancellor of the Exchequer in producing a five-year rolling programme of expenditure, a task which required discipline among the spending departments. As in all Cabinets, there was a strong sense of hierarchy, the ministers without portfolio, Lord Carrington and Mr. Deedes (at the end of the Government) sitting at the very bottom of the table and being expected to listen rather than speak. While Mr. Macmillan managed his Cabinet with charm and geniality, once the broad lines of policy were set or if there was an element of political tension in an issue, to seek to raise discussion was in effect to challenge the Prime Minister and this

---

[32] Called " Magpie " after its initials, M.P.E.

meant taking one's life in one's hands. One tough and independent-minded minister used to look across at the Prime Minister and say to himself "There is Henry VIII—he cannot send me to the Tower but politically he can have me beheaded at any moment."

By 1962, Mr. Macmillan's success and capacity both began to decline. There are several explanations but the major one is the failure of his policies. Successive British leaders have grappled with the painful problem of readjusting British foreign, defence and economic policy to the reduced or altered role necessary for a moderate-sized European nation with no Empire and no inherent economic advantage over other countries. Mr. Macmillan faced the failure of his attempt to enter the Common Market, the collapse of the summit meeting he had worked hard to produce (with Britain totally ignored when a really serious crisis arose over Cuba in October 1962), while a deteriorating balance of payments led to deflation and a "pay pause" at home. On top of the disillusion and unpopularity caused by these setbacks came a series of by-election reverses. Mr. Macmillan responded to these by deciding that his government needed a fresh look and dismissed seven of the Cabinet. He only intended to fire six but Mr. (now Lord) Eccles refused to be moved, he would either stay at Education or resign, the total thus reaching seven. It does not appear that the Prime Minister consulted anyone in making these decisions except Mr. Martin Redmayne, the Chief Whip. Lord Kilmuir, one of those axed, has said "I got the impression that he was extremely alarmed about his own position and was determined to eliminate any risk for himself by a massive change of Government." [33] The result was to bring some able younger men into the Cabinet, but it also caused bewilderment and resentment among Conservative back-benchers. It was a too cynical casting aside of colleagues and it made the relations within the Cabinet too openly a question of the personal power and advantage of the Prime Minister.

A further blow to Mr. Macmillan came over the revelations of the private life of Mr. Profumo, the Minister of War, who compounded his offence by lying to his colleagues and to the House. As a result, by early 1963 the Conservatives were trailing up to a maximum of twenty points behind Labour in the Gallup poll, there

[33] Lord Kilmuir, *Political Adventure*, p. 324.

were abstentions by back-benchers on important votes, open
grumbling in the Party and talk of a change of leadership. Yet
despite all, Mr. Macmillan continued in office and (as has been
discussed at length above (pp. 432–433) could not have been
driven from the leadership had he not decided to resign when
an operation was necessary on his prostate gland.

After a lengthy and very public contest for the succession,
Mr. Macmillan advised the Queen to send for Lord (soon to
become Sir Alec Douglas) Home. He faced a series of handicaps
throughout his year as Prime Minister. The first was the extent
of the contest before his selection and the refusal of Mr. Macleod
and Mr. Powell to serve in his government. The second was the
knowledge that an election was necessary within twelve months
and that unless the political situation changed dramatically, his
tenure of the office was purely temporary. The third was that he
had some difficulty with the mass media which had been exploited
so effectively by Mr. Macmillan and by the Leader of the Opposition, Mr. Wilson. As a result Sir Alec Douglas-Home's style as
Prime Minister was not fully revealed as it would have been had
he won the 1964 election and had a full period of office with the
endorsement of the electorate.

Yet despite these handicaps, his conduct of the Cabinet and
the Government did not differ markedly from that of his predecessors. Sir Alec lacked a wide experience of home ministries and
was clearly more positive on foreign policy but he was able to
push through the abolition of resale price maintenance when
Mr. Macmillan, who favoured the same policy, preferred to leave
it alone. Sir Alec's strength was first in his integrity, his word was
trusted, and secondly in the knowledge among all Conservatives
that if he failed, the Party would be defeated. Besides resale price
maintenance, the only serious dispute (which did not take place
in the Cabinet) was over the timing of the election. Mr. Maudling
favoured June as the economic situation was rapidly deteriorating
and action, especially if it was unpalatable, was difficult just on the
eve of a poll. But the Whips, the Central Office and some Ministers said defeat in June was certain, while in October the issue was
open so that Sir Alec decided to wait till the Autumn of 1964.

Few Prime Ministers can have given as much thought to the
mechanics of government prior to their election as Mr. Wilson.

Yet his views were a mixture. On the one hand he wanted to build up the staff of the private office in No. 10 Downing Street and of the Cabinet Secretariat so that the Premier would be better equipped. "My conception of the Prime Minister is that if he's not managing director, he is at any rate and should be very much a full-time executive chairman." [34] Mr. Wilson expanded the system of senior ministers without portfolio presiding over Cabinet Committees; Mr. Douglas Houghton, for instance, chairing the Committee on the Social Services and the Home Affairs Committee. At the same time, the Prime Minister wanted an Attlee-Ernest Bevin type relationship with Mr. Gordon-Walker at the Foreign Office. Mr. Wilson did not try to pack committees with like-minded ministers but operated on the Civil Service principle of asking only those whose departments were affected.

In the early days of the government, when the senior ministers were exhilarated with power and worried by the economic situation, many rapid decisions were taken by Mr. Wilson, Mr. George Brown and Mr. Callaghan. This was not, however, an inner Cabinet on the Attlee model as it was not based on the same type of trust and Mr. Wilson had far more positive ideas than his Labour predecessor. As time went on, the Prime Minister tended to deal bilaterally with individual colleagues and, on key issues, to take over more himself. From the time of Gordon-Walker's resignation, he supervised foreign policy. He had at once become chairman of the Cabinet Committee on Rhodesia and he conducted the main negotiations with the illegal régime. When industrial disputes assumed major proportions—the seamen's strike and the threat of a national railway stoppage—Mr. Wilson intervened, while in August 1967 he announced that he had taken over personal control of the economy and had assumed overall responsibility for the work of the D.E.A.

At Cabinet, Mr. Wilson tended to introduce most subjects and often to comment on the contributions of each minister. He did not wait for the senior men to speak and content himself with summing up. Finally, he developed a tendency to go round the table for a last word, the Prime Minister ticking off "Fors" and "Againsts" so that something very like a vote took place. The result was that when there were leaks to the Press, it often took

---

[34] *Whitehall and Beyond* (B.B.C. Publications), p. 20.

the form of " Selective Benefits carried by one vote " or " Common Market, eight for, six against, seven with qualifications " and so on. It was even said that the package of cuts announced in January 1968 was settled by a series of Treasury proposals and departmental counter-proposals being " spoken to " in turn and then a vote taken. The explanation for this procedure is probably threefold. First, as has been said, there was no inner Cabinet on which Mr. Wilson could rely to set the right tone, leaving him to sum up. Second, the older procedure meant a definite point at which the card of collective responsibility was played; this was the decision, like it or resign. Mr. Wilson wished to avoid resignations both when he had only a tiny majority and later when the political going was hard. By going round the table all were in a sense involved; they had had their say and the minority had lost. Lastly, there is, on long-term issues, a certain indecisiveness in Mr. Wilson's make-up, perhaps because he sees too many options and does not wish to move till it is certain which one is correct (or till only one possibility is left).

While on issues on which he is convinced and on threats to his position, no Prime Minister has been tougher than Mr. Wilson, his kindliness and his desire to avoid Mr. Macmillan's errors has led to a reluctance to be " a good butcher." Mr. Wilson prefers to neutralise opponents by keeping them inside the government, and when some ministers have had to be relieved of their duties he has done all he can to find them alternative posts inside or outside Parliament. Essentially a rather lonely man, Mr. Wilson worked closely with Mr. Callaghan till devaluation in November 1967, the early influence of the ebullient Mr. Brown declining as his conduct aroused criticism. Mr. Crossman as Leader of the House and Mr. Silkin as Chief Whip were close to Mr. Wilson on matters of political tactics though, like other senior ministers, they felt they had to compete for Mr. Wilson's ear. The kind of issue which tended to be decided by the Prime Minister alone or after only one or two consultations was the policy of maintaining the parity of the pound or of making a further offer to Mr. Smith in Rhodesia. Once the general line was settled, it was not reopened at Cabinet. On the other hand proposals of a more technical nature where there were serious disputes were gone over again and again—the cancellation of TSR II aeroplane, the future of Stansted airport or whether there should be random breath tests for drivers.

Mr. Wilson's loneliness comes out in his readiness to believe in conspiracies, an example being the fear that there had been a plot while he was in Moscow in July 1966. On his return, Mr. Wilson saw the principal members of the Cabinet individually. Meanwhile he and a team of officials drew up the list of deflationary measures which he also announced personally to the House. Thereafter, the Prime Minister appeared to have re-established complete control of the Cabinet (if it had ever been in any way shaken) and he completed the process by a reshuffle designed to see that there would be no crown prince. By moving Mr. Brown to the Foreign Office, Mr. Stewart to the D.E.A., leaving Mr. Jenkins at the Home Office and refusing Mr. Callaghan's pleas to be released from the Exchequer, he ensured that there was no leading alternative. In the reshuffle after devaluation caused by Mr. Callaghan's insistence on resigning, Mr. Wilson would have preferred Mr. Crosland as his replacement at the Exchequer on the same grounds. However, when Mr. Callaghan said he would take the Home Office or go on the back-benches, the Prime Minister decided the switch with Mr. Jenkins would be the lesser threat. In fact, once again, Mr. Wilson soon resumed control though some of his power had to be shared with Mr. Jenkins. The state of sterling and the stability of the Labour Party could not have withstood a resignation by Mr. Jenkins and in this sense, for the first time since 1964, someone was indispensable and therefore had a measure of independent authority.

Even when this is said, Mr. Wilson retained great power and the only effect of the talk of a leadership crisis in January 1968 was that those involved looked round and realised that they were facing an impregnable position with no rival leader and very few troops. The cases of Mr. Macmillan and Mr. Wilson at their weakest reveal the strength inherent in the position of a British Prime Minister.

THE CABINET SECRETARIAT AND NO. 10 OFFICE

Although Mr. Wilson contemplated an increased staff at No. 10 Downing Street before he won the 1964 election, in fact it rose by only one. The role of this office of eight must be clearly distinguished from that of the Cabinet Secretariat which has been in continuous existence since the time of Lloyd George and had expanded into a highly skilled office of a hundred civil servants under Sir Burke Trend. The latter's task is to prepare the agenda for the Cabinet, to take minutes, circulate decisions, follow up and see that action has been taken and to brief the Premier. While the office serves all ministers bringing business to the Cabinet, those with departments have their own briefs. The Secretariat works much more for those without a team of civil servants, that is for the Prime Minister and the ministers without portfolio. To get information, the Secretariat can reach into the ministries. If a particular department is trying to maintain a special case, it may feel a little reluctant to divulge all the arguments but resistance is not wise and there have been few complaints that anyone from the Prime Minister down has lacked information; the usual complaints are that there is too much paperwork, though it is sometimes added that the advice is not always unbiased.

Besides the Secretariat, since the Second World War there has been the No. 10 Office. It deals exclusively with the Prime Minister and his immediate needs. The staff is small; a Press agent and his assistant, a Principal Private Secretary and his assistant, a specialist in foreign affairs, an expert on the Commons who watches over the Prime Minister's questions and speeches in the House, a person to keep the diary and a rather separate official whose sole task is Church and other patronage. This office has included some remarkable men in recent years. They have to be more political than most civil servants with a sympathetic understanding of the Prime Minister's views. Their job is to provide information and briefs for the Premier, they must find out what others will be proposing on committees and prepare the answers and they can on occasion slip into the position of actual advisers. Such advice usually consists not so much of positive recommendations as in pointing out gaps in the evidence submitted by departments and urging the study of this or that problem. Mr. Wilson soon found that this Office and the Secretariat provided him with as much material and arguments as he could assimilate in the time available.

Mr. Wilson's one innovation was a personal political office

to deal with his constituency and political correspondence. There was some friction at first but once the demarcation lines were clear, most civil servants accustomed to the central machinery could not imagine how previous Prime Ministers managed without such aid.

So it is agreed that there is sufficient advice and support. Indeed, there are elements of danger in that some modern Prime Ministers have had something like a private court in which they live, a body of confidants giving advice in a sympathetic manner so that Premiers become cut off from other sections of the government and their party and unduly reliant on this one source of advice. It has sometimes been said that a reason for the decline of Mr. Macmillan was the drop in the quality of his entourage. Lord Normanbrook, as head of the Cabinet Secretariat, suddenly found his health failing. The brilliant Mr. Frederick Bishop ceased to be head of the No. 10 staff and an able Parliamentary Private Secretary, Mr. Barber, was replaced by Mr. Knox Cunningham. While Mr. Wilson's central machine has worked overtime and well since he took office, it cannot provide contact with the Parliamentary Party and there is resentment among senior ministers if it is suspected that the counsel of non-elected persons is preferred to theirs. Yet a Prime Minister has to have this backing. He cannot hang around the smokeroom in the Commons or chat regularly with even the most senior of his hundred ministerial colleagues. So long as the staff do staff work while political advice comes from other politicians, there will be little jealousy, and relations with M.P.s and the party outside Parliament depend more on the success of the Government's policies than on any tactics suggested or hints dropped about the Prime Minister's views by his go-betweens.

CABINET COMMITTEES

Below the Prime Minister and his senior and junior colleagues in the Cabinet, there are the widening rings of Ministers of Cabinet rank who are not actually members, Ministers of State, and the many Cabinet Committees. The latter are appointed for different purposes. Ad hoc committees have been set up to by-pass or control a particular minister as when Sidney Webb (then Lord Passfield) found the Palestine problem passed to a committee under

Arthur Henderson. More often the purpose is to study a particular question, such as unemployment in 1930, or to carry through a particular interdepartmental project.[35] For instance a Cabinet Committee was set up after the 1959 election to examine and recommend suitable steps to increase the University population and in the winter of 1965–66 a Winter Emergency Fuel Supplies Committee was announced. These are termed " Miscs " as short for anything on the Cabinet Office's long list of " Miscellaneous Committees." Some look after a special branch of policy, as in the case of Mr. Attlee's India and Burma Committee while others have been constituted just to fill in the gap in August and September so that the rest of the Cabinet can have a holiday. One minister told Tom Jones that the tendency " to breed committees like rabbits . . . is only proof of feebleness in reaching decisions in Cabinet," [36] but no government or Cabinet could operate nowadays without the sifting process and preparatory work done by such committees. Sometimes, as has been shown, committees set up to handle difficult and vital developments— the Chanak Crisis; the Economy proposals of August 1931; Foreign Policy at the time of Munich; the loss of the Suez Canal in 1956—take control of the major lines of policy and for a period become the effective centre of government.

In the case of standing committees, the Economic Defence and Development Committee (see p. 378, above) had lapsed soon after the end of the First World War, but the Home Affairs Committee (H.A.C.) continued to operate. During the Labour Government of 1924, Haldane acted as chairman of the H.A.C. and the committee considered all items of domestic legislation, though more emphasis was being placed on the drafting than on the content of Bills.[37] Serious disputes (as over the Guardianship of Infants Bill in May 1924) were referred to the Cabinet. This aspect of the committee's work remained under the Conservative and National Governments, though it still occasionally stepped across the rather obscure line between points of law and points of policy. In 1940 Mr. Attlee separated the two functions by

---

[35] While civil servants (other than the Secretariat) never attend the Cabinet, they are often attached to and speak at Cabinet Committees.

[36] Tom Jones, *op. cit.*, p. 176.

[37] Beatrice Webb was amazed that the clumsy wording (and muddled thought) of the Evictions Bill had passed Haldane's Committee. B. Webb, *op. cit.*, p. 19.

creating a separate Legislation Committee on which lawyers looked at the drafting, while the Lord President's Committee discussed the merits of proposals and tried to reconcile departmental divisions. This committee managed the major part of internal policy during the war under the chairmanship successively of Neville Chamberlain, Sir John Anderson and Mr. Attlee. Its powers can be gauged from the fact that Mr. Butler's Education Bill of 1944, one of the most sweeping reforms of this generation, was settled in the Lord President's Committee, and, as all members were agreed, it did not go before the War Cabinet. Mr. Churchill sometimes referred to the committee by its old title of the Home Affairs Committee.[38] This name was revived in 1947 when economic policy was handed to a separate committee and the task of co-ordinating the departments working on domestic matters was left to the new Home Affairs Committee. Because so many topics have been hived off from home affairs and given to other committees, the H.A.C. has tended to be left a rather odd assortment of relatively minor issues. For a while it was chaired by the Home Secretary, but after the advent of the 1964 Labour Government it went to a minister without portfolio (Mr. Douglas Houghton, and later Mr. Gordon Walker) so that the Home Secretary could be a member and state his department's case. After a few months, so many ministers were asking their Ministers of State or Parliamentary Under-Secretaries to deputise for them that the Chairman asked the Prime Minister to send round a note objecting to this practice. The sense of hierarchy evident in the Cabinet is even more marked on Cabinet Committees, and a minister present at the H.A.C. would not accept a refusal from a Parliamentary Under-Secretary from another department. Thus unless sufficient heads of departments came, the committee was not able to perform its function of taking decisions on the kind of issue which need not go to full Cabinet.

On May 25, 1924, Lord Esher wrote to the *Sunday Times* suggesting a civilian equivalent of the Committee of Imperial Defence. The Cabinet took up the idea and wanted a committee to examine such matters as taxation, the machinery for keeping in touch with the governments of the Dominions, and the position of sheltered trades. Various memoranda were circulated, but no one

[38] Churchill, *op. cit.*, Vol. II, p. 326.

was clear what Ramsay MacDonald had in mind except that he wanted to be able to say something about unemployment. Haldane took up the plan for what he was now calling the Committee of Economic Enquiry, and by July 1924 a Treasury Minute had been drafted and the Cabinet had approved. MacDonald, however, did not find time to give his final authorisation and the committee was launched by Baldwin's government on June 13, 1925. Under the new title of the Committee of Civil Research, Balfour announced that it was " an additional wheel required to complete the mechanism of Cabinet Government," and would consider inter-departmental questions, problems that fitted no special category, and matters raised by the Dominions.[39] The only individual mentioned in the Minute was the Prime Minister, and in this way he was left free to call any who might help and to delegate the task of chairmanship. It was made clear that the committee had no executive power. Though the idea was excellent, the results were poor, because the committee had no definite duties and there was no economic doctrine which would have guided it in any long-term study of unemployment, trade or investment problems. Meetings were held in a desultory fashion in the late 1920s with Balfour as Chairman. In 1929 Willie Graham asked the com-mittee to investigate the Cotton and Iron and Steel Industries, but by the end of the year Ramsay MacDonald was talking of a change in its functions. He now wanted, attached to the Prime Minister as an advisory body, an " Economic General Staff " which would include civil servants and outside experts. Its task would be to examine various industries and to make public pro-nouncements " with the object of putting faith and spirit into the industrialist." (J. H. Thomas dubiously remarked that such a body " would have stopped many of our impossible election promises.") By January 1930, the matter was settled and the Committee of Civil Research was reconstituted as the Economic Advisory Committee. It failed, in part for the reasons already given, but chiefly because Snowden was unshakable in his financial orthodoxy and ruled out of court suggestions by R. H. Tawney and G. D. H. Cole for government spending policies similar to those later adopted by President Roosevelt. The committee did

[39] See the full discussion in the House of Lords: H.L. Debates, Vol. 61, cols. *872–879*, 1925.

not survive the collapse of the Labour Government.[40] During the war, when the Government again contemplated economic planning (and this time had the theoretical equipment to make it possible), the task was given to the Lord President's Committee. After a short period (1945–47) when there were two committees, one for internal and the other for external policy, both facets were given to the Economic Policy Committee. From 1947 to 1951 the Committee considered the central questions of balance of payments policy and of the state of British industry but in 1951, when the Conservatives took over, its character altered for a while. Consisting of Lord Swinton, Lord Woolton, Lord Leathers and Sir David Eccles, its task was to scrutinise (" to rag " was the expression used by one member) Mr. (now Lord) Butler, whose Conservatism was slightly suspect among the Prime Minister's circle. Gradually, as the Conservatives encountered the balance of payments problems of 1957–58 and of 1962–63 it returned to the task of co-ordinating the attempts to build up exports, to watch over wages and public expenditure totals.

As has been said, one aspect of this was handed to the new standing committee on the Management of Public Expenditure after 1961. This was renamed the Public Expenditure Scrutiny Committee in 1965. Chaired by a Treasury Minister, it went over the estimates of every department trying to make cuts and help the Chancellor of the Exchequer preserve his overall totals of future public expenditure.

The Economic Policy Committee after 1964 worked largely on the inter-departmental side of the National Plan and was chaired by the First Secretary (at the Department for Economic Affairs). There were sub-committees of this Committee, for instance on Transport Policy. This was created partly because of the political and economic significance of railway closures, partly because the Ministry of Transport would not produce a plan and partly to bolster up the Minister, Mr. Tom Fraser. When he was replaced by Mrs. Barbara Castle, one of her first actions was to repudiate the Committee and insist on going direct to the Economic Policy Committee with all her proposals.

---

[40] It did, however, lead to the formation of a non-ministerial body, the Committee of Economic Information, under Lord Stamp. This committee lasted till 1941, when it evolved into the Central Statistical Office and the Economic Section of the Cabinet Secretariat.

When the Labour Government encountered the sterling crisis of July 1966 and all its economic policies seemed to be in jeopardy, a new Economic Policy Committee was formed in addition to the old one to look at long-term planning. This was a high-powered group chaired by the Prime Minister and including the Foreign Secretary, the Chancellor of the Exchequer, the First Secretary (D.E.A.), the Ministers of Technology and Labour and the Minister without Portfolio (then Mr. Douglas Houghton). Thus by 1968 there were three standing committees of the Cabinet working on economic policy and public expenditure.

In November 1919 when the full Cabinet was restored after the war, the Committee of Imperial Defence was also re-created. Its weaknesses have been discussed above (in Chapter 10) and they were apparent to most contemporary observers. A sub-committee of the Committee of Imperial Defence under Lord Salisbury reported in favour of combining defence planning in a single professional committee of the three Chiefs of Staff. Haldane, who regretted that before 1914 plans had been made in the War Office and the Admiralty rather than in the Committee of Imperial Defence, was anxious lest " an unrivalled opportunity for getting the machinery for the formulation of defence policy effectively at work would lapse." [41] Ramsay MacDonald had agreed that Haldane should act as Chairman of the Committee of Imperial Defence and the latter now instituted the Chiefs of Staff Committee over which he presided. The point about this committee was that it changed the direction of professional activity. Before, the habitual and most natural method was for each Service to make its own plans and estimates and urge them on the minister in question, and through him appeal to the Cabinet. After 1918, all the armed forces were in eclipse and none of the Service ministers carried much weight. But the Chiefs of Staff found that while the Cabinet might not listen to the relatively low-ranking politicians who were appointed to the Service ministries in these years, it was less easy to ignore point-blank warnings from the officers responsible for the defence of the country. For a while the Chiefs of Staff tended to dispute among themselves (the R.A.F. wrested the defence of Iraq and Aden from the other Services), but they soon found that it paid to work together. In

---

[41] D. Sommer, *Haldane of Cloan*, p. 396.

1927 Joint Planning and Joint Intelligence Committees were added and the Chiefs of Staff began the custom of making an annual survey of military needs for the full Committee of Imperial Defence, the Foreign Office and the Cabinet. The Report for 1932 laid great stress on the weakness of the forces—" we had no real Army except in India; . . . our Air Force . . . was a wreck of its former self; our Navy . . . was just keeping itself alive." [42] This had the very important effect of terminating the Treasury rule that planning must be based on the assumption that there was no likelihood of hostilities for ten years. In 1933 the Report was even stronger and the Chief of the Naval Staff put in " a last paragraph . . . to the effect that we could not, with the arms we had, accept our present responsibilities as they were laid down " and it asked " for new and clearer instructions of the Government's intentions as to the defence of this Country and the Empire." [43] During the 1930s all the major decisions to rearm, to start talks with the French about sending an expeditionary force and to introduce conscription were, quite rightly, taken by the Cabinet or by its directing coterie. But the value of tendering united advice and the habit of combined planning was fully established, and the only question that remained was the best way of linking the Chiefs of Staff and their organisation to the political leadership. The method of appointing a Minister to co-ordinate defence had mixed motives and was not a success.[44] After 1945, the Chiefs of Staff were built into a Ministry of Defence having direct access to the Prime Minister through the Defence Committee of the Cabinet. By stages, the Service ministries were drawn together till in 1963 there was complete amalgamation, the framing of policy being retained by a Committee of the Cabinet. Till that year there had been no regular Committee on Foreign Affairs though one was set up in 1956. When this had occurred it was evidence either of a desire by the Prime Minister to formalise his control over a weak or little trusted Foreign Secretary or it might be a device for withdrawing a topic from the full Cabinet. But by 1963 it was appreciated that defence and foreign policy could not be separated so the Committee of the

---

[42] This is the paraphrase of Lord Chatfield, then Chief of the Naval Staff; Chatfield *op. cit.*, pp. 77–78.

[43] *Ibid.*, p. 79.

[44] See p. 442, above.

Cabinet was renamed the Defence and Oversea Policy Committee. Its membership and functions were set out in the White Paper (Cmnd. 2097 of 1963) and the ministerial committee chaired by the Prime Minister had beneath it a Defence Council presided over by the Secretary of State for Defence.[45]

Since 1964 there has been a standing committee to co-ordinate and review policy in the social services. Whether this, as in the case of defence, is a sign that in time the ministries concerned will be amalgamated cannot be said, but it is clearly necessary for common policies to be pursued and there is information collected in some departments which can be of great use to others working in this field.

Finally there are the two standing committees which deal with the legislative programme. One is the Legislation Committee (again formerly a function of the H.A.C.) which goes over all Bills to see that they accord with the decisions of the Cabinet. At one time this Committee did try to reopen policy matters in the guise of making drafting easier. For instance, it said that it was so difficult to frame and carry a clause providing for random breath tests, that the Cabinet reconsidered and went back on the idea. But there have been instructions which are on the whole observed that this Committee deals only with drafting. The second committee with a very similar title is the Future Legislation Committee which prepares the programme for each parliamentary session. This came into existence in 1945 and has been essential in view of the crowded timetables the House has had to face in recent years.

The one standing committee that has gone out of existence has been the Atomic Energy Committee.[46] By the early 1960s, the policy decisions had been taken and the work could be handed on to the appropriate departments. So this completes the list of standing committees on Defence, Economic Policy, Home Affairs, Social Services, Legislation and Future Legislation. In addition there are committees which recur, such as the one on agriculture revived for every annual price review, and some that last for several years and are very important, examples being the

---

45 It is the only Committee of Cabinet to have a publicly acknowledged existence and membership.

46 For a description of this committee, see R. Darcy Best, "The United Kingdom Atomic Energy Authority," *Public Administration*, Spring 1956.

committees on the Rhodesian problem and on the British application to join the Common Market. Further, there are the many "Miscs" set up to consider specific problems and questions of interdepartmental co-ordination.

All this is now and has been since the 1930s a regular part of the machinery of government. Many issues are settled in these committees and never reach the Cabinet. They go up if the matter is of crucial importance or if one or more ministers has refused to agree or has, in the language normally used, "reserved his position." Some questions start at the top with the Prime Minister or his senior colleagues and only go into the machine when they have been thoroughly explored. The Cabinet is the Court of Appeal in this system, it is the body which has a right to be informed of vital matters but it cannot enforce this right against the Prime Minister or some senior ministers. It sees all the most important issues at some stage but it cannot be held to be the only decision-making body in the British system of government.

INDIVIDUAL AND COLLECTIVE RESPONSIBILITY

Much has been said and written about the responsibility of ministers. The discussion can easily become confused because of the different meanings that are attached to the word "responsible." Collective responsibility will be discussed below, and the first task is to consider whether there is any separate element of individual responsibility. The most common political meaning is that a certain minister will answer parliamentary questions on a given subject. A second sense arises when those in political circles appreciate that a particular policy is largely the idea of the minister, rather than the traditional policy of the party in power, and they may single out the minister for attack. For instance, in 1903–05 Wyndham was pursuing his land purchase schemes for Ireland in a manner which alarmed many Conservatives and would certainly have been unlikely under any other Chief Secretary. A third sense is simply that a minister is responsible even if a policy is the work of the Cabinet as a whole but his colleagues choose to place the burden upon him. Thus Sir Samuel Hoare thought he was acting in accordance with the views of the ministry in concluding the Hoare-Laval Pact and his decisions were subsequently endorsed by the Cabinet till opposition became acute. He was then asked to disavow and denounce his actions but preferred, "accepting his responsibility," to resign. There is, in addition, the normal moral sense of the word meaning "culpable" and a minister may, like a private individual, feel responsible if he could by greater wisdom or exertion have prevented some unfortunate occurrence.

The one aspect that remains is the alleged obligation on a minister to resign when he or one of his subordinates has blundered. The origin of this notion is fairly clear. It dates from the 1850s and 1860s when it was reasonable to assume that a minister could watch over every significant action of his department. Even then, there would have been no need to acknowledge errors in this way but for the power of the House of Commons to move and carry a motion censuring the individual in question without necessarily dislodging the government. When Lord Chancellor Westbury was censured for jobbery in 1865 Palmerston stood by him, but the House of Commons drove him from office. By the 1890s it was no longer possible to remove an individual by a hostile vote without defeating the government and ministers either resigned because they were morally culpable as individuals (as J. H. Thomas was in 1936) or because the Cabinet had abandoned them. But there remained the one intermediate case where the fault lay with a subordinate and the Cabinet was prepared to stand by the minister. In this situation there had never been any constitutional obligation to resign. Once the hardening of the party system prevented dismissal by the House of Commons, the minister was responsible only in the senses that he answered questions on this field and that the action lay within his department. If the Cabinet was prepared to wrap him in the blanket of collective responsibility, he was safe. The only remaining reason for resignation was the point of honour or of punctilio that after all, this had happened in his department and therefore some degree of moral culpability should be accepted, even if not deserved.

It was for this rather vague sentiment that "someone must own up" that Austen Chamberlain resigned when the Commission on the campaign in Mesopotamia blamed him and the War

Cabinet for not making more careful official inquiries about conditions in the Persian Gulf.[47]   The most recent case was the resignation of Sir Thomas Dugdale, when officials of his ministry were censured over the Crichel Down Case in 1954. Sir Thomas Dugdale was a popular minister who had the support of the Premier and there was no question of the latter asking for his resignation. He decided to leave because he felt that if he stayed, the whole matter would be smoothed over, whereas a ministerial resignation would administer a profound and salutary shock to the whole Civil Service. There is the added point that this was not a matter in dispute between the parties and Sir Thomas Dugdale could act without fear of any political repercussions.

A government may simply refuse to recognise any form of responsibility. It was evident that some officials had blundered over the circumstances in which Commander Crabb met his death in Portsmouth Harbour in 1956, but Sir Anthony Eden refused to answer questions, to say that this was the work of any department, or to accept any moral culpability. In 1958 the Colonial Secretary, Mr. Lennox-Boyd, was to some degree censured (at least by implication) in the Devlin Report on the disturbances in Nyasaland and in the inquiry into the deaths of eleven men in Hola detention camp. Mr. Lennox-Boyd was responsible in the sense that he was the minister who answered (or had refused to answer) questions on these subjects and that the matters were dealt with by his department. But the Cabinet accepted a collective responsibility for his actions, the House of Commons were unable (even if they had been willing) to take action against him as an individual and there was certainly no constitutional obligation on him to resign. The only reasons for resignation could have been a sense of some degree of moral culpability for errors of judgment, or a desire, like Sir Thomas Dugdale's, to give his officials a jolt. Whether Mr. Lennox-Boyd had any such feelings is not known, but there was the added problem that this was a matter of acute political controversy and it has become a fashion for governments to refuse to admit to any errors either collective or individual, on the eve of a general election.

Collective responsibility likewise has several meanings which

---

[47] The conduct of operations had been entirely in the hands of the Indian Government and Chamberlain had made all his inquiries and voiced his doubts in his private letters.

become entangled. In one sense, it refers to the fact that all members of a government are expected to be unanimous in support of its policies on all public occasions. This is in part because divergencies among leading members of a government afford such wonderful openings to its opponents and are such evidence of disharmony that they cannot be tolerated. But there was and is a feeling that men working together to guide national affairs ought either to be in sufficient agreement to give genuine advocacy to collective decisions (despite differences at the formative stage) or should resign. For minor members of the government whose views are of little consequence and who may play no part in taking decisions, these contentions have clearly less force. Some Parliamentary Private Secretaries were only warned when they abstained during the 1945–50 Labour Government, but when this happened in 1967, seven were dismissed though the ban on their employment was lifted after a few months. The precise position of a P.P.S. has long been in doubt for they receive no salaries and are not listed as members of the government. Yet they should be and usually are close to their minister and dissent by a P.P.S. may be taken to indicate that his master has disagreed in Cabinet but been overruled. This situation occurred in 1967 when the Labour Cabinet was debating a possible British application to join the Common Market. Not only were the divergent views of members of the Cabinet widely publicised in the Press but the P.P.S.s to Mr. Douglas Jay and Mr. Frederick Peart were vigorously organising the anti-Common Market campaign in the House of Commons and in the country. These activities were continued after the application to join had been agreed upon by the Cabinet and endorsed by the House of Commons. After Mr. Jay had been relieved of his post later in the year it became only too evident that he had been in fundamental disagreement with his colleagues.

There have been one or two other similar instances in recent years. Mr. Frank Cousins, while a senior member of the Labour Cabinet publicly expressed his " delight " at resolutions by his Union condemning the government's policies on prices and incomes and on the war in Vietnam. Although Mr. Enoch Powell never openly criticised the policies of Conservative administrations of which he was a member, his extreme reverence for the operation of " the free market " was well known and most observers appreciated how deeply he disagreed with the regional development and planning policies adopted in the last years of Mr. Macmillan's Government.

There are deplorable features of these developments but they must be recognised as the outcome of the tendencies already noted: — the power of the Prime Minister to dismiss and to refuse, if he so wants, to reinstate a politician who has annoyed him; the strong feeling that life on the back-benches of the House of Commons has little to offer and the feeling that since major policy is determined mainly by the senior members of the Cabinet, the rest have some excuse for disagreeing but staying. The other side of the problem is the very weak position of resigners which has already been discussed on pp. 444–446, above.

The bad features of this tendency are that if informed opponents of a policy remain in the government, there may be no proper argument about the merits of a policy, particularly if the Opposition is not concerned. Secondly, it means that if the Prime Minister and his closest associates misjudge a situation, they may go a long way before one of the principal remaining checks on them begins to operate, the fear of resignation adding to the opposition to their policies.

Although this problem has only come out into the open recently, it has worried ministers for many years. When Lord Maugham, who was Lord Chancellor in 1938–39, was attacked as an appeaser, he said, " I have a complete answer to the charge, for I was never an intimate adviser in the matter, or indeed in any other purely political matter, and had no opportunity of displaying complacency or intransigence or disregard of warnings . . . I was not at any time a member of any inner group of the Cabinet if there was one." [48] Lord Woolton found he was worried by the great scope accorded to the Chancellor of the Exchequer: " Other members of the Cabinet are placed in considerable difficulty by this problem, since they become politically committed to financial decisions with which they may not agree." [49] Some ministers have tried to avoid personal implication in major decisions while accepting the obligation not to differ in public. Lord Curzon did not accept the Report on which the Montagu-Chelmsford Reforms were based and so he refused to serve on the Cabinet Committee

---

[48] Viscount Maugham, *At the End of the Day*, p. 383.
[49] Woolton, *op. cit.*, p. 375.

which drew up the Bill and gave only lukewarm support in the Lords. When Sir Stafford Cripps came to doubt Mr. Churchill's system of war control, he asked to be moved out of the Cabinet to the Ministry of Aircraft Production. Sir Walter Monckton remained a member of the Cabinet during the Suez Crisis but withdrew from any active participation by taking the post of Pay-master-General. The most extreme example of such dissociation occurred when Mr. Attlee and Vernon Hartshorn were asked, as ministers, to wind up debates on unemployment in the 1929–31 Labour Government. They declined to do so until they saw signs of a more vigorous policy.

The only accepted method of making such reservations, and it is extremely rare, is when a minister dissents very strongly from the majority in the Cabinet and asks that his dissent be recorded.[50] There may be embarrassment in reconciling such private dissents (be they recorded or purely personal) with collective unanimity in public when politicians have taken strong and well-known stands before they enter a government. It was soon evident that the National Government of 1931 was moving towards tariffs though several members were life-long Free Traders. No one expects all members of a Cabinet to be in complete agreement, and the public has often been aware that ministers differ over major issues (as the Liberal leaders were known to disagree over women's suffrage before 1914 and Labour ministers were divided over capital punishment after 1945). In the instance of the National Government of 1931, a formula was found by which four Cabinet Ministers stated that they regarded the continuance of the ministry as paramount but they were free to speak and vote against tariffs. As Tom Jones observed: " what the ministers have done is really to carry the expression of their dissent a step further than the practice of placing it on record in the Cabinet minutes. And just as you drop your dissent once you record it, so they should drop it after stating it to the House." [51]   This episode also serves to show that collective responsibility covers as much as the Prime Minister and Cabinet determine it shall cover. Similarly in the case of individuals like Sir Samuel Hoare in 1935, it was left to Stanley Baldwin and the

50 Snowden refers to such occasions, *op. cit.*, Vol. II, p. 619, and there were a few during the latter years of the 1945–51 Labour Cabinets.
51 Tom Jones, *op. cit.*, p. 26.

Cabinet to decide whether his actions were to be laid at his own door or were to be covered by collective responsibility.

Most of the cases in the 1930s and 1940s did not cause alarm because (apart from the special circumstances of the free traders in 1931) the disagreements were not revealed to the public. The objector entered his caveat in his own mind or in the Cabinet minutes [52] and then proceeded to support the government. Also there were sufficient resignations on disagreements of principle for the public to assume that fundamental divisions were brought out into the open. (There were fourteen such resignations between the wars, eleven in the years 1945 to 1958 and four in the decade since 1958).[53] Now the fear is that however much ministers may disagree or have had to reverse their policies, they will remain until asked to leave by the Prime Minister, a situation which leads to the dangers mentioned and decreases public respect for politicians.

SHADOW CABINETS

The old practice of holding Shadow Cabinets has continued and undergone changes of emphasis which reflect the developments in government. The chief task of a Shadow Cabinet is to determine policy and plan parliamentary tactics. As it is free of the great bulk of administrative work, there is much more time to consider policy, though even then much is inevitably settled by the Leader of the Opposition and his chief advisers. The Shadow Cabinet is most useful in bringing ideas together, and determining the precise line which is to be explained to the rank and file of the party and put forward in the House. The Conservative strategy over the Campbell case in 1924 was worked out in their Shadow Cabinet (Consultative Committee is the official title), as was the party's policy on protection earlier in the same year. Relations with the Liberals after the Conservative defeat in 1929 were handled by the same body. Labour Shadow Cabinets (officially called the Parliamentary Committee) meet regularly in the Leader of the Opposition's room in Parliament to conduct their business.[54]

[52] It is hard to find out whether such reservations are recorded. The Cabinet Office have refused to declare their practice but some of the ministers who have indicated their objection believe that this was recorded.

[53] These figures are taken from R. K. Anderson and J. A. Cross, *The Tactics of Resignation*, pp. 80–83.

[54] When the Liberals had enough members to warrant such a body its title was the Advisory Committee.

To try to cope with the growing complexity of government and to offset the advantage Civil Service briefing gives to those in office, Shadow Cabinets have used committees to work out policies and have developed a secretariat to aid with research. In 1923, Stanley Baldwin's administration set up a committee under Sir John Anderson to study the future of National Insurance. When the Conservatives went into opposition, the Shadow Cabinet continued the work and were ready with a project should they return to office. Neville Chamberlain and L. S. Amery took advantage of their defeat in November 1923 to create a policy secretariat and it was ready with proposals for the Conservative election programme a year later. Part of the work had been organised by Neville Chamberlain himself and he was able to produce a series of twenty-five Bills for the reform of local government services, " each . . . based on the report of a party committee aided by chosen experts." [55] On the Labour side, the Shadow Cabinet was aware of its acute lack of assistance and background information between 1931 and 1935. To meet this, the various study groups that were set up by the National Executive Committee helped to brief front-benchers and a rudimentary service was provided by the staff in Transport House. Mr. Attlee regarded it as a step forward in Labour thinking and practice when he persuaded his party to form a committee on defence policy in 1935. In 1929, the Conservatives had started a Research Department and after 1945 it was revitalised by Mr. Butler, and a separate Parliamentary Secretariat was formed under Mr. Henry Hopkinson to provide raw material for the Opposition Front Bench. The Shadow Cabinet, backed after 1948 by a Parliamentary Secretariat, and a Library and Information as well as a Research Department, set up committees on an Industrial and an Agricultural Charter. All this material was used in the work of opposition and went into the 1950 election programme, *The Right Road for Britain.* The Labour Party has always expected its leading members to do more for themselves, but since 1951 it has had policy committees of the National Executive and a Research and Parliamentary Secretariat to aid its official spokesmen.[56]

55 Viscount Templewood, *op. cit.*, p. 37.
56 The Leader of the Opposition quite often receives information from the Prime Minister on important foreign and defence matters but this cannot

On the Conservative side, the membership of Shadow Cabinets is determined by the Party Leader though it is usually assumed that all ex-Cabinet Ministers will be called. When Austen Chamberlain, Birkenhead and A. J. Balfour were readmitted to the fold in early 1924, they resumed their places at the Shadow Cabinet. Sir Samuel Hoare's prominence and abilities were rewarded by an invitation to attend in 1929. The same year L. S. Amery, who sympathised with Beaverbrook and Rothermere's campaign for Empire Free Trade, found himself excluded, but he was readmitted in 1931 after the Imperial Conference. Disagreement with Baldwin's policy towards India led Mr. Churchill to resign and Duff Cooper, among others, saw this as a great mistake. It meant that Baldwin could pass him over more easily when the National Government was formed and, without office, Mr. Churchill was largely impotent. When the Labour Cabinet was formed in 1929, MacDonald wanted to exclude all left-wingers but it was made simpler for him in the case of John Wheatley, as the latter had recently resigned from the Shadow Cabinet. The Labour Shadow Cabinet (or Parliamentary Committee) consists of five *ex officio* members—the Leader in both Houses, the Deputy Leader in the Commons and the Chief Whip in both Houses—and twelve M.P.s elected by the Parliamentary Labour Party. (One peer is also selected.) Presence at either Conservative or Labour Shadow Cabinets has never constituted any claim for inclusion when an actual Cabinet was formed. Mr. Attlee left out several of the Parliamentary Committee of the day when he selected his Cabinet in 1945.

With a written constitution, the Labour Parliamentary Committee meets regularly but the Conservative equivalent is less definite. In 1924, Neville Chamberlain wanted more Shadow Cabinets " though Stanley Baldwin struggles like a bronco to avoid them." [57] The next period of opposition found the Conservatives badly divided. Some of the Shadow Cabinet were angry when Baldwin gave Conservative backing to Irwin's Indian policy (Dominion status as the ultimate goal) without consulting them. The disagreement occurred in October 1929 and Baldwin retaliated

be included as part of the normal equipment of a Shadow Cabinet. Bad personal relations or acute controversy may lead to the severance of all such contacts.

[57] Feiling, *op. cit.*, p. 114.

by refusing to call the Shadow Cabinet. Neville Chamberlain found this situation when he returned from a tour abroad in January 1930 and persuaded Baldwin to circumvent the problem by calling a smaller body called " the Business Committee." The membership consisted of Neville Chamberlain, Churchill, Hailsham, Peel, Oliver Stanley and Hoare and it was " a sort of inner shadow cabinet." [58] Both the Shadow Cabinet and the Business Committee met in late 1930 and 1931. Between 1945 and 1951, the term "Business Committee" was applied to a larger body composed of the principal officers of the committees of the Parliamentary Party and its duty was to advise the Leader.

The Leader of the Opposition is never in quite the same position of power as a Prime Minister: he has either led his Party to defeat or has yet to show that he can win. Conservative opposition leaders have tended to have a rough passage. Balfour was dismissed in 1911, Austen Chamberlain had his advice rejected in 1922, Baldwin only just survived in 1930 and there were mutterings that Mr. Churchill did not do enough in the early years after the 1945 defeat. Sir Alec Douglas-Home resigned as Leader of the Opposition in July 1966. It was his own decision taken without consulting the Shadow Cabinet (and some members were angry at his methods and at the decision). But he had not done well enough in the 1964 election. While liked and respected among Conservative M.P.s, his support in the constituency parties ebbed. Then came a Press campaign insisting that this was " The Right Moment to Change," a campaign which led Sir Alec to consult the Whips and get the reports that the constituencies no longer backed him. This had spread to over a hundred M.P.s and he decided to resign, joining A. J. Balfour as an ousted Conservative statesman whose failing was to lead the Party to defeat. His successor, Mr. Edward Heath, took over and not only led the Party to a greater defeat but faced the continual accusations that he could not stand up to the Prime Minister in the House, that his television image was poor and that he was failing to make an impact on the public. Such objections reached a climax at the Conservative Annual Conference in October 1967 but were stilled by the evidence of Labour's declining electoral popularity. The greater help to a Leader of the Opposition is the prospect of

58 *Ibid.*, p. 177, and Templewood, *op. cit.*, p. 48.

becoming Prime Minister with all the power and patronage that it carries. The closer this comes, the more criticism declines. Also leaders such as A. J. Balfour and Sir Alec Douglas-Home were aristocrats with an alternative and entirely satisfying position and way of life available. If the party did not want them as leaders and they felt the party would do better in other hands, they resigned. Mr. Heath is a grammar school product and the first leader to be elected. He is a career politician similar to Mr. Wilson in the sense that this is his whole life and he would not relinquish his position without a stiff fight. Removing unsuccessful Conservative leaders of the opposition may be a very different matter in the future. There is no doubt that if the Labour Party and Mr. Wilson's fortunes revive after 1968, the grumbling about Mr. Heath will return but it is unlikely to have any effect so long as there is any prospect of victory at the next general election.

In measuring the effectiveness of a Shadow Cabinet, many factors such as the quality of leadership, the morale of the Government, the tide of national opinion and the nature of Government policy have all to be considered. But it is a noticeable fact that Labour Cabinets, though often reasonably harmonious politically, have not been as friendly, and Labour Shadow Cabinets have not been as united or determined, as their Conservative counterparts.

In Labour Shadow Cabinets much excellent work is done, but there is more acceptance of the role of opposition and sometimes the observer may detect a feeling that Conservatives, who are able if misguided, are better in office than a Labour leader of the wrong school. Interviews with Labour front-benchers and a study of their memoirs reveal antipathies which, though they may be overlaid by the absorption of office, cannot but tend to weaken a government, and reappear with renewed edge in opposition.[59] There was evidence of these clashes in the 1930s when Bevin attacked Lansbury with great bitterness at the 1935 Labour Party Conference and virtually drove him from the leadership. Yet Attlee provided a fairly quiet guidance and managed most of his colleagues well. Neither then nor in his period as Leader of the Opposition from 1951 to 1955 did he face the problems encountered by Mr. Hugh Gaitskell. Some of these were due to

---

[59] There are many examples but perhaps the most telling, if over-drawn, illustrations are in L. Hunter, *The Road to Brighton Pier*. It is significant that Mr. Shinwell calls his autobiography *Conflict Without Malice*.

Mr. Gaitskell's tendency to lay down principles, insist on a debate, a vote and adherence to the decision reached. In an essentially federal party, such tactics underlined differences. But he had also special problems to face in that the Party seemed to be out of office for an indefinite period, its doctrines seemed less relevant, the Conservatives had struck a period of economic prosperity and outside pressures, particularly from the Campaign for Nuclear Disarmament, intensified the divisions within the Party. Yet Mr. Gaitskell survived both a direct challenge for the leadership by Mr. Harold Wilson in 1961 and the overruling of his defence policy by the Party's Annual Conference at Scarborough in that year. In fact his struggle to reassert himself did much to make him a national figure and his stock in the Labour Party and in the country was rising at the time of his death in 1963. Mr. Wilson, who succeeded him, was a much more tactful Opposition leader. He gave old opponents important shadow posts when they were elected to the Parliamentary Committee, he established an ascendancy in the House and as the election approached looked more and more like the next Prime Minister, an impression which is the major factor in creating and maintaining the authority of the Leader of the Opposition.

CONCLUSION

While British government in the latter half of the nineteenth century can be described simply as Cabinet government, such a description would be misleading today. Now the country is governed by the Prime Minister, who leads, co-ordinates and maintains a series of ministers all of whom are advised and backed by the Civil Service. Some decisions are taken by the Premier alone, some in consultations between him and the senior ministers, while others are left to heads of departments, to the full Cabinet, one of the many Cabinet Committees, or to the permanent officials. Of these bodies the Cabinet holds the central position because, though it does not often initiate policy or govern in that sense,[60] it is the place where disputes are settled, where major policies are endorsed and where the balance of forces emerges if there is a disagreement. In the end, most decisions have to be reported to the Cabinet and

---

[60] It was Beatrice Webb who concluded that " the Cabinet does not govern "; *Diaries*, 1924–1932, p. 213.

Cabinet Ministers are the only ones who have the right to complain if they have not been informed or consulted. The precise amount of power held by each agency and the use made of the Cabinet depends on the ideas of the Premier and the personnel and situattion with which he has to deal. Lloyd George, Neville Chamberlain, Mr. Churchill during the war, Mr. Attlee, Sir Anthony Eden and Mr. Wilson have all adapted the machinery to suit their own tastes and purposes. Bonar Law, Ramsay MacDonald, Stanley Baldwin and Mr. Macmillan, on the other hand, have tended to accept the existing pattern, but they have all imposed their stamp on the governments they have led. Too much must not be made of the talk of inner Cabinets. There is no group of offices which confer any special status on their occupants and no machinery which formally separates an inner from an outer ring. The point about men who are said to be in an inner Cabinet is that they are markedly and regularly consulted (often one by one rather than as a group) by the Prime Minister. The reason for such a development, when it occurs, is the loneliness of the Premier and his desire for support. The criterion for admission to the inner circle is that the Premier finds the individual's views or abilities a help. Such prior or special consultations often create feelings of jealousy among those who are excluded but Cabinet Ministers still have a great advantage over non-Cabinet ministers.[61] Ultimately they will be told what has happened and they have a right to express their views. However, the real sphere in which Cabinet Ministers in charge of the less important offices can act is not in the Cabinet itself but in the committees covering their field of interest and in their own departments. Prime Ministers do not have the legal security granted by an American President's fixed term of office but in this century Prime Ministers have only been removed in times of national emergency during a world war or when leading a coalition the majority of which was drawn from supporters of another party. This indicates, despite fluctuations in the power of Prime Ministers (as of Presidents), a very great measure of security. There is no single catchphrase that can describe this form of government, but it may be pictured as a cone. The Prime Minister

[61] Lord Woolton explains that Mr. Churchill's tendency to see only his cronies did cause jealousy. " The truth is that ambitious ministers are anxious to be both seen and heard by the Prime Minister—how else can he recognise and judge their competence and value?" *Memoirs*, p. 377.

stands at the apex supported by and giving point to a widening series of rings of senior ministers, the Cabinet, its committees, non-Cabinet ministers, and departments. Of these rings, the only one above the level of the Civil Service that has formal existence and acts as a court of appeal for the lower tiers is the Cabinet.

CHAPTER 22

LIMITATIONS ON GOVERNMENT ACTION

THE limitations on the freedom of action of a British Government have multiplied. In the nineteenth century the Cabinet's decisions were largely concerned with matters of foreign policy, taxation and domestic regulation. These were not difficult to carry through though there were some problems of controlling colonial officials and co-ordinating departments at home. Then, in the early twentieth century, as governments turned to more positive social policies and defence became more complicated, it was appreciated that some ideas might come from civil servants and that new tasks might require new machinery. After the First World War, the size of the Civil Service grew and, for the first time, there were discussions about how far a Cabinet could impose its will on such a large bureaucratic machine. Some left-wing writers and politicians feared Whitehall as a stumbling block to their policies while some Conservatives felt the existence of such an apparatus led to an inbuilt propensity to interfere, to aggregate power.

Since the Second World War there have been new difficulties for British Governments seeking to carry out their policies. The principal difficulty has been the elimination of the country's economic and political supremacy as revealed in the recurrence of balance of payments crises, the lack of bargaining power to achieve such objectives as entry to the European Common Market and the need, at intervals, to cut back on internal development. At the same time, successive ministries have asked the Civil Service not merely to regulate factories or to intervene by building schools and providing social benefits but positively to create new economic growth in development areas, to increase the output of industry and agriculture and to conduct research and apply the results. Lack of success in some of these activities may have been due to external factors or to features of British society outside the immediate control of any government. (It may be hard to prevent rural depopulation in Wales and the Highlands or to make certain industries export-minded whatever the merits of the civil servants or the machinery available.) Part of the problem is that the constitutional requirements of being answerable through ministers to the House of Commons impose restraints that are not always compatible with rapid decisions and risk-taking. But it is also true that the machinery of government was not prepared for this kind of positive intervention. In many ministries data were not collected, there was little operational research and few specialists in economics or sociology so that policy was sometimes made and carried out against a background of inadequate information. The insistence, particularly after the Report of the Committee on Administrative Tribunals and Enquiries (the Franks Report, Cmnd. 218, of 1957) on elaborate, careful and long-drawn out procedures for the protection of private rights slowed down government action in acquiring land and all forms of construction at a time when adequate infrastructure was essential if rapid economic growth was to be achieved. Many government policies fall to be implemented in part at least by local authorities and the capacity of many local councils and their staff has been found to be inadequate.

It is necessary to examine these limitations in turn to see how far they have affected the working of successive Cabinets or conditioned ministers' approaches to the problems of government, the most important the capacity, conduct and control of the Civil Service.

THE CIVIL SERVICE

The traditional view of British Government was that all decisions on matters of policy were taken by the Cabinet or by individual ministers so that the Civil Service merely carried out instructions. In the mid and late nineteenth century this was the case, or could have been so if ministers had desired it. In several senses the theory still applies. It is formally maintained in that civil servants are never said to take decisions and letters always begin: " I am instructed by the Secretary of State to inform you. . . . " It is also true in that a Cabinet minute outranks all other orders and a definite pronouncement from this source cannot be ignored. On the other hand, the administration is not conducted on two distinct planes, matters of discretion being in the hands of ministers while detailed execution is left to the officials. To continue the analogy of a cone-shaped executive, a number of senior civil servants in each department will work with and advise the minister, attend

Cabinet Committees and come into contact with other ministers. A
Permanent Under-Secretary in a major department will probably
have more influence than a Parliamentary Under-Secretary in a
minor department.

As a result, there have been commentators who argue that
power has to a large extent passed to the Civil Service; they say
that the Cabinet can deal only with a very limited field and that
even there its action is circumscribed by the kind of information
and advice offered by the officials. The first systematic and
powerful exposition of this view was by Ramsay Muir in his book
How Britain is Governed, published in 1930. Extending his
examples to cover recent developments, the course of the argument remains clear. In the 1960s there were over 750,000 civil
servants, headed by an Administrative Grade of some 4,400 highly
trained and able individuals. Even if thinking and planning goes
no further down the scale than the level of Assistant Secretary,
there are 800 people in this position. The President of the Board
of Trade probably deals regularly with a dozen of the senior men
of his department but he cannot know and watch over the seventy
Assistant Secretaries who work nominally under his supervision.
These men are full-time experts anxious to do their duty and to
smooth out kinks in the various tasks allotted to them. To overcome a series of obstacles may require new legislation which they
devise and recommend to their superiors. In many cases all that
is needed is a new Statutory Order, code, or circular of instructions to the local authorities. The present output of Statutory
Instruments exceeds 2,000 a year and these are largely the work
of officials. In giving evidence to the Tomlin Commission in 1930,
the Association of First Division Civil Servants stated that:

> " Almost any administrative decision may be expected to
> have consequences which will endure or emerge long after
> the period of office of the government by which or under
> whose authority it is taken. It is the . . . special duty of the
> administrative class . . . in their day-to-day work to set these
> wider and more enduring considerations against the exigencies
> of the moment. . . ."

Even at the level of full-scale legislation, there are many examples
of Bills being passed on from governments of one political complexion to another without any change of form or substance.

Yet all these points only cause alarm if they are set against the old premiss that no official should exercise any element of discretion. Once this assumption is cast aside, Ramsay Muir's argument that government has fallen into the hands of the civil servants becomes merely a demonstration that policy is made at all levels. What matters in this case is that the political top tiers can create the appropriate atmosphere in administration, encourage certain schemes and restrain others and, on occasion, introduce into the thinking of departments changes of direction or emphasis.

It is now fully accepted that civil servants should recommend what seems to them to be the correct course of action. The Civil Service Commission's note to entrants says that one of the tasks of the Administrative Class is to " advise ministers on the formation of policy." Sir Edward Bridges has described how " there has been built up in every department a store of knowledge and experience in the subjects handled, something which eventually takes shape as a practical philosophy, or may merit the title of a departmental point of view." The distinction between policy and administration cannot be pushed too far and " these departmental philosophies are of the essence of a civil servant's work." [1] Lord Strang accepts the evidence put above (pp. 267–8) that the Foreign Office was nothing more than the Foreign Secretary's clerical organisation till about 1900. Since that date there has been an enormous expansion in the volume and complexity of its work. Officials cannot just pass information through to the Secretary of State: it has to be weighed and evaluated and " usually he will want a definite recommendation." [2] So a senior civil servant gives life and direction to existing legislation or policies, acquires a deep knowledge of the field, and promotes new solutions.

This situation has long been recognised by ministers when they talk of the views of the Treasury, the Foreign Office or the Admiralty. Often the political head of a department is included in this description or it is assumed that he agrees with his officials, but it is also used to refer to the long-term attitudes of a department. The Foreign Office, for example, disliked the special position and attitudes of the High Commissioners in Egypt after the First World War, had doubts about the policy of appeasement in the 1930s, and has advocated British entry to the Common

1 Sir Edward Bridges, " Portrait of a Profession," *Rede Lecture* for 1950.
2 Lord Strang, *The Foreign Office*, p. 18.

Market since it was formed. The Treasury's belief in Free Trade in the 1920s, its constant interest in economy, and its post-war preoccupation with the balance of payments, come into the same category.

Normally civil servants, who are wedded to a departmental policy, will change their actions if not their beliefs on the instruction of the minister. But if not there have been occasions when alternative posts have been found for them or the date of retirement advanced. Arthur Henderson did not find Sir Ronald Lindsay, the Permanent Under-Secretary at the Foreign Office, satisfactory and facilitated his appointment as Ambassador in Washington. His successor, Vansittart, was moved out of the main current of business by Neville Chamberlain. Hore-Belisha decided that he could not operate with the older members of the Army Council and asked for the resignations of the C.I.G.S. and the Adjutant-General in late 1937. On the whole, the Civil and Armed Services tended to be more rigid in the inter-war years. The Second World War broke down many departmental barriers, brought in a new generation and showed how much was possible to those who try. Mr. Attlee was as definite in his handling of officials as of ministers and on the rare occasions when a civil servant was disloyal or arrogant, he was left in no doubt as to the nature of his offence. The only Prime Minister who has himself been a civil servant is Mr. Wilson and this has given not only a special respect for and understanding of the service but also an unwavering insistence on loyalty to and support for ministers.

On the question of giving advice to the Prime Minister or senior ministers, the No. 10 Downing Street staff and the Cabinet Secretariat play a special role. In the first case, it is inevitable that the bonds of trust and sympathetic understanding which must link a Prime Minister and his staff inevitably allow the latter some influence. They draw the Premier's attention to weaknesses in a departmental case, they report on conditions in other ministries and whether work is progressing well and relations between the minister and his staff are good. Originally Lloyd George's Garden Suburb had this function and though it was dissolved in 1922, Horace Wilson in the 1930s and Professor Lindemann in the 1940s had the same special relationship to Neville Chamberlain and Mr. Churchill. The No. 10 staff is in fact a help to the

Prime Minister not only in dealing with policy questions and with the Cabinet but in controlling the Civil Service. Their activities are often resented by the other departments. One of the senior members of Mr. Macmillan's staff was a convinced economic expansionist and wanted to reconsider sterling's role as a reserve currency. Whenever the Prime Minister began on one of these themes, Treasury officials used to groan and say, " Here goes old X again."

The same applies in a more modified degree to the Cabinet Secretariat. It helps in the exercise of political control by chasing up Cabinet decisions and insisting on action. There can also be an element of direct advice to the Prime Minister. Sir Norman Brook accompanied Mr. Macmillan on his tour of India in 1958 and his function was clearly to give advice rather than to act as a secretary. The recommendations of such men as Sir Norman Brook, Sir Edward (now Lord) Bridges or Sir Burke Trend, are based on the experience they have gathered by a life-time of public service and constant attendance at the Cabinet, its committees and endless conferences, and while they would not seek to undermine departmental advice, it is the duty of the Secretariat to see that the decisions of the Prime Minister and the Cabinet are carried out.

Working with the Cabinet Secretariat, there is the network (often called by this actual word) of senior officials from the departments. In the late 1930s it was the practice for every Cabinet or ministerial committee to have a parallel committee of officials which met before to compare briefs and even to prepare a minute of what was to be decided later by the ministers.[3] This practice was stopped by Mr. Churchill in the early part of the war as he felt it prejudged the outcome of the ministerial dis-cussions. The practice crept back under the later years of Mr. Macmillan's administration and by 1964 it was normal for every meeting to be preceded by a discussion among the senior officials from the same departments. Some ministers regard this as essen-tial to clear the ground and establish the points in dispute. Others have been worried by a tendency for things to " jell " too early. A minister can feel that however well he makes his case at a Cabinet committee, a fellow minister who lacks knowledge of this

---

[3] Francis Williams, *A Prime Minister Remembers*, p. 40.

subject or self-confidence and has a brief marked " resist " will go on doing so and the minister may wish he could put his case direct to the real stumbling-block, the official in the resisting ministry. There have even been cases of a ministerial meeting deciding to do X and when one of the participants has scrutinised the minute he has found it recording a decision to do Y because that had been the outcome of the preliminary official discussion.

Despite the obvious dangers of such a system these arrangements and attitudes on the part of the Civil Service have usually been accepted by the leaders of the major parties, especially after they have had experience of office. Indeed, they realise that government without a stream of suggestions and comment would be totally impossible. There have, however, been one or two instances when politicians considered that the relationship operated in a particular way. During the 1929–31 Labour Government Beatrice Webb observed that " of course the usual accusation brought by the outside enthusiasts is that the minister is the tool of the Civil Service and that the Permanent Heads of Departments are always against progress along the lines of political democracy and social and economic equality." [4] There was some truth in the first part of the accusation. In 1924 Haldane had complained about the trade unionists in the Cabinet. " They are unintelligent and timid, and never grapple with anything that needs thought . . . [and] simply accept everything their officials tell them." " Fortunately we have a first rate and progressive Civil Service." [5] MacDonald added to the impression that he and his colleagues were overawed by the professional experts when he defended himself against charges of doing nothing about unemployment.

> " Until you have been in office, until you have seen those files warning Cabinet Ministers of the dangers of legislation, or that sort of thing, you have not had the experience of trying to carry out what seems to be a simple thing, but which becomes a complex, an exceedingly difficult, and a laborious and almost heartbreaking thing when you come to be a member of a Cabinet in a responsible government." [6]

There was no need for Labour ministers to be run by their officials or to give this impression, but experience does show that when

4 B. Webb, *Diaries, 1924–32*, p. 227.
5 *Ibid.,* p. 37.
6 Lyman, *The First Labour Government*, 1924, p. 138.

the views of ministers and civil servants are intermingled at this high level, the outcome depends more on personality, confidence and ability, than on constitutional proprieties. Arthur Henderson, for example, took hold of the Foreign Office in 1929, refused to be rushed into quick decisions, and sent round copies of *Labour and the Nation* (the 1929 election manifesto) so that officials could appreciate the spirit in which advice and replies to questions should be drafted. The result was excellent and he soon built up a spirit of loyalty and enthusiasm for his ideas in the office.[7] After some observation of the 1929–31 Labour Cabinet, Beatrice Webb concluded that J. H. Thomas and Margaret Bondfield were completely " in the hands of that arch-reactionary Horace Wilson." [8] The evidence suggests that in addition to these two ministers, who were in the centre of the controversy over unemployment policy, Clynes at the Home Office, Shaw at the War Office, Buxton as Minister of Agriculture and Fisheries, and Adamson as Secretary of State for Scotland, were carried by their staff.[9] It was this situation (and stories like that of the arch-conservative who voted Labour because he considered it was the only party that would not dare to argue with the officials) that gave colour to opinions of the kind put forward by Ramsay Muir.

It is interesting that the only other occasion on which the Civil Service has been accused of participating too actively was when some Conservatives felt that it showed an undue enthusiasm for the policies of the Labour Governments of 1945–51. In part this was due to dislike among business circles for certain controls administered by the Civil Service. There was a special distaste for the Ministry of Supply after it became evident that the senior officials in that department were in favour of the nationalisation of the iron and steel industry. Chiefly, however, it arose from Conservative propaganda which sought to identify the Labour Government with a heartless, idle and inefficient bureaucracy, and from a genuine failure to appreciate how far the internal and external position of the country had altered since 1939. This attitude was epitomised by Lord Woolton's opening question when a committee of the Conservative Cabinet first met the senior

[7] He told Mr. Dalton that " The first forty-eight hours decide whether a new minister is going to run his office or, whether his office is going to run him." H. Dalton, *Call Back Yesterday*, p. 219.
[8] B. Webb, *op. cit.*, pp. 210 and 232.
[9] R. Postgate, *George Lansbury*, p. 245.

Treasury officials in 1951. " I asked . . . whether the financial trouble into which the country had fallen was due to the advice that the civil servants had given to the previous Chancellor, or due to the fact that the ministers had not taken their advice." [10] Mr. Attlee records that " there were certainly some people in the Labour Party who doubted whether the civil servants would give fair play to a socialist government, but all doubts disappeared with experience." [11] Likewise, after 1951 the Conservatives soon came to the conclusion that since 1945 the permanent officials had been grappling with realities rather than falling victim to false theories.

Apart from these few occasions when the politicians have either formed or suspected the existence of a rather special relationship with the Civil Service, they have found the system entirely satisfactory. It is hard, if not impossible, to work with a department which is incapable of analysing its experience and providing advice. But if a minister wants to receive recommendations, he must also be prepared to listen to objections to his own proposals. Whether the minister takes the right advice, or rises above the warnings, is largely a matter of the balance of ability and personality between himself and his senior officials. He can gain support from his colleagues individually or formally by asking for a Cabinet decision. Lord Stansgate, as Secretary of State for India in the Second Labour Government, had some difficulty with the tougher elements in the India Office, who wanted to send a punitive expedition to Lhasa. His solution was to march them along the corridor to see Arthur Henderson. As the procession advanced, its confidence receded and by the time the Secretary of State for Foreign Affairs had read out the treaties with Tibet making Britain's rights in the matter clear, the fight was over. On the other hand it is proper that a minister takes great care before overruling his experts, and one senior ex-minister has estimated that, looking back on the times when he did so, on four out of five occasions the officials were right. Whatever the outcome of an argument, the civil servant will loyally carry out the final decision. Sir Arthur Street strenuously opposed Addison's

---

10 Lord Woolton, *Memoirs*, p. 372. Lord Woolton received no answer to this intriguing question but very shortly he, like his predecessors, was explaining the end of Britain's overseas investments, the dollar gap, and so on.

11 Lord Attlee, " Civil Servants, Ministers, Parliament and the Public," p. 16. An Essay in *The Civil Service in Britain and France*, edited by W. A. Robson.

Agricultural Marketing Bill while it was being shaped (between 1929 and 1931) but, once it was announced, he made every effort to ensure its passage through Parliament and faithfully put the Act into practice.

To appreciate the character and strength of professional advice, it is best to examine three departments with the strongest corporate traditions, the Foreign Office, the Service Departments and the Treasury. Lord Strang has described how " the Foreign Office itself has in recent times acquired perforce a certain influence in the making of foreign policy." [12] He and his successors among the senior officials try to exclude all internal considerations and deal with matters " on their merits " as they arise.[13] In the 1920s the Foreign Office tended to regard the League of Nations as being of little value, and preferred to safeguard British interests by unilateral action or agreements with individual Powers. On British rights in Egypt and China, men like Amery and Mr. Churchill considered " The Office " was " soft " but the officials argued that it was best in the long run to reach a reasonable accommodation with nationalist movements. In the late 1930s there was a desire to take a stronger line with the Fascist dictators. Neville Chamberlain thought that moderate rearmament and the cultivation of better relations with Germany " will carry us safely through the danger period, if only the F.O. will play up." [14] A section actively sympathised with Mr. Anthony Eden's position and Halifax had to ask for complete support for the government's policies. Later, in 1956, the Foreign Office disagreed strongly with the attack on Egypt. Sir Anthony Eden referred to their intransigence in very similar terms to the remarks just quoted of Neville Chamberlain. It was with difficulty that Mr. Anthony Nutting prevented a number of senior Foreign Office officials from resigning in protest.[15] By the 1960s the Office was strongly in favour of British entry to the Common Market, so much so by 1967 that certain anti-Common Market ministers alleged it had become a pressure group rather than a Department of State

---

[12] Lord Strang, *op. cit.*, p. 170.
[13] Lord Strang explains that to exclude any outside influences or partisanship, he avoided talking about foreign policy at his club and did not study the debates in *Hansard*. He relied on the incoming telegrams, his own reactions and a careful reading of *The Times*.
[14] K. Feiling, *Neville Chamberlain*, p. 319.
[15] Anthony Nutting, *No End of a Lesson*, p. 138.

and that its enthusiasm about the prospects of British entry had outrun its judgment.

The Service Ministries, as has been mentioned, tended to work together through the Chiefs of Staff Committee after 1924, and from 1932 pressed the case for rearmament. The impetus which produced the 1934 White Paper on Defence came from the Defence Requirements Committee which consisted of the three Chiefs of Staff, Vansittart for the Foreign Office, Sir Warren Fisher for the Treasury, and Sir Maurice Hankey. Of the Services, the Navy did best in terms of funds in these years because it had stated levels or objectives—departmental policies hardened into maxims like the two-power standard (excluding the United States) and the Washington Conference ratios. A second Defence Requirements Committee was formed in late 1934 and provided most of the pressure for rearmament up to 1937. When ministers wanted to resist such demands, they could simply say " No " (Neville Chamberlain cut the Committee's first programme from £76 million to £50 million) or they could turn another Department, the Treasury, on to the job. It pruned all requests for money, especially from the Army, on the grounds that national strength depended on economic recovery and this required a balanced Budget. The Service Chiefs, having had their requirements cut and being thoroughly alarmed about the state of Britain's defences, were then brought to the Foreign Affairs Committee. There they could be used to combat the Foreign Office's views, on the grounds that it was not safe to antagonise Germany or Italy. And while the international situation remained precarious, the Treasury was able to intensify its drive for economy to ensure stability and a more rapid industrial recovery.

After the war the Chiefs of Staff led by Field-Marshal Montgomery pressed for conscription. Mr. Alexander, the Minister of Defence, obtained Service agreement to a reduction in the period of national service from eighteen months to a year in order to appease Labour back-bench criticis. In 1948 Field-Marshal Montgomery persuaded the entire Army Council to say they would resign unless the eighteen-month period was restored. This was accepted by the government soon after Field-Marshal Sir William Slim had taken over as Chief of the Imperial General Staff.[16] In

[16] See Montgomery of Alamein, *Memoirs*, pp. 477–480.

the 1960s there was renewed tension as Service Chiefs tried to insist that re-equipment was with the most modern weapons while the Treasury imposed a ceiling on expenditure. The R.A.F. demanded a low level supersonic reconnaissance-strike plane while the Navy fought to retain an aircraft carrier fleet. On some issues after 1964 they could count on the aid of the Minister of Defence but he was firm in maintaining a ceiling on arms expenditure of £2,000 million at 1964 prices. Up till 1966 each service had its own junior minister but while the Minister for the Army was a member of the Defence and Oversea Policy Committee of the Cabinet, the Navy and Air Force Ministers were not. The Minister for the Navy, Mr. Christopher Mayhew, and Admiral Sir David Luce, the First Sea Lord, struggled either to keep a carrier fleet or to cut commitments. They lost and both resigned in January 1966. Since then the overall economic needs and capacities of the country have been the paramount consideration of the Cabinet, the Services have had to cut their requirements to meet these needs and in January 1968 the historic decision was taken that Britain should withdraw from the Far East, the Indian Ocean and the Persian Gulf reverting to her seventeenth-century role as a purely European Power.

In handling ministers, the Service Chiefs have always held that they have a higher duty to the sovereign and the general safety of the country, though in fact their position is precisely that of the other senior civil servants. The only possible difference is that the Service Chiefs have contacts with brother officers who are still on the active list but outside Whitehall, and through them with those former officers who have been elected to Parliament. As a result, ministers or departments who resist Service demands have found apposite questions being asked in the Commons and well-informed articles appearing in the Press. The Air Force, having fewer and poorer connections, is a comparative novice at this compared with the Admiralty. Snowden observed that " the leakage of information from the Admiralty was a common occurrence, and it caused embarrassment to every government which was making an effort to reduce the Navy Estimates." [17] Yet too much must not be

---

[17] Viscount Snowden, *An Autobiography*, Vol. II, p. 623. P. J. Grigg noted that in Mr. Churchill's battle over the Navy in the 1920s " the swaying fortunes . . . [were] bruited in the newspapers in accordance with the usual Admiralty plan of controlled leakages." *Prejudice and Judgment*, p. 202.

made of such practices. There is no evidence that they have had any material effect on policy, and after his experiences in the 1930s, one of Chatfield's chief laments is that the experts have no means of explaining their case to Parliament or to the public.[18] Since the retirement of the senior officers who became public figures in the Second World War, the capacity of Service Chiefs to rally outside opinion has virtually disappeared and the remarkable fact about the defence reductions of 1966–68 was how little political difficulty they caused for the government.

In the Treasury, the distinction between policy and administration is probably less clear than in any other department. The official heads after the 1962 reorganisation were two joint Permanent Secretaries, one of whom deals with the pay and management of the entire Civil Service, the other with finance, resources and expenditure while a third official of equal rank is the Secretary to the Cabinet and is strictly speaking outside the Treasury network.[19] The Joint Permanent Secretary who works with the Chancellor of the Exchequer and supervises the expenditure of the various departments is not supposed to form any opinion of the objectives of these ministries. He must not, for example, decide that Civil Defence is nonsense and refuse all money. If the policy of the government is to provide for Civil Defence, this must be accepted and then, in theory, the Treasury knows the right questions to ask about whether the money is needed at this moment, or whether the same thing has not been done more economically in the past, and so on. There is a double check at this level in that any requests for more staff must go to the other Joint Permanent Secretary of the Treasury. In practice, on both counts of money and staff, it is hard for the Treasury not to take some view of the urgency or sufficiency of the proposals put before them. Government policy was to provide adequate forces for defence in the 1920s, but the rule that no major war should be anticipated for ten years was in fact the imposition of a Treasury estimate of the international situation on the Service Departments. This is not to suggest that there was any serious study of foreign

---

[18] Chatfield, *It Might Happen Again*, p. 85.
[19] These reforms were carried out after the Report of the Plowden Committee (Cmnd. 1432, H.M.S.O. 1961) and are described in Lord Bridges, *The Treasury*, Chapters XIV and XV. In 1964 further changes were made when the section of the Treasury dealing with economic planning was transferred to the D.E.A.

affairs in the Treasury. It was an extension of the old maxim that
" if you begin to argue with each department about each item,
they will always get the better of you." [20] " The Ten Year Rule "
was a simple device, which was endorsed by the Cabinet and
allowed the Treasury to pare defence costs to a minimum just as
was the 1964 rule that there was a £2,000 million ceiling (at 1964
prices) on defence expenditure.   Similar questions of principle
are raised by applications for new staff.   L. S. Amery had stipu-
lated that a separate Dominions Office be created when he
accepted the Secretaryship of State for the Colonies.   The proposal
would have gone through but for the Treasury's refusal to pay
the full £3,000 a year for a Permanent Under-Secretary.[21]   Amery
could have raised the matter at a higher level and ultimately he
would probably have had a decision in his favour.   Similarly when
the Cabinet agreed in the 1960s that certain nationalised industries should be made more competitive it was still possible for the
Treasury to refuse to pay the salary needed to entice the leaders
of private industry to accept such posts.   A strong Chancellor
backed by the Treasury can thus delay or even veto policies from
other departments, particularly if the Minister concerned lacks
weight or the Cabinet is not very concerned about the issue.

There is a strong corporate feeling in the Treasury which may
affect ministers who have no very firm experience of economics or
finance.[22]   Yet the atmosphere can be resisted.   In 1921 at a
Cabinet Council on the Safeguarding of Industries Bill, " the
Treasury pundits had expounded at length the fallacies of protection and the virtues of free trade." Sir Philip Lloyd-Greame
remarked that the theory just did not work in fact, and the only
retort was the surprised exclamation that " It ought to." [23]   Several
contemporaries (L. S. Amery and Lord Beaverbrook) asserted that
Mr. Churchill as Chancellor of the Exchequer, was held to free
trade and bounced into a return to the Gold Standard in 1925

20 This was Sir Joseph Maclay's advice to the Geddes Committee in *Lord
   Riddell's Intimate Diary of the Peace Conference and After*, p. 321.
21 L. S. Amery, *My Political Life*, Vol. II, p. 336.
22 This argument has been most cogently put forward by Samuel Brittan in
   The Treasury under the Tories, 1951–1964, though after 1964 there was little
   evidence that the Treasury's influence was in any way altered under Labour,
   though the existence of the D.E.A. did, for a while, offer a source of
   countervailing advice.
23 Lord Swinton (then Lloyd-Greame), *I Remember*, p. 15.

by the officials of the Treasury and by Montagu Norman, Governor of the Bank of England. Sir James Grigg, who was Mr. Churchill's Private Secretary, declares that "nothing could be farther from the truth." His detailed account proves not that Mr. Churchill himself studied the facts and formed an independent opinion, but that all his advisers, almost all outside experts, and the financial spokesmen in the House of Commons concurred in their advice.[24] It would have required an economist of great knowledge and originality with exceptional self-confidence to have enforced any other policy. In the 1930s events and the views of Neville Chamberlain carried the country off the Gold Standard and into protection, but in every other respect the views of Chamberlain, and later Sir John Simon, entirely coincided with those of their officials. Treasury policy since the 1950s has come under fire from diverse quarters but there has been little evidence that an official doctrine has been imposed on reluctant ministers. On the other hand, this field requires such expertise that it is hard to imagine any minister imposing his views on the Treasury. There has been a combination between Chancellors and officials to defend the balance of payments at all costs, to damp down domestic demand if either the reserves fell or inflation seemed to be excessive. The agreement to defend sterling's position as a world reserve currency has never been in doubt in the Treasury. One of the major virtues of creating the Department of Economic Affairs in 1964 was to obtain an altogether fresh source of advice but the outcome was that the Prime Minister solidly supported the Treasury views, indeed he appeared to take an even stronger view that there was no question of devaluing the pound than some officials. It is, therefore, hard to maintain that the politicians were overborne by Treasury advice, the complexity of modern government and the magnitude and persistence of the economic problems facing Britain tending to draw ministers and officials into a common thraldom.

These ministries—the Foreign Office, Service Departments and the Treasury—are among the most satisfactory from a ministerial point of view precisely because they have a traditional approach and order of priorities. The incoming minister knows what his task is, he can see how his predecessors have approached it, and

[24] P. J. Grigg, *op. cit.*, pp. 180–185.

either pursue the same policies or try a new tack. The least
satisfactory departments are those that have never really worked
out what they are supposed to do. For instance, the Ministry of
Agriculture has never formulated a clear policy on how far first-
class land should be kept for agriculture or be sacrificed to roads
or housing estates. The Ministry of Transport has never established a definite order of priorities as between road building and
other forms of transport. In a slightly different situation, the
Scottish Office has not been able to decide whether its task is
simply to repeat in Scotland what the various ministries are doing
South of the Border, or whether it should strike out on some
positive policies of its own. As a result the new minister taking
over one of the departments receives either muddled advice, or no
advice, and he can hardly conduct the kind of research and
original thinking that is required, as well as run the day-to-day
work of the department.

With the growth in the number of departments and the ambit
of government policies, the number of issues that can be settled
inside one ministry has declined and the amount of inter-
departmental consultation has increased. Naturally the more
departments that have to be consulted in framing a proposal or
have to give their consent, the longer the process takes. In discussing the decision to sign the Optional Clause of the Statute of the
Permanent Court of International Justice, Mr. Dalton says

> " this was my first experience, as a minister, of . . . the White-
> hall obstacle race—of trying to push or pull some piece of
> policy over, or through, a long series of obstacles. These
> included, in this case, first, some of our own officials in the
> F.O.; second, some other departments, particularly the Service
> Departments; third, some members of the Cabinet; fourth,
> some of the Dominion Governments." [25]

Yet all this is reasonable if many interests are affected and
ministers as well as departments have to be won over.

This system of government works less satisfactorily when
problems come up that are not the concern of any ministry or
are not simple disputes between ministries—that is if there is no
group of officials with the duty assigned to them. Yet when a new
task or problem arises, it may be difficult to rearrange the

[25] H. Dalton, *Call Back Yesterday*, p. 328.

machinery of administration. Several departments usually have a strong interest in preventing the creation of a new office or are ready to lay claim to a new function while there may be no one to put sufficient weight behind the case for a change.

One of the best examples is the struggle over the creation of an Air Ministry. A joint War Air Committee was set up in February 1916 and went through four chairmen and four different constitutions before a ministry was established in early 1918. The War Office had not been happy about this, but the chief resistance had come from the Admiralty. In 1923 the Fleet Air Arm was included in the R.A.F. and confirmed in this position by the Salisbury Committee in 1929. The Admiralty were determined to reopen the question and did so in 1936. After a battle lasting two years and two months in which there were two changes in the post of First Lord of the Admiralty (one of them, Sir Samuel Hoare, said he " felt he could not take an active part in the discussions ") [26] the Navy won back control of all carrier and seaborne planes. The infant Ministry of Information set up in February 1918 survived the initial hostility to its first minister, Lord Beaverbrook, but " the War Office, the Admiralty and the Foreign Office all joined together in determined resistance " and the project collapsed, Beaverbrook resigning for health reasons in October 1918. [27] A proposal for a Ministry of Health was first circulated in March 1917, the problem being that it would involve gathering together a medley of health services run by the Board of Trade, the Home Office, the Privy Council, the Insurance Commissioners and the Local Government Board. These bodies, and especially the last, put up a strong resistance and kept suggesting that outside agencies (the Approved Societies, the County, Borough and District Councils, the B.M.A., the Royal Colleges of Physicians and Surgeons, and the Society of Medical Officers of Health) had not been fully consulted. It required incredible work and persistence for a year and eight months before opposition, which had no Press or political support, could be overcome and the Bill introduced. [28] In such cases, if there is deadlock, the only agency that can provide the authority to push through a solution is the Prime Minister, but when he supports a reorganisation it can be carried.

[26] Chatfield, *op. cit.*, p. 105.
[27] Lord Beaverbrook, *Men and Power, 1917–1918*, pp. 265–303.
[28] Addison, *Politics from Within*, Vol. II, pp. 221–232.

Mr. Wilson has abolished the Colonial Office and the Ministry of Aviation and created the Department of Economic Affairs, the Ministry of Technology and sub-sections of departments to supervise sport and the arts.

When the balance between political and professional influence is being assessed, the question must also be considered from the angle of the Premier and the other ministers. Most politicians who reach Cabinet level have a fair measure of ability. They are ambitious men, eager to make a reputation and win advancement. This is not to be achieved simply by letting a department run itself, as sweeping or original schemes are unlikely to come up. Also Prime Ministers (according to Lord Attlee) soon detect the minister who is completely dependent on his brief and his stock falls. Civil servants have been accustomed all their lives to taking orders and they also wish advancement. A reputation for being headstrong or stubborn can do a civil servant great harm. On the whole, a government which wants to mark time has little difficulty as ministers have simply to say "No." An innovating ministry is more dependent on its officials but they, at least since the Second World War, have on the whole been ready to add to their spheres of action. All these factors combine to put the minister in a very strong position. When the second Labour Government decided to recognise Soviet Russia, some of its adherents thought that it must have been difficult to secure professional support for the proposal. Yet the Foreign Service at once appreciated that an Ambassadorship and five or six senior posts were being created and there was widespread enthusiasm combined with a sudden rise in the numbers claiming to speak Russian.

On the other hand difficulties arise where a minister of moderate capacity is working in a field which may be comparatively new to him, the party policy and the Cabinet may have no formed views and his advice from officials all points in a certain direction. In this type of situation a minister can do little to equip himself with new ideas or to review existing practices. For instance both parties proceeded on the same assumptions on agricultural policy after the 1947 Agriculture Act. It inaugurated a system which became accepted by and congenial to both the Ministry and the National Farmers' Union, there being no change till a vigorous minister, Mr. Christopher Soames, changed his mind, a step which he took only after going into opposition. Similarly, as has been said, a series of fairly or very able Chancellors of the Exchequer have established a symbiotic relationship with Treasury officials so that a rethinking of the basic assumptions or priorities becomes very difficult.

It is, therefore, hard to be precise about the degree of restriction the Civil Service imposes on ministers while the help it gives them is readily apparent. The machinery is constructed to make political control a reality and a Cabinet which meets twice a week with all its various committees can pour out a stream of decisions which reach fairly far down into the administrative grade of the Service. Yet this political control can only operate properly if adequate information and advice comes up from those who are putting past policy decisions into practice. The result in practice is that every variety of relationship exists between ministers and the half-dozen or so leading officials with whom they deal. Mr. Arthur Henderson (junior), as Air Minister in 1947, was disturbed by any disputes with the Chief of the Air Staff and preferred to give way.[29] George Tomlinson at the Ministry of Education in the same government was quite content to let his officials run the office while he told them of any Cabinet decisions.[30] Sir Stafford Cripps, in contrast, liked to be surrounded by advisers of all viewpoints. After he had heard them all, he broke down the briefs and memoranda till he had considered and mastered every point.[31] Sir James Grigg was one of the few men who passed from the position of Permanent Under-Secretary to that of a minister. He says that as the senior civil servant in the War Office

" I could get nothing done without persuading those whose primary concern it was that it was the right thing to do. After that we had to go hand in hand to the Secretary of State and convince him that it was the right thing to do. But once he had decided . . . to adopt our suggestions, they became his own and he assumed the entire responsibility for them *urbi et orbi*. . . . Now I was myself Secretary of State. I had no longer to go through a whole chain of private persuasions.

[29] E. Shinwell, *Conflict Without Malice*, p. 215.
[30] F. Blackburn, *George Tomlinson*, p. 151.
[31] Six months before he was informed that he had a mortal illness and would have to resign, Sir Stafford Cripps told a close friend that he thought he would soon have to go as he was getting too tired to unravel the briefs put up to him.

In the administrative sphere I could decide things for myself and I could give orders in any sense and at any time I liked. But I had to recognise that I might be called on to justify what I had done to the Prime Minister and the War Cabinet or to defend it publicly in the House of Commons." [32]

The vast majority of civil servants have a keen appreciation of what matters are " political " and these they are eager to push up to the minister. As Grigg recorded at an earlier stage, Philip Snowden " was the ideal of what a minister should be in that he gave a clear lead on all questions of policy, interfered rarely, if at all, in matters of administration, gave decisions quickly and unequivocally, and then defended his decisions against all comers with confidence and vigour—and nearly always with success." [33] The last thing a civil servant wants is a man who cannot make up his mind or who will wobble under pressure. And nothing raises the morale of a department more than to know that its head is capable of winning appeals that are pushed up to the Cabinet and that he has the ear of the Prime Minister. Any crude theories that the permanent officials run the politicians must be discarded. Many decisions are taken at levels below that of the minister, but what matters is that the tone of the department can be altered and different schemes given a chance when the political top tiers of the administration change. Sometimes departments fall into fixed habits or attitudes and it may be necessary to jerk them into a new approach, but a strong minister backed by the Cabinet has sufficient authority—provided the new line is feasible.

The question of feasibility introduces a new series of limitations which have only been remarked on since the 1950s. Then criticism of the Civil Service arose on several grounds. One was that it did not do proper research. A policy, say, for new hospitals was drawn up without a study of the anticipated pattern and incidence of illness in the years when these hospitals would come into service. Home ownership was encouraged by the Conservatives without research into the rent and price levels at which citizens preferred to buy rather than rent. When the Robbins Committee studied future requirements in higher education, the

---

[32] P. J. Grigg, *op. cit.*, p. 352.
[33] *Ibid.*, p. 136.

necessary statistics had to be collected as they did not exist in the Ministry and the Newsom Committee was faced with the same task in reporting on secondary education. Sometimes these deficiencies could lead to ministers receiving misleading advice. For instance the Ministry of Housing estimated 750,000 houses would be affected if rent control was removed on all houses with £30 rateable value or above when the figure turned out to be 414,000. An official at the Commonwealth Relations Office advised Mr. Wilson that if economic sanctions were applied to Rhodesia, the economic system of that country would collapse within weeks. The Foreign Office may well have misled Mr. Brown in 1967 in their reports on the French attitude should Britain make a second application to join the Common Market.

In considering this lack of research and accurate information leading in some cases to bad advice being tendered, several further criticisms have been made of the Civil Service and of the structure of government.[34] It has been argued that British officials have lacked specialist training and outside contacts, that they have had a too-cloistered life inside Whitehall with all their training being on administration in general. As far as relations with ministers are concerned, the result has been to weaken the relevance of their policies and to lead to positive errors of judgment. After years of inactivity on university building, an outcry arises among the public, a Cabinet committee is appointed, a high-level outside body studies the question and reports. Thus after a long delay there is a sudden burst of activity which may be hasty and ill-conceived. A fuel policy needs the most careful research and forecasting and, again, inaccuracies may lead to mistaken conclusions, misdirected investment and false hopes in parts of the energy-providing industries.

A further weakness has lain in the actual machinery for carrying out decisions. Central government departments act directly in the case of the Foreign Office, the Inland Revenue or the Ministry of Labour. But there is a great reluctance to act in a constructive rather than a regulatory way, the tendency being to give the actual task of building and staffing schools, conducting certain health and welfare services or maintaining roads to the local authorities. Yet many of these bodies have neither the staff,

[34] The leading exponent of these views has been Brian Chapman in *British Government Observed*.

the resources nor the imagination to act on their own. They may then either be controlled by central government or intermediate agencies are formed between local and central government to execute these tasks. The trouble with hospital boards, electricity boards, river pollution boards, regional planning councils, countryside commissions, the White Fish Authority and the Forestry Commission is that each has its *amour propre*, and projects which may involve the co-operation of several of these bodies in addition to local councils and several ministries become inordinately complicated and desperately slow. To delay matters further, there are the elaborate defences of private rights that have been mentioned. The result is that ministers may struggle to carry a motorway programme through the Cabinet to find that it takes eight years for the paperwork before the London-Birmingham stretch (the M1) can begin. On average secondary schools take five years for the paperwork and construction to be completed while a major redevelopment in the centre of an old city may stretch over twenty years.

To take a random example, the *Fifth Report from the Committee of Public Accounts* for 1966–67 lists a series of cases where government policies have broken down or been warped or delayed, from inadequate cost control over aircraft ordered for the services to inadequate information about the specialised requirements of a new police headquarters or the twenty-one years taken to build a teaching hospital at Dundee. A series of committees and commissions were appointed in the 1960s to examine and report on the machinery of government (the Fulton Committee on central government and Royal Commissions on English and Scottish local government) and these defects may be partly or wholly remedied by the 1970s. Once again the able and energetic minister faced with such problems might get round those aspects that were purely administrative. Reducing time taken by planning procedures would require legislation in certain cases while some deficiencies could only be solved by long-term changes in Civil Service recruitment and procedure.

The deficiencies mentioned must be considered in relation to the many unpublicised successful operations of government and it must be added that these weaknesses have only become evident since government has undertaken positive but difficult policies and since the country has found itself confronted by a series of foreign and domestic problems of adjustment which might well have proved too much for any administrative machine or Civil Service.

THE NATIONALISED INDUSTRIES

It has usually been accepted that the government has sufficient powers to control the nationalised industries and public boards. In 1955 the Select Committee on Nationalised Industries was asked to inquire into the policy and practices of those industries except where the policies " have been decided by or clearly engage the responsibility of any ministers." [35] After obtaining lists of the ministers' powers over each industry, they concluded that there was no area left for them to investigate. On the other hand, it is obvious that no men of ability will consent to run major industries if the threat of dismissal or repeated use of the statutory power to issue directives is made. As Hore-Belisha had found in dealing with the Army Council, he could dismiss them once but not a second time. The problem becomes more difficult if the Chairman is a public figure who commands real support either in the industry or with the public. Dr. Beeching, who was appointed Chairman of the Railways Board by Mr. Macmillan, was widely known, but his policies did not strengthen his hand in dealings with the Minister of Transport. Lord Robens at the National Coal Board offered to resign after the publication of the Report on the Aberfan disaster in 1967. He was asked to stay by the Minister, an invitation which greatly strengthened his hand when he had an open dispute with Mr. Marsh (the Minister of Fuel and Power) over the government's fuel policy. Lord Robens became identified with the miners and the policy of saving a sizeable mining industry, so that to dismiss him would have had very serious repercussions. Nevertheless Mr. Wilson's government has persisted with its Fuel Policy.

Normally ministers do not make use of their statutory powers but prefer to influence the boards by private discussions and conferences on policy and by control over the level of investment.[36] So far these financial controls have largely involved cutting programmes, and some doubts have been raised as to whether it would

---

[35] The terms of reference also excluded day-to-day matters, consumers' grievances and wage negotiations. *Report of the Select Committee on Nationalised Industries*, 1955-56, Vol. IX, p. 441.

[36] See E. Davies, "Ministerial Control and Parliamentary Responsibility of Nationalised Industries," *Political Quarterly*, 1950.

be so easy to force the boards to invest more if they were unwilling to do so or if the plans did not exist.[37] This situation is unlikely, since in those industries where demand is increasing, there is always a fairly evident line of advance. But should it occur, this would be a case where the power to change the membership of the board would soon lead to the desired result.

INTEREST GROUPS

Sir Edward Bridges has said that " it is a cardinal feature of British administration that no attempt should be made to formulate a new policy in any matter without the fullest consultation with those who have practical experience in that field, and with those who will be called upon to carry it out." [38] The question is how far the existence and activities of the various professional, economic and ideological interest groups influence or hamper the actions of the government. Sir Edward Bridges' remark brings out the fact that such bodies can often be useful. They have expert knowledge, so that fixing a change in the beer duty, for instance, is best done by asking the Brewers' Association whether the proposed sum would break down into a workable increase per pint and half pint. The National Farmers' Union has an elaborate organisation of committees which are virtually parallel to those in the Department of Agriculture and each side helps and informs the other.

Further, it is a mark of good administration that proposals are not only workable but acceptable to those who are chiefly affected. It is a legitimate ground for complaint by any considerable body that they have not been consulted. From the government's angle, it is important to prepare the public mind for any change, and this may involve special care in informing those who will have to administer the new system. In these ways, the interest groups can be of assistance to the government in preparing and carrying through its ideas. But there is the added element that most of these organisations wish to protect certain elements, or further certain objectives, and they may refuse their services or put up a resistance if their claims are disregarded. The opposition can vary from a tendency to grumble to raising questions in

[37] See S. Please, " Government Control of the Capital Expenditure of the Nationalised Industries," *Public Administration*, 1955.
[38] Sir Edward Bridges, " Portrait of a Profession," *Rede Lecture* for 1950.

Parliament, a public campaign, or even a threat to strike or boycott the new service.

It is hard to assess the precise weight of such bodies, but it is important not to treat them in isolation. The public consists of a large number of groups with varying degrees of cohesion, and any government elected to carry out certain policies knows that it will antagonise some elements, please others and create a general impression on the rest of the community. The assertion of minority or special interests cannot go too far without raising the question of attempts to dictate to the government and the electorate—a position which few groups are ready to accept. As a result, most associations prefer to concede the points of principle and to reserve their efforts to ensure that the details are as satisfactory as possible. If their objective is to contest the principle, they must either appeal direct to the public or line themselves up with one or other of the major parties. Then their actions become part of the conflict of interests that constitutes regular political life. (This aspect of pressure group activity, being more political and resting on appeals to the public, is discussed in the next chapter.)

To take one major field of action, if the government decide on a policy which affects economic conditions or a particular industry, it encounters the trade unions, the employers and, very occasionally, the consumers. The old attitude of the unions was that they required legal protection and the passage of statutes dealing with such matters as employers' liability and factory conditions. To obtain legislation of this kind, the T.U.C. was formed and its Executive was named the Parliamentary Committee, as lobbying was its main function. When the results of these efforts became increasingly unsatisfactory in the 1890s, the unions slowly associated themselves with the Labour Party which, among many wider aims, promised to press the larger parties to remedy such grievances. After the First World War the unions emerged as a major and self-confident force whose economic aims were to be achieved by negotiation with employers while the political objectives were to be gained by putting the Labour Party in power. There followed disappointments on both fronts, and after 1926 Sir Walter (now Lord) Citrine established the principle that the T.U.C. should deal with whatever administration was in office. The governments of the 1930s were unsympathetic to the unions but consultation did take place. After Ernest Bevin as Minister of Labour during the War had brought the unions into consultation at every level, it became the practice to go directly to the ministries rather than to raise detailed matters in Parliament and this habit continued after the Conservatives returned to power in 1951, Mr. (later Lord) Monckton, their first Minister of Labour, being particularly ready to deal with the trade union leaders. As a result, this relationship developed, the House of Commons was increasingly by-passed, a typical complaint by a trade union M.P. being voiced by Mr. Roy Mason in November 1958. He said that

"on occasions trade union M.P.s are actually gagged. When a deputation from a trade union is in negotiation with a Government Department, all too often a hint is passed to the union's M.P.—'No questions in the House on this issue, please. They might be embarrassing.'"

After 1964, when Labour returned to power and then turned to enforce a wages freeze, a linkage arose between trade union leaders outside the House and most of the trade union group of M.P.s so that joint pressure could be exerted on the government. Nevertheless the main connection has remained a direct one between the T.U.C. and individual union leaders and ministers, the reason being that this gives both sides the best chance of being understood and of getting the desired results.

Thus as a pressure group the T.U.C. operates at various levels. In the broadest sphere it would like to see the Labour Party in power, as it would expect to receive more sympathy from Labour ministers and because such a government would fulfil many of the T.U.C.'s larger aims in the fields of pensions, health and technical education.[39] For these purposes the unions contribute funds, attend conferences, and operate as part of the Labour Party. In a narrower sphere, the T.U.C. claims to be consulted on all matters affecting its members and it has representatives scattered across innumerable government committees and advisory bodies. Here, its views may be taken into consideration if it is simply a matter of expert information or convenience. On more restricted issues affecting hours and wages, the T.U.C. and the unions concerned

---

39 The sympathy would only be very general. In January 1930 the T.U.C. asked the Labour Government if it could see advance copies of some Bills. The answer was that it could see the original proposals and some clauses in draft as it had done in 1924, but not whole Bills, as this would then have to be conceded to other organisations.

become principal parties to the dispute. If the government is drawn in, it has to set the problem against the background of its overall economic policy and conditions in the industry. Whatever the attitude of the unions, the Ministry of Labour finds it essential to have a group of men with whom to negotiate. Finally there are a limited number of topics connected with the right to bargain and the legal position of unions and their members, which the T.U.C. regard as impinging on their very existence but which have been raised by legislation on prices and incomes and may arise out of the Report of the Royal Commission on the Trade Unions. (Report due in late 1968.) The Conservative Party abandoned the Industrial Charter they had drafted and a promise to restore " contracting in " (for those who wished to pay the political levy) just before the 1951 general election and they did not respond to calls for legislation to curb abuses in the unions till after they lost office in 1964. Since then public resentment at unofficial strikes has grown and the Conservative Party is committed to legal changes which would make unofficial industrial action difficult. But whatever solution they adopted would be settled or at least carefully discussed between the government and the trade union leaders.

Another fairly well-documented example of an interest group is the British Medical Association. Founded in 1832 for scientific purposes, it has grown and been drawn into public affairs as government policy has impinged on the medical profession. On major issues such as the formation of a Health Service, the B.M.A. had to concede to public opinion. Though officials of the Ministry of Health conferred on some twenty occasions during the preparation of the National Health Service Bill, they refused to regard these discussions as negotiations. As in the case of the 1911 Insurance proposals, the Bill was published and the doctors were left to ask for modifications to a broad scheme, which they could not resist. But once this stage was passed, the B.M.A. and the civil servants had many meetings over the Statutory Instruments needed to give effect to the Act and the former were fully consulted over the National Health Service Amendment Act of 1949. Here again, the political decisions were taken in the normal manner and the doctors were on the same level as the rest of the public. But neither Aneurin Bevan nor his officials wished to start work with a bitter or disgruntled force of doctors and, once the principle was conceded, they were ready to make concessions. Whether or not the information provided by the B.M.A. was of any value, the Ministry of Health was able to say that they had engaged in full consultations and accepted professional advice.[40] As in the case of the T.U.C., the B.M.A. wields little power in the sense that it is unable to bend a reluctant government to its will or thwart positive policies that have been endorsed by the electorate. It can, however, obtain changes of detail when a new measure is being framed. In addition it has an entrenched position which is revealed when a government decides to economise on the Health Service, as happened during the anti-inflationary measures of 1957–58. Then there was no question of cutting doctors' salaries and indeed they were shortly awarded an interim rise. The solution was to cut the moneys available for hospital building as this affected no organised body, many medical men subscribed to the argument that the Service cost too much and patients who were kept waiting for beds would grumble about the Health Service rather than criticise the government.

This assessment covers most of the groups such as the National Farmers' Union or the National Union of Teachers, which have some broad semi-political objectives and a close relationship with the appropriate government department in order to safeguard their particular interests. These groups usually have one or two fundamental positions which successive governments have in fact conceded, but which they are always ready to defend to the last gasp. This discussion has not dealt with those organisations which are devoted to a cause or a viewpoint such as the Lord's Day Observance Society, the League against Cruel Sports or the Campaign for Nuclear Disarmament. Their efforts are bent on convincing Members of Parliament and the public and they have few direct contacts with the administration but their efforts can have some effect. Their propaganda may, for instance, deflect a government from introducing a Bill itself (say to prohibit hare coursing) which may then be left to a private Member. Or they

40 In his *Pressure Group Politics—The Case of the B.M.A.*, Professor Eckstein says " the Association has become indispensable to the Government as a source of technical knowledge. . . ." There is no evidence for this, and the information and specialised resources for research available to the Ministry of Health make anything the B.M.A. can do in this field merely a helpful adjunct. See also J. S. Ross, *The National Health Service in Great Britain*, and A. Bevan, *In Place of Fear*.

may rouse a special group of M.P.s, such as the Welsh who had the Principality excluded from the 1968 Sunday Observance Bill. These pressure groups can have such an influence largely because the matters at issue are not of critical importance to any government and seldom feature in party programmes. The pressure groups promoting causes which are nearer to the centre of political controversy have to adopt rather different techniques. The campaign to establish commercial television worked on ministers because the Cabinet was divided and on M.P.s in order to influence ministers and on the Press and the public in order to interest M.P.s and succeeded. The large-scale drive by the iron and steel companies to avert nationalisation was so political that it could not escape acting in liaison with the Conservative Party and losing when that party lost the 1964 and 1966 elections.

In dealing with the professional and economic pressure groups already mentioned, there have been variations in the general reactions of governments. The Conservatives in the 1930s were exceptionally open to pressure from industrial interests. In the war there were greater efforts at consultation with all groups and Ernest Bevin resisted compulsion in labour matters till he was subject to severe criticism. After 1951 Conservative leaders, particularly Walter Monckton and R. A. Butler, regarded it as a virtue to seek accommodation with outside interests, an attitude which hardened a little as Conservative rule continued and became more confident. By 1964 the public were much less sympathetic to sectional pressures and despite his narrow majority, Mr. Harold Wilson felt it added to the impression that he was providing " the smack of firm government " to refuse to concede and even to slap down the farmers, the teachers, the aircraft industry and the unions.

The one set of organised interests which the Labour Government did not handle in quite this fashion were those representing the City and Big Business (with their links with foreign banks and financial agencies). This was largely a matter of choice but the experience of the government reopened the old question of whether these groups possess a peculiar overriding power which puts them in a different category. Mr. R. H. S. Crossman has said that " in the Affluent Society *no* Government is able to give orders to Big Business. After one Budget a Labour Chancellor who tried to squeeze private industry too hard would soon discover that he was not master in his own house. . . ." [41] Mr. A. A. Rogow concluded his study of *The Labour Government and British Industry* between 1945 and 1951 with the verdict that "the continued co-operation of vested power groups in measures of social change designed to reduce their power and influence can no longer be taken for granted." [42]

It is certainly true that finance and industry have always been well represented in Parliament and have wielded considerable power, but when ministers have been tough and sure of their political and popular support, they have usually won. Austen Chamberlain put up the profits tax from 40 per cent. to 60 per cent. in 1919. "The F.B.I. is very strong in the House and its clamours are being echoed by the *Daily Telegraph*, *Chronicle*, *Express*, and *Pall Mall*, whilst the *Daily News* and *Manchester Guardian* continue to support me." "They are a selfish swollen lot, and if they think that they can bully this Chancellor because there are so many of them in the House, they will find that they are mistaken." [43] Chamberlain took the F.B.I. into consultation and asked them to produce an alternative method of taxing war fortunes. After fourteen months they produced a scheme for what was, in effect, an additional income tax. The whole episode was related by Chamberlain to the House and he easily secured a vote of confidence.

An almost identical situation arose in 1937 when Neville Chamberlain proposed to help meet the rearmament bill by a National Defence Contribution levied either on a firm's capital or its profits. There was a furious outcry and the F.B.I. and the other business organisations were up in arms. Chamberlain was worried lest he had "risked the Premiership" but held on till the following year when he and Sir John Simon abandoned the Defence Contribution in favour of a simple 5 per cent. profits tax. [44]

Lord Cunliffe had acquired unusual powers as Governor of the Bank of England while Asquith was Prime Minister. He insisted that he would only meet the Chancellor of the Exchequer in the presence of the Premier and that he should have control over the London Exchange Committee. When Bonar Law became

---

[41] R. H. S. Crossman, *Labour in the Affluent Society* (Fabian Tract, No. 325), pp. 21–22.   [42] A. A. Rogow, *op. cit.*, p. 176.
[43] Sir Charles Petrie, *The Life and Letters of Austen Chamberlain*, Vol. II, pp. 149–150.
[44] K. Feiling, *op. cit.*, p. 292.

Chancellor, he arranged a loan against Cunliffe's advice and let Treasury officials (Sir Robert Chalmers and J. M. Keynes) influence exchange policy. Cunliffe retaliated by asking for the dismissal of these men and closed Bank of England gold reserves in Ottawa to the government. Bonar Law then went to Lloyd George and insisted that the Bank must be subordinate to the Treasury and obtained an apology and forced Cunliffe's resignation. In November 1917 he was replaced by Sir Brian Cockayne.[45] Mr. Churchill's disputes with Montagu Norman, the Governor of the Bank of England from 1920 to 1944, arose largely from his annoyance at the results of the return to the Gold Standard. On one occasion he ordered the Governor to suspend a rise in the Bank Rate but this had been recommended by the Treasury Committee of the Bank and Norman was within his rights in refusing.[46] Later, in December 1925, Montagu Norman raised the Bank Rate despite the protests of Mr. Churchill and his threat to tell the House of Commons that the increase had been made without consultation and against his wishes. Had Mr. Churchill had a stronger position in the ministry—that is if Baldwin had agreed with him and been concerned about economic policy—Norman could have been made to concede or have been replaced. As it was, Mr. Churchill had to let these matters go. The Nationalisation of the Bank of England in 1946 put in writing powers which the Prime Minister had held in reserve and had used in forcing Cunliffe to go. Nevertheless Governors of the Bank since 1946 have occasionally made pronouncements on financial and economic policy that have led to questions in the House of Commons, one particularly sharp outcry occurring in 1967 when Sir Leslie O'Brien said that the British economy could not be run successfully without a larger pool of unemployment than had been the case till 1966.

In the case of the inter-war Labour Governments, the two most important measures, Wheatley's Housing Act and the Coal Mines Act of 1930, were carefully negotiated with the unions and the employers. In both cases, however, the Government's position was so weak that it could only hope to proceed with legislation that

---

45 See Lord Beaverbrook, *Men and Power, 1917–1918*, pp. 93–111 and R. Blake, *The Unknown Prime Minister*, pp. 252–253.

46 P. G. Grigg, *op. cit.*, p. 193. The account in R. Blake's *The Unknown Prime Minister* says that Cunliffe was forced to sign a letter of resignation but in a letter to *The Times*, October 10, 1955, Lord Beaverbrook corrects this and says that he refused to resign and had to be dismissed.

was acceptable to all the parties concerned. One of the arguments used by Labour speakers to explain the demise of the second Labour Government was that it had been killed by an international bankers' conspiracy. In fact it was hamstrung by its own decision to borrow gold in order to remain on the Gold Standard. When the Federal Reserve Bank had lent the maximum permitted by law, the government could only raise further reserves by a loan from Messrs. J. P. Morgan. In asking for a guarantee that the policies of the Labour Government were sound in the eyes of the City of London, Morgan and Company were only asking for the sort of assurances that would be required of any borrower, capitalist, liberal, labour or socialist. The second Labour Government was destroyed by its own failure to grapple with unemployment and the economic crisis in a manner which would have avoided dependence on funds from Wall Street.

In the years immediately after the war, the Labour Party received reasonable co-operation from industry. The only problem was that the government found it could not simultaneously coerce business and obtain its wholehearted assistance. Sir Stafford Cripps wanted to eliminate inefficient firms and introduced the idea of Development Councils for this purpose. He also tried to force industry to build in what had been the Distressed Areas of the 1930s. The various industrial organisations objected to both policies (especially the former as it threatened to undermine their own Trade Associations) but the reason why the government relaxed pressure was that it had to ask for the assistance of the same industrialists in mounting an export drive. There was nothing peculiarly sinister about this reaction and the same motives led Aneurin Bevan to make minor concessions to the doctors. There were also protests against the Chancellor's later requests for dividend limitation but the response on the part of business organisations was not markedly less favourable than those of the unions or professional associations which were asked to hold back wage or salary claims. The one attempt at positive resistance to the government was the boycott of the Iron and Steel Board by the leading ironmasters and it was a dismal failure.

Conservative governments had far fewer reasons for conflict with these interests, but when they occurred, there was no less intensity. Conservative Chancellors watched the reactions of the City and the international bankers (by then known as " the gnomes

of Zurich ") with equal care. When Mr. (later Lord) Heathcoat-
Amory introduced a retrospective tax on dividend stripping, he was
attacked with great intensity and, lacking the Prime Minister's
backing, gave way and soon thereafter resigned.

The same non-political reactions were evident in the last
years of Conservative administration. Some City elements felt that
from 1963 decisions were put aside because senior politicians
were too absorbed with election tactics and in particular the postponement of the election date from June to October 1964 which
prevented action to meet a growing balance of payments deficit
was resented. There was, therefore, considerable relief amounting
even to good will when Mr. Wilson became Prime Minister in
October 1964. The first blow to this harmony came at once
when some of those in the City thought that Labour leaders
laid too much emphasis on Britain's economic plight and thus
accelerated the sterling crisis of that autumn. Then the capital
gains and corporation taxes led to a further breach which was
widened by the 1966 Selective Employment Tax. For some time
after July 1966 there was admiration for the Government's toughness on wages but increased doubts about its economic management, doubts which became general with the third sterling crisis
and forced devaluation of November 1967. In order to obtain an
international loan to guard against further runs on the pound, the
Chancellor had to issue a Letter of Intent to the International
Monetary Fund which stated certain objectives of increasing exports
and reducing home demand to make such an increase possible.
Some Government spokesmen said that the cuts in government
expenditure (or increases in charges) had to include reversals
of Labour Party policy on a number of items such as prescription
charges in order to " restore confidence." It is clear that a combination of industrial and financial interests in Britain and banking
institutions abroad can exercise very considerable influence over
the policy of a British Cabinet.

However such an influence is not inescapable. The need to
consider foreign bankers would not arise if Britain had a satisfactory balance of payments and if either reserves were much
higher or sterling ceased to be a reserve currency. Both these
conditions can be achieved by British governments. Within the
country, there is evidence that private businessmen may dislike
a Labour Government and resent some of its policies of control

and taxation. But such resentment does not counter the normal desire to make money and provided a Labour Government can create conditions of economic expansion and increasing rewards for all kinds of labour, the necessary minimum co-operation will be forthcoming. If a Labour Government's economic policy fails and there is a general lack of confidence, it may be harder for Labour ministers to get back any measure of trust, but there is little sign that British businessmen respond to exhortation whatever its political origins. Finally, among the financial firms, government control through the Bank of England remains effective on domestic matters and if there is still freedom to invest or send capital abroad in an embarrassing volume, this is because successive governments have not thought fit to try to establish tighter regulation or prohibition.

There is a tendency when Labour Governments run into difficulties to blame international speculators or the " sell Britain short brigade " at home. Yet these men, though more powerful than any other pressure group, can only exercise this power if the economic climate is unfavourable, and recent experience suggests they do not alter their conduct deliberately to make a Labour Government fail—if only because they also are damaged. Their reactions are consequent on, rather than a cause of, economic difficulties but once there is a shaky financial position and a lack of confidence at home, their powers, even though largely negative, do become formidable.

Any British government also faces limitations on its power by virtue of its international political position, the Treaties it has signed and the commitments it has accepted. The United Nations Organisation places certain obligations upon members caring to observe them while membership of N.A.T.O., S.E.A.T.O., C.E.N.T.O. and G.A.T.T. all impose more precise obligations. Yet so much does international freedom of manoeuvre depend on economic strength that it is possible that further limitations on sovereignty, for instance by joining the Common Market, might, if the result was a strong balance of payments, actually strengthen Britain's hand. Conversely, maintaining land bases and forces in the Near, Middle and Far East may have weakened this country in the 1950s and early 1960s if the cost led to more serious balance of payments deficits and the need to ask for help from the World Bank or the International Monetary Fund.

Thus British governments are fortunate in having a unified central administrative system to operate and their only problems at this level are those of managing such a large, complex and expert Civil Service and of adapting it to a more positive interventionist role in society. Facing the nationalised industries, private industry and the many pressure groups interested in political decisions, the government has great power in the knowledge and capacity of the Civil Service and in its own firm political position, and ministers can usually rely on widespread support provided it is evident that the government is acting on behalf of the public interest. Recent British governments have had to reverse their economic policies and admit failures in foreign policy not because of the opposition or non-co-operation of big business and international finance but because failure to readjust internal and external policies to the country's new and diminished world role has left it in a vulnerable condition, a prolonged vulnerability which has undermined Conservative and Labour Governments alike.

CHAPTER 23

CONTROL BY THE PUBLIC

THE OPPOSITION IN THE HOUSE OF COMMONS

THE second major limitation on the freedom of action of the Prime
Minister and his colleagues is the need to carry public support
as institutionalised in the House of Commons and the majority
party. While a government does not need to have the backing of
the Press or of the public as revealed in opinion polls or by-
elections, evident lack of support is a source of weakness which
becomes greater with the approach of a general election at which
the government may be defeated. For these reasons all ministers
pay close attention to both the House of Commons and the other
indicators of public feeling, the task in this chapter being to
estimate how far this need to pay attention has affected the conduct
of successive British governments both in form and in content and
the ways in which this constraint is felt.

In the older books about British government it was often said
that the chief constraint on any Cabinet was the opposition in the
House of Commons and fear of defeat in the lobbies. The degree
of control exercised by individual M.P.s and by the opposition in
the nineteenth century has been examined in the earlier sections of
this book but it is important to recall that no government in
Britain has been defeated by its own supporters deciding that they
have lost confidence in the Cabinet since the summer of 1885.
There have been splits since then, snap defeats, the break-up of
coalitions and bouts of abstentions but no opposition facing a
government with a clear majority in the House can expect to
detach sufficient government supporters to win a major division.
The one claim that has sometimes been made for a determined
opposition has been that the Conservatives so harried and worried
the Labour Government of 1950–51 that its fall was precipitated. This government had a majority of only six and its existence
was bound to be precarious, but it lasted far longer than most
people expected. Mr. Attlee was able to choose his own time for
going to the country and while the date selected may have been

567

a bad one, it was not forced on him by defeats in the House. At one point, Conservative back-benchers attempted to wear their opponents down by moving prayers against ministerial orders. There was no fixed end to debates arising on such prayers, but after two weeks of all-night sittings, the government Whips solved the problem by carrying the customary motion for adjournment (at the end of the scheduled business) to a division. Mr. Attlee had indeed to consider the difficulty of conducting some aspects of foreign and economic policy in an atmosphere of uncertainty and the Conservatives' attacks did hearten their followers in the country, but there is no evidence that the government could not have carried on beyond October 1951.[1] The proof that it is possible to govern with the most slender majority was given by Mr. Wilson and the 1964–66 Labour Government. It had a majority of four (after December 1964 down to three) and lasted for seventeen months, the Prime Minister being free to choose his own date for a general election.

The other cases when the House of Commons took a part in destroying a government were in 1886, 1895, 1916, 1922 and 1940. Of these the only case where the result of an actual division in the House played a major, if not a decisive, part was in May 1940. Then, Neville Chamberlain's conduct of the Norwegian campaign was upheld by a majority of only eighty-one, thirty-three of his normal supporters voting against him and some sixty abstaining.[2] This was clear evidence that confidence in his government had collapsed and yet it is not quite true to say that he personally was dismissed by the House of Commons. After the debate, Mr. Churchill advised him to hang on with the reminder that "you have a good majority."[3] The Prime Minister realised that he would have to reconstruct his ministry, but he considered that he might well remain as its head.[4] Whether this was possible depended on Mr. Attlee and the Labour Party. It was

---

[1] The fact that the Labour Government post office rather than that the Conservatives wrested it from them is brought out in J. D. Hoffman's study, *The Conservative Party in Opposition, 1945–51*.

[2] The division can be described in these personal terms because not only was it Chamberlain's policy and tone that were under fire but he himself said "I accept the challenge . . . and I call on my friends." K. Feiling, *The Life of Neville Chamberlain*, p. 443.

[3] Sir Winston Churchill, *The Second World War*, Vol. I, p. 522.

[4] He reported in this sense to King George VI. See J. W. Wheeler-Bennett, *King George VI, His Life and Reign*, p. 522.

their decision not to join any government under Neville Chamberlain's leadership that forced a change in the Premiership though the original action of the House of Commons had shown that a reconstructed government with a new verve was required. In a somewhat different way, the 1918–22 Coalition under Lloyd George was brought to an end when Conservative back-benchers carried their motion to withdraw support, but this was at a meeting in the Carlton Club. The location was significant because though the disgruntlement was felt by M.P.s, the place they chose to show it emphasises that the situation where such changes of opinion are least likely to be revealed is on the floor of the House or in divisions. On the rare occasions when Premiers or ministries totally lose the confidence of their followers, they may be dismissed, but such a decision is more likely to be reached in conclaves within the governing party or, if it is a Coalition Government, in discussions between the party leaders. The atmosphere on the government benches and perhaps a number of abstentions may contribute to the feeling that something has to be done, but the action is more likely to take place elsewhere. For example, the temper of Conservative back-benchers was a major factor in Bonar Law's decision to oust Asquith in 1916 though the Commons heard nothing but a few rumours before they were presented with a new ministry under Lloyd George. The case of 1895 was a special one since the Liberal Cabinet accepted a tactical reverse in the House as a suitable moment for leaving office, while Gladstone was defeated in 1886 by the departure of a definite section of his followers to form a new party, the Liberal Unionists.

It is therefore accepted that the opposition cannot dislodge a ministry with a working majority. The only defeats which have been inflicted on governments in this century have been entirely trivial or otherwise have been due to some laxity on the part of the Whips. On the one or two occasions when a government has lost, the Premier has demanded and obtained an immediate reversal of the decision.[5] It has sometimes been assumed that the House of Commons recovered its power during the two inter-war Labour Governments because neither of them possessed an overall

---

[5] For example, in April 1936, the government was beaten on equal pay for women teachers and the same happened in committee on the 1944 Education Bill. In each case Baldwin and Mr. Churchill went to the House and insisted on an immediate restoration of the government's clause.

majority.[6] Yet their position only serves to illustrate the forces which make for party cohesion in the House and the importance of the modern system of Standing Orders. The Liberals both in 1924 and 1929 decided to support a Labour ministry for tactical reasons. Since defeat on any important issue would have been followed by the Premier's resignation, Members had no choice open to them. Labour M.P.s were bound to vote with the government, Conservatives against, while Liberals were tied by the knowledge that unless they could create a situation which left them as the radical alternative to Conservatism, they faced destruction at the next election.[7] The first Labour Government was defeated ten times on minor points before the negotiations with Russia seemed to give the Liberals the sort of issue they wanted. On October 1, 1924, Asquith declared that his party would vote against the Russian Treaty, thereby announcing the end of the Labour Government, though this came a little sooner than expected over the Campbell case. After the elections of 1929 the Liberals were again bound to the Labour Government. Relations became precarious in 1931 yet fear of a general election was even greater than in 1924 and a committee was set up to ensure the necessary minimum of co-operation.

The one thing which the Liberals (and, of course, the Conservatives) denied to both Labour Governments was the power to impose the closure. This meant that Liberals might have to vote for social legislation put before the House, but they could do so safe in the knowledge that if they disapproved there was no power to carry a Bill through all its stages. When the National Government was formed in August 1931 one of its first actions was to resume control of the timetable of the Commons.

So, under normal circumstances, governments are not disturbed by the immediate pressure of the opposition. Indeed, if the government is a Coalition, there may be some advantage in having a strong opposition. Both Austen Chamberlain and Lloyd George thought (in 1918 and 1920) that the Coalition would have been

---

[6] One of the arguments in favour of Proportional Representation has been that it would be unlikely to give any one party an absolute majority and so would restore some life and power to the House of Commons.

[7] P. J. Grigg records an occasion in 1924 when a Liberal came into the House to find a division taking place and hastened to ask his colleagues: "is it safe to vote against the Government?" *Prejudice and Judgment*, p. 131.

healthier if it had faced a party putting forward a genuine alternative policy.[8]

This, in fact, is all that an opposition can do. Between 1906 and 1914, governments lengthened the working hours of the House, started the modern system of standing committees and made more drastic use of the closure rule and the guillotine. Since 1918 there has been little change except that after the Second World War the guillotine was applied in standing committees. The opposition has been left with, on average 30 per cent. of the time of each session when it can choose the issues on which it wishes to criticise the government.[9] Lord Morrison has said that a government ought and often does listen to the views of its opponents. How far this happens is hard to assess but there is no evidence that a confident Ministry has altered its views to meet opposition pressure. It is just possible that when a government is weak and worried, as the Conservatives were in the twelve months after the attack on Suez, persistent and able opposition pressure might accentuate a sense of despair and dismay and thus contribute to the weakness of a government. In day-to-day affairs in the House an able opposition can keep government supporters up later and cause the odd revision in the order of business. On some issues of an administrative character, ideas may be borrowed from across the House and some opposition spokesmen have claimed that amendments pressed by them in debates on the Finance Bill and rejected by the government have reappeared as clauses in the next year's Finance Bill, but all this is of little significance.

For most political proposals, the government expects opposition from the other side of the House and, though some ministers may feel the need to win the argument, the opposition has no means of pressing its point home. Lord Morrison was clear that " the function of examining and challenging important government policy is reserved to Parliament as a whole." [10] Proposals for making criticism more potent—such as standing committees of

---

[8] Lord Riddell's *Intimate Diary of the Peace Conference and After*, p. 240, and Sir C. Petrie, *The Life and Letters of Austen Chamberlain*, Vol. II, p. 132.

[9] Sir Gilbert Campion in *British Government Since 1918*. The 30 per cent. share has been fairly constant since 1906.

[10] Herbert Morrison, *Government and Parliament*, p. 154. Lord Morrison, like Sir Gilbert Campion, felt that the essence of the parliamentary spirit in Britain lay in the refusal by successive governments to encroach on the 26 (now 29) supply days set aside for the opposition.

specialists on each subject, or the provision of expert advice for the opposition have been regarded with suspicion because the idea that the House, including the opposition, could actually make the government change any significant item of its policy is foreign to the modern British political system. This is what Lloyd George meant when he said : " Parliament has no control over the Executive; it is pure fiction." [11] The indignation many ministers and back-bench M.P.s would feel at such a statement arises because they confuse the desire of both the government and the opposition to make a good case, the desire of individual ministers to score a success, the eager attention of the Press looking for news and the constant effort of Members to gain recognition, with actual control of what the government does. The House of Commons matters a great deal to politicians but not in this sense. It matters in that members' reactions can affect a minister's position if he is a candidate for promotion or is vulnerable. If a minister is secure in the Premier's estimation, then he can, like Mr. Selwyn Lloyd in 1957, appear to have lost all grip of the House without being in any danger. On the other hand a superb performance in the Commons such as Mr. Macleod's spectacular attack on the then invincible Aneurin Bevan almost certainly hastened his promotion to Cabinet office by six months while Mr. Richard Marsh advanced his claims for Cabinet rank in 1965 by very able speeches on steel nationalisation. Yet there is no suggestion that the conduct of or the reception accorded to these individuals in any way influenced the policy of the government or of the opposition.

In effect the opposition takes advantage of its share of parliamentary time to speak to the electorate and to build up a case which it hopes to press home at the next general election. Whether this can be done depends on several factors. An opposition hoping to improve its position must appear to be competent and vigorous and be capable of maintaining an attack on a few telling themes. Secondly there must be the means of communicating these arguments to the public. Cobden's remark that " the best place from which to address the people of England is the floor of the House of Commons " is only true if the Press, Radio or Television will report what is said and if the public is prepared to pay some attention. There is an obvious connection in that a declining

[11] Quoted in F. Williams, *Press, Parliament and People*, p. 107.

interest in politics and in Parliament has been both a cause and an effect of the end of regular reports of debates in the popular Press. Yet despite these obstacles in the path of the government's critics, opposition leaders have usually drawn comfort from the widespread belief that there was a normal tendency for support to swing away from the party in office and that an opposition had every ground for assuming that in time it would return to power.

THE GOVERNMENT'S ADVANTAGE OVER THE OPPOSITION

The theory that there is a regular swing of the pendulum has been widely accepted both by students of the British political system and by statesmen. R. S. Milne and H. C. Mackenzie, who conducted constituency surveys in the general elections of 1951 and 1955, considered that " it is a necessary feature of British representative government that the parties should alternate in office." They also assumed that " usually at a general election the familiar ' pendulum,' symbolised in the slogan ' time for a change,' swings to a government's disadvantage." [12] In his account of the 1955 election, D. E. Butler looked for reasons " why the customary swing ' agin ' the government did not take place." [13]

There were no systematic expositions of this theory of a swing in popular support from one political party to the other. The underlying assumption appeared to be that a government was bound to alienate voters or fail to fulfil expectations and so the opposition would gain strength. When the modern studies of elections confirmed what most politicians knew: that a large part of the electorate habitually voted the same way, attention was concentrated on the small percentage of " floaters " who changed sides. (It was more of a surprise to find that the " floaters " tended to be those least interested in and least well informed about politics. It had been assumed that these electors were attentive but open-minded, and parties and candidates had framed their election campaigns in the hope of winning over such voters.) In 1958 Milne and Mackenzie re-stated the theory in the light of their findings:

" It is probably the same group of people who switch their support from time to time. In other words, there is a block

[12] R. S. Milne and H. C. Mackenzie, *Marginal Seat*, 1955, pp. 194 and 1.
[13] D. E. Butler, *The British General Election of 1955*, p. 164. For other statements showing a general acceptance of the pendulum theory, see S. E. Finer, *Anonymous Empire*, p. 91, and R. B. MacCallum and A. Readman, *The British General Election of 1945*, p. 263.

of voters who are almost as consistent as the ' regulars ' in their irregularity." [14]

By 1966, there had been further work on the subject but it proved to be impossible to find or analyse the conduct of such a group of " swinging floaters." G. N. Sanderson in a review article speculated on the possibility of a " slow swing " lasting for a twelve- to fifteen-year period as one party appeared to exhibit more competence than the other.[15] However, this was more a surmise drawn from the results than an explanation of voters' behaviour and no evidence was produced to show that any electors had acted in this way for these reasons. The point was well put by J. Rasmussen:

" The use of swing in political analysis favours conceiving of the electorate as an immortal group which from one election to the next gives to one party exactly the amount of support that it takes away from the other party." [16]

This notion does not allow for new voters coming on to the register, elderly voters dying, relative rates of abstention or the effect of more or less third party candidates. In the sense being considered here, what matters is first whether there is an inbuilt tendency for oppositions to succeed governments in power and secondly whether current politicians believe this to be the case.

The academic studies by 1968 had established no such tendency, D. E. Butler, the most authoritative scholar in this field, accepting that " swing " is a purely statistical concept useful in explaining the relationship between votes cast and seats won or lost.[17] As a result it is only possible, for purposes of generalisation, to turn to the actual historical events. The beliefs of the politicians follow on these events; they are the product of their experience and are not inaccurate, allowing for the time lag between new evidence and the adjustment of accepted maxims.

Between 1868 and 1885 there was a regular swing in terms of seats and of governments between Liberals and Conservatives. After 1886 the situation was affected by the split in the Liberal

[14] R. S. Milne and H. C. Mackenzie, *Marginal Seat*, 1955, p. 80.
[15] G. N. Sanderson, " The Swing of the Pendulum in British Politics," *Political Studies*, Vol. 2. (1966), pp. 349–360.
[16] J. Rasmussen, " The Disutility of the Swing Concept in British Psephology," *Parliamentary Affairs*, Vol. 18, 1964–65, p. 444.
[17] D. E. Butler, " A Comment on Professor Rasmussen's Article," *ibid.*, pp. 455–457.

Party and the drift of sections of middle-class voters over to the Conservatives. Apart from three years of weak Liberal rule between 1892 and 1895 Conservative governments dominated British politics for twenty years. It might have been thought that this experience would have modified generalisations about " swings " based on the 1868–85 period but doubts were removed by the Liberal landslide of 1906. The Liberals held on till the war and then the political situation was altered by the collapse of the Liberals and the rise of the Labour Party. However, the notion of a " swing " could still be regarded as having some validity in that the decline of the Coalition and tactical errors of Baldwin allowed Labour to form a minority government in 1923. Then after a resounding Conservative victory in 1924, the self-confidence and capacity of that party steadily declined till Labour was again able to form a government, albeit dependent on Liberal votes, in 1929.

It is from the time of the overwhelming Conservative (officially National) victory of 1931 that events have made it hard to go on talking about " the swing of the political pendulum " and that politicians have begun to act and later to talk as if a swing in favour of the opposition was by no means likely. The National Government formed in 1931 went off the Gold Standard and turned to a policy of tariffs and state aid for industry. British recovery from the slump was uneven and slow but outside the areas dependent on heavy industry there was a steady improvement. On the other hand the Labour Party failed to present a very clear or reassuring alternative and was saddled with its disastrous failure in its last period of office. Labour did win some hundred seats in the election of 1935 but this was only a partial restoration of what had been lost in 1931. Moreover, there was no great optimism among Labour leaders that the party would win an absolute majority in 1935 nor was there any evidence of better prospects for the next election due in 1940. D. E. Butler has pointed out that the view that the swing to Labour was likely only arose after the war and the 1945 landslide. " Once the electorate had recovered from the shock of 1931 there appears to have been a very sharp swing in favour of the Labour Party, but from 1933 onwards their support seems, if anything, to have declined." [18] The war cut right across these lines of development, and did much to raise political interest and to foster the idea that both men and measures had been woefully inadequate between the wars. With the electorate wishing to make a break with the past, the Labour Party won the 1945 election and seemed to be firmly in office, despite rationing and restrictions. There was full employment and the improvement in basic living standards that had taken place during the war was maintained. Had the Labour Government been able to last into the favourable terms of trade and consumer boom of the early 1950s (and if it had been able to adjust its outlook to these conditions) there is little doubt that it would have remained in power. Like all victors, the Conservatives have taken credit for their achievement in regaining office. But a major factor in their success was the way in which the Labour Administration failed to find new ideas or talent and drifted into a state of fatigue, division and gloom till its chief characteristic seemed to be a "death wish." The great advantage which Labour (like all governments) held, was the right to choose the date of the election. In both 1950 and 1951, there was no attempt to set the scene, to keep their opponents baffled, to raise the hopes of the country—in a legitimate fashion—and then dissolve. The government "drifted on from month to month in the hope that the electoral situation would take a turn for the better, until finally, that hope abandoned, Parliament was dissolved lest it should get any worse." [19]

Back in power, the Conservatives went on to win the 1955 and 1959 general elections. Although the party lost ground between elections, particularly in 1957–58 it rallied in the last year of office not only to hold its position but even to improve on the number of seats won at the previous election. The same pattern occurred between 1959 and 1964 when, after being behind by 17 per cent. on the National Opinion Poll and 16 per cent. on the Gallup Poll, the Conservatives pulled back to a mere 0·7 per cent. behind on polling day. These electoral facts have been supplemented by the realisation that the governing party has many advantages. The activities of its leaders have much greater news value than any of the reactions or pronouncements of the opposition unless the latter is splitting or quarrelling over its leadership. The Prime Minister

[18] D. E. Butler, *The Electoral System in Britain, 1918–1951*, pp. 183–184.
[19] D. E. Butler, *The British General Election of 1951*, p. 21.

naturally appears more often on television than any of his opponents and he can time his activities and announcements so as to steal the headlines almost at will.[20] Most voters are interested in domestic problems and in their own sense of well-being, modern economic management usually making it possible for competent politicians to ensure that a boom takes place in the nine months preceding an election. It is concrete acts that weigh most heavily in the public's estimation of a party and here again the government can do more and change its image more readily than the opposition which is left saddled with the memories of its last failures in government. Also in terms of the party in power, this capacity to alter conditions, to have an easy budget, together with the shortness of the public's memory, means that changes in the political climate in favour of the government are not too difficult to engineer. In April 1955 Mr. Butler as Chancellor of the Exchequer was able to distribute £150 million in tax relief followed by a further tax reduction on non-woollen textiles which was of special interest to those in the marginal seats in Lancashire. (Most of the tax reliefs were withdrawn at an autumn budget after the general election.) In 1959, the public had forgotten about the Suez crisis, the Cyprus problem was dead directly an agreement was signed between the Greeks and the Turks, while even the patches of unemployment in the winter of 1958–59 were forgotten directly the economy picked up. The Budget of that year conceded £300 million in tax relief and the Conservatives won the general election six months later. Preparations for the 1964 general election were hampered by the greater depth of dissatisfaction with the Conservatives, the aftermath of the Profumo scandal and the difficulty in establishing Sir Alec Douglas-Home as a national leader. Yet Conservative support rallied as the economic boom continued and it can be argued that all that beat the government was that it ran out of time. The five-year limit to the Parliament expired and had it been possible to delay the election even a further six weeks, the Conservatives might have won by four rather than have lost by that number.

Once in office in 1964, Mr. Wilson simply had to play the cards in his hand properly in order to secure his position. He

[20] Mr. Wilson was a past-master at this technique and managed, for instance, to prevent any major coverage of the 1965 Conservative Party Conference by flying to visit the Queen at Balmoral the day the Conference started.

received great and sympathetic Press attention, his government rapidly carried a series of measures which more than any number of speeches made in opposition convinced the electorate that Labour could govern, the Conservatives shorn of power suddenly looked insignificant and then with economic prosperity advancing in the spring of 1966, Mr. Wilson took his chance. Despite a tired campaign in which the Prime Minister miscalculated by holding his fire for far too long, Labour romped home with a majority of ninety-seven. Before very long, the government was in difficulties and by the winter of 1967–68 had reached as low a level in the opinion polls as the Conservatives had touched in mid-1963. Yet the memories of the come-backs of 1959 and 1964 could not be eradicated. No opposition in modern circumstances can imagine that there is any inherent tendency to a swing which will restore it to power. Even worse, no opposition, however well it is doing (or to be more realistic, however badly the government is doing), can be confident of victory unless it has this lead in the last twelve months before an election must be held. In the mid-1960s it is accepted in British politics that governments lose elections rather than oppositions win them, that the advantages lie almost entirely with those in power and that it requires serious political blunders, ill luck or tactical miscalculation if these advantages do not yield the expected results.

THE INFLUENCE OF THE PARTIES AND BACK-BENCHERS

Thus governments pay little attention to the views of the opposition other than in the debating sense of being able to answer their arguments and score points. But they do react if there are signs that the public and particularly their own voters are becoming restless and one of the indications of such disaffection is the attitude of government back-benchers.

There are several channels through which a government tries to keep in contact with its Members in the House and its friends in the country and these connections naturally permit a degree of reciprocal influence. Most of these channels have a connection with Parliament and with the political machine built up to contest parliamentary elections. The source of influence which is both most obscure and most difficult to classify is the direct dealings between the party leaders and their principal backers. As was pointed out in the discussion of pressure groups (pp. 555–566, above), some of these bodies have interests which can only be safeguarded, or objects which can only be furthered, by continuous political activity and groups in this position tend to identify themselves with one of the major parties. M. Harrison starts his study of *The Trade Unions and the Labour Party* by saying that " the most important single source of pressure is exercised directly on the party leadership by the General Council of the T.U.C. quite outside the party's normal constitutional circuits." [21] It was clear that in the discussions about a statutory limit on wage increases in 1966 and 1967, the government was more concerned to get T.U.C. support than to meet any other objections, for instance from trade union M.P.s. Similarly Labour leaders deal directly with the senior members of the Co-operative Movement when a matter of mutual concern arises. In 1949 the Labour Party indicated that industrial assurance would be taken under public control in the next period of office but after lengthy talks with the Co-operators, nationalisation was altered to " mutualisation " which would have safeguarded the position of Co-operative insurance. The same situation almost certainly exists on the Conservative side, though little is known of either the financial or personal contacts that are involved. Over a long period the drink trade has looked to the Conservative Party. In 1916 Bonar Law favoured Lloyd George's scheme of nationalisation as " it would free us as a party from the incubus of being tied to the Trade, which has done us far more harm than good." [22] Yet the National Trade Defence Association was still in close liaison with the party when it came to resisting the 1948 Licensing Bill and directly the Conservatives returned to power the Trade obtained the concessions it wanted: no state ownership of public houses in new towns.

The better-known methods of influence are through the back-benchers in Parliament and through the party machine—chiefly the annual conference—outside Parliament. Sometimes powerful interests combine with back-benchers and sympathetic ministers to press for specific objectives. In the campaign to end the monopoly of the B.B.C. and permit the introduction of commercial television all these elements aided by the Conservative Central

---

[21] M. Harrison, *op. cit.*, p. 17. A good example of this direct dealing was when the Labour Cabinet put their economy proposals before the General Council of the T.U.C. in August 1931.

[22] R. Blake, *The Unknown Prime Minister, The Life and Times of Andrew Bonar Law*, p. 239.

Office built up a most effective lobby and won over the undecided section in the Cabinet.

In Parliament, pressure is exerted in two directions. Back-bench Members explain their views to the Whips who give their general impressions to the leaders. The Whips in turn persuade and reason with M.P.s. In addition, there are the meetings of the parliamentary party and of its committees at which Members can express worries which they might not care to mention in public. In the Conservative Party, the back-benchers' meeting is known as the 1922 Committee as it was started in 1922–23 after a period of acute dissatisfaction over the poor relations between the leadership and the rank and file. Its essential purpose is to discuss political problems and no resolutions are put or votes taken, though the sense of the meeting and the views of sub-committees can be of considerable importance. Conservative leaders quite often describe the 1922 Committee simply as a method of " quietening the boys " but the degree of activity it has shown and the part it has played has varied markedly with different leaders of the party. Normally the object is to test Members' reactions to government proposals but such reactions have sometimes had a definite effect. Austen Chamberlain's speech to the Foreign Affairs Committee of the Conservative Party probably prevented genuine alarm over the proposed Hoare-Laval pact breaking into open dissension. In 1957 the Housing and Local Government Sub-committee of the 1922 Committee suggested an amendment to the Rent Act and the 1958 Landlord and Tenant Act was introduced to meet Conservative back-bench views of the hardship that might be caused by increased rents. Again in 1957 rank and file pressure led the government to withdraw clauses of an Electricity Bill which would have given the Central Electricity Authority power to manufacture electrical equipment. An attempt to give judges a tax-free increase in salary in 1953, the Teachers' Superannuation and Industrial Organisation Bills of 1954, and the Shops Bill (1957) were all dropped because various interests were well represented among Conservative M.P.s and because some of the provisions offended back-bench opinion. On one occasion, the Home Affairs Committee of the Cabinet was unsure how a certain proposal would be received and asked the Minister of Housing to consult the Housing Sub-committee of the 1922 Committee before taking the matter any further. Sir Anthony

Eden has explained that ministers were doubtful about the negotiations granting independence to the Sudan in late 1952.

"I therefore undertook to explain the agreement to a
meeting of Government supporters that evening. My colleagues accepted that if I were satisfied that I could command
enough support, they would authorise the conclusion of the
agreement. At my request, the final decision was to be taken
that night after I had addressed the meeting." [23]

The Annual Conference of the National Union of Conservative
Associations has never tried to assert any direct control over
Conservative Governments but it has indicated that it would like
to see more action along certain lines. Determined pressure for
restrictions on the political activities of trade unions was ultimately
successful when the Trade Disputes Act of 1927 was passed,
though a long series of resolutions asking for a reform and
restoration of some of the former powers of the House of Lords
was persistently ignored.[24] Between 1924 and 1929 the Conference
repeatedly recorded its exasperation with Stanley Baldwin and
his government, an example being the unanimous acceptance of a
resolution calling for tariffs to safeguard industry in 1928.[25]

Later, when the National Ministry was in office in 1933 the
Conference voted for an immediate increase in the strength of the
armed services. The same happened in 1934 and in 1935 Mr.
Churchill carried a resolution urging the government "forthwith
to repair the serious deficiencies in the defence forces of the
Crown." [26] An amendment asking for tariffs on non-Empire food-
stuffs was also put forward at the 1935 meeting. Walter Elliot,
the Minister of Agriculture, persuaded the delegates to reject it
though he was unable to defeat a similar resolution in 1936. In
many ways the fiercest struggle was over the policy of progressive
self-government for India.[27] The official view was upheld in 1933

23 Sir Anthony Eden, *Full Circle*, p. 246.
24 No less than 12 Conservative Conferences passed resolutions in favour of
   House of Lords reform between 1923 and 1936. See R. T. Mackenzie, *British
   Political Parties*, pp. 221–229.
25 Mr. Mackenzie sums up its attitude by quoting a delegate. "Our loyalty is
   the same as ever, but it has got to be 'On Stanley, On,'" *ibid.*, p. 227.
26 *Ibid.*, p. 229.
27 It is interesting that Mr. Churchill, whose instincts date from an earlier era,
   preferred open attack on the floor of the House to working in private or
   through the party machine, though he did use these methods. His attack
   on the Government of India Bill was the last great filibuster of a private

and squeezed through in 1934 by the narrow margin 543 to 520. The die-hards then took the matter to the Central Council of the National Union where they lost decisively.[28]   After 1951 the Annual Conference did not reveal so many of these gusts of feeling though there has been some alarm over such issues as legislation on restrictive practices (see below) immigration, capital punishment, resale price maintenance and comprehensive schools. From 1951 to 1964 the Conference's loyalty was excited by the fact that the party was in power, in 1965 an election was imminent while in 1967 there had been so much speculation about the future of the leader, Mr. Heath, that the Conference took care not to reveal any internal dissension.

If there is any dissatisfaction in the constituencies, it rapidly reaches some M.P.s who tell the Whips or try to see the appropriate Parliamentary Private Secretary.   If this fails and feeling grows, the matter will be raised in the party committees and only when no progress is made at this level will the matter come up at the Annual Conference.   Disagreement has to be serious before M.P.s will seek to prove that ministers are not in touch with opinion in the party outside Parliament.   Signs that the political standing of the government is satisfactory combined with careful explanations and timing of less palatable items are usually sufficient to ensure complete harmony.   Some members of the Conservative Cabinet doubted whether they could ever persuade the party to accept the Restrictive Trade Practices Bill in 1956. L. S. Amery, by then an elder statesman, opposed the Bill at the Annual Conference and defeat would have been a serious blow. However the proposal was skilfully defended and carried.   The Government then tackled the Federation of British Industries and pointed out that the Press (very conveniently) was exercised over the problem of monopolies.   Would it not be better for the matter to be tackled in a friendly way by ministers who understood the

M.P. against a major government measure. The acceptance of a " voluntary timetable " meant that Mr. Churchill could not hold up the Bill by the older parliamentary methods of his father's day. He had to bring masses of evidence before the Joint Select Committee and make diversionary charges that the government had tampered with the evidence. (This took two months to clear up.) Once, however, the Joint Select Committee reported, the timetable came into operation and the Bill was passed.

28 The Central Council is the governing body of the National Union. It normally has no critical functions and meets once a year, the membership being the party leaders, all Conservative M.P.s, peers and candidates, and four representatives from each constituency.

position of industrialists? At this point the Monopolies Commission brought out some rather sharp suggestions for control. The 1922 Committee was split from top to bottom over whether to legislate in favour of competition or to defend monopoly. The Labour Party helped by demanding a debate and the government seized its chance to bring in its Restrictive Practices Bill—which was accepted by the party and took the wind out of the opposition's sails.

Labour leaders have tended to pay less attention than the Conservatives do to their back-benchers. One reason is that ministers are only seriously worried by back-bench pressure if they consider that it represents a real dissatisfaction in the constituencies. Among the Conservatives back-bench dissent is rare and the party is relatively homogeneous so that if M.P.s are agitated, this is usually a sign of genuine pressure on them by supporters. Also the Conservative Party is less bound to a programme based on ideology so that if there are objections to a course of action, this is a good reason for dropping it. In the Labour Party, on the other hand, there is a broad spectrum of opinion with some left-wingers who will object to many policies any Labour Cabinet is likely to produce.[29] As a result their objections tend to be discounted, they are seen as representing only themselves, and far more attention is paid if normal loyalists or centre members grow alarmed or threaten to abstain. A second reason is that while the Conservatives tend to have the mores of a gentlemen's club in that those involved in bad behaviour are ostracised, reasonable people making objections do not have reflections cast on their motives. In the Labour Party, communications across a series of class and occupational barriers are poorer and order has tended to be maintained after the fashion of a trade union branch with a tendency to keep quoting standing orders and calling for discipline.

In the minority Labour Governments of 1923–24 and 1929–31 relations between ministers and back-benchers were bad or non-existent and one of Snowden's reasons for appointing the May

---

29 See S. Finer, H. Berrington and Bartholemew, *Back Bench Opinion in the Parliament of 1955–9*. The weakness of this brave attempt to assess back-bench opinion lies in the weight it gives to signatures on early day motions without appreciating that many sign because they do not wish to appear churlish when asked while others who may agree never sign such motions on principle.

Committee was that he knew he could not carry the party with him in cutting unemployment relief. Between 1945 and 1951 there was both better organisation and a greater sense of purpose. The Parliamentary Party held fortnightly meetings and set up a series of committees, that on Civil Aviation playing a useful part in preparing for the nationalisation of the industry. The one occasion on which back-bench opinion influenced the government on an important matter was when Mr. Attlee told the Parliamentary Party that an eighteen-month period of conscription was required. At the party meeting, the proposal was carried with a substantial minority in opposition. When it came before the House in March 1947 seventy-two M.P.s voted against the Bill and as many were absent. The government thereupon agreed to reduce the period to twelve months and the Bill was carried by 368 to 17. On winning office in 1964, Labour found any difficulties between the front-benches and back-benches smoothed over by the need to maintain a majority of three and the comradeship this enforced. Yet this narrow margin allowed Mr. Desmond Donelly and Mr. Woodrow Wyatt to persist with their objections to the Iron and Steel Bill to the last minute, their presence in the government lobby being obtained by a promise by Mr. George Brown that he would listen to any further representations from the steel owners. But the government conceded little to back-bench pressure in this Parliament except possibly to postpone legislation on wage-restraint.

After the 1966 election, with an initial majority of ninety-seven, back-bench pressure reappeared. At meetings of the Parliamentary Labour Party there were debates (and votes) on proposals that the government should retire from its commitments East of Suez and give up its support for American policy in Vietnam. The Prime Minister spoke at one such meeting and deplored these attempts to exert pressure by forcing divisions at the Parliamentary Labour Party. Relations grew worse after the economy measures of July 1966 and back-bench criticism of the prices and incomes policy. When sixty-three Labour members abstained over a defence White Paper in February 1967, Mr. Wilson attended the Parliamentary Labour Party meeting and said:

> "All I say is 'watch it.' Every dog is allowed one bite, but a different view is taken of a dog that goes on biting all the time. If there are doubts that the dog is biting not

because of the dictates of conscience but because he is considered vicious then things happen to that dog. He may not get his licence renewed when it falls due." [30]

The speech did not alter relations and there was continued back-bench pressure on the same issues culminating in twenty-five abstentions on a motion of confidence in the government and in a series of cuts in public expenditure which had been announced in January 1968. The result was a considerable controversy on discipline and the introduction of a modified code of conduct defining the powers of the Chief Whip later in the same month.

These pressures on the Labour Government should afford a measure of back-bench influence as they could scarcely have been carried further. Yet it is clear that the abstainers kept down the numbers (or other potential abstainers refrained from doing so) in order that the existence of the government should not be endangered. These episodes were demonstrations of feeling when all the other approaches through the Whips, early day motions and deputations to see the Prime Minister had failed. It is hard to estimate whether this pressure had any effect. Probably the indications that normally reliable members of the trade union group would join the Left in abstaining over renewed statutory restrictions on wage increases had an influence in preventing such legislation in the summer of 1967 but the Cabinet were divided on the question and the T.U.C. was exercising the maximum pressure. The decision in 1966 to dissociate Britain from American action in bombing Hanoi and Haiphong may have been to avert back-bench complaints and Mr. Wilson almost certainly anticipated trouble if he had reached an agreement with Mr. Ian Smith about Rhodesian self-government. On certain aspects of minor Bills, the government gave way to suggestions while the Selective Employment Tax was amended in its effect on agriculture and on charities (but not on retail co-operative concerns). One back-bench M.P., Mr. Tam Dalyell, mounted elaborate attacks on the Anglo-French variable geometry aeroplane and on a proposed island base at Aldabra and both were abandoned. Dr. Dunwoody successfully pressed for a government decision to ban free gift coupons being included in cigarette packets. A strong group, the miners' M.P.s, were so incensed at the government's fuel policy that they were able to prevent a vote being taken actually to approve of the minister's White Paper and were able to postpone the closure of certain pits though they were unable to change the actual fuel policy. It is also possible that in the confused dispute over the sale of arms to South Africa back-bench opinion, which was being mobilised by several sections in the Cabinet, may have had some effect. In all these instances apart from the minor amendments referred to, senior ministers can be found who deny, quite sincerely, that back-bench pressure played any part and they assert that to have given way to such pressure would have been to have abandoned their task of governing—a concept which would have seemed strange before 1914 or even, perhaps, before 1939.

In Labour's first periods of government, its leaders were treated with respect and even awe by the Party's Annual Conference while on their side, there was an attempt to implement Conference resolutions. In 1924 Arthur Henderson " pointed out (to his fellow ministers) that we should be bound by Conference resolutions, and particularly by the resolution to increase unemployment pay to £2 per week," [31] but both then and in 1929, the fact that the government was in a minority was held to absolve it from any such obligations. On the issue of unemployment, the 1929 and 1930 Conferences almost succeeded in " referring back " the report of the Parliamentary Party. Between 1945 and 1951 there was greater harmony and though official views were rejected on seven occasions, they were on relatively minor issues such as the tied-cottage. After 1964 the Annual Conference (held in 1965) was so pleased that Labour was back in office that there was no friction, but in both 1966 and 1967 it was evident that there would be sharp criticism of Mr. Wilson and of some of the government's policies. In the event the platform was defeated in 1966 over a motion calling for a reduction of defence expenditure and on an emergency resolution on unemployment. In 1967 there were defeats over Vietnam, Greek despotism and one of several resolutions on prices and incomes. Yet the real point was not so much individual items as the tone of the conferences and the reception given to the Prime Minister, though concessions were made behind

[31] P. Snowden, *An Autobiography*, Vol. II, p. 596.

the scenes to certain unions (*e.g.*, the miners over pit closures) in order to secure the passage of some of the key motions.

Thus there is no evidence that Labour M.P.s or the party at large have had any direct influence on the major policies of Mr. Wilson's government though it is possible to detect minor adjustments made to meet pressure, particularly if it is associated with a powerful outside group such as the T.U.C. or an individual big union. There have been a number of small concessions to particular demands either because this has helped general progress or because the minister or the government was moving in this direction in any case.

In the case of a party in opposition, the activities of M.P.s have little effect on future governments but the annual conferences do sometimes try to press for the adoption of certain policies if and when their party comes to power. In the 1930s the Conservative party organisation was always more definitely in favour of tariffs than the leadership and the 1930 Conference " urgently demand[ed] that the Conservative Party at the next General Election shall place a wider programme of safeguarding as the principal and foremost item in the Party Programme." [32] In 1950 the Conference was debating a resolution which condemned the Labour Government's housing policy and one delegate said a Conservative Ministry could well build 300,000 houses a year. Other speakers took up the suggestion and at the end of the debate Lord Woolton accepted the target on behalf of the leadership of the party.

The line to be taken by the Labour leadership when in opposition (which may commit the party if it later wins office) is settled in theory at meetings of the Parliamentary Party. Under normal conditions, however, the Leader of the Opposition and the relevant members of the Shadow Cabinet work out their ideas. They may hear the views of the appropriate committee of the Parliamentary Party or of a policy sub-committee of the National Executive and then, if there is time, the matter goes to a full meeting of the party. The Annual Conference ostensibly plays a larger role in opposition in that its decisions constitute the objectives of the party and proposals carried by a two-thirds majority have to be included in the party programme. R. T. Mackenzie has argued

[32] R. T. Mackenzie, *op. cit.*, p. 202.

that the Conferences of the two parties have much the same degree
of influence.[33] It is true that when the Labour Movement has
been divided, as over the sanctions question in 1935, or deeply
disturbed as it was about the Spanish Civil War in 1936, the
Conference has been able to resolve the matter or has genuinely
reflected the state of party feeling. In 1944 the Conference asked
why specific industries had not been put on the list for nationalisation and when the programme *Let Us Face the Future* appeared,
this had been done. The most serious issue between the Conference and the parliamentary leadership arose in 1960 when the
official statement on defence was rejected in favour of a motion
embodying the policy of unilateral nuclear disarmament. This
episode has raised many points but it does show that relations
between the trade union leadership and the parliamentary spokesmen of the party have to break down before there is a set battle
on the floor of the Conference. The influence of the unions and
of the Conference as a whole cannot be measured by the few
occasions on which matters have come to a head in this fashion.[34]
The particular issue of unilateral nuclear disarmament led Hugh
Gaitskell to set out his view of the situation when a clash took
place. He argued that once the Parliamentary Party has taken
a decision, the Conference cannot insist on a reversal nor bind
the Shadow Cabinet but they in turn are bound to take notice of
Conference decisions and a serious divergence over a number of
years will not be permitted. It is implicit in this argument that
if the Conference does not change its mind or show that it will
return to the policy of the Parliamentary Party within a reasonable
time, the leadership in the House of Commons will have to alter
its views or retire. So it would appear that the delegates of the
trade unions and of the constituencies who come together at the
Annual Conference have more influence over the Labour Party
while in opposition than the Conference has on the Conservative
Party in similar circumstances, because they care about certain
issues and about their right to decide on policy to a larger extent
than their Conservative counterparts. For the latter, policy formation is not of great importance, there is a deeper trust in the
parliamentary leadership and a stronger desire to win or hold

---

[33] *Op. cit.*, pp. 486–490.
[34] This case is argued by Martin Harrison in his *Trade Unions and the Labour Party*, pp. 196–260.

power which is made easier if the party presents a united and confident front to the public, a motive which was very much in evidence in the 1966 and 1967 Conferences. It is these differences of ethos and objective which account for the greater degree of influence exerted by the body of the Labour Party over its leadership, though this influence dwindles to the same low level as that exercised by the Conservative Party directly a Labour government takes office and its leader becomes Prime Minister.

While both the Prime Minister and the Leader of the Opposition are always aware that they have a numerous following whose interests and convictions must be borne in mind, they have various methods of bringing pressure to bear on their adherents in Parliament. As has been mentioned, the Whips reason with M.P.s who are dissatisfied and urge them to consider the damage done by open dissension. Between 1945 and 1951 the Labour Party suspended its internal Standing Orders (which govern discipline) but Members were still expected to obey the Whips. In opposition the Standing Orders were reintroduced, making it an offence to vote against the policy of the party. These Standing Orders were reintroduced at the start of the 1964 Parliament but not after the general election of 1966. Then, after the occurrence of various clashes over back-bench abstentions, a modified Code of Conduct was adopted in January 1968. This allowed the Chief Whip to reprimand and to recommend suspension from attendance at party meetings as stages on the way to the full penalty of having the Whip withdrawn. Should this occur, the M.P. would not be able to stand as a Labour candidate at the following election. An official candidate would then be nominated in his place and no sitting Member has triumphed over such opposition since the election of 1945.

On the Conservative side, there is not the same insistence that Members should accept official policy and withdrawal of the Whip or expulsion does not normally take place.[35] Mr. Churchill was in open revolt against his party for long periods in the 1930s but there was no question of expulsion. None of the eight Conservative Members who opposed the attack on Suez in 1956 suffered any penalties from the Conservative organisation within

---

[35] The Whip has in fact been withdrawn on only one occasion from a Conservative M.P. between 1920 and 1968.

the House of Commons. But there is a strong chance that deviations other than those of the extreme right—that is, any that involve an element of agreement with the party's Labour or Liberal opponents—will bring down the wrath of the Member's constituency association. When Lord Cranborne (now Lord Salisbury) resigned his post as Under-Secretary of State for Foreign Affairs in 1938 because he disagreed with the Prime Minister's handling of foreign policy, his local association refused to allow him to speak in the constituency. His position might have become precarious had events not rapidly vindicated his stand. Of the eight anti-Suez rebels mentioned above, only Sir Robert Boothby escaped without any censure from his local association while Mr. Nigel Nicolson was disavowed and refused renomination.[36]

Normally coercion in these forms is not required. Members vote with their party because they realise that they were elected on the party ticket and because they want it to succeed. If there are doubts, the most powerful restraints are not the Standing Orders (in the Labour Party) but much more subtle influences. Many of the younger and more ambitious M.P.s wish for office and a leader, who is or will become Prime Minister, can make or break a Member's career. In recent years the Leader of the Opposition has appointed not only a Shadow Cabinet but a full Shadow Ministry so that thirty or forty M.P.s know their exact standing in the party and think of themselves as working with and behind their front bench. On each side there are back-benchers who know that they are not ministerial timber but they are usually the more solid and reliable Members. In the Labour Party, the older trade union M.P.s have been brought up in organisations which place a great premium on loyalty while Conservative back-benchers find no glory in rebellion and may lose their chance of a knighthood or a peerage. The use of political honours to keep the parliamentary rank and file happy and united cannot be ignored. Between 1945 and 1951 Mr. Attlee distributed twenty-three peerages and knighthoods among his 393 followers and there is no evidence that Hugh Gaitskell or Mr. Wilson have ever been short of candidates for their quota of life peerages. In the six years between 1951 and 1957 Conservative Prime Ministers awarded

---

[36] See Nigel Nicolson's account in *People and Parliament.*

104 peerages and knighthoods to the 340 M.P.s who were elected in 1951.[37]

An older method of control has been cited by the late Lord Morrison. He considered that " governments are often saved from parliamentary defeat by the back-benchers' fear of a dissolution "[38] and in January 1968 Mr. Wilson told a meeting of the Parliamentary Labour Party that numerous abstentions could force a general election. It is true that in the mid-nineteenth century, when Members paid their own election expenses and fought more or less single-handed for their seats, there was a genuine abhorrence of premature elections.[39] But in modern conditions Members face far more immediate penalties for voting against their party than a dissolution. And if abstention or cross-voting is being considered, what worries a Member is the risk of expulsion or refusal of renomination, not the possibility of having to fight an election campaign as an accredited party candidate. Indeed, an election is just the time when politicians pull together and no parliamentary leader is likely to play into the hands of his opponents by asking the public to defeat troublesome members of his own party. Any party leader with a desire to survive will settle or smooth over a rebellion before going to the country and while Mr. Wilson in the instance just quoted may have been stating a fact—too many abstentions could theoretically have led to a defeat, his resignation, a Conservative Government and an immediate election—none of the Parliamentary Labour Party took this seriously as a disciplinary threat. The one situation in which a Premier might consider a dissolution as an aid to discipline is when he is confident of winning and wishes to show grumblers that his policies have popular support. In December 1938, Neville Chamberlain " was wondering whether he could ever shake down with this ' uneasy and disgruntled House ' without an election."[40] But there is no sign that he had to use such a threat to save

---

[37] Mr. Anthony Wedgwood Benn, H.C. Debates, Vol. 582, col. 495, February 12, 1958. He concluded that " this is the secret of discipline in the Conservative Party." I am very grateful to Mr. Benn for letting me see the detailed break-down of these figures.

[38] H. Morrison, *Government and Parliament*, p. 94. Mr. Attlee has made a similar statement. The argument against such a view is put by W. G. Andrews, " Some Thoughts on the Power of Dissolution," *Parliamentary Affairs* (1960), Vol. XIII, No. 3.

[39] See above, pp. 92–96.

[40] K. Feiling, *op. cit.*, p. 390.

himself from defeat. Had Chamberlain announced a dissolution, the small band of Conservative M.P.s who were alarmed at his foreign policies would have turned to attack socialism and the "pacifism" of the Labour Party. After the election they would have had to go on expressing their worries about German policy in the face of a Prime Minister fortified by a victory at the polls.

Any discussion of Parliament as a check on the Executive must take into consideration the standing of the House of Commons in the country. In the intense and self-regarding atmosphere of Westminster, some M.P.s and even senior statesmen can still hold that the institution has in no way lost ground. They can argue, quite correctly, that nowadays all M.P.s have to be able to make some kind of a speech and that one hundred and fifty regularly take part in debates while a further two hundred and fifty speak occasionally. The standard and activities of M.P.s have increased in every sense, and yet none of these points affects the evidence that Parliament is no longer the forum of the nation.[41] Basically this is because the House of Commons lacks power and the public soon lose interest in debates, however acute, and personalities, however forceful, once it is believed that they have no effect on policy.[42] When power goes and public attention turns elsewhere, the vitality of an elected Chamber fades away. Only a few senior statesmen are in the public eye and even well-informed citizens who read the "quality" Press find it hard to name the junior members of the Cabinet. The days when a vigorous back-bencher could make a national reputation which would then constitute his claim for office have come to an end, probably the last case being that of Aneurin Bevan. Now the aspirant for office hopes

[41] The standard has risen in terms of educational achievements and specialist knowledge while after 1966 the working of procedure was made harder by the sheer pressure of Members wishing to participate, sometimes as many as 300 questions being tabled in a single day.

[42] There have been many proposals for the reform of the House of Commons. In his *Reform of the Commons* (Fabian Tract, No. 319) Mr. Bernard Crick has produced a valuable series of suggestions for offices, research facilities, specialised standing committees, etc. But he, like most of the reformers, considers that the House can be revitalised without in any way weakening the power of the government. Such a view makes all the rest worthless, for if the government is left in its present position reforms may make life easier for M.P.s but nothing will result from the use of these facilities, the role of the House of Commons will remain unaltered, and the public will continue to ignore it.

to catch the eye of the Premier or of a senior minister and to make his wider reputation after he has been appointed.[43]

A further difficulty for Members has been the dwindling sources of information. One senior Foreign Office official has said that he felt no less well informed after he had retired. But he had had expert training and knew which lines to read between. It was noticeable that the Labour Opposition was much more effective in 1951 and 1952 when its leaders were still living on the hump of information they had acquired in office.[44] The old practice of publishing blue books containing the correspondence between Britain and a given foreign Power was dying away before 1914 and ceased after 1918. The attack on Suez would have remained shrouded in mystery had a junior minister (Mr. Anthony Nutting) not chosen to write an account and corroborate information published by some of the French participants. Perhaps the most serious lack of information has been in the field of defence. Discussing the position in the 1930s Lord Chatfield complained that "Parliament is never fully confided in"[45] and so had no basis on which to form its opinions. Since 1945 there has been the same dearth of information and few, outside official circles, have been competent to discuss the policies open to Britain or to judge if and when mistakes have been made.

Members of Parliament are left to make what use they can of their average of one and a half hours of debating time a head each session and to ask questions. The latter serve a purpose in that they give M.P.s some satisfaction and some publicity but if action is wanted, it is always preferable to raise the matter privately with the minister. Civil servants are expert at producing answers which convey the minimum of information and are rounded off so as to leave no openings for supplementaries. Yet question time is valuable in that it focuses attention on current

---

[43] An impression of the conditions and atmosphere of the House as seen by an ambitious back-bencher can be gained from W. Fienburgh's novel, *No Love for Johnnie.*

[44] Lord Eustace Percy considers that "In England Ministers have for generations been so accustomed to rely for technical knowledge on the Crown Services. . . . This makes for a dangerous weakness in English parliamentary oppositions; for a political leader who has been used to command expert opinion while in office feels lost when in opposition he has to manufacture it for himself . . .": *Some Memories,* p. 154.

[45] Lord Chatfield, *It Might Happen Again,* p. 197.

grievances and keeps civil servants on their toes though it is no substitute for the older methods of parliamentary control.

It is often said that apart from question time and the ministerial statements and cross-questioning that can occur at the "focal point" of 3.30 p.m. the House lacks the excitement of the pre-1914 era and that the opposition does not oppose in the old vigorous fashion. It is clear that debating has altered since the era when ministers were in constant attendance and made every effort to rebut their critics and win over the doubtful.[46] On the other hand, some debates still reach a high quality both in content and in drama, yet they are barely reported in the popular Press and have little effect on political opinion outside the House. Lord Woolton, reflecting on the period between 1951 and 1955, observes that " whilst the parliamentary life of the government was vigorous and not lacking in excitement, the public showed little interest in it." [47] Lord Kilmuir observed that in 1958 "time and again the Labour Party would enjoy a great parliamentary triumph, only to discover as the weeks passed that it had had absolutely no effect upon public opinion." [48] What happens in the House has an effect on the morale of Members and on the standing of individual politicians but the public judges a government by results, by what happens, partially modified or emphasised by the impressions gathered from television coverage and newspaper headlines.

Against this background, it would not be surprising if the standard of M.P.s had declined. In fact it has almost certainly risen absolutely in terms of the standards of the last century, but the real question is whether there are opportunities for putting these talents into effective use, and whether the public will take any notice. In 1935 Austen Chamberlain thought " that in some respects the present House is superior and that the average of ability and knowledge is greater . . . but its debates excite less interest among its members and have less influence on the country than in earlier days." [49] The attraction of a parliamentary career

---

[46] This can occur still on odd occasions when the Whips are off or lose control at times of great passion as over the Immigration Bill in February 1968.

[47] Lord Woolton, *op. cit.*, p. 379.   [48] Lord Kilmuir, *Political Adventure*, p. 291.

[49] *Down the Years*, p. 75. Earlier in May 1929 a diarist records that " Austen was interesting about the very rare occasions on which in recent Parliaments there have been what he called real ding-dong debates between the two front-benches. In the old days you had Gladstone and Morley, Balfour and Hicks-Beach making swift punching speeches to the huge enjoyment of everybody."

depends on many factors but in part on the public's estimation of its value. In the past one of the great strengths of the House of Commons was the general opinion that a life of service in politics was among the highest aspirations open to a Briton. Yet this is fading and any prospective candidate who proposes to leave a reasonable post in the professions or in industry for Parliament becomes accustomed to the kindly view that he is eccentric and the less charitable one that he is crazy. Among the trade unions, the most capable leaders tend to prefer to remain on the industrial side, a view confirmed by Frank Cousins' evident pleasure at leaving the Cabinet to resume his post as General Secretary of the Transport and General Workers' Union. M. Harrison concludes in his study of the trade unions and the Labour Party that "the militant's reluctance to make sacrifices to maintain their union's position in the House of Commons reflects their assessment of the value of parliamentary representation. This has probably never been lower." [50] The same is true of the attitude of industry which became so critical that some senior industrialists in late 1967 argued that it would be better if Britain was run by businessmen on a business basis. It is clear that the leading men do not regard the House of Commons as a final goal of their careers. A few are willing to accept ministerial posts because these clearly carry some power; it is the life and influence of a back-bench M.P. that is so unenviable. Among those who have sought entry to the House but wish to have something to show for their lives there is a tendency to leave if there is no prospect of office. In the 1950s and early 1960s the Labour Party lost Lord Shawcross, Lord Robens, Sir Geoffrey de Freitas, Hilary Marquand, Kenneth Younger and George Chetwynd, while Mr. Roy Jenkins contemplated an alternative career. The Conservatives lost Oliver Lyttelton (now Lord Chandos), Lord Monckton and Aubrey Jones. Some of their Opposition Front Bench after 1964 took posts in the City and if the party was defeated at the general election due in 1970–71, it is likely that there would be a large-scale exodus of the more able men.

Despite all this, there is a certain grandeur about the House of Commons that can never be removed. Its Members may not still feel that they are at the hub of the universe but they have

[50] M. Harrison, *op. cit.*, p. 292.

ringside seats for events that are absorbing and important by any standards. The House and the opportunities it offers will always draw a number of men of real ability who are fascinated by public life. But it remains true that the Commons no longer retains its dominating position in the life of the country or in the machinery of government.

The House of Lords has played no significant part in influencing the conduct of modern governments. After the Home Rule and Welsh Disestablishment Bills had been forced through by the Liberals, it did not intervene again till the second Labour Government when the Lords made substantial alterations in the Coal Mines Bill of 1930. When the Labour Party was returned with its large majority in 1945 Lord Samuel characterised the attitude of Lord Salisbury and the Conservative peers: " he recognises to the full the obligations which lie upon this House not to intervene in any factious or party spirit with a programme which has been clearly endorsed by the people." [51] The Labour Government found the Lords "fulfilled a useful role as a debating forum and revising Chamber," [52] and the only doubt was whether the Upper House might not join the Commons in welcoming the policy of withdrawal from India by a definite date. Lord Halifax, however, made a speech of great statesmanship and there was no division. By 1948, the vigour of the ministry was waning and a clash came over the Iron and Steel Nationalisation Bill, Lord Salisbury holding out for postponement of the vesting day till after the next general election. Foreseeing a struggle the Labour Government had introduced a Parliament Bill which reduced the period by which the Upper House could delay measures to two sessions or one year. This Bill was passed over the Lords veto in December 1949 but the government accepted the idea of a further election before the Iron and Steel Act came into operation.

After the creation of life peers and peeresses, the use of the Lords to strike out the clause in the 1948 Criminal Justice Bill for a trial suspension of capital punishment, and the appointment of Lord Home as Foreign Secretary in 1960,[53] there was some talk

---

[51] Quoted by R. J. Minney in *Viscount Addison: Leader of the Lords*, p. 48.
[52] C. R. Attlee, *As it Happened*, p. 169.
[53] It is interesting that as recently as 1955, Sir Anthony Eden contemplated making Lord Salisbury Foreign Secretary but refrained on the grounds that

of a revival on the part of the Lords but its real position was emphasised when the Peerage Act of 1963 allowed peers to relinquish their titles and thus stand for election to the Commons. In fact the peers have no more than minor tidying-up functions and by 1967–68 there were renewed discussions of how to remove the hereditary element and leave a group of appointed life peers with these tasks of assisting the Commons in the details of legislation.

Taking the two Houses together it would be more accurate to say that the Prime Minister and his colleagues govern through Parliament rather than to talk of parliamentary control of the executive. Once a government is in office, Parliament and the party outside Parliament stand in the position of highly important pressure groups whose support must be retained and who therefore have direct and recognised avenues for approaching the Premier and his colleagues. Ministers try to keep in touch with M.P.s but no government can foresee every reaction to a proposal. There is, therefore, a record of occasional adjustments to meet the views of the party stalwarts from the constituencies and a much larger number of cases where ministers take in the views of their back-benchers in framing measures and adjust their schemes to suggestions from the party committees. This is not so much power as a high degree of influence and it does much to make the lives of M.P.s worthwhile. But such influence is seldom exercised in the open in free debate and it fails to attract attention, so that Parliament has tended to fall in public estimation a little further than its position, as the leading source of political pressure in the country, merits.

The Press and Television

The Press acts as a link between the government, Parliament and the public, interpreting each section to the other and, at times urging its own views on both. The most direct influence the Press exerts is on ministers who read and may pay attention to the views of certain newspapers. Mr. Attlee used to read *The Times* and the *Daily Herald* as a matter of duty but took no real notice of

the House of Commons would never take an important statement on foreign affairs from anyone but the Foreign Secretary or the Prime Minister. (*Full Circle*, p. 273.)

what the Press was saying. He relied much more on personal contacts and on the atmosphere in the House of Commons. Sir Alec Douglas-Home likewise was largely impervious to Press criticism. Mr. Churchill read all the first editions at midnight before he went to bed and paid special attention, perhaps because of his Liberal past, to the *Manchester Guardian.* Ramsay Mac-Donald and Sir Anthony Eden were hypersensitive to newspaper attacks and both men could be seriously unnerved by the kind of assaults launched on MacDonald over the Daimler given him by Sir Alexander Grant,[54] and on Sir Anthony Eden over the Suez episode. Mr. Wilson has always been an avid newspaper reader and though much tougher than MacDonald or Eden, he has, like many politicians, attached a considerable amount of importance to the line taken by particular papers. At times of real political pressure the most resilient politician—even Mr. Churchill—could be shaken. The only explanation of his amazing action in threatening to ban the *Daily Mirror* in March 1942 was that he had had a very bad day with news of many sinkings, saw an offending cartoon, and made an irrational decision which he would not reverse.[55]

When Ministers are sensitive in this way, it is natural that they should try to gain and hold the support of what they consider to be influential newspapers. Stanley Baldwin had been severely criticised by the Rothermere and Beaverbrook Press (largely for his part in the American debt settlement). When he became Prime Minister, he asked for their support, using Stanley Jackson and J. C. C. Davidson as intermediaries.[56] Both Mr. Macmillan and Mr. Wilson in their own ways have prided themselves in their capacity to manage the Press which may mean offering posts or awards to editors or proprietors or simply treating them with courtesy. This management only began to decline when the

---

[54] Ramsay MacDonald had been given a Daimler and the interest on £30,000 worth of shares for its upkeep by an old friend, Sir Alexander Grant, who was subsequently given a baronetcy.

[55] This was a slightly ambiguous cartoon by Zec showing a sailor in direst straits clinging to a raft in a threatening sea with the caption " The price of petrol has been increased by one penny—Official." For a full account of the episode see H. Cudlipp, *Publish and be Damned.*

[56] In this case, both the Press magnates were offended at not being approached in person by the Prime Minister and remained critical of Baldwin's administration. L. S. Amery, *My Political Life*, Vol. II, p. 282.

respective government's policies encountered difficulties and the papers turned to reflect the popular mood of disaffection, though in the case of Mr. Wilson the estrangement was accelerated by a clash in mid-1967 over the D-Notice system of classifying material as secret.

A second way in which the Press enters the arena is that papers largely identified with one party can create considerable trouble by suggesting that there are divisions in the ranks, or by actively stirring up disaffection. When the *Daily Herald* or *Reynolds News* attacked Stanley Baldwin it was normal opposition criticism and could be ignored. But when Beaverbrook and Rothermere, whose papers were the staple diet of rank and file Conservative voters, kept repeating that unless Baldwin adopted Empire Free Trade the country and the party were heading for disaster, it had a definite impact. In large part this impact was only possible because there were doubts about the economic situation and about Baldwin's leadership. Both had shown signs of serious weakness between 1924 and 1929 and against this background the Press campaign began to have some effect. In the end, the Press magnates overreached themselves. Baldwin held a party meeting in June 1930 and read out a letter from Rothermere saying he could only support a Conservative Ministry if he knew the names of eight or ten of the members and approved of the general lines of policy. This gross piece of arrogance roused the ready dislike of Conservatives for such newly arrived Press lords and swung the meeting behind Baldwin, the continued opposition of these papers becoming, if anything, a source of strength. The capacity of normally sympathetic papers to create alarm was revealed again in January 1956 when the *Daily Telegraph* indicated its dissatisfaction with the leadership of Sir Anthony Eden. As in the case of Baldwin there were grounds, though not nearly such serious ones, for doubt. The Summit meetings of 1955 had solved nothing, fighting had flared up in Cyprus, while an Autumn Budget and some credit restrictions cancelled tax concessions made just before the election. Such setbacks occur in the life of any ministry, but when the *Daily Telegraph* lent its authority to the discontented, Sir Anthony was stung into an attack on " certain papers " and to an announcement denying that he had any intention of resigning.[57] On the left, the *Daily Herald* and the *Daily Mirror* did not indulge in such inter-party warfare before 1964 though Hugh Gaitskell's standing in certain small but articulate sections of the Labour Party suffered from the unremitting offensive waged against him in 1960–61 by *The New Statesman*. After 1966, the Mirror Group (by then owning the former *Daily Herald* under its new title of *The Sun*) remained pro-Labour but indicated a lack of confidence in Mr. Wilson in a manner which must have added to his difficulties in the winter of 1967–68.

Inasmuch as newspapers have been used to try to win political power or posts for their proprietors or editors, they have been a failure. Rothermere offered his support to Bonar Law in 1922 in return for an earldom for himself and a Cabinet post for his son. In 1923 he asked for a place in Baldwin's Cabinet. Both requests were ignored. When newspapermen have been taken into the inner circle, it has been because of personal friendships or their own capacities. Geoffrey Dawson was, as Sir Robert Boothby has said, the Secretary-General of the 20th Century Establishment, and though his services as Editor of *The Times* were valuable, he achieved this position more by virtue of his connections and outlook. When Beaverbrook was admitted to the Cabinet and performed his great services in the war, it was his abilities and Mr. Churchill's friendship that won him his place. In 1966 Mr. Cecil King was made a member of the Court of the Bank of England but this was in recognition of his business abilities.

The impact of the Press on the public in terms of its capacity to alter political attitudes is very slight. The term " quality " papers carry a fair amount of comment and yet are dealing with a section of the community whose views are not easily swayed. There is no evidence that the persistent criticism of Mr. Macmillan's 1957–59 Ministry and the ultimate decision of *The Guardian*, the *Observer* and the *Spectator*, to back Labour in the 1959 general election, had any noticeable effect. A committed paper such as the *Daily Telegraph* can be useful to Conservative Premiers by " flying kites " about Cabinet reshuffles or policy changes to test reactions among the upper ranks of the faithful. It is often said that

---

[57] Mr. Randolph Churchill has an interesting account of the origins of this quarrel in a dispute between Lady Pamela Berry (wife of the Editor of the *Daily Telegraph*) and Lady Eden, but there was already a strong undercurrent of criticism of the Premier in Conservative circles. See *The Rise and Fall of Sir Anthony Eden*, pp. 207–211.

Dawson's assiduous advocacy of Chamberlain's foreign policy was of great importance in the 1930s. But the Prime Minister and his closest colleagues were bent on this policy, they had the ardent support of the vast majority of their party, and it is unlikely that even under a different editor *The Times* would ever have done more than indicate reservations. The government made great efforts in 1938 and 1939 to keep the Press in line with their policies. Proprietors and editors were given special briefings by ministers and Cabinet assurances that all would be well.[58] Since 1945 there has grown up the practice of a regular weekly " off the record " briefing for the Parliamentary Press Lobby usually undertaken by the Leader of the House on behalf of the Government, a practice which spread to the Opposition in the 1960s which now has its weekly " counter-briefing."

Among the general public, the Press's pursuit of anything that is bright, entertaining and exciting has brought a mass circulation but almost total disbelief in its opinions or reliability. In 1945 there was virtually an even balance of support for the Labour and Conservative Parties among the London dailies, though the *Daily Mirror* tuned in with the sincere and serious desire for improved conditions better than the *Daily Express*. The studies of the 1950 and 1951 elections use the same words to describe the part played by the Press. Its " treatment . . . was overwhelmingly partisan, relatively demure, and, so far as can be judged, politically ineffective." [59] The national Press took little interest in the 1955 election and though in 1959 much more attention was paid to the campaign, there was also more straight reporting, a tendency which continued in the campaigns of 1964 and 1966. In part this was due to extensive television coverage which gave most citizens some impression of the policies and personalities of leading politicians, impressions which could not be unduly distorted by Press coverage. On the whole, electors seem to judge by the broad facts of their own experience and by the general climate of opinion in the country reacting on their established attitudes and voting patterns. While explicit political propaganda by newspapers has virtually no effect, the overall impression of a party as conveyed by the Press may

---

58 For a description of these conferences, see F. Williams, *Dangerous Estate*, pp. 271–278.
59 H. G. Nicholas, *The General Election of 1950*, p. 145, and D. E. Butler, *The British General Election of 1951*, p. 136.

in time influence the public's image of that party. It cannot be good for the Labour Movement that a fairly large section of the working class electorate derives its few scraps of political information from sources that are hostile to the Labour Party. On the other hand while Mr. Wilson and his government were in the ascendant, he had a very fair Press and far more coverage than his opponents, many newspapermen clearly being fascinated by his capacities and style of government.

The effect, in political terms, of the Press is therefore surprisingly subtle and consists mainly of accelerating and spreading existing trends. While it is almost impossible to create an opinion where there is no initial response, much can be done to confirm and magnify a movement of opinion. While little attention was paid to complaints about conditions in Scotland in the 1950s, once the Scottish National Party began to score electoral successes (such as winning the Hamilton by-election in 1967), the widespread support given by the Scottish Press undoubtedly helped to build up that party. In somewhat the same way, when there began to be talk about replacing Sir Alec Douglas-Home as leader of the Conservative Party, this might have remained private had it not been taken up by the Press and it was an article in the *Sunday Times* by Mr. William Rees-Mogg entitled " Times for a Change " that led Sir Alec to consult his Whips, find out what was happening and decide to go. It is also possible that this " accelerator effect " may be carried too far and the car may stall. If a campaign based on some genuine feeling is pushed to extremes because of the particular involvement of sections of the Press, it may rebound and there is some evidence that the virulence of the attacks on Mr. Wilson in early 1968 may have produced a slight revulsion.

The one other situation in which the popular Press can have some influence is in the exposure of particular instances of bureaucratic negligence or in the conduct of campaigns to remedy a single grievance. Government departments are extremely reluctant to be exposed to newspaper criticism which may stir up questions in Parliament and irritate the minister. Often the Press concentrates on relatively minor matters or on individual cases but there have been some exceptions. The officials in the Service Ministries were very grateful to the Rothermere Press's campaign for rearmament in the 1930s as it was almost the only wind in their sails.[60] Using the same technique, papers can try to weaken an individual politician. Aneurin Bevan lived on controversy, but at times his real views and character were distorted by the sort of publicity he received. On rather a different level, the report of Duff Cooper's impressive resignation speech in 1938 was suppressed by *The Times* and a story substituted under the heading " a damp squib." The safeguard against unfair treatment of individuals is that a person who is newsworthy (and recently much more important, television worthy) cannot be unduly neglected or distorted. On particular events the Press is well aware that it has nothing to gain from so overplaying a situation that readers merely shrug their shoulders.

While most observers agree that popular newspapers have no direct influence on political fortunes some, like Sir William Haley, hold that " indirectly, cumulatively, they are building up an attitude of mind in the new generation which can be disastrous unless it is counteracted." [61] The only research on this subject has been the impressionistic survey by Mr. Richard Hoggart in his *Uses of Literacy*. It seems to show that in catering for the interests of the widest possible numbers, the Press has cultivated the natural and strong desires for material possessions and the " What's in it for me?" reaction to questions affecting the public as a whole. Television has added its influence. The companies inform potential advertisers that people feel comfortable while viewing, they do so as a family when their mutual needs are in mind, and the total effect is to make " Mrs. Smith " all the more eager to buy goods next morning. At recent elections the political parties have tended to concentrate their campaigns not so much on political issues as on what they can do for the voter. The only reservation that can be made about such an argument is that, when a society is dominated by commercial values, it is scarcely fair to ask the Press and television to be the sole bodies to swim against the tide. In one other respect, already mentioned, newspaper techniques may have had an effect on political practices. The constant production of headlines and stories, each of the same vital importance, has probably helped to shorten the public's memory. Each day's sensational

[60] Lord Chatfield repeatedly asserts that it was this campaign that enabled a measure of rearmament to be achieved; *op. cit.*, pp. 83, 192.
[61] Sir William Haley, Clayton Memorial Lecture on *The Public Influence of Broadcasting and the Press*.

stories blot out yesterday's news and "unflappable" politicians have come to realise that it is only necessary to ride out today's storm—it is forgotten tomorrow.

Less space has been devoted to television because it cannot editorialise or slant reporting in the manner of the Press. The B.B.C. is committed to impartiality while the I.T.A. watches over the independent television companies to see that there is complete fairness. Despite this there has been friction. The Conservatives complained about satire programmes in the early 1960s which pilloried Conservative ministers more than their Labour opponents (largely because the ministers were better known and better targets). When Labour came to power in 1964, relations between the Prime Minister and the B.B.C. showed some signs of strain but the main effect of television has been to reduce the disadvantage of the Labour Party in terms of its poorer support in the Press and to give the public a greater first-hand impression of politics and a return to political controversy. It was to bring the House of Commons back into the centre of political controversy from the public's point of view, to make it rather than the television studio the forum of debate, that a proposal was made to televise and show parts of the proceedings of the House. On a free vote this was lost by one in 1966 but it is hard to imagine that in time the more exciting and informative exchanges in the House will not be televised, a change which would help to restore the reputation of the House and revive the importance as opinion-formers of the exchanges and arguments that take place there.

THE PUBLIC

The great objective of any government is to increase its standing with the electorate, but its methods of finding out how it is being regarded and where it is erring were haphazard or non-existent before the advent of opinion polls. Usually governments relied on the general atmosphere in the country, the tone of certain newspapers and the reports coming up from M.P.s and constituency associations. During the early stages of the war the Home Intelligence Division submitted a weekly report on the state of public feeling. This was soon found to be worthless if not misleading. It was collected by a panel of informants (like the B.B.C.'s listener research system) and tended to exaggerate petty grievances. The only thing that did worry the British public was the occasional suspicion that they were not being told the truth or that unpalatable facts were being suppressed.

Most politicians worked on their own contacts and a " hunch " as to the public's reactions. Mr. Attlee used to consider that George Tomlinson had an intuitive knowledge of what the people of Lancashire would accept. Asked for his opinion in Cabinet, Tomlinson would say that he had tried to convince his wife on this point but had failed and that was the end of the matter. The trouble with such inspired guesses is that they can be wildly wrong. Neville Chamberlain tended to plant his views on *The Times* and then convince himself that the paper was an accurate reflection of public opinion. In the early years of the war, it became evident that Conservative politicians and senior civil servants were completely mistaken in their estimate of what the average citizen would accept in the shape of discomfort and disappointment just as Labour Ministers erred in the late 1940s in neglecting the widespread weariness over rationing and austerity.

One opportunity of testing the political temperature is at by-elections and these often assume considerable importance. The news of the failure of the Coalition candidate at Newport came just in time to exercise some influence at the Carlton Club meeting in October 1922. Stanley Baldwin's leadership was at issue in the St. George's by-election in 1930 and the defeat of the official candidate (Duff Cooper) would have been a serious blow to him. At the East Fulham by-election, the Labour vote rose by 10,000, the Conservative's fell by 9,000, and G. M. Young considered that " the shock had broken Baldwin's nerve." [62] But here again, much depends on the state of the politician's nerves. Baldwin knew that by-elections tend to show a bigger swing against the government than general elections. The Conservative candidate at Twickenham in June 1934 advocated rearmament and increased his majority, yet there was no sign of a resurgence of confidence on the part of the Prime Minister. Bad by-election results can be and are discounted between general elections but they do have an effect on the morale of the parties and, going beyond a certain level, may begin to look like omens for the next general election. It was a startling by-election victory at Orpington in 1962 that

---

[62] G. M. Young, *Stanley Baldwin*, p. 177. The Labour candidate advocated collective security and general disarmament.

gave some short semblance of credibility to the Liberal revival while it was news that the Conservative vote was likely to fall catastrophically in the North East Leicester by-election that precipitated Mr. Macmillan's purge of his Cabinet. In the same way an increased majority at North Hull gave Mr. Wilson the signal to hold the 1966 General Election while the mood of the Labour Party in 1967–68 and Mr. Wilson's difficulties were due not just to the outcome of government policies but to their reception in the form of a series of disastrous by-election defeats.

Very occasionally a section of the public have manifested their views by open activity or demonstration. In early 1935 the unemployed in certain areas put up such a resistance to the rates proposed by the Unemployment Board that they had to be postponed and introduced later in slow stages. The Campaign for Nuclear Disarmament in the late 1950s developed its own techniques of drawing and manifesting large-scale support but it has proved extremely hard to affect politics by such campaigns. Outside agencies or pressure groups have tended to find it easier to ally with the main parties unless they have a corner in a particular electorate (such as the Welsh and Scottish nationalists) where it is a less enormous task to make an impact and overcome the loyalties and habits of voters.

The one instance in this century when some politicians have claimed that public opinion actually diverted them from the policies they would have preferred to follow was over the matter of rearmament between 1934 and 1938. On November 12, 1936, Stanley Baldwin in a reflective speech asked himself this question:

> " Supposing I had gone to the country and said that Germany was rearming and we must rearm, does anybody think that this pacific democracy would have rallied to that cry at that moment? I cannot think of anything that would have made the loss of the election from any point of view more certain."

The time to which Baldwin was referring was October 1933 when the East Fulham by-election took place. Those who defend Baldwin and Chamberlain argue that they wanted to rearm but that the country would not look at such a policy. This is true in that at any given moment between 1933 and 1938, a sudden announcement that defence was now going to receive the highest priority would have aroused an outcry. Yet governments with large and loyal majorities can survive momentary unpopularity, provided they keep educating the public and provided that events justify their stand. Conservative ministers could not claim that they lacked support among party enthusiasts in the constituencies, for the Annual Conference had regarded the state of the nation's defences with " grave anxiety " since 1933. Nor can they say that they lacked professional advice, for the Service Chiefs pressed their case to the verge of resignation. Virtually every major event in international politics could have been used, with regret and proper reluctance, to show that " this pacific democracy " was being driven to prepare its own defences. Lord Templewood (then Sir Samuel Hoare) has argued that there was no mandate for rearmament in 1933 and 1934. Yet this did not stop an increase in money spent on the Air Force in 1934, and when Neville Chamberlain cut the requirements of the Service Chiefs from £78 million to £50 million, it was because he did not think the extra arms were necessary. Even on Hoare's theory a partial mandate existed after the general election of 1935 and no real rearmament took place till 1938.

To plead the pressure of public opinion is only possible on the grounds that the Labour Opposition, which was far more hostile to rearmament, would have gathered all the uncommitted voters and swept the country if the government had undertaken a major defence programme. Put most clearly by A. W. Baldwin, this case presents the Prime Minister in a most unfavourable light, forced to follow a policy he did not like for fear of the public reaction.[63] The imputation is not really fair to Baldwin and is certainly not true of Neville Chamberlain, who never lacked courage.

The real explanation of the refusal to rearm was not public opinion but that neither Baldwin nor Chamberlain was convinced of the reality of the German menace and neither was prepared to give defence first priority. It was Chamberlain who scaled down the programme of 1934. Then the Service experts proposed a White Paper in order to educate the public to the danger. The ministers, however, did not accept the need for such a process and they re-edited the paper. One official protested to Baldwin that " the chief trend of the Cabinet variations is to weaken the warning which I have always imagined it is common ground that our public

63 In *My Father, The True Story*.

badly needs." [64] Both Tom Jones and G. M. Young point out that in 1935 Baldwin still did not believe that rearmament was necessary.[65] Neville Chamberlain agreed to some more money being spent on aircraft in the spring of 1935 but wrote: "I have been greatly alarmed at some of the proposals, which appeared to me panicky and wasteful." [66]

In such a frame of mind, episodes that could have several interpretations all served to confirm the views of senior ministers. The Peace Ballot was quoted to show the ingrained pacifism of the country, though ten out of eleven million answers favoured economic sanctions against an aggressor and over six million were prepared for military sanctions. The East Fulham by-election remained "a nightmare" for Baldwin while the much steadier results (from a Conservative viewpoint) of 1934 counted for nothing. The outburst of public indignation over the Hoare-Laval pact showed that there was a great reservoir of resentment against the claims of the dictators which could have been tapped by a Premier wishing to rearm. After the 1935 election, there were five clear years in which a government with a massive majority could have developed its policies.

In fact it did so, and the policy, based on the genuine beliefs of the senior ministers, was that there should be only a limited degree of rearmament and that it should have a low priority in the government's programme. In February 1936 Chamberlain recorded that "I have had to do most of the work on the [defence] programme, which has been materially modified as a result...." [67] Lord Ismay says that nothing was possible in 1936 since defence was not a matter of concern to the Cabinet nor did it have the support of the Prime Minister.[68] Duff Cooper spoke on the need to stand in close support of France and had an unfavourable reaction as "minds had not been prepared by the Government or by the Press to accept the idea that any immediate danger existed." [69] As Mr. Churchill has observed, "the government adhered to their policy of moderation, half-measures, and keeping things quiet." [70] Not till 1938 did the policy of the Prime Minister

---

[64] G. M. Young, *op. cit.*, p. 194.
[65] *Ibid.*, p. 200, and Tom Jones, *Diary with Letters*, p. 156.
[66] K. Feiling, *op. cit.*, p. 259.
[67] *Ibid.*, p. 313.
[68] Lord Ismay, *Memoirs*, p. 75.
[69] D. Cooper, *Old Men Forget*, p. 204.
[70] Churchill, *op. cit.*, Vol. I, p. 147.

(by then Neville Chamberlain) begin to change, and though re-armament was reluctant and not emphasised, a positive start was made.

The point of this analysis has been to repudiate the quite false picture of a dominant and opinionated public forcing a British government to suppress facts and avoid policies it would have liked to pursue. Tom Jones, who entirely sympathised with Baldwin, was sure that he "might have confronted the pacifists in all parties with a more vigorous and earlier policy of rearmament" had he so desired.[71] The Chairman of the Chiefs of Staff Committee realised that "to lead the country into rearmament publicly and with determination, the first thing necessary was conviction in the Government's mind that the moment for rearmament had not only arrived but was urgent. . . . As far as I can judge, there was insufficient conviction."[72] The defence of Baldwin and Chamberlain is not that they were unable to act for fear of hostile reactions, but that they had their own assessment as to what were the correct policies to be pursued, and were wrong.

CONCLUSION

Governments in Britain have a wide area of action open to them and the electorate judges by the total record and by their own recent conditions of life. Governments watch their conduct constantly in order to improve their standing, though unpopularity can easily be survived if policies are justified by events. Relatively little attention is paid to the arguments of the opposition. The main factors influencing governments are the views of the men and organisations which contribute the ideas, the personnel and the finances of the party. Apart from this, rank-and-file members in the constituencies have to be kept, as far as possible, united and enthusiastic, and most governments pay close attention to the reactions of their supporters in the House of Commons. Governments which fall totally out of step with their own voters or whose policies have a disastrous effect on a substantial section of the electorate can expect retribution but each ministry knows that provided it has a majority in the House of Commons, it has upwards of five years with substantial scope to carry out its policies.

---

[71] Tom Jones, *op. cit.*, p. 35.   [72] Lord Chatfield, *op. cit.*, p. 195.

CHAPTER 24

CONCLUSION AND CRITICISMS

THIS book has tried to present a picture of the decision-making process at the top of British government, of who has power and what limitations are encountered in its exercise. The views put forward are accepted by almost all present and past members of the Cabinet. Sir Anthony Eden has said that

"A Prime Minister is still nominally *primus inter pares*, but in fact his authority is stronger than that. The right to choose his colleagues, to ask for a dissolution of Parliament and, if he is a Conservative, to appoint the chairman of the party organisation, add up to a formidable total of power." [1]

Tom Jones who, as Assistant Secretary to the Cabinet, had worked closely with four Premiers concluded that " the step from being a Cabinet Minister to being a Prime Minister is a long one." [2]

Lord Butler, asked about this specific point said

" I think that on the whole the Prime Minister has tended to stop being an equal among equals. There is a tendency not exactly to dictatorship . . . but to be the leader who does control everything, and things are getting more and more into his own hands." [3]

The same point put to Sir Alec Douglas-Home (then Lord Home) produced this response:

" Every Cabinet Minister is in a sense the Prime Minister's agent—his assistant. There's no question about that. It is the Prime Minister's Cabinet, and he is the one person who is directly responsible to the Queen for what the Cabinet does. If the Cabinet discusses anything it is the Prime Minister who decides what the collective view of the Cabinet is. A Minister's job is to save the Prime Minister all the work he can. But no Minister could make a really important move without consulting the Prime Minister, and if the Prime

[1] Sir Anthony Eden, *op. cit.*, p. 269.
[2] Tom Jones, *op. cit.*
[3] *The Listener*, September 16, 1965.

Minister wanted to take a certain step the Cabinet Minister concerned would either have to agree, argue it out in Cabinet, or resign." [4]

This analysis does not belittle the position of the Cabinet or write off its importance as a group. Mr. Crossman goes far too far when he says that

"with the coming of Prime Ministerial government, the Cabinet, in obedience to the law that Bagehot discovered, joins the other dignified elements in the Constitution." [5]

The point is that the Cabinet is no longer the nineteenth-century body which took virtually all decisions, where legislation was worked out, the parliamentary programme devised and in which ministers could raise any issue. The changes in party organisation, the volume of business and the subject-matter of politics have put great powers in the hands of the Prime Minister and have introduced a series of levels at which decisions are made. The Prime Minister may share much with an inner group varying in membership, depending on the issue in question, or he may deal directly with individual ministers or the Cabinet.

In this structure, the Cabinet is the place where certain categories of decisions are taken, disagreements ironed out and compromises registered but the principal policies of a government may not be and often are not originated in Cabinet. The key decisions of Mr. Macmillan's government to seek a summit meeting with Russia, America and France, to try to enter the Common Market and to go for industrial expansion, though shared with certain key ministers, were in a real sense his own. Similarly the central policies of Mr. Wilson's first three years, again to mediate on Vietnam, to retain a presence East of Suez, to enter Europe and to defend the existing parity of the pound, though concerted with Mr. Brown or Mr. Callaghan, were his policies rather than those of the whole Cabinet. When a member of the Cabinet who wished to devalue the pound soon after Labour took office and in July 1966 was later asked if a change of economic strategy was ever discussed in the Cabinet, he said "No. And in any case I am keeping my head below the parapet." This was one of the policies that was above or beyond the Cabinet and when it was

4 *The Observer*, August 23, 1961.
5 R. H. S. Crossman ed., *Walter Bagehot: The English Constitution*, Fontana, 1963, p. 54.

adopted in November 1967, the decision was taken by Mr. Wilson and Mr. Callaghan and reported to the Cabinet.

The importance of the Cabinet is, as has been indicated, that it reconciles, records and authorises. It is the place where Mr. Douglas Jay and the anti-Common Market members made their last stand and where the cuts in public spending were allocated in January 1968. While there is a marked hierarchy within the Cabinet, not to be a member is a very big step down. The non-Cabinet minister coming in to make his case does not know the atmosphere and cannot detect whether a laugh is because he has gone for far too much or far too little. He feels an outsider. The minister with a major department, especially if it needs little new money or inter-departmental consultation, feels, quite rightly, that he has an empire to rule over where his untrammelled word is law. These are the men who have little experience of the take-overs when the Prime Minister moves in to handle foreign affairs, economic development or the negotiations in a key labour dispute. Below the ministers of all kinds and ranks, there are the civil servants who are the full time experts, who know that they have only to last till the next reshuffle in a year or two when a new, less experienced and perhaps less opinionated minister may take over. Not that they always want such a person. If they have schemes they want to further, they may be hoping for the able, determined type of politician.

This then is the distribution of power at the upper reaches of government in Britain. It is quite misleading to call it Presidential because this draws in American analogies where the party system is looser, there is a fixed term of office and no immediate dependence on Congress. It is a comparison which obscures and misleads rather than helps any understanding of the position. On the other hand, to pretend that nothing has changed since the days of Gladstone and Disraeli is equally misleading. Only Mr. Ronald Butt in his *The Power of Parliament* [6] has challenged the account of nineteenth-century Parliaments given in this book. He tries to argue that Parliament never had as much power as has been suggested in the 1830 to 1880 period, the object of the argument being largely to support his later assertion that its position has not declined.

[6] Constable, 1967.

The difficulty with this case is the facts. In that half century, the House of Commons sacked Cabinets, it removed individual ministers, it forced the government to disclose information, it set up select committees to carry out investigations and frame Bills and it rewrote government Bills on the floor of the House. Disraeli, it is true, in the 1840s claimed that this was an aberration and that party ties were neglected. But this was special pleading unacceptable to most of his contemporaries, put forward simply because the only accusation he could level at Sir Robert Peel, who had sought the best interests of the country, was that he was guilty of betraying his party.

All the other criticisms of the first edition of this book concentrated on the analysis of the Cabinet itself or the modern role of the House of Commons. The first objections came from the late Lord Morrison and Mr. D. N. Chester who were replying to comments on their own earlier work. The comments were that:

> The only authorities who present a markedly different picture (to that of *The British Cabinet*) are Mr. D. N. Chester in Chapter 2 of *British Government Since 1918* and Lord Morrison in his *Government and Parliament*. The similarity between the views of these two authors is striking and differs from that presented in this book less on matters of fact than of emphasis. The reason for the difference is that Mr. Chester and Lord Morrison both set out to describe the machinery of the Cabinet rather than to ask where power lies. They outline the membership of the Cabinet, the tasks of the various ministers and standing committees, and the history of the Secretariat, the total effect being to supplement but not in any way revise the traditional view of the Cabinet as the effective centre of government. A description like that of Mr. Chester which focuses attention on actual bodies can be correct in every item and yet tend to omit matters of influence, of relative weight, and of informal practice. It neglects the power of the Prime Minister and the importance of such habits as talks on an informal basis to settle matters outside or before Cabinet meetings. It is curious that Lord Morrison, who in his political career showed such a brilliant intuitive appreciation of where power lay, should write in the same way. He does not try and estimate just what the function of the Cabinet is,

how much it sees, and at what stage, or whether it actually takes the major decisions. Lord Morrison, however, goes further than neglecting the power of the Prime Minister. He positively rates the Premier as essentially a co-ordinating minister whose position differs only in degree from that of other non-departmental ministers like the Lord President of the Council. He repeats the old estimate that the Premier is *primus inter pares.*[7]

Mr. Chester replied [8] by defending Lord Morrison's account of what business should or should not go to the Cabinet, arguing that it would have applied equally well in the 1850s or 1860s. This is not surprising as Morrison's criterion was simply that important matters should be referred to the Cabinet. The real issue here is that in the earlier period all such questions could be and usually were talked over and settled in Cabinet (Gladstone's agenda for Cabinets confirm this point) while recently some important measures and policies, such as the 1944 Education Bill and the Munich and Suez negotiations, either were not put to the Cabinet or were referred to it simply for confirmation. In addition to these major lines of policy, many other issues which would previously have merited Cabinet deliberation are now settled in the departments or in Cabinet Committees. Another historical objection of a rather different kind was put by R. T. Mackenzie who has said that Gladstone and Disraeli may well have exercised an ascendancy equal to that of a modern Premier. But this raises the question of the kind of ascendancy;—was it over the machinery of government, over Cabinet colleagues, over the House of Commons or over the electorate? Only in the last instance is there any evidence to support the case. Time and again both these Prime Ministers had to make policies in the Cabinet and have them remade there by the interaction of other ministers. Disraeli's inability to formulate a policy on the Eastern Question in 1877 was because of the differences in the Cabinet, his need to take every step in full meetings contrasts with Sir Anthony Eden's capacity to act either on his own or through a like-minded Cabinet Committee at the time of Suez. Premiers a hundred years ago had to consult over promotions and the timing of dissolutions,

[7] Herbert Morrison, *op. cit.*, p. 37.
[8] D. N. Chester, "Who Governs Britain?" *Parliamentary Affairs*, Vol. XV, No. 4, p. 522.

Gladstone had to collect voices over Irish problems and the 1870 Education Bill in a manner which made the Cabinet the real centre of policy-making. Finally, despite all their oratorical gifts and the beginnings of party organisation, both of them had to listen to the views of the House of Commons. Disraeli recast the 1867 Reform Bill on the floor of the House, the Fourth Party chivied and obstructed Gladstone in a manner only exceeded by the Irish and he was the last Premier who had to resign because a number of his normal back-bench supporters decided (in the summer of 1885) that they would rather have another ministry in office.

In fact, Chester and Morrison almost completely accepted the historical argument and concentrated their criticisms on two aspects of the account of the modern relations and roles of the Prime Minister, the Cabinet and the other relevant institutions of central government. Both argued that the description of Prime Ministerial government underestimated the powers of the House of Commons. Morrison in his review in *The Daily Herald* first made the old formal point that the Commons "can force resignation (of a government) or even dissolution," [9] and his two examples were the resignations of Neville Chamberlain in 1940 and of Lloyd George in 1922. These have both been discussed in detail above (pp. 429–31) and in fact Morrison conceded that these are rare occurrences and that the real question is the influence of individual M.P.s, groups, party meetings and the opposition on the government. D. N. Chester did not go into the question in detail (in *Parliamentary Affairs*, Autumn 1962), simply saying that there was not enough evidence presented to allow a comparison of the 1890s with the 1950s. If this is a criticism of *The British Cabinet* as a book, it is fair to point out that Chester was only referring to the treatment of the contemporary House of Commons and appears to neglect the lengthy examination of the power or influence of Parliament in the 1832–67 and 1867–1914 periods.

If this is a more general statement that there have not been enough detailed studies of the impact of Parliament on government now or in the nineteenth century, it has some force. Too many of the standard works are still legalistic and discuss how the two Houses work rather than take up the more difficult question of what difference having to govern in part through the House of

---

[9] *The Daily Herald*, March 23, 1962.

Commons has made to the policies of particular governments. Important contributions have, however, been made by P. G. Richards, Professors Crick, Hanson and Wiseman among others and the estimate of the power of the Commons which they produce fits in with the general thesis advanced in *The British Cabinet*. They accept that the opposition has little direct influence and that to estimate the influence of the House, it is necessary to collect a list of instances of the kind above (pp. 585–6). Some students, such as Mr. Ronald Butt in the second section of his *Power of Parliament* may collect a few more or less, but the general assumptions about the way Parliament operates is the same. If the future analysis of the two Houses of Parliament continues in these terms, whether a few more or a few less instances of influence are discovered and even when other aspects of the parliamentary system, such as the effect of good or bad performances by individual politicians on their own careers, are added in, the total result is entirely compatible with, indeed is a cause of the changes in, the position of the Cabinet and of the Prime Minister's increased authority which were described in *The British Cabinet*.

The other main criticism by D. N. Chester is of lack of precision. He asserts that it is not clear exactly what is being said in *The British Cabinet* and quotes the first phrase (" the country is governed by the Prime Minister . . .") of a paragraph originally on page 451 to summarise the position. Similarly he takes a single phrase out of the one other paragraph-long description of the general argument which was on the dust cover of the book " that Britain is not governed by the Cabinet . . ." and can then submit with little difficulty that, having excluded all the qualifying sentences and clauses, much remains to be said. Indeed he then places these few words taken out of context alongside the qualifications that a Prime Minister is not " the master of his Cabinet " and that Premiers have to " consider the views of . . . colleagues and work with them " and effects surprise at a contrast which is entirely of his own devising. The core of this accusation of imprecision, which is intended to cast doubt on the whole argument of the book, comes out in the comments on the sentence that " this is not Presidential Government because the Premier can, in exceptional circumstances, be removed and he will collapse if deserted by all his colleagues or by his party." Mr. Chester says " the use of the word ' removed ' is strange." He asks " What is meant by

' exceptional circumstances '? Why must he be deserted by ' all ' his colleagues before he collapses?"

The criticism is easy to make because, in dealing with any complex series of inter-relationships of this kind, no precise answer can be given. But when all the available examples have been examined (as on pp. 428–35, above) the weight of evidence does suggest that British Prime Ministers are in a position of very great strength as against their colleagues and within the whole framework of British Government. The meaning of " exceptional circumstances " is as precise as the words can be. Since 1900 Prime Ministers have resigned either after electoral defeat or because of ill-health on fifteen occasions, they have only been driven from office on three occasions. These were Asquith's replacement by Lloyd George in 1916, Lloyd George's by Baldwin in 1922 and Chamberlain's resignation in 1940. Two occurred at moments of national crisis in wartime and the third when the Prime Minister was leading a Coalition, a majority of whom belonged to another party. It would be hard to find a better brief method of characterising these three as compared with the fifteen regular or normal changes of Prime Minister except by saying that they occurred under " exceptional circumstances."

In Chapter Twenty, above, the difficulty, indeed the virtual impossibility of removing a Prime Minister who has a majority and is in good health has been analysed. A coup would require a background of national crisis or disaster and a quite extraordinary measure of agreement and solidarity among the other members of the Cabinet or among back-bench supporters of the government. It is reasonable to point out that " all " Mr. Wilson's colleagues need not threaten to resign to force his hand. If Mr. Shore was not among the resigners, this would make little difference and on the precise number needed no figure can be given. If all did desert, it would be fatal. If three ministers resign over a given policy it can be dismissed as " a little local difficulty." Under pressure of adverse circumstances, a Prime Minister can sack seven of the twenty-one members of his Cabinet. Who can then be precise about how many ministers would have had to have resigned or to have threatened resignation to bring down Macmillan in 1963 or Wilson in 1968? It would depend on the political situation and who the ministers were, but there would have to be such a combination in such desperate circumstances that it is barely possible to imagine the situation. This is not precise but is it not an adequate indication of the strength of a modern Prime Minister?

A later and elaborate criticism has come from G. W. Jones (in *Parliamentary Affairs*, Spring 1965) who takes all the points made by any author in supporting the case that Prime Ministers' powers have increased, lumps them all together, exaggerates them and then claims that this is going too far. But in demolishing the edifice thus created, Mr. Jones does not wish simply to remove extravagant claims but goes much further arguing that " the restraints on his (the Prime Minister's) ascendancy are as strong as ever, and in some ways even stronger." [10]

The exaggerated version of the Prime Minister's powers starts with the view that general elections are a plebiscite for one party leader or another and " thus the only mandate given to an M.P. is to support his leader." [11] The power to distribute patronage, to hold a dissolution and the whipping system all ensure total support for the Premier by a subservient majority; " his will becomes an Act of Parliament." [12] The same means enable the Prime Minister to " master his Cabinet " and " to have a free hand in managing its operations." [13] Each individual minister has become " the public relations man for his department, and the errand boy for the Prime Minister " while the latter's position as the First Lord of the Treasury provides further patronage which " enables his will to prevail in Whitehall." [14]

Having given this extreme account, which corresponds to the views of no single author, Mr. Jones has no difficulty in showing its errors. But, after demonstrating that this series of propositions is exaggerated, it is suggested that this disproves even a moderate or reasonable statement of the case and further, Mr. Jones introduces a series of new errors. For instance, election studies agree that the voter has a compound image of each party in which the leader plays a variable but not predominant part. But to conclude from this that " there is no mandate on the M.P.s to support their leaders " does not follow. [15] M.P.s know they are

[10] G. W. Jones, " The Prime Minister's Power," *Parliamentary Affairs*, Spring 1965, p. 167.
[11] *Ibid.*, p. 175.
[12] *Ibid.*, p. 169.
[13] *Ibid.*, p. 170.
[14] *Ibid.*, pp. 172–173.
[15] *Ibid.*, p. 175.

elected primarily because they carry a party label, not for their own opinions, and they feel an obligation and a necessity of supporting the party unless once again there are " exceptional circumstances." The effect is to give tremendous strength to the leaders of the party and to the Prime Minister. It is reasonable to state that " neither inside nor outside Parliament are the parties tamely sub-servient to the will of the Prime Minister " [16] (why use a loaded word like " tamely "?), but this does not alter the fact that skilful management usually gets its way so that the Labour Party can be persuaded to take Part IV of the Prices and Incomes Bill and the Conservatives to abolish Resale Price Maintenance. Mr. Jones says " a revolt is not completely out of the question." [17] No political observer could possibly suggest that party revolts were " out of the question," indeed they occur regularly. The real issue is how far they form an effective means of checking or changing the policies of the executive. No Prime Minister wants revolts and he will head them off, meet the objectors and ask ministers to explain particular points, but if the disagreement persists, those running the revolt may decide to stage a public demonstration. Yet it is significant that if this involves abstentions in an important division, the critics usually will organise and keep the number of abstentions down to a level which will allow them to make their point without in any way endangering the Government. Once again this is not personal loyalty to the Prime Minister but as he is the head of the Government, it strengthens his hand.

It is moving from exaggeration to positive error to say that " the most important factions in both parties are those which coalesce around the main figures . . . the Prime Minister's colleagues are his rivals, eager to replace him, and he is engaged in a constant battle to fend them off." [18] This is far too reminiscent of eighteenth-century politics and the groups which gather round individual politicians nowadays seldom outlast particular situations. In part this is because the Prime Minister's drawing power is too great and the others have no patronage to offer, in part because support is in terms of capacity to fill a job. Three months after Wilson beat Brown for the Labour leadership, there was no Brown party or group, the Callaghan support had disappeared overnight and

[16] *Idem.*
[17] *Idem.*
[18] *Ibid.*, p. 176.

this situation has not changed. The explanation in part was that Mr. Wilson's performance was very good but also that most members' loyalties are not to individuals but to the party. It is legitimate to gather round one of three candidates for the leadership while it is open for election, but once Wilson was chosen, loyalty to the party and success in the struggle for power with the Tories meant backing the existing, chosen leader.

A few backbenchers could be found in late 1967 who would declare that Roy Jenkins should be the next Prime Minister, but they were literally thinking of the time when Mr. Wilson's health failed or a further economic disaster occurred. They would not have marched or counter-marched at that time on the orders of Mr. Jenkins and he would not have tried to command them. If ministerial revolts are ever considered, they do not count up their back-bench supporters. No one can tell how the vast majority of non-committed M.P.s, whose chief loyalty is to the party, would react. The few revolts of this kind that have been contemplated (such as the discussion to to whether Attlee should go in 1947) assumed that there would be no appeal to the back-benches. The extreme difficulties of coups of this kind have been discussed and none have succeeded since 1916.

Mr. Jones's suggestion that television allows front-benchers " to win, consolidate and encourage a personal following " in the country which can be used against the Prime Minister can equally be scouted.[19] The Prime Minister (and the Leader of the Opposition) control who appears on behalf of their parties and each appears far more often than their senior colleagues. The comparison with the past here is also revealing. A hundred years ago with verbatim reporting of the Commons debates, front-benchers and some back-benchers were household names. Now, unless an M.P. is given a post, it is hard to become prominent and one of Mr. Heath's problems is that the members of his Shadow Cabinet who were not senior ministers before 1964 remain virtually unknown.

The combination of this exaggerated emphasis on constant ministerial manoeuvring to replace the Prime Minister, of the overestimate of the powers of the House of Commons and of the readiness of back-benchers to give steady support to possible claimants for the Premiership leads to such remarks as " if a

[19] *Ibid.*, p. 177.

back-bench revolt found a spokesman of leadership calibre, who could win the backing of his other close colleagues, then the Prime Minister would be in a very insecure position." [20]

To form an accurate estimate of how far this possibility exists and is a normal check on the powers of the Prime Minister, the mechanics of the procedure have to be examined. Spokesmen who constitute real threats cannot today arise from the back-benchers. Mr. Michael Foot and Mr. Woodrow Wyatt, Sir Gerald Nabarro and Lord Lambton are listened to but are no great danger. The only possible start for such an operation is when a minister resigns on a major issue. But when this happens all the forces of party loyalty (which are not personal loyalty to the Prime Minister but which aid him so long as he is leader) turn on the resigner. Realising this, most of those who leave do not even try to press the issue. Mr. Thorneycroft, who was "the little local difficulty" in early 1958, remained very quiet. When resigning ministers do raise a storm, the effect is to press a case and not necessarily to menace the Prime Minister. The Bevanite group in its early days while Labour was still in power wanted certain policy concessions. To have got them might have led to Gaitskell's resignation as Chancellor of the Exchequer but not necessarily or even probably to Attlee's replacement. Since March 1966 Mr. Christopher Mayhew has tried to rouse the Parliamentary Labour Party to an appreciation of his case against the East of Suez defence policy. Some ministers almost certainly agreed with him, but they were arguing the matter at appropriate times within the Government, they had no intention of starting a "Wilson-must-go" movement. Nor did Mr. Mayhew and the rather mixed group of back-benchers who agreed with him have any such desire. They simply wanted to modify either expenditure or commitments east of Suez and were glad when economic necessity proved them right. In the late 1930s when Mr. Eden resigned from Neville Chamberlain's Cabinet, he did not add his weight to that of the critics but even if he had, there is no evidence that a Churchill-Eden combination could have deflected the Prime Minister from his policy or have threatened his personal position. The last time when a leading party figure might have combined with back-bench support to threaten the leadership of his party was when Austen Chamberlain had doubts about the Hoare-Laval pact and the conduct of Stanley Baldwin in dismissing Sir Samuel Hoare. Had he been willing to press his criticisms at a meeting of the 1922 Committee, this might well have had an effect, but the efficacy of this type of proceeding as a regular check on Prime Ministers must be estimated in the light of the fact that this was the last occasion when it was a serious possibility.

A similar analysis has to be undertaken for each of a series of statements such as " The Prime Minister is not the master of his party. Leaders can lose their parties' support and be toppled. They lead only with the sufference and by the courtesy of their followers. A Prime Minister is only as strong as his party, and particularly his chief colleagues, lets him be." [21] Such statements may be legally correct—for instance, the House of Commons *can* topple a government just as the monarch *can* refuse a request for a dissolution. The last statement is a truism in that leaders who are as strong as their parties allow them to be may be very strong. Moreover, the suggestion that the degree of power is what is permitted by colleagues or the party, though true in one sense, gives a very wrong impression of the balance of forces involved. Finally, as a description of the realities of political power such statements are worthless unless backed by examples, for one must know when and how often these limitations have been imposed and how far they are present as serious possibilities in the minds of current political leaders.

The lack of concrete examples comes out when Mr. Jones says that Prime Ministers may be forced to give " careerists . . . who argue with great force " office to quieten down their attacks.[22] It is true that Prime Ministers sometimes like to spread their patronage, giving a little to different sections in the party, but there is not a single case in this century of a man whom the Prime Minister wishes to exclude from office forcing his way in, the concession being made to stop his attacks in the House or at party meetings. Such attacks are simply not that dangerous.

On the assertion that " through their specialist Committees M.P.s have opportunities for gaining expertise in the work of particular departments and can therefore keep significant checks on the policy of the Government," the evidence has been scarce

[21] *Ibid.*, p. 178.
[22] *Idem.*

because the committees are supposed to operate in private.[23]
However, these committees have been seriously overestimated in
the recent literature on Parliament (see particularly Hill and
Whichelow, *What's Wrong with Parliament?*) and this overestimate
is carried somewhat further by Mr. Jones. Back-bench committees
are open to all members of the parties not merely in the sense of
joining in the first instance but in that meetings are listed on the
Whip and any member can turn up at any committee. Without a
fixed membership, the committee engage on no fixed course of
study or investigation and merely have odd persons to talk to them,
the attendance shooting up if a minister comes and dropping away
if it is some non-political expert. On the Conservative side they
are better served in that each committee has a full-time secretary
who will prepare briefs for those interested and some Conservative
ministers have handled their back-benchers carefully. On the
Labour side two officials share the task of taking minutes at all
the committees and no briefing or documentation is provided.
Some of the most able and ambitious back-benchers on both sides
refuse to attend any of these gatherings, regarding them simply as
a waste of time. By no stretch of the imagination could they be
described as offering " opportunities for gaining expertise in the
work of particular departments."

As a third example, where some evidence is given, but the
deductions are weak, Mr. Jones argues that because an incoming
Prime Minister usually appoints to ministries the persons who
watched over these subjects in the Shadow Cabinet, this indicates
a lack of freedom of manoeuvre. In fact the Prime Minister, when
Leader of the Opposition, himself allocated these men to their
various tasks and since he wants the most effective team possible,
then and after entering office, it is not surprising that few changes
are made. What is significant is that even when the most powerful lieutenants make their desires absolutely plain, they can be
chopped and changed at will by the Prime Minister. Thus Mr.
Attlee planned to put Ernest Bevin at the Exchequer and Dalton
at the Foreign Office (a disposition which both of them expected)
and then reversed this a few hours later without consultation. Mr.
Wilson on taking office in 1964 swopped Mr. Stewart and Mr.
Crossman, each of whom had anticipated getting the subject they

23 *Ibid.*, p. 180.

had dealt with in the Shadow Cabinet and when Mr. Callaghan in July 1966 made it quite clear he wanted to leave the Exchequer for the Foreign Office, Mr. Wilson flatly refused and made his own dispositions. Mr. Jones seeks to belittle the revelation of Prime Ministerial authority when Mr. Macmillan sacked seven of the twenty-one members of his Cabinet in July 1962 by saying that " none of those axed had a reputation for being awkward or nuisances or opponents of the Prime Minister. They were removed because they were easy targets and appeared to have no significant following among the remaining leading Cabinet Ministers or the M.P.s generally." [24] But the motive for removal was not the capricious one of " lack of following." Mr. Macmillan removed those who, he felt, gave the Government a tired air although Mr. Selwyn Lloyd was among the most personally popular members of the Cabinet. Had a further batch insisted on resigning in sympathy, Mr. Macmillan's position might have become difficult; but in the end his colleagues and the Party accepted this extreme demonstration of personal power.

The same type of criticism applies to Mr. Jones' account of the internal balance of power within and conduct of Cabinet meetings. Of course no Prime Minister requires obedience from his Cabinet. These are men drawn from the same party working together towards the same end and the real issue is not a crude one of the Premier bulldozing or hoodwinking or ignoring members. The question is how far decisions are taken in the departments, in smaller meetings and in committees and are merely reported to the Cabinet. And the suggestion is not that the Cabinet would rise in wrath if it heard what had happened—it would almost always agree—but the point is that the role of the Cabinet and the way decisions are taken have changed and changed in a manner which leaves more influence and power of initiative with the Prime Minister. Thus the fact that the decision to produce atomic weapons was taken in the Defence Committee of the Cabinet and passed as an agreed item through the full Cabinet (so rapidly that most members did not recall it being discussed) supports rather than disproves the revised account of how the Cabinet works. Similarly to say that a majority of the Conservative Cabinet accepted the Suez policy is beside the point, the

[24] *Ibid.*, p. 180.

significant fact is that the planning and execution of the policy was taken into the hands of a special Committee of the Cabinet.

Mr. Jones seeks to discount Sir Alec Douglas-Home's remark quoted above (pp. 610–11) from his interview with Mr. Harris in *The Observer*.[25] He says this statement may say something about the then Earl of Home's relations with Mr. Macmillan but little more and that " it has long been the custom for the Prime Minister to be virtually his own Foreign Minister." [26] Whatever Mr. Jones may think, when Sir Alec Douglas-Home said "*Every* Cabinet Minister is in a sense the Prime Minister's agent . . ." he meant *every minister* and was describing the relationship between the Premier and all the other ministers, a description which he does not withdraw after a further year as Foreign Secretary and another year as Prime Minister.[27] And the significant point about Prime Ministers often taking over the conduct of foreign affairs is not that this is in some way customary, but that they do so because of the importance of the subject. And when they so desire, they can take over other issues as when Mr. Wilson turned to handle the seamen's strike in place of the Minister of Labour, the Rhodesian problem in the place of the Secretary of State for Commonwealth Relations, the Productivity Conferences in place of one of the economics ministers or the deflationary measures of July 1966 in place of the Chancellor of the Exchequer. And while some might try to describe this as an idiosyncrasy of Mr. Wilson's Mr. Macmillan and Sir Alec Douglas-Home both intervened in a similar manner in threatened national strikes and in the formation of economic policy.

The final point that a Prime Minister is weak and defenceless in dealing with departmental ministers because he has no department to brief him has little substance. The Prime Minister can call for any information and he can at once see everything that is available to other members of the Cabinet. To argue that Mr.

---

[25] *The Observer*, September 16, 1962.
[26] G. W. Jones, *art. cit.*, p. 183.
[27] Confirmed in an interview with the author on March 7, 1967. This quotation was put before 15 out of the 23 members of Sir Alec Douglas-Home's Cabinet for their comments. It is interesting that all the senior ministers and those non-departmental ministers who chaired Cabinet Committees accepted the statement as entirely true. Departmental ministers whose affairs (education, health, housing) seldom were of such importance to the credit of the entire Government as to merit occasional intrusions or a steady oversight by the Prime Minister accepted the general implications but felt the words " agent," " assistant " were " a little too royal " as one of them put it.

Wilson strengthened the Cabinet office rather than build up his private office because he feared the displeasure of his ministers and their officials is simply incorrect. Increasingly Mr. Wilson has not found it necessary to develop new machinery because he has realised that the Cabinet Secretariat and No. 10 staff can between them supply him with all he needs. Before every ministerial meeting, there is an equivalent meeting of officials at which the points to be made on behalf of each department are gone over and Mr. Wilson has found he can enter any conference or confrontation with all the information his quick mind is able to absorb. Mr. Jones says " Prime Ministers have had little success when fighting the entrenched departments, who remain impervious to take-over bids," [28] yet on the previous page he has admitted that Prime Ministers are repeatedly successful in overcoming a department with one of the strongest *esprit de corps*, the Foreign Office. The appeasement policy in the 1930s and the Suez policy in the 1950s were both run against the solid opposition of the majority of the Foreign Office and there is considerable evidence that the Selective Employment Tax was imposed by Mr. Wilson on the Treasury. More than this, the Prime Minister can decide to create ministries such as the Department of Economic Affairs or the Ministry of Technology and destroy others such as the Ministry of Aviation or the Colonial Office.

It is carrying legalism to the point of absurdity to conclude that " the Prime Minister has no executive powers vested in him." [29] He has to work through other ministries, but an order from No. 10 Downing Street outranks any other instruction and the Cabinet Secretariat are there to follow up such commands so that the attempts to defeat by delay or endless consultation are harder in this situation than when departmental ministers issue instructions that may not be welcomed by their officials.

The difficulty (and the interest) in studying institutions at this level is that the problem cannot be quantified; it is impossible to establish conclusively the precise weight or influence of one office or body out of an elaborate series all of which have some share in the decision-making process. There is also the constant confusion between what is legally or formally the situation, what has happened in the past and could conceivably still happen today,

[28] G. W. Jones, *art. cit.*, p. 184.
[29] *Ibid.*, p. 185.

with the prevalent contemporary practice. This is exacerbated by the fact that some practising politicians, while operating the machine most skilfully, may still use outdated descriptions, either because they have not thought about the process or because this offers a certain protection (as when the Prime Minister says he cannot reveal information in a recess because his first duty is to report to the House of Commons). Even the fact that all the memoirs of those concerned with this aspect of the machinery of government have accepted the increased power of the Prime Minister and the altered and diminished role of the Cabinet is not a final or conclusive argument. It is possible that the Earl of Avon, Sir Alec Douglas-Home and Lord Butler as quoted above may all have erred in their emphasis. The only method of checking is to describe instance after instance, to analyse the factors affecting one decision after another and to compare these not only with the comments but the actual conduct of the ministers, M.P.s, civil servants and pressure groups when faced with specific problems. Out of this there should emerge a spectrum of possibilities which will allow the observer to identify the preponderant or normal situation. The process needs to be constantly repeated or reviewed. Factors may change. Something may come of present efforts to give a little more power to the House of Commons. Entry to Europe would produce some new limitations on the freedom of action in certain ministries and might also bring the economic strength on which a more independent foreign policy can be based. But so far, the politics of the 1960s have strengthened rather than weakened or altered the lines of development which have led contemporary British Government to be described as Prime Ministerial rather than Cabinet Government.

CABINET MINUTES

THERE is a little confusion about the term "minute" in the period covered by Section Four. The *Gladstone Papers, Add. MSS.,* 44,636 to 44,648 are described as Cabinet Minutes. In fact they contain many different types of document, most of them being agenda lists jotted down by Gladstone on half sheets of paper or on the back of the printed summons to the meeting. There are also printed memoranda, notes for statements, answers to questions and the odd remarks tossed across the table to other ministers. The term was more precisely used to describe either specially solemn advice to the Crown which was desired in writing or definite instructions which the Cabinet wanted to have on record. In the second category there was the Minute of 1869 instructing all departments to clear every proposal costing money with the Treasury, a Minute embodying a decision in 1877 over which Derby might have resigned, and a further case in 1892 when the Cabinet decided to give the Uganda Company three months to evacuate. There are three examples of the first type. Queen Victoria agreed to cancel the Royal Warrant authorising the purchase of commissions in the Army but asked for a Cabinet Minute requesting her to do so. When the Cabinet informed Edward VII on February 11, 1910, that the Budget would be reintroduced and that the King would only be asked to give an assurance that he would create peers after the government's plans had been put to Parliament, this was done in a Minute. The Cabinet used the same form on November 15, 1910, for asking George V to promise to create peers if the Lords finally rejected the Parliament Bill. The Committee of Imperial Defence had its proceedings recorded in regular Minutes from December 18, 1902, and it was in this form that Cabinet Minutes were resumed after December, 1916.

INDEX